The
Contentious
French

The
Contentious
French

CHARLES TILLY

The Belknap Press of
Harvard University Press
Cambridge, Massachusetts, and
London, England 1986

Library of Congress Cataloging-in-Publication Data

Tilly, Charles.
    The contentious French.

    Bibliography: p.
    Includes index.
    1. France—Politics and government—1589-1789.
2. France—Politics and government—1789-1900.
3. France—Politics and government—20th century.
4. Demonstrations—France—History. I. Title.
DC55.T55 1986   944   85-9137
ISBN 0-674-16695-7 (alk. paper)

To Franc and Peg Smith,
who helped me start

Preface

WHEN DID MY WORK on this book begin? Depending on the definition of "begin," it could be any time from my first exposure to French history in graduate school over thirty years ago to the wet, wet winter of 1974–75, when I first found myself laboring in the archives with this specific book in mind.

In any case, it is easy to say when and how my research ended. I returned to the Archives Nationales in January 1984 to read material in the boxes concerning strikes, meetings, and demonstrations of the Popular Front. These crucial boxes had been "out for microfilming" the previous June. Appropriately, a strike of the *magasiniers* at the archives cut short my effort. No more documents for that trip! No way to know now whether in those last three boxes lurks the one document that sets everything straight, or refutes some major argument of the book. That uncertainty adds exactly the tension that ought to accompany an inquiry like this one; it can never really end.

Through those many years, a host of people have helped me find the necessary material, organize the evidence, and put this book together. Judith William-Powlett started the long file of helpers in Princeton during 1962–63. The following year, Lutz Berkner, James Doty, Lynn Lees, Ted Margadant, Andrejs Plakans, James Rule, Edward Shorter, Gerald Soliday, Cyrus Stewart, and I labored together in the library above Sage's grocery store in Cambridge. (David Landes sent most of that first group of collaborators my way; I have always been thankful to him for that favor.) Since then, at least a few people have always been involved in collecting, organizing, or analyzing the evidence. There is no way to single out a few of those dozens of collaborators without being unfair to the rest. Thanks to them all.

I do, however, want to pay tribute to an institution. The University of Michigan's Center for Research on Social Organization, in the shabby-genteel Perry School building, housed my research projects for fifteen years. My colleagues, collaborators, and friends at CRSO pitched in to create a marvelous setting for research, discussion, and learning. In recent years, Mayer Zald, in his double role as center member and chair of Michigan's sociology department, has given CRSO indispensable aid. Within the center, Sheila Wilder dealt with its daily problems graciously; she also helped me repeatedly in the production of this book. Dozens of other staff members, faculty, and graduate students poured their efforts into seminars, fundraising efforts, volleyball, midnight discussions, and research. Let me express my affection and gratitude to the people of CRSO.

For criticism of various sections of this book, I am grateful to Ron Aminzade, Rod Aya, William Beik, David Bien, Julian Dent, Lynn Eden, Steve Fraser, Sharon Kettering, Michael Kimmel, M. J. Maynes, Leslie Moch, Robert Schneider, and Eugen Weber. (None of these critics has seen anything approaching the whole text; none of them therefore bears any responsibility for its blunders.) Franc Smith set aside his own writing—and an urgent stack of student papers—to give me a splendid writer's reaction to the book. Aida Donald provided superb editorial guidance. Ann Hawthorne deftly combed the errors from my text. Tessie Liu, John Merriman, and Louise Tilly lent me valuable notes on their work in the archives of Maine-et-Loire, the army, and the Nord respectively. For financial support, I am happy to thank the John Simon Guggenheim Foundation; the National Science Foundation; the German Marshall Fund of the United States; the Department of History, University of Michigan; and the Horace Rackham School of Graduate Studies, University of Michigan.

A very preliminary version of Chapters 1 and 2 appeared as "Getting It Together in Burgundy," *Theory and Society* 4 (1977), 479–504. Some material from Chapter 5 appeared in "Routine Conflicts and Peasant Rebellions in Seventeenth-Century France," in Robert Weller and Scott Guggenheim, eds., *Power and Protest in the Countryside* (Durham, N.C.: Duke University Press, 1982). In Chapter 12 I have adapted some passages from material in my "Violenza e azione colletiva in Europa. Riflessioni storico-comparate," in Donatella della Porta and Gianfranco Pasquino, eds., *Terrorismo e violenza politica. Tre casi a confronto: Stati Uniti, Germania e Giappone* (Bologna: Il Mulino, 1983), and "Speaking Your Mind without Elections, Surveys, or

Social Movements," *Public Opinion Quarterly* 47 (1983), 461–478. All translations of French sources are my own unless otherwise indicated.

Louise Tilly was too busy with her own work to give this opus much direct attention. She and I know, however, how much it owes to her tolerance, cooperation, and moral support. For that, and for much more, I am grateful to her.

Contents

1. The Challenge of Popular Struggle *I*

2. Burgundy Battles *13*

3. France over Four Centuries *41*

4. Anjou's Crises *79*

5. Purse, Sword, Loaf, and Cross *119*

6. Toulouse, Languedoc, and Enlightenment
France *162*

7. Statemaking, Capitalism, and Contention *201*

8. Flanders from the Revolution to the
Great War *245*

9. Revolutions and Social Movements *274*

10. Festivals and Fights in the Ile-de-France *313*

11. Parties, Regimes, and Wars *351*

12. Four Centuries of Struggle *380*

A Note on the Evidence *407*

Bibliography *414*

Index *443*

Illustrations

		Facing page
1.	France by region in the seventeenth century	*14*
2.	Burgundy in the seventeenth century	*15*
3.	Dijon in the seventeenth century	*18*
4.	A seventeenth-century warning against collective action	*19*
5.	The neighborhood of the Place de Grève in the seventeenth century	*42*
6.	Aerial perspective of Paris in the seventeenth century	*43*
7.	Paris and its surroundings in the seventeenth century	*46*
8.	A celebration in the Place de Grève, 1615	*47*
9.	The masons' hiring fair at the Place de l'Hôtel de Ville, about 1868	*56*
10.	The Place de l'Hôtel de Ville in the twentieth century	*57*
11.	Twentieth-century France and the five regions	*66*
12.	The Ile-de-France in the seventeenth century	*67*
13.	Flanders and Picardy in the seventeenth century	*68*
14.	Languedoc in the seventeenth century	*69*
15.	The region of Anjou in the seventeenth century	*80*
16.	Aerial perspective of Angers in the seventeenth century	*81*
17.	Toulouse in the eighteenth century	*198*
18.	Hardy's description of the taking of the Bastille	*199*
19.	Lille in the nineteenth century	*246*

20. Flanders in the nineteenth century   *247*
21. Proclamation of the Commune at the Place de l'Hôtel de
    Ville, 18 March 1871   *306*
22. Père-Lachaise demonstration, 25 May 1885   *307*
23. Paris and the Ile-de-France in the twentieth century   *314*
24. Père Peinard poster about May Day 1890   *315*
25. Old workers demonstrate at the Hôtel de Ville, 1947   *372*
26. Farmers' demonstration in the Nord, 1955   *373*
27. May Day 1983, Paris   *390*
28. Peace march, Paris, June 1982   *391*

Credits

Special thanks are due to the following for providing photographs and for granting permission to reproduce them: Bibliothèque Nationale Cartes et Plans, 1, 2, 3, 5, 6, 7, 12, 13, 14, 15, 16, 17, 19, 20, 23; Archives Municipales, Dijon, 4; Bibliothèque Nationale Estampes, 8, 9, 21, 22, 25, 26; Bibliothèque Nationale Manuscrits, 18; Archives Nationales, 24. Photographs 10, 27, and 28 are by Charles Tilly.

The
Contentious
French

Abbreviations

AA   Archives Historiques de l'Armée, Vincennes
ADA   Archives Départmentales de l'Ariège, Foix
ADCO   Archives Départmentales de la Côte d'Or, Dijon
ADH   Archives Départmentales de l'Hérault, Montpellier
ADHG   Archives Départmentales de la Haute-Garonne, Toulouse
ADIL   Archives Départmentales de l'Indre-et-Loire, Tours
ADML   Archives Départmentales de Maine-et-Loire, Angers
ADN   Archives Départmentales du Nord, Lille
ADPO   Archives Départmentales des Pyrénées-Orientales, Perpignan
AMA   Archives Municipales, Angers
AMD   Archives Municipales, Dijon
AML   Archives Municipales, Lille
AMT   Archives Municipales, Toulouse
AN   Archives Nationales, Paris
BN   Bibliothèque Nationale, Paris
Fr   Fonds Français (Bibliothèque Nationale)
NA   Nouvelles Acquisitions Françaises (Bibliothèque Nationale)

The set of numbers after the archives designation is the series, and the number after the solidus is the folio. Thus AMA BB 72/97 designates Archives Municipales, Angers, series BB 72, folio 97.

I

The Challenge
of Popular Struggle

*D*IJON'S MUNICIPAL ARCHIVES occupy several cluttered rooms in the grand old palace of the dukes of Burgundy. The archives' main doors look out onto the elegant semicircle of the Place de la Libération, built in the late seventeenth century as the Place Royale. Researchers in the lofty reading room have no trouble tallying arrivals and departures. So long as the outside door is open, a strident bell sounds in the room. The interruption usually lasts five to ten seconds, as the newcomer closes the street door, crosses the anteroom, fumbles with the inner door, and enters. In bad weather, arrivals disrupt more; after the long bell stops sounding, visitors stomp their feet unseen, remove their boots, and hang up their raincoats before presenting themselves for inspection. Exits are equally distracting, for they mirror the entries precisely: thud, shuffle, stomp, ring.

The bell does not ring often. On an average day, readers include a few city employees, an antiquarian or two, an occasional student from the university, now and then an itinerant historian. Those few people, nevertheless, have riches before them. They have the surviving papers of the capital of Burgundy, both as an independent power and as a major French province. The archives remain ample up to the point at which the centralization of the Revolution shifted the balance of power, and of paperwork, toward the state's own bureaucracy.

Among the thousands of bundles in the prerevolutionary collection, some 167 deal with "police," in the broad old-regime meaning of defense against all manner of public ills. Their concerns include sanitation, public health, fire protection, and asylums; the pursuit of beggars, vagrants, and criminals; and the control of games, gatherings, and public ceremonies. Nineteenth-century archivists sorted the papers by subject matter, by rough time period, and then usually by affair, event, session, or whatever other subdivision the organization producing the records had used in its own work.

The series contains reports of the activities of the *chassecoquins,* the seventeenth-century officials assigned, literally, to chase *coquins*—scalawags and ne'er-do-wells—from the city. It includes more details than most people care to read concerning the official surveillance of the grape harvest, in that great wine region, from 1290 onward. It has a great mass of reports (and, especially, of invoices) from four centuries of publicly sponsored celebrations. Reading those documents, we see the elaborate preparations for the annual fireworks of Saint John the Baptist Eve, the city's feast-day, as well as election day for the mayor (*vicomte-mayeur*). A note from 1642 mentions the "malefactors who set off the fireworks when the mayor was, as usual, going to light them himself" (AMD I 43). We watch the great funeral processions, including the sixty musicians who played and sang the funeral mass composed for the dauphin in 1711. We attend splendid municipal celebrations, such as the 1766 city hall concert in honor of the prince of Condé, featuring the prodigious Mozart children from Salzburg (AMD I 48, B 400). We witness incessant pompous entries into the city: King Charles VI in 1387, Duke Charles the Bold in 1470, King Henry IV in 1595, Louis XIV and the queen in 1674, and dozens of others up to the Revolution (AMD I 5-36). (At the entry of Charles IX in 1564, no fewer than twenty-three painters were among the hundreds of people paid for helping prepare the "works and mysteries necessary for the arrival and entry of the King": AMD I 18). We observe, in short, the very tapestry of Dijon's public life.

Readers concerned less with kings and more with the participation of ordinary people in public life also find much to think about in those dossiers. One bundle, for example, deals with "seditions" and other serious offenses against public order between 1639 and 1775. In the century before the Revolution, "sedition," "emotion," and "mutiny" were common terms for events that later observers would have called "riots" or "disturbances." Unsympathetic observers, that is. "Sedition," "emotion," "mutiny," "riot," and "disturbances" are terms of disapproval, powerholders' words.

One day in the spring of 1975, I sat in the reading room of Dijon's archives. As I pored over those seventeenth-century reports, Monsieur Savouret, Madame Jacquette, and Monsieur Benoist, the archivists, were busy about their work. Gradually a muffled noise resolved itself into chanting, crescendo. "What is it?" I asked my companions. We went to the tall windows, which gave us a view through the great barred gate of the palace into the Place de la Libération. People were marching outside.

I rushed to the exit. The indefatigable bell announced my translation from the seventeenth century to the twentieth. Up the street came several hundred young men and women, in uneven ranks. Some carried an effigy of a man, while others hoisted signs and banners. They continued to chant loudly. A marcher thrust a handbill at me. The issue, it turned out, was the future of students preparing to teach sports and physical education. The dummy represented M. Mazeaud, secretary of youth, sports, and leisure, who was proposing a tiny budget for physical education and the removal of compulsory sports from public schools. That would seriously curtail these students' job prospects. Like students in other French cities, the demonstrators were on their way to the Place de la République for a rally. An hour or so later they passed the archives again, on their way back to the university area. The undisciplined ranks and disciplined chants had dissolved, but the demonstrators still shouted and cheered. Gradually their voices gave way to the ordinary noises of the street. My thoughts turned back three centuries to 1675.

Do the turbulent events of 1675 and 1975 form knots in the same long thread? Both the event in the archives and the event on the street consisted in people's banding together to act on their shared grievances, hopes, and interests. That banding together—let's call it *collective action* for short—has its own history. As people's grievances, hopes, interests, and opportunities for acting on them change, so do their ways of acting collectively.

In between interests and opportunity comes a third factor: organization. Whether the people involved are seventeenth-century winegrowers or twentieth-century students, they don't seize every opportunity to act on their interests. Nor do they react to every opportunity in the same way. How they are tied to each other, what ways of acting together are already familiar to them, to which sorts of news they have alerted themselves—all these factors affect how often people act, in what manner, and how effectively.

The events of 1675 and 1975 represent a particular class of collective action: discontinuous, contentious collective action. We may simply call it *contention.* On these occasions people not only band together to act on their interests but also act in ways that directly, visibly, and significantly affect other people's realization of their interests. What is more, people act discontinuously: they put in a considerable effort, then stop. If we concentrate on seditions, mutinies, riots, and demonstrations, we neglect collective action for the purposes of sociability, entertainment, self-improvement, or ritual obligation, except when it spills over into contention. We likewise neglect routine ways of getting things done through workshops, churches, confraternities, and other organizations, unless they become contentious. The study of contention still requires us to pay some attention to these routine and self-centered forms of collective action; they form an important part of the context. But we focus on conflict.

Conflict, not disorder. Authorities and thoughtless historians commonly describe popular contention as disorderly. In seventeenth-century Burgundy they used words such as *sédition, émotion,* and, yes, *désordre* to describe the means by which ordinary people made claims. But the more closely we look at that same contention, the more we discover order. We discover order created by the rooting of collective action in the routines and organization of everyday social life, and by its involvement in a continuous process of signaling, negotiation, and struggle with other parties whose interests the collective action touches.

The forms of contention themselves display that order. In following the very same actions that authorities call disorders, we see the repetition of a limited number of actions. In seventeenth-century France, ordinary people did not know how to demonstrate, rally, or strike. But they had standard routines for expelling a tax collector from town, withdrawing their allegiance from corrupt officials, and shaming moral offenders. The following pages abound with descriptions of those routines.

Each of these forms of action links some concrete group of people to some other individual, group, or groups. Each originates and changes as a function of continuing interaction—struggle, collaboration, competition, or some combination of them—among groups. With regard to any particular group, we can think of the whole set of means it has for making claims of different kinds on different individuals or groups as its *repertoire* of contention. Because similar groups generally have similar repertoires, we can speak more loosely of a general repertoire that is available for contention to the population of a time and place. That includes a time, place, and population as broad as seventeenth-century France.

The repertoire actually constrains people's action; people generally turn to familiar routines and innovate within them, even when in principle some unfamiliar form of action would serve their interests much better. Roughly speaking, then, we can think of a repertoire of various forms of contention connecting real people to each other, a repertoire that comes into use and changes as a function of fluctuations in interests, opportunity, and organization.

Capitalism, Statemaking, and Popular Contention

This book, however, does not propose a general account of all contention. It asks a narrower question: In the case of France from the seventeenth century to the present, how did the development of capitalism and the concentration of power in the national state affect the ways that ordinary people contended—or failed to contend—for their interests? No single place, population, or event can provide the answers to such a question. But a thoughtful comparison of popular contention in different regions over the years from 1598 to 1984 can give us a grip on the answers. *The Contentious French* undertakes that comparison.

With respect to capitalism and statemaking alike, our problem is to trace how the big changes affected the interests, opportunities, and organization of different groups of ordinary people during the centuries since 1598, then to see how those alterations of interest, opportunities, and organization reshaped the contention of those people. We follow change: not a complete explanation of all contention, much less of all collective action, but an effort to understand the specific impact of two large, interdependent transformations on collective action. That is the book's major task.

Capitalist production meant that people who controlled capital made the basic decisions concerning the use of land, labor, and capital and produced goods by means of labor drawn from workers who survived through the sale of their labor power. In short: concentrated capital and wage labor. The national state's growth entailed increasing control of the resources in a contiguous territory by an organization that was formally autonomous, differentiated from other organizations, centralized, internally coordinated, and in possession of major concentrated means of coercion. In short: centralized and territorial control.

Both the development of capitalism and the growth of the national state implied or caused a complex of other social changes. When it came to the quality of everyday experience, for example, the most important single change in French life over our four centuries was probably the proletarianization of work—the declining control of households over their own means of production, and the increasing dependence of those households on the sale of their labor power. Proletarianization was part and parcel of the development of capitalism. In one way or another, the development of national labor and commodity markets, the shift to factory production, the class segregation of the urban population, and numerous other changes in the texture of social life resulted, at least in part, from the process of proletarianization.

With regard to statemaking, it is hard to decide which aspect of the process had the more profound effect, on everyday life: the growth of the state's bulk and complexity, or the penetration of its coercive and extractive power. Since the two reinforced each other, it may be idle to pose the question. The growth in scale increased the likely impact of any state action on the welfare of millions of ordinary people. The increasing penetration made it more and more difficult to insulate small-scale social life from state surveillance and intervention. The routinization of policing, the generalization of military service, the creation of fiscal and demographic reporting, the emergence of parties and pressure groups are among the varied changes in day-to-day experience that stemmed more or less directly from the growth of the national state.

Neither the development of capitalism nor the growth of the national state ran linear, continuous, and smooth. Both proceeded through fits, starts, crises, reversals, and great surges. That is the main reason why the history of contention itself is so irregular. For, more than anything else, the major changes and fluctuations in French contention responded to the ups and downs of statemaking and capitalism. Rapid seventeenth-century construction of a belligerent state incited broad resistance from people whose rights and resources that state began to preempt. The nineteenth-century boom in production via disciplined, subdivided labor in large shops helped bring the firm-by-firm strike into prominence. In these instances and many others, the links between waves of contention and surges of capitalism and statemaking were direct and strong.

Not all contention, to be sure, responded so directly to statemaking and capitalism. No doubt the rise of Breton and Occitan nationalism in the 1970s, for example, had something to do with statemaking and capitalism. Yet regional and ethnic movements do not follow as directly from the logic of statemaking and capitalism as do, say, workers' organizations and taxpayers' resistance movements.

What are those logics? In what ways do the very structures of statemaking and capitalism promote certain forms of contention? To frame a short answer to that demanding question, we must smooth out time and ignore the quirks of French history. To the extent that contention has its own historical memory, with the outcome of one struggle influencing the shape of the next, such a simplification is full of risk. Yet a simplified analysis will provide a baseline against which we can measure the historical reality. That return justifies the risk.

In general terms, the development of capitalism entails three fundamental conflicts. All tend to produce open contention. The first is the most obvious: the opposition of capital and labor. All other things being equal, the fuller the development of capitalism, the sharper that opposition. (That all other things do *not* remain equal—for example, that organized workers and organized capitalists commonly work out bargaining procedures as the proletarianization of the labor force proceeds—is the usual objection to Marxist predictions of increasing polarization.) The second conflict results from concentration of control over the factors of production, which is likewise intrinsic to capitalism; in this regard, capitalists face the opposition of others whose existing claims on land, labor, commodities, and capital compete with the effort to consolidate. The third conflict pits participants in the same markets against each other. To the extent that the buyers or the sellers of commodities, labor power, or land are competing in the same markets, their interests set them one against the other.

As for statemaking, its logic is likewise three-faced. Face one: extraction of resources from the subject population, which typically involves some sort of struggle between the operators of the state and members of the other organizations, households, firms, communities, and others that already have claims on those resources. Face two: competition between the state, both within and outside its territory, and rival governments (including would-be or quasi-governments) for control of population, territory, and resources. Face three: competition among organizations nominally subject to a given state for resources and facilities that are already under control of that state's agents.

Historically, the development of capitalism and the growth of national states have overlapped and interacted. Yet one does not follow automatically from the other. At the extreme, indeed, the two contradict each other: an extreme version of capitalism puts all factors of production at the disposal of capitalists and leaves no resources for the state, whereas an extreme version of statemaking squeezes all resources from other social units and leaves no autonomy for capitalists. Nevertheless, if capitalism and statemaking were to proceed simultaneously, we might expect some sort of accommodation between capitalists and statemakers to develop. We might then imagine a sequence of the following sort:

Early: Capitalist property being created as statemakers struggle to extract resources and to beat off rivals; major themes of contention are expropriation, imposition of state control, imposition of capitalist control, and resistance to all of them.

Late: Within the framework of capitalist property and an existing state, major themes of contention are capital-labor struggles, competition within markets, attempts to control the state and its resources.

These are relative matters; we have no reason, for example, to expect the play of extraction and resistance ever to end, and we have every reason to expect some capital-labor struggle from the earliest days of capitalism. Furthermore, to the extent that capitalism and statemaking are out of phase, different patterns should result; in a case in which statemaking comes early and capitalism late, for instance, we may well find more intense resistance to the state's extraction of resources, simply because capitalists are not facilitating that extraction by means of their own expropriation of the factors of production. Later in this book we shall see contrasts among French regions that follow just such a pattern. As a broad summary, nevertheless, the two-phase scheme applies quite well to the history of France since 1500 or so; the transition to the second phase occurred within the century after 1789.

The permutations and possibilities never end. In tracing the impact of statemaking and capitalism on changing patterns of contention, we confront an interesting choice: a choice between (1) working out the likely patterns theoretically before going to the historical record and (2) letting the historical record guide our theoretical inquiry. This book takes the latter approach: seeking to enrich our understanding of the transformations wrought by capitalism and statemaking by staying close to the historical record of ordinary people's contention.

Yet I shall be disappointed if the book makes no contribution to two other sorts of understanding. The study of French contention should spark insight into the particular times, places, groups, and events it takes up—help us see, for instance, what was at issue in the great seventeenth-century political struggles. It should also improve our comprehension of contention in general—making it clearer, for instance, in what ways we ought to mend existing models of protest that present it as a consequence of anxiety, or of anger, or of ideology. In all these regards we have much to gain from an analysis that singles out the effects of large social changes on ordinary people's interests, opportunities, and organization, then examines how changing interest, opportunity, and organization influence their prevailing modes of collective action.

Interest, opportunity, organization, and action: a large, rich historical agenda. The turbulent events whose traces survive in seventeenth-century police archives are obviously a peculiar sample of all the country's contention, and therefore of the interests, opportunities, and organization at work. Nevertheless, those events immediately identify lineaments of seventeenth-century contention that differ significantly from those of the twentieth century.

A Challenge to Historical Analysis

France's experience with contention since the seventeenth century sets a challenge for historical analysis. We must survey from the ground the same terrain that high-flying historians have mapped into regimes, wars, crises, and transitions. Our materials will often be the standard materials of political history: reports by police and regional administrators, narratives of rebellions, descriptions by powerholders. Yet the point of reference will differ greatly from that of most political history. We shall know that a new era has begun not when a new elite holds power or a new constitution appears, but when ordinary people begin contending for their interests in new ways. Of course, changes in contention *could* occur mainly as effects of changes in elites or constitutions. The historical challenge is to try out that hypothesis, not to take its validity for granted.

The narratives to come will raise doubts about the overriding effects of regimes and constitutions. The doubts arise from the historical record as well as from general reflections on the character of contention. On strict historical grounds, there is too much continuity across major political crises and changes of regime for us to suppose a simple cause-and-effect relationship between regime and contention; continuities across the Revolution of 1789 will provide a clear case in point. There is likewise too much change in the pattern of contention corresponding to alterations in the relations of production rather than to constitutions, regimes, and revolutions; the rise and fall of anticapitalist contention will illustrate that fact abundantly.

General reflections on the character of contention likewise give us reasons to look beyond narrowly political explanations. If it is true that contention changes as a function of interest, organization, and opportunity, then it is implausible that all three should shift simultaneously, and even more implausible that all three should shift mainly as a consequence of changes in regime. On general grounds, we might expect the arrival of new regimes and new powerholders to have fairly immediate and powerful impacts on ordinary people's opportunities to act. But interest and organization? In those regards we should expect the impact of regime changes to be weaker, slower, and more indirect. Changes in the relations of production ought to have powerful and immediate effects. There are also other factors, not readily reducible either to immediate effects of regime changes or to changes in the relations of production, whose influence we must at least consider: transformations in the ways people think about themselves and the world, population growth or decline, technological innovations.

Moreover, if it is true that the available repertoire of collective action itself limits who can act and how, then it is unlikely that regime changes alone account for alterations in those means. More likely the existing repertoire grows out of the following factors:

1. The population's daily routines and internal organization (example: the grain seizure depends on the existence of periodic public markets and on a population that relies on those markets for survival)

2. Prevailing standards of rights and justice (example: the firm-by-firm strike depends on the presumption that people have the right to dispose of their own labor)

3. The population's accumulated experience with collective action (example: the appearance of the demonstration as a standard form of contention depends on the discovery that some sorts of officials are more likely than others to listen to demands that have the visible backing of large numbers of determined people)

4. Current patterns of repression (example: the adoption of the public meeting as a vehicle for protest depends on the vigor with which the authorities have been breaking up public meetings)

These points are not self-evident. It could be that "repertoire" is simply a name for whatever people do to achieve common ends, and that people are perfectly ready to adopt new tactics as the need or opportunity arises. Furthermore, even if there *is* a repertoire that constrains people's actions, it could be that regimes design and set repertoires in much the way that they establish rules for voting or holding office. Part of the historical challenge, then, is to determine whether repertoires of contention really do limit the alternatives open to potential contenders; whether they do, indeed, change as a result of struggles among contenders; and to what degree the limits they set depend on the character of the regime.

If a narrowly political analysis fails to account for the ebb and flow of collective action, that is not because politics is unimportant. On the contrary. We need a broader view of politics, one that looks beyond parties, factions, and national leaders. Politics concerns power in all its guises. We have to examine the everyday use of power, the continuing struggle for power, the changing structure of power as it has involved the fates of local communities and ordinary people.

Sometimes those features of power coincide with national politics in the narrow sense of the word. More often the connection is complex and indirect: from a national perspective, the struggles of local communities and ordinary people are problems and opportunities that must be dealt with, but those struggles are not the core of politics. From the viewpoint of local communities and ordinary people, national governments make demands and monopolize resources in ways that commonly aggravate the difficulties of everyday life but occasionally offer the chance for a strategic alliance or a lucrative payoff. Another statement of the historical challenge, then, is this: to follow the impact of large transformations of social life on collective action without blurring the complexity and specificity of everyday struggles for power.

This book responds to the historical challenge by tracing the history of contention in five regions of France from the seventeenth into the twentieth century. Most of all, it asks how the development of capitalism and the rise of a strong national state impinged upon the contention of ordinary people. In order to ask that question sensibly, we must consider the effects of capitalism and the national state on people's interests, organization, and opportunity to act. We shall certainly have occasion to ask about the effects of industrialization as such, urbanization as such, changes in the politics of the French state as such, and so on. The dominant question will remain: *How did statemaking and capitalism alter the ways in which ordinary French people acted together—or, for that matter, failed to act together—on their shared interests?*

The inquiry is broadly chronological. For convenience, it begins with Henry IV's accession to national power in 1598. It then divides French history since 1598 into four blocks:

a "seventeenth century" running from 1598 to about 1715, dominated by struggles over the expansion of the national state

a short "eighteenth century" ending around 1789, characterized by sharpening resistance to the imposition of capitalist property relations

a longer "nineteenth century" extending from the early Revolution to about 1906, marked by revolutionary struggles and the emergence of a new repertoire of contention

a "twentieth century" from then to the present, involving a continuation of struggles initiated in the nineteenth century, with increases in the scale of capital, coercion, and contention

We shall see that these chronological divisions are not precise but do mark off contrasting experiences in French popular contention. They will, for example, make it easier to see important transformations in the basic repertoires of contention that occurred around the middle of the seventeenth century and, even more dramatically, around the middle of the nineteenth.

Within each broadly defined century, we shall concentrate on the comparison of several major French regions: Burgundy, Anjou, Languedoc, Flanders, and the region of Paris. The book's twelve chapters function as six pairs. Complementing Chapter 1, Chapter 12 reviews the same problems in the light of the intervening historical analysis. The ten chapters in between pair off by period, one chapter dealing with a particular region, the other comparing the experiences of all five regions during the same period. Chapter 2 takes Burgundy from the beginning of the seventeenth century to near the end of the twentieth. Chapter 3 follows the five regions, and France as a whole, through the same four centuries. These two chapters provide an overview of the changes in social organization and in popular contention that later chapters discuss in detail. Chapter 4 concentrates on Anjou during the seventeenth century; Chapter 5 compares the seventeenth-century experiences of Anjou, Burgundy, Flanders, the Ile-de-France, and Languedoc. And so on through three more chronologically matched pairs.

The overlapping of time spans and regions means that we encounter the same events more than once; the Fronde of 1648–1653, the Revolution of 1789–1799, the struggle over separation of church and state in 1905–06, and a number of less notable happenings all recur at different points in the story. They reappear, however, in new perspectives, with fresh detail; the sacrifice of strict chronology will, I hope, enrich our understanding of the connections among events. The final chapter knits the chronology and geography back together—first by reviewing long-run changes in contention in France as a whole, then by reflecting on the teachings of all this contentious history.

2 ∽⌣

Burgundy Battles

IJON, 1668. Louis XIV had taken full control of the national government at Cardinal Mazarin's death seven years earlier. Louis's aggressive chief minister, J. C. Colbert, was helping him formulate and execute plans to extend the state's power and make war. The formidable pair was currently pursuing Louis's continental ambitions in the War of Devolution, the struggle with Spain resulting from Louis's claims, through his Spanish wife, to the Spanish Netherlands. The war was fought largely in Spanish-held Flanders and Franche-Comté, and paid for mainly by the villagers and townspeople of France. The great rebellions and civil wars that had raged twenty to thirty years earlier had now subsided, although mountaineers in parts of the Pyrenees recently wrested from Spain were fighting the imposition of a salt tax. Louis XIV and Colbert were assembling the wherewithal of warfare by tightening and expanding the national system of taxation.

Royal Power and Local Conflict

Dijon, capital of Burgundy, did not escape. In 1668 the royal council struck one of its periodic blows at the municipal council's autonomy. Up to that point, Dijon's municipality had been large, self-perpetuating, and exempt from many taxes. What is more, each of the twenty aldermen (*échevins*) had been responsible for assessing royal taxes within his own district. The decree halved the municipality's size, reduced the aldermen's terms of office, put the current appointments to office in royal hands, and centralized the collection of taxes. All, of course, in the name of efficiency.

The royally appointed municipal council then issued a warning against unnamed people who had spread rumors that the major property tax, the _taille,_ was to be increased, and forbade the populace to "assemble or form a crowd day or night on any pretext, or to incite the people to sedition, on pain of death." Rumormongers had allegedly said "they needed a Lanturelu" (AMD I 119).

Lanturelu was a song of the 1620s that gave its name to a popular rebellion of February 1630. Back then, Richelieu and Louis XIII had announced the elimination of Burgundy's privileged tax status. A hundred-odd armed men led by winegrower Anatoire Changenet, plus a crowd of unarmed women, men, and children (_gens de bas étage_—lowly folk—city officials called them later), gathered in the streets of Dijon. Anatoire Changenet himself had just served as King of Fools in the city's Mardi Gras festivities; he wore his gaudy costume into an assault on symbols and representatives of the crown.

A contemporary newspaper, _Le Mercure François,_ relayed the news to the rest of France:

> Toward evening on 28 February there began in the city of Dijon a sedition, carried out by a troop of winegrowers, who attacked the house of a certain individual, but settled for breaking in the outside door and threatening to come back the next day, Friday 1 March. On that day, easily and without resistance, they went to the houses of many royal officers, even that of the parlementary court's first president, opened them up, and burned the furniture they found inside. (_Le Mercure François_ 1630: 148–149)

Dijon's crowd is supposed to have burned a portrait of Louis XIII and shouted "Long live the Emperor!"—meaning the Holy Roman emperor, Hasburg descendant of Burgundian Charles the Bold and mortal rival of the French king. Dijon's mayor hesitated a day before calling out the militia. As they dispersed the crowd, militiamen killed ten or twelve of the rebels. The king retaliated by imposing a state of siege. He required a large payment to the victims of property damage, further abridged the city's privileges, and in April 1630 staged a humiliating confrontation with local dignitaries. The parlement of Burgundy did its part: it sentenced two leaders of the rebellion to hang. That was a Lanturelu.

The Lanturelu threatened in 1668 did not occur. Women of St.-Nicolas parish attacked one of the local tax collectors and threatened to burn his

Fig. 1. France by region in the seventeenth century

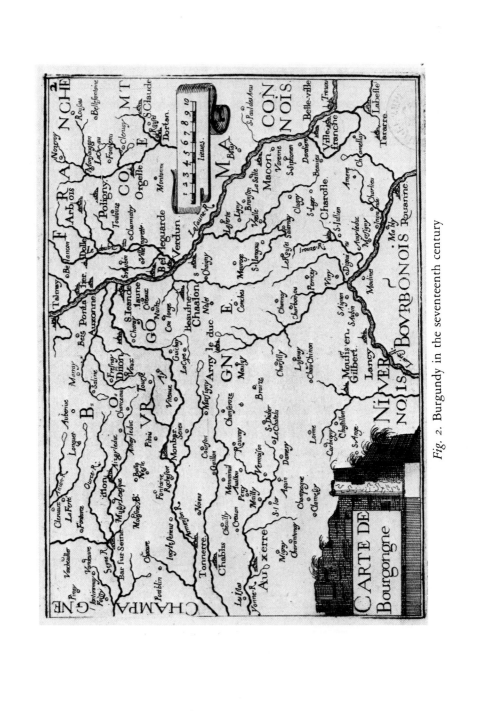

Fig. 2. Burgundy in the seventeenth century

house, but then the movement subsided into grumbles and rumors. Dijon's authorities easily put down the new flurries of resistance.

Yet seventeenth-century Dijon had its share of "seditions, emotions, and mutinies," as authorities of the time called concerted public demands. In February 1684 winegrowers again took their turn. As Dijon's public prosecutor described the event:

> A large number of winegrowers [300 or 400 in another of his accounts] of this city have had the nerve to assemble and not only to go around the city with beating drum but also they have been rash and insolent enough to proceed in the same way to a great oak in a wood belonging to the Carthusian prior of this city. The mutiny and boldness of these insolent winegrowers are so great that they have continued to make the same disturbance and scandal in the city, with drums still beating, without any permission whatsoever. Since their behavior deserves the severest punishment, the prosecutor requests that he be given authorization to proceed.   (AMD I 119)

Later details in the prosecutor's account set the number of marchers at something over a hundred. His exaggerated estimate may well reflect another fact: in an encounter between city officials and winegrowers at the Guillaume Gate, as the prosecutor tells the story, "it was only by some sort of miracle that none of them was assaulted, notably the said public prosecutor by one of the seditioners, who was at the head of the crowd and got ready to strike him with his pruning-knife" (AMD I 119).

The rebellious winegrowers assembled to a drumroll, elected sergeants, and marched in good order. Among the leaders, as in 1630, was a winegrower named Changenet. (This one, Jean Changenet, described himself as "winegrower in Dijon, rue Chanoine, twenty-nine years old, professing the Apostolic Roman Catholic religion": AMD I 119). The group went en masse to Champmoron Wood, which belonged to the nearby Carthusian monastery. There they gathered firewood, then returned to the city. On their way back through the gate they met a small band of officials who had come to stop them. Hilaire Edouard Demouchy (*conseiller du roi, trésorier de France,* and, most important, leaseholder of Champmoron Wood) filed a formal complaint asking for redress, prosecutions, and official rejection of the winegrowers' claim to the firewood. The authorities clapped a dozen leaders of the march, including Jean Changenet, in jail.

The invaders of the forest claimed they had the right to cut firewood at Champmoron "as a result of concessions to the winegrowers by the duke of Burgundy, as has often been practiced in the past when required by bad weather and hard winter, as in the present year when the need is great" (AMD I 119). Part of the transcript from the interrogation of forty-year-old Pierre Reignaut runs:

> Asked why they banded together thus to go to the wood if they already had the right to cut there.

> Replies that the reason they went to said wood in large numbers was that the first persons to go had been chased out by the valets of the Carthusian fathers and in the fear that the same thing would happen again the greater part of the winegrowers had assembled in order to maintain their right to cut in said wood.   (AMD I 119)

After some weeks in jail, the twelve prisoners went free on their promise of good behavior. Their action apparently stirred the municipality: the following year the city itself sued the Carthusians for enforcement of the winegrowers' right to gather wood.

Dijon's city fathers had reason to be concerned. Wood shortage was becoming a critical problem in all of Burgundy, as forests passed into private hands and small woodburning forges multiplied. In 1661, at the very start of Louis XIV's personal reign, for example, Burgundy's new intendant, Bouchu, had written to Colbert that "it would be a task worthy of your attention to restore the province's forests, which are on their way to complete ruin, and which will be of greater and greater importance, given the need for wood people here are beginning to have" (BN Mélanges Colbert 103, letter of 21 October 1661). Compared with other groups of poor people in Dijon, winegrowers not only played a crucial part in the local economy but also had the advantage of coherent organization: extensive ties sustained by daily contact, relatively effective leadership, previous experience in acting together. Although the prosecutor called the winegrowers' march a "sedition," the municipal officers had to take its substance seriously.

So do we. For the winegrowers' invasion of Champmoron Wood in 1684 shows a classic interaction of interest, opportunity, and organization in popular response to the development of capitalism. The leasing of church and noble property to bourgeois managers, the annihilation of common-use rights in favor of exclusive ownership, and the proliferation of small industrial enterprises such as woodburning forges in the countryside all played significant parts in France's early capitalist development. The growth of capitalism thus threatened the winegrowers' interests in more ways than one.

To say so, we need not deny that some winegrowers benefited from the expansion of urban markets. We need not claim that winegrowers were waging a self-conscious battle against the development of capitalist property relations. We need not assert that cold weather, Carthusian avarice, and other factors leading up to the confrontation of the winegrowers with the monastery's valets all constituted, in some sense, consequences of capitalism. We need only ask whether, to the extent that the development of capitalism *was* involved, ordinary people found their interests threatened in characteristic ways and adopted some common means of responding to those threats.

The answer: Yes, they did. Dijon's seventeenth-century records of "seditions, emotions, and disorders" portray a Dijon in which some issue brought crowds to the streets and into confrontation with authorities every three or four years. Most of the issues involved resistance to the extension of capitalist property relations, to increasing demands of the state, or to both.

Contention in Seventeenth-Century Burgundy

Dijon and Burgundy had come to the French crown with Louis XI's defeat of Charles the Bold, duke of Burgundy, at the end of the fifteenth century. Charles's successors, the Habsburg emperors, continued to press their claims by word and sword. Adjacent to the Habsburg lands of Franche-Comté, Burgundy was a military frontier and a favorite sixteenth-century battleground. After the decline of direct military threat from outside came a division from within; Burgundy ran red with the blood of sixteenth-century Protestant-Catholic wars. After the Wars of Religion, dynastic struggles for control of the duchy blended into the Thirty Years' War. Thereafter popular insurrections continued through the tumultuous time of Lanturelu to the mid-seventeenth-century rebellion of the Fronde.

During the early years of the Fronde, many Burgundian notables sympathized, and even conspired, with the insurgent governor of Burgundy, the prince of Condé; he stood as their bulwark against an ambitious, centralizing monarchy. From 1651 to 1653 Condé's supporters raised an armed rebellion that ended only with the royal siege of Dijon and the conquest of the fort of Bellegarde, at Seurre. The victory of Louis XIV and Mazarin over the *Frondeurs* ended Burgundy's age of war and large-scale rebellion.

The middle of the seventeenth century, then, marks an important transition that shaped popular contention in Burgundy as well as the province's general political history. Before, every popular movement provided an opportunity for some fragment of the ruling classes to press its advantage against the crown. The clientele of one great noble or another often formed the basic units among warriors or rebels. Crowds that moved against royal exactions, such as the crowd led by Anatoire Changenet in 1630, found sympathy or even support among local authorities.

With decisive subordination of local officials to royal power in the later seventeenth century, the chances for implicit or explicit alliance between officials and plebeian rebels greatly diminished. Ordinary people continued to act. But as royal power grew, the chances for cross-class alliances declined. The shift left ordinary people to contend alone in the name of their particular rights and privileges. Local authorities, quelled or co-opted, increasingly treated popular gatherings as dangerous sources of "sedition."

During the seventeenth century, then, the interests, opportunities, organization, and contentious collective action of Burgundy's ordinary people were all changing. Their interests shifted as a warmaking monarchy pressed them increasingly for taxes to support its growing armies and as the bourgeoisie of Dijon increased their domination of the region's land and economic activity. Their opportunities to act on these interests altered, mostly for the worse, as the importance of patronage and the possibility of alliance with regional powerholders declined. Their organization changed as the proportion of landless workers rose and the stratification of rural communities increased. As a result, the contention of ordinary people also changed.

Popular resistance to demands of the state continued in the years after the winegrowers' invasion of Champmoron Wood. In 1690 a royal edict prescribed yet another creation and sale of offices for the profit of the crown. This time there were two offices of *jurés crieurs des obsèques et enterrements:* public registrars of funerals and burials. They sold for 6,000 livres each. In 1691 the new officeholders maneuvered, with some success, to make their purchases profitable. They sought to extend their monopoly to all public announcements, to collect on all phases of funerals—"graves, caskets, and transportation"—to cash in on all burials whether publicly announced or not, and to exact very high prices for their so-called services. Word spread that the funeral fees of the poor would therefore rise prohibitively. A "few poor women" complained that the new registrars had seized the corpses of their children and husbands and held the bodies hostage to the uncollected fees. Menacing crowds formed outside the homes of the registrars. The crowd insulted them and called again for a Lanturelu (AMD B 329; AN G[7] 158).

In 1696 firewood was again the issue, Guillaume Gate once more the site of the crucial confrontation. This time, however, countrymen delivering wood to the city were the chief actors. As the city's indictment described the affair:

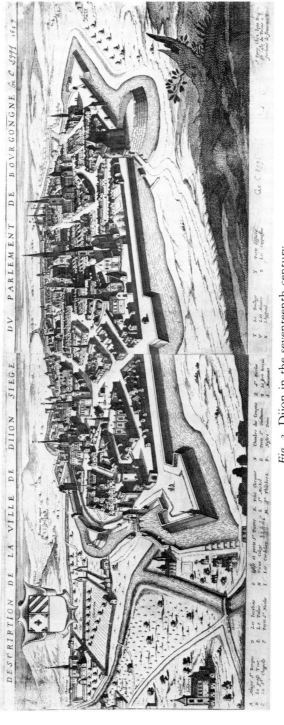

Fig. 3. Dijon in the seventeenth century

EXTRAIT DES REGISTRES
DE PARLEMENT.

 EU la Requéte du Procureur Syndic de Ville de Dijon, à ce qu'atendu que le jour d'hier, depuis les huit
heures du foir jufqu'a dix, plufieurs femmes de Vignerons & Manouvriers s'étoient atroupées, menaffant de
tuer & mettre le feu dans les maifons parce qu'il n'y
avoit que trez peu de blés en ladite Ville, qui ne pou-
voient être fuffifants pour nourrir tous les Habitants, qu'il plut à la
Cour faire défenfes aux Habitans de ladite Ville, hommes, femmes
& enfants de s'atrouper par les rûes de jour & de nuit, ni d'ufer de
menaffes & violences, à peine de la vie contre les contrevenans ; &
ordonner que le prefent Arrét feroit lû, publié & affiché. Conclu-
fions du Procureur General du Roi : LA COUR a fait & fait
trez-expreffes inhibitions & défenfes à tous les Habitans de cette Ville
de Dijon de tous fexes & âges de s'atrouper par les rûes ni en quel-
qu'autre lieu que ce foit de jour ou de nuit, ni d'ufer d'aucune menaffes, violences & paroles tendantes à émotion, à peine de la vie ;
& Ordonne que le prefent Arrét fera lû, publié & affiché aux Car-
refourgs de ladite Ville, à ce qu'aucun n'en prétende caufe d'igno-
rance. Fait en Parlement à Dijon le vingtiéme Août mil fix cents
quatre-vingts-treize. *Signé*, J O L Y : *Collationné*, GRILLOT.

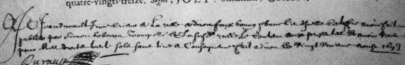

Fig. 4. A seventeenth-century warning against collective action: Edict by the
Dijon parlement, August 1683

On Wednesday 30 May, a number of peasants who had brought wagons of firewood gathered at the Guillaume Gate and made themselves masters of the tollgate there. Having broken the lock with pokers and clubs, they passed through violently, refusing to pay the toll of eight sous that his majesty had ordered paid on each bundle of wood by his edict of last March, which was ratified by the parlement. A few people from the city were at the Guillaume Gate and said things that encouraged the peasants not to pay the toll and incited a popular emotion.   (AMD I 119)

Two people were highly visible and were seized immediately. The first was Estienne Piot, twenty-one-year-old son of a plowman from nearby Fleury; he stood out because he had red hair and was driving a wagon. The second was Andriette Chalet, widow of a carter and day-laborer; she was beating a child's drum, which she claimed had fallen into her hands "by chance." Others jailed in the immediate aftermath included Antoine Vollant (a sedan-chair porter of Dijon), Philippe Fiet (a gardener of the faubourg St.-Pierre), Jean Gilbert (a farmer of Perrigny), Elizabeth Boisselier ("niece and servant" of Dijon's postmaster), François Caupin (likewise the postmaster's servant), Antoinette Devaux (wife of a Dijon tailor), and Pierre Gomeruet (a plowman from Laye). Judging from the arrests, the authorities seem to have been more concerned about their opponents within the city than about the peasants outside.

The parlement, under pressure from intendant Bouchu, issued the following sentences:

> Andriette Chalet to be whipped, branded with the *fleur-de-lis,* fined 100 livres, and banished permanently from the kingdom
> Estienne Piot: sentenced to nine years in the galleys and fined 100 livres
> Pierre Royer (a coachman from Dijon who had escaped): sentenced in absentia to be hanged in effigy, to have all his goods confiscated, and to pay 100 livres

All the others seem to have been freed. The intendant had wanted stiff sentences both to frighten the populace and to show the reluctant parlement that it had to take the enforcement of the king's taxes seriously. Once he had accomplished that, he recommended clemency for Chalet and Piot (AN G^7 159).

As Louis XIV pursued his wars against the Habsburgs, the tax on wood was only one of many new exactions by the crown. In the last years of the century, Burgundy saw rising complaints and resistance against conscription, impressment, billeting, and military foraging amid its pompous *Te Deums* for royal victories at the front. Most of the resistance was small in scale, like the occasion in 1696 on which Captain Hussieu d'Angencourt of the Dauphin regiment put three "recruits" into the royal jail at Sémur for safekeeping until he received authorization to march them off; at his return, the three barricaded themselves in the jail, with the apparent complicity of the jailer, and refused to go until overwhelmed by force (ADCO C 114). In those years, however, new exactions were common, while open resistance to royal demands was rare. The monarchy was gaining strength.

Anticapitalism and Rural Contention

In rural Burgundy the contention of the eighteenth century had a strong anticapitalist orientation. The most frequent and visible expression of popular anticapitalism was the grain seizure: the sort of event authorities and historians called a food riot. From the 1690s to the 1840s, some form of struggle for control of marketed food was no doubt the most common setting for violent conflict above the scale of the barroom brawl in Burgundy, as in the rest of France. In 1693–94 Burgundy experienced numerous instances of the struggle in all three of its major forms: the popular inventory and seizure of grain held in storage by dealers and private parties; the forced sale of grain or bread at a price below the current market; the blockage of grain shipments destined to leave or pass through on their way to other markets.

In 1693–94 the combination of an inferior harvest and the pressure to supply French armies at war in Germany emptied Burgundian markets, drove prices up, and squeezed the poor. In response, authorities of Dijon and other cities, when they could, did the same as so-called rioters: they inventoried and commandeered the grain on hand, blocked shipments, and arranged public sale of food below the market price. The main differences between the action of authorities and that of crowds were two. First, authorities also typically ordered poor people, beggars, and vagabonds who had not acquired the right of residence to leave town. Second, authorities had the legal right and obligation to apply these measures; crowds did not.

For the most part, the "rioters" were either substituting themselves for authorities or forcing authorities to do their duty. Sometimes, however, crowds fought or threatened vengeance. A declaration of Dijon's parlement posted on 20 August 1693 stated that "last night from eight to ten, many wives of winegrowers and laborers gathered together and threatened to kill and to set fire to houses because there is only a small amount of grain in said city, and it cannot be enough to feed all the residents." As usual, the poster went on to forbid "all residents of Dijon, of whatever sex or age, to gather in the streets or any place else by day or night, or to use threats, violence, or inflammatory language, on pain of death" (AMD I 119).

Conflicts over food flourished in the next century. Only sixteen years later, in 1709, came one of the greatest struggles over food in French history. Again the coincidence of a bad harvest and extraordinary demand from armies abroad put acute pressure on local supplies. Again the crisis gave merchants and local officials a hard choice: (1) concede priority to the indigenous poor by commandeering the local stocks and selling them at controlled and subsidized prices, or (2) accede to the higher-priced, and officially backed, demand from outside. In Burgundy the squeeze came from militias under arms in Bugey, Bresse, and Gex; from the armies campaigning in nearby Dauphiné; and from the insatiable market of Lyon. "Hardly had I registered the royal declaration forbidding people to gather and to stop the shipment of grain," reported the attorney general of Dijon's parlement in May 1709, "when a great many people from Lyon came to St.-Jean-de-Losne . . . and bought up all the grain. That could cause a very large disturbance" (AN G^7 1641). As it happened, Burgundy's "disturbances" of 1709 and 1710 remained small and local. Yet the threat continued.

As the eighteenth century wore on, royal policy favored the armies and the national market with increasing zeal and effectiveness. The desire of merchants and officials to favor the local poor wilted obligingly. On 9 May 1770 "a large number of women" seized five wagons of grain that were on their way from Bar-le-Duc to Chalon-sur-Saône via Dijon. The women dragged the wagons to Dijon's central market. The market's manager refused to open the gate—fearing, he said later, that the women might grab other merchandise that was stored inside. The women threatened to break the door down and began to throw paving stones at it; the manager finally gave in. The women, over two thousand strong, dragged in the wagons, then left to find more. When they returned, the manager again refused to open up. Again they threatened, and again he gave in (AMD I 119).

That apparently ended the incident. But five days later, on 14 May, the parlement of Burgundy issued an edict. Like so many other edicts of the period, it forbade anyone "to gather and stop wagons loaded with wheat or other grain, on roads, in cities, towns, or villages, on pain of special prosecution" (ADCO C 81). Blockage of grain expressed the demand of ordinary people that the needs of the community take priority over the requirements of the market. By the same token, it called for restraints on what royal officials were beginning to call "freedom of trade": the right of producer or merchant to sell his grain where it would fetch the highest price.

This act of parlement has an ironic edge. Through much of the century the parlement itself engaged in a rearguard action against the efforts by the king's ministers to "free" the grain trade. In times of shortage such as 1770, the parlement sought to forbid the exportation of grain from the province. The royal intendant in Dijon and the *contrôleur général* in Versailles, on the other hand, strove to see that Burgundian grain would be available to feed Lyon, Paris, and the armies stationed along the eastern frontier. In order to do so, they challenged the doctrine that each locality had a prior right to the food on hand; as a substitute, they promoted the belief that a national market in grain would serve the national weal. Larger merchants were ready to subscribe to this convenient and profitable belief. Thus the crown promoted mercantile capitalism. And thus both the parlement and ordinary people fought the rise of mercantile capitalism.

In the same period the landless poor were increasing in proportion to the general population. As a result, pressure on local communities increased despite a slow rise in agricultural productivity. The eighteenth century's widespread struggles over food replied to that pressure. The structure of the classic grain seizure—commandeering, blocking, and/or selling below market—makes it clear that the action was a means of forcing merchants and officials to favor the locality over armies and the national market.

During the great national subsistence crisis of April 1775, Dijon's Wednesday markets produced repeated small conflicts between bakers and citizens. The contrôleur général, writing from the comfortable distance of Paris, blamed the city's "imprudent searches" of bakers' premises for some of these troubles (AN H^1 187). The largest conflict, at the market of 19 April, broke through the conventional bounds of the grain seizure. Word had spread that Carré, a miller, and Fijan, a counselor at the parlement, had leagued to manipulate the grain market. As Carré was walking down the rue de Bourbon at two in the afternoon,

> he was chased by a considerable number of women, who forced him to take shelter in the house of the prosecutor, Potel . . . [After the mayor arrived with troops to disperse the crowd] a bunch of men joined the women, and the guard was hit so hard with pebbles and cobblestones that it had to withdraw. Immediately Potel's house was forced and sacked. Then the prodigiously enlarged crowd divided into two bands, one of which went to the house of M. Fijan, counselor at the parlement, whom they suspected of being associated with Carré, and the other to

Carré's mill. They sacked and broke everything they found in both places . . . The same bands of desperadoes had the nerve, during the disturbance, to threaten to pillage the headquarters of the military commander, the house of the mayor, and those of all the municipal officers. The common people shouted that they were driven to riot by the high price of grain.   (AMD B 409)

The crowd knew their enemies. Furthermore, their threats were crudely effective. In the conflict of April 1775, the city soon suspended all taxes on grains and flour, as well as imposing controls on bread prices (AMD B 409, 26 April 1775).

The structure of the individual event does not make it clear that the seizure of grain also blocked the advance of mercantile capitalism. Not that people who seized grain put it in those terms; they simply saw that merchants and officials were not doing their duty, that the rights of the poor were being violated, that it was time for the poor to defend themselves. Only in retrospect do we realize that they were attacking the most visible piece of an expanding system, the system of property relations we now call capitalism. In the face of the inexorable advance of capitalism, the grain seizure was at most a minor delay.

The form of struggle over food that grew up in the late seventeenth century nicely illustrates the place of changing interests, opportunities, and organization in alterations of contention. The interest of the local poor (and, to some extent, of their patrons) in local priority over the food supply was growing as the interest of the crown and larger merchants in freeing that supply from the local group increased. The opportunities of the poor were mainly negative; they consisted of official failures to intervene in the local market as local authorities were supposed to. The change in organization in this case is relatively unimportant, although there are some signs that groups such as Dijon's winegrowers were becoming more clearly aware of their distinctive and threatened class position. What is important is the *persistence* of local organization on the basis of which poor people pressed their claims to the food supply. This changing combination of interests, opportunities, and organization produced the grain seizure as naturally as other combinations of interest, opportunity, and organization produced tax rebellions, concerted resistance to conscription, and attacks on enclosing landlords.

The second common form of anticapitalist action was less routine and more puzzling. It was local resistance to landlords' consolidation of lands and of rights in the land. The puzzle lies in our normal readiness to place landlords themselves in the anticapitalist camp. As the great regional histo-

rian Pierre de Saint-Jacob has shown, Burgundian landlords of the period—
including both the "old" nobility and ennobled officials and merchants—
played the capitalist game by seizing forests, usurping common lands, enclosing fields, and insisting on collecting all the use fees to which their
manors gave them claim. Rural people fought back. Suits against landlords
multiplied, a fact that Saint-Jacob interprets as evidence not only of seigneurial aggression but also of increasing peasant liberation from traditional
respect.

Where lawsuits were impossible or ineffective, peasants resisted the seizure of commons by occupying them, resisted enclosures by breaking the
hedges or fences. As Saint-Jacob describes it:

> The wardens of Athie were attacked by the people of Viserny for trying
> to forbid entry to a shepherd. On the lands of Bernard de Fontette,
> Pierre César du Crest, lord of Saint-Aubin, organized an unusual expe-
> dition. He went with 17 men armed with "guns, stakes and staves" to
> break down the enclosures. They led in 40 cattle under the protection of
> two guards "with guns and hunting dogs," and kept the tenants of Ber-
> nard de Fontette from bringing in their cattle. In Charmois, at the urg-
> ing of two women, a band of peasants went to break down a fence set
> up by the overseer of Grenand, who could do nothing but watch and
> receive the jeers of the crowd. In Panthier, a merchant wanted to en-
> close his meadow; he got authorization from the local court. People as-
> sembled in the square and decided to break the hedges, which was done
> that night. They led in horses. The merchant wanted to chase them
> away, but young people who were guarding them stopped him, "saying
> that they were on their own property, in a public meadow, that they had
> broken the enclosures and that they would break them again." (Saint-
> Jacob 1960: 370–371)

Popular opposition did not aim specifically at the landed nobility. It aimed
at the landlords of any order who chewed up the rural community's collective rights. If in Longecourt (1764) it was the lord who demanded his share
of the commons, in Darois two years later the Chapter of Sainte-Chapelle, in
Dijon, tried to take a share of the communal woods. At Villy-le-Brûlé
(1769) it was a farmer-notary who enclosed a meadow, only to see the
ditches filled in by the local people (ADCO C 509, C 543, C 1553).

To the Revolution

Much of the anticapitalist struggle continued into the Revolution of 1789.
Grain seizures in standard eighteenth-century form took on new signifi-

cance in 1789, for now they threatened to overturn the old authorities or to topple the new. Rural people stepped up their efforts to regain their common rights. Attacks on enclosing landlords accelerated. Many of the popular raids on chateaux combined a search for hoarded grain with a bonfire of legal documents the landlord had used to justify his rents, fees, privileges, and demands for services.

In the little village of Sercy, south of Mâcon, the struggle pitted villagers against the local lord, Claude Perroy de la Forestille. Perroy de la Forestille, a master counselor at Burgundy's Chambre des Comptes (a purchased office that conferred nobility), bought the fief in 1787. Ten years before, his predecessor, Viard de Sercy, had wanted to make a clear cut of a major section of his forest in Epinay and to sell the oaks in that part of the forest. No one contested his right to dispose of the oaks, but the village claimed a collective right to gather wood, acorns, and plants in the forest. Through a series of maneuvers, Viard de Sercy and his successor chipped away at that right; the villagers fought back. Their new lord went further: he sought to enclose the forest and exclude the villagers. Similar fights arose over access to the lord's meadows and fields—the lord seeking to turn them into private property, the villagers fighting to retain their rights to pasture and glean.

With the Revolution, the villagers, backed by their parish priest, used control of the municipal government and alliances with revolutionary authorities at higher levels to narrow Perroy de la Forestille's room for maneuver. He, in his turn, made no secret of his hostility to the Revolution. By Germinal of Year II (spring 1794), he was answering for his counterrevolutionary opinions to hearings of revolutionary committees. Arrested and sent to Paris, Perroy appeared before the revolutionary tribunal. He went to the guillotine at the Porte Antoine (the secularized Porte St.-Antoine) on 21 Prairial—9 June 1794 (Rebouillat 1964). The parties had switched sides: the lord had begun by trying to take advantage of opportunities for gain provided by expanding capitalism, and had ended up strongly committed to the privileges of the old regime. The villagers had begun by defending particular rights, and ended up strongly committed to a revolution against privilege.

In this case, the interests of the parties changed little with the Revolution's coming. Nor did their organization alter greatly: the villagers still acted as members of the same village, and the lord still acted as a big landlord, although the presence of local revolutionary committees and a reorganized municipality made some difference in both parties' ability to act. Their respective *opportunities* to act on their interests, on the other hand, shifted enormously: revolutionary legislation against privilege, an increasingly radical government in Paris, and a growing web of revolutionary committees, clubs, and military units gave villagers sources of support they had never before enjoyed.

Elsewhere, local organizational changes brought on by the Revolution played a large part in the reshaping of contention. Consider Dijon in the early Revolution. A national guard report informs us:

> Today, 23 August 1790, on the complaints brought by a number of citizens to the commander of the Volunteers' post at the Logis du Roy around 11:00 P..M. that someone (to the great scandal of right-thinking folk) had just sung, to the accompaniment of several instruments, a romance or complaint containing a funeral ode to the marquis de Favras, outside the home of M. Frantin, a city official. We, Jean-Baptiste Rey, captain of Volunteers commanding said post at the Logis du Roy, thought proper to form immediately a patrol to follow the group of musicians, who, we had been informed, were heading toward the rue du Gouvernement, and therefore led said patrol to that street, where we did in fact find said group of musicians at the hour of midnight, stopped before the door of M. Chartraire, mayor of this city. Among them we recognized, and heard, M. Roche, a lawyer, singing to the accompaniment of a guitar and of several violins in the hands of MM. Propiac, Pasquier, and a number of others unknown to us, the complaint of said Favras, in which we noticed the language of the enemies of the Revolution, in that the author of the complaint in his delirium dares to accuse the Parisian people of madness, and taking a prophetic tone announces that the people will get rid of the new system. Considering that a text of that type, in which one is not ashamed to favor a traitor to the people such as the king's friend, sung at improper times in the most frequented neighborhoods of the city could only have for its object to incite the people to insurrection, and considering that it is urgent to prevent that mishap, we thought it was our duty to report the event to the general staff. (ADCO L 386)

The comrade-in-arms of the commander at the city hall post reported that "a number of citizens of the city of Dijon, following a musical ensemble, passed before the city hall; eight of the riflemen of the post of said city hall, drawn by the melody, followed the line of march, which ended in front of the home of the mayor; there the musicians, seating themselves, sang a complaint or romance that seemed quite improper to the riflemen, in that they heard some words which could upset public order" (ADCO L 386). And that "seditious song" itself? The surviving text includes this verse:

> Since you must have a victim,
> Blind and cruel people,
> Strike. I forgive your crime.
> But fear eternal remorse;
> You will recover from madness;
> And tired of a new system
> You will see my innocence.
> You will cry on my tomb.

The marquis de Favras had helped form a plot to seize the king and spirit him away from the Revolution's grasp. Betrayed by his fellow conspirators, Favras was hanged in the Place de Grève, in Paris, on 19 February 1790. A more counterrevolutionary hero would be hard to find. Confronted with such evidence of subversive activity, the national guard's general staff leap-frogged the city council to report on the incident directly to the department's administration; among the nocturnal singers, it appears, were some members of the city council itself.

The counterrevolutionary musicale connected with a whole series of demonstrations of opposition to the leaders and the symbols of the revolutionary movement in Dijon. There is, for example, that group of forty-odd citizens who "struck down the national cockade" (that is, their red, white, and blue ribbons) in November and "provoked all the citizens" at the Café Richard (ADCO L 386). There is the group of customers at the Old Monastery cabaret who, two days later, insisted that three young men take off their national cockades before being served (ADCO L 386). At that time the national guard, municipal guardian not only of public safety but also of revolutionary sentiment, was campaigning for the obligatory wearing of the cockade. (The city council, at its meeting of 8 November 1790, declared the request that its members wear the cockade on their chests "illegal and harassing": AMD 1 D.)

We should not conclude from these little run-ins, however, that Dijon was simply a counterrevolutionary haven. The capital of Burgundy had undergone a local revolution in 1789. On 15 July, before the news of the taking of the Bastille in Paris the previous day had reached Dijon:

> the tocsin sounded in St.-Philibert, the most populous parish, the parish of the winegrowers ... At once the people assembled and armed themselves. The youth of the city, who seem already to have had a rudimentary organization, lined up behind fiery leaders such as Basire, a clerk at the provincial Estates, and the lawyer Viardot. The military commander, M. de Gouvernet, tried to calm people down and restore order. But he

was powerless: He had no troops at hand ... Gouvernet was insulted, called on to turn over the weapons in the military depot, and brought back to his townhouse, where a guard of thirty men was given him, less to protect him than to keep him from fleeing; he was a prisoner. Meanwhile the people seized the St.-Nicolas Tower, the castle, and all the ammunition they contained. A general staff formed, with Viardot at its head. They laid the foundation for a municipal militia. Nobles and priests (in a move that does not seem to have occurred anywhere else) were required to stay in their homes. Although it is impossible to tell exactly when he left, the intendant fled. Nothing remained of the local authorities. The entire city was in the hands of the triumphant Third Estate. (Millot 1925: 41–42)

An impeccably bourgeois revolutionary committee, with strong support from the city's workers, seized power from a council that was closely attached to the parlement, and therefore to old-regime institutions. All that paralleled municipal revolutions in many other parts of France.

A conservative municipality came to office in the elections of January 1790. It faced an active Patriotic Club speaking for the national guard's leaders and for the revolutionary committee of 1789. Other events displayed the revolutionary spirit in Dijon: popular gatherings of April 1790 against the so-called Amis de la Paix, a reactionary club; similar street meetings against the Fifth Section of the Amis de la Constitution in December 1790; workers' gatherings around the municipal offices at the opening of a work-relief program in March 1791; crowds in April 1791 that "formed in front of the churches of la Madeleine and la Visitation and went through the city to tear down coats of arms, pillars, and ornaments attached to private houses and public buildings" (AMD 1 D; see also ADCO L 444); the crowd of May 1791 that paraded a dummy of the Pope, then burned it ceremoniously at the Place Morimont. As late as Fructidor Year III, crowds in Dijon were crying "Long live the Mountain! Long live the Jacobins!"—which by that time had become "seditious cries" (ADCO L 387).

Yet conservative forces had not disappeared. In December 1792 angry gatherings had opposed the seminary's closing. During the intensification of the Terror in December 1793, people of Dijon had taken to the streets to demand the release from jail of Chartraire, the conservative mayor who had been elected in January 1790. The "sedition" began with complaints over high prices at the market, where some of the people present began to abuse the new mayor, who had come to calm things down. Then the crowd "went to the Conciergerie, where they called for Chartraire. On the refusal of the jailer to deliver him without an order, they forced the department to give

the order. Chartraire was released and carried in triumph. But the municipality called out its armed force, dispersed the rebels, and arrested many of
them. They were locked up in the same prison as Chartraire, who was also
put back in jail" (AMD 1 D). In short, Dijon was a divided city, like many
other French cities of its time. Rather than flowing from a unanimous desire of the French people, the Revolution emerged from ferocious struggles
in place after place. Their form, their combatants, and their results varied
with local social structure. The revolution that occurred in Paris during July
1789 started a vast effort to centralize political power, opened up great opportunities for organized segments of the bourgeoisie, stirred an unprecedented popular mobilization, and encouraged a politicization of all sorts of
conflicts. But the ramifications of the Revolution outside Paris posed particular problems in each locality, depending on existing interests and organization.

In the Loire, for example, the fundamental cleavage that led to the department's participation in the anti-Jacobin Federalist revolt separated two
well-defined groups: the Montagnards, composed largely of workers and a
bourgeois fragment, and a moderate majority coalition led mainly by the region's landholders (Lucas 1973). In Champagne, judicial officers of Troyes
who retained local power into the early Revolution faced the opposition of
a broad popular coalition, while at Reims a common hostility to the great
local power of the Church united bourgeoisie and workers in support of the
Revolution (Hunt 1976a, 1976b, 1978). In the Vendée, a compact nucleus
of merchants and manufacturers faced a formidable coalition of nobles,
priests, peasants, and rural workers (Mitchell 1968). In Burgundy, the
bourgeoisie fought at once against the resistance of the parlement's adher-
ents and against the relatively radical demands of winegrowers.

From these alignments, diverse though they were, developed deep,
common consequences: several years of intense political participation by the
general population; a long-term decline in the influence (and especially the
official position) of priests and nobles; a rise in the political significance of
the regional bourgeoisie; the promotion of conditions favoring capitalist
property and production; a sharpening awareness of connections between
local conflicts and national power struggles; and a concentration of power
in a growing, increasingly centralized state. In Dijon's serenade of 1790 we
hear a small reaction to a very large transformation.

Although the serenade was clearly part of the revolutionary struggle, it
was just as clearly a piece of the preceding centuries. We have already noticed the importance of song to the public displays of sentiment in the Lanturelu. We have not yet examined the widespread form of action that the

1790 night music most closely resembled. It is the *charivari*—often corrupted into "shivaree" in American English, and often called "rough music" in England.

Charivaris and Serenades

The charivari deserves special attention because it illustrates the displacement of an established form of collective action from its home territory to new ground; during the first half of the nineteenth century French people often used the charivari and related routines to state positions on national politics. The innovation endured until more powerful forms such as the demonstration and the public meeting made it obsolete.

The basic action of the charivari runs like this: assemble in the street outside a house; make a racket with songs, shouts, and improvised instruments such as saucepans and washtubs; require a payoff from the people inside the house; then leave if and when the people pay. The words and action are mocking, often obscene. They describe and condemn the misdeeds of the house's residents. In its essential form, the eighteenth-century charivari was the work of a well-defined group that bore some special responsibility for moral rules that the targets of the action had violated.

The best-known, and probably most widespread, examples concerned familial, sexual, and marital morality. One standard case was the noisy public criticism of an old widower who married a young woman. In such a case the makers of the charivari were ordinarily young, unmarried men of the community. Often they were members of a defined, exclusive association: the youth abbey or its equivalent. In the case of moral offenses, the payoff required was not always a simple gift or round of drinks. Sometimes the serenaders demanded the departure from the community of the tainted individual or couple. Sometimes the victims of a charivari actually left town.

Like most other regions of Europe, Burgundy had its own version of the charivari, linked to a complex of local institutions. In Burgundian villages the "bachelors' guilds" (*compagnies de garçons*) included all the unmarried males age twenty or older. The local bachelors' guild required a cash payment from young men when they reached the minimum age, kept an eye on their love affairs, and even told them which girls they had a right to court; it also defended the village maidens from the attentions of men outside the guild. The bachelors' guild collected a substantial payment, in cash or in the form of a festival, from the young men who married, and especially from outsiders and otherwise unsuitable men who dared to marry women from the locality. This last category of marriages provided a common incentive for charivaris and brawls.

In Burgundy the same bachelors' guild often had responsibility for public bonfires in Lent and at other sacred moments of the year. It typically gathered wood for that purpose and had the right to collect a contribution from each household in compensation for its efforts. At the local scale, it was thus a significant institution that provided services, bound the young people together, and exercised genuine social control. The charivari, for all its apparent quaintness and triviality, had profound roots in the regional culture.

Under the old regime, local authorities had generally tolerated charivaris but watched them closely to make sure they did not get out of hand. In 1655, for example, the parlement of Burgundy had declared that

> François Buvée, Sebastian Theilley, clerics currently in jail; Pierre Léger, Louis Vachet, Louis Quarré, and the lackey of Mr. Dordaud, fugitives from justice; Pierre Guyot, Guillaume des Varennes, Nicolas Buisson, Charles Brun, and Gaspard Malgrat, all accused of insults, violence, and other actions at night while armed, charivaris and popular emotions in front of the house of the apothecary Petit, breaking into his shop, wounding his person, excesses and outrages to the person of his wife, and atrocious calumnies against the honor of the household of Master Nicolas, the prosecutor, and Anne Jazu, his wife. The court sentences Léger, Vacher [*sic*], Quarré, and the lackey to banishment from Burgundy and 60 livres fine. It sentences Buvée and Thalley [*sic*] to 30 livres fine, the others to 20 livres, and all of them to 600 livres damages and interest for M. Petit. (AMD I 106)

Other sentences of the same nature punctuated the century before the Revolution. For example, at the end of April 1757 Dijon's city council sat as a court and tried "Marie Baland, servant of widow Dumont; the servant of Lanoix the panemaker; the servant of Tillier the tailor, Tillier's son; Françoise Gueland; Bénigne and Charlotte Gendarme and the servant of Durand the engraver for having caused a disorder by means of the charivari they conducted outside the house of Sieur Cageot, prosecutor at the Bailliage, on Monday the twenty-fifth." (Servants were mainly young, almost by definition unmarried, and therefore likely participants in charivaris.) Baland and Lanoix's servant were sentenced to indefinite jail terms and fined twenty livres, for which they were jointly liable (AMD B 391). In the well-documented cases of 1655 and 1757, the celebrants had the nerve to give charivaris to government prosecutors. That was a good way to get yourself prosecuted. A great many more charivaris must have passed without attracting much attention from the authorities, and therefore without leaving much trace in the official records.

During the Revolution, use of the charivari seems to have declined; at least the papers that have survived from that time barely mention it. Perhaps the revolutionary authorities paid less attention to this ostensibly apolitical form of action, or people shifted their energies to other forms of contention. In any case, the charivari survived the Revolution unimpaired. Under the July Monarchy (1830–1848), reports on charivaris jammed Dijon's police files. In July 1834, for example, "on the twenty-second instant, toward nine at night, some youngsters gave a charivari to the newlyweds—Baudry, a tailor, and Mlle. Ody—who did not give a ball; that fact occasioned a rather large gathering on the rue St.-Nicolas but did not produce any disorder, and the *charivariseurs* fled at the sight of the gendarmes" (ADCO 8 M 29). The charivari's being considered police business was not entirely new, since even in the seventeenth century the municipal police intervened when a charivari was too raucous, too long, or too close to the seats of power. The intervention of police in a nonviolent charivari nevertheless shows the opening of a breach between bourgeois law and the law of popular custom.

Under the July Monarchy the charivari also came into use for explicitly political purposes. A police report from 8 September 1833 states that

> yesterday evening the seventh instant, toward nine o'clock, a charivari took place outside the Hôtel du Parc on the occasion of the stopping in this city of a deputy named M. Delachaume, coming from Paris on his way to Chalon-sur-Saône, whither he went at four o'clock this morning. The charivari lasted only a few moments. It began on the rue des Bons Enfans, where the organizers, known to be republicans, assumed that M. Delachaume was having supper with one of his friends. But having learned differently, they went to the Hôtel du Parc, where a crowd of more than 300 persons gathered at the racket they made. The noise soon stopped at the request of one of them, a certain Garrot, known to be a fiery republican. He raised various cries: "A bas le rogneur de budget, le con de député," etc., and other indecent words we could not make out. After those cries they left, along with the people whom the scandalous spectacle had attracted. With M. Garrot at the head of all these young people, most of them workers and disguised some in work clothes and others in straw hats, the group scattered and later gathered at the Republican Club located at the Place d'Armes over the Thousand Columns Café. (ADCO 8 M 29)

A charivari? Certainly a transplanted one. The event retains some traditional features but aims at a political enemy and operates under the guidance of a republican club with its headquarters a private room in a café. Those are nineteenth-century stigmata. Nevertheless, to the expert eyes of Dijon's captain of gendarmes, it is a charivari.

Another police report ten days later likewise sheds a revealing light on the charivari's nineteenth-century form: "On the evening of the eighteenth, it was said that a serenade would be given to M. Petit, deputy royal prosecutor, who had just resigned on refusing to make a search that took place at the offices of the *Patriot,* and also that a charivari would be given to the royal prosecutor, who ordered that search. The gendarme patrol was therefore sent to the homes of M. Petit and the royal prosecutor, but no disorder was seen" (ADCO 8 M 29). This juxtaposition of the serenade and the charivari reveals another significant feature of these means of action: the existence of gradations of the performance, running from very negative to very positive. One could organize a friendly charivari: a serenade. Both types, unlike the demonstrations that proliferated later in the century, ordinarily took place at night and at the residence, not the workplace, of their targets. When the deputy-philosopher Etienne Cabet arrived in Dijon in November 1833, "many young people" immediately gave him a serenade. During the festivities the innkeeper Mortureux was arrested for "seditious cries"; he had shouted "Long Live the Republic!" (ADCO 8 M 29).

For another twenty years the charivari continued to fill the police dossiers of Dijon—and, for that matter, of other French cities. After the Revolution of 1848 its irrevocable decline began. The dossiers of the Third Republic contain plenty of actions of workers and peasants that attract police attention, but almost no trace of that once-flourishing ritual, in either its moral or its political form. The charivari was a form of action that the ordinary people of the old regime often put to use, a form that adapted to different circumstances and to broad social changes, an essential element of the old collective-action repertoire. Yet the charivari went into retirement in the age of unions, associations, and political parties.

The existence of that range of application for a musical sanction raises an interesting series of problems. First, there is the paradoxical combination of ritual and flexibility. As in every well-defined, familiar game, the players know how to modify, improvise, elaborate, even innovate while respecting the ground rules. From the Revolution on, the players extend the charivari from its moral base into the world of national politics. The charivari is an established means of collective contention, parallel in that regard to demonstrating, petitioning, striking, and voting. Like every other means of collective action, the charivari has its own applications and a specific history. But at a given point in time it belongs to the familiar repertoire of collective actions that are at the disposition of ordinary people. The repertoire evolves in two different ways: big structural changes reshape the means of collective action that are available to people, as people themselves refashion each individual means of action in response to new interests and new opportunities. In Burgundy's cities we see both processes at work.

Changing Repertoires

Burgundy's rural areas likewise saw important alterations in their forms of contention, coupled with some persistence of earlier forms, from the eighteenth century to the nineteenth. Grain seizures survived until the middle of the nineteenth century. In April 1829, for example, a crowd in Châtillon forced M. Beaudoin, operator of a flour mill, to sell his wheat at 5 francs 25 centimes per double bushel, when he had posted the price at 5 francs 30 centimes (ADCO M 8 II 4). At the next market, several brigades of gendarmes were on hand to prevent such "disorders" (ADCO 8 M 27).

Although seizures of grain continued to flourish, postrevolutionary struggles bore hardly a trace of resistance against landlords. Instead they concerned the policies, and especially the fiscal policies, of the state. The active groups of the nineteenth century came especially from the small landholders and the workers of the commercialized, fully capitalist vineyards. Just after the Revolution of 1830:

> in September, the announcement of the resumption of the inventory of wine on the premises of winegrowers started turbulent demonstrations, near-riots, in Beaune. On 12 September at the time of the national guard review "cries of anger against the Revenue Administration [la Régie] rose from its very ranks." Told that the residents of the suburbs planned to go to the tax offices in order to burn the registers as they had in 1814, the mayor thought it prudent that evening to call the artillery company to arms and convoke part of the national guard for 5 the next morning. On the 13th, toward 8 A.M., "a huge crowd of winegrowers and workers," shouting "down with the wolves," "down with excise taxes," occupied the city hall square. To calm the demonstrators the mayor had to send the national guard home at once. "The crowd then dispersed gradually." (Laurent 1957: I, 484–485)

Despite that peaceful dispersion, the authorities had to delay the inventory of wine. In Meursault it was less peaceful: winegrowers actually drove out the tax men.

Resistance to taxation persisted after 1830, as it did in the immediate aftermath of every French revolution. In Beaune on 3 September 1831 a gathering formed outside the excise offices, "and soon a pile of papers and registers was set on fire." The group then went to another tax office in the city, but the mayor and the subprefect talked them out of their incendiary plans (*Journal Politique et Littéraire de la Côte d'Or* 7 September 1831: 2). In Burgundy, none of the July Monarchy's movements against taxes went beyond that standard routine. Yet winegrowers' resistance to taxation was a major theme of rural contention in Burgundy throughout the nineteenth century. It was a major component of Burgundy's conflicts during the Revolution of 1848.

What is more, the antitax movement connected directly to national political movements. The winegrowing area stood out for its republicanism, especially the hinterlands of Dijon and Beaune. In fact we have already had a foretaste of the Burgundian flavor. The search of newspaper offices that incited the serenade and the charivari of September 1833 concerned the *Patriote de la Côte d'Or*. That newspaper was being prosecuted for promoting resistance to tax collection. Etienne Cabet, deputy of the vineyard region, took up the newspaper's defense. And during the Cabetian serenade of November 1833 described earlier, people shouted not only "Long live the Republic!" but also "Down with excise taxes!"

All things considered, there was a significant transformation of Burgundy's repertoire of contention. To be sure, the early nineteenth century showed important continuities with the old regime: survival of the charivari, the grain seizure, the classic antitax rebellion; persistent orientation to the protection of local interests against the claims of the state and the market rather than to the creation of a better future. Yet the forms of action themselves altered and adapted to new conditions; there was, among other things, a partial politicization of all forms of contention. New forms of contention arose; most notably, the demonstration and the strike came into their own as established ways of pressing contested interests. The hundred years spanning the Revolution marked a period of transformation and of growth in the means of contention.

The evolution of contention, however, did not end in 1850. Although the Dijon winegrowers' demonstrations of the 1830s certainly displayed many more familiar features than the Lanturelus of the 1630s, they also showed their age. Nowadays, the successors of those winegrowers typically assemble outside the departmental capital, grouped around placards and banners identifying their organizations and summarizing their demands. The vintage charivari and grain seizure have vanished, along with a number of other forms of action that persisted into the nineteenth century. Today's large-scale actions are even more heavily concentrated in Dijon, Beaune, and other cities than they were in the 1830s. Labor unions and political parties often appear in the action. Although prices and taxes continue to be frequent causes for complaint, such exotic issues as American warmaking in Vietnam and the future of students in sports and physical education animate many a crowd. As the world has changed, so have its forms of contention.

A Twentieth-Century Repertoire

With the Revolution, and especially with the building of a national police apparatus under Napoleon, three important changes occurred. First, the surveillance, control, and repression of popular collective action became the business of the national government's specialized local representatives: police, prosecutors, spies, and others. Second, the procedures of surveillance, control, and repression, bureaucratized and routinized, became objects of regular reporting and inspection. Third, *anticipatory* surveillance increased greatly: authorities watched groups carefully to see what collective action they might take in the future, and to be ready for it.

The papers of Dijon's regional police inspector (*commissaire de police*) from 1914 to 1922 illustrate all these points. On the whole they are much less exotic, to twentieth-century eyes, than their old-regime predecessors. In contrast to the cramped handwritten minutes and elegantly penned proclamations of the seventeenth century, these twentieth-century dossiers contain many typewritten reports, some telegrams, occasional notes of telephone conversations, scattered newspaper clippings, and a few standard printed forms. As archaeological specimens, they clearly belong to our own era.

Those are only their most superficial ties to the twentieth century. The police dossiers provide clear traces of great events: World War I manifests itself in the antiwar demonstrations of 1914 and in the ceremonies, on 4 July 1918, renaming the Place du Peuple the Place du Président Wilson. The Russian Revolution shows up in the form of "Bolshevist propaganda" spread by the detachment of 220 Russian soldiers in Dijon and by a few Russian civilians in the city. The national split of the labor movement into Communist and Socialist branches leaves its mark in the 1922 fractionation of the departmental labor federation. Major events of political history have immediate counterparts in the stream of contention gauged by the local police. Reports of 28 July 1914 convey a familiar tone:

> This evening toward six, a group of about a hundred workers, composed
> mainly of Spaniards and Italians and also of young people from the city
> age sixteen to eighteen, almost all of them workers at the Petit Bernard
> glassworks, formed spontaneously into a parade at the Place du Peuple
> and, passing through Chabot Charny and Liberté streets, went to the
> Place Darcy, shouting "Down with war! We want peace!" Because the
> demonstration was growing from moment to moment and because it
> seemed to be of a kind that would produce disorder in the streets and
> agitate popular feeling, I immediately took the necessary measures to
> stop the demonstration and, with the aid of a number of the available
> police, I managed to disperse the demonstrators at the Place Darcy and
> on the boulevard de Sévigné, and by 7:20 calm had returned.

The inspector's helpers had picked up the group's marching orders. They
read: "Calm. Don't resist the police, disperse. In case of breakup, reform at
the corner of *Le Miroir*. If broken up again, reform in front of *Le Progrès*,
then in front of *Le Bien Public*. No shouts, no singing. In front of *Le
Progrès*, only one shout: Vive la paix!" (ADCO SM 3530).

To anyone who has taken part in twentieth-century demonstrations,
both sides of the story are drearily familiar. Despite his allusion to "sponta-
neity," Dijon's police inspector recognizes the event as an unauthorized
demonstration and takes the standard steps to check it. The glassworkers,
on their side, anticipate the police reaction and make contingency plans;
what is more, they try to make sure that sympathetic newspapers will carry
word of their action. The players know their stage directions, although the
script leaves plenty of room for improvisation, and no one is sure how it
will end. The demonstrators want to assemble as many people as possible in
a visible and symbolically significant public place. They want to display
their common devotion to a single well-defined program. The event shares
some properties with the Lanturelu of 1630, the serenade of 1790, the political charivari of 1833. It bears a much greater resemblance to the winegrowers' tax protest of 1830. It is a full-fledged demonstration, a variety of
contention that germinated in the nineteenth century and flowered in the
twentieth.

By Bastille Day 1921 the themes of peace and internationalism had regained prominence after dissolving in World War I. On the morning of
that holiday Dijon's "communist socialists" organized a march to the city's
cemetery. One hundred fifty to two hundred people (including some
twenty women) gathered at the Place du Président Wilson. Young people
distributed handbills as they paraded. At the head of the procession came

three dignitaries from the labor exchange, the editor of the socialist newspaper, a former deputy, and a departmental council member. "Next came twenty children carrying flowers and three red flags representing the A.R.A.C. [the Association Républicaine des Anciens Combattants, a Communist-affiliated veterans' group], the union federation, and the socialist party, then six signs saying WAR AGAINST WAR, WE HATE HATRED, AMNESTY, HANDS ACROSS THE BORDER, THOU SHALT NOT KILL (JESUS), THEY HAVE CLAIMS ON US (CLEMENCEAU)." Leaders of the movement gave speeches at the 1870–71 war monument, and members of the crowd ceremoniously laid out three bouquets—one each for the French, Italian, and German dead. "The banners were folded up," the inspector reported, "and the crowd left the cemetery without incident at 11:30 A.M." (ADCO SM 3530).

In the midst of this series of reports come periodic appraisals of local "public spirit." *Esprit public* refers specifically to the likely intensity and direction of contentious collective action by different parts of the population. "Good" public spirit is one that will make little trouble for the authorities, "bad" public spirit a threat of widespread contention. The job of the spies, informers, and observers employed by the police is to gauge and document those likelihoods. In 1918 the inspector reported to the public prosecutor that

> the world of factory and shop workers is complaining about the cost of living but has not been too hard hit so far by the new controls. In any case, they are willing to do their part ... The three groups of railroad workers (trains, roadbed, and operations) are holding secret meetings and talking about occupational questions; they expect a follow-through on the promises made to them; this looks to me like a sore point that could bring on some agitation in the future if they don't receive satisfaction. In my opinion it would be a good idea to resolve the question of special compensation as soon as possible. (ADCO SM 3530)

Nothing unusual about all this. That is the point: by 1918, a police force routinely scans the world of workers, students, and political activists for any sign of "agitation," any predictors of concerted action. That same police force has developed standard procedures for monitoring, containing, and, on occasion, breaking up meetings, demonstrations, and strikes when they do occur. Its business is repression.

Compared with those of the nineteenth century, these twentieth-century actions are large in scale, strongly tied to formal organizations pursuing defined public programs, closely monitored by the police. Their variety and color appear to have diminished: the charivari and its companion forms of street theater, for example, have disappeared from the popular repertoire without replacement. Popular contention has channeled itself into meetings, strikes, demonstrations, and a few related types of gathering. These recent changes have all continued trends that were clearly visible by the middle of the nineteenth century. The same sorts of changes of interest, organization, and opportunity that we have seen occurring in the nineteenth century have continued in the twentieth: increasing state control of essential decisions and resources, the expanding importance of special-interest associations, a growing range of governmental surveillance, and so on. In the perspective of the last three or four centuries, the period since the Revolution of 1848 is definitely of a piece.

Long-Run Changes in Contention

Burgundy's chronology of contention has some surprises in it. We commonly think of great revolutions as points of major historical transition and expect most aspects of life to be quite different before and after. Surely that expectation should apply to the form and content of collective contention. With the French Revolution of 1789 to 1799, we do discover a considerable alteration in the parties to contention, and some alteration in their objectives. During the early years of the Revolution there was a burst of innovation in collective action; in retrospect, the meetings and marches of those years seem to anticipate the late nineteenth century. Yet the innovation ceased rapidly, and the new forms disappeared. All in all, the forms of contention—the repertoire of means available for acting on contested interests, grievances, and aspirations—show impressive continuities from the eighteenth to the nineteenth century.

In that regard, the less momentous Revolution of 1848 marked a greater point of transition; it practically eradicated older forms of contention such as the grain seizure and the tax rebellion, while greatly accelerating the use of such means as the meeting, the demonstration, and the strike. To find a comparable transition, we must look back to the mid-seventeenth century, the period of the Fronde. Then, as in the nineteenth century, a great expansion and centralization of state power altered the character of contention for a wide range of interests.

In Burgundy, as elsewhere, the transition showed up first and most visibly as a series of rebellions against new and increased taxation. The Lanturelu of 1630 is a case in point. From that time on, Burgundy and most of the rest of France moved into two centuries of intermittent popular resistance to the expansion of state power and to the growth of capitalist property relations. Anticonscription movements, grain seizures, invasions of fields, and further tax rebellions stated that popular resistance.

People had fought taxes and military service long before 1650. Nevertheless the mid-seventeenth century served as a hinge in the history of contention. Before that point, local authorities and regional magnates often made themselves available as allies; in popular rebellion they saw the means of retaining their liberties or expanding their power. The great rebellions of the seventeenth century all built on the complicity or active support of local authorities and regional magnates. Largely for that reason, they sometimes united virtually the entire population of a city or a region against the crown.

Starting with the repression of the Fronde, Louis XIV and his ministers managed to check, co-opt, replace, or liquidate most of their regional rivals. After swelling in the seventeenth century, with considerable support from authorities and magnates, popular resistance continued on its own for two centuries more. It changed form as interests, organization, and opportunities shifted. Grain seizures, for example, increased persistently at the end of the seventeenth century, as the pressure on communities to surrender local grain reserves to demands of the national market increased, and as that pressure gained the support of royal officials. Rural efforts to defend communal rights of gleaning and pasturage rose and fell against the efforts of landlords to consolidate their holdings and make their property claims exclusive. This sort of resistance to claims of the state and demands of capitalism continued unabated into the nineteenth century.

The nineteenth-century transition brought a great decline in the two-century-old resistance to statemaking and capitalism. Although the mobilization and politicization of the 1789 Revolution anticipated some of its effects, the Revolution of 1848 marked—and helped produce—a major swing away from the defense of local interests against expansion of the state and of capitalism, toward popular efforts to organize around interests on a relatively large scale and to seize some control over the state and over the means of production. Witness the virtual disappearance of the grain seizure and the old style of tax rebellion, the flourishing of the strike, of the demonstration, and of the public meeting as means of contention. In our own time, the great movement of students and workers in May–June 1968 and the intermittent protests of Bretons and other cultural minorities have provided glimpses of further possible alterations in the pattern of contention in France. But the Burgundy and France of the 1980s have continued to act within a framework that had become clearly visible in the middle of the nineteenth century.

3

France over
Four Centuries

A SUBWAY RIDER elbows his way out of the blue, rubber-tired train at the Hôtel de Ville station. He climbs the littered stairs, blinks his way into the sunshine and exhaust fumes of a summer noon, and stands at the edge of a square half again as large as a football field. Taxis, buses, trucks, and motorcycles swirl around the oblong flower beds in mid-square, turning in from the Quai de Gesvres, which borders the Seine just to the south of the square, speeding west along the rue de Rivoli at the top of the square, or heading down toward the river from the rue du Renard. Many of the vehicles are tour buses—German, English, Belgian, Dutch, Italian, sometimes provincial French—which stop momentarily while their occupants gawk out the windows. They have plenty to see.

Our pedestrian stations himself on the curb of the rue de Rivoli, facing south toward the river. An unceasing stream of shoppers, salespeople, and lunchtime strollers threatens to bump him off the sidewalk into the path of the fast-moving traffic. The strollers are passing between our observer and a large block of cafés and shops. Many of them are coming to or from the Bazar de l'Hôtel de Ville, the big department store just up the street to his left. In that direction, our traveler notices rows of offices, shops, and cafés lining the rue de Rivoli up to the point where it melts into the rue St.-Antoine; farther east, out of sight, he knows, the road leads past the Place des Vosges and then to the Place de la Bastille. Over the rooftops of the rue St.-Antoine, in fact, he catches sight of the winged figures atop the Bastille column.

Straight ahead, beyond the river and over the tops of six-story buildings on the Ile de la Cité, our spectator sees the towers of Notre Dame. If he turns to his right, he can look up the broad avenue, past the Tour St.-Jacques, toward the Louvre. He has only to walk thirty steps in that direction, stop at the corner of the rue du Renard, turn his back on the square, look north, and he will see the garish blue, red, and green surfaces of the Centre Georges Pompidou. The huge exposition center is roughly the same 500 meters north that Notre Dame is south, the streets from one to the other balancing on the rue de Rivoli like a crooked teeter-totter.

A Place in Paris

Here at the square, the Pont d'Arcole and the stone walls of the riverbank occupy the far side. On the right sit two large blocks of office buildings, separated by a tree-shaded street. And on the left, to the east, looms the ornate mass of the Hôtel de Ville—the Paris city hall. If it is a day of ceremony, the great building is decked with bunting, movable barriers stand ready for use, and a dozen policemen wait in clusters before the city hall's doorways. The traveler senses at once that the Place de l'Hôtel de Ville is a center of communication, ceremony, and command.

Habitués of Paris can fix our subway rider's view of the Place quite precisely in time: no earlier than 1977, when the Centre Pompidou opened its doors. No later than 1980, when Mayor Jacques Chirac of Paris succeeded in banning motor vehicles from most of the square, and in starting the construction of a spacious pedestrian mall. Thus the Place de l'Hôtel de Ville began one more transformation—this one a return to the pedestrian traffic that had prevailed over most of its history.

For the better part of its existence, the square was much smaller and went by another name. The Place de Grève, Parisians called it. The name came from the beach (*grève*) that was until the nineteenth century the chief port of entry for the city's waterborne food supply. The name has its own history: the French word for strike (likewise *grève*) may derive from the action of workers, who ordinarily showed up in the morning at the Place de Grève for hiring. They gathered in bands near the river when there was too little work or when the offered price was too low. To stand apart from work was therefore to *faire la grève*; strikers became *grévistes*. At least so the story goes.

During the Revolution the square was rebaptized Place de la Maison Commune, to match the city hall's revolutionary title. That name never really stuck; it remained Place de Grève. In 1802 the old label officially gave

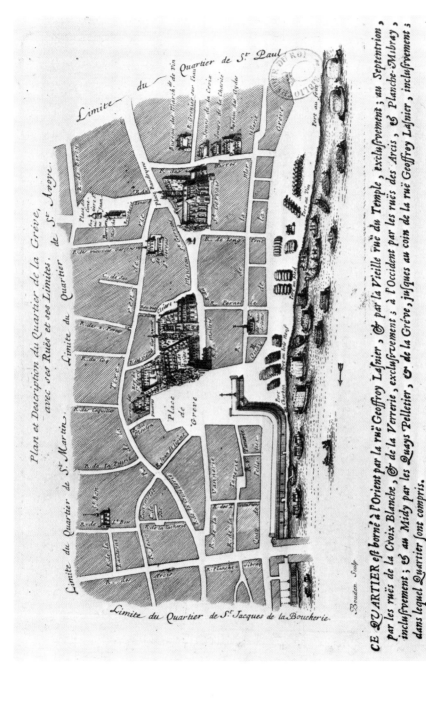

Fig. 5. The neighborhood of the Place de Grève in the seventeenth century

Fig. 6. Aerial perspective of Paris in the seventeenth century

way to Place de l'Hôtel de Ville. Half a century passed before the new name began to catch on. In the 1850s, the old streets and houses that had covered three-quarters of the area vanished to realize the grand designs of Louis Napoleon's planner-prefect Georges Eugène Haussmann. From then on, the city hall faced an oversized, traffic-laden public square. The Place de Grève had disappeared.

The Hôtel de Ville itself served for centuries as the seat of the city's closest equivalent to a mayor and council: the *prévôt des marchands* and the échevins. As their names imply, they were simultaneously the executive officers of the merchant community and the chief persons responsible for the day-to-day policing and maintenance of the city. This overlap of mercantile organization and city government did not distinguish Paris from hundreds of other European trading centers; in those cities, the merchants usually ran things. The distinction of Paris—aside from its sheer size and influence—lay in the coexistence of the merchants with the chief agents of a powerful, expanding kingdom and with the dignitaries of a wealthy church. In the city, that church operated great sanctuaries, large monasteries, and a world-famous university. The city's geography gave a rough representation of the division: royal institutions concentrated on the Ile de la Cité and the western part of the Right Bank, church and university especially prominent on the Left Bank and on one corner of the Cité, mercantile and municipal institutions grouped on the central and eastern sections of the Right Bank. The Grève came as close as any spot in Paris to forming the junction of royal, ecclesiastical, mercantile, and municipal activity.

This combination of commerce, administration, and intellectual activity made seventeenth-century Paris one of the dominant cities of Europe. It also made Paris a big, sprawling place for its time. A seventeenth-century booster, closing a building-by-building inventory of the entire city, summed it up this way:

> In the city and faubourgs of Paris there are 656 streets; 190 churches and convents; 12 hospitals; 42 noble residences; 4 palaces; 38 colleges; 11 bridges, including the boat-bridge of the Isle Louviers; 23, 223 houses, not including those in back off the street; 92,892 inhabitants on the basis of only 4 persons for each house, and on the basis of 10 persons capable of bearing arms for each residence, house, academy, college, inn, and religious community, 232,230 persons; 45 public fountains; a water tower; pumps at the Pont Notre-Dame and at the Pont-Neuf, whose water fed into the city and faubourgs by lead pipes containing 11,640 *toises* [a toise, or fathom, was about six feet] runs into and through the streets of the city and faubourgs via both open and covered sewers ex-

tending over a distance of 6,600 toises. (BN Fr 22388: "Estat et
Répartition de la Ville de Paris," vol. 2, 1684)

The statistical intoxication is no doubt forgivable in an author who has just
finished enumerating every one of those 23,000 houses, not to mention
the churches, colleges, bridges, and water pumps. The Paris of 1684 did in
fact have on the order of 400,000 residents. It was one of the world's great
cities.

Meeting and Passing Through

Within the great city, the Place de Grève served as a major meeting-place.
Visitors to the city often entered through the nearby Porte St.-Antoine,
next to the Bastille, and proceeded down the rue St.-Antoine to the Hôtel
de Ville. That was the standard itinerary of ambassadors and princes. Royal
troops customarily met them with ceremony somewhere on the road outside the capital, then accompanied them through the walls, past the Hôtel
de Ville, and into the presence of the king.

The way from the Bastille to the Hôtel de Ville led past many imposing town houses. The neighborhood—the Marais—was once the chief
dwelling area of the *grande noblesse*. From the fourteenth to the sixteenth
centuries, the kings of France themselves resided in the Hôtel St.-Paul, then
in the Hôtel des Tournelles, neither one far east of the Hôtel de Ville. Later
kings lavished attention on the Place Royale (now the Place des Vosges),
farther out on a spur from the rue St.-Antoine. During the 1650s, Catherine
Bellier built the elegant Hôtel de Beauvais on the rue St.-Antoine, near the
Hôtel de Ville. Bellier was Queen Anne's personal servant. She was reputed
to be both Anne's reliable aide in the queen's affairs with Cardinal Mazarin,
and the woman who ended the virginity of the queen's son, Louis XIV. In
seventeenth-century Paris, servitude and turpitude apparently had their rewards.

Catherine Bellier's Hôtel de Beauvais still graces the Marais, although
nineteenth-century urban renewal renamed its section of the old main
street; people now call it the rue François Miron. Not only the Hôtel de
Beauvais, but also the imposing Hôtel Béthune-Sully, the handsome Hôtel
de Sens, and the spectacular Hôtel de Carnavalet now testify to the neighborhood's old grandeur. St.-Gervais, just east of the Hôtel de Ville, was an
aristocratic church in the seventeenth century; beginning in mid-century, a
long line of Couperins served as its organists. Only toward 1700, with the
exodus to Versailles, did the areas north and east of the Hôtel de Ville begin
to lose their elite character.

The aristocratic neighborhoods contrasted sharply with the commercial and proletarian cast of the Place de Grève itself. The Grève hosted an important part of the city's wholesale trade, while the nearby St.-Jean market supplied a good share of Parisian fruits and vegetables. Emile Magne offers a dramatic reconstruction of the Place as it looked in 1644:

> On the left, beyond the stone cross with its Gothic shaft on a pyramidal pedestal, the Wine Market brought together, all the way over to the bank of the Seine, tight ranks of wagons loaded with barrels, kegs, and demijohns. Around the licensed brokers and measurers, the master vendors begin the auction amid a great crowd of merchants and tavernkeepers, who compete stridently for Burgundies, Bourbonnais, Spanish wines, and Malmseys. Beggars in rags, mean-faced rascals, loafers, and pamphleteers wander from group to group looking for a handout, a purse to snatch, a piece of news to seize in flight. (Magne 1960: 10–11)

Farther on there are coachmen, petty merchants, water carriers, servants, and errand boys. Through the middle of this human mass, in Emile Magne's tableau, march the solemn black-robed municipal officers. Seventeenth-century etchings likewise portray a Place de Grève teeming with travelers, peddlers, workers, merchants, officials, and spectators.

Workers of the Grève included plenty of casual laborers hired by the day, but they also included a variety of established trades, each with its permanent claim on some corner of the neighborhood. When it came time for the workers of a trade to assemble and consider making collective demands on their masters, they commonly gathered at the Grève. Early in the eighteenth century, fifteen different incorporated trades had their headquarters on the square or in its immediate vicinity: the *bourreliers, boursiers, cordiers, ceinturiers, maîtres chandeliers, maîtres charons, maîtres cordonniers, maîtres corroyeurs, maîtres garniers, huissiers à cheval, marchands de vins, peaussiers, potiers de terre, maîtres tonnelliers,* and *maîtres tourneurs* (Constant 1974: 9). All of them, plus many more workers from the construction trade, met, drank, hired, organized, and debated their interests at the Place de Grève. For work, play, and politics, the square brought together people from all walks of life and all quarters of the city.

The coincidence of municipal power, commercial activity, and everyday gathering made the Place an ideal location for parades, ceremonies, and insurrections. Within Paris, the Hôtel de Ville and the Place de Grève were the foci of the Fronde. Mazarin's seizure, and very slow payment, of bonds secured by the Hôtel de Ville's revenues turned many of the city's *rentiers* against the government and precipitated a series of rebellious gatherings in 1648 and 1649. The rebel princes and princesses themselves lodged at the Hôtel de Ville in 1649. There the duchess of Longueville gave birth to a son, baptized him Charles-Paris, and enlisted the city's magistrates as the boy's godfathers. When, in 1649, Morlot was sentenced to hang in the Grève for having printed a *mazarinade* (a handbill criticizing the beleaguered Mazarin), the crowd in the square freed the prisoner, breaking the gallows and its ladder in the assault. Later in the Fronde, when divisions opened up among the municipal officers, the bourgeois of Paris, and the princes, control of the Hôtel de Ville continued to be a prime objective of the rebels. When the rebellion had failed, the city brought the Fronde to its symbolic close, in July 1653, with a great festival celebrating the reestablishment of royal authority. It took place, naturally, at the Hôtel de Ville.

After the fright of the Fronde, the king himself avoided the Hôtel de Ville for twenty-five years. But he did ride through the square. On 25 August 1660 Louis XIV and his bride, the Spanish Infanta Maria Theresa, made their formal entry into the city: their gala procession moved through triumphal arches and past admiring throngs via the rue St.-Antoine, the Place Baudoyer, and the rue de la Tisseranderie to the Place de Grève. Among the great lords and ladies on the balconies of the Hôtel de Beauvais, the newlyweds saw Queen Mother Anne of Austria, her aging friend Mazarin, Marshal Turenne, Queen Henrietta of England, Marie Mancini, and Mme. Scarron—who would eventually become the marquise de Maintenon and Louis's last wife. The procession moved from the Grève over the river to Notre Dame before finally making its way to the Louvre.

Waterborne voyagers took a variant of the same path. They often debarked at the Port St.-Paul, just upstream from the Place de Grève. Then they passed through the square on their way to other parts of the city. When Restif de la Bretonne wrote *La Paysanne pervertie,* his eighteenth-century tale of the peasant maiden corrupted by Parisian life, he had his innocent Ursule arrive by water coach at the Port St.-Paul, then proceed immediately to her encounters with the wicked city.

The Place also launched many a procession, parade, and popular movement. The city's register of festivals and ceremonies for the seventeenth and eighteenth centuries shows, for example, the municipality assembling in the square each New Year's Day to pay a call on the king. Once the king built his splendid new castle in Versailles, visiting him meant a long procession by coach to the suburbs. The minutes for 1 January 1783 list the

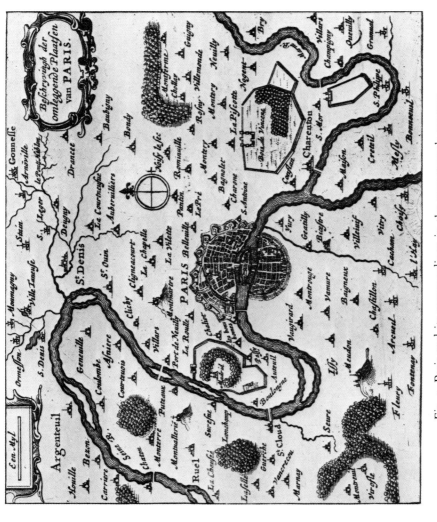

Fig. 7. Paris and its surroundings in the seventeenth century

Fig. 8. A celebration in the Place de Grève, 1615

major city officials: "invited by warrant, they assembled in black robes at 6:00 A.M. at the Hôtel de Ville, where the first city clerk and two other clerks (likewise in black robes) and the colonel of the municipal guard (in dress uniform) had also reported. After hearing Mass, they left for Versailles at 7:00 A.M." (AN K 1018).

Toward the end of the same year the American war ended, and France celebrated the conclusion of the peace treaty. On 23 November at 9:00 A.M., another procession left the Place de Grève. Led by fifteen inspectors and deputy inspectors of police, four companies of the municipal guard, two detachments of the city's watch, and clerks of the royal administration at the Hôtel de Ville came the city's major officials—exquisitely balanced, with seventeen royal officers on the left, seventeen municipal officers on the right, their rear protected by horse guards and by another company of police inspectors.

From the Hôtel de Ville, the impressive parade went to proclaim the peace at the Carrousel of the Louvre, in the court of the Palais de Justice, back at the Hôtel de Ville, over on the Pont Neuf, and at the Croix du Trahoir by the rue St.-Honoré, across from the pillory at the central market (La Halle). Next they read their declarations in the Place des Victoires, in the Place Louis le Grand (now the Place Vendôme), in the Place Louis XV (now the Place de la Concorde, and then at the city's very western edge) and by the Pont St.-Michel. For their last round they proceeded to the Place Maubert, to the Place Royale (now the Place des Vosges), and to the Place Baudoyer, near St.-Gervais. From there they returned—no doubt footsore and thirsty from their ten-mile tramp—to the nearby Hôtel de Ville. More celebrations occurred during the next few weeks: the singing of *Te Deums,* the illumination of the city, the fireworks at the Place de Grève (AN K 1018).

The square was, in fact, the standard locale for fireworks, and for public celebrations in general, during the seventeenth and eighteenth centuries. As in Dijon, St. John's Eve (23 June) was in Paris the annual moment for fire and fireworks. It was the Christian successor of pagan Midsummer's Eve, a sort of Bastille Day *avant la lettre.* The huge bonfire and the display took place in the square. "In the midst of a pile of faggots," according to Augustin Challamel, "was planted a May tree thirty meters high, graciously decorated with bouquets, crowns, and garlands of roses. On 22 June three companies of archers, the guards of the Hôtel de Ville, the general staff, and the authorities went in procession to present the official invitations. To the king belonged the honor of lighting the fire" (Challamel 1879:20). Legend has it that sixteenth-century celebrants customarily hung a cageful of cats on the May tree and watched them burn. By the later seventeenth century, that gruesome entertainment had disappeared, but fireworks and petards lay stacked inside the woodpile to give the crowd its own *spectacle de son et lumière*. After the Fronde, the king abandoned the honor of lighting the bonfire to his deputy, the governor of Paris. Even after the royal withdrawal from the festivities, St. John's Eve and many other holidays continued each year to draw the rich (in carriages) and the poor (on foot) to the Place de Grève.

The square likewise attracted spectators to its many public executions. There, from the fourteenth century onward, heretics had burned, gentlemen-rebels had lost their heads, and common criminals had hanged, all in public view at the Place de Grève. In his bawdy *Histoire comique de Francion,* published in 1623, Charles Sorel says of a thief, "They sent him to the Grève, where his head learned how much the rest of his body weighed." About the same time, the irreverent poet Théophile de Viau went to prison in the Conciergerie on the initiative of the Jesuits. When the troops came for him, wrote Théophile, he wasn't sure whether it was for incarceration or decapitation ("Requeste de Théophile AU ROY," 1624):

> In the name of the king, people use
> Both force and trickery.
> As if Lucifer had undertaken
> To give me justice.
> As soon as I was in Paris
> I heard vague rumors
> That everything was set to do me in
> And I rightly wondered
> Whether these people were going to take me
> To the Grève or to jail.

Nor was the square's bloody reputation a mere literary expression. In 1610 Ravaillac, Henry IV's mad assassin, was tortured, drawn, and quartered at the Grève. "Finally," runs a contemporary account,

> the horses having tugged for a good hour, Ravaillac gave up the ghost before having been dismembered. After the executioner had cut him into quarters, people of every class went at the four parts with swords, knives and staves. They took the pieces away from the executioner so eagerly that after hitting, cutting, and tearing the hunks of flesh they dragged them through the streets in all directions, with such rage that nothing could stop them. (*Le Mercure François* 1610: 457).

Then the crowds burned their shares of the battered corpse in different neighborhoods of the city.

During that same century, the Grève saw Catherine Voisin and Leonora Galigai burned; the count of Montmorency-Bouteville, the count of Chapelles, Marshal Marillac, and the marquise de Brinvilliers decapitated; three rebel gentlemen of Poitou (du Jarrage, Chef-Bobin, and Champ-Martin) degraded by being hanged rather than beheaded; poets Durant and Siti broken and burned along with their seditious writings; the missing Joseph Palmier and Jean Antoine Jourdan (both profiteers of Agde) hanged in effigy; and dozens of other rebels, heretics, magicians, and ordinary felons executed—in the flesh or in effigy—by one means or another. Montmorency-Bouteville lost his head the day before the St. John's fireworks of 1627, thus providing the city with two holidays in a row. In 1655, in his *Chronique scandaleuse ou Paris ridicule,* the poet, murderer, and sometime pornographer Claude Le Petit wrote of that

> unhappy piece of ground
> consecrated to the public gallows
> where they have massacred
> a hundred times more men than in war.

Claude Le Petit was unwittingly writing his own epitaph. On 26 August 1662 at the Place de Grève, he paid the price for *lèse-majesté* and *écrits séditieux:* right hand amputated, burned alive, ashes scattered to the winds, property confiscated.

"They" who massacred at the Grève were the royal executioner, his family, and their employees. From 1688 to the middle of the nineteenth century—and right through the murderous years of the Revolution—that executioner ordinarily belonged to the family of Charles Sanson, a lieutenant from Abbéville cashiered from his regiment for his love affair with the daughter of Rouen's executioner, and thereby recruited into the separate world of the hangman. In Paris it was usually a Sanson who set the sword, the noose, the wheel, the pillory, or, eventually, the guillotine. For the most part, the Sansons did their killing at the Grève.

The eighteenth century brought its share of famous brigands, assassins, traitors, and rebels, although the quota of executions for impiety seems to have declined. The dead included Horn, Cartouche, Damiens, Lally-Tollendal, and the marquis de Favras. Jacques-Louis Menétra, the Parisian glazier, noted in his journal for 1750 the consequences of a rumor that kidnappers were taking young boys for their blood: "The rumor was so effective that the police officers' windows were broken, people beat up several suspects and even burned one at the Place de Grève. No one let children out any more. Three poor fellows hanged in the Place de Grève for the sake of justice and Parisian peace of mind" (Menétra 1982: 34). The execution itself caused several incidents at the Place.

Riotous or not, all these executions were grand public spectacles. One time in the 1780s, Restif de la Bretonne went to the Grève to watch the breaking of three malefactors on the wheel. The spectators, he reported, "chatted and laughed as if they were attending a parade" (Restif 1930: 171). Under the old regime, the greater the victim, the more colorful the show.

A Revolutionary Square

In 1790, however, the marquis de Favras—convicted of conspiring to arrange the royal family's escape—was hanged like a common criminal. True, some features of the old-regime execution remained: the display of the marquis in a tumbril, clad in a nightshirt, with a knotted rope around his neck and a sign reading CONSPIRATOR AGAINST THE STATE on his chest; the public repentance (the *honorable amende*) to God, the nation, the king, and justice before the doors of Notre Dame; the dictation of a long last statement in which the marquis continued to protest his innocence (Cléray 1932: 102–110). Still, Favras was one of the few nobles ever to hang at the Place de Grève. The early revolution leveled downward, hanging its noble enemies.

Later, the Revolution leveled upward, decapitating noble and commoner alike. The newly invented guillotine took its first victim, in April 1792, at the Place de Grève. Although the major executions of the Revolution generally occurred at the Place de la Révolution (earlier Place Louis XV, later Place de la Concorde), public guillotining of felons continued at the Place de Grève until the Revolution of July 1830. Then the government decided the blood of criminals should not sully a square that had played such a glorious part in the nation's recent revolutions.

During the revolution that began in 1789, the customary separations among spectators, authorities, and victims blurred, then shifted. The Place de Grève retained its symbolic importance as a locus of public celebration and retribution, but popular initiative played a far larger role than before. Repeatedly, ordinary people took the law into their own hands.

The first major occasion of 1789 came during the so-called Reveillon Riots of April. After Reveillon and Henriot (manufacturers, respectively, of decorative paper and of gunpowder) had allegedly stirred up a local political assembly by making rash remarks about the desirability of holding down wages, knots of angry workers began to form in the streets of eastern Paris. The twenty-seventh of April was a Monday, a free day for most skilled workers. That afternoon, a crowd formed on the Left Bank around a drummer and a marcher; the marcher carried a makeshift gallows bearing the cardboard images of two men. The crowd, according to the officer on guard at the Palace of Justice, were all "workers from the faubourg St.-Antoine, armed with sticks and clubs." Playing town criers, members of the procession announced a "decree of the Third Estate of the faubourg St.-Antoine, which sentences Anriot and Revillon to be hanged" (BN Joly de Fleury 1103).

After a certain amount of confrontation and maneuvering with the authorities, the workers arrived at the Place de Grève. "People said," reported bookseller Sébastien Hardy, "more than three thousand of them were there to set up the gallows that had marched with them so long" (BN Fr 6687). There they did, as announced, hang and burn their effigies. The crowd then tramped up the rue St.-Antoine, through the city gate, past the Bastille, into the faubourg beyond—thus reversing the path of ceremonial entries into Paris. Unable to get through the troops who guarded Reveillon's house and shop, they went to Henriot's place and sacked it. The next day a crowd of workers returned to the faubourg after another rendezvous at the Place de Grève. This time they managed to break through the troops; then they gutted the house and shop of Reveillon as well. In the battle some three hundred persons, including a few soldiers and a great many demonstrators, died (Godechot 1965: 187).

At that point, by most definitions of revolution, the Revolution had not yet begun. Nevertheless, the popular assemblies that were to play so prominent a part in subsequent revolutionary events were already in action. One of the most important, the assembly of the electors of Paris, met at the Hôtel de Ville. (Indeed, on the very day Reveillon's house was sacked, the assembly was electing him a member of its commission to draft a program statement, a *cahier,* for the Third Estate.) On 13 July it was at the Hôtel de Ville that the assembly responded to the crisis created by the king's firing of his minister Necker; the assembly created a Permanent Committee and declared the establishment of a citizens' militia.

From his Left Bank window, Hardy saw the hastily formed companies of *milice bourgeoise* marching to the Place de Grève:

> A little after 7:00 P.M. yet another detachment of militia went up the rue St.-Jacques. This one was composed of about 120 individuals, who were going to the Hôtel de Ville three by three, and who made sure not

to frighten anyone along the way, by announcing that it was the Third
Estate that was going to the Hôtel de Ville. One was surprised to see
that a day that should have been a day of public mourning seemed to be
a day of rejoicing, judging by the shouts and indecent laughter on every
side, and by the shenanigans people were performing in the street; as if
it were a day of carnival.   (BN Fr 6687)

Eighty members of the National Assembly joined the militiamen at the
Hôtel de Ville, and thus gave a national meaning to the city's action. "The
prévôt des marchands and other city officers," noted Hardy, "assured the
electors of Paris that they would not budge from the Hôtel de Ville, so long
as their presence was necessary for consultations on the means of remedying
the current difficulties and securing public order" (BN Fr 6687).

They had their hands full. The decision to create a militia was fateful,
for a militia needed arms. Great crowds sought those arms at the Hôtel de
Ville, at the Arsenal, at the Invalides, and, finally, at the Bastille. Jacques de
Flesselles, the recently appointed interim prévôt des marchands, had continued in his leadership of the city government by becoming head of the Permanent Committee. In that capacity, he distributed a few hundred muskets
to the crowd in the Place de Grève and fended off their demands for more.
As he temporized, a widespread belief in his treachery arose.

Flesselles paid for his new reputation the very next day. On the fourteenth, a crowd went to seek gunpowder stored at the Bastille, at the other
end of the rue St.-Antoine from the Hôtel de Ville. The powder-seekers
broke into the fortress, took it over, and seized its governor, de Launey.
Some of the official delegates from the Permanent Committee managed to
march de Launey through taunting crowds back to the Place de Grève. But
there, before de Launey's guards could get him into the building to face the
committee, members of the crowd bayoneted, sabered, and shot him. They
then beheaded the corpse and displayed the severed head, as the heads of executed traitors had always been displayed. Soon afterward Flesselles left the
Hôtel de Ville and entered the Place de Grève. He, too, was shot and decapitated, his head paraded through the street.

The Place continued for some time to be the focus of revolutionary activity. The day after the taking of the Bastille, members of the National Assembly again symbolized the unity of the city and the nation by marching
to the Hôtel de Ville amid a militia escort. At the moment of their entry
into the Place de Grève, the great bells of the city's churches rang out. On
17 July, when Louis XVI gave in to popular pressure and came to Paris
from Versailles, his parade proceeded to the Hôtel de Ville. That was per-

haps the king's last moment of general popularity. "They had eliminated the shouts of 'Long live the king' at the arrival of the monarch," reported Restif de la Bretonne, "but at his departure from the Hôtel de Ville, the barriers of the heart broke. All at once, every voice cried 'Long live the king.' The sound spread from neighbor to neighbor throughout the city, and those who had stayed in the most distant quarters of the city repeated it. The women, the sick opened their windows and replied to people in the street: 'Long live the king!'" (Restif 1930: 215). Royalist enthusiasm did not last long. On 22 July, when the Parisian crowd massacred Berthier de Sauvigny (the intendant of Paris) and Foulon (his father-in-law, the king's councilor), it was in the Place de Grève that they did so, and that they began their dragging of the battered bodies through the city. Restif, who witnessed the botched execution of Berthier, returned home shaken and ill.

Disciplined or riotous, the Grève's revolutionary events continued. On 5 September, when the Swiss Guard itself took the national oath en masse, the ceremony occurred at the Place de Grève. On 5 and 6 October, when the crowd of women set off to Versailles to fetch the royal family, they departed from the Place de Grève and led "the baker, the baker's wife, and the baker's lad" back to the Place de Grève. (By this time the decreasingly democratic Restif was prepared to believe that those women in the crowd who were not actually armed men in disguise were mostly brothel-keepers rather than the rough but honest fishwives they claimed to be.) Throughout the second half of 1789 the Hôtel de Ville figured in almost every major revolutionary action.

No doubt 1789 marked the all-time high point of national significance for the Place de Grève. For a while the Hôtel de Ville regained the centrality it had lost as the Sun King had eclipsed the City of Light. As the Revolution nationalized, such public spaces as the Place de la Révolution (now the Place de la Concorde, and then as now an easy stroll—or a quick march—from the National Assembly) assumed greater importance. The last political executions at the Grève were the guillotinings of nine émigré officers in October 1792. The Terror took its victims in other public places. The great parades of the later Revolution focused on those newly important spaces rather than on the Place de Grève. City and square lost out to nation.

Exceptions were still important. The ninth of Thermidor, the great day of reaction, was exceptional—and symbolically the more powerful—in featuring an attack of the counterrevolutionary crowd on the Hôtel de Ville, where Robespierre and his few remaining allies had fled. Throughout the eighteenth-century revolution, and again throughout the revolutions of the nineteenth century, the Place de Grève and the Hôtel de Ville were repeatedly the sites of great moments in which sovereignty passed temporarily from the national government to the people of Paris and their representatives. What could be more natural for a place that was at once the seat of the city's government, the place of retribution, and the standard setting for public gatherings? The Place de Grève was for centuries the locale par excellence of popular politics.

Of that, the authorities were perfectly aware. They concentrated their surveillance of workers' movements in the square, in the nearby streets, and in the many local wineshops that served, in effect, as working-class clubs. The prefectoral surveillance report for 7 October 1830, for example, states that

> for several days, the heads of the combination among the city's blacksmiths have been meeting in a wineshop at no. 6 Quai de Gesvres. After agreeing on the means to their goal (the raising of salaries), they fanned out into different neighborhoods and entered every shop in their trade, seeking to turn out their comrades either by seduction or by threat. Since they were being watched and were well aware that the authorities, who knew about their activities, were prepared to repress any disorder, they moved very cautiously. (AN F^7 3884)

Nevertheless, the blacksmiths' leaders turned out several hundred workers and got them to the Champ de Mars before the national guard and the cavalry herded the demonstrators back to the prefecture of police: "They did not resist; in fact, throughout the trip they continued to sing *La Parisienne*" (AN F^7 3884). The strike, as we know it in the twentieth century, had not yet crystallized. This turnout-demonstration was then a standard way of concerting action within a trade. Movement after movement of this kind originated on the corners and in the wineshops around the Place de Grève.

Workers at the Grève

Well into the nineteenth century, the Place de Grève and the nearby Place du Châtelet were also the prime locations for the shape-up: the morning gathering of workers seeking a day's employment on the docks, in other rough labor, or especially in construction. By the early nineteenth century, and probably before, the authorities were regularly sending spies to mingle with the waiting workers and to report back on their concerns. Under the Restoration and the July Monarchy, the reports of the prefect of police included summaries of how many workers had shown up, how many had been hired, and what they had talked about. On 7 September 1831, for example, the report ran: "More than 500 workers assembled at the Place de Grève this morning. Not one was hired. They said they were going to go to the rue du Cadran [where a major labor dispute was under way]. Some said it was time to build barricades." Five days later, "About 600 workers gathered on the Place de Grève, the Place du Châtelet, and the adjacent quais. At most 30 were hired. The others complained bitterly of their hard lot. Some said that since the government clearly didn't want to take care of them, the whole thing was going to turn bad" (AN F^{1c} I 33, 12 September 1831).

Authorities could not dismiss such threats as idle grumbling. After all, on 27 and 28 July 1830 crowds of armed workers had gathered in the square, fought off the royal guards sent to disperse them, forced the Hôtel de Ville's guards to disband, broken into the building, and raised the revolutionary tricolor on its heights. During the next few days yet another provisional committee governed Paris from the Hôtel de Ville. On the thirty-first the marquis de Lafayette stood in a balcony of the city hall to present the duke of Orléans to the public as lieutenant general of the realm; soon Louis-Philippe would be king. Although the Place de Grève was not the site of another full-fledged revolution until February 1848, the insurrections and street-fighting of the 1830s and 1840s commonly involved the workers of the surrounding area, and often spilled into the Place itself. A threat from workers there commanded attention.

Workers who dwelt nearby included a wide range of the city's skilled and semiskilled. In the streets just to the east lived many craftsmen from Paris' large construction industry. The rue de la Mortellerie, which led to the back of the Hôtel de Ville, concealed in its name the word "mortar." For centuries, the street served as the headquarters of Paris' masons. Masons who worked farms in the Limousin during the winter, then tramped to construction work in Paris for the rest of the year, were prominent among them. When mason (later deputy and author) Martin Nadaud first walked to Paris from the Creuse in 1830, he and his father lodged with other workers from their region in a boardinghouse at 62 rue de la Tisseranderie, just behind the Hôtel de Ville and just north of the rue de la Mortellerie.

Much of the masons' life pivoted on the Place de Grève, and much of their leisure went by in the wineshops of the neighborhood. Before the day's hiring, construction workers typically met to drink a glass together. If they were hired, they would take their wine breaks in the cabarets near the job. If they were not hired yet still had money, they would often stay at the Place de Grève to drink and complain; it was then that the police spies picked up their choicest evidence. If they were penniless, the Place de Grève still served as their headquarters. When Martin Nadaud returned to Paris in the spring of 1833, his friends told him the winter had been disastrous. When he went out the next morning, "That Place de Grève, the last vestige of the slave markets of antiquity, was crowded with men who were pale and gaunt but coped with their starvation without too much sadness. One saw them shivering with cold in their cheap smocks or threadbare jackets, stomping their feet against the cobblestones to warm themselves" (Nadaud 1976: 77). Nadaud himself was more fortunate, or more enterprising. He found work, and returned to Paris from the Limousin year after year. Eventually, like many other seasonal migrants, he settled more or less permanently in the city.

As he became a skilled mason and a Parisian veteran, Nadaud became deeply involved in workers' organizations and republican politics. There, too, he resembled his fellows. During the repression of the June Days (the huge workers' insurrection of 1848), the authorities compiled detailed dossiers on the roughly 12,000 persons charged with involvement in the rebellion. Those dossiers give a picture of the working-class activists in different sections of the city. In the *quartier* of the Hôtel de Ville, 272 people were arrested. A full 135 of them, including 94 masons, worked in construction. There were also 18 garment workers, 13 from retail trade, 11 from metalworking, 10 from transport, and 85 from a scattering of other trades (AN F^7 2586). By that time, workers from large-scale manufacturing lived out in more peripheral locations such as St.-Denis, Belleville, and the faubourg St.-Antoine. The Hôtel de Ville remained the center of a neighborhood housing workers in small shops and petty trades.

Nineteenth-Century Renewal

Two large changes of the 1850s shifted the center of working-class Paris away from the Place de Grève. The first was the accelerated growth of large-scale industry. That growth concentrated, as urban industrial growth usually does, in the areas of relatively cheap and open land near the edges of the city. Meanwhile, the small shops in the center stagnated or declined. Services and retail trade, on the other hand, prospered downtown. On the Place de l'Hôtel de Ville—as the Place de Grève was finally coming to be called—the opening of the great department store, the Bazar de l'Hôtel de Ville, around 1860, epitomized both the shift of the central city away from manufacturing and the rise of big, capital-intensive organizations.

A second change was the national government's deliberate reshaping of the city's physical plant. Many called it Haussmannization, to stress the im-

Fig. 9. The masons' hiring fair at the Place de l'Hôtel de Ville, about 1868

Fig. 10. The Place de l'Hôtel de Ville in the twentieth century

portance of Baron Haussmann, prefect of the Seine, in the transformation. Haussmann lived at the Hôtel de Ville, in a grand apartment at the corner of the quai and the Place de Grève. One of his early projects for the renewal of Paris was the razing of whole blocks of nearby buildings to expand the old Place de Grève into the vast Place de l'Hôtel de Ville we know today.

There was more: a similar clearing of streets behind the Hôtel de Ville to the east, alterations in the city hall itself, and the laying down of the ostentatious rue de Rivoli—the broad, nearly straight band that eventually led from the Place de la Concorde past the Tuileries, the Louvre, the Palais Royal, the Châtelet, and the Hôtel de Ville to the rue St-Antoine, and thereby to the site of the razed Bastille. The rue de Rivoli now formed the northern boundary of the Place de l'Hôtel de Ville and linked it the more firmly to the other crossroads of Paris.

These combined changes in the Parisian economy and geography diluted the working-class character of the quartier and diminished its importance as a rallying point for working-class activists. The Hôtel de Ville did not yet, however, lose its significance as the seat of Parisian government and, by extension, of popular sovereignty. During the mild revolution of September 1870, when a left-wing crowd invaded the National Assembly from the Place de la Concorde, it still made sense for Jules Favre to divert the invaders into a march on the Hôtel de Ville. There, a left-center coalition created a provisional government.

France's nominal government (or, sometimes, one of the country's two nominal governments) sat at the Hôtel de Ville for almost all of the next eight months. A whirlpool of reforms, expedients, and revolutionary experiments churned through the city, with its vortex at the Hôtel de Ville. "Revolutionaries were everywhere," wrote Louise Michel, herself one of the most prominent among them, later on. "They multiplied; we felt a tremendous life force; it seemed we were the revolution itself" (Michel 1970: I, 72). As the provisional seat of government, the Place de l'Hôtel de Ville again became a favored locale for rallies, demonstrations, delegations, and attempted coups.

The high point of activity was, to be sure, the Paris Commune. The Commune began, in effect, with the occupation of the Hôtel de Ville by the national guard's Central Committee on 18 March 1871. It ended, in effect, with the evacuation and burning of the building on 24 May. In between, revolutionary activity and the defense of the city against the Germans and against the rival national government filled the old Place de Grève.

On 19 March, according to a participant in the Commune, "twenty thousand men camped in the Place de l'Hôtel de Ville, their bread lashed to their guns" (Lissagaray 1969: 121). On the twenty-eighth, after Thiers had declared that the *misérables* of the Commune could not win:

> two hundred thousand misérables came to the Hotel de Ville to install their elected representatives. The battalions—drums beating, flags topped with liberty caps, red tassels on the guns, augmented by infantrymen, artillerymen, and sailors who were faithful to Paris—flowed from every street into the Place de Grève, like the tributaries of a mighty river. In the middle of the Hôtel de Ville, opposite the main entryway, stood a large reviewing stand. The bust of the Republic, a red sash around her neck, gleaming with red trim, stood guard above. Huge banners on the facade and the tower mapped out their message of salvation to France. A hundred battalions presented glinting bayonets before the Hôtel de Ville. Those who could not get into the square spread out along the quais, the rue de Rivoli, and the boulevard Sebastopol. The flags grouped before the reviewing stand—mostly red, some tricolor, all decked with red—symbolized the presence of the people. While the battalions took their places, songs broke out, bands played the *Marseillaise* and the *Chant du Départ,* bugles sounded the charge, and the cannon of the 1792 Commune thundered on the quai. (Lissagaray 1969: 151)

Later came such festivals as that of 29 April, when a great, colorful procession of Freemasons marched gravely from the Louvre to the Hôtel de Ville in order to dramatize the adherence of the previously secret society to the Commune. (After the ceremonies and speechmaking at the Place, the procession moved on to the Bastille, around the boulevards, and back to the Champs-Elysées. That later itinerary anticipated the large alteration in the geography of public ritual that was to occur after the Commune. But in this case the central encounter of citizens and authorities still took place at the Hôtel de Ville.)

The Hôtel de Ville served, finally, as the headquarters for the last vain defense of Paris against the troops of the rival government in Versailles. Versaillais artillery pounded the city, national troops fought their way into the city, and the Communards burned to cover their retreat. As Eugene Vermersch wrote from his London exile in September 1871 ("Les Incendiaires"):

> Then all at once a gigantic fire, emerging
> From amid the fearsome city, dwarfs
> The great horror of the cannon and the mine,
> Sending whole neighborhoods skyward in its bursts.
> Walls shiver and fall to pieces

> With the long roar of thunder.
> Voices, tears, footsteps, war cries.
> Leaping toward the startled stars
> We see the great soul of the city that was Paris ...
> The pitiless flame is choking the Hôtel de Ville!

As the Hôtel de Ville burned, the Commune turned to ashes.

From that point on, the Place de Grève/Place de l'Hôtel de Ville lost much of its old importance as a focus of Parisian and national political life. The government of Paris remained a significant force in the experience of France as a whole, but for most purposes the national state eclipsed it. The geography of ceremony and confrontation recorded that change in the political balance. The Place de l'Hôtel de Ville became merely one of many way stations in the city's center: a place for the prefect and council to greet visiting dignitaries, a break in the march up the rue de Rivoli, the logical location for a demonstration directed specifically at the city administration, but nothing to match the Arc de Triomphe, the Place de la Concorde, the Champs-Elysées, the National Assembly, or even the *grands boulevards*.

The struggles of right and left in the 1930s, for example, generally bypassed the Hôtel de Ville in favor of locations closer to the center of power. When the Jeunesses Patriotes rallied there before the fateful right-wing demonstration of 6 February 1934, they were deliberately choosing an archaic connection. The exceptions were such occasions as the municipal employees' strike of December 1936, when some four thousand demonstrators (with signs reading NOS SALAIRES and BLUM A L'ACTION) broke through police barricades and occupied the square until their delegates reported they had gained a "favorable reception" from the authorities (*Le Journal des Débats* 31 December 1936). In the great confrontations of workers and students with the state in May and June 1968, Paris streets filled with barricades and demonstrators as they rarely had in the previous hundred years. Yet the Hôtel de Ville was the scene of only minor skirmishes, and the sidewash of workers' marches along the rue de Rivoli.

A new symbolic geography had taken over. When right-wing and Jewish activists staged separate protests of Soviet Premier Brezhnev's visit to France in October 1971, a bit of action occurred at the Hôtel de Ville, but the chief clashes took place on the Champs-Elysées. In 1974, when President Giscard d'Estaing sought to give the Fourteenth of July a more popular flavor, he displaced the principal ceremonies from the Champs-Elysées. But instead of choosing the Hôtel de Ville he moved the ceremonies to the boulevards between the Place de la Bastille and the Place de la République. When Giscard changed the itinerary again in 1978, the line of march turned back to the Champs-Elysées. François Mitterrand's inauguration as Giscard's successor in 1981 included a brief stop at the Hôtel de Ville, but the main events took place on the Champs-Elysées and the Panthéon. That was the general pattern of the 1960s and 1970s. As the relative importance of the municipal government declined, so did the prominence of the Place de l'Hôtel de Ville as a site for celebration or contention.

The Grève as Microcosm

The general significance of the Place de Grève/Place de l'Hôtel de Ville in the history of French contention is evident. Another side of its experience is less obvious: the slowly-changing routine life of the square recorded major changes in the social structure of France as a whole. As we follow the ebb and flow of crowds in the Place de Grève, we detect the emergence of our own world: urban, industrial, commercial, bureaucratic, oriented to rapid communication and quick consumption. Royal processions give way to popular demonstrations, weekly markets yield to department stores, carriages and sedan chairs make way for buses and taxis, household workshops disappear with the rise of large commercial and industrial organizations.

Not all the major changes in France as a whole were equally visible from the Place de Grève. Through most of the period from the seventeenth century onward, Paris grew ever larger and ever more dominant in the affairs of the nation; but a long-lived observer who stuck to the Place de Grève would have had trouble detecting that change. The commercialization of agriculture and the increase in scale of industry affected life in the Place profoundly, but only indirectly. There were very few traces of the conquest and loss of a French overseas empire, the creation and decay of a great army, the building of a railroad network, the exodus from the countryside, the alteration of regional patterns of urban influence and prosperity. To see these changes in operation we must travel to the edges of Paris, then through the rest of the country.

Nevertheless, the two master processes of change in France as a whole dominate the experience of the Place de Grève as well. Those processes are the growth of capitalism and the rising importance of the national state. The Place de Grève was already a locus of petty capitalism in the seventeenth century: small merchants and craftsmen made many of the important production decisions, and wageworkers may well have formed a majority of the people who passed through the square on an average day. Yet in the subsequent three centuries the power of people who controlled capital multiplied, the concentration of capital increased greatly, and the proletarianization of work proceeded apace. These changes added up to the growth of a deeply capitalist economy.

From our vantage point in the Place de Grève, we can also follow the rising importance of the national state. We see it in the shrinking scope of municipal government, the nationalization of the police, the disappearance of the city's independent military force, the prefect's part in replanning the city, and a dozen other signs. French statemaking provided an example to all the world. The royal statemakers built armed forces; extended their fiscal power; created a large, durable national bureaucracy; acquired a near-monopoly over the making, adjudication, and enforcement of law; and formed a centralized structure that reached far into the individual life of every French person.

Taxes and Statemaking

The mountainous growth of the national state appears clearly in the long-run rise of taxes. Exhibit 1 combines fragmentary evidence from old-regime budgets with official figures for the nineteenth and twentieth centuries. Using Fourastié's series of estimated wages of a semiskilled provincial worker (a *manoeuvre de province*), we can express the total tax burden as hours of work, then as hours of work per capita. These are conservative measures; because real wages rose greatly in the long run, they greatly understate the increase in the state's purchasing power. On the other hand, by using personal worktime as a standard, they give a sense of the state's rising impact on the daily life of the average citizen.

The statistic in question is gross receipts from regular taxes. It has a larger margin of error for the old regime than for recent decades. Old-regime sources are flimsier and less reliable. Before 1750 or so, a large share of state revenue came from so-called extraordinary sources such as forced loans and the sale of offices. A significant portion of the taxes collected never reached the state treasury, because they went into the pockets of tax farmers, creditors, and sticky-fingered officials instead. Finally, the commercialization of the French economy made it easier to assess, to collect, and even to pay taxes; the disruption of social life caused by a given amount of taxation therefore surely declined as time went on (see Ardant 1975). As a result of all these factors, the earlier figures tend to overestimate the revenues directly available to the central government, but to underestimate the weight of the exactions borne by the French public. Nevertheless the two curves give a good sense of the general trend. It runs upward, almost continuously upward.

The curves show a breathtaking rise in the state's demands from the end of the sixteenth century to the 1640s, followed by a slower growth up to the time of the Seven Years' War (1756–1763). The flattening of the

Exhibit 1. Total French taxes, 1597–1966 (Clamagéran 1867–1876: *Annuaire Statistique* 1966: Fourastié 1969: 44–49). This and several other exhibits use a logarithmic scale, which foreshortens higher values.

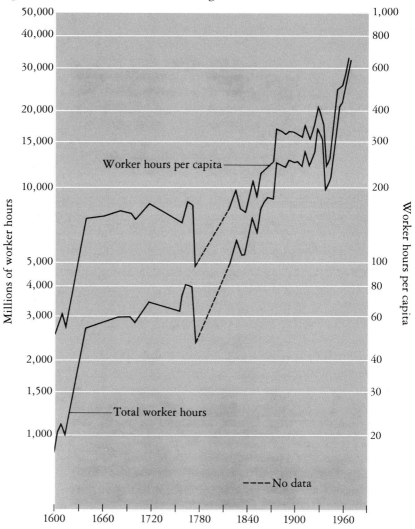

curve after 1650 is a bit misleading; it covers the great age of expedients: making do by mortgaging future income, repudiating debts, devaluating currency, forcing "gifts" and special payments, as well as creating and selling offices. (The selling of offices amounted to long-term borrowing, since the offices carried salaries and/or fees, and often provided tax exemptions to boot.) The flattening of the curve probably *does* correspond, however, to some shift of the expenses of the state toward the merchants, officials, corporations, and property owners who loaned the money and bought the offices.

The evidence leaves a regrettable gap for the period of the Revolution. France emerged from the Revolution with a tax burden at least as great as at the end of the old regime. From the early nineteenth century on, the growth of the state's demands was rapid and nearly continuous: accelerating in times of war, slowing or even declining in depressions, but frequently matching the dizzy expansion of the early seventeenth century. In the earlier centuries, the money that actually reached Paris or Versailles went largely into armed forces and the expenses of the court. During the nineteenth and twentieth centuries, military expenditures and the central bureaucracy continued to absorb large shares of the state's revenue, but more and more of it paid for expanding state services, education, welfare, and policing.

Per capita taxation rose like a mountain: in 1600 our hypothetical average citizen worked some 50 hours for the state each year (the actual worker put in much more, of course, since the per capita estimate includes the entire population of children, old people, and other unemployed persons). The figure stood at 150 hours of work in the 1640s, about the same in the 1760s, around 200 hours per year a century later, over 300 at the start of the twentieth century, and at nearly 700 worker hours per person per year in recent times. So far, the curves show no slowing of the state's growth.

France Defines Itself

If the French budget kept expanding, French territory eventually stabilized. At the end of the sixteenth century the ideas of "France" and "the French" were sharp at the center, but blurred indeed at the edges. A well-bounded French world, neatly distinct from the worlds of Spain, Italy, or Switzerland, emerged only from the heroic statemaking of the following centuries. Speakers of Breton occupied a large western arm of the territory claimed by the French crown, speakers of various *langues d'oc* the southern half of the land. The Pope ruled a large enclave around Avignon. The entire eastern frontier consisted of duchies and principalities of uncertain loyalty. About one-fifth of what would become the continental France of the twentieth century—including Artois, Flanders, Alsace, Lorraine, Franche-Comté, the French Alps, and much of Provence—lay under the control of Habsburgs or dukes of Savoy. Burgundy, which now sits comfortably distant from Swiss and German borders, was then a troubled frontier province, vulnerable to invasion, insurrection, and smuggling.

In the interior, the subordination of great lords to the French crown was grudging and intermittent, punctuated by conspiracies, rebellions, and foreign alliances. Protestant magnates who feared the Catholic crown and treasured their own autonomy maintained effective control of major cities and substantial regions in Guyenne, Languedoc, Saintonge, and Poitou. The Edict of Nantes (1598) had confirmed the claims to survival of that series of Protestant states within the Catholic state. As of 1600, France was less a centralized monarchy than an uneasy confederation coordinated from Paris.

Yet all is relative. In that world of Elizabeth I, Philip II, and Henri IV, of Shakespeare, Cervantes, and Théophile de Viau, the French kingdom was exceptionally unified, its territory unusually continuous, its crown surprisingly powerful. What is more, in its seventeenth-century context, France was rich and populous. Some 18 million people inhabited its 450,000 square kilometers, compared with the 11 million of the sprawling Russian empire, the 8 million of Spain, the 4.5 million of England, the single million of the Netherlands. Via the great fairs of Lyon the woolens and linens of France journeyed throughout the Mediterranean. Wines of Bordeaux graced the meals of prosperous Flemings; salt from the Bay of Bourgneuf streamed to the Baltic. Marseille, Bordeaux, La Rochelle, Nantes, and Rouen stood among the most important European ports. Inside the kingdom, the bustling markets of Paris and Lyon drew upon the agriculture and manufacturing of broad hinterlands. France was starting to overcome the commercial advantage of Spain and appeared to be holding off the mercantile challenges of England and Holland.

A century later, in 1700, much had changed. Relative to England and Holland, if not to Spain, the economic and political importance of France had receded. While England was experiencing population growth on the order of one-third from 1600 to 1700, and thus nearing 6 million inhabitants, France was edging up only about one-twentieth, to 19 or 20 million. It began to look as if Louis XIV—just after the War of the League of Augsburg, and soon to undertake the War of the Spanish Succession— would keep France in a state of perpetual combat. Parts of the country had suffered acute food shortages in the 1690s and would face them again in the next decade. The century as a whole had been a time of massive popular rebellions, including the Fronde. The prosperous, powerful France of 1600 had certainly not evolved into a stable, placid state.

Yet, again, all is relative. By comparison with the start of the seventeenth century, French manufacturing had multiplied. Nantes and other Atlantic ports were shipping French textiles widely through Africa and the Americas. French artists such as Molière and Couperin set standards for all of Europe. The drive of Richelieu, Mazarin, Colbert, and Louis XIV had built up an army and a state apparatus that were much stronger, and several times larger, than they had been in 1600. That army and that state had conquered and incorporated Franche-Comté, Alsace, Lorraine, Artois, and some of Flanders; on the eastern frontier, substantial numbers of people speaking Germanic languages now lived under French control. The beginning of the eighteenth century was a time of vigorous economic and political expansion.

In sheer territorial terms, the French expansion was nearing its peak a century later, in 1800. By that year Napoleon's conquests had pushed the boundaries of the French Republic to the Rhine and into Savoy and brought much of Italy under the power of France. Within a few year after 1800 France and its satellites governed all Italy, all Spain, Illyria, and, beyond the Rhine, Holland and Westphalia as well. Although the Revolution had shaken and transformed that expanding French government, for its time it was a marvel of centralization and extractive power. The French economy had likewise felt the weight of the Revolution, with the increasing demand for military goods not compensating the loss of markets for export industries.

Nevertheless the eighteenth century as a whole brought great expansion to French agriculture and industry: a likely rise of 25–40 percent in agricultural production (Le Roy Ladurie 1975: 395), a plausible annual growth rate of 1.5–1.9 percent in the industrial sector (Labrousse et al. 1970: 521). The population of France (excluding the new territories seized by its revolutionary armies) had risen to 27 million. That figure still towered over the 10 or 11 million of Spain and the combined 16 million of England, Wales, Scotland, and Ireland. However, the German empire-in-the-making visible in and around the Prussian territories contained some 20 million people, a disciplined military force, and important industrial nuclei. As a commercial and industrial power, France had lost ground to England. As a large, centralized national state, France found others, including Britain and Prussia, threatening her preeminence.

In another century, by 1900, a great simplification of the European map had occurred. Just nine states—Spain, Italy, Austria-Hungary, Germany, Russia, Sweden, Norway, Great Britain, and France—occupied the great bulk of the European land mass and population. The French state, for its part, had ballooned: during the nineteenth century, in real terms, the national budget had quadrupled, while France's economy was growing a bit less rapidly than that; the effect, according to Jean Marczewski, was to raise the ratio of the state budget to the gross physical product slightly: from 13.7 percent (1803–1812) to 14.7 percent (1905–1913) (Marczewski 1965: lxx). France had lost its demographic superiority: to its 39 million people, Germany now had 56 million, Britain and Ireland 42 million, Italy 34 million. At that point France had given up Alsace-Lorraine to Germany but had gained a chunk of Savoy, plus the regions around Avignon and Nice. During the century France had likewise acquired vast areas of northern and western Africa, as the European powers divided up the continent.

Although agriculture still played an important part in French national life at the start of the twentieth century, France had become a recognizably urban-industrial country. In 1800 some 15 percent of the French population had lived in urban places (by which French census-takers meant communes with 2,000 or more people in their chief agglomeration); by 1900 that figure had risen to 41 percent. In labor force terms, agriculture, forestry, and fishing had declined from about 55 percent of all employment in 1800 to about 40 percent in 1900; the labor force shift was less dramatic than the population shift because an important part of France's nineteenth-century urbanization consisted in a transfer of industry and services from countryside to city; the countryside was more purely agricultural in 1900 than it had been for centuries before.

In the 1980s the European map of 1900 was still visible. The Austro-Hungarian Empire, it is true, had cracked into a series of states, most of them under direct or indirect control of Russia's successor state, the Soviet Union. In the Balkans, areas such as Bulgaria and South Serbia had shaken loose from the Ottoman Empire, spent some time in or under the shadow of Austria-Hungary, and eventually reformed into new states. A separate Poland had reappeared in what had previously been western Russia and eastern Germany, while Germany itself had been split into two hostile states. Ireland and Finland had become independent. France itself had recovered Alsace-Lorraine from Germany. Yet the alterations of the European map from 1900 to 1980 were much less dramatic than those of the nineteenth century.

Within the boundaries of France, change continued. A population

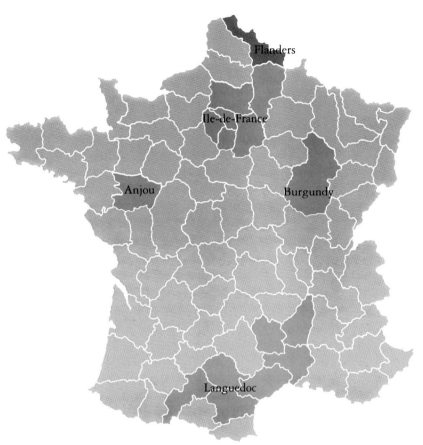

Fig. 11. Twentieth-century France and the five regions

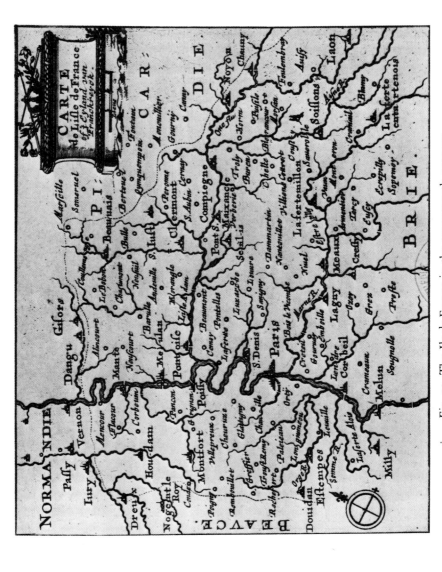

Fig. 12. The Ile-de-France in the seventeenth century

whose total numbers increased only slowly (from 39 million in 1900 to 52 million in 1976, including the effect of regaining Alsace-Lorraine) nevertheless redistributed radically. The French moved out from the interior, especially toward the north and east, piling up in cities as never before: 16 million people in urban places in 1901, 21.5 million in 1946, 28.5 million in 1962, 37 million in 1975. During the first three-quarters of the twentieth century, real per capita income rose, according to Alfred Sauvy's measurements, from 58 francs in 1901 to 78 in 1946, 167 in 1962, and 315 in 1974 (*Annuaire Statistique* 1966, 1975). Whereas up to the beginning of the century agriculture, forestry, and fishing had merely declined relatively, changing little while manufacturing and services increased much, as the twentieth century moved on agriculture declined absolutely: a little under 9 million workers in 1901, still around 9 million in 1921, about 7.5 million in 1946, just under 4 million in 1962, fewer than 2 million in 1975.

Equally important, but harder to illustrate with simple statistics, was the knitting together of the country by roads, trains, airplanes, and mass communications—all systems centering on Paris to such an extent that it is often difficult to pass from one secondary point to another without going through the capital. The rhetoric of decentralization becomes an indispensable tool of administrations that nevertheless continue to concentrate their activity at the center. What people call decentralization is actually an increasing division of labor: surveillance and decision making the growing specialties of Paris and its region; production, extraction, and amusement the expanding functions of other cities and other regions of France.

Five Cities, Five Regions

In the last analysis, then, a view of French social change from the Place de Grève, or even from Paris as a whole, is bound to be myopic. The French Hexagon has many angles, some of them invisible from the rue de Rivoli. Let us correct our vision by continuing to examine the same processes from several different vantage points. So far we have looked at Dijon and Burgundy, then at Paris, but without much attention to the Parisian hinterland. Let us regularize: Dijon and Burgundy, Paris and its Ile-de-France, then Angers with Anjou, Lille with Flanders (and sometimes pieces of Hainaut, Cambrésis, and Artois as well), Toulouse with the Toulousain (and sometimes the whole of Languedoc).

In 1652 Peter Heylyn published a book demurely titled *Cosmographie in Four Bookes. Containing the Chorographie and Historie of the Whole World, And all the principall Kingdomes, Provinces, Seas, and Isles Thereof.* The section titled "FRANCE, Properly so called," runs:

> The first place which the *Franks* or *French* had for their fixt habitation, was by that people honoured with the name of FRANCE; the first *green turf* of *Gallick* ground, by which they took *livery* and *seisin* of all the rest. A Province now bounded on the East with *Champagne,* on the North with *Normandie,* on the West and South with *La Beausse.* To difference it from the main Continent of *France,* it is called the *Isle of France;* as being circled almost round with severall Rivers, that is to say the *Oise* on the North, the *Eure* on the West, the *Velle* on the East, and a vein-Riveret of the *Seine* toward the South. A Countrie not so large as many of the *French* Provinces, but such as hath given name unto all the rest, it being the fate of many small, but puissant Provinces, to give their name to others which are greater than they, if conquered and brought under by them . . . A Countrey generally so fruitfull and delectable (except in *Gastinois*) that the very hills thereof are equally to the vallies in most places of *Europe;* but the Vale of *Monmorencie* (wherein *Paris* standeth) scarce to be fellowed in the Wor[l]d. An Argument whereof may be, that when the Dukes of Berry, Burgundie, and their Confederates, besieged that City with an Armie of 100000 men; neither the Assailants without, nor the Citizens within, found any scarcitie of victuals; and yet the Citizens, besides Souldiers, were reckoned at 700000. (Heylyn 1652a: 154)

Thus the Fronde, just ending, provided Heylyn with evidence of both the centrality and the richness of the Ile-de-France.

When he came to the duchy of Anjou, rather enlarged in his account, Heylyn remarked that "the Countrey for the most part is very fruitful and pleasant, especially in *Tourein;* as is the whole tract upon the *Loir. Anjou* is somewhat the more hilly, but otherwise little inferiour to *Tourein,* affording plenty of white wines, the best in *France:* and yielding from those Hills above 40 Riverets, falling into the *Loire* from thence" (Heylyn 1652a: 167).

Languedoc was different:

> The Countrie in those parts which lie next to *Auvergne,* is like the *higher* parts thereof, mountainous and not very fruitfull; in all the rest, as rich and pleasant as the best provinces in *France* and having the advantages of Olives, Raisins, Figs, Orenges, and other fruits not ordinary but here, and in the neighboring *Provence.* In that participating the commodities both of *France* and *Spain.* The people have somewhat in them of the ancient *Gothes,* and draw neerer to the temper of the *Spaniards,* than any

Fig. 13. Flanders and Picardy in the seventeenth century

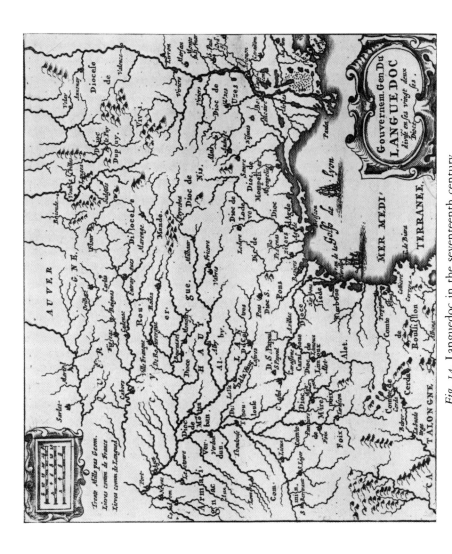

Fig. 14. Languedoc in the seventeenth century

other of the *French,* as being accounted very devout, great vaunters of themselves, affecting bravery above their condition and estates; not caring how they pinch it on the working days, or at home in private, so they may flaunt it in the street, and be fine on *holydays.* The humour also of the Women, and in them more pardonable. (Heylyn 1652a: 183)

Peter Heylyn found Burgundy rather less appealing:

A province so well watred with pleasant and profitable Rivers, that as Qu. *Catherine de Medices* used to say of *France,* That it had more fair rivers than all *Europe;* so we may say of this Countrie, That it hath more fine Riverets than all *France;* here being the Rivers of 1 *Armacan,* 2 *Serum,* 3 *Curi,* 4 *Terney,* 5 *Valence,* 6 *Dove,* 7 *Brune,* 8 *Sein,* 9 *Louche,* and 10 *Soasne,* (the *Araxis* of the antient Writers) this last dividing the two *Burgundies* from one another. Yet, notwithstanding this great plentie of waters, the Country generally is less fruitfull than the rest of *France:* hardly yeelding sufficient for its own inhabitants, except wines only. (Heylyn 1652a: 193)

Heylyn reserved his description of Flanders for his second volume, and the section on Belgium; in 1652 Flanders was not French, but Spanish, territory:

The Soyle indifferently fruitfull in corn and pastures; the aire healthfull, temperate and pleasant. The whole Countrey not in length above 90. miles, and in breadth but sixty; and yet containing in that compasse above thirty Cities (for they reckon all Cities which be walled) 1154 Villages; which stand so thick (as needs they must in so narrow a compasse) that the *Spaniards* at their first coming in with King *Philip* the second, took the whole Province for one Town. (Heylyn 1652b: 7)

Five regions, then, quite different in character: a capital and its hinterland, an old agricultural district, a vast and culturally distinctive southern province, a relatively poor frontier area blessed with a rich vineyard, a thickly-settled commercial region just beyond the border. These are the five sections whose experience with contention we are exploring and, in the measure possible, attempting to explain.

The selection of five regions from the fifteen or twenty that easily suggest themselves is necessarily arbitrary. Dare we neglect Lyon, Marseille, Bordeaux, Nantes, Le Havre, or even Limoges? Can we let those five provinces speak for Alsace, Provence, Corsica, Berry, Brittany? No: there is no way to choose five areas that sum up all of France, especially when we have four centuries to survey. Yet the attempt to follow the ebb and flow of contention throughout the entire country over nearly four centuries would be even more futile than the search for a scientific microcosm. The point of scrutinizing five cities and their regions is to keep the analysis manageable, yet to assure some differences among the points of observation. If common patterns emerge, we gain confidence that they hold for the country as a whole. If persistent differences appear, we acquire a sense of the factors that underlie those differences.

The history of French contention that follows concentrates on Dijon, Angers, Lille, Toulouse, and Paris; on Burgundy, Anjou, Flanders, Langue-doc, and the Ile-de-France. At each stage the chief materials will come from these five areas, and the chief comparisons will set these five areas against one another. Nevertheless, when rich evidence, revealing events, exceptional work by other scholars, or the simple need to round out the story call for it, I will not hesitate to call in material from other parts of France. My aim is disciplined reflection, not rigid symmetry.

We already have an idea of the places of Dijon and Burgundy. For most purposes our "Burgundy" will be a shrunken relic of its historic self, the territory of the present-day department of Côte d'Or. Now and then we will stray into the adjacent department of Saône-et-Loire, which includes the lower portion of the Burgundy incorporated by France in the fifteenth century, and which extends almost to Lyon. In addition to Dijon, Châtillon-sur-Seine, Sémur-en-Auxois, Beaune, and other Burgundian cities will figure repeatedly in the account.

Paris we know, too, but not necessarily the Ile-de-France. The "island" consists of the territory blocked out by the rivers Eure, Yonne, Marne, Aisne, and Epte, cut through by the greatest river of them all, the Seine. Beauvais, Compiègne, Fontainebleau, and Chartres mark its outer limits, its areas of competition with Maine, Normandy, Picardy, Champagne, and the Orléanais. Since the 1960s the administration of the Ile-de-France has fallen into seven separate departments: Val-d'Oise (capital: Pontoise), Yvelines (Versailles), Essonne (Evry), Val-de-Marne (Créteil), Hauts-de-Seine (Nanterre), Seine-St.-Denis (Bobigny), and Paris itself. Today's Seine-et-Marne (Melun), plus significant chunks of Oise (Beauvais) and Aisne (Laon), also belonged to the old-regime province.

From a commercial and political viewpoint, Paris has dominated this entire region since the later Middle Ages. Until recently, however, the area outside the great walled capital divided into three quite different sorts of places: estates of great magnates (ecclesiastical, noble, and bourgeois alike); zones of intensive cash-crop farming, sometimes overlapping with the estates; towns and small cities having their own commercial rationales. During the century before the Revolution, Versailles partly displaced Paris as the effective capital of France. In the twentieth century, despite repeated attempts at comprehensive planning and despite the survival of gorgeous forests, parks, and castles, the entire region has coalesced increasingly into a single built-up metropolis centered somewhere between the Eiffel Tower and the Hôtel de Ville.

Angers today is a city of 100,000 straddling the Maine River, a few kilometers north of the Loire, with a metropolitan area reaching down to the Loire. When the Constituent Assembly of 1790 blocked out France's departments, it did a fairly good job of approximating the old duchy of Anjou with the new department of Maine-et-Loire and of separating it from the adjacent territories of Brittany, Poitou, Touraine, and Maine. Thus for most purposes the contemporary limits of Maine-et-Loire will serve as our Anjou. Under the old regime, Angers stood only in the third echelon of French political structure: it had no parlement or Estates and was administratively subordinate to an intendant based in Tours. Saumur, Beaufort-en-Vallée, Baugé, Segré, and other small cities play parts in the history of Angevin contention, although by comparison with Burgundy or the Ile-de-France, Anjou's experience of the last four centuries is rather rural.

For a major part of that period, the province's fate depended especially on the fortunes of the Loire. The river carried Angevin wheat elsewhere in France, and the wines of its valleys—Saumur, Layon, Muscadet, Cabernet, rosé d'Anjou—into the export market. As the slave trade of Nantes flourished in the eighteenth century, a vast, export-oriented textile industry grew up in rural areas both north and south of the Loire. As a result of the nineteenth-century decline of slaving and the acute competition of cotton fabrics with the linens of Anjou, that Angevin textile industry contracted and concentrated in a few small cities such as Cholet.

Lille and Flanders present quite a different picture. Wrested definitively from the Habsburgs only in the seventeenth century, on the Belgian frontier to this day, partly Flemish-speaking and strongly tied by culture, trade, and population movements to portions of the Low Countries that remained outside France, the region was conquered foreign territory to a much larger degree than any portion of Anjou, Burgundy, or the Ile-de-France. The department of the Nord, which will serve as our practical definition of Lille's region, does not approximate any previously existing unit, social or political, very accurately. It corresponds roughly to the northern territories France acquired from the Habsburgs in the 1678 Treaty of Nijmegen, by which Franche-Comté also became French. The name Flanders is an inaccurate shorthand, since after centuries of struggle and transfers between France and its neighbors a major part of the Flemish territory remained outside of French control, and since the Nord not only touches Picardy but also contains sections of the historical provinces of Cambrésis, Artois, and Hainaut.

None of this means the region of Lille was insignificant. It was one of France's earliest and most important manufacturing regions. Lille was a great textile city, and its countryside hummed with small-scale spinning and weaving long before the Revolution. During the nineteenth century, coal mining brought dust and prosperity to such centers as Anzin, while cotton spinning brought smoke and prosperity to such centers as Roubaix. The industrial triangle of Lille–Roubaix–Tourcoing began to coalesce and to grow in that same century. Cambrai, Dunkerque, Valenciennes, Armentières, and other cities also participated in the expansion of manufacturing and commerce. Yet agriculture survived, and even prospered, in the Nord: among French departments, says Michel Morineau, only the Nord and the adjacent Pas-de-Calais "stand up to comparison with England, Belgium, and the Netherlands, the pioneers of European agriculture" (Morineau 1971: 30).

To go from Lille to Toulouse takes us almost from the English Channel to the Mediterranean, into a different world. The counts of Toulouse came under the control of the French crown long before 1600, yet the region maintained a distinctly Mediterranean language and culture long afterward. A commercial and political capital since Roman times, Toulouse retained its exceptionally autonomous municipal institutions, the Capitoulat, against the claims of lords, bishops, judges, and kings. Nevertheless, the generality (and therefore the intendant) of Languedoc was quartered not in Toulouse, but in Montpellier. The modern-day department of Haute-Garonne, on which we shall focus, approximates the Toulousain, heart of old Languedoc. Languedoc as a whole is large; the province extends from the Mediterranean to fill an area west of the Rhône and northeast of the Pyrenees; Roussillon, Gascony, Périgord, Auvergne, the Lyonnais, Dauphiné, and Provence are all its neighbors. The Toulousain itself is Mediterranean and Roman: settled in large towns, raising olives and grapes in addition to its wheat.

Dijon, Angers, and Toulouse resemble each other as commercial and administrative headquarters for large rural regions. They also differ in important ways: because their regions differ in culture and in geopolitical significance; because Angers lost its political autonomy and influence to the French crown very early, while in different ways Toulouse and Dijon held onto important levers of power until the Revolution; because the fine wines of Burgundy, the textiles of Anjou, and the polycultures of the Toulousain, not to mention other economic differences among the regions, pulled their capitals in different directions. Paris and Lille have in common their major industrial concentrations but differ dramatically in many other respects. If

the histories of contention in these diverse regions display common characteristics, we will have some assurance that they result from processes that
operated very generally in France. If they differ significantly, we will have
some hope of identifying the bases of their differences.

Of course there are some common trends. In all these regions we witness the rise of the state and the expansion of capitalism. We also see the
impact of the two great changes on the contention of ordinary people. In all
of them during the seventeenth and eighteenth centuries the state was
reaching incessantly into local affairs and resources, and the contention of
ordinary people often aimed at fending off the insatiable demand of royal
officials for men, for money, for food, for services. The fending off continued in the nineteenth and twentieth centuries, but an increasing share of
the action consisted of demanding something *from* the state; that new trend
correlated with a nationalization of political power, a centralization of decision making.

In all the regions we also notice the growing prevalence of capitalist
property relations: the destruction of common-use rights; the shift toward
production for sale; the setting of prices for all factors of production, including land; the growing dominance of wage labor; the increasing power
of owners of capital relative to those who owned land or labor or technical
expertise. These trends continued into the nineteenth century, when a new
trend joined them: an increasing concentration of capital, and a corresponding rise in the scale of producing units. Not all these trends were unilinear.
By the middle of the nineteenth century, for example, there were few common-use rights left to destroy, and the government was moving slowly toward the creation of new common facilities such as schools and hospitals;
again, the family farm regained a measure of importance as wage laborers
began to flee the countryside toward 1900.

It is also possible that since World War II, with the nationalization of
a few industries and the increasing deliberate involvement of the state in
economic policy, the power of capitalists with respect to government officials has declined. Possible, but not self-evident; the sticky question is how
much government officials continue to serve capitalist interests. In any case,
the drift of our period as a whole runs powerfully toward capitalism, more
capitalism. On the whole, we find ordinary people resisting that drift, but
ineffectually—attempting to hold off the increasing power of the capitalists
among them; attempting to hold on to their prior collective rights to land,
labor, crops, and goods; resisting proletarianization; fighting the growth of
disciplined large-scale production. Now and then we find them attempting
to deflect the process, as in the sporadic nineteenth-century visions of small-

scale socialism. The great revolutionary moments involve a temporary synthesis of the resistance to the present with an alternative vision of the future. In 1789, for example, we discover a coalescence of resistance to the rising exactions of the state with a vision of a world in which property is the only basis of privilege.

In all the regions, finally, the bases on which people acted together, when they did act collectively, altered greatly. In very general terms, they moved from community to association. When seventeenth-century Angevins, Toulousans, Burgundians, Flemings, and Parisians got together, it was generally as members of groups that included a large round of life: villages, guilds, age-grades, and the like. Those communities frequently had a recognized collective identity and distinctive privileges, but they usually encompassed a broader range of shared interests and less often resulted from a deliberate decision to organize than is the case with the collective action of our own time. With the nineteenth century we observe a great increase in the deliberate creation and use of special-interest organizations: firms, unions, clubs, parties, and the like. Communities did not disappear, but they lost their dominance as the bases of collective action. In the process, the sheer scale on which people organized and acted tended to increase. On the average, it became more common for thousands of people from dozens of localities to take part in the same action: a strike, a demonstration, a boycott, an electoral campaign. Specialized associations and large-scale collective action rose together.

Specialized associations that organized action frequently drew their memberships from a single social class and represented the interests of that class. Although unions and parties provide the salient examples, clubs, citizens' associations, and even recreational groups often worked the same way. Why not, then, speak of the emergence of a society of classes? After all, many observers have read the nineteenth century that way.

The reason for rejecting that label is simple: social classes also existed and acted in earlier centuries. They did not, however, bear the names capitalist and worker. They called each other landlord, rentier, peasant, agricultural laborer, artisan, and so on. In a world in which relationships to land made the profound sort of difference that relationship to capital makes in our own world, people who bore a common relationship to a given chunk of land were likely to build a whole round of life around that common relationship; classes were likely to form communities. Common relationship to the same land tended to mean not only common work but also common residence, common means of subsistence, common privileges, common access to services, common religious identity, common marriage pool, common subjection to political authority. Interlaced, those common ties formed communities.

Because of the fluidity and spatial discontinuity of capital, a common relationship to a given block of capital does not generate communities as regularly as common relationship to a given block of land does. To be sure, the difference is a matter of degree: the capital fixed in a single large factory promotes the creation of homogeneous communities of owners, managers, and workers, unified by shared work and shared residence. But on the average, capital generates fewer communities than land. When people having a common relationship to capital organize, they almost necessarily do so on a larger scale than do people who already belong to class-based communities. They frequently do so through the deliberate creation of specialized associations. The rise of capital as the great divider promotes the proliferation of associations and an increase in the scale of collective action. Changing patterns of contention in Anjou, Burgundy, Flanders, Languedoc, and the Ile-de-France showed the net shift from community to association, from small scale to large, quite clearly.

Not only the scale, but also the character of collective action changed. Some features of the change should already be clear. For one thing, the relationship of collective action to daily, weekly, or annual routines altered. Back in the seventeenth century, a large share of all collective action went on in the context of routine, authorized public gatherings such as markets, fairs, processions, festivals, hangings, and local electoral assemblies. As the twentieth century approached, the relative importance of routine, authorized public gatherings declined. Instead, deliberately called meetings, rallies, strikes, demonstrations, and other prepared actions became common means of getting together to act on shared interests. They broke with everyday routine. As a result, they gave the average individual a sharper choice between joining or not joining a collective action than his seventeenth-century ancestors faced. The organizer of a meeting or a demonstration cannot count on the membership's being there as a matter of course.

If we look only at the nineteenth- and twentieth-century end of the continuum, the change is easy to misconstrue. From the point of view of a contemporary organizer, it looks as though ordinary people used to be passive, unmobilized, uninvolved in politics—as though it took the strenuous organizing of the last century to mobilize the masses. What actually happened was quite different: centralization of power tended to *de*mobilize ordinary people and to make their ordinary routines irrelevant and ineffective as means of collective action. The nationalization of politics that eventually grew from the centralization of power did create new opportunities for collective action built around elections and similar institutions. It created the "problem" of mobilization, and an unprecedented opportunity for professional organizers to work at solving that problem. The social movement—the sustained, organized challenge to the existing structure or exercise of power in the name of some large interest—took shape. The whole repertoire of collective action changed.

As the repertoire of collective action detached itself from local daily routines, some of its quality as folklore disappeared. The ritual mockery, the effigies, the fifes and drums, the songs, the garish symbols faded from the forms of contention. The matter is not easy to sort out: part of the reason that a Lanturelu or the parading of a dummy on a gallows now looks like folklore is that twentieth-century observers see an antique sheen on almost _any_ feature of seventeenth- or eighteenth-century life: the language is quaint, the clothing is museumlike, the names of people, shops, and trades are unfamiliar. A twenty-second-century student of American demonstrations in the 1960s will undoubtedly be impressed with the folklore of Yippies and flower children. Yet by virtue of its specialization and its detachment from everyday routine, the contemporary repertoire carries over less of the ritual and symbolism shared by particular local populations than did now-forgotten forms of contention such as grain seizures and charivaris. In that sense, at least, the history of French contention shows us a decline of folklore.

The same change has another side. Many of the older forms of action consisted of a crowd's carrying out—sometimes in parody, sometimes in deadly earnest—a routine that normally belonged to the authorities. Hanging in effigy, seizing stored grain and selling it below the current market price, decapitating a traitor and displaying his head, refusing to permit the collection of a tax until the collector produced full documentation of his right to collect it were all standard governmental routines; they also became significant features of "seditions" and "emotions." That borrowing of the place and the action of the authorities did not disappear in the nineteenth and twentieth centuries, but it became less common and less salient. In a sense, the autonomy of the crowd and of the action increased. The power of the crowd and the efficacy of the action did not necessarily grow as a consequence; patronage and the borrowing of established routines were often very effective ways of pursuing common interests. The crucial change was the creation of autonomous, specialized forms and organizations for collective action.

What was the role of alterations in our three major factors—interests, organization, and opportunities—in these basic changes? The remaining chapters attempt a full answer to that question. We can see already that the rise of the national state and the expansion of capitalism greatly altered what sets of people had pressing common *interests* in collective action as well as the character of the interests they shared. The corporate trade and the self-sustained religious community, for example, virtually disappeared as the political coalition and the specialized occupational group became prominent interests. There is no doubt that the characteristic *organization* of such interests has changed. The most obvious change has been the rise of various forms of special-purpose association. Along with that change has come the increasing importance of professional organizers, running from committed revolutionaries to sleek fund-raisers.

The *opportunities* for collective action, too, have shifted dramatically. So far, the aspect of that shift we have seen most clearly has been the nationalization of power and politics. Increasingly the action (or, for that matter, the inaction) of large organizations and of national states has created the threats and opportunities to which any interested actor has to respond. Increasingly, national politics have provided the channels within which an actor can deal effectively with the interest in question. Increasingly, the repression or facilitation applied to a particular actor by organizations of national scope—and especially by the national state itself—has determined whether the actor could act effectively at all.

For the moment, it would be idle to weigh the relative importance of changes in interests, organization, and opportunity. It would be premature to specify the ways they influenced each other. It is enough for now to realize that they were profound changes, that they occurred together and interdependently, and that they constitute much of what people have in mind when they talk about the modernization of politics or about political development.

In one perspective, these changes signify the creation of a bureaucratic, capitalist, specialized world dominated by powerful governments, large organizations, and big cities. In another perspective, they amount to fundamental changes in the interests, organization, and opportunities that together govern the intensity and character of collective action. In yet a third perspective, they mean a profound alteration in the repertoires of contention employed by ordinary people. The three perspectives converge. It is our task in the remaining chapters to see how they converge.

Our comparison of five regions will serve to document and to specify the grand trends. It will help us understand how they work and how they interact. There are, for example, strong correlations among the concentration of power in the state, the nationalization of politics, the enlargement of the electorate, the rise of the association as the chief vehicle of political action, and the increasing use of the meeting and the demonstration as means of collective action. Why, how, and with what regularity did those correlations occur? That is not so clear; a close look at the eighteenth and nineteenth centuries will clarify the connections.

Consider another problem. We have all too many plausible explanations of the food conflict's rise and fall: the changing cost of food, the changing policies of local officials, the changing beliefs and organization of poor people, the changing practices of merchants, and others. All of them probably played their parts in the seventeenth-century rise and the nineteenth-century fall of the grain seizure; but in what proportions, and in what connection with each other? Observation of food supply and of conflicts over food in the five regions should make the proportions and connections easier to grasp.

Comparisons will also identify significant differences. We shall notice, for instance, a contrast between the more or less artisanal producers of fine Burgundies, who supplied plenty of republican activists during the nineteenth century but remained aloof from large winegrowers' movements in the twentieth, and the increasingly proletarian winegrowers of Languedoc, who at one time supplied many recruits to anarcho-syndicalism, and later mounted large strikes and demonstrations aimed simultaneously at large distributors and at the state. We shall see associations becoming prominent bases of contention in Paris and the Ile-de-France earlier than in the other four regions, and will have occasion to wonder why. Thus the differences, as well as the similarities, will lead us to further reflection on the relationships among capitalism, statemaking, and changing forms of contention.

4

Anjou's Crises

HE TOWN OF Ponts-de-Cé arches across the shifting islands and shores of the Loire just south of Angers, halfway from Saumur to the border of Brittany. These days the road from Angers to the Ponts-de-Cé passes through nearly unbroken ranks of drab shops and apartments. Although the willows along the river offer a refreshing break from the roadway's stone, slate, and carbon monoxide, the town itself now seems no more than a commercial suburb of Angers. At the start of the seventeenth century, however, four kilometers of open country separated the walls of the old city of Angers from the north bank parish of St.-Aubin-des-Ponts-de-Cé. St.-Maurille, the twin of St.-Aubin, occupied an island in midriver.

At high water the meandering Loire often flooded the nearby islands, the adjacent plains, and part of St.-Maurille's island as well. But the Ponts-de-Cé, as their name implies, stood on high enough ground to hold the series of wooden drawbridges that crossed the Loire to connect Angers with southern Anjou. A seventeenth-century journalist described the city as

> a long street on an island in the Loire River, with two big bridges that span a half-quarter league. The one on the side toward Brissac is longer by a third than the one on the Angers side. Within the bridges there are drawbridges, so that when they are up you can enter the city only by boat. The city has for its defense a good castle on the high part of the island, which commands all the roads across the bridges; the lower part contains a few houses. Except for the castle the whole place [is] without walls. At the ends of the two bridges there are also a good many houses, which serve the city as suburbs. (*Le Mercure François* 1620: 331)

The twin towns were Angers's chief port for goods moving up or down the river: her "nurse in grain, wheat, and bread," according to another seventeenth-century observer (Louvet 1854–1856: 4 pt. 1, 36). That was no doubt why Angers's customs area (*octroi*) bulged out to include the Ponts-de-Cé. By water, the river town was Angers's chief connection with the rest of the world. By land, the road across the Ponts-de-Cé was Angers's principal link with Poitou and with the regions farther south.

The Frolic of Ponts-de-Cé

In 1620 that link was vital to Marie de Medici. Marie (widow of Henry IV and mother of the nineteen-year-old king Louis XIII) had become governor of Angers in 1619. Her appointment helped settle a three-year war against her son. She had marked her entry into Anjou by spending the night of 15 October 1619 in the castle of Ponts-de-Cé. The next day she had ridden in her litter past six thousand armed burghers in regular ranks, passed through four triumphal arches erected in her honor, and endured repeated flowery speeches from Angers's officials (*Le Mercure François* 1619: 313–332).

Now, nine months later, Marie was settled in Angers, and at the center of another vast conspiracy. It aligned Marie, her adviser Richelieu, and a whole web of great lords against Louis XIII and his minister de Luynes. Many of Marie's noble co-conspirators had joined her in Angers. Some nine thousand soldiers were in the city under their command. Marie's allies held strong positions in a number of cities in northwestern France, including Rouen, Caen, and Vendôme. But several of Marie's most important allies, including the dukes of Epernon and Mayenne, kept their troops in readiness south of the Loire. The Ponts-de-Cé provided the sole practical line of communication between the queen mother and her armed supporters outside Angers.

During much of July the young king and his sometime ally the prince of Condé were marching their armies from stronghold to stronghold in Normandy, Perche, and Maine. There they chased away the queen's allies and extracted guarantees of loyalty from the local authorities. Then they headed for Anjou. Dread seized the Angevins; after all, many of them could still remember the sieges and sacking of the recent wars of religion.

Jehan Louvet was there. The modest clerk at Angers's Présidial Court kept a journal in which he recorded the city's everyday events—especially its legal events—from 1560 to 1634. (The journal, properly speaking, began in 1583; the earlier entries were retrospective.) We can imagine Jehan Louvet

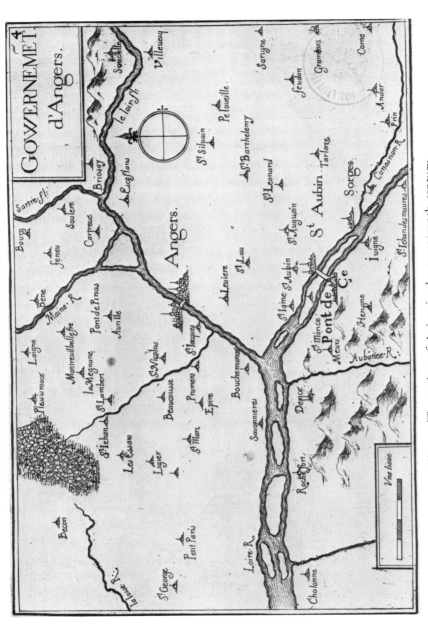

Fig. 15. The region of Anjou in the seventeenth century

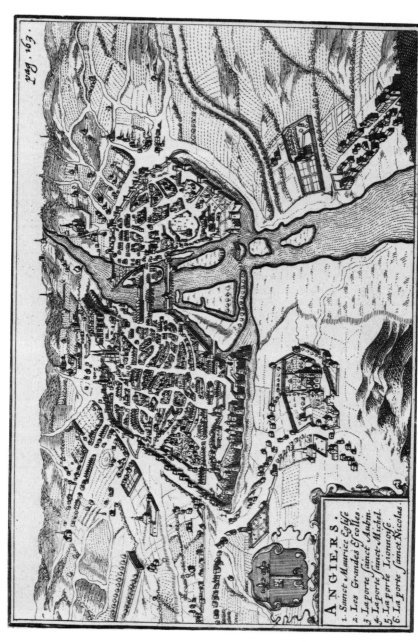

Fig. 16. Aerial perspective of Angers in the seventeenth century

on the evening of 24 July 1620 lighting his candle, opening his notebook, sharpening a goose quill, dipping it into his inkwell, and scratching these words into the journal:

> Le vendredy, vingt-quatrième jour dudict mois de juillet, audict an 1620, M. le duc de Vendosme est arrivé Angers de La Flesche, où il estoit avec la royne . . . Comme aussy cedict jour, M. Le Grand, M. le président Janin et aultres depputez, qui estoient venuz de la part du roy Angers vers la royne, mère de Sa Majesté, pour conférer avec elle sur le traitté de la paix, s'en sont allez et sortiz d'Angers, où ilz estoient venuz le douzième de ce présent mois, sans avoir faict aulcune conference, faict ny arresté aulcune chose, dont les habitants de la ville d'Angers ont esté grandement faschez et marriz, prévoyant que c'estoit signe de grande guerre, maulx et afflictions que Dieu préparoit envoyer auldicts habitants, M. Lasnier, maire de la ville d'Angers, n'a voullu bailler les clefs des portes de Boisnet pour les ouvrir.   (Louvet 1854–1856: 4 pt. 1, 30)

> On Friday, the twenty-fourth day of said month of July of said year 1620, the Duke of Vendôme arrived in Angers from La Flèche, where he had been with the queen . . . On the same day M. Le Grand, the President Janin, and other deputies who had come to Angers on the king's behalf to see the queen, the king's mother, to confer with her about a peace treaty, left and departed from Angers, where they had arrived on the twelfth of this month, without making any announcement, without any decree, because of which the residents of the city of Angers were greatly angered and upset, foreseeing that it was the sign of a great war, of evils and afflictions that God was preparing to send the said residents. And to increase the fright and fear of said inhabitants, M. Lasnier, mayor of the city of Angers, did not want to hand over the keys of the Boisnet gates for them to be opened.

The fears, negotiations, and preparations for war continued.

In Angers, Marie de Medici drafted the inhabitants to work on the ramparts as rumors of treason and destruction ran from door to door. When the king's forces came close, the queen mother imposed a rigid curfew, made the inhabitants surrender all their arms, and released the prisoners from Angers's jail to serve in her army. Meanwhile Marie's troops fortified the Ponts-de-Cé and lived off the nearby land. In an age-old routine, people from the defenseless countryside fled to the relative safety of Angers's city walls. According to Jehan Louvet,

> the poor people of the fields and faubourgs left and abandoned everything, carrying and dragging into Angers anything they could bring

away. It was a piteous and frightful thing to see them, and to hear them cry and lament, saying that the queen mother's companies and soldiers had greatly pillaged, beaten, and ransomed them, leaving some of them nothing, and that they had been forced to leave grain they had just begun to cut, and that where people had already cut and stacked their grain, the soldiers—led by the devil, spiteful and full of anger—lighted the stacks and burned them.   (Louvet 1854–1856: 4 pt. 1, 36–37)

As the king's armies approached, fear and anger mounted.

Passing through Le Mans and La Flèche, the royal forces feinted toward Angers, then rushed toward Ponts-de-Cé. The battle, such as it was, took place on Friday 7 August. Near the river the royal army confronted a rebel garrison reinforced by several thousand troops dispatched from Angers. The front-line rebel troops stood along a trench that ran parallel to the river for about 500 meters. The remainder of the force spread from there to the town of St.-Aubin, across the bridge, and to the castle. "The unlucky cavalry," reported Marshal Marillac, "was placed on the city's parapet in the broiling sun, in no position to serve" (Pavie 1899: 678). As one of the rebel commanders who bore the brunt of the royal attack, Marillac had strong reasons for complaint.

The condition of the cavalry set the tone for the day: for one reason or another, many of the rebel troops on hand never entered the action, and many more left before a serious battle had begun. The most important defection was that of the duke of Retz, who led some seventeen hundred men south across the bridges "in a single file so long the enemy could easily see half of it" (Marillac in Pavie 1899: 679). Apparently the duke was furious at signs that the queen mother and the king were discussing peace terms without consulting him. That loss of more than two regiments opened a gap in the middle of the line of defense and made it easier for the royal forces to attack and to rout the rebel army. The battle was so unequal that it entered history as the "drôlerie des Ponts-de-Cé": the Ponts-de-Cé Frolic. "A two-hour skirmish," wrote du Plessis–Mornay, "broke up the largest dissident group that had formed in France for several centuries" (Bazin 1838: 115).

Battle, skirmish, or frolic, the clash at the Loire brought Louis XIII into the castle at Ponts-de-Cé and started several days of negotiations. It produced the Peace of Angers. On 13 August Marie de Medici and Louis XIII sealed their agreement in a tearful reunion at the chateau of Brissac, ten kilometers south of the Loire on the road to Poitiers. Thus ended the so-called Second War of the Mother and the Son. All that remained was to bury the dead, nurse the wounded, pay off and dismiss the troops, make sure they left the region quickly without marauding, and then rebuild the city's burned, bombarded suburbs.

No: There was one more thing to do. That was to pay for the war. War has always been one of mankind's most expensive activities, and wars have usually strained the finances of the states that have waged them. It is nevertheless impressive to see how the rapid expansion of European war-making in the seventeenth century overran the capacities of existing governments, and how much every statemaker scurried from expedient to expedient, seeking to squeeze more out of established sources of revenue, to invent and enforce new forms of taxation, to beg, borrow, and steal. The French state was no exception. The civil wars that racked France between 1614 and 1622 elevated the national budget from about 27 million livres to about 50 million (Clamagéran 1868: II, 453–454). That meant an increase of 85 percent in eight years.

To raise that enormously expanded sum, the royal ministers stepped up the basic property tax (the taille), augmented the salt tax, increased all sorts of internal customs and sales taxes, sold offices and more offices, borrowed money, forced loans, devalued old debts by one trick or another, and re-sorted to such nasty old reliables as formally expelling Jews from the king-dom in order to extort special residence fees from Jews who could afford to remain. In the process, the crown relied increasingly on financiers and tax-farmers who had the ruthlessness and ingenuity to bring in money fast in return for broad powers, large profits, and extensive claims on future royal revenues. The growing power of these *traitants* and *partisans* threatened the perquisites of established officeholders as it increased the oppression of ordi-nary taxpayers.

Yet the treasury was often empty. On his very way to Ponts-de-Cé in 1620, Louis XIII had to stop in Le Mans and declare the reestablishment of the annual tax on venal offices (the *droit annuel*), designed "to bring in very quickly the large sums he needed" (Mousnier 1971: 636). Louis's edict pre-cipitated an eight-month struggle with the high courts of the land. No new money arrived without struggle.

Thus the machinery of war ground away at the resources of the coun-try. The machinery often broke down, whether bent by its own weight, im-mobilized by the cracks in its structure, stopped by the sheer exhaustion of its fuel, or blocked by outside resistance. Despite their apparent mutual contradiction, the pretentions of absolutism, the growth of the war ma-chine, the rise of tax-farmers, the proliferation of fiscal makeshifts and out-break of fierce popular rebellion were part and parcel of the same process of statemaking.

From Civil War to Popular Rebellion

The War of the Mother and the Son was anything but a popular rebellion. Even the word "rebellion" sits on it uneasily; the term presumes all too readily that the king was the rightful authority and his mother on illegitimate challenger. And "popular"? The queen mother and her co-conspirators had enthusiastic supporters in some cities, but those supporters were for the most part magnates who brought their own clienteles into the antiroyalist party. As for the rest of the people, wars among the great of the land meant forced labor, burned fields, requisitioned cattle, billeting, rape . . . and taxes, ever more taxes. The armies, like all armies of the time, consisted of mercenaries, clients, and retainers of the great lords. The wars pitted elite against elite, at the expense of ordinary people.

Yet, by a nice negation, the closing battle of this elite civil war produced a small popular rebellion. On 5 August, as the king's armies approached Angers, Marie de Medici had ordered the city's inhabitants to surrender their arms to the civic guards. More exactly, they were to deposit them at the homes of their parish captains or at the castle. Marie wanted to keep the populace out of the fighting that was likely to occur in the city— and, no doubt, to deprive them of the means of collaborating with the enemy outside the walls. When it finally came time for the citizens to reclaim their muskets and swords nearly three weeks later, word spread that one of the captains was planning to keep some of the arms, probably to sell them to the occupying armies. The rumor was true; the scoundrels were an échevin, Pierre Marchant, and his son-in-law Mathurin Leferon, lord of la Barbée. They had already sent some of the impounded guns off to Leferon's estate outside the city. A delegation of outraged citizens went to the mayor, complained, and asked permission to chase after the horse carrying the weapons and bring them back to Angers. Permission granted.

While the citizens went for the horse, the mayor sent a formal warning to Pierre Marchant; Marchant laughed and denied everything. Denial was harder when a crowd brought his servant and a gun-laden horse back through the city gate. As the mayor wrote an affidavit—a *procès-verbal,* the necessary preliminary to an old-regime criminal proceeding—people came from all over the city to the square outside Marchant's house. It was no longer a laughing matter. The mayor's affidavit, according to Jehan Louvet,

> did not prevent a great emotion and popular uproar of the people, who gathered in front of M. Marchant's dwelling, shouting that all the inhabitants' weapons had been put in the dwelling. On that cry and up-

roar a great many inhabitants took up the belief (justified by what has been said before and by other true reasons yet to be stated), and on that belief all or most of the people who were assembled in the said Pillory Square wanted to enter by force into the dwelling of said Marchant, saying loudly that said Marchant and said M. de la Barbée, his son-in-law, were robbers and thieves of the king, of the queen his mother, as well as of the city's inhabitants and the public. (Louvet 1854–1856: 4 pt. 1, 131)

As the crowd milled before Marchant's door, various people stated grievances against him: he had used his judicial powers to enrich himself, he had judged people cruelly and arbitrarily, and so on. The crowd, Louvet noted, consisted almost entirely of artisans. Off to the side gathered a number of "inhabitants and honorable persons" who worried about the threat to the person and property of one of Angers's dignitaries but were held in check by some mysterious, intriguing "lords and gentlemen who were there, and made a point of criticizing and threatening them" (Louvet 1854–1856: 4 pt. 1, 133).

The workmen took stones, smashed every window they could reach from Pillory Square, then threatened to break down the door and burn down the house. Only the intervention of the city's mayor, its military commander, and other dignitaries saved the house. Although the crowd finally dispersed around six that evening, the discontent continued for days. A group of citizens filed suit against Marchant. The queen mother herself, in her farewell address to the people of Angers, made a point of guaranteeing that every householder would get back the weapons he or she had surrendered before the battle at Ponts-de-Cé.

Angers's attack on Pierre Marchant made an exceptionally direct connection between war and popular contention. Ordinary people, it is true, also resisted war rather directly when they fought against billeting; against the requisitioning of food, animals, and other supplies for the military; and, later on, against the impressment or conscription of young men for military service. By and large, however, the seventeenth-century connection between war and popular contention was more indirect. It took the form of resistance—passive, active, or even collective—to the new and expanded taxes with which French statemakers sought to raise the money for their larger wars and growing armies. The seventeenth century became the classic time of large-scale popular rebellions against taxation. The Croquants, the Nu-Pieds, and the Bonnets Rouges were only the most visible insurrections of the series.

Taxes, Tax Collectors, and Protest

The big rebellions burst out from a backdrop of repeated local protests about taxes and tax collectors. Most of them ended with no more than an indignant but restrained complaint to local authorities by some group of aggrieved citizens; in most cases the complaint produced no more than a fearful, vague promise of action by the authorities. On the morning of 19 September 1623, for example, "a large number of poor baker women from Bouchemaine and Ruzebourg came to the royal palace in Angers and raised a great clamor and complaint before M. Jouet, the city's mayor, and the échevins about the bad treatment, cruelty, and tyranny they were getting from the salt-tax guards" (Louvet 1854–1856: 5 pt. 1, 4). But the authorities did nothing. The citizens, according to Jehan Louvet, "greatly murmured against the mayor and magistrates" (Louvet 1854–1856: 5 pt. 1, 4).

Not surprisingly, the mayor and council tended to act when new taxes or fiscal officials threatened their own privileges, competed with their own sources of income, or affected some major group of local powerholders. In Angers, judicial officers held a near-monopoly of public offices. They sought to fill existing offices by co-optation and to resist the creation of new positions. Thus in 1626, when the crown farmed out the 5 percent sales tax (the *pancarte*) in Angers to a certain Guillaume Abraham, the city fathers staged an extraordinary assembly, stated their opposition, and chose two of their most distinguished citizens as a delegation. The delegation went to Paris to plead with Marie de Medici and Richelieu for intervention on behalf of the city.

Fiscal innovations and injustices were the most consistent bases of contention in the Angers of the 1620s, but they were not the only ones. Louvet's journal provides a running account of the long struggle for precedence between the new bishop and the cathedral chapter, a struggle that sometimes divided the city's whole elite into bitter factions. Louvet chronicles the maneuvering between the local Huguenots (who were already confined by royal edict to one place of public worship in a village outside the city) and the city authorities, who were reluctant to grant them any privileges at all. There are more quarrels over precedence, brawls, processions to mobilize sentiment against the English, assemblies of trades to air particular grievances. There are hard times for the executioner: in July 1625 a crowd massacred a hangman who botched his job; seven months later a group of lackeys snatched one of their own from the hangman's hands, and the hangman went to jail for it. And there is the Merchants' Mardi Gras of 1629.

On Jeudi Gras (Thursday 22 February) of that year, the city's law clerks had held their mock court, with the son of the city's chief judge presiding. In the course of their pleading, the clerks had insulted many of Angers's leading citizens, including the wife of a prominent merchant. On Mardi Gras (Tuesday 27 February), more than four hundred members of the merchants' guilds gathered at St.-Nicolas field, just outside the city. They donned masks and elaborate costumes made for the occasion, mounted fine horses "that a large number of nobles and lords had loaned them," and entered the city two by two. Passing through the city's major streets and squares,

> they tossed a dummy wearing a long robe, a square bonnet, with bags
> and writing-board attached to its belt. People said it was a trial lawyer
> they were mocking. They did the same thing in front on the law court
> in the rue St.-Michel. They went out the St.-Michel Gate and proceeded
> along the moats. A great many people gathered in the shops and at the
> windows of houses in order to see them. Because of the mock pleading,
> the masquerade, and the display of the dummy a great many divisions
> and hostilities developed among numerous families in the city.   (Lou-
> vet 1854–1856: 5 pt. 2, 54)

Mutual mockery reinforced the existing division between the legal officials on the one side and the merchants and artisans on the other.

Even local power struggles, however, became more acute when compounded with new and increasing taxes. During the 1620s, although Louis XIII was not yet heavily involved in international wars, his reduction of the principal Huguenot strongholds in France required large armies, and therefore a rapid increase in revenue. (The siege of Protestant La Rochelle alone cost more than 40 million livres, at a time when a laborer's daily wage, at 20 sous per livre, was 10 or 12 sous and a bushel of wheat generally ran to around one livre; Clamagéran 1868: II, 478.) Toward the end of the decade, furthermore, Louis was organizing campaigns in Italy against the Habsburgs and the dukes of Savoy. As usual, the expanded military effort meant more taxes.

As taxes rose from the late 1620s on, the tempo of protest also increased. The cluster of conflicts that beset Angers in 1629 and 1630 were tame affairs compared with the bloody insurrections elsewhere in France, but they illustrate the smaller-scale versions of contention about taxation. The sequence was impressively standard: royal officials announced a new or increased tax, the people most affected by the tax (typically the workers in a given trade) protested the impropriety of the new action by petition or declaration, the protest was rejected or ignored. The tax collectors then arrived

with their commissions, a crowd formed outside the tax collectors' premises, the people involved restated their protest and then attacked the homes
or persons of the tax collectors.

The tanners of Angers, for example, protested vociferously the levying
of a new tax on hides and skins. Around 10:00 P.M. on 5 September 1629,
sixty to eighty of them went to the inn "where the image of Saint Julian
hangs as its sign." They found the hotel locked, then "made a great noise
and uproar and threatened to throw said tax collectors into the water and
even to burn down the inn, and made a point of breaking down the doors
to get into the hostelry, broke the lower windows with stones, and went
away" (Louvet 1854–1856: 5 pt. 2, 136). The judges to whom the tax collectors complained the next day advised them to leave town in order to
avoid greater violence.

In April 1630 another variant of the tax rebellion took place in Angers.
After placards attacking the magistrates for their role in the collection of
new taxes had appeared in the city, the company of trial lawyers assembled
to debate their own fiscal problems. The lawyers—confronted both with
new fees and with the necessity of buying off the appointment of prosecutors the crown was otherwise threatening to impose on them—resolved not
to show up for work again until they had brought their case against the
greedy tax-farmers to the king and to the parlement of Paris.

Three days later, on 9 April, a crowd gathered to block the bailiffs sent
to enforce the payment of delinquent taxes in one of Angers's faubourgs.
When a bailiff injured a recalcitrant tavernkeeper with a blow of his sword,
the crowd chased away the lot of them. (One of the bailiffs had the bad
judgment to flee for protection to the city's jail; there the authorities held
him, tried him for assault, and sentenced him to hang.) The next day another crowd besieged in his home a local dignitary "suspected of tax gouging" (AMA BB 72/97).

Not all the action was negative. On 21 May the civic militia honored
the mayor of Angers for his opposition to the tax-farmers. The militia companies marched through the streets with banners, drums, and trumpets, firing their muskets and carrying a May tree. They finally planted the tree at
the mayor's door. After that the ordinary militiamen received ten sous each
to dine on the town together, while their officers enjoyed a banquet at the
mayor's house. On 30 May the tribute continued with the citizens' building
of an elaborate tableau. On the river they constructed a fort, a stage, and a
giant figure representing, in effect, the French people resisting tyranny. In a
mock battle on the river, the giant Alastor and his forces repelled attack
after attack. Gunsmoke clouded the river, fireworks sprayed from the fort,

orators declaimed verses written for the tableau, and everyone who saw the show (according to the ever-observant Jehan Louvet) "went away pleased" (Louvet 1854–1856: 5 pt. 2, 162).

In June 1630 it was again the turn of the salt-tax guards, the *archers de la gabelle,* to feel the people's anger. Two of the guards had been arrested for murder and theft in a village near Angers. On the thirteenth, as the popular mayor (who was also a judge at the Présidial) took his two prisoners to hear witnesses at the scene of the crimes, the captain of the salt-tax forces came up with more of his guards. Brandishing a pistol, he threatened the mayor. The mayor sent to Angers for help. Help came, in the form of a swarm of people who rushed out the city gates bearing all sorts of weapons. The attack on the guards ended with two archers dead, the captain's house in Angers sacked, his wine drunk, and his household goods consumed in a giant bonfire (Louvet 1854–8566: 5 pt. 2, 167–170).

As it happened, St. John's Eve (23 June) was only ten days away. While the people of Paris gathered for fireworks at the Place de Grève, the youths of Angers organized their own spectacle. They were, said Louvet, accustomed since time immemorial "to light fires in honor and reverence of the holiday in the squares and other places and locations of the city" (Louvet 1854–1856: 5 pt. 2, 171). This time, according to the royal prosecutor, the participants were residents "of base and vile condition"; that probably means journeymen, apprentices, and servants. They made a dummy of the hated captain, a sword in his hand and a sign on his back. They took their staves and halberds, bearing the dummy through the streets with drums and banners, drubbing the effigy as they went, shouting taunts, and eventually tossing the figure into the flames.

The citizens of Angers soon suffered for their enthusiastic opposition; no matter how badly he behaved, after all, a *capitaine des gabelles* embodied royal authority. For the events of April and June, thirty-odd people went to jail in the castle, five were shipped to Tours for trial, two were hanged, and the city had to reimburse the archers' captain for his losses.

These protests were, to be sure, minor compared with Dijon's Lanturelu, which occurred earlier the same year. But the grievances of Dijon were greater. There, the king was trying to abolish the city's special tax exemption and to establish a local tax administration (an *élection*) directly responsible to the crown. By 1630, Anjou already had an élection. It had long since lost the protection of its own provincial Estates. The province had seen much of its fiscal independence disappear in earlier centuries.

Yet the struggles over taxation in Dijon and Angers had important traits in common. They had the common background of war-induced demand for greater royal revenue. They also shared a standard sequence of popular resistance running from principled formal protest (when possible) to direct attacks on the collectors (when necessary); the importance of corporate trades and professions such as the trial lawyers and the tanners as nuclei of resistance; the special hatred reserved for local officials who made money on new taxes or abused the authority given them by their appointment as tax collectors; the frequent hesitancy or complicity of local officials when it came to overcoming popular objections to royal taxes; the brutal but highly selective repression that arrived when royal authorities entered on the scene.

The forms of popular action also had much in common: the attack on a miscreant's house, the ritual mockery, the costumed parade, the borrowing of legal forms such as burning in effigy, the recurrent threat to throw enemies into the water. Antitax actions drew on a standard repertoire. In general, they conveyed a popular attitude we might call aggressive supplication. "Give us our rights," people said, in effect, "and we will stay in our place; deny us our rights and we will fight." Ordinary people saw more or less clearly that royal taxes were cutting deeper and deeper into their own lives, local authorities saw their own power and autonomy being circumscribed as royal officers multiplied, and both realized that the new levies often violated long-standing, legally sanctioned rights and privileges.

With the end of Jehan Louvet's journal in 1634, we lose some of the texture of contention in Anjou. The official proceedings of Angers's city council for the period (AMA BB 28–74) mention most of the events in the journal, but soberly and laconically; they lack the loving detail prized by a gossipy clerk of the court. Yet the official record makes it clear that the basic conflicts of the 1620s recurred throughout the 1630s and 1640s: running battles with the salt-tax guards, an intensifying struggle between the judicial officers and the bourgeoisie of the city, an unceasing effort by royal officials to pry more taxes from Anjou, an unceasing effort by Angevins to keep from paying.

Between the end of Louvet's journal in 1634 and the start of the Fronde in 1648, the largest struggles came in 1641 and 1643. Both were antitax movements, but they took different forms. In 1641 crowds attacked the collectors stationed at the city gates to collect the new royal *subvention* of one sou per livre (that is, 5 percent) on the value of goods entering the city. Although the people in the streets were poor and obscure, the intendant reported that "a number of merchants are encouraging the sedition. I cannot find a single person to make a deposition, do what I may; everyone tells me, 'I don't know those folks.' These people have reached such a high degree

of insolence that they are threatening to burn the house of anyone who testifies; they haven't the least concern for the magistrates" (Mousnier 1964:
487).

Two years later, in 1643, the tax in question was the *subsistances,* a levy
designed to pay for feeding the royal troops who were then attacking the
Habsburgs in Catalonia and Flanders. When the military governor pressed
for payment of past-due amounts, the Angevins refused. Unauthorized parish assemblies named speakers (*syndics*) and declared they would not pay the
illegal tax. Although the intendant boasted in August that he had "broken
their syndicate" (Porchnev 1963: 619–620), in one form or another the alliances that appeared in the near-rebellion of 1643 continued through the rest
of the 1640s. They aligned the city's workers, many of the clergy, and a
cluster of lawyers not only against royal fiscal officers but also against the
magistrates who monopolized city offices and did the dirty work of the
crown (Lebrun 1966: 129–130).

The Fronde

At the local level, the Fronde continued the same struggles but complicated
and aggravated them. In its simplest terms, the Fronde amounted to a series
of challenges to royal authority. The challenges ranged from passive resistance to remonstrance to open rebellion, and lasted from 1648 to 1652.
There were four major clusters of actors:

> the king, the queen mother, Cardinal Mazarin, and their agents
> the high judiciary, clustered around the parlements, especially the
> parlement of Paris
> a shifting coalition of great magnates such as the prince of Condé,
> aligned against the crown most of the time but constantly vulnerable to
> defection, co-optation, and internal rivalry
> a set of local popular parties, variously drawn from merchants, profes-
> sionals, artisans, and rentiers

The complexities of the Fronde resulted partly from the changing positions
of the individual actors (for example, the great princes moved to open rebellion only well after the popular insurrections of 1648), partly from the
changing alliances *among* the actors (for example, when the Fronde began,
Condé was the king's chief military supporter, but when it ended he was the
king's chief enemy), and partly from tensions and splits within the big
clusters (for example, when the workers and shopkeepers threw up barricades throughout central Paris in August 1648, the big merchants and municipal officers first did nothing, then turned against the rebels).

Fortunately, we do not have to retrace all the intricacies of the Fronde. As a broad framework, we can accept the conventional chronology: a parlementary Fronde (1648-1649), a princely Fronde (1650), a coalition of princes and parlements (1650-1651), a Fronde of Condé (1651-1653). Within that chronology, Table 1 situates the major events of the Fronde in Anjou and in France as a whole.

As the chronology indicates, Angers and Anjou were heavily involved in the various rebellions of 1648 to 1652. From the viewpoint of popular contention, the Fronde consisted of many separate events, most of them having a good deal in common with the tax rebellions and factional struggles of the 1620s and 1630s. The Fronde impinged on Anjou's ordinary people as a series of occasions on which troops were billeted or removed, as a set of changes in taxes, as an intermittent opportunity to resist taxation or billeting with an unusual likelihood of support from some group of powerful people and, now and then, a chance to reshape government by organizing militias, holding local assemblies, and choosing deputies to present popular demands.

The solemn journal of Mathurin Jousselin, curé of Sainte-Croix in Angers, recorded many of the crucial events. (Jousselin began jotting notes in his parish register when he took office in 1621, and continued his observations until 1662; but he came close to a day-to-day chronicle only during the years of the Fronde.) His first entry for 1648 described a typical grievance, the provincial governor's billeting of a company of Scottish soldiers and several companies of French troops, to force the payment of back taxes. Those troops, he reported,

> cost more than 12,000 livres a day, not counting their thieving and violence; to avoid that expense, a number of people bought off their liability for large sums, not daring to show the slightest resistance for fear of irritating Marshal Brézé, governor of the province, who had been angered by the indiscreet words of a few hotheads; besides which the troops had come to press for the payment of the subsistances of 1644, 1645, and 1646, delayed by the stubbornness of a few. As a result, instead of the 32,000 livres the inhabitants had arranged to pay each year, it was necessary to pay more than 57,000 livres, plus 2 sous per livre and 8 sous per tax bill for each year of arrears. All this completely stripped the city of money, to such a point that many people had to melt down their silver and sell or pawn their pearls. (Jousselin 1861:431-432)

No open, concerted resistance occurred during the six weeks the troops were living on the town. The clergy, however, created opportunities for subtle symbolic opposition by sponsoring "continuous prayers for the protec-

Table 1.   The period of the Fronde in Anjou and in France as a whole

Year	France as a whole	Anjou
1635	Beginning of open war with Spain and Austria; rebellion of Guyenne and Languedoc	
1636	Croquant rebellion in southwest begins	Plague epidemic in Angers and vicinity (to 1639); *August:* parishes of Angers voluntarily raise money for troops to defend Picardy
1638		Increasing resistance to a variety of war-linked taxes
1639	Nu-Pieds rebellion in Normandy, further insurrections in Languedoc	
1640	Rebellions in Rennes, Moulins, and their regions	City residents imprisoned for failure to pay forced loans to crown
1641	French crown allies with Catalans and Portuguese after their successful anti-Spanish rebellions of 1640; rebellion of count of Soissons; other rebellions in Poitou, Saintonge	*October:* attacks on collectors of subvention in Angers
1642	Conspiracy of royal favorite Cinq-Mars with Spanish; Cinq-Mars executed	
1643	Louis XIII dies; regency for five-year-old Louis XIV includes Anne of Austria, Mazarin; multiple insurrections in western and southern France (continuing in south to 1645)	Parish assemblies in Angers to resist subsistances
1644		*August:* warm reception of exiled Queen Henrietta of England in Angers, Saumur, and elsewhere
1645	Uprising in Montpellier	
1647		Attacks on agents of pancarte lead to stationing of troops in Angers
1648	*June–July:* assembly of high courts (parlements and *chambres*) demands major reforms, including recall of in-	*September:* citizens of Angers boycott troops sent through the city

Table 1. (continued)

Year	France as a whole	Anjou
	tendants, high court control of new taxes, and sales of offices; peasants assemble in Paris to demand reduction of taille; insurrection in Pau; *August:* Mazarin arrests leaders of parlementary movement; barricades erected in central Paris; Mazarin releases prisoners; *October:* Mazarin accepts parlementary demands; treaties of Westphalia end Thirty Years' War, although French war with Spain continues intermittently until 1659	
1649	*January:* Mazarin and royal family flee Paris, order exile of high courts; parlement of Paris seizes government; popular pressure against royalist municipality; movements of support for parlement in many provinces; Condé blockades the capital for king; *March:* provisional settlement (opposed by popular protest in Paris); *August:* royal family reenters Paris	*February–March:* merchants, artisans, and minor officials form autonomous militia in Angers; barricades, alliances with La Trémouille and other Frondeurs; attacks on tax collectors; *April:* militia attacks royal forces in Angers; later, reconciliation of inhabitants with royal governor
1650	*January:* queen has Condé and his allies, who seek to displace Mazarin, imprisoned; *February–August:* duchess of Longueville, princess of Condé, and other allies of prince of Condé organize resistance and rebellion in provinces, especially in Bordeaux and Flanders; popular movements in Tulle, Bordeaux, and elsewhere; rebellions defeated by December; *September–December:* Paris rentiers press claims against the government	*March:* civic assemblies in Angers oppose royal policy; royal siege of rebels in castle of Saumur; *April:* numerous nobles of the province declare for the Frondeur princes; *May:* popular party in Angers names its own deputies
1651	*February:* parlement of Paris, allied with princely opposition, demands removal of Mazarin; Mazarin liberates princes and leaves France; *February–September:* numerous conflicts between royal troops and residents in	*January:* deputies of Angers's popular assemblies attempt to exclude judiciary from municipal offices; *February:* bonfires in Angers for release of princes; *May:* Angers elections bring in popular-party mayor and council;

Table 1. (continued)

Year	France as a whole	Anjou
	Paris region; *spring:* the Ormée (a dissident assembly of artisans, shopkeepers, petty officials, etc.) forms in Bordeaux; beginning of open rivalry among Frondeurs, many of whom reconcile with queen; *September:* Condé leaves Paris for the southwest; *Fall:* Condé organizes support in south and west; *December:* Mazarin reenters France with his own troops	widespread resistance to tax collectors; *December:* governor of Anjou (duke of Rohan) refuses to turn over Ponts-de-Cé to royal forces, sides with Condé, courts Angers's popular party
1652	*May–July:* Condé advances on Paris, seizes the city; *June:* the Ormée takes power in Bordeaux; *summer:* displays of popular support and popular opposition to Mazarin in Paris; *July:* anti-Mazarin crowd attacks the Hôtel de Ville; *August:* next exile of Mazarin; *October:* Condé, beset by increasing resistance, leaves for the Low Countries; Louis XIV and Anne of Austria make triumphant reentry into Paris; repression of Frondeurs begins throughout France	*January:* duke of Rohan keeps royalist bishop (Henry Arnauld) from returning to Angers, breaks up assembly of judiciary called to condemn him; *February:* people of Angers attack royal sympathizers; *February–March:* royal armies besiege and capture Angers and Ponts-de-Cé, pillage the region, reorganize the municipality and militia; factional fighting ensues within city, and popular party regains some strength; *April–July:* popular party revives assemblies and maneuvers to regain power but finally capitulates at approach of new royal army; *August:* banishment from Angers of leaders of popular party
1653	*February:* Mazarin returns to Paris; *August:* the Ormée capitulates in Bordeaux	*April:* crown names new municipality for Angers, with severe restriction of municipal rights

tion of the oppressed" and organizing a general procession to attract divine mercy.

Some priests went further. Gaultier, curé of La Trinité, was one. A "tumult" had arisen when two officials chased a bailiff into the curé's church during a service, and the congregation attacked the officials. At the entrance to the castle, the bailiff in question had posted a set of legal charges against one of the occupying soldiers. The curé was convicted of aiding and abetting his congregation in their protection of the daring bailiff. He paid a fine of 240 livres (it was to be used, conveniently enough, for the costs of lodging a military officer billeted on the judge in the case: Jousselin 1861: 432–433). Few others dared resist at all. The governor and the occupying troops did what they would with the city. Arriving at the start of January, they decamped only in mid-February, when the city had yielded the bulk of its delinquent taxes.

Royal pressure for taxes had not ended; nor had Angevin resistance to royal demands. By the end of April 1648 the city was having to collect a new version of the old royal sales tax, the pancarte, on wine, hay, and other goods entering its walls. The governor's granting of tax exemptions to a number of his friends and then to the clergy as a whole added indignation to despair. Repeated deputations to the governor did nothing but increase his threats to impose the tax and the exemptions by force. By the end of June, however, the opposition that the parlement of Paris was showing to royal demands encouraged the people of Angers to draw the line; although the parish assemblies called to answer the governor reluctantly confirmed the clergy's exemption, they did so with the clear reservation that the exemption would not serve as a precedent for other taxes (Débidour 1877: 62). The governor's sword-rattling did not shake the city from that position. At the same time, wholesale evasion of the pancarte began and a move to challenge the tax on the ground of illegal ratification gained strength. After having been completely subjugated in February of 1648, the people of Angers lined up against royal authority once more in July.

From July 1648 to the beginning of 1649, the Angevin commitment to the opposition deepened. No open protest in Angers accompanied the Day of the Barricades in Paris (26 August 1648, when the queen ordered members of the parlement of Paris arrested, saw barricades spring up all over central Paris, and then released the _parlementaires_ under popular pressure). But on 30 September the people of Angers blocked the gates, ignored the orders of a frightened city council, and temporarily kept a royal regiment from marching through the city. That flouting of royal authority, as the mayor and council well knew, brought the city within a hair's breadth of punishable rebellion.

Still, the city's visible, durable break with the king did not come until February 1649. In mid-January the parlement of Paris had issued an appeal for support from the country as a whole. Angers's high courts and council avoided any official recognition of the appeal, but word eventually seeped out into the city. In February a great crowd gathered at the city hall and demanded the creation of an armed civic militia. The council gave in. Armed civilians manned the city gates and ringed the castle, with its royal garrison. Municipal sentries marked the limits of royal power.

Yet the city authorities hedged. They failed to answer the Paris parlement's call for support. On 6 March the officers of two major courts (the Sénéchaussée and the Présidial) wrote to Paris on their own, declaring that "they would never falter in their fidelity and obedience due to his majesty's service, nor in their respect for the rulings of your court, under whose authority we count it an honor to continue to fulfill our functions" (BN Cinq Cents de Colbert 3). That amounted to an elaborate but definite statement of alignment with the parlement. A still-hesitant city council temporized; it tried to reduce the civic guard, but, according to Jousselin,

> at once the anticipation of a trick obliged the people to demand a major, [that is, a head of the civic militia]; since that was not to everyone's taste, the people came to the city hall on 16 March; they all unanimously named M. de Lespine Lemarié, a counselor at the Présidial, as major. His excuses, his protestations about his youth and inexperience in war, did not keep the people from carrying him off and taking him to the city hall to take the oath before the mayor, whom they forced to come back from his house to the city hall for that purpose. (Jousselin 1861: 435)

Lemarié, the new major, was one of the two signers of the 6 March message to the parlement of Paris.

This naming of a major who was not the council's creature—who was in fact the nominee of a self-selected popular assembly—was at once a rebellion against the municipal authorities and a heavy step toward open alliance with the Fronde. For the next three years, Lemarié and his ally Claude Voisin (professor at the law faculty) led a popular party within Angers. The party sometimes dominated the city government and almost always pushed it to demand municipal autonomy, to resist royal taxation and the billeting of troops, and to align itself with the national opposition to Mazarin and the queen. So far as we can tell from the passing references in city council proceedings, Jousselin's journal, and similar sources, the heart of the popular party was the same coalition of merchants, artisans, and minor officials that had led the antitax movements before the Fronde. Their methods, too, were much the same: the solemn convocation of unauthorized parish assemblies, the defiant election of chiefs and delegates, the direct attack on the persons and premises of tax collectors, and so on. The difference was that they now had powerful potential allies outside the city.

Angers continued its advance toward the Fronde. On 25 March a general assembly of the city's parishes ceremoniously opened letters from two great Frondeurs, the marquis de la Boulaye and the duke of La Trémouille, asking for recognition of the authority granted the two chiefs by the parlement of Paris. After due deliberation the assembly sent delegates to grant that recognition. In the meantime began attacks on royal salt-tax officers and skirmishes with the royal garrison at the castle. The collection of taxes virtually ended, and citizens treated themselves to the luxury of importing their own untaxed salt. After the duke of La Trémouille and the marquis de la Boulaye formally entered the city, the residents pledged moral, financial, and military support for a siege of the castle. At that point they had committed themselves willy-nilly to armed rebellion against the crown. So had a great many other towns throughout France.

Much more was to come: attacks on the royal garrison in Angers, running a weak-kneed mayor out of town, reconciliation with the royal governor after a truce had checked the parlementary rebellion in Paris, intercession by Angers's bishop, Henry Arnauld, to prevent brutal punishment of the city after its capitulation, more billeting of troops to enforce collection of delinquent taxes, more struggles between troops and townsmen, tilting of a new royal governor (the duke of Rohan) toward the princely Fronde, repeated swings of Angers's popular party toward insurrection when the national situation looked promising, intermittent alliances between the city's popular party and the insurgent nobles of the surrounding region, frequent tergiversation by the city's judicial elite.

Anjou's Fronde was complex, tumultuous, and changeable. Yet it returned again and again to the same themes: preservation of local and regional privileges against an omnivorous monarchy; hostility to everyone who profited personally from the royal expansion; opposition to the billeting of unruly, demanding troops on the citizenry; resistance to arbitrary taxation, especially when farmed out to financiers, and particularly when applied to the necessaries of life.

Smaller cities joined in Angers's Fronde. In Saumur, for example, people resisted the salt tax in March 1651. The rhyming *Muze Historique* recorded the events (II: letter 8, 25 March 1651, 103):

> La populace de Saumur
> Trouvant le joug un peu trop dur
> Et menaçant d'etre rebelle
> touchant les droits de la gabelle,
> Comminge, gouverneur du lieu
> Sans presque pouvoir dire adieu
> Sans mesme avoir loizir de boire,

Alla vitement vers la Loire
Pour au peuple séditieux
D'abord faire un peu les doux yeux;
Et, s'il s'abstinoit d'aventure
En son sot et brutal murmure
Agir après comme un lion
Pour punir la rébellion.

The people of Saumur
finding their burden hard to bear
and threatening to resist
the salt tax,
Comminge, governor of the region,
hardly saying goodby,
without time for a stirrup cup,
rushed off to the Loire
to give the seditious people
a bit of sweet talk
and if by some chance
they kept up their murmuring
then to strike like a lion
and punish the rebellion.

In Saumur, too, resistance to arbitrary taxation joined other forms of opposition to the regime and compounded into a local version of the Fronde.

One moment of the Fronde in Anjou shows the joining of many of these themes. When the hesitant duke of Rohan finally took possession of his new governorship in March 1650 and made his first ambiguous gestures of sympathy toward the regional movement of resistance, the city gave him an old-style hero's welcome, complete with processions, cavalcades, *Te Deum,* banquets, and balls. The day after his pompous entry into the city, "he released a number of poor tax collectors, whom the poverty of the people had kept from paying their quotas, leaving in jail only those who had received more money than they had turned in" (Jousselin 1861: 448). The contrast with the previous governor, who had billeted troops and jailed hapless collectors who did not deliver their quotas, could not have been sharper . . . or, no doubt, more deliberately contrived. Still, Rohan managed to keep from putting himself into obvious personal rebellion against royal authority until December 1651. Then, summoned to turn over the fortress of Ponts-de-Cé to an emissary of the crown, he refused. He thereby aligned himself with the prince of Condé.

Anjou's Fronde ended effectively in March 1652 with the capitulation of Rohan and the surrender of Ponts-de-Cé. Then began the conventional retribution. The occupying troops, declared curé Jousselin, "committed previously unheard of excesses and violence, such that one would not have expected of the Turks: houses burned with their furnishings, all the provisions ruined, murders, rapes, sacrileges extending to chalices and monstrances, churches converted into stables" (Jousselin 1861: 470).

Yet for four months the popular party held together in the city, and even bid to regain power over the municipality; only the approach of a new mass of royal troops in July put them down for the last time. Their leaders were banished, and in the spring of 1653 Angers lost the tattered remnants of her municipal liberties. By that time Mazarin and the fifteen-year-old Louis XIV were again masters of France.

After Anjou's Fronde

Anjou's history had reached a fateful moment. Two linked changes were occurring whose profound importance would be clear only in restrospect. On the one hand, the province's great nobles were never again available for alliance with a popular rebellion—not, at least, until the great counterrevolution of the Vendée, in 1793. On the other hand, continuous and direct royal administration of the province really began at that point, with the absorption of the municipality into the royal bureaucracy and the definitive installation of an intendant at Tours with jurisdiction over Anjou. Those two changes greatly altered the odds and opportunities for popular resistance to royal demands.

How did those changes shape popular involvement in contention? The most obvious break with the past was the virtual disappearance of the popular rebellion headed by, or allied with, the region's great magnates. Such rebellions had flowered in Anjou during the sixteenth and seventeenth centuries, but now they withered away. Closely related to the decline of the elite-led rebellion were three other important departures: of armed combat by organized military units as a primary means for deciding the outcome of popular protests; of the clienteles of important nobles and officials as major actors in insurrections and other struggles; of that recurrent routine in which the members of a community assembled, stated their grievances, elected a captain (or major, or syndic) as a substitute for the duly constituted authorities, and refused to obey the orders of those authorities until they had reached some agreement about their grievances and demands. We witness, that is, the decline of war, clientelism, and mutiny as means of collective action.

Both the lords and the commons, however, took a while to recognize the great transformation. In 1654, for example, the Frondeur Cardinal de Retz escaped from imprisonment in the castle of Nantes, fled to the castle of Beaupréau in southern Anjou, and gathered around him a small army of sympathetic nobles. In the fall, after the cardinal's capture, his faithful in southern Anjou tried to raise troops for an expedition to free him. Over the next two years a veritable league of potentially rebellious nobles formed in the province; they divided Anjou into ten "cantons" for the purpose of organizing the nobility and collecting their grievances. The language of their act of association was that of the Fronde: "All the gentlemen and others undersigned, obedient to the authority of the king, have promised support, aid, protection, and maintenance against those who are abusing the authority of his majesty and who want to abolish the immunities, prerogatives, and freedoms possessed by gentlemen" (Débidour 1877: 303). A canny Frondeur did not, of course, blame the king himself when there was a Mazarin around to hate; one blamed the king's advisers, executors, and clients. The nobles knew the seventeenth-century rules of rebellion by heart. Yet that league of nobles disbanded, checked by a judicious mixture of threats and concessions. The nobles of Anjou had been neutralized or coopted.

The rest of the population did not see their privileges so well treated. Angers's city council struck at the guilds in the name of economic advancement: in 1653 they set up a municipal cloth works that competed with the local masters; in 1655 they appealed successfully to the parlement of Paris for an edict dissolving the weavers' guild and permitting any weaver to come to the city and set up in the trade. (It may not be coincidental that a major element of the popular opposition to Angers's civic and judicial elite during the Fronde had been the organized trades.) They also reinstated the old taxes.

The reinstatement of taxes revived two old cycles of conflict. The first was the familiar sequence in which the city fell into arrears on its royal tax bill, the provincial governor billeted troops to force payment, the citizens fell to squabbling over the burden of lodging the troops, while the soldiers themselves robbed, stole, caroused, and raped until the burghers finally bought them off. As early as the spring of 1655, Angers's city council was conducting a major inquiry into the thefts committed by soldiers billeted in the faubourgs St.-Jacques and St.-Lazare, and into "the violence committed by their lieutenant against the sieur Herbereau, échevin of Angers" (AMA BB 86/16). The second cycle was the one in which the city or the crown, hard pressed for cash, farmed out one of its taxes to a local capitalist who would advance the necessary sum, then permitted him to tighten and broaden the collection of the tax in question, only to confront wide, indignant resistance from those expected to pay, and once again to call in military force against the city's population.

In 1656 the city council made that second cycle worse by agreeing to farm out all the city's taxes to one of their own number. He was bound to squeeze hard in order to make his profit on the lease. He even dared to extend the pancarte to everyday foods entering the city. On 2 October 1656, the day after the tax-farmer's lease began, a crowd destroyed his guardhouses at the city gates. That routine had already become familiar before the Fronde. The arrival of the province's royal military commander did not end the agitation. At an emergency meeting of the city council on 22 October, according to the council minutes, "so large a number of unknown people, mutinous and angry, entered the council chamber that it was filled immediately; they began to shout that they wanted no more tax profiteers, no more pancarte, and no more sou per pot [the entry tax on wine], no more guardhouses and salt-tax collectors at the city gates; that they would have to kill and exterminate all the profiteers, starting with those on the city council" (AMA BB 86/170). After much shouting and some negotiation, they extracted from the royal prosecutor, de Souvigné, a written declaration that the taxes would be abolished; at its reading, the crowd roared, "Long live the king and M. de Souvigné." In the ensuing discussion, members of the crowd took up the city officials' other derelictions. At one point, according to the vice-mayor's minutes, a man said to him, "There you are, you who don't want us to be master weavers. Ha! There will be master weavers in Angers when you're long gone from this world!" (AMA BB 86/170).

Neither that abolition of taxes nor the triumph of the weavers lasted beyond the one happy day in October. Far from it. A few weeks later the inevitable occupying force of royal soldiers marched into Angers; they were not to leave until February 1657. Once more the city council began hearing citizens' complaints about the "exactions of the soldiers lodged in the city" (AMA BB 86/205). This time the soldiers brought with them an ominous figure: the royal intendant from Tours. An improvised court, including some members of the city's old judicial elite, cranked into action. Three people were hanged for their parts in the rebellion of 22 October. And in the spring of 1657 the king once again took away the few privileges he had restored to the apparently docile city in 1656. If there had been any doubt that the Fronde was over, the wisp of uncertainty had blown away.

The coalition that had made the region's Fronde shook apart well before the end of the 1650s. The nobles, artisans, merchants, and secondary officials who had sometimes worked together against Mazarin between 1648 and 1652 occasionally conducted their own little wars against royal or municipal authority in the following decades. But after the crushing of the Fronde they never again showed signs of consolidating against the crown. Furthermore, the decline of the parlement of Paris as a model, locus, and rallying point of opposition greatly diminished the chances of coordination between Anjou's aggrieved parties and their counterparts elsewhere.

When it came to local conflict, Anjou returned to some of the class alignments that had prevailed before the Fronde. After Charles Colbert (brother and agent of the king's great minister) visited Angers in 1664, he reported that the city

> is divided into two parties: that of the magistrates and officers, both of the city and of the Présidial, Prévôté, and salt administration; and that of the ordinary bourgeois such as attorneys, barristers, merchants, and artisans. The enmities of the two parties cause great trouble in the city. The latter party complain that ... the others never let anyone into the city administration but the law officers, who are almost all relatives and confederates, all powerful people who, out of common interest, join with the other officials to exempt themselves from all taxes and to push them onto the people, and furthermore eat up public revenues, which were once 75,000 livres each year; nor can they ever provide justification or receipts for their expenditures. And not satisfied with that, they persecute in different ways individuals who complain about this state of affairs, and dismiss them as mutinous and seditious with respect to the powerful.
>
> The other party says that the leaders of the people are composed of very proud and disrespectful characters, lacking subordination to their superiors, that all they want is independence, that they have never failed to embrace the party of novelties when the opportunity arose, and have often called exemplary punishment upon themselves as a result. ("Estat de la Généralité de Tours," BN Fr 18608)

The veiled reference to popular support for the Fronde ("the party of novelties") should not mislead us: large-scale rebellion had disappeared. Contention on a smaller scale was apparently declining as well.

From Hurricanes to Summer Squalls

The decline of contention did not mean that grievances evaporated and conflict vanished. Louis XIV continued to make war; he therefore continued to require men, money, and food for his growing armies. Taxes continued to rise after the middle of the seventeenth century, though at a slower rate than before the Fronde. The crown drew an increasing share of its income from forced loans, currency depreciations, the sale of offices, and other complements to the regular tax burden. Ordinary people, for their part, continued to fight the new exactions when they could—especially when the royal demands gave large profits to middlemen, appeared without due show of legality, or threatened people's ability to survive as contributing members of their communities. All three circumstances revived old conditions for resistance to taxation and other governmental demands.

Despite the decline of civil war, clientelism, and mutiny as means of collective action, many of Anjou's conflicts of the later seventeenth century ran along familiar lines. The nearly unbroken series of wars in Spain, on the eastern frontiers, and in the Low Countries kept large armies on the move, living on the towns and villages through which they passed. Furthermore, the intendants maintained the practice of billeting soldiers in order to speed the payment of delinquent taxes. The two sorts of billeting imposed similar costs: the basic expenses of food and lodging, the additional pain of raping and brawling. Through the victorious French campaigns of the 1670s in Flanders and Franche-Comté, the minutes of Angers's city council follow an insistent counterpoint between *Te Deums* and bonfires for battles won in the east, on the one hand, and complaints and contestations about the local troops, on the other. In December 1675 the city fathers debated how to pay the *ustensile,* yet another assessment for troops stationed in the region. "It seems that the regular way to take care of it," declared the mayor, "would be to impose a head tax. But that looks impossible, since most residents of the city and its suburbs have been ruined both by the frequent passing of cavalry and infantry and by the soldiers who are here in winter quarters and who have to be fed entirely at the expense of the residents. In addition, head taxes have always caused divisions within the city" (AMA BB 94/129). They chose instead to take the money out of the entry taxes—which was a way of pushing the burden toward the poor.

The échevins must have calculated correctly. No more that century did the people of Angers mount a major attack on tollbooths and tax collectors. The only notable struggle with the salt-tax officers during the next few decades, for example, came in November 1663; then soldiers of Captain Brette's company, Champagne regiment, attacked the archers who had been blocking their repeated attempts to smuggle salt into Angers. Captain Sanche of the salt-tax forces, declining a duel but finding himself backed into a sword fight with the company's sergeant, then set upon by other soldiers, drew his pistol and killed the sergeant. Captain Sanche, "retreating with his men,

pursued by twelve men armed with swords and by a stone-throwing populace, after standing them off four or five times, was forced to fire a shot,
which killed someone." Only then did the salt-tax clerk (who told the story
just quoted) and the soldiers' officers manage to restore order (BN
Mélanges Colbert 118, report of 12 November 1663).

Again in 1669, five men who appear to have been soldier-smugglers
broke into the jail at Pouancé, rescued a colleague, attacked a salt-tax guard,
and sped away (BN Mélanges Colbert 151, letter of 7 April 1669). With
soldiers on their side, Angevins still struck at the hated salt-tax guards. On
their own, however, they no longer dared.

Perhaps enforcement had simply become more severe. When John
Locke visited Angers in 1678, he was impressed with the weight of the salt
tax:

> Here a boisseau of Salt costs a Luis d'or & about 10 livres of it is sold for
> 10s. This makes them here very strict in examining all things that enter
> into towne, there being at each gate two officers of the Gabelle who
> serch all things where they suspect may be any salt. They have also in
> their hands iron bodkins about 2 foot long which have a litle hollow in
> them neare the point, which they thrust into any packs where they sus-
> pect there may be salt concealed, & if there be any, by that means dis-
> cover it. The penalty for any one that brings in any salt that is not a
> Gabeller, pays 100 ecus or goes to the galleys. It is also as dangerous to
> buy any salt but of them ... I saw a Gabeller at the gate serch a litle
> girle at her entrance, who seemed only to have gon out to see a funerall
> that was prepareing without the gate, which had drawn thither a great
> number of people.   (Locke 1953: 222)

Yet salt smugglers continued to ply their trade and to run into occasional
confrontations with the salt-tax guards.

As the salt tax rose, the profitability of smuggling—for those who
weren't caught—increased as well. Soldiers found the supplementary income from salt smuggling more attractive, and more regular, than their
meager and tardy wages. As smugglers, they had several advantages: location
near the frontiers, a degree of invulnerability to search and seizure, the right
to bear arms. Whole military units seem to have made a practice of riding
off to areas of low-priced salt and bringing it back in their saddlebags. The
tax-farmers were not, to be sure, amused; they sent out their own armed
forces, the salt-tax guards, to apprehend the lawbreakers. These lawbreakers,
however, not only thought they had a right to a little smuggling, but also
were armed. Bloody battles ensued.

In Anjou toward the end of the century, the regiments of Arsfeld and

St.-Simon joined enthusiastically in the salt smuggling. In March 1693 the dragoons of Arsfeld were bringing twenty-five horses loaded with salt back from the province of Brittany, where the price was low, when they met the archers de la gabelle. The outcome of that encounter was one dead on each side. (The intendant collected compensation for the family of the dead salt-tax guard by deducting the money from the salary due the regiment's officers: AN G^7 521.) Five horsemen of the St.-Simon regiment were tried for salt smuggling in January 1693. All were convicted, and two were chosen by lot to serve life sentences in the galleys; the other three were held "at the king's disposition" (which ordinarily meant they would find their way back into military service after symbolic punishment). The comrades of the two unlucky convicts broke into the St.-Florent jail and rescued them, then attacked their own officers when the latter tried to arrest the perpetrators of the jailbreak (AN G^7 521). Around 1700, Anjou's larger struggles over the salt tax usually involved military men as well as the armed guards of the gabelle.

Other conflicts persisted as well. Fights between soldiers and civilians, sometimes amounting to pitched battles, seem to have been more common than before the Fronde. Plenty of bitter arguments and attacks on officials grew out of billeting. Now and then forced enlistments in the local regiments became bitter issues. Units of the civic militia and other corporate groups continued to jostle each other for precedence at public ceremonies, as in the fracas of July 1686 at the dedication of the statue of Louis XIV; there units of the civic guard fired at each other in a disagreement over who should lead the parade (AMA BB 97/33). Still, the once-ample capacity of Angers's ordinary people for rebellion seems to have dwindled in the later decades of the century.

During this period the region's Protestants (a mighty political force one hundred years earlier) gave an outstanding example of acquiescence. True, they faced overwhelming odds: a few hundred people in a province of 400,000, with the face of royal authority set against them. In 1685, with the revocation of the Edict of Nantes, Angers's Presidial decreed the destruction of the region's one Protestant church at Sorges, not far outside the city; 5,000 Angevins went to tear the church down (Lehoreau 1967: 58–59). A few months later, royal officials turned an old tool to new tasks: "the king sent an order to oblige the Huguenots of his city to abjure their faith. They sent a great many soldiers from the Alsace regiment to live in their houses at will. The great expense forced all [the Protestants] to embrace our religion right away. God grant that it be for His glory!" (Saché 1930–1931: no. 5, 239). Although there were plenty of later complaints about the "insincerity" and "incompleteness" of the Protestant conversions, the Huguenots dared not offer open resistance to the royal drive against them.

There are two significant exceptions to the general decline of open rebellion in the later seventeenth century: industrial conflict and struggles over the food supply. The sources I have examined document only one clear-cut major movement of workers against employers in Angers, at the very end of the century. In 1697 the master serge-weavers complained that

> the journeymen in their trade are gathering each day to insult them and to make other journeymen leave work by force and violence, and to leave the city as well; they call that "hitting the road"; when one of the journeymen displeases them or agrees to work for a lower wage than the one they want to earn, they threaten the masters, insult them, and mistreat their women. It is important to stop these conspiracies and assemblies, since they will lead to sedition.   (AMA BB 101/25)

Angers's city council agreed. They ordered the arrest of the two "most mutinous" journeymen, and the end of these riotous assemblies. The gatherings amounted to an old-fashioned strike; the antiquated English word "turnout" describes the journeymen's actual behavior better. It probably followed a wage cut agreed upon by the masters. In any case, the fact that the masters complained to the city council gives a momentary glimpse of a struggle that was probably much more continuous than the record tells us.

Food and Contention in Anjou

Another ground over which people were struggling toward the end of the seventeenth century was control of the food supply. After the Fronde, the monarchy became increasingly involved in efforts to influence the distribution of food in France. The crown had several reasons for increasing concern about the supply of food, especially of grain: the need to feed growing armies, which often marched far from their bases and outside the country; the difficulty of supplying the expanding capital cities in which the royal bureaucracies were stationed; the side effect of regularizing and extending the powers of the intendants, which was to enmesh the central government in pressing provincial affairs, especially affairs affecting the province's capacity to produce revenues; that emphatically included the price and supply of grain.

Through most of the seventeenth century in Anjou, taxation was the principal way in which problems of food supply generated open conflict. As we have already seen, when the hard-pressed authorities decided to tax everyday victuals, they almost always encountered outraged resistance from producers and consumers alike. That was one of the implicit rules of the age: don't tax the necessaries. (The salt tax was a hated exception that people evaded whenever they dared.) But violations of that rule produced smuggling and attacks on tax collectors, not grain seizures. Seizures of grain, after all, consisted of blocking shipments, breaking into storehouses to seize hoarded grain, or forcing the sale of foodstuffs below the current market price. It was only at the end of the seventeenth century that the grain seizure, in the full old-regime sense of the term, became common in Anjou. For 150 years thereafter, it remained one of the most frequent forms of violent contention in Anjou, as elsewhere in France.

One important reason why seizures of grain were rare through most of the seventeenth century was that local authorities themselves took the responsibility for blocking shipments, seizing hoarded grain, and controlling prices. To twentieth-century eyes, it is surprising how much of the old-regime public administration consisted of watching, regulating, or promoting the distribution of grain. The archives are jammed with information on prices and supplies; they contain, among other things, the voluminous *mercuriales* that make it possible to gauge price fluctuations from year to year, sometimes even from week to week, for most of France over most of the seventeenth and eighteenth centuries. When Nicolas de la Mare summed up the seventeenth-century wisdom concerning routine public administration (that is, what was then called "police," in the large sense of the term) in his *Traité de la police,* a good half of his reflections dealt with control of the food supply.

The distribution of food required continuous attention because the statemakers were anxious to assure the state's own supply, because the margin between survival and disaster was both slim and hard to guarantee, and because food shortages and high prices figured so frequently in conflicts at the local level. The tie between conflict and food supply was more complex than we might think, since the intensity of contention over food did not vary simply as a function of the badness of harvests or even the steepness of price rises. Shipping grain among regions aggravated or mitigated the effects of harvest failures; along with public subsidies and controls, the shipping of grain significantly affected local prices. When prices *did* rise to impossible heights, open conflict was still unlikely in the absence of a profiteering miller, a merchant shipping needed grain elsewhere, a royal official commandeering part of the local supply, a speculator waiting for an even better price, or a city administration unprepared to take the standard remedies against shortage.

Because these stimuli to struggles over food became more common in the eighteenth century, let us save the full story for later chapters. The headings will do here. First: Despite modest increases in agricultural productivity, the accelerating urbanization and proletarianization of the population in the eighteenth century meant that a declining proportion of Frenchmen raised their own food, that more and more people depended on the purchase of food for their own survival, and that the transportation of grain from one place to another became more active and crucial. Second: Grain merchants became increasingly enterprising, prosperous, and sensitive to price differentials among regions or between city and country. Third: The state (in implicit collaboration with merchants) involved itself increasingly in promoting the delivery of grain to cities and armies; that meant taking the grain away from communities that often had both acute needs for food and prior claims on the local supply. During the century, the state leaned more and more toward a policy of "freeing" the grain trade—that is, encouraging and protecting merchants who would buy up grain in lower-price areas for delivery to the starving, high-priced cities. These shifts all increased the frequency with which merchants and local citizens found themselves at loggerheads over the disposition of the grain on hand, while the authorities refused to activate the old controls and subsidies. Those were the conditions for grain seizures.

This set of mediating factors helps us understand the weak correspondence in Anjou between acute food shortages and struggles over the food supply. During the seventeenth and eighteenth centuries, some years of exceedingly high prices (such as 1699) followed harvests that were not disastrous, but merely mediocre. In terms of prices, Anjou's most acute crises of the two centuries occurred in 1630-31, 1661-62, 1693-94, 1708-1710, 1713-14, 1724-25, 1752, 1771-1773, and 1788-89. Crises arose thicker and faster during the eighteenth century. Nevertheless, the famine of 1661-62 was "the most serious one to occur in Anjou during the seventeenth and eighteenth centuries" (Lebrun 1971: 134).

As Louvet's journal has already told us, 1630 and 1631 were turbulent years in Anjou. In Angers, repeated general assemblies discussed measures for assuring food supplies, decided to control prices, and took the standard preventive measure: expelling "outside paupers" from the city to reduce the number of mouths that had to be fed (AMA BB 73). Yet compared to tax gouging, food supply was a relatively minor theme in the contention of those years. Some attacks on bakers occurred in Angers, and some minor battles broke out between hinterland villagers and city dwellers who wanted to cart off part of the village food stocks (AMA BB 73). But that was all.

Historians sometimes call the great hunger of 1661–62 the "crisis of
the accession" to mark its coincidence with Louis XIV's personal assumption of power after the death of Mazarin. It was one of the great Mortalities,
as people said back then: one of those recurrent shocks of famine and devastation that battered the old regime. Early in 1662 the intendant of the
generality of Tours reported of the three provinces in his jurisdiction—
Touraine, Maine, and Anjou—that they were

> more miserable than one can imagine. They harvested no fruit in 1661,
> and very little grain; grain is extremely dear. The extreme famine and
> high prices result, first of all, from the crop failure, which was universal
> this year, and then from the resistance of the leaders of Nantes to letting
> pass the grains required for the subsistence of Tours and surrounding
> areas . . . Famine is even worse in the countryside, where the peasants
> have no grain at all, and only live on charity.   (BN Mélanges Colbert
> 107)

By June 1662 the intendant was reporting that "misery is greater than ever:
purpurant fever and fatal illness are so prevalent, especially at Le Mans, that
the officers of the Présidial have decided to close the courthouse, thus cutting off trade completely" (BN Mélanges Colbert 102). In Anjou death
rates rose to several times their normal level (Lebrun 1971: 334–338).

The great crisis focused renewed administrative attention on the distribution and pricing of grain. With official approval, Angers imported grain
from Holland. The intendant reported that he had offered grain from the
royal supply to the mayors of Angers and Saumur, who unexpectedly refused: "Since they had thought the grain would be supplied free, and since
they had no cash for payment, they preferred to take grain on credit from
their own merchants" (BN Mélanges Colbert 109). Despite this sort of administrative maneuvering, there was even less popular contention over the
problem in 1661–62 than in 1630–31 (AMA BB 89). The whole province
simply devoted its undernourished energy to survival.

The year 1693–94 was different. As early as 3 June 1693, a general police
assembly met in Angers to discuss subsistence problems. (The assembly, a
sort of all-city welfare council, brought together representatives of the
church, the courts, and other major institutions with city officials.) The assembly proposed that the city buy "a quantity of wheat for the provision of
the city's residents, in order to prevent the utter famine and dearness with
which we are threatened because of the bad weather and harshness of the
season" (AMA BB 100/10). The city council decided on a cash purchase of
fifty or sixty septiers (some 100 hectoliters) from the leaseholder of the

abbey at St.-Georges-sur-Loire. But when a member of the council, the city assessor, two guards, and a wagon driver went off to St.-Georges to fetch the grain, "they were blocked by a number of people, gathered together and armed, who sounded the tocsin for two hours and made a great sedition and emotion" (AMA BB 100/10).

Intendant Miroménil glowered. "I have reprimanded the mayor of Angers," he wrote to Paris, "for trying thoughtlessly to show the common people his zeal by sending to St.-Georges-sur-Loire for grain at a time when he knew that some was coming from Nantes and when there surely was some left in Angers, where there were a number of granaries that could have been opened up" (AN G^7 1632, 15 June 1693). The mayor of Angers had not only caused an "emotion" at St.-Georges but also violated royal policy in the process.

Over the next year the struggle with the countryside only intensified. By May 1694 merchants of Angers were unable to carry off grain they had bought in the vicinity of Craon, a small city to the north. Angers dispatched its city attorney with forty gendarmes. Then, according to the journal of a lawyer at the Présidial, "they met with resistance. A large number of peasants and woodsmen armed with guns, picks, and hatchets ambushed them; one of the soldiers had his hat punctured with a bullet. That blow stunned him. Nevertheless, he advanced and killed his man. There were two others mortally wounded and four prisoners. If the peasants had not retreated, there would have been real butchery. They brought back fifty loads of grain" (Saché 1930–31: 5, 307–308). The expedition from Angers, and the resistance it encountered, anticipated militia marches into the countryside during the Revolution, almost exactly a century later. Although within the city we have evidence of great concern but no major confrontations, the struggle over food in the province as a whole had reached a new level of bitterness.

From that point until the Revolution, each subsistence crisis—even the minor ones—renewed the struggle. The second-rank shortage of 1698–99, for example, became serious mainly because merchants began buying up the region's grain for consumption in Paris. We see Angers's city council, in the fall of 1698, shackled by the intendant's recent declaration of the "freedom of the grain trade" in and from Anjou. The problem drove them to the official equivalent of a grain seizure. "At the word that was going around the people at the city hall and the market," read the minutes, "that there was no grain, not a setier, available," the council asked the royal military governor for authorization to call a general police assembly; he refused, on the grounds that a regular assembly was already scheduled for five days later,

that a special assembly would alarm the people, and that anyway the intendant had decreed the freedom of the grain trade (AMA BB 101/99–100).

Having heard that some grain was stored in a house in Bouchemaine
(where, as the village's name indicates, the Maine River flows into the
Loire) the council dispatched two officials, the échevin Poulard and the *procureur* Gasté, to check out the rumor and commandeer what they could.
Poulard and Gasté did indeed find a securely padlocked house bulging with
grain. They peeped through the windows longingly but found no one to open
the door for them. Walking down the riverbank, they came on three big boats
of wheat. Since the wheat was earmarked for shipment to Paris, they dared
not touch it. They put it somewhat differently: "Considering that they
were only looking for rye in order to give help quickly to the common
people," they moved on the next village (AMA BB 101/101). There they
found another locked storehouse, again could get no one to open it for them,
and again trudged on. At the river was a barge loaded with rye: at last!

After asking around, the two delegates duly concluded that the barge
was being smuggled into Brittany, and seized it in the name of the city. The
bargemen refused to bring the shipment to Angers for them, so Poulard and
Gasté hired their own wagoner to tow in the barge. They returned in triumph, only to have the barge hit submerged piles as it approached the dock;
it began to sink. The city council, apprised of its emissaries' victories, decided to rescue the barge and put the boatload of rye into a storehouse to
dry (AMA BB 101/101–102). The city's impotence opened the way to popular initiative: during the spring and summer of 1699, Angers experienced
many threats and at least one substantial conflict over food.

Monsieur de Miroménil, the intendant, frowned again. In his reports of
January 1699 he denounced the frequent blockages of grain shipments and
the widespread use of the excuse that the grain was illegally destined for
Brittany. "We will spare nothing," he warned, "to guarantee the freedom of
trade, despite the bad will of certain judges who, in order to make themselves popular, invent their own arguments, saying that people may not buy
grain in the vicinity of cities or ship it down the river from one city to another, since the king wants only boats loaded for the upstream passage to
Paris and Orléans to be let through" (AN G^7 524).

Thus in the waning years of the seventeenth century judges and municipal officers faced a hard choice. Both administrative tradition and popular
pressure called for them to assure the local food supply before letting grain
escape their grasp. But if they sided with local people and defended what
remained of the old system of controls, they risked the wrath of the crown.

We can conveniently, if unconventionally, end Anjou's seventeenth

century in 1710. The acute subsistence crisis of 1708–1710, again compounded by the pressure to supply armies of the eastern frontiers, incited
grain seizures all over France. In Anjou, the seesaw swung: conflicts within
the cities because the merchants and officials did not bring in enough cheap
grain; struggles outside the cities because merchants and officials were trying to ship out needed grain. One of the earliest "popular emotions" in the
series occurred in Saumur at the end of July 1708. There a crowd broke into
a stock of grain that was being readied for shipment to French colonies in
the Caribbean. The intendant's report on the trial conveys the texture of the
event and shows that he took it seriously:

> We had six people in the jails of Saumur. The first was a woman named
> Bottereau, who incited the others—more by words than by actions—as
> she returned from washing clothes at the port. She served as an example.
> She was sentenced to undergo the full routine of public apology for her
> wrongs before the court, since its judges' authority had been violated by
> the riot; then to be whipped there; next to be taken for whipping to the
> site of the crime and to the three suburbs where the most common peo-
> ple live; finally to be branded with a fleur-de-lis and banished for life.
>
> There was a crippled beggar who had eagerly smashed the contain-
> ers with his crutches, divided up the flour, and incited the others by his
> talk. He was put in the stocks, whipped in the public square, and ban-
> ished for nine years.
>
> Three other women, who had taken a few bushels of flour, were
> sentenced to be given a lecture in court and to pay three pounds to char-
> ity; I proposed adding that they be required to attend the public apology
> and punishment [of Bottereau], for the sake of the example.
>
> Finally, a journeyman woodworker, who was at the six o'clock
> émotion and rolled away some empty barrels: held over for further in-
> vestigation.   (AN G[7] 1651, 31 August 1708)

Conflict over the food supply, however, did not reach its height until eight
months later, during the spring of 1709. Then, the attempts of Angers to
supply itself incited resistance in the countryside, the failure of those attempts produced commotions in Angers, and both sorts of conflicts agitated
the region's medium-sized cities.

Of that spring's many grain seizures, one of the biggest occurred in
Angers. The chaplain of Angers's cathedral tells the story:

> the people rose up on 18 and 19 March 1709; they stopped the boats
> loaded with grain that someone was shipping to Laval . . . The police
> judges and others went to the site in their official robes but did nothing,
> because the mutinous people threatened to do them in and drown them.

> Finally, people calmed down at the agreement that the grain would re-
> main and be sold here, which was done. Not content with that, the
> people forced open the storehouses of several grain merchants in the city
> and broke into the shops of bakers suspected of having grain. Many
> people were killed. The stirred-up populace guarded the city gates so
> well that it was impossible to take out any grain; they even stopped
> shipments of bran that poor people from the country came to buy
> here. (Lehoreau 1967: 191–192; cf. AN G^7 1651)

They kept that watch more than a month. The mobilization of the "populace" inspired the city council to take every opportunity for the purchase or
forced sale of grain.

City officials even became willing to benefit by other people's grain seizures. On 27 March the mayor reported to his colleagues that

> a few merchants who were having boats loaded with grain shipped
> down the Loire and who wanted to move them under the Ponts-de-Cé
> were blocked and stopped by the residents of that city, who asked that
> the grain, being there for their subsistence, be sold and distributed to
> them, since they couldn't find any grain elsewhere and since the markets
> of nearby cities didn't have enough for everyone who needed it. The
> merchants refused, on the pretext that they had passports validated by
> the intendant that permitted them to take their grain to Nantes and
> Bordeaux. (AMA BB 104/44)

Insufficiently impressed by these arguments, the citizens of Ponts-de-Cé let
eight boatloads go but seized three others. They sold off the contents, below
the current market price, to poor people who had been certified by their
curés as needy (Lehoreau 1967: 191).

Officials of Angers, noting the success of their suburban counterparts,
sent a delegation to the intendant in Tours to ask that part of the grain
seized at Ponts-de-Cé be sold to the poor of Angers (AMA BB 104/44). The
intendant ratified that arrangement, although he also delivered a stern sermon on maintaining the freedom of trade (AN G^7 1651). The distinction
between riot and sound municipal management blurs before our very eyes.

Anjou and France

From the Ponts-de-Cé Frolic of 1620 to the Ponts-de-Cé grain blockage of
1709, nearly a century of social change had transformed the character of
popular contention in Anjou and in France as a whole. Well into the seventeenth century, the rivalries and armed combats of elite clienteles had inter-
woven with the competition of corporate groups and the recurrent

insurrections of taxpayers to give Anjou's contention a rough, tangled texture: each new mutiny had the chance of attracting aristocratic protectors, each new elite faction the chance of encouraging a popular movement. The century's greatest change, in this regard, was the blocking of the opportunity for alliance between elite and popular opposition to an expanding monarchy. The failure and repression of the Fronde marked the most important moment in that transformation.

Why did the Fronde make such a difference in Anjou? Two pieces of the answer are fairly clear. The first is that the outcome of the Fronde cowed and co-opted the chief elite supporters—notably the great landlords and the second-echelon officials—of popular resistance to royal demands. The stripping away of municipal liberties, the strengthening of the intendant, the retreat of nobles to the court or to their rural properties all reduced the chances for a conjunction between elite maneuvering and popular rebellion. The second part of the explanation concerns the crown itself: despite the continuing increases in the national budget, royal fiscal policy shifted away from the brutal, abrupt imposition of new levies toward a more subtle (though just as potent) blend of indirect taxation, currency manipulation, sale of privileges, and borrowing. It is likewise possible that after Colbert supplanted Fouquet at Louis XIV's assumption of personal power in 1661, the visible inefficiencies and inequities of the fiscal system declined. It may also be that the intendants' more nearly continuous control of tax collection began to break up the old cycles linking unrealistic assessments, large arrears, municipal complicity, the billeting of troops to enforce payment, and popular rebellion.

In any event, the period after the Fronde brought a general decline in Angevin rebelliousness. Yet there was an important exception: the rise, at the very end of the seventeenth century, of struggles over the food supply. Whereas the earlier fluctuations in contention had followed the rhythm of statemaking, this time the expansion of mercantile capitalism combined with changes in governmental policy to reshape popular contention. For centuries local wageworkers had been vulnerable to sudden food shortages and price rises. Local authorities had ordinarily responded to the threat of dearth with a complex of control measures; their essence was to administer the distribution of whatever food was already on hand, to increase the stocks through public action when possible, and to subsidize the cost of food to the deserving poor.

Toward the end of the seventeenth century we find the crown fighting that old system in order to assure the food supply of its armies, bureaucracies, and capital cities. The new program's slogan was "Free the grain trade," its executors the intendants and the big grain merchants. Local officials found themselves increasingly torn between royal demands and local needs at a time when the crown was steadily eating into their power and autonomy. Confronted with unwilling or incompetent local authorities, ordinary people responded to food shortage by taking the law into their own hands.

Taking the law into their own hands. In the case of grain seizures, the words leave the realm of metaphor and enter that of concrete social life. Poor consumers who on their own initiative inventoried grain in private hands, blocked shipments, or forced sales below the current market price were substituting themselves for local authorities. They thereby criticized the authorities for dereliction of duty. They did not claim to *be* authorities; their regulatory work done, they resumed their previous identities: ordinary members of the local market.

The elements of criticism and substitution in the grain seizure reflect a general feature of the collective-action repertoire prevailing in France from the seventeenth to the mid-nineteenth century: a strong affinity between the forms of popular contention and the ways of doing public business that were ordinarily organized by powerholders. The range of modeling on authorized behavior ran from satire to subversion to substitution. In a satirical mode, people took advantage of an authorized festival, ceremony, or procession to display symbols, parade effigies, or mime solemnities; thereby they mocked delinquent powerholders. Under the heading of subversion, they turned an execution, assembly, or public rite intended to awe common people into a declaration of official iniquity. As for substitution, people actually sat themselves in the places of the powerful and did what the powerful should have done: seized grain, executed a criminal, opened an illegally closed field.

Then they stepped back into line. Even in great rebellions, the ordinary people who substituted themselves for authorities generally sought to bargain their way back to their previous positions after redress of the wrongs they had suffered; rarely did they try to make the substitution permanent.

Notice how faithfully many of these routines mimicked established procedures. When grave judges, for example, convicted a felon in absentia, they commonly paraded a dummy labeled to represent the culprit and his crime; a crowd that tossed a labeled effigy into a fire followed essentially the same routine. The public display of a convicted traitor's head united the frequent action of old-regime courts and the rare action of old-regime rebels. Even the popular destruction of a public enemy's dwelling echoed an infrequent but eloquent judicial ritual.

Sometimes, however, imitation was not the point; ordinary people simply played their regular roles, but without authorization, or in unexpected ways. The Angevins who held unauthorized assemblies and elected their own syndics did the first, those who used Mardi Gras to satirize their rivals did the second. All these varied forms of action built on established official routines to voice complaints or claims. If authorities still called those popular actions *séditions* or *émotions*, they had to recognize in them the lineaments of their own standard procedures.

People who make claims in our own time do not mimic official procedures—whether as satire, subversion, or substitution—nearly so often as their seventeenth-century counterparts did. Officials and powerholders do not usually strike, demonstrate, or organize social movements; certainly not in the line of duty. Ordinary people do. But in the seventeenth century, almost all ordinary protesters stayed close to sanctioned routines, even in acts that authorities regarded as flagrant rebellion. Using authorized procedures to press unauthorized claims has three large advantages over a more autonomous, innovative strategy. First, at least their first stages give a claim of legitimacy to the actions of people who otherwise would be subject to repression from the very outset: Can people be punished for gathering and talking at a parish festival? Second, the participants themselves do not have to plan, organize, and practice the routine; they already know how to hold a procession or inventory grain. Third, the adoption or mockery of powerholders' procedures sends an unmistakable message to those powerholders; they see opprobrium coming their way. Faced with expanding capitalism and a growing state, seventeenth-century Angevins took all those advantages.

We might sum up the great themes of Anjou's seventeenth-century contention with three catchwords: sword, purse, and loaf. The sword figured both directly and indirectly in Anjou's conflicts: the armies of great lords crossed and recrossed the province during the first half of the century; the lodging and feeding of troops imposed on the province was the source of acute disagreement throughout the century; the troops sent to punish nonconformity or to force conformity to the royal will generated new grievances by their plundering, raping, and brawling; and the bulk of the other royal demands that called up popular resistance had their origins in the drive to build larger armies and bigger wars. The purse had its own logic: royal officials and financiers sought to increase the crown's revenues by any possible expedient, and ordinary Angevins resisted exactions that violated their rights or cut into the necessaries of life. The loaf was, of course, one of those necessaries; when local officials ceased to be willing or able to guarantee fair access to whatever bread and grain were available in times of shortage, people acted on their own against merchants, bakers, and the officials themselves.

Sword, purse, and loaf were three of the great themes of seventeenth-century contention throughout France. Outside Anjou, a fourth theme loomed large as well: the cross. At the beginning of the century, the struggles between Protestants and Catholics that had torn France apart in the 1500s continued in diminishing form. As the seventeenth century moved on, the kings (and especially Louis XIV) shifted from containing the Protestants to dominating them, and finally to eliminating them from France's public life. We have seen only the faintest traces of that series of battles so far. In seventeenth-century Anjou, despite the presence of a famous Protestant academy in Saumur, Huguenots were a small, unimportant, largely foreign population. Elsewhere in France, however, Protestants were sometimes crucial members of the regional elite, a majority of the population, or both. In those areas, contention over religious rights and privileges absorbed a great deal of energy. We shall have to look elsewhere among our regions, especially to Languedoc, to observe those conflicts in action.

Despite Anjou's repeated insurrections and despite the Fronde, the province did not produce one of those great regional rebellions that racked seventeenth-century Normandy, Périgord, and other parts of France. In order to understand why it has been so easy for historians, as well as for contemporary observers, to think of the century as one continuous crisis, we must consider those repeated, massive challenges to the central power. Having squinted at Anjou, we must widen our gaze to the rest of France.

5

Purse, Sword,
Loaf, and Cross

POETS ARE NOT PROPHETS. In the fall of 1622, while Louis XIII
was busy crushing the Protestant lords of Languedoc, Théophile de
Viau thought it politic to write the king these lines ("Au Roy, sur son re-
tour de Languedoc"):

> Young, victorious monarch
> Whose glorious exploits
> Have made the gods jealous
> And the Fates afraid
> What more do you want from destiny?
> You've punished enough rebels.
> You've razed enough cities.
> We know that henceforth
> The rage of civil wars
> Will rob our peace no longer.

Théophile should have known what he was rhyming about. After all, hadn't
he joined the early part of the Languedoc campaign as "professor of lan-
gauges"? Furthermore, his hometown, Clérac, was one of the many places
that fell to the Protestant rebels that year; in fact his brother Paul was one
of the local rebel chiefs.

Perhaps the prediction of peace was wishful thinking. Théophile himself was a Protestant, an alumnus of the famous Protestant academy of Saumur. He might well have wished the warrior-king would turn his sword to
other enemies than France's Huguenots. Or perhaps Théophile's mind was
on more mundane things, such as the writing of his pornographic *Le Parnasse*

satyrique, published the next year. (*Le Parnasse* was one of the creations that turned Paris' Jesuits against Théophile and soon got him into jail.) At any rate, when he forecast peace he misjudged his sovereign and his century.

His sovereign was not an easy man to know. Three years earlier, in 1619, Sir Edward Herbert had come to Louis XIII as England's ambassador. As Herbert later recalled the king:

> His words were never many as being so extream a Stutterer, that he would sometimes hold his Tongue out of his Mouth a good while before he could speak so much as one word. He had besides a double Row of teeth, and was observed seldom or never to spit or blow his Nose, or to sweat much though he were very laborious and almost indefatigable in his exercises of Hunting and Hawking to which He was much addicted. Neither did it hinder him though he was burst in his body, as we call it, or Herniosus, for he was noted in those his sports though often times on foot to tire not only his Courtiers but even his Lackies; being equally insensible as was thought either of heat or cold; His Understanding and natural parts were as good as could be expected in one that was brought up in so much ignorance, which was on purpose so done that he might be the longer governed; howbeit he acquired in time a great knowledge in Affairs as conversing for the most part with wise and active Persons. He was noted to have two Qualities incident to all who were ignorantly brought up, Suspicion and Dissimulation . . . neither his fears did [*sic*] take away his courage, when there was occasion to use it, nor his dissimulation extend itself to the doing of private mischiefs to his Subjects either of the one or the other Religion.   (Herbert 1976: 93–94)

Nevertheless this complex king, son of a monarch converted from Protestantism, became a scourge to France's Protestants.

The stuttering, hypochondriacal king was only twenty-one in 1622, but he already had five years of rule behind him. They had not been easy years: two civil wars with his mother and her entourage, two seasons of campaigns against France's Protestant strongholds, foreign conflicts drumming up in Germany and Italy. Memories of the long wars of religion, ended only twenty-five years earlier, reminded France what ravages continuous combat could wreak. The nation and its poets might well pray for peace, but the past gave them every reason to believe that the gods preferred war.

War and Pacification under Louis XIII

The rest of the century saw little peace. Every year from 1623 until Louis XIII's death in 1643 brought at least one substantial insurrection somewhere in France. Rebellions continued in annual cadence well into the reign of his son and successor, Louis XIV. Chief minister Richelieu began to build up France's military forces and to intervene discreetly in the European war from 1629 on, although France did not enter the conflict openly until Louis XIII declared war on Spain in 1635. That burst the dam. During most of the next eighty years, France was fighting somewhere: along her eastern frontier, in Italy, or in Spain.

In his *Traité de l'économie politique,* published seven years before Théophile's ode to the king, Antoine Montchrestien had reflected on the cost of war. "It is impossible," he mused, "to make war without arms, to support men without pay, to pay them without tribute, to collect tribute without trade. Thus the exercise of trade, which makes up a large part of political action, has always been pursued by those peoples who flourished in glory and power, and these days more diligently than ever by those who seek strength and growth" (Montchrestien 1889 [1615]: 142). That money was the sinew of war was by then an old saw. Machiavelli had already felt compelled to combat the idea a century before Montchrestien's dictum: he turned the trick by arguing that although good money could not always buy valiant warriors, valiant warriors could always capture good money. Even then, many a monarch thought good money a better bet, and found unpaid warriors a source of mutiny. But the full argument from war back to trade became the standard sermon only during the seventeenth century.

Montchrestien and his contemporaries did not draw the obvious conclusion: that cutting off trade would therefore be desirable, since it would prevent war. French conventional wisdom became, instead, that: (1) in order to make war, the government had to raise taxes; and (2) to make raising taxes easier, the government should promote taxable commerce. A large share of what we call mercantilism flowed from these simple premises. Both the raising of taxes and the promotion of commerce infringed on some people's established rights and interests; they therefore produced determined resistance. Thus began a century of army building, tax gathering, warmaking, rebellion, and repression.

Internal Enemies

Part of the royal domestic program consisted, in effect, of undoing the Edict of Nantes. The 1598 edict had pacified the chief internal rivals of the crown—the Catholic and Protestant lords who had estabished nearly independent fiefdoms during the turmoil of the religious wars—while Henry IV was bargaining for peace with a still-strong Spain. The edict had granted

Huguenots the rights to gather and to practice their faith, even to arm themselves and to govern a number of cities in southern, western, and southwestern France. It had also absolved those officials who had raised troops, arms, taxes, and supplies in the name of one or another of the rebel authorities (Wolfe 1972: 225–230). The Edict of Nantes had frozen in place the structure of forces that prevailed in the France of 1598, while restoring the ultimate powers—including the powers to raise troops, arms, taxes, and supplies—to the crown. For a century, subsequent kings and ministers sought to unfreeze the structure, to dissolve the autonomous centers of organized power that remained within the kingdom.

Louis XIII had reason to worry about the Protestants: armed Huguenots had supported the rebellion of the prince of Condé in 1616 and his mother's in 1619. As soon as the young king had checked his mother and her counselors, he began a series of military campaigns against Protestant strongholds: La Rochelle, Rochefort, St.-Jean-d'Angély, Montauban, Privas, and many others. Sir Edward Herbert reported that the duke of Luynes,

> continuing still the Kings favorite, advised him to War against his Subjects of the reform'd Religion in France, saying he would neither be a great Prince as long as he suffered to Puissant a Part to remaine within his Dominions, nor could justly stile himself the most Christian King, as long as he permitted such Hereticks to be in that great number they were, or to hold those strong Places which by publick Edict were assigned to them, and therefore that he should extirpate them as the Spaniards had done the Moors, who are all banished into other Countreys as we may find in their Histories. (Herbert 1976: 104)

Herbert reported making a prophetic remark to the duke of Guise: "Whensoever those of the Religion were put down, the turn of the Great Persons and Governors of the Provinces of that Kingdome would be next" (Herbert 1976: 105). The prophecy fell on deaf ears.

The distinction between "Great Persons" and "those of the Religion" was then far from absolute; many magnates were also Protestants. When Louis XIII went off on his campaign of 1622 against Protestant strongholds in the southwest, he faced multiple revolts allying influential nobles with rank-and-file followers of the religion. "There were few of that religion," reported *Le Mercure François,*

> who last year had sworn oaths of fidelity to the king who did not this year revolt and again take up arms against him: some of them unhappy *because they had not been compensated for the military governorships they had*

lost, the others on the specious pretext of the *defense of their churches,*
which was, they said, a matter of *honor and conscience.* One finds enough
soldiers when one gives them the freedom to live off the land, and allowing them to pillage supports them without pay. Nevertheless, a
party cannot survive without some sort of established order, and without having the means of paying the costs of war: that was why the sieur
de la Force established at Ste.-Foy a Council of the Churches of Lower
Guyenne. That council, which he ran, was a miniature version of the
Protestant Assembly, which . . . decided and decreed all political, military, and financial questions. Thus the first thing they decided was a levy
of three hundred thousand livres, which would be divided among all the
cities and towns of Lower Guyenne, and for which some average peasant
or other resident would be seized and made a prisoner in St.-Foy, so that
he would act to collect from the other people of his parish. (*Le Mercure François* 1622: 446)

That technique, long employed by royal tax collectors, served equally well
for the crown's opponents.

   Indeed, the conquest of Protestant areas in France had much in common with war against foreign powers. For example, when the duke of Soubise went to besiege Protestant Sables-d'Olonne, on the coast of Poitou, the
city's leaders gave him 20 million ecus, some cannons, and three ships in
order to avoid the sack of the city by his troops. Yet as soon as the troops
entered Les Sables-d'Olonne, they began pillaging. Soubise explained, "I
had promised them booty before you and I worked out the peace settlement" (*Le Mercure François* 1622: 530–531).

   The crucial difference between international wars and these campaigns
against internal enemies was no doubt the treatment given the enemies. The
domestic opponents of the crown qualified as rebels, their actions as treason.
Not for them—except for the great powerholders among them—treaties,
ransoms, and the courtesies of war. Jean-Paul de Lescun had been an official
of Pau and had helped organize the Protestant resistance of 1622 in the
southwest. When Lescun was captured in battle, he went to Bordeaux for
trial. This was his sentence:

   to be dragged on a frame through the streets and squares of this city,
   with a sign at his head (GUILTY OF LÈSE-MAJESTÉ, AND PRESIDENT OF
   THE ASSEMBLY OF LA ROCHELLE), and from there to be led to the front of
   the royal palace of Lombrière, there to do penance in a plain shirt, noose
   around his neck, head and feet bare, and kneeling with a two-pound
   torch of burning wax, to declare that with evil and malice he had at-

tended and presided over said assembly of La Rochelle, and that in his role as president he had signed commissions to levy troops against the service and authority of the king, and attended the council of justice set up in said city of La Rochelle by said assembly to judge in a sovereign manner with respect to the lives and goods of subjects of the king; together with other people to have prepared the book called *The Persecution of the Reformed Churches of Béarn,* and that he asks forgiveness of God, the king, and justice. And nevertheless this court commands that both said book and said commissions will be burned by the executioner for high justice in the presence of said Lescun; and this done, said executioner will cut off his head and his four limbs on a scaffold to be built for this purpose. And after the execution, we order the head of said Lescun to be taken to the city of Royan, to be placed on top of a tower or gate of the city, pointing toward said city of La Rochelle. The court furthermore declares the offspring of said Lescun ignoble and common, and all his goods in any place whatsoever to be confiscated and surrendered to the king, from which however the sum of 3,000 livres will first be deducted, half for the feeding and maintenance of the poor of the Hospital St.-André of this city, the other half for the repair of the palace. The costs of the trial will likewise be deducted. (*Le Mercure François* 1622: 602–604)

Thus did rebels—when captured and vulnerable—suffer for braving royal authority. When those captured rebels were Protestant, they were more likely to be vulnerable.

In striking against Protestant autonomy, Louis XIII could count on popular support. Although the Wars of Religion, as a matter of state, had ended with treaties and with the crowning of a converted Protestant, Catholic hostility to Protestants survived in many parts of France. Very likely the officially enforced segregation of the religious minority accentuated the hostility. That included the religious segregation of Paris. There, Protestants could practice in only one church—in Charenton, outside the city walls. In 1611

> the Protestants went to bury a small child in their Trinity Cemetery, near the rue St.-Denis; they went in the evening, but before sunset. Two members of the watch officially led the procession. A vinegar-maker's helper began to throw stones at them and was imitated by his master and by several others. One of the watchmen was wounded. The *lieutenant criminel* of the Châtelet had them arrested, and on 1 July the helper was whipped outside of the Trinity Cemetery. But on Sunday 21 August, Protestants coming back from Charenton were insulted. (Mousnier 1978: 75)

In Paris, the Sunday trips of Protestants to Charenton were frequent occasions for abuse from Catholics. Sometimes they turned into occasions for violence. When the news of the death of the (Catholic) duke of Mayenne at the 1621 siege of (Protestant) Montauban arrived in the city, crowds attacked the carriages of Protestants, battled with the watchmen stationed at the St.-Antoine Gate to protect them, and rushed out to burn down the church. Later, "the other clerics and common people who had busied themselves with setting the fire and burning the temple and drinking eight or ten kegs of wine that were in the concierge's cellar, and eating the provisions, after making a flag of a white sheet, came back to Paris through the St.-Antoine Gate, 400 strong, shouting 'Vive le roy' " (*Le Mercure François* 1621: 854). That "Vive le roy" should remind us of the connection between popular hostility and official policy. In this instance the stationing of armed guards to prevent an attack on the Protestants makes it dubious that royal officials directly instigated the violence. Yet from early in his reign Louis XIII sought to cow his Huguenots, to demilitarize them, and to circumscribe their activities.

Local groups of Protestants and Catholics also fought intermittently. Where the Protestants were relatively strong, as in Nîmes, Montpellier, and much of urban Languedoc, there was a series of struggles over control of public offices. In the mainly Protestant city of Pamiers, the consuls sought to exclude all Catholics from the consulate. In March 1623, Catholics demanded a voice; they persuaded the parlement to decree equal representation of the two religious groups. The consuls closed the city gates to the parlement's emissary, and then to the envoy who brought confirmation of the decree by the king's council. Only when the king sent troops did the consuls give in (*Le Mercure François* 1624: 381–385). Later the same year, the emboldened Catholics complained against the stay in the planned destruction of local Protestant churches and demanded a division of the city keys—two per gate—between Protestants and Catholics.

By that time Pamiers actually had three competing factions: (1) Protestants, (2) Catholics who had remained in the town during Languedoc's Protestant-Catholic wars of the previous years, and (3) the bishop, priests, and (presumably wealthier) Catholics who had fled Pamiers when the wars came too close (*Le Mercure François* 1624: 871–877). In 1625 the Pamiers Protestants joined those of a number of other cities of Languedoc in a new rebellion against the crown. In this case, as in most, the national conflict and the local one reinforced each other.

When French warmaking on an international scale resumed in the 1630s, the crown had two additional reasons for intervening against Protestants: France's claim to lead Europe's Catholic powers, and her conquest of territory from her chief Catholic rival, Spain. As French troops entered Spanish territory, her cardinal-ministers redoubled the prohibitions on Protestant religious services and proselytization in the army. At the same time, it became an implicit national policy to encourage Protestant conversions to Catholicism, and to keep the remaining Protestants from retaliating against their turncoat brethren. Although the French crown took another half-century to arrive at a complete legal ban on Protestant worship, by the later 1630s it was already treating Protestants—individually and collectively—as a threat to the state's integrity.

Protestants were by no means the only threat. Great Catholic lords also caused trouble. As seen from the top down, seventeenth-century France was a complex of patron-client chains. Every petty lord had his *gens,* the retainers and dependents who owed their livelihood to his "goodwill," to his "protection" against their "enemies" (to use three key words of the time). Some of the gens were always armed men who could swagger in public on the lord's behalf, avenge the injuries he received, and protect him from his own enemies.

The country's great magnates played the same games on a larger scale. They maintained huge clienteles, including their own private armies. They held France's regional military governorships, and kept order with a combination of royal troops and their own. Indeed, at the century's start France did not really have a national army in the later sense of the word. In time of war or rebellion the king fielded his own personal troops plus those of the great lords he could both trust and persuade to take the field on his behalf.

Great Catholic lords, including such members of the royal family as the successive princes of Condé, tried repeatedly to strengthen their holds on different pieces of the kingdom. In the summer of 1605, according to a contemporary account,

> The king, being in Paris, was warned by a certain Captain Belin that in Limousin, Périgord, Quercy, and other surrounding provinces many gentlemen were getting together to rebuild the foundations of rebellion that the late Marshal Biron had laid down. Their pretext was the usual one: to reduce the people's burdens and to improve the administration of justice. In any case, their plan was simply to fish in troubled waters and, while appearing to serve the public good, to fatten themselves on the ruin of the poor people. (*Le Mercure François* 1605: 12)

The king gave Belin a 1,200-livre reward, then rushed to Limoges. There he convoked the nobles and hunted down the rebels. Five were decapitated in person, six more in effigy. That stilled the threat of noble rebellion in the southwest for a few years.

Limousin's abortive rebellion never reached the stage of popular insurrection. Only half of the potent seventeenth-century combination—noble conspiracy plus popular response to royal exactions—came into play. But in those insurrectionary years the gentlemen-conspirators had a reasonable hope that if they kept on stirring their region's troubled waters, people's grievances against royal taxes, troops, laws, and officials would sooner or later coalesce into disciplined resistance. More than anything else, the popular contention of the seventeenth century swirled around the efforts of ordinary people to preserve or advance their interests in the face of a determined royal drive to build up the power of the state.

The France of 1598 was, then, a weakened country—weakened by internal strife, but also by threats from outside. Three remarkable kings spent the next century reshaping the French state into an incomparable force within its own borders and a powerful presence in the word as a whole. Henry IV, Louis XIII, and Louis XIV accomplished the transformation of a leaky, creaking, wind-rocked vessel maneuvering among mutiny, piracy, and open war, with either too many hands on the wheel or practically no steering at all, into a formidable, tight man of war.

War Prevails

Remember how much war the seventeenth century brought. A list of only the major foreign conflicts in which French kings engaged includes:

> 1635–1659: war with Spain, ending with the Treaty of the Pyrenees
> 1636–1648: war with the Holy Roman Empire, ending with the Treaty of Westphalia
> 1664: an expedition against the Turks at St. Gotthard
> 1667–1668: the War of Devolution, ending with the Treaty of Aachen
> 1672–1679: the Dutch War, ending with the Treaty of Nijmegen
> 1688–1697: the War of the League of Augsburg, ending with the Peace of Ryswick

If we included the minor flurries, the list would grow much longer. In 1627 and 1628, for example, the English temporarily occupied the Ile de Ré, on France's Atlantic coast, and sent a fleet to support besieged La Rochelle. In 1629 and 1630, while still battling domestic rebels, Louis XIII was sending expeditionary forces into Italy. In 1634 the king occupied and annexed Lorraine. War had long been one of the normal affairs of the state. Now it was becoming the normal state of affairs.

As they fashioned an organization for making war, the king's servants inadvertently created a centralized state. First the framework of an army, then a government built around that framework—and in its shape. The wherewithal of war included soldiers and arms, to be sure. It also included food for the soldiers, money to pay them, lodgings on the march and in the long off-season, wagons and draft animals, food and shelter for the animals and for cavalry horses. As a practical matter, if not as a logical necessity, the wherewithal of war likewise included drink, sex, and sociability, not to mention the policing of the "disorder" occasioned by those activities. All this came from a population which often harvested barely enough food to survive, which converted a significant part of its production into rents, tithes, and local taxes, and for which the loss of an ox, the occupation of a bed, or the increase of taxes could mean a family crisis.

In order to squeeze these precious resources from a reluctant population, the crown's agents adopted a series of expedients. They increased existing taxes, farmed them out to entrepreneurs who knew how to collect those taxes profitably, and backed the tax-farmers with armed force and judicial sanction. They created new taxes and ensured their collection in the same way. They issued money to military commanders for the purchase of soldiers, food, lodging, and so on—often by establishing yet another special tax on the local population. They allowed military chiefs to commandeer, within limits, the goods and services their armies required. Within more stringent limits, they also let the troops themselves commandeer food, labor, sex, drink, and sociability from the local population.

As the seventeenth century moved on, however, royal officials increasingly adopted three means of regularizing the entire support of military operations: first, creating a staff of specialists in supply and support linked to a geographically stable civil administration spread through the entire country; second, relying on large-scale purchases of goods and services in the national market, purchases carried out by agents of the central administration; third, constructing a well-defined national standing army with a relatively clear and stable hierarchy of command reaching up to the king's ministers. Combined with the growth of the apparatus for taxation and its enforcement, these innovations created most of the structure of a centralized national state. Among the major national institutions, only the courts and the church escaped a fundamental reorganization as a consequence of preparation for war. They escaped, in essence, by collaborating with the warmakers.

The chief countercurrent to centralization was an important one. The whole system (if the word is not too strong) erected by warmaking ministers relied on raising cash quickly. They had neither the power nor the administrative apparatus to raise the cash directly. Instead, they relied on specialists in credit who had substantial funds at their disposal, and who— for a good price—were willing to advance money to the crown. They fell into two overlapping classes: the *munitionnaires,* who supplied the armed forces directly; and the various sorts of tax-farmers, who collected taxes on the basis of contracts (*traités*) that compensated them amply for their risks.

To be strictly accurate, we would have to distinguish among tax-farmers in the narrow sense—those who took control of regular indirect taxes— and the traitants who took contracts for "extraordinary" revenues. We would likewise have to remember that those who actually signed the contracts were frequently *prête-noms,* front men for syndicates of capitalists; to review the seventeenth-century use of rich pejorative terms such as *partisan* and *maltôtier* for these fiscal entrepreneurs; and to make allowance for the significant changes of vocabulary that occurred as the process unfolded; for present purposes, the broad distinction between munitionnaires and tax-farmers will do.

The greatest of these profit-making creditors became known as "financiers." A circle of a few hundred financiers formed a sort of parallel government, often holding offices but nonetheless putting a major part of their effort into the mobilization of capital. They were, in fact, the great capitalists of their day: the Fouquets, Colberts, and Maupéous who, in the short run, raised the cash to keep the French monarchy going. The munitionnaires, tax-farmers, and great financiers depended closely on one another and made their money on the making of war. Indeed, the families involved in raising capital for the crown originated disproportionately in Burgundy and Champagne, where warmaking had long provided opportunities for profit to those who knew how to supply grain, fodder, arms, and advances in pay to troops of the monarchy (Dent 1973: 115–118; Dessert 1984: 107). There, waxing capitalism and growing state power walked hand in hand.

For collectors of irony, the French seventeenth century is a treasure trove. One of the century's ironies is that the great guides in the early decades of French militarization were men of the cloth. Cardinals Richelieu and Mazarin hammered out a policy of conquest; that policy required in its turn the recruiting, organizing, supplying, and paying of unprecedented armies. The effort brought to prominence such financiers as Fouquet, adept at the creation of *combinazioni* and the quick mobilization of credit. It called forth such administrative virtuosos as Le Tellier, indefatigable in the creation of armies and the large support structures required to keep them going. Its consequence was the reshaping of the state into an administrative apparatus oriented increasingly toward the production and use of armed force.

Here is another irony. If the dominant process in seventeenth-century France was the militarization of the state, its effect was a civilianization of royal administration. Increasingly the representatives of the crown with whom local people had to deal were full-time civilian administrators. Royal administrators owed their livelihood not to the protection of a great regional lord but to the support of a minister in Paris and the sustenance of the royal apparatus as a whole.

That happened in two ways. The first was the long drive to disarm every place, person, and group that was not under reliable royal control; the drive took the form of bans on dueling, dismantling of fortresses, and dissolutions of civic militias as well as the incorporation of private forces into the royal army. The second was the expansion of the numbers and powers of royal officials—most obviously, the intendants and their staffs—who were charged with raising the revenues, controlling the supplies, and securing the day-to-day compliance necessary to build and maintain a big military establishment. Over the century as a whole, the crown was successful in both regards: it greatly reduced the possibility of armed resistance within the kingdom, and it enormously increased the resources available for royal warmaking. Yet success came at the price of bloody rebellion, of brutal repression, of expedients and compromises that committed the crown to an immense, exigent clientele of creditors and officials. These statemaking processes stimulated the large-scale contention of the seventeenth century.

The ultimate irony is this: By and large, the people who built that increasingly bulky and centralized seventeenth-century state did not seek to create a more effective government, but to extend their personal power and that of their allies. Yet they found themselves ever more implicated in their own design. Ministers of finance forced rich men to buy offices, only to find that the officeholders now needed military force to back their claims on the revenues assigned to those offices. Nobles aligned themselves with the king, and against other nobles, in civil war, only to find that the king was a demanding and tenacious ally. Artists and authors dipped into the royal treasury, only to find that subventions were habit-forming. Ordinary people, it is true, got little _quid_ for their _quo;_ but as their sometime supporters slipped into the state's grasp, ordinary people's capacity to resist the state's exactions slipped away as well.

Given the formidable growth of state power and the decreasing sup-

port of opposition movements by great lords, the persistence of popular rebellion and resistance through the seventeenth century offers a measure of
the interests at stake. That ordinary people had the urge to resist is easy to
understand. They could see their lives threatened; warmaking and statemaking proceeded at their expense. Warmaking and statemaking placed demands on land, labor, capital, and commodities that were already
committed: grain earmarked for the local poor or next year's seed, manpower required for a farm's operation, savings promised for a dowry. The
commitments were not merely fond hopes or pious intentions, but matters
of right and obligation. Not meeting those commitments, or impeding
their fulfillment, violated established rights of real people.

In addition to encroaching on local and customary rights, raising new
resources often meant abridging or rescinding privileges the state itself had
ratified. Exemptions from taxation, rights to name local officers, established
means of consent, and bargaining over financial support to the crown—all
gave way as statemakers made the claims of the government supplant the
rights of individuals and communities. Popular indignation was the greater
because of a standard seventeenth-century tactic: offering privileges and
profits to the tax-farmer, officeholder, or entrepreneur who was prepared to
give the crown ready cash in exchange for the opportunity to draw future
revenues from the local population. It was bad enough that a rich man
should profit from other people's sacrifices. When his privileges actually increased the local burden (as regularly happened when a newly exempted official stopped paying his share of the local tax quota, or when the office in
question involved new or expanded fees), the rich man's neighbors were
commonly outraged.

Not that middlemen were the only objects of popular resistance. Ordinary people often felt the military effort quite directly. Soldiers and officials
wrested from them the means of war: food, lodging, draft animals, unwilling recruits. People hid those resources when they could, and defended
them against seizure when they dared. On the whole, however, the military
got what they wanted.

The direct seizure of the means of war from the people lagged a distant
second behind the extraction of money. In a relatively uncommercialized
economy, demands for cash contributions were often more painful than demands for goods. They required people either to dig into the small stores of
coin they had saved for great occasions or to market goods and labor they
would ordinarily have used at home. The less commercialized the local
economy, the more difficult the marketing. Taxes, forced loans, the sale of
offices, and other means of raising money for the state and its armies all

multiplied during the seventeenth century. Directly or indirectly, all of them forced poor people to convert short resources into cash at the current market's terms, and then to surrender that cash to the state.

When rights were at issue and the force available to the state was not overwhelming, ordinary people resisted the new exactions as best they could. Tax rebellions, attacks on new officeholders, and similar forms of resistance filled the seventeenth century. Nevertheless, French statemakers managed to override rights and resistance alike; they succeeded in increasing enormously the financial burden borne by the population as a whole.

Extracting the Means of War

How did statemakers succeed? By dividing their opposition, by using force, by expanding the number of people and groups having a financial interest in the state's survival, by routinizing the collection of revenues, and by multiplying the specialists devoted to the extraction of those revenues. The definitive settling of the intendants in the provinces, accomplished after the Fronde had forced the temporary withdrawal of the intendants from the land, was no doubt the single most important stratagem. Intendants of Richelieu and Mazarin were still serving, by and large, as temporary troubleshooters. After the Fronde, however, things changed. Mazarin, and then Colbert, expanded and regularized their service. Intendants supervised the collection of revenues, applied coercion when necessary and feasible, kept watch over the local expenditure of state funds, and stayed alert for new opportunities to tax, to sell offices, to preempt local revenues, and to borrow, borrow, and borrow again.

Although the borrowing eventually increased the share of state revenues that went to service debts, it also expanded the number of people who had financial interests in the state's survival. It created a large class of officials and financiers who served their own advantage by helping to pay the expense of the state. A tax-farmer advanced cash to the crown in return for the right to collect taxes at a profit. The purchaser of a new office made a substantial payment to the crown in return for the right to collect the office's revenues and, frequently, for some form of exemption from taxation. A local guild borrowed money on its own credit or levied contributions from its members, paid a "loan," a "gift," or a "tax" to the royal treasury, and gained confirmation of its monopoly over the production and sale of a certain commodity.

That became the standard royal expedient: in order to raise current revenue, the king's agents found someone with capital, then induced or coerced him to advance money now in return for a claim on future income and the assurance of governmental support in collecting that income. This routine deflected the indignation of ordinary people from the statemakers themselves to tax-farmers, officeholders, and other profiteers who fattened themselves at the people's expense.

Well might the people complain. The burden was heavy and growing heavier, uneven and becoming more uneven. Not long after the Fronde, Peter Heylyn (building on the knowledge he had accumulated for his multivolume *Cosmographie*) published his delightfully opinionated *France Painted to the Life*. "To go over all those impositions, which this miserable people are afflicted withal," wrote Heylyn, "were almost as wretched as the payment of them. I will therefore speak onely of the principal" (Heylyn 1656: 238). And so he enumerated the salt tax (gabelle), the taille, the *taillon,* and the pancarte or *aides*. Of the taillon, Heylyn reported:

> In former times, the Kings Souldiers lay all upon the charge of the Villages, the poor people being fain to find them diet, lodging and all necessaries for themselves, their horses and their harlots, which they brought with them. If they were not well pleased with their entertainment, they used commonly to beat their Host, abuse his family, and rob him of that small provision which he had laid up for his Children, and all this *cum privilegio*. Thus did they move from one Village to another, and at the last returned unto them from whence they came ... To redress this mischeif [*sic*], King Henry the second, *Anno* 1549, raised his imposition called the *Taillon,* issuing out of the lands and goods of the poor Country man; whereby he was at the first somewhat eased: but now all is again out of order, the miserable paisant being oppressed by the Souldier as much as ever, and yet he still payeth both taxes the *Taille* and the *Taillon*. (Heylyn 1656: 242–243)

Heylyn went on to enumerate the innumerable inequalities and exemptions: nobles, clerics, officeholders, provinces that had bargained for special treatment, and so on. He concluded, quite properly, that the "miserable paisant" ultimately bore the French fiscal burden. He declared that the long chain of tax-farming intermediaries guaranteed two additional pernicious results: that only a fraction of the revenues collected in the king's name ever arrived in the royal coffers, and that those most involved in the collection of taxes had the least interest in justice, compassion, or moderation. "Were the people but so happy," reflected Heylyn,

> as to have a certain rate set upon their miseries, it could not but be a great ease to them, and would well defend them from the tyranny of

these theeves: but, which is not the least part of their wretchedness, their taxings and assemblings are left arbitrary, and are exacted according as these *Publicans* will give out of the *Kings* necessities. So that the Country man hath no other remedy, than to give *Cerberus* a crust, as the saying is, and to kiss his rod and hug his punishment. By this meanes the *Quaestors* thrive abundantly, it being commonly said of them, *Fari bouvier au jourd huy Chevalier,* to day a Swineheard, to morrow a Gentleman.   (Heylyn 1656: 248)

What is more, when Heylyn wrote in 1656, the rise of taxes had slowed for a while, the age of fiscal expedients was just beginning, and another half-century of surging taxation was in store. If the post-Fronde installation of the intendants regularized the fiscal system to some extent, it certainly did not lighten the burden, remove its cruelties, or eliminate its inequities.

Exhibit 2, showing France's seventeenth-century tax burden, records the growth of a greedy state. Net royal revenue displays the spectacular rise of the 1630s and 1640s, the decline of the Fronde, the recovery of the 1650s, then the new acceleration after 1660; only after 1700 does it again show a decline. In short, the curve of royal revenue follows the timetable of war: mobilization under Louis XIII and Richelieu, a lull (though certainly no decline) with the Fronde and the slowing of the war against Spain, renewed armament with Louis XIV.

The line for royal expenditure in days' wages per capita per year (computed from Guéry 1978 as a multiple of the standard construction worker's wage in Paris, from Baulant 1971, adjusted for total population by interpolation from the estimates in Reinhard, Armengaud, and Dupâquier 1968) shows roughly the same rhythm as gross tax revenue; the main differences are a stronger increase from 1620 onward, a lesser decline with the Fronde, signs of plummeting expenditure in the late 1650s, and evidence of temporary drops in spending during Louis XIV's rare intervals of peace. But the second curve gives an idea of the rhythm's effects on the lives of ordinary French people. In these terms, the rising expenditures of the seventeenth century nearly sextupled the annual effort a hypothetical average worker put in for the state: from the equivalent of two or three days' wages in the decade after 1600 to between ten and fourteen days' wages in most years of the 1690s.

These figures for expenditures and for net revenues count only money that actually reached and then left royal hands; collection costs added more to the burden. Since many nobles, clergy, and officials were exempted, since local authorities who had borrowed to meet royal demands for loans likewise imposed new taxes, and since the tax-farmers took their cuts over and above the state's net tax revenue, Heylyn's "miserable paisant" could easily have felt a tenfold increase of his load. By the time Louis XIII, Louis XIV, and their agents had finished the job, the average French family were paying many times the royal taxes they had paid in 1600.

Coming from Commonwealth England to Bourbon France, Peter Heylyn could well be impressed with French fiscal oppression. With the Civil War, England had more or less definitively established the principle of parliamentary consent to taxation. English taxes involved fewer exemptions

Exhibit 2.   French central government expenditures and net revenues in millions of livres, 1600–1715 (Guéry 1978; Baulant 1971; Reinhard, Armengaud, and Dupâquier 1968)

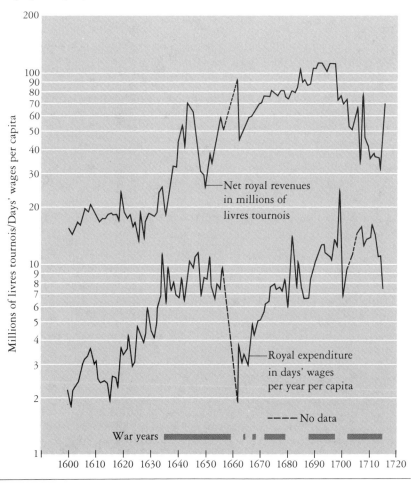

and inequities than the French. They bore more heavily on customs—hence on international trade—and less heavily on the land. And the overall weight of English taxation was significantly lower. Furthermore, the French growth curve does not show the struggle between crown and commoners it represents. The crown won its struggle by exempting the strong and taxing the weak.

To reduce the political risks of this fiscal strategy, however, the crown had to tame and supplant its internal rivals. Otherwise, each new round of popular resistance would provide an opportunity for some set of magnates to offer themselves as champions of the people's rights. In parallel with its external warmaking and its internal fund-raising, the crown undertook a massive effort of co-optation, neutralization, and suppression. After the failure of the Fronde, the great princes and their clienteles fell into line. With some important exceptions, the major blocs of Protestant autonomy gave way under the continued grinding and blasting of Louis XIII and Louis XIV. The parlements, the other "sovereign courts," the provincial Estates, the guilds, the municipalities all finally lost significant shares of their ability to resist royal demands and to ally themselves with ordinary people against the crown as the intendants used a combination of force, fragmentation, and fiscal advantage to bring them to acquiescence. Thus the intendants and other royal officials became freer to use their growing repressive power when ordinary people dared to resist governmental demands directly.

These changes had predictable effects on the character of popular contention: a decline in the involvement of major powerholders in big rebellions, an increasing focus of popular resistance on the exactions of tax-farmers and officeholders, a decreasing readiness of royal officials to negotiate with groups protesting violations of their rights. The word "absolutism" describes such an incomplete and contested process quite badly. But it accurately conveys the claims the king's agents began to make on their master's behalf. They claimed an absolute right to override local privileges and individual rights in the interest of the crown. And they did so largely to pay for war.

Seventeenth-Century Repertoires

The pervasiveness of war's influence and the variable character of that influence with distance from war show up emphatically in a comparison of the Ile-de-France and Languedoc during the 1640s. In the six years from 1640 through 1645, for example, the Ile-de-France stood at the very edge of the French campaigns in Artois, Picardy, and Champagne, while Languedoc was reluctantly helping to pay the rapidly mounting cost of war and saw troops marching through to and from the fighting in Catalonia, but was relatively distant from major battlefields.

In the Ile-de-France, 1640 was a great year for attacks by local residents on billeted military units: at Champagne-sur-Oise, at Villeneuve-le-Roi and nearby villages, and in the vicinity of Senlis; near St.-Quentin and Guise, at the northeast corner of the Ile-de-France, peasants fought off the attempt to make them cart military supplies to the siege of Arras. That same year brought an attack on the salt stores at Vesles, on the border of Picardy, by an Irish mercenary regiment; an illegal assembly to levy arms in Mantes (modern-day Mantes-la-Jolie); and rebellions against tax collectors in Proisy and the élection of Château-Thierry (AA A[1] 57, 58, 59, 60). The next five years brought more contention (Bonney 1978b: 329; Mousnier 1964: I, 534–536; AA A[1] 81, 82; BN Fr 18432; Hillairet 1970: 53):

1641: violent resistance to the *sol pour livre* surtax in Nemours
1643: attack on light cavalrymen at St.-Germain-près-Montargis
1644: expulsion of a tax-farmer from Argenteuil
     attacks on troops in Bourg-sur-Aisne (now part of Bourg-et-Comin), Vinsouet(?), and Garancière
     violence against the mayor of Etampes by troops stationed there
     disorderly march of workers in Paris
1645: "sedition" against salt-tax guards and officers in St.-Denis
     barricades in the streets of Paris to defend the parlement against a rumored attack by royal troops

In addition, during those years Paris saw at least one extraordinary assembly of Protestants, and at least one brush between the law and a group of Frondeurs—in the pre-Fronde meaning of young men who fought for the sake of adventure outside the walls of the city.

In Languedoc during the same period we find a "seditious assembly" at Gimon for which ten people hanged (1640), then no major contention for the next two years (*La Gazette de France* 1640: 630). In 1643 the featured events were attacks on tax collectors in Valence, Lavaur, and Toulouse and an armed Protestant gathering in Ribaute (Mousnier 1964: I, 589; Devic & Vaissète 1876, XIII: 143; Liublinskaya 1966: 36–38, 40–47). Sixteen forty-four brought another fiscal rebellion in Figeac; a public confrontation between the Cour des Comptes and the intendant, with undertones of local opposition to taxes for the military, in Montpellier; and a turbulent assembly in Nîmes on behalf of local notables accused of shaving coins (BN Fr 18830; Porchnev 1963: 639–640; Beik 1974b; Liublinskaya 1966: 77–82).

And 1645 was the year of a large insurrection against taxes in Montpellier, the forceful freeing of a young man imprisoned for tax evasion in Nîmes, illegal Protestant assemblies in Aubenas, and attacks on bishops in Carcassonne and Mende (Porchnev 1963: 242–260, 654; Liublinskaya 1966: 133–137; Mousnier 1964: II, 737–738, 763–772; BN Fr 18432; Barrière-Flavy 1926: 18–21). The incomplete calendars of contention for both regions contain a great deal of resistance to taxes. But the struggles between soldiers and civilians were concentrated in that corner of the Ile-de-France crisscrossed by troops sent to conquer Spanish territory to the northeast.

Of all these conflicts, only the Montpellier insurrection of 1645 has found much of a place in history books. In that insurrection, as a memoir written for Chancellor Séguier summed it up,

> the dregs of the common people and the weaker sex had the nerve to take arms and to seize the city gates; to break into the houses of royal officials and tax collectors; to mark for pillage the houses of persons suspected of being tax-farmers and to threaten those same persons with death; to attack a duke, peer, and marshal of France who is governor of the province in a city to which he has devoted his friendship, personal establishment, and time; to make him risk his life; to burn, sack, and massacre to the sound of the tocsin; to run down an intendant; to brave the cannons of the fortress; in fact to push back the cannons, beat down the soldiers, and plan to attack and raze the fortress.   (BN Fr 18432)

And why all this? Bosquet, one of Languedoc's two intendants, declared that the artisans of Montpellier had encouraged their wives to act against a new tax because they were "extremely surprised both by the unprecedented character of the tax and by the large assessments levied on them" (Coquelle 1908: 69).

The judicial inquiry of 30 June 1645 began with the judge's declaration that he had heard "word from various sources that many women of the city as well as artisans and workers of said city had gathered, two or three hundred in number, complaining about a certain tax on artisans organized in guilds within the city, a tax levied for the happy accession [of Louis XIV] to the crown and other taxes imposed upon them" (BN Fr 18432). The "two or three hundred" swelled to several thousand, took over the city, sacked the elegant houses of a tax-farmer and an official of the provincial Estates, defeated the troops of the viceroy (Marshal Schomberg, previously governor, but now lieutenant general), and forced the viceroy to expel the tax-farmers.

It appears that city officials, already at odds with the money-starved royal government, sat on their hands for a day or two before moving decisively to the side of repression. That implicit assent from the bourgeoisie, plus bitter continuing rivalry between the two intendants then assigned to Languedoc, most likely gave the city's people more than the usual hope that they would succeed (Porchnev 1963: 251–254; Beik 1974b). Indeed, they did succeed—temporarily. Eventually, however, two women hanged for their involvement in the uprising, and a man died in prison. Such victories were always temporary.

Despite the profusion of conflicts, seventeenth-century French people employed a limited number of ways to make their demands and grievances known. They assembled solemnly, itemized their grievances, and elected leaders or delegates. They gathered to attack oppressive officials or tax collectors and their premises. They ganged up on marauding soldiers, stripped them of their baggage, and ran them out of town. They conducted mocking ceremonies and stoned or beat moral offenders. Occasionally they formed their own militias and patrolled their towns, or even marched off to punish some enemy. Those forms and a few others constituted the seventeenth-century repertoire of contention. When people did several of the same things on a large scale, with leaders linking a number of localities, they created a popular revolt. When they did the same things in conjunction with nobles who fielded private armies, the result was a great rebellion. Although the consequences were very different, the forms of popular action were much the same.

Before mid-century, popular revolts and great rebellions occurred with remarkable frequency. In the Ile-de-France, Languedoc, Burgundy, and Anjou, we would certainly want to include these events:

1614–1616: rebellion of the princes in Ile-de-France and elsewhere

1620: rebellion of Marie de Medici in Anjou and elsewhere

1621–1629: war of Protestants with royal forces in Languedoc and elsewhere

1623: uprising against merchants of Angers in Beaufort (Anjou) and surrounding area

1630: rebellion against tax-farmer in Angers

1630: "Lanturelu" rebellion against establishment of élection in Dijon

1632: partial involvement of Burgundy in rebellion of Gaston d'Orléans

1632: greater involvement of Languedoc in rebellion of Gaston, coupled with rebellion of duke of Montmorency

1643: rebellion against subsistances tax in Angers

1645: tax rebellion in Montpellier

> 1648–1653: the Fronde, concentrated in the Ile-de-France, but with important repercussions in all other provinces

Other, lesser conflicts have sometimes figured in maps and inventories of rebellions leading up to the Fronde; in Languedoc, for example, the beginnings of an antigabelle revolt in Toulouse (1635) and two more movements against taxes in Montpellier (1639, 1644) have served as exemplary cases. But the list above gives a sense of the major moments in which people who were clearly challenging established authorities exercised sustained control over a city or a group of towns despite the efforts of authorities to use force against them.

Not *all* the authorities, in the usual case. One requisite for large-scale popular rebellion was division among established authorities. That division could run from covert to flagrant: at one extreme, reluctance to repress people who made demands in the streets or sacked the premises of tax collectors; further along, visible sympathy with people's grievances; at the other extreme, outright declaration of opposition to the crown. Dijon's Lanturelu of 1630 showed the effects of local authority's visible sympathy with some of the winegrowers' complaints; so, at least, thought Richelieu.

Montpellier's rebellion of 1645 fell somewhere between the first two categories; some authorities merely hesitated, but others visibly opposed the crown's imposition of taxation without representation. The rebellions of 1632, on the other hand, gave rancorous commoners a clear chance to wrap their grievances in noble cloth—at the risk, to be sure, of eventual hanging for their effrontery. Joining in lèse-majesté always brought the risk of sudden, painful death.

Our select list of major revolts displays a shift away from dynastic struggles to tax rebellion, and a corresponding shift from the Ile-de-France to outlying provinces. It also reflects a decline in the relative importance of battles between beleaguered Protestants and the crown. None of these shifts was permanent. Toward the century's end, both royal efforts to subdue Protestants and Protestant efforts to hold off royal threats reached new heights. Before that, the Fronde of 1648–1653 swept the Ile-de-France back into action, and combined dynastic struggles with tax rebellion. In that combination, the Fronde summed up the conflicts of the first half of the century.

The Fronde

Event for event, the Fronde brought nothing new to the forms of French contention. Assemblies of rebellious nobles had formed before, princes had declared their readiness to battle the king, creditors and officeholders had gathered to protest reductions in their privileges and payments, great cities and whole regions had risen against the crown. During the 1630s and 1640s, as preparations for war gouged the goods and privileges of more and more French people, the frequency of such conflicts probably rose. The later rebellions show an overextended, capital-hungry state threatening the interests of many of its clients and subjects, shaking the very structure of social relations within which those clients and subjects lived. And in the Fronde we discover a convergence of previously separate conflicts, a repeated slipping of previously contained areas and peoples into the control of opponents of royal authority, and a real, if temporary, check to royal expansion.

For a half-century, French kings and their ministers had operated on a narrow margin. They could survive only by squeezing acquiescence from a half-dozen different parties: existing creditors, potential sources of credit, royal officeholders, municipal and provincial officials, regional magnates, and the hapless households that paid taxes, performed corvée labor, and supplied men for the armies. The parties overlapped, to be sure. Existing creditors who still had cash reserves or borrowing power became attractive sources for new advances to the crown. Furthermore, the seventeenth-century fiscal strategy regularly transformed potential creditors and municipal officials into royal officeholders. Nevertheless, on the whole the parties had conflicting interests.

Conflicts of interest could work either for or against the crown. They produced barriers to effective coalitions against royal demands. Yet conflicts of interest also meant that by favoring any one party the crown was sure to harm at least one other. Sometimes, as we have seen, royal power rode an upward spiral: borrowing, farming taxes, and selling offices expanded current royal revenues, decreased the crown's reliance on the direct seizure of the means of war, and increased the number of people dependent on the crown's success; the increased revenues bought armed force that could be used against domestic opposition as well as external foes; and the presence of that armed force weakened resistance to mounting royal demands for taxes.

The spiral could, however, unwind. If royal demands rose much faster than royal coercive power, opponents joined and became formidable. Much of the time, the most the king could hope for was to keep the parties at each other's throats, to aim the greatest harm at the least powerful, and to contain the discontent of the strong.

Although they differed enormously in power, each party had both an implicit program and a limit beyond which, if pressed, it was more likely to resist or to rebel than to cooperate. We have already surveyed the variety of ways in which ordinary people resisted demands for the wherewithal of war—when they could. Merchants and rentiers who invested their reserves in bonds (*rentes*) secured by Parisian municipal revenues did not willingly suffer reductions or delays in the income from those bonds. Great nobles who served as provincial governors and lieutenants-general did not cheerfully see their regional hegemony challenged by intendants and other officeholders. Potential creditors, officeholders, and municipal or provincial officials likewise had their programs and limits. Add to the situation a nine-year-old king, a regency, large numbers of royal troops tied up in Flanders and Catalonia, and a chief minister—Mazarin—who was a foreigner still building his networks of patronage within France; those circumstances gave the great nobles additional hope of checking the monarchy's threats to their power.

During the 1640s the monarchy was not merely maintaining itself, but aggrandizing. To win its wars with Spain and the Holy Roman Empire, it was pressing every available resource, mortgaging the future, disregarding inconvenient rights and obligations. The result was to push every one of the parties beyond the margin of its acquiescence to royal demands, and to create temporary but powerful coalitions of the parties against the crown. Each party resisted more or less as it always had. The old links between urban fiscal insurrections and rebellions of regional nobles reappeared. But this time both the resistance and the coalitions were more widespread, intense, and durable. That was the Fronde.

Remember the Fronde's bare chronology. In mid-1648 an assembly of regional parlements and high courts demanded a rollback of many measures Mazarin and his agents had taken to build up royal military strength; they asked for control of the sale of offices, regular parlementary review of taxation, recall of the intendants from the provinces, and other drastic steps. An insurrection sprang up in Pau as peasants gathered in Paris to state their opposition to the taille. When Mazarin had leaders of the parlementary movement arrested, Parisians erected barricades in the streets and forced the cardinal to release the prisoners; later, Mazarin acceded to most of the high courts' demands.

Meanwhile Mazarin and the royal family slipped out of Paris, preferring to issue orders to a fractious parlement from the comfortable distance of St.-Germain. They returned to Paris briefly, then decamped again at the start of 1649, leaving behind orders for the exile of the high courts. The parlement

of Paris took over the national government, and the city's populace bad-
gered the royalist municipality while the prince of Condé, still aligned with
the king, blockaded the city. A provisional settlement brought protest from
Parisians but eventually permitted the return of the king, the queen mother,
and the royal entourage to the capital.

By 1650 Condé and fellow magnates were seeking to displace Mazarin.
The queen had Condé and others imprisoned. The movement of opposition
by great nobles spread, and coupled with popular rebellion against the
crown in many cities and their hinterlands. Although most of the rebellious
cities came back under royal control by the end of the year, Parisian creditors of the government stepped up their complaints, while the parlement of
Paris moved increasingly against Mazarin and for his princely opposition.
Early in 1651 Mazarin freed the imprisoned princes and went into exile.
During that year Parisians battled royal troops in the streets, a rebellious coalition (the Ormée) arose in Bordeaux, and divisions opened up among the
great Frondeurs, some of whom rejoined the royal side, others following the
prince of Condé to the southwestern provinces. At the end of the year Mazarin returned to France with troops of his own.

The following year, 1652, turned the tide against the Fronde. During
the first eight months the shift was not obvious: Condé took Paris, the
Ormée seized control of Bordeaux, and the people of Paris repeatedly acted
against Mazarin. At summer's end, Mazarin again fled the country. Yet during the rest of the year, military defeats and defections weakened Condé's
cause, Louis XIV and his mother returned triumphantly to Paris, and the
Frondeurs began to lose everywhere. In 1653 Mazarin himself made a definitive return to the capital, the Ormée gave up Bordeaux, and royal agents
reinstated their authority throughout the country. The great Fronde was
over.

The Fronde included the full range of seventeenth-century conflicts.
When the prince of Condé allied himself with the Spanish and sent his
troops into Flanders against the armies of Louis XIV, the civil war melted
into the international struggle. Even when foreigners were not so directly
involved, many actions of the Fronde followed the routines of war: pitched
battles, sieges, campaigns, treaties. During the first exile of the king and his
party from Paris, for example, royal forces ringed Paris and attempted to cut
off the city's food supplies. Throughout the Ile-de-France, troop movements
brought the usual pillage and the usual scattered resistance from the pillaged population. The versifying commentary of *La Muze Historique* (II,
letter 21, May 1651, 121) has a familiar ring:

> In many places, the men of war
> Displayed such fury
> Did so many insolent things
> That, in order to check the evil
> The parlement indicted
> These infamous mercenaries
> Oppressors of women and girls
> Wild executioners and blowhards
> Less soldiers than thieves.

In place after place, furthermore, conquerors imposed corvées and taxes on the local population in order to support the costs of warmaking. In response to that pressure, other conflicts of the Fronde took the classic forms of rebellion: chasing out the tax collector, attacking the profiteer's premises, and so on. The combination of war and regional rebellion made the Fronde formidable.

In all five of our regions, officials and magnates had to choose sides repeatedly: whether to send messages of support to the parlement of Paris, whether to swear allegiance to the king, whether to snuff out Condé's local supporters, and so on. Beyond that common ground, however, the five provinces built starkly different relationships to the Fronde. The Ile-de-France served as both prize and arena: locus of assemblies, street-fighting, and power struggles in 1648, divided between a rebellious, besieged Paris and a royally controlled hinterland for the first part of 1649, relatively untroubled the second half of that year, scene of maneuvers between supporters of the king and the imprisoned princes (plus protests by unpaid royal creditors) in 1650, site of insurrection and tumultuous assemblies in 1651, object of open warfare in 1652, stage for the triumphant return of the king and his followers from late 1652 into 1653.

Anjou remained in turmoil throughout the Fronde by tying existing conflicts within the region to the national divisions of successive years. Burgundy became more heavily involved in the Fronde during the later years of princely warfare, when troops fought for control of Bellegarde and other military outposts in the province. Flanders, though still mainly in Spanish hands, likewise figured as a battlefield where royal troops were unavoidably detained and dissident Frenchmen joined the side of the enemy. Languedoc, finally, offers something of a surprise: in that once-rebellious province, few powerful people took open stands against the king or Mazarin, and military action on behalf of the princes never spread very wide.

Like any civil war, the Fronde left a zigzag trail. Yet its main path had a fairly clear logic. The central facts to grasp are, first, the intermittent action

of several distinct groups—the members of the high courts, Parisian rentiers, great nobles, residents of major cities, and others—who had seen the
warmaking growth of royal power attacking their autonomy, rights, and
welfare; second, the making and breaking of temporary coalitions among
different sets of those aggrieved parties. Unfortunately for the popularity of
their cause, the nobles who warred against the crown's forces likewise taxed
the citizenry, impressed soldiers, grabbed supplies where they could find
them, and used their military power to advance their personal advantages.
As the struggle ground on, princely power and return to the rule of regional
magnates looked no more enticing to ordinary people—or to the officeholders of the high courts—than did the restoration of royal authority. At that
point, the linked rebellions had lost.

     What if the Fronde had not occurred? Paradoxically, without the great
rebellion the monarchy would most likely have consolidated its power less
quickly. First, Louis XIV never forgot the turmoil that beset him as a child-
king, nine years old in 1648; it became a high priority of his regime to detect, co-opt, and preempt potential rebels. Second, at the same time that it
demonstrated the vulnerability of the crown, the Fronde displayed even
more visibly the inability of all the crown's opponents to unite in a program
or an effective military force. Third, the rebellion gave Mazarin and the
queen mother license and incentive to repress their enemies. If the defeated
prince of Condé could rush into service for the Spaniards as a general
against the French, his independence of action now became exceptional;
even dukes and major cities now felt royal vengeance.

Divide and Conquer, Conquer and Divide

Quelling the Fronde did not eliminate resistance to royal demands; it displaced and fragmented that resistance. Alliances between ordinary people
(typically aggrieved by taxation or other forms of extraction) and important nobles (typically aggrieved by checks to their power) became both less
likely and less effective. As the crown turned increasingly to the sale of offices and other indirect ways of raising revenue, fewer occasions arose for
confrontations between citizens and direct representatives of the national
state. As intendants and other disciplined royal officials in the provinces extended their knowledge and control, the chances of an inviting breakdown
in official surveillance dwindled. All these changes diminished the frequency, and especially the scale, of open resistance.

     In the decade following the Fronde, all five of our provinces showed
signs of diminished capacity for action against the crown, especially action

requiring a broad coalition of classes. Anjou saw the rallying of a few nobles around the Frondeur Cardinal de Retz (1654), a large tax rebellion in Angers (1656), assemblies of nobles who still hoped to band together against Mazarin (1658–1659), and a few more conflicts over taxes in the early 1660s. In Burgundy, despite a drumroll of local resistance to tax collectors, the only concerted attacks on officials were an insurrection in Chalon (1657) and a smaller "rebellion" in Commarin (1661). After the frenzy of the Fronde, Paris and the Ile-de-France remained dutifully calm: a flurry of protest over the selection of a parish priest, a brawl or two, scattered resistance to increased taxation at the end of 1661, and an assembly of angry rentiers the following year. In those provinces, the Fronde's defeat seems to have made people lower their estimates of their chances to win concessions from the crown by outright rebellion. Cross-class coalitions became especially rare.

Flanders and Languedoc, however, behaved somewhat differently. Flanders, a war zone still largely in Spanish hands, had the usual run-ins between soldiers and civilians. In the borderland of Flanders and Artois under French rule, a few vigorous reactions to the royal imposition of new taxes occurred. The most important came in 1662, when the same borderland produced a major revolt—the Lustucru rebellion—after the king revoked its war-linked fiscal privileges. Languedoc had unruly Protestants assembling and arming in the Vivarais (1653, 1656), a struggle for power in Carcassonne (1656) drawing many citizens into the streets, a mutiny, destruction of a Protestant church, and several struggles over taxes in 1662; if we count adjacent Roussillon, that section of France also experienced the long struggle between authorities and the Angelets of the Pyrenees (1663–1672). Only Lustucru and the Angelets approached the scale of great rebellions before the Fronde, and neither of them involved the open alliance between provincial powerholders and commoners that had characterized the sustained struggles of the 1620s, 1630s, and 1640s.

At the edges of France, events followed a different timetable from those in the center. On the whole, the peripheral provinces were the last to come under central control, the slowest to lose particular privileges and exemptions. Frontier and coastal provinces commonly enjoyed fiscal advantages, either in exchange for special military services such as coastal defense or in recognition of the hopelessness of policing the flows of persons and goods across coastlines and mountain passes. Furthermore, important parts of France came to the crown only as prizes of seventeenth-century wars; Béarn, Roussillon, Flanders, and Lorraine are outstanding examples. Yet in all these peripheral places Louis XIV, Colbert, and their collaborators kicked at the barriers to increasing royal revenues. Inevitably, that meant revoking or bypassing rights certified by treaty and decree. In those circumstances large rebellions involving several social classes, many localities, and open opposition to royal authority still occurred from time to time.

After the Fronde, France's great seventeenth-century rebellions included the Tardanizats (Guyenne, 1655–1656), Sabotiers (Sologne, 1658), Bénauge (Guyenne, 1661–1662), Lustucru (Boulonnais, 1662), Audijos (Gascony, 1663), Angelets (Roussillon, intermittently from 1663 to 1672), Roure (Vivarais, 1670), Papier Timbré and Bonnets Rouges (also known as Torrében; Brittany, 1675), and Camisards (Cévennes and Vivarais, intermittently from 1685 to about 1710, especially 1702–1704). In those events, groups of people openly defied royal authority and maintained control over multiple localities for many days.

Note the geography of the major rebellions. The Sabotiers of Sologne were the only people to mount a large, sustained insurrection against the crown in the central regions of France. The southwest still contributed the rebellions of the Tardanizats, Bénauge, and Audijos, but its preeminence was shaken. Once-rebellious Poitou and Normandy produced only relatively local movements of resistance to taxation, such as the guerrilla activity organized by the swamp dwellers near Les Sables-d'Olonne in the late 1650s, when the crown sought to impose an exceptional tax for the draining of the land in addition to the *quartier d'hiver,* the levy for maintenance of troops in garrison. ("Thus you see," wrote Jean-Baptiste Colbert's cousin Colbert de Terron, "that we have to establish the quartier d'hiver by acts of war, as if we were in enemy territory": BN Mélanges Colbert 101, 17 March 1658.)

Languedoc took at least as prominent a part in the post-Fronde rebellions as it had before. Nevertheless, the hearts of those rebellions were no longer Montpellier, Toulouse, and other important cities, but the province's mountainous edges, the Cévennes and Vivarais. In Brittany the crown faced a forbidding province that had long benefited from special status, including exemption from the salt tax. In the Boulonnais and Roussillon, the king's agents were trying to extend routine fiscal administration into war zones, one of which received gentle treatment in return for its loyalty and military service, the other having become French territory only with the Treaty of the Pyrenees in 1659.

How Rebellions Happened

After the devastation of the Fronde, the slowing of the Spanish war, and a pause for the treaty with Spain, 1661 marked the royal return to serious preparation for war. In that year Mazarin died, Louis XIV took over full direction of the state, Colbert became the king's chief financial aide, and—not coincidentally—Colbert's competitor Fouquet went to prison for his derelictions. Soon Colbert turned his attention to raising new revenue, with special emphasis on making taxation more "uniform" throughout France. That meant abolishing special agreements and particular privileges, extending the same basic taxes everywhere in the country.

As we might expect, people in the peripheral provinces did not relinquish their advantages joyfully. Near Bordeaux the reaction came quickly, in December 1661. The insurrection of Bénauge was the largest of a series of struggles with tax collectors, and with soldiers sent to support the tax collectors, that took place in the region of Bordeaux after the Fronde. When Colbert decided to collect back taxes from all those years, and a company of cavalry rode out from Bordeaux to enforce his call for payment, the tocsin rang in the villages of the Bénauge region. A few hundred peasants occupied the chateau of Bénauge, seat of the county, and a few hundred more besieged the royal troops in the mill to which they had fled. A "Captain Straw" (*capitaine La Paille*) appeared among the rebels; straw had served as an emblem for the rebel Croquants of the southwest during the sixteenth and seventeenth centuries. But that mock captain was the closest they came to noble support; with the exception of a surgeon and a few rural artisans, the rebellion remained wholly plebeian. It received the plebeian treatment: dispatch of seven or eight hundred troops, hanging of two chiefs, sentencing of four more likely participants to the galleys, assessment of fines on the region's villages to compensate court costs and the families of cavalrymen killed in the rebellion, and, of course, payment of the long-due taxes (BN Mélanges Colbert 105–107 bis; Loirette 1966).

The Lustucru rebellion took place the following year, 1662, at the opposite end of France. The region of Boulogne, at the edges of Artois, Picardy, and Flanders, had a long experience of war on land and sea. The region enjoyed exemption from all major taxes but had the obligation to supply able-bodied men for a frontier guard. Louis XIV had imposed "extraordinary" taxes on the region during the 1650s on the grounds of war emergency, but in 1661 his council announced the regularization of taxes there. Protests from the Estates of the Boulonnais and the Estates of Artois went unheard.

Forewarned, the government sent 250 troops to accompany the new tax collectors on their village rounds. Nonetheless the villagers fought off the troops where they could, formed bands that attacked both troops and

local gentlemen who were exempt from taxation, and eventually regrouped in a barricaded town under the nominal leadership of the one petty noble they had been able to recruit. (*La Muze Historique* claimed that "more than five thousand five hundred" peasants took part: XIII, letter 27, July 1662, 527.) Once a strong royal force tracked them down and surrounded the town, the rebels were easy work for professional troops. As the rough-talking duke of Elbeuf reported:

> I arrived Monday noon at Montreuil, where I learned that the marquis de Montpezat and M. de Machault were scheduled to arrive that very evening. I used the rest of the day having bread made, getting four cannons ready to move, and doing everything else that I thought useful for punishing these miserable rebels. When they arrived, I ordered the commander of Montreuil's fort to give the marquis de Montpezat and M. de Machault whatever they asked for. I had eighty horse from the government of Montreuil made ready, with carts and wagons to carry ammunition and supplies ... The troops went five leagues like Basques, and the rangers of the guards and the Swiss, without even waiting for their battalions, attacked a thousand of these scum who were in a well-barricaded village on a good site, and forced them to retreat to the castle of Heudin, where we took them at will. We had four of them hanged immediately. All the chiefs are taken. We have found only a few soldiers of fortune who once served in the royal armies. (BN Mélanges Colbert 109 bis, 11 July 1662)

On this occasion *La Muze Historique* praised Elbeuf for "preventing ... an excessive number of deaths, and saving the women and girls from assault by the mercenaries" (*La Muze Historique* XIII, letter 27, July 1662, 527). Instead, the troops took prisoners. The captives included the one petty noble, who escaped for a while but was recaptured, drunk on the eau-de-vie of a cellar in which he had hidden. After show trials, 365 men went to the galleys, 1 hanged, and 3 died broken on the wheel (BN Mélanges Colbert 108–110; Héliot 1935).

At both ends of the Pyrenees, the royal effort to raise revenue by farming out a new salt tax soon incited sustained rebellions. At the Atlantic end, the Basque-toned foothills produced the rebellion of Audijos, named for the petty noble who darted to and fro with his armed band, attacking tax collectors and royal forces when they were vulnerable. Using the mountains and Spanish territory as his refuge, Audijos managed to impede the region's tax-farmers and to encourage urban rebellions during much of 1663, 1664, and 1665. He escaped capture; indeed, in 1676 Louis XIV finally rewarded his prowess by giving him a regiment to command (AA A[1] 247, 249; AN Z[1a] 890; BN Mélanges Colbert 120–133; Clément 1866: 289–293; Communay 1893).

At the Mediterranean end of the Pyrenees, the farming of the salt tax aroused the armed mountain dwellers who plied the passes of the Vallespir. These Catalans found themselves transferred from a distant Spain to a rather more vigilant France by the 1659 treaty. Their region produced metals, cloth, and—significantly—salt, which mule drivers carried down both slopes of the mountains. When Roussillon's Sovereign Council (the regional body empowered by the French to govern on their behalf) discovered that its salaries would depend on salt-tax revenues, it authorized the collection of the tax.

That was, however, to reckon without the mountaineers. As soon as the tax-farmer's guards arrived in that part of the Pyrenees in 1663, the local bands began to attack them. Raids and slayings on both sides continued for years, until the mountain people, the Sovereign Council, the tax-farmer, and the king's ministers worked out a compromise in 1669.

Soon, however, skirmishes began again. One of the mountaineers' leaders, nicknamed "Hereu Just," fell into royal hands. At that point guerrilla activity gave way to general insurrection. At royal instruction, the Sovereign Council issued a decree

> as a result of the riots, arson, sacrilege, homicide, armed gatherings, and other violence committed in the villages and mountains of the Vallespir and in a few parts of the Conflent by the seditious people commonly called *Angelets* . . . who after entering by force into the city of Prats-de-Mollo, whose gates they broke open, forced the governor and bailiff of said city to free a certain Jean-Michel Mestre, called *Hereu Just,* of Vallestavia, one of the chiefs of said sedition, and one of his accomplices, both of them legally constituted prisoners, disturbed trade and public order for more than three months, occupied cities and villages of the mountains, took arms against troops and officers of the law, blocked the collection and administration of royal taxes, especially the salt tax, besieged the city of Céret, resisted . . . M. de Chastillon, viceroy in the province of Roussillon, when he came with royal troops to aid that city, and continued said sedition in various places, opposing an army commanded by the comte de Chamilly, marshal of the king's armies.   (ADPO C 1395, *criée* of 4 September 1670)

It took two more years to put down the Angelets by a combination of bargaining and military force. Then those Pyrenean passes became a favorite route for salt smugglers, who thus made their fortune from the tax they had previously fought (AA A¹ 246–247; BN Mélanges Colbert 144–151; ADPO C 1366, 1367, 1395; Clément 1861–1869: IV, lxxvii–lxxxviii, 337–347: Depping 1850–1855: I, 620, 652–654, 803–804; Marcet 1974, 1977a, 1977b).

About the same time that the Angelets were renewing their battles to the south of Languedoc, another fiscal rebellion was forming on the province's hilly northern flanks. The Roure rebellion took its name from the demi-noble Jean-Antoine du Roure, whom the region's people drafted as its chief. Roure became a rebel commander only after a crowd of artisans and peasants, acting on the rumor that a new head tax was to be established, fell upon a tax collector in the city of Aubenas, threatened the city council, and inspired a rising of villages in the nearby countryside of the Vivarais. They ruled the territory for much of the time from April to July 1670.

Roure is said to have had 4,000 men under arms at one point. But once regular troops under the command of the count of Roure (no relation) and Marshal Lebret set out after them, toward the end of July, the beginning of the end was in sight. As the *Gazette de France* tells the tale:

> They resisted at first, but once they saw the rest of the musketeers, supported by the Choiseul Squadron, they fired and fled . . . The rebels were pursued right up into the rocks, where the royal forces killed 140 and took 80 prisoners. That evening the army went back to camp, and the next day it marched to Aubenas, which the rebels had abandoned at the news of the rout. The inhabitants told the count of Roure of their joy at being freed from these insurgents. We have learned that since then most of the gentlemen who had left their houses have returned, and have forced the rebels to lay down their arms, put them into the hands of their curés, and seek the mercy of the king. (*La Gazette de France* 1670: 766–767)

Gentlemen apparently had good reason to skip town. In addition to their manifest opposition to profiteering tax collectors, the peasants and artisans sacked the houses of the rich. They had likewise sacked the rich in Privas when they overran the town on 22 July (ADH C 162). Still, their battle cry fell far short of outright class warfare. "Vive le roy, Fy des elus!" it ran: "Long live the king, and down with revenue officers!" (AA A¹ 247; BN Mélanges Colbert 155; Le Roy Ladurie 1966: I, 607–610).

A stronger strain of class antagonism appeared in the last great series of seventeenth-century fiscal rebellions, the 1675 events in Brittany variously called the Révolte du Papier Timbré, the Bonnets Rouges, and Torrében. Roughly speaking the "stamped paper revolt" took place in the cities, while the "red caps" or Torrében belonged to the Breton countryside. To finance the Dutch War, begun in 1672, Colbert had not only pumped up the regular taxes and bargained for special allocations from the provinces but also enacted a series of excise taxes on merchandise and official paper—ninety years before a similar stamp act set American colonists against their mother country. When imposed in 1675, those excise taxes roused serious popular movements in many parts of France: Le Mans, Poitiers, Agen, and elsewhere. A generation after the Ormée, an insurgent force again took over Bordeaux: in late March 1675, after people attacked excise agents and pewterers who had let their wares be marked by the excise agents, antitax rebels controlled the city for a week. In August, crowds burned bundles of stamped paper and the boat bearing them, then besieged Bordeaux's city hall (BN Mélanges Colbert 171-172; Bercé 1974: I, 517-518).

Nevertheless, the largest series of rebellions by far occurred in Rennes and its hinterland. There, in April 1675, people attacked the newly established tobacco sales office, then went on a round of other excise and registry offices, sacking as they went. Shortly afterward the people of Nantes did likewise. Then it was the turn of Brittany's rural areas, where excise taxes were a relatively minor concern.

In the countryside, peasants went after landlords and their agents. "It is certain," wrote the duke of Chaulnes, military governor, to Colbert, "that nobles here have treated peasants badly; the peasants are now taking their revenge; they have dealt with five or six of the nobles barbarously, assaulting them, sacking their houses, and even burning a few houses down" (Depping 1850-1855: I, 547, letter of 30 June 1675). The marquis de Lavardin shared that opinion:

> The peasants are still gathered in various places around Quimper and Corentin, and have even threatened Quimper. It seems that their anger is aimed at the gentlemen rather than at the authority of the king. They have returned to the gentlemen some of the beatings the gentlemen have given them. Since they live under a very hard custom we call the Usage of Broerek, which takes inheritance rights away from the peasants, they are forcing the landlords to give them receipts for their back rents on these properties.   (BN Mélanges Colbert 172, letter of 5 July 1675)

In some parts of rural Brittany, indeed, rebellious peasants went so far as to draft "peasant codes" in counterimages of the hard customs under which they had been living, and to force signatures of those codes from their landlords. The code ratified under duress by the Carmelite monks of Pont-l'Abbé addressed the "noble city dwellers" on behalf of the "well-intentioned" people of surrounding parishes. It included these items:

1. The inhabitants promise on pain of death to give aid, men, arms, and food to said well-intentioned people whenever called to do so by deputy or by sounding of the tocsin.

2. They will have their syndic publish in their cities the revocation of all edicts contravening the rights and privileges of our province.

3. Neither they nor their associates will pay corvées, *champart,* or rents shown on the old rolls of 1625. On pain of a beating.

4. All innkeepers are forbidden to sell wine at more than 10 sous a pot, at the same penalty.

5. Judges are forbidden to charge more than 45 sous for an inventory.

6. Notaries are forbidden to use stamped paper, to charge more than 5 sous for a lease, or 13 sous for any transaction whatsoever, under the same penalty.

7. Clerks and officers of the official registry are forbidden to use stamped paper and to charge more than 10 sous for an attestation. Nothing for an attestation from one lawyer to another.

8. The same prohibitions for lawyers as to stamped paper, and to finish all cases, however difficult, within a month, on pain of a beating.

9. Judges must announce their judgments free, not charge for them, and judge by common sense rather than by trickery.

10. All sorts of residents may hunt on the lands of their lords, outside game preserves.

11. Everyone may shoot the lord's pigeons when they are off the lord's land.

12. Rectors, vicars, curés, and all priests are forbidden to take more than 5 sous for a mass, and they must do burials for 8 sous.

13. Said rectors, municipal syndics, and vestrymen will be deputies to the Estates to complain to his majesty's agents about the misery of his people and to obtain the privileges stated in this document.

Enacted in the assembly of the well-intentioned on this happy day of a miserable year. (Garlan and Nières 1975: 99–100)

The enactment of a peasant paradise—never realized, one need hardly add—marks a significant shift in the emphasis of seventeenth-century rebellions. At this point, hostility to landlords and to petty officials outweighed opposition to new taxes. In that sense, at least, the Bonnets Rouges anticipated the eighteenth century.

"So-Called Reformed Religion" and Its Defenders

The century's last great series of rebellions, however, grew from a century-old struggle. From the 1630s to the 1670s the government ground away at the "so-called Reformed Religion" intermittently and without drama. By the 1670s the Protestants of Languedoc had lost their noble leaders and great protectors but still dominated the Cévennes and Vivarais, and still had a considerable following among the artisans and small merchants of the cities. Without patricians or patrons, they organized strenuous resistance to the long, long royal campaign against them.

Local battles with Catholics continued. A case in point occurred in the Protestant stronghold of Le Mas-d'Azil, near Pamiers, in October 1671. According to the testimony of witnesses, a day-laborer who had recently converted to Catholicism

> was attacked in the middle of the fair by François and David Cave, former Huguenots ... and many others armed with swords and staves. They wounded him so badly that he was left for dead ... The brother prior and a Benedictine monk who happened by complained to them ... and they shouted against the day-laborer "Get the rebel, get the rebel, for taking a religion that is worthless to its supporters" and other words forbidden by law on pain of death. (Wemyss 1961: 36)

But no sustained, large-scale conflict developed at Le Mas-d'Azil or elsewhere until a few years later, when the government of Louis XIV began to intensify its campaign to squeeze out Protestants. Traveling through Languedoc in 1676, John Locke noted in his journal that the Protestants of Uzès "have an order from the King to choose noe more consuls of the town of the Religion, and their Temple is ordered to be puld down, the only one they had left there, though ¾ of the town be Protestants" (Locke 1953: 22–23). That pressure on Protestant municipalities continued until all of them were crushed.

At the provincial level, intendant d'Aguesseau was encouraging compliance by the simple expedient of suspending payments to Protestant officeholders: a "sure way to multiply conversions," he called it (AN G^7 295, letter of 8 March 1680). In Le Mas-d'Azil the campaign started in earnest with the decree of 29 April 1680, which forbade Protestants to sit on a city council they had previously divided equally with the Catholic minority. In 1685, after the revocation of the Edict of Nantes, local people went through the mechanics of conversion to Catholicism en masse and without open resistance. A trickle of emigration began. The "New Converts" of Le Mas-d'Azil survived by stratagem and subterfuge. The first serious confrontations there began after the Peace of Ryswick (1697), when word spread that royal policy toward Protestants was going to relax. Local Protestants—not nearly so converted as it had seemed—began holding secret "assemblies," or church services, in the countryside. Royal persecution drove Protestant religious practice back underground very quickly that time. But whenever royal authorities and Catholic clergy turned their attention elsewhere, the hidden organization of local Protestants started to reemerge (Wemyss 1961: 96–107).

Elsewhere in Languedoc the struggle between Protestants and royal authorities turned to open rebellion, to civil war. The cockpits were the mountain regions of Vivarais and Cévennes. Since the 1620s of Louis XIII's anti-Protestant campaigns and the 1630s of the Montmorency rebellion, Cévennes and Vivarais had often mounted substantial opposition to the crown. When the duke of Rohan had lost to the royal offensive of 1622, for example, his troops received permission to retreat into the Protestant safety of the Cévennes. The new element later in the century was the exchange of noble leaders and private armies for assemblies of common people protected by their own improvised militias.

As early as 1653 "a band of seven or eight thousand Protestants tried to establish by force of arms the right to hold services at Vals in the Vivarais" (Bonney 1978b: 398). That became the standard pattern: Protestants assembled to hold forbidden services in the countryside, royal officials sent troops to stop them, the "assemblies in the desert" evolved into armed rebellions. By August 1683 d'Aguesseau was reporting that the Huguenots of the Vivarais "are organized by companies under designated leaders. They have taken various castles, have dug in, have ammunition and weapons, and, in a word, show every sign of intending to resist the king's troops, aroused as they are by ministers who preach nothing but sedition and rebellion" (AN G[7] 296).

With the revocation of the Edict of Nantes in 1685, a new intendant came in, bringing a mandate to clear out Languedoc's Protestants. The famous intendant Basville began his work with energy and cautious optimism. After losing two officers in the course of a cavalry charge on an assembly of "New Converts" near Le Vigan, Basville wrote:

> I have been in the mountains for six days and have set a strong example; it cost the life of a gentleman named Saint-Julien who was at the assembly; he had his head cut off. I also sentenced seven other defendants to be hanged. That and the movement of troops into the communities responsible for the assembly have worried the country. In any other region one might hope that such a punishment would put people on their good behavior, but these people are so crazy and stupid that I'm afraid they won't remember it very long. For the moment, they are off their heads with the ridiculous rumor that a league has formed in Germany

against our king, to reestablish the Edict of Nantes. Nevertheless all the
assemblies have been broken up. No regular ministers are preaching; the
preachers are only miserable carders and peasants who lack common
sense; I hope to arrest two or three of them but haven't yet managed to
find them.   (AN G^7 297, 15 October 1686)

As it happened, there were many lay preachers, plus a nearly inexhaustible
supply of inspired men, women, boys, and girls. And they had defenders.
Soon Basville was sending armies into the hills to search out and exterminate Protestant guerrilla forces, who eventually became known as Camisards. With many interruptions and changes of fortune, the War of the
Camisards lasted twenty-five years.

Bread Nexus versus Cash Nexus

As the hills of Languedoc blazed, elsewhere in France the grain seizure came
into its own. Around the end of the seventeenth century, the seizure of
grains displaced the tax rebellion as the most frequent occasion on which
ordinary people collectively and openly attacked their enemies. Conflicts
over food had, of course, arisen repeatedly before. Tax rebellions themselves
sometimes concerned food indirectly: rank-and-file participants in tax rebellions rarely had the chance to explain themselves for the record; when they
did, however, they commonly pointed out that in times of scarce food, high
prices, and hunger, demands for new taxes added insult to injury (cf. Le
Roy Ladurie 1966: I, 499–502, on the Croquants of 1643). When authorities dared to raise money by taxing grain, as they did with the _cosse_ tax at
Narbonne in 1682, they almost always faced determined resistance; at Narbonne, that resistance reached the scale of sedition (AN G^7 296–298). But
seizures of food, in the strict sense—capture and redirection of stored or
transported food, with or without attacks on the food's owners or their
premises—were rare before the 1690s, and common for 150 years after that.

Not that hunger became more intense: throughout France as a whole,
the famines of 1630–31 and 1661–62 were probably even more acute than
the shortage of 1693–94; yet only the 1690s brought the grain seizure to
center stage. Nor did rising expectations make officials and ordinary people
more sensitive to the suffering brought on by high prices and short supplies.
During the crisis of 1661–62, for example, we find officials through much of
France busy making pleas and inventing expedients to hold off hunger and
its consequences: the Estates of Burgundy asking Colbert to "consider the
universal famine and the terrible conditions for tax collection" and to grant
them a delay in their payments, the officers of Paris exercising meticulous

control over grain sales and distributing bread to the poor at the Tuileries, and so on (BN Mélanges Colbert 109, 109 bis).

Paris is an important case: great city, brain and belly of the national market, stimulus to market gardening and large-scale capitalist agriculture over a large region, troublemaker by reputation, yet relatively free of public conflicts over food in 1661–62. In Paris during that famine, the royal courts and the city administration collaborated in enforcing tight controls over the purchase, shipment, and distribution of food for, to, and in the city (BN Joly de Fleury 2531; Saint-Germain 1962: 269). Under those conditions, people did not collectively seize food and attack its holders.

What changed between then and the 1690s? The growth of cities and of wage labor increased the number of people dependent on the purchase of food; perhaps it also made supplying them more difficult. The moderation of overall price levels for grains in the later seventeenth century, however, throws doubt on that factor as a major explanation. The diversion of marketed grain to the army on the eastern front surely put a severe strain on the national market from the 1660s to the 1690s. But the big change was the national state's promotion of marketing.

From the time of Colbert's rise to chief minister, the government strove to assure French prosperity, and the crown's tax revenues, by encouraging trade. The encouragement certainly included the production and shipping of grain for sale. It gave profits to merchants who could assure a supply to Paris or the army. And it began to define all the old parochial controls over the grain trade—inventorying, withholding, distributing locally at a fixed price, giving priority to local people, especially the local poor—as retrograde. As a result, local and regional officials who tried to feed their own people first, and only then to let commodities enter the national market, found themselves at odds with ministers, intendants, and merchants who argued that national needs should take priority. Given that policy, shortages, and high prices, officials hesitated to impose the old controls. Then it was up to ordinary people to create their own controls. The various popular efforts to control the food supply, and to coerce officials and merchants into restoring the old rules, came to be known as food riots.

In Paris, 1692 and 1693 brought the century's first great wave of grain seizures. More often than not, a crowd of women, plus a few men and children, broke into a baker's shop, seized the bread, and sacked the premises. When that happened in May 1693, for example, city police commissioner La Reynie had a worker who led the attack on a baker's shop in the rue de Lourcine hanged at the St.-Marcel Gate the very next day (Clément 1866: 255). Still attacks on bakers continued in Paris, as people in the city's hinterland continued to block shipments when they could. Flanders was again a battleground, where it was hard to distinguish conflicts over food from the usual turmoil of war. But in Languedoc, Burgundy, and Anjou the crisis and the grain seizures lasted up to the harvest of 1694. One of the more dramatic confrontations occurred in Toulouse at the beginning of May 1694. As touring royal official Abrancourt reported from Toulouse on 5 May:

> Being here for the purposes of royal tax collection, I thought I should tell you what is going on. The common people here have been mutinous for five days without good reason. There have been such large mobs gathered to massacre the mayor that last Sunday, coming back from a meeting of the Hôtel Dieu by the Garonne bridge, only by a miracle did he escape from the hands of two thousand women with daggers, clubs, and stones. The soldiers of the watch who were escorting him suffered wounds from the stones, and his carriage door was broken. The bakers, claiming that the official bread price was too low for the cost of grain, did not bake as much as usual. The beggars took that pretext to pillage the bread they found in a few shops. Then the mayor raised the price of bread to get rid of the problem and give the bakers their due. Then the little folk took the excuse of that increase, and, knowing yesterday morning that the mayor had gone to the courthouse, the same number of women went to occupy the courthouse while the *Grande Chambre de la Tournelle* was meeting. They asked for the mayor's head, saying they wanted that, not bread.　(AN G[7] 302)

Both Abrancourt and Toulouse's mayor claimed the protest occurred because of an earlier dispute between the mayor and the parlement, so serious that the women might well have thought the parlement would back them. In any case, the mayor and council, sitting as a court, sentenced Catherine Thémines, wife of Pierre Alibert, who worked at the tobacco office called "La Rouergue," to hang, and three other women to be banished from Toulouse. According to his letter on the subject, the mayor thought that the parlement would mitigate the sentences on review (AN G[7] 302). After all, the judges still had a score to settle with him. In this way the lowly grain seizure acquired connections with high politics.

　　As the great crisis of the 1690s ended, the crown resumed its policy of promoting the national market and assuring food to the capital and the army. The policy itself required important choices, as we learn from Burgundy's intendant Ferrant. When the harvest of 1694 was approaching, he commented on a request to send some sixty thousand 200-pound sacks of grain to Lyon: "The problem is not to supply that much, but to be sure that the shipment wouldn't mean a significant decrease in the amount available for the armies of the king and the city of Paris" (AN G^7 1634, letter of 24 August 1694). The intendant understood national priorities. He increasingly had the means to make them prevail.

A Fateful Century

From the rubble prevailing at the start of the seventeenth century—the debris left by the Wars of Religion, the weakness of the crown, the maneuvers of dukes and princes—it would have been hard to predict the growth of a powerful, centralized state. Nevertheless it happened. Henry IV, Louis XIII, Louis XIV, and their mighty ministers squeezed, cajoled, and stomped the means of warmaking from a reluctant population; built a powerful national army; conquered territory to their north, east, and south; quelled or coopted their greatest internal enemies; and in the process created the far-reaching apparatus of a national state. In doing so, they built an uneasy alliance with France's capitalists. On the one side, the kings relied on capitalists to mobilize and advance the money required for all this expensive activity, to generate trade that would produce taxable revenue, to buy the offices and privileges that secured long-term loans to the crown. On the other side, the kings made wars that hampered international trade, seized and taxed accumulations of capital wherever they could find them, regulated economic life in the interests of royal revenues, and borrowed so heavily as to undermine the government's credit.

If the government those great kings had created by 1700 was far more potent than the one of 1600, the kings had to some extent exchanged a parceling out of sovereignty among regional magnates for a parceling out of sovereignty among thousands of officeholders. If they had enormously increased the resources at the disposal of their ministers, they had also multiplied the royally certified claims on those resources. By straining the economy to its limit, they had committed themselves to constant worry, surveillance, and intervention. The vast apparatus was far from self-regulating; any relaxation of centralized control produced a new crisis, as claimants helped themselves and ordinary citizens stiffened their resistance.

Those turbulent, contradictory processes created the common features of the century's collective action. Those processes explain the extraordinary impact of war and preparations for war on ordinary people's collective action. They explain the overwhelmingly defensive character of that collective action—the defense of crucial rights against violation, the defense of precious goods and services against expropriation. They explain the prevalence of tax rebellion, in one form or another, through most of the century. They explain the remarkable readiness of villagers and city dwellers alike to join rebellions against royal authority, despite recurrent losses and spectacular repression. They explain the domination of the collective-action repertoire by routines resembling those of mutiny.

Among the recurrent protests and rebellions, however, some critical changes occurred. During the first half of the seventeenth century, it was common to see a set of people who had an established right to gather—at least under some circumstances—assembling, deliberating, appointing a leader or deputy, and then declaring by word or deed their unwillingness to comply with a demand from authorities."Seditions" and "rebellions" often began in just that way.

As the century moved on and the state sapped local autonomies, such deliberative assemblies lost much of their importance as bases of resistance. Embattled Huguenots continued their own form of assembly, while provincial Estates and sovereign courts kept on deliberating, but for most Frenchmen that form of action became either impossible or ineffectual as a means of redressing their greatest grievances. Instead, ordinary people found themselves banging on the doors and windows of those who had retained or acquired the right to deliberate effectively. They used authorized assemblies of the whole population, such as festivals and public ceremonies, to convey their opinions. They undertook direct action, sometimes including guerrilla, against their oppressors and their delinquent protectors. They stepped in to impose the controls and punishments authorities had failed to deliver. They took the law into their own hands. As the deliberately rebellious assembly declined, the grain seizure and the popular avenging action rose.

These changes linked to another fundamental seventeenth-century alteration: the withdrawal of regional powerholders from popular rebellion. Until the Fronde, great lords were often available—at a price—as protectors and allies against royal authority. The price could easily rise too high, as it did during the Fronde. But in the meantime noble protection and alliance offered access to military expertise and a chance to bargain from strength. With the defeat of the Fronde, the absorption of nobles into the royal party, the increasing dependence of those nobles on privileges (not the least of which was relative exemption from ever-increasing taxes), and the systematic undermining of autonomous power bases within the country, nobles great and small became less and less available as partners in rebellion. War, mutiny, and patron-client action became rare forms of contention.

By the time of England's Revolution of 1688, one of Louis XIV's advisers could say, rather smugly: "If England had as many officials supported by the king as France does, the revolution would never have occurred. For it is certain that so many officials means so many committed people attached to the maintenance of royal authority. Without that authority they would be naught. If it were destroyed they would instantly lose the large sums of money with which they bought their positions" (BN Fr 7009).

By the end of the century, plenty of officeholders understood what was happening. One of them was Jean de la Bruyère, who in 1673 bought the office of treasurer in Caen's Bureau des Finances (income: 2,350 livres per year) and in 1686 became *gentilhomme ordinaire* (income: 3,000 livres per year). "One has nothing to lose by becoming noble," declared La Bruyère in 1688. "Freedoms, immunities, exemptions, privileges, what do people with titles lack? Do you think that it is for nobility itself that [the *secrétaires du roi*] had themselves ennobled? They are not so vain: it's for the profit they gain. Anyway, doesn't that look better than going into salt-tax farming?" ("De Quelques Usages," *Les Caractères,* paragraph 13). The kings had arranged to make honor and interest coincide rather neatly. The apparent fragmentation of sovereignty for mere money by Louis XIII and Louis XIV had a potent political outcome: it ensnared some of the monarchy's most dangerous potential opponents.

Rebellion, however, did not disappear. It became less frequent, and less dangerous to the government's survival. It changed character, becoming more plebeian, creating its own leaders, relying more heavily on existing community structure, aiming even more directly at the oppressors and oppressions endured by ordinary people. Class war was on its way.

6 ↝

Toulouse, Languedoc, and Enlightenment France

N 1700 AN AGING Louis XIV set up one of his last great coups. When Charles II of Spain died, Louis instantly took advantage of Charles's last testament: he had his own grandson, Philip of Anjou, assume the title of king of Spain. Almost as quickly, Louis dispatched Philip to Madrid in order to give him a strong grip on the crown before any rival claimants appeared. Philip of Anjou, now dubbed Philip V of Spain, departed ceremoniously for his new kingdom with his two brothers, the dukes of Burgundy and Berry. As if that studied challenge to other European rulers were not enough, Louis XIV soon arranged for the parlement of Paris to declare that Philip had retained his rights of succession to the French crown. His declaration not only contradicted the terms of Charles II's will but also held out the threat of an overpowering French-Spanish state. What is more, Louis had his seventeen-year-old grandson deputize him to rule the Spanish Netherlands. Once deputized, Louis wasted no time. He immediately sent French troops to oust the Dutch from forts along the French frontier. In his sixties, Louis XIV still hurried to make his mark.

After a delay for consternation, coalition building, and calling up of troops, the other European powers engaged France in the War of the Spanish Succession. Louis XIV's last war dragged on for a dozen years. France eventually had to settle for a reduction of Philip's domain to a Spanish kingdom still holding overseas colonies, but severed from the rest of its European territories and from the succession to the French crown. Nevertheless, the Treaty of Utrecht, which ended the war, fixed the French royal family on the Spanish throne.

Displaying Royal Power

Near the beginning of this adventure, Philip's two brothers slowly made their way back to Versailles after accompanying him to Spain. Toward the end of January 1701 they sent word to Toulouse that they would stop there for a few days en route. The city provided an ostentatious welcome for princes of the blood and—as the *Relation* of 1701 put it—"worthy grandsons of Louis the Great."

All the provincial magnates joined the preparations. The archbishop of Albi, eager to please, convened the grand old court of the Sénéchaussée in order to propose an appropriation for road repairs "so that the princes will find nothing in their path that will hinder or inconvenience them" (Devic and Vaissète 1872–1896: XIV, 1526). The elite of Toulouse planned a parade of militias created especially for the occasion: one hundred infantrymen per ward drawn from the city's chartered crafts, plus four companies of young merchants, for a total of five or six thousand troops in elegant new uniforms. The militias drilled with the city's watch to the tune of fifes, drums, and trumpets. For two whole weeks they polished their sabers and honed their skills. The city council planned fireworks at the Place St.-Etienne and set out fountains of wine at four locations in the city. Monsieur de Basville (intendant since 1685) and the count of Broglie (military governor and, not incidentally, Basville's brother-in-law) reviewed the preparations two weeks before the princes' arrival. "They approved of everything that had been done, and had all the troops pass in review" (*Relation* 1701: 5).

On the great day, 14 February, the troops were out at seven in the morning to form ranks on each side of the street, from St.-Cyprien Gate to the princes' lodgings in the archbishop's palace—a distance of exactly 1,226 toises (about 2.25 kilometers), reported the meticulous *Relation*. Behind and above the two files of militia hung the city's richest tapestries. When everything was in place, Broglie and Basville rode their carriages out to St.-Cyprien Gate. Close behind followed the watch and the *capitouls*—noble city councilors—present and past. Toward three o'clock the princes and their entourage finally reached the gate. Toulouse sounded its guns and rang its bells, and its spokesman, the capitoul Gardel, launched his oratory. After thanking Gardel politely, the princes entered the faubourg St.-Cyprien, across the Garonne River from the city's center:

> Since they could see the bridge, surely one of Europe's most beautiful, they stopped with pleasure to see the many people on it; companies of merchant militias lined the walkway. The falls of Castle mill, the tree-filled islands that seem to leap from the water, the great mirror of water between the bridge and the Basacle mill, the full skyline of that great city, the square at the end of the bridge with its balconies hung with tapestries and thronged with spectators; all these things provided a show no other city of the kingdom could offer.   (*Relation* 1701: 6–7)

The duke of Burgundy, the duke of Berry, and their retinue rode at a stately pace—three-quarters of an hour for just over two kilometers—past the troops, tapestries, and Toulousans to the archbishop's palace, where "they did the archbishop the honor of not removing the furniture from their rooms and of sleeping in the beds that had been prepared for them" (*Relation* 1701: 7).

That first night in Toulouse the city provided gifts, illuminations, and fireworks designed by a Jesuit professor of mathematics. So the visit continued: archbishop's mass and "harangue"; receptions of delegates from royal courts, religious orders, and academy; military parade of the lawyers' guild; visits to the cathedral, city hall, and other public buildings; concerts; more illuminations and fireworks—four full days of honors in seventeenth-century style. During those festive days intendant Basville sponsored fireworks in honor of the princes and laid out tables of food for all comers. Riquet, president of the parlement, matched Basville by offering illuminations, banquets, fountains of wine on either side of the main gate to his house, and seven brand-new boats. Riquet's agents had built those boats especially for the excursion the princes would take a few days later on the Canal des Deux Mers, or Canal du Midi, which linked the Atlantic to the Mediterranean via the Garonne.

Riquet did not choose the canal on a whim. The president's father had been the Languedoc salt-tax farmer who, with Colbert's blessing, organized the construction of the canal. Although Riquet père died in risky financial condition, the canal's profits eventually made his family rich. His son's purchase of one of Languedoc's most distinguished offices—the presidency of the parlement—testified to the family's wealth. The elder Riquet was also the tax-farmer whose efforts to install the gabelle and to stamp out salt smuggling in Roussillon (and especially in the Pyrenees) incited the sustained rebellion of the Angelets in the 1660s.

Intendant Basville was, for his part, the same Basville who had for fifteen years been trying to eradicate Languedoc's Protestants. He was soon to face the major rebellion of the Camisards. "Would you believe," he wrote not long after the princes had gone, "that the prophets say the king's grandson is on their side, and they know it because he said nothing about religion when he was in the region?" (Armogathe and Joutard 1972: 61). When they claimed the king's grandson for their ally, the prophets engaged in wishful thinking. Yet Philip V and Languedoc's Protestants did have a peculiar strategic link: withdrawal of royal troops from the Protestant country in preparation for war with the European powers on Philip's behalf facilitated the Camisards' rebellion.

The slow-paced pomp of February 1701 and the violent conflicts of the seventeenth century therefore had many connections. Forty years of Louis XIV's personal rule had wrought an enormous transformation in the forms and risks of rebellion in France. By 1701 the king had gained greater power relative to other contenders than ever before. But not all was calm.

Over the previous four decades, intendants such as Basville had done much of the day-to-day construction of royal power. They now served as the front line of resistance to challenges from within the kingdom, and as the chief agents of royal encroachment on provincial liberty, privilege, and power. Languedoc differed from other provinces only in being larger and richer (and therefore more crucial to royal designs) than most, and in retaining relatively strong provincial and municipal institutions with which an intendant had little choice but to bargain. Bargain he did, using whatever threats and enticements he could deploy.

Aside from ceremonial occasions, Basville was much involved in assuring royal influence among the powerful, and royal control among the rest. His routine correspondence makes that clear. In 1701, for example, we find him reporting nervously about the proliferation of Protestant preachers in the Cévennes and requesting support for repressive measures against them. We notice his defense of the abbé de Chayla, charged with converting the Protestants of the Cévennes and widely accused of profiteering from his post. (The massacre of the same abbé by hymn-singing Protestants at Pont-de-Montvert the following year was to precipitate the open rebellion of the Camisards.) We see Basville trying to aid the bishop of Viviers, who faced two knotty problems: determined resistance to his collection of the tithe from his tenants in the diocese, and the spread of ecstatic preaching among his region's Protestants.

Basville's careful containment of the provincial Estates, his steady reorganization of the grain trade, and his attentive surveillance of disputes involving the nobility illustrate his sustained effort to subject powerholders, and thus all who depended on them, to royal supervision. His invention and promotion of the *capitation*—a tax covering noble and commoner alike, and crudely proportioned to income—displayed his willingness to innovate on the crown's behalf. Over his thirty-five years of effort, the "king of Languedoc" (as the duke of Saint-Simon called Basville) forwarded royal power with extraordinary success.

Languedoc at the Start of the Eighteenth Century

Three years earlier, in 1698, Basville had joined his fellow intendants in submitting an essay on his province for the instruction of the duke of Burgundy, heir apparent to the crown. His "Mémoire concernant la province de Languedoc" discusses provincial history and geography, administration, fiscal structure, economic activity, and public works. From beginning to end Basville's essay reveals an administrator who knew the royal interest in keeping his region under control, in stimulating activity that would generate royal revenue, and in drawing off all the income to which the crown could claim title.

Basville provided detailed estimates of goods produced for sale in the province, exported, or imported. Table 2 summarizes them. It shows the importance of textiles as an item of trade both for export and for consumption within the region. Textiles far outweighed the grain trade within Lan-

Table 2. Estimated annual sales of various goods in Languedoc, 1698 (in livres)

Item	Local sales	Exports	Imports
Grain	1,160,000	40,000	—
Wine	—	830,000	—
Eaux-de-vie	—	440,000	—
Silk	300,000	1,500,000	—
Wool	—	—	650,000
Leather	958,000	1,180,000	—
Textiles	12,875,000	1,985,000	1,790,000
Livestock	400,000	600,000	1,240,000
Spices	—	—	471,000
Fish	40,000	60,000	349,225
Other	2,860,000	1,440,000	290,000
Total	18,593,000	8,075,000	4,790,225

Source: Basville, "Mémoire concernant la province de Languedoc" (1698), AN H[1] 1588[26].

guedoc. In the export market textiles, raw silk, leather, wine, and distilled liquor outranked all other products. Lodève and other industrial centers exported great quantities of woolen cloth to the Levant. As for imports, finished cloth, sheep, and wool dominated Languedoc's trade.

Basville's figures provide one surprise: the trivial amount of revenue generated by Languedoc's exports of grain. The plain of Toulouse was one of France's major breadbaskets, an important supplier of Marseille and the Mediterranean. A "wheat machine," Roger Brunet (1965: 329) has called it. The region's peasants ate maize and shipped wheat for income. During the eighteenth century, Languedoc's nobles grew rich on the wheat they exported, and cemented their new wealth by squeezing out peasant rights to graze animals and to forage on cultivated land. According to a memorandum from the crisis year 1709, Upper Languedoc "has no other way to pay its taxes but the export of wheat grown here. It is the only crop raised in the region, and even mediocre harvests supply the needs of the whole province. That is why it has always been the practice to allow the export of wheat from France, and to set a fixed quantity or a fixed period for exports when the harvest has been mediocre" (AN G^7 1644).

These facts suggest a vigorous export trade in wheat. Yet according to the intendant's report the bulk of the wheat sold ended up within the province, and even there fell far short of the trade in textiles. In any case, the intendant's figures reveal the central position of wool and silk in the region's commercial economy. If the silk production of Nîmes and its surrounding region was declining fast, and if its Protestant workers were emigrating to textile areas of England, Holland, and Switzerland, woolen cloth was flowing to the Levant as never before. From his rough estimates, Basville concluded that "it is easy to see the wealth and strength of this province, which has plenty of every staple; it can easily get by without depending on foreign countries and neighboring provinces" (AN H^1 1588 26/106). For that reason, Basville recommended the reduction of tariff barriers and the removal of impediments to trade.

Clearly, Basville wanted trade to increase royal revenues. Over the nine years from 1689 through 1697, he estimated the average annual royal return in the categories listed in Table 3. Thus Basville and his fellows were extracting almost 14 million livres per year from a province whose total annual trade, by his own estimates, ran in the vicinity of 32 million. Small wonder that he wanted to promote more trade.

Not all was orderly commerce and peaceful administration in Languedoc, however. Basville used the label "New Converts" to describe the prov-

Table 3. Average annual royal revenues from Languedoc, 1689–1697

Item	Millions of livres
Farmed indirect taxes	4.0
Direct taxes	6.5
Sale of offices, privileges	2.1
Surtax	0.2
Capitation	0.7
Total	13.5

Source: Basville, "Mémoire concernant la province de Languedoc" (1698), AN H[1] 1588[26].

ince's Protestants but knew that it did not stick very well. He claimed to have more former Protestants than any other intendant. Basville counted precisely 198,483 New Converts in a total provincial population of roughly 1.5 million; that meant about 13 percent of Languedoc's people. After a century of conversions, voluntary and forced, in the lowland areas, Protestants remained numerous in the mountains. "One ought to note," remarked Basville, "that the New Converts dominate the Cévennes, the Pontine mountains, the Vivarais, and the mountains near Castres, an area that used to be nearly impenetrable; that makes the inhabitants seditious and inclined to rebellion" (AN H[1] 1588 26/30).

Exhibit 3 maps Basville's figures by diocese. The map records the concentration of Protestants in Languedoc's northeast corner. It also shows, however, the imperfect correspondence of Protestantism and open resistance. The dioceses of Nîmes and Montpellier, for example, had considerable Protestant populations but little concerted resistance. Basville suggested two reasons for the difference between these lower-lying areas and their highland neighbors. The first was simply tactical: it was easier for the mountain Protestants to escape royal surveillance and control. The second was economic: on the average, the lowland Protestants were wealthier and more heavily involved in trade. They had a great deal to lose in futile resistance. It was more practical for them to feign conversion.

Well aware of the difference, Basville outlined the strategy he had followed. In the lowlands he had used persuasion and economic pressure. In the highlands he had adopted two main measures. The first was to build twelve-foot roads into the Cévennes and Vivarais; that would, he thought, promote communications and speed the movement of armies. The second was to recruit a Catholic provincial militia to supplement the regular troops at his disposal. The two measures combined in a campaign of military occupation and destruction.

Over the longer run, nevertheless, Basville hoped that the exile of all the Protestant pastors and the installation of good Catholic priests would wean the younger mountain people from heresy. "The New Converts," he concluded, "will go to confession and take Communion all you want so long as they are pressed and threatened by secular power; but that only produces sacrilege. We must attack their hearts; that is where religion lives;

Exhibit 3. Protestants in the dioceses of Languedoc, 1697 (Basville, "Mémoire concernant la province de Languedoc," AN H[1] 1588[26])

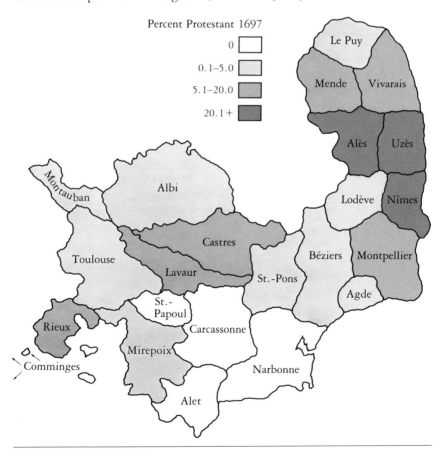

one will never establish it solidly without winning those hearts" (AN H^1 1588 26/34).

Louis XIV Wins His Wagers

Nicolas de Lamoignon de Basville was one of those proud, tyrannical officials who established Louis XIV's hold on the fractious hinterland. The duke of Saint-Simon credited Basville with great shrewdness but lost little love on the upstart. "Languedoc," he recalled,

> had groaned for many years under the tyranny of intendant Basville, who after blocking Cardinal Bonzi . . . seized all power . . . Basville was very smart, quick, enlightened, active, and hardworking. He was also clever, scheming, and implacable. He knew how to help his friends and acquire clients: a person who above all sought power, who broke any resistance, and for whom no cost was too great, since he was willing to use any means whatsoever. He had greatly increased royal revenues from the province, and the invention of the capitation had given him a great reputation. The ministers feared his broad, bright, imperious genius, kept him away from the court, and, in order to keep him in Languedoc, let him have all the power there. He used it ruthlessly.   (Saint-Simon 1873–1876: III, 404)

At the price of allowing Basville enormous discretion, however, Louis XIV and his ministers secured the subjugation of a once-rebellious province.

The provincial Estates offered one large challenge. The Estates of Languedoc were the most formidable of all France. With their double representation of the Third Estate and their inclusion of bishops who played major parts in the political administration of their dioceses, the Estates claimed a broader base and closer contact with workaday politics than did their counterparts elsewhere. Basville therefore continued to handle the Estates with care, but he did so adeptly; they received few bargains or concessions for their regular authorization of royal taxes.

Toulouse's proud capitouls likewise proved unable to resist integration into the royal apparatus. In the 1680s the king had acquired the power to name the capitouls from among a panel of candidates nominated by various groups in Toulouse. By the early decades of the eighteenth century the capitouls found themselves increasingly confined to ceremonial display and the administration of local affairs. If it had not been for the stubborn Protestants of the mountains, Basville would have established royal priority in every major region of Languedoc and in every important sphere of life. At

Basville's death in 1718, the Protestants, too, had given up their effort at sustained armed rebellion.

Eighteenth-century Languedoc lay under the control of a small number of seasoned intendants. That brought a genuine change from the seventeenth century. Richelieu had sent out his first intendant, Robert Le Miron, in 1631. From then to Basville's arrival in 1685, the average term of an intendant or commissaire was three or four years. Basville's thirty-three-year term introduced the great change. From 1685 to the Revolution, a mere seven intendants ran Languedoc, and the average term rose to fifteen years. In two of those cases, furthermore, a son groomed for the job succeeded his own father as intendant: a Bernage replaced a Bernage in 1725, and in 1785 a Saint-Priest who had already been deputy intendant for twenty-one years replaced his father as full-fledged intendant. Basville's death in 1718 did not end dynastic control over Languedoc.

Louis XIV died three years before Basville. Up to his death, Louis made war. His ministers kept at their expedients for raising the wherewithal of war, under the increased pressure of a rising royal debt; borrowing cumulated even faster than taxes. Taxes themselves reached a temporary ceiling. After the rapid growth of Languedoc's taxes from Louis XIV's accession in 1661 to the century's end, they remained at around the same level until after 1750. Then the Seven Years' War (1756–1763) and the American war (1776–1783) again pushed up both debt and taxes (Frêche 1974: 502–505).

Among France's provinces, Languedoc had a relatively equitable distribution of taxes. That for two reasons. First, with a "real" rather than a "personal" taille (royal land tax) nobles paid taxes on at least some of their land, and newly ennobled men remained subject to the same land taxes. Second, Languedoc's assessors actually used income from the land, rather than surface area or broad type of land use, as the base for levying the taille; in its *compoix,* which enumerated property parcel by parcel, they had at their disposal provincewide land registers. Wealthy men's incentive to claim nobility and royal incentive to track down false claims of nobility both diminished accordingly (Frêche 1974: 140–141). Under these circumstances, to be sure, nobility-bestowing offices did not sell fast. In fact, when the costs of office went up and its revenues went down, Languedoc's officeholders were inclined to abandon their appointments; in 1708, for example, the officers of Carcassonne's Présidial were giving up their posts for that very reason (AN G[7] 310). Thus in Languedoc the crown's fiscal stranglehold weakened to something like an aggressive hug.

No need to exaggerate. Even in Languedoc, eighteenth-century France showed a cruel, exploitative face. Even in Languedoc, inequalities among communities or regions that had been equitable at one point in time tended to endure until they were clearly unjust (Frêche 1974: 501). Even in Languedoc, the exemption of noble lands gave the old land-owning caste a decisive advantage. Even in Languedoc, the intendant sometimes had to arrange loans to pay current provincial taxes; Basville, for example, resorted to Genoese lenders for just that purpose in 1701 (AN G^7 305).

Even in Languedoc, all things considered, taxes arrived only with difficulty. In 1702 we find Basville reporting that he had "prosecuted those who resisted the capitation in Capestan. Nothing more has come of it. The Bonafoux, who attacked the collector, are on the run. I tried them in absentia. The ones who shouted in the streets that people shouldn't pay, I had arrested. That place is now setting a good example: it doesn't owe any of its capitation" (AN G^7 305). In 1707 we witness Basville threatening to send a regiment to Toulouse in order to force the capitouls to pay their city's capitation (AMT BB 188). The intendant remained in control, but that control required sustained effort.

With a bit of force, a dollop of bribery, and an abundance of patient maneuvering, most of Languedoc's nobles and municipal officers fell into line. Part of the reason was the intendant's caution in creating new offices. To pay for the War of the Spanish Succession, Louis XIV's ministers rolled out the old expedients, including the creation and sale of offices. In 1704 Basville stated his reasons for opposing the establishment of officeholding administrative courts for the taille, municipal tolls, and other special taxes: "It was really the creation of élections in Languedoc that stirred up so much disorder in 1632 and caused the formation of M. de Montmorency's party. That creation was revoked in 1649. There is no doubt that such an effort would be the most odious one could undertake in this province, and the most likely to cause great disturbances" (AN G^7 307). Some new offices—most of them soon bought up by the corporate bodies they threatened—did come into being in Languedoc. By and large, however, Basville and his successors held back on that source of revenue in favor of regular negotiation with the Estates. If Louis XIV won most of his bets in Languedoc, it was by dint of his agents' knowing combination of surveillance, patronage, persuasion, bargaining, and force.

Down with the Camisards

Some wagers lost, however, or became very expensive to win. In its attempt to eliminate Protestants from Languedoc, the crown confronted a tough, locally based, and ideologically unified organization. With the luxury of hindsight, we can easily see that Louis's agents miscalculated their approach to Protestants. The seventeenth-century anti-Protestant campaign had operated implicitly on these premises:

1. that French Protestants, like other major opposition parties, were organized in patron-client networks around great lords
2. that the checking and conversion of those great lords would therefore eliminate most of the Protestant threat
3. that Protestant ministers were supplying the local and regional leadership
4. that the exile of those ministers would therefore dismantle the rest of Protestant organization
5. that for the more powerful and wealthier Protestants, the threat to deprive them of office, municipal power, and the right to pursue their businesses would suffice to bring them round
6. that for the poor and weak, a realistic threat of force would do

Every one of these premises touched part of the truth. In some respects the threat posed by the Protestants resembled the threat of any extensive seventeenth-century party formed in opposition to the crown: they might block the execution of domestic policies, including the collection of royal revenues. They might league with the king's other domestic enemies. They might ally with enemies abroad. In July 1710, after all, the duke of Roquelaure reported a landing of more than a thousand enemy troops near Sète and supposed that "they had no doubt concerted their action with the ill-intentioned Protestants of the region" (AN G^7 314). From one perspective, then, the same tactics that had brought dissident seventeenth-century nobles into line should have worked for eighteenth-century heretics. From that perspective, the seventeenth-century program of military conquest, co-optation, exile, exclusion, and terror made sense. It greatly reduced Protestant power in France and greatly accelerated the rate of (at least nominal) conversion to Catholicism.

The program as a whole, nevertheless, rested on a large underestimate of the toughness of Protestant local organization. Especially where Protestants formed self-sufficient communities in forbidding terrain, they proved capable of producing new leaders to replace the old, of creating communication networks among distant locations, and of organizing guerrilla activity the likes of which French troops had never seen. Deprived of nobles, ministers, and bourgeois leaders, moreover, they behaved like people whose very selves were at stake: they assembled to preach and pray, created armed camps in the hills, came into battle singing hymns, refused to back down or inform under torture. They became, as Basville and his colleagues put it, "fanatics." By the start of the eighteenth century the king's representatives in Languedoc realized they had a very stubborn enemy up in the Cévennes and Vivarais.

Unlike the classic seventeenth-century rebellion, the Camisard resistance lacked noble and bourgeois leadership. The fighting forces and their immediate supporters consisted almost entirely of rural and small-town people; perhaps half of them were artisans, mainly from the rural wool trade (Joutard 1976: 50). They belonged to the hill people. They melted back into the population at large when they were not under arms. They formed a guerrilla force.

The action did not begin with military rebellion in any usual sense of the word. Up to the middle of 1702, most of the action consisted of clandestine assemblies and religious services, in defiance of the royal ban on Protestant practice. But that was precisely what Basville, Broglie, and their aides were trying to stop. One of those aides was the abbé de Chayla, inspector-general of the diocese of Mende. The abbé had the chief ecclesiastical responsibility for conversion—forced or otherwise—of Protestants in the Cévennes. Chayla, according to Camisard chief Abraham Mazel, "was just as cruel within his own sphere as Basville was in his" (Joutard 1965: 33). Chayla had taken over the house of a Protestant sentenced to the galleys and had converted part of it into a jail for captured heretics. Isolated in the mountains at Pont-de-Montvert, he became a visible symbol of Catholic intrusion into a Protestant world.

Inspired by divine messages, Mazel and about fifty of his fellow believers gathered in the hills on 23 July 1702. Singing psalms, they marched to Chayla's house. They summoned the abbé to release his Protestant prisoners. He feigned agreement but failed to open the door. Growing impatient, Mazel and the others chopped their way in. Chayla gave up all the prisoners but one. When the Protestant troop asked for that last prisoner, someone fired on them from upstairs. At that, Mazel and his lieutenants retired to pray. "Start a fire at the bottom of the stairs and block the house," came instructions from on high. They followed orders, and the house burned like straw. The one remaining prisoner escaped miraculously, so Mazel reported. Then Chayla jumped out a window and tried to flee the back way, only to be captured and hacked to death (Joutard 1965: 34–37).

With the murder of Chayla, royal forces moved toward the aggressive pursuit of Protestant bands, as the Protestants shifted into full-fledged guerrilla warfare. By March 1703 the *Gazette de France* was summing up in these terms:

A few months ago the fanatical Protestants of the Cévennes, seduced by their so-called prophets, rose up. Under the command of a few criminals they chose to lead them, they killed a few priests and burned many churches. People hoped at first that punishing a few of their chiefs would bring them back into line; but that indulgence having instead increased their insolence and madness, they grew in number, burned a large number of churches, villages, and houses, and killed men, women, and children with incredible inhumanity, boasting that they would exterminate all the old Catholics of the region.   (*La Gazette de France* 24 March 1703: 144)

Widespread warfare in the highlands continued into 1704, accompanied in the lowlands by intermittent struggles over taxation and occasional Protestant assemblies. Royal troops and militias burned and killed. The Camisards replied in kind.

Chasing down the Protestant enemy disrupted the normal flow of provincial business, including the crucial business of taxation. During the early decades of the eighteenth century, military campaigns against the Camisards disrupted Languedoc's fiscal machine in several different ways. First, they cost money—money in the urgent form of pay for troops. In 1706 Basville found himself forced to pay the local troops by touching the untouchable: borrowing from the salt-tax revenues (AN G^7 309, 310). But the crown also wanted those revenues. By 1710 the competition for salt-tax returns had become so intense that the provincial Maréchaussée (the regional mounted police) went unpaid. "The archers of this province," Basville wrote to Desmaretz on 25 February 1710, "have not been paid because their pay is charged to the salt-farm's account, and on your orders we sent everything in the till to Paris ... This situation poses a serious threat to public order, since the Maréchaussée is now out of service" (AN G^7 313).

A second difficulty came from the necessity of giving tax rebates to people whose property the war had damaged; after Basville adopted a scorched-earth policy in the Protestant hills, those rebates cut significantly into his tax revenues. Indeed, forty-one parishes of the dioceses of Mende and Uzès suffered so much damage that they received general tax exemptions from 1705 to 1730 (AN H^1 1071).

Finally, resistance to taxation blended into the general resistance of the Camisards. In 1703 the bishop of Mende wrote that the rebellion made it impossible to collect the taille and capitation in a large part of his diocese (AN G^7 306). Nor were the clergy's own revenues sacrosanct. In the diocese of Nîmes, handbills appeared in many villages the same year forbidding anyone, in the name of God and the Camisard military commanders, to collect or pay the tithe (AN G^7 306). Where taxable, tithable property survived the burning and shooting, "fanatics" often made life dangerous for the tax or tithe collectors. Salt smuggling, furthermore, gave rebellious Protestants the satisfaction of making money by depriving the hated authorities of tax revenue. In the Cévennes and Vivarais, tax evasion took on the glow of a divine mission.

In Camisard country, Basville had ideas about how to proceed. At the start of 1708, he mapped out a fiscal strategy for the Cévennes:

> Since the inhabitants of the Cévennes are resisting the payment of the taille and the capitation, and since it is necessary in any case to make them bear the full cost of their rebellion (which they can certainly end when they want to), I think it would be quite appropriate to order that the richest people of each community advance the total amount of both taxes, with the right to collect from the other taxpayers. That would be a better strategy because the local collectors say they can't prosecute debtors, and the royal receivers say they can't find bailiffs who dare to go into the mountains. (AN G^7 310)

By means of these and other divide-and-conquer tactics, Basville and his successors eventually assured a steady flow of tax money from Languedoc's Protestant households to the coffers of the crown.

During other years, the calm was only relative. The major war of the Camisards raged from 1702 to 1704. Before it was over, Marshal de Montrevel replaced Broglie, then Marshal de Villars replaced Montrevel; the royal armies did not establish control easily. After the end of open war, small bands of Camisards continued to harass royal forces from their secret positions in the highlands. In 1705 Camisard leaders attempted to coordinate a new general rebellion with France's enemies, only to fail once more. In 1709 Abraham Mazel sought to raise the Vivarais, and a new flurry of fighting arose. Thereafter, royal forces gradually drove the armed Protestants into defeat, dispersal, and despair. Languedoc's last great old-regime rebellion had collapsed.

From 1709 until the relaxation of controls over Protestant practice in 1786, Languedoc's Protestants rarely showed a public face—and never in open rebellion. In 1723, for example, the new intendant Bernage reported that royal forces had captured "a famous preacher named Vesson and twelve other preachers or fanatical women at the home of widow Verchant in Montpellier." He had arranged for the preachers to do penance and be hanged, the male members of the congregation to go to the galleys and the women to go to prison, the house to be razed, a cross to be erected, and the widow's goods to be confiscated. Bernage felt that the "good effect" of his exemplary punishment justified its severity (AN H^1 1066). As the memory of foreign war and the Camisard rebellion receded, however, a modus vivendi emerged: the authorities tolerated assemblies of Protestants so long as they didn't cause trouble or meddle with France's enemies (Wemyss 1961: 144-150).

"Tolerated" is not exactly the right word. "Exploited" would be better. In the 1740s royal officials actually stepped up the prosecution of Protestant assemblies, but with two innovations. First, so long as the New Converts dispersed peacefully, they paid stiff fines and costs but rarely went to trial. The intendant and governor became much more reluctant to arrest anyone—especially children and old people—merely suspected of attending a clandestine service. Second, the intendant levied the fine on all Protestants of the area in which the assembly occurred, rather than on the few people known to have attended.

When Protestants gathered near the mountain village of Molandier on 21 May 1752, for example, the intendant slapped a fine of 1,000 livres (plus 269 livres 18 sous in costs) on all members of the faith living in the surrounding district of Calmont (ADH C 234, judgment of 29 June 1752). A regular accounting system, quite similar to the one used for regular taxes, grew up and flourished through the 1740s and 1750s. What is more, the cases came to judgment in a few weeks, instead of the months usually consumed by criminal proceedings. In effect, Languedoc's royal officials were converting the levies into a tax on known Protestant meetings.

At the same time, other strategies of control shifted. In 1753 the intendant announced a four-point policy: (1) to drive all Protestant ministers from the country; (2) to watch assemblies carefully, but to distinguish sharply between armed and unarmed gatherings; (3) to make it easier for New Converts to marry in the church; to stop insisting that they prove their fidelity beyond any doubt; (4) likewise, to encourage them to baptize their children (AN H^1 1093). By the 1760s, in any case, all systems of control over Protestants were weakening. Judging from the volume of prosecutions brought by royal officers, the decline continued right to the Revolution (ADH C 163-489). Except for the stir caused by an occasional superzealous Catholic bishop or official, the more tolerant and profitable arrangements almost eliminated serious confrontations with Languedoc's Protestants.

Toulouse and Castres were, perhaps, the chief exceptions. The officials of Toulouse gave little room to Protestants. In 1762, on the flimsiest of circumstantial evidence, capitouls and parlement rammed through the execution of Protestant Jean Calas for the murder of his son. In 1764 their counterparts in Castres convicted the Protestant Sirven family for the murder of their daughter; this time the authorities had to settle for execution in effigy, since the Sirvens had fled to Switzerland. In each case, the child in question had most likely committed suicide. In each case, that child had previously taken steps toward conversion to Catholicism. Thus the rumor spread that Protestant parents had killed their children to keep them from leaving the faith. Voltaire made the parlement's conviction of Calas notorious as an example of intolerance, then beat the drum for the Sirvens. The Toulousans soon recanted, Calas received his posthumous rehabilitation in 1765, and a renewed parlement acquitted the Sirvens in 1771. No significant Catholic-Protestant conflict stirred up Toulouse or Castres for the rest of the century.

Brawls and Tax Rebellions

The seventeenth century died, in a sense, with the demise of the Camisard rebellion. The great regional rebellions had lost their noble heads with the Fronde. Later in the seventeenth century, however, whole populations of commoners had continued to rise at the sign of the government's violation of its contract with the people. After the Protestants fell into line, whole populations rose no more.

With the decline of open conflict across religious divisions, Languedoc's people settled into struggles that involved more patent material interests. Up to mid-eighteenth century, tax rebellions, though not on the grand regional scale of the seventeenth century, continued to shake Languedoc. During the second half of the century they virtually disappeared. After that the focus of contention shifted from the state to the market, and to capital. Grain seizures reached their historical apogee after 1700. Fights over control of land and its products likewise intensified.

The chief apparent eighteenth-century exceptions to the predominance of material interests were battles among artisans, soldiers, students, and other specialized communities; they continued from previous centuries and persisted into the next. In Toulouse, for example, pitched battles between students and the city's watch rocked the whole city in 1721, 1737, 1739, 1740, and 1750. In 1740 the parlement took formal note that

> bills were posted at the gates of the university schools, of the colleges of this city, and elsewhere, calling an assembly of youths and scholars outside the city gates, as a result of which the city's scholars gathered yes-

terday, Thursday the last of March, bearing swords and other weapons; so that when the capitouls went to the site with their armed force to disperse that seditious assembly they met complete rebellion and disobedience, their legitimate authority was disregarded, and people threw stones at them, wounding one of the capitouls seriously on the right cheek; the disorder having been ended, and some of the crowd having been disarmed and made prisoner, despite the proceedings against some of them, that riotous troop dared today to invade the city hall. (ADHG C 316; see also Dumas 1907)

The events of March 1740 had begun with the usual heckling in the theater, called up an intervention by the watch, activated long-standing grievances of students against the watch, spilled over into marches through the streets, continued with some 800 young people assembling at the Seven-Penny Meadow, and ended with a series of confrontations between youngsters and authorities in the streets of Toulouse. The sentences of a number of participants to banishment or fines were overturned on appeal, but those participants did spend time in jail. Despite the repression, the same drama (and the same admonition from the parlement) played again just ten years later, in June 1750 (ADHG C 316).

Although authorities often called those communal battles "brawls" or something equally demeaning, the fighting often broke out over serious issues. Groups of artisans fought each other over precedence within a town, young men from adjacent villages over control of courtship and marriage, soldiers and civilians over the depredations of the troops. In 1750 Toulouse's watch (egged on by the capitouls) and the seneschal's military escort (backed by the seneschal himself) battled over precedence in the seneschal's court (d'Aldéguier 1830–1835: IV, 274–275). On 5 May 1751 the sedan-chair porters of Toulouse attacked soldiers of the watch who were arresting another porter, a fugitive from conscription into the regional militia (ADHG C 316). In 1758 at Florensac two former captains of the regional coast guard led an armed rebellion against the taking of local men for the militia (ADH C 626, 1319, 6572). Two days later the same thing happened in nearby Vias (ADH C 1319).

La jeunesse (as organized local groups of unmarried men were commonly called in Languedoc) frequently had communal battles of one sort or another. They generally conducted charivaris against widowers who married young women and against other offenders—such as the husband at Buzet who, in 1751, stood for his wife's beating him (ADH C 6851). They provided the shock troops for intervillage fights. In 1779, for example, the young men of St.-Thibéry and Bessan chose to battle over the removal of a tree the Bessanites had bought for their May Day celebration; the youths of Bessan had made the mistake of picking out a tree growing on the turf of St.-Thibéry's jeunesse (ADH C 6666).

Organized young men likewise defended their own interest in fending off military conscription. In Gévaudan, according to the intendant's edict of 1782, la jeunesse was collecting forced contributions from the parents of other young men who had acquired exemptions from the drawing for military service; the contributions went to compensate the winners of that frightful lottery (ADH C 626). Although these matters involved only the most parochial of interests, they greatly affected the participants.

On other occasions an essentially communal fight took a different turn when the authorities intervened. Writing on behalf of himself and his city's consuls, Esquirol, mayor of Montgaillard, complained to the intendant on 20 February 1754 that

> on Sunday the third toward nine at night a large number of peasants and artisans gathered in the square of our little city and started fighting. Someone called us in to settle things. Seeing no better and quicker remedy, we ordered everyone to go home. But the mutinous troop turned its anger against us, cursed and insulted us, jostled us, and even grabbed some of us by the collar. At that we retired. More for the sake of form than for any other reason we filed a complaint with the seneschal. Despite that, these rebels continue to challenge us, gathering almost every day with fifes and drums, wearing laurel in their hats while singing and shouting in the streets, and making a point of doing it more loudly in front of our doors than anywhere else. All this no doubt in hopes of trying our patience, getting us to come out, and then perhaps to take out their anger on us—all at the instigation of Jacques [Maynent?], the former consul you threw out. (ADHG C 91)

Then, more or less predictably, the mayor asked the intendant to send an infantry company to defend him and his colleagues from the "mutineers."

"Peasants and artisans" were not the only people resisting royal authority. At the close of the Seven Years' War, in 1763, Louis XV attempted to pay for some of the war's great expense by extending some of the "emergency" taxes enacted in wartime and by establishing some new levies as well. Led by the parlement of Paris, a number of provincial parlements, including that of Toulouse, formally opposed the war taxes. Prolonged negotiations between Toulouse and Versailles began in July. By the end of August the parlement was overruling the capitouls' decision to give the duke of Fitz-James (the provincial lieutenant general) a reception befitting a royal envoy. It was also refusing to give formal recognition to Fitz-James's installation as Languedoc's commander-in-chief. On 15 September 1763 the parlement circumvented its first president (François de Bastard) and the province's lieutenant general (the duke of Fitz-James) by issuing an edict that forbade collection of the war taxes. Two days later, when bills announcing the edict appeared on the city's walls, the lieutenant general put the members of the parlement under house arrest. The parlementary resistance of 1763 recalled the Fronde of 1648, but with three crucial differences: no private armies remained; no genuine rivals to the king appeared; and no large popular rebellions formed.

After almost two months of further maneuvering in concert with parlements elsewhere, the parlement of Toulouse in its turn issued a warrant for the arrest of the duke of Fitz-James. Since he, not they, had the necessary troops, their gesture was mainly symbolic. They followed up by declaring that the duke had no right to the title of commander-in-chief in Languedoc. Later the parlement initiated a series of legal actions against its first president, Bastard, who had worked too closely with the lieutenant general. In this case the parlement won: neither Fitz-James nor Bastard returned to Toulouse (BN Fr 6828; ADH C 6544; Egret 1970: 152–154).

By no means, however, did all resistance to taxation follow the niceties of courtroom procedure. Despite the leveling off of taxes after Louis XIV's death, smuggling remained attractive and profitable in the Cévennes, the Vivarais, and the Pyrenees; smuggling meant occasional open battles between revenue officers and purveyors of contraband. Likewise, taxes on production, sales, and business transactions periodically incited resistance; witness the "sedition" brought on at Joyeuse in 1735 by the attempt to collect fees for the registry of personal documents (ADH C 1253) or the "revolt" at Sommières in 1738 against the attempt by the tax-farmer's agents to deliver summonses to people convicted of possessing untaxed cotton goods (ADH C 1270).

By the 1780s, tax rebellion had practically disappeared from Languedoc's conflicts. The chief events occurred at the province's mountainous margins. A series of confrontations in Foix, Goulier, and elsewhere in the Pyrenees once again pitted citizens against tax-farmers. In 1783 the royal council decreed new taxes on wine to pay for road construction. When one of the two tax-farmers showed up in Foix at the end of March 1784, children hooted him; women and children stoned him; men, women, and children chased him out of town; and someone posted bills forbidding payment of the tax (AN H[1] 7111). It did not help matters that the tax-farmer's commission to collect the tax was suspect.

The marquis d'Usson, sent by the crown to investigate the trouble, saw a broader significance in Pyrenean resistance to taxes. In a letter to Marshal Ségur, minister of war and military governor in the region, he described the region's people as "poor in money and rich in crops" and concluded that they therefore "lived in abundance but had no means of paying their taxes"—a situation obviously not to be tolerated in a tax-starved country. The marquis then came up with a fresh idea: "The greatest and most useful thing for them would be the presence, at least for a year or two, of a body of troops who would spread money through the province. Soldiers, being professionals, would stimulate industriousness and train the region's workers. By increasing the number of men available for road construction, the soldiers could also increase the region's well-being and repair some rundown roads" (AN H^1 7221). Thus the cure for the diseases of a peripheral area was to open it up, develop trade, monetize the economy, expand its involvement in capitalism. In short: the standard capitalist remedy for backwardness.

The nearly contemporaneous Revolt of the Armed Masks, in the Vivarais, took quite a different shape from the tax rebellions around Foix. But it illustrated the other side of capitalism's advance. Up in the Vivarais in 1783, the self-styled Honest Legion of the Vivarais blackened their faces, donned women's clothing, and attacked the homes of judges, lawyers, grain merchants, and tax collectors—all those who collected or enforced debts incurred by small-town workers. The bandits seized the money, burned the papers, drank the wine, and feasted on what they could find; then they decamped. Although the main rebellion spent itself before the end of 1783, attacks on local capitalists and officials by armed, masked men continued into the next year. Authorities convicted about twenty people and executed three of them (ADH C 6564, C 6886, C 6870, and C 6889; N. Castan 1980a: 229–231 and 1980b: 186–190, 199).

The Honest Legion had not dreamed up its enemies. In 1785 the parlement of Toulouse instituted a formal commission of inquiry into "swindling" by village lawyers (AN H^1 1103). By this point the popular enemy was no longer the state; it was the local capitalist class.

Food for Proletarians

France's local capitalists often made their money, one way or another, on the grain trade. Although Languedoc as a whole grew plenty of grain, not everyone had direct access to it. In the Cévennes, poor people had long eaten chestnuts and shipped out what grain they could grow (Le Roy Ladurie 1966: I, 211–221). In all of Languedoc, the number of people who depended on the purchase of grain or bread for household survival increased rapidly during the eighteenth century. Around Toulouse the population increased 50 or 60 percent, while food production rose from 5 to 15 percent (Frêche 1974: 311). At the same time, grain prices shot up. Toulouse's average price, benefiting from the city's proximity to grain-growing areas, had long been lower than the price in Paris, despite the fact that the two prices moved in close cadence. But after about 1740 the average price in Toulouse rose much faster than the Paris price, reaching about the same level (Frêche 1974: 692–693; cf. Tilly 1972: 743-745). In Upper Languedoc wheat grew so valuable that peasants shifted to selling all of it and growing maize for their own consumption. Noble and bourgeois property expanded, reducing peasants to tiny plots or none at all (Frêche 1974: 164-166, 213-224). The region of Toulouse became a prime area of agricultural capitalism.

Wage labor increased accordingly. The population underwent proletarianization. By 1734 agricultural wageworkers formed a majority of the rural population around Toulouse (Frêche 1974: 351). Later in the century, as "day-laborers and unemployed people multiplied," proletarian migration from the countryside accelerated (Godechot and Moncassin 1965: 47, 48). The contrast grew sharper between a relatively high-wage region around Montpellier (Lower Languedoc) and a distinctively low-wage region around Toulouse (Upper Languedoc). Georges Frêche lays out the reasons:

> In the region of Toulouse, the concentration of property, which turned many smallholders and sharecroppers into landless laborers, put pressure on wages by increasing the supply of workers who had no choice but agricultural labor. In Lower Languedoc the fragmentation of property worked in the opposite direction. There were many smallholders who preferred to live on their own, however modestly, instead of hiring themselves out. What is more, workers of Lower Languedoc who got only occasional income from the land earned money in manufacturing or public works. (Frêche 1974: 556)

There, seasonal migrants descended from the hills for harvests.

Judging from the situation in the early nineteenth century, people of the Cévennes likewise migrated regularly to the lowlands for seasonal work in agriculture (Lamorisse 1975: 98-100). But before Languedoc's woolen industry suffered its great decline, late in the eighteenth century, a higher proportion of the *cévenols* surely stayed on the land, alternating agricultural and industrial work. In 1726 Pichol, inspector of manufacturing for the region of Nîmes, excused himself from providing statistical data on the ground that the organization of production made any such effort hopeless.

"The majority of the producers of my region," he explained, "are peasants of the Cévennes who live in villages and hamlets scattered through the mountains and who make imperial serge, caddis, or other woolens when they aren't working on the land." The peasants, he continued, sold their goods to merchants from Nîmes, Montpellier, and elsewhere; the merchants usually supervised the final processing before sending the cloth on to the market (AN F^{12} 673, letter of 19 August 1726).

In the Causses, above Lodève and adjacent to the Cévennes, perhaps half the rural population were proletarians; they pieced together an existence from various combinations of agricultural day-labor, textile production, transport work, and seasonal migration (Marres 1935–1936: II, 64). The broad contrast within Languedoc, then, separated the rapidly increasing landless agricultural laborers of Toulouse's Upper Languedoc from the smallholders–cum–industrial workers of Montpellier's Lower Languedoc, and from the smallholders, shepherds, and industrial workers of the Cévennes and Vivarais.

In Upper Languedoc, ordinary people therefore became increasingly vulnerable to subsistence crises just when merchants, authorities, and propertyholders were developing a greater interest in shipping the region's food to national and international markets. Ordinary people had no trouble detecting subsistence crises; all they needed to know was that the price of grain or bread rose quickly while wages remained the same. That was likely to happen as a result of some combination of bad harvests and increasing exports. As real income plummeted, and as people cut back their food consumption, shortage was likely to increase the death rate while slowing both marriages and births. Major crises of this sort came to Languedoc in 1709–1713, 1719–20, 1750–1752, and 1788–1790; the region also experienced important subsistence crises in 1739–1743, 1771–1774, and 1781–1783 (Godechot and Moncassin 1965: 26–36; Frêche 1974: 107–110, 677). Twenty-five of the 90 years from 1701 to 1790 were crisis years, an average of 1.8 per decade before 1740, and 3.5 per decade from 1740 on. Times were hard, and getting harder.

By themselves, however, hard times did not necessarily precipitate intense conflicts over food supply. Languedoc's crises of 1709–1713, 1771–1774, and 1788–1790 produced far more open struggle than those of 1719–20, 1750–1752, and 1781–1783, although on balance all hurt people equally badly.

The year 1752 is a case in point. It brought the "worst crisis since 1713" (Frêche 1974: 109). Trouble started with the awful weather of the preceding fall. In October 1751, intendant Saint-Priest wrote that the upper

Vivarais was devastated: "storms have been so terrible and so much rain mixed with hail has fallen in some places, that a large number of communities . . . will never recover. The soil suitable for seeding has washed away down to a considerable depth, many mills have been destroyed, many bridges washed out, roads ruined, so that all communication is cut off" (AN H^1 1093). In that miserable year, maize ran short and rose disastrously in price. From Levignac, beset by five months of miserable weather, came the report that "consuming hunger has left people looking barely human, and the roads are unsafe"; at Lescure, desperate people stole from each other and from the lord as acts of destruction multiplied (Bastier 1975: 84). Yet in Levignac, Lescure, and the province as a whole, collective contention over the supply of food simply did not occur.

The relatively minor shortages of 1746–1748, 1764–1766, and 1777–78, in contrast, incited widespread popular intervention in markets and shipments of food (Bourderon 1953, 1954; Viala 1909). The big differences between times of small-scale misery and those of large-scale action lay in the ways merchants and authorities responded to the rise in prices. People began to fight over food when someone profited visibly from the crisis, and when authorities failed to meet their obligations to reserve a share of the shrunken supply for the poor at a price they could afford. They also complained—hard times or not—whenever authorities sought to tax staple foods, and thus to drive up prices.

Languedoc suffered one of its greatest subsistence crises during the national shortage of 1709. The "great winter" of 1708–09 brought killing frosts, then hail; wheat, maize, and chestnuts all suffered immensely. By the beginning of April the syndics of Languedoc were declaring that it would be impossible to collect the taille, the capitation, and the tithe in 1709. By 18 April the bishop of Carcassonne was writing:

> We have worked on the capitation rolls. There is no one on them but professed paupers, certified as such by unanimous agreement. We have already had three or four years without a harvest. The exceedingly high price of wheat means it is no longer within the reach of ordinary folk. Their usual resource was maize, but none has come to market for quite a while, and before that it was, proportionately speaking, even higher priced than wheat. Last winter, which came and went three times the same year, finished off all our communities. The seed is completely rotten in the ground.   (Boislisle 1874–1896: III, 130–131)

If the good bishop dramatized his flock's plight just a bit, who could blame him? The intendant, too, found the situation critical.

Basville raised his first warning note at the start of February 1709, when a thaw without rain threatened the year's crop (AN G^7 1644). During the following weeks, as the ground froze again and grain prices jumped, the threat became clearer. People along trade routes began to block shipments. In a semilegal move, for example, inhabitants of Tournon seized a grain barge loaded in Languedoc without passport and headed for Lyon; they paid both the going price and the transport costs (AN G^7 1644, letter of 9 April 1709). Basville himself bought back 3,000 *sétiers* (about 6,000 hectoliters) of grain that Genoan merchants had acquired in Béziers; but when his agents began to move the grain into the city's barracks, he had to send troops to hold off the people of Béziers (AN G^7 1644, second letter of 9 April 1709).

Nevertheless, threats to public order did not unduly concern the hardy intendant. Something else did. He began to sound the alarm in a letter of 23 April 1709 (AN G^7 311). Two ominous changes worried him. First, people in each region of Languedoc were starting to resist the shipment of grain elsewhere. Second, the bishops of Languedoc's various dioceses were pleading for suspension of royal taxes, on the ground that no one had the means to pay.

Basville had reasons to be worried. A month later he was writing that "the loss of olive trees is irreparable and that of livestock very worrisome. In the worst cases the problem is what to do about paying the first installment of the taille, which is now past due. It certainly can't be collected in many places where the inhabitants are completely preoccupied with avoiding starvation; any of the pressures we are used to exerting on the local collectors would be completely useless" (AN G^7 311, 24 May 1709); on 29 June, Basville explained that in ordinary times the peasants of different regions raised the money to pay taxes from the sale of olive oil, wheat, and fattened cattle; the loss of all three amounted to a fiscal disaster (AN G^7 311).

In 1709, when he could turn his attention from the renewed Camisard war to questions of subsistence, Basville did the conventional things. He consulted with bishops and municipal authorities, inventoried the grain on hand, assured the food supply of military posts, controlled the shipments of grain from region to region, bought Mediterranean rice for the poor. He even arrested a noble hoarder: "The sieur de Maisonseule," he wrote late in 1709, "is a gentleman of the Vivarais, an odd sort and a bad example. During the last famine he had a stock of grain in his house. The duke of Roquelaure ordered in someone to inspect, so the grain could be brought to market. He resisted, saying he did not recognize the provincial commander, or the intendant, or M. Courteu, who commands in the Vivarais ... We had to send troops to enter his castle" (AN G^7 312, 12 November 1709).

But he could not prevent such incidents as the one in early June in which a "considerable number of women, accompanied by a few men," stopped the grand vicar of Toulouse's archbishop, gave "insolent speeches" on their misery and their need for charity, extorted four louis d'or from the grand vicar, then went off and demanded a similar amount from the curé of a nearby parish (AN G^7 311, 12 June 1709). Nor could he forestall the "emotions" and "seditions" in which the people of Pradelles, Narbonne, Le Puy, Castelnaudary, and other places—but not, it seems, well-stocked Toulouse—blocked shipments or large purchases of grain.

Hungry Toulouse

If Toulouse's people remained quiet in 1709, it was not because they lacked a voice. The capitouls and Basville heard them shout during the city's next subsistence crisis, in 1713. On 17 June, when two capitouls went to the parlement on a routine mission, a crowd of women blocked their way, called for bread, and blamed the capitouls for the shortage. "I found the parlement's courtyard full of women," reported Riquet, "who demanded with great cries that we give them bread and turn the capitouls over to them." The parlement huddled in the adjacent hall, deliberated solemnly, passed a decree threatening the women with "corporal punishment" if they did not disperse, then sent a bailiff with troops to read the decree to the crowd in the courtyard. They prudently declined to accompany their spokesman.

When the bailiff got there, a "large number of men, along with sedan-chair porters and lackeys," joined the crowd, stoned the troops and the bailiff, and drove them back—though not before the troops fired, killing one woman and wounding others. The capitouls fled (AN G^7 319, letter of 18 June 1713). Basville blamed the "insolent lackeys" of the parlement, who, he reported, had not only joined the angry crowd, but also tried to break open the door of the Great Hall, where the capitouls had taken refuge. The affray should not have taken place, he reasoned, since prices had not risen as much at Toulouse as elsewhere. Nevertheless, he was taking the precaution of having his son (now conveniently placed as intendant in Bordeaux) ship in enough grain to tide the city over until harvest time (AN G^7 319, letter of 19 June 1713).

Although the capitouls had not caused the bad harvest of 1712, the women and "lackeys" of Toulouse had some legitimate reasons for suspecting them. As early as 1710 the capitouls, pressed for revenue, had proposed a tax on grain earmarked for the army; the intendant's deputy (the *subdélégué*) had blocked that move (AMT BB 181). In May 1715 they finally got their tax and farmed it out to a contractor (AMT BB 186). They soon paid the consequences. Basville showed little patience with the capitouls' explanations and excuses for the trouble that ensued:

> I am very surprised that you were unable to find the means of quieting an assembly of thirty women. One has difficulty believing that the riot was not stimulated by the merchants or the artisans, since it served them perfectly. So it was women of the city's dregs, incited by persons of bad will who don't understand the true needs of the city? I think that if you had taken the trouble to install the tax-collector yourselves, as one might have expected you to, no disorder would have occurred; your very presence would have held back the little people, and they would have understood that a legitimate authority had established the tax.

Basville also blamed them for sending only a lieutenant and four soldiers to break up the crowd, and staying away themselves. They could, he pointed out, have sent the whole watch, called out the city militia ("composed of merchants and artisans, who will march willingly"), and asked for royal troops (AMT BB 188 31 May 1715). The capitouls got the message; a week later Basville was congratulating them, perhaps with a touch of acid, on "having done, this time, everything one might have expected from your zeal and attention for the public welfare" (AMT BB 188, 7 June 1715).

Somehow, when it came to food supply, those "women of the city's dregs" always got involved. On 30 November 1747, for example, Toulouse's women began the day's action by seizing three wagonloads of grain while another group organized the free distribution of grain that had been offered for sale in the market. Later in the day, crowds broke into the grain stores of merchants they accused of hoarding. For those events two men hanged, and the authorities whipped and imprisoned two women and gave others lesser punishments (d'Aldéguier 1830–1835: IV, 268–270; Bourderon 1954: 160–161; Viala 1909: 54–55; ADH C 2875, C 5419, C 6850).

In April 1773 the women of Toulouse again started the action. This time they went to the president of the parlement in a delegation sixty to eighty strong and demanded a reduction in bread prices. In subsequent action women threatened the president and the royal prosecutor with an invasion of grain stores, temporarily forced the capitouls to reduce the grain price from twenty to sixteen livres per sétier, and joined with the men of the civic militia in demanding the release of a woman arrested in the course of these encounters. In its declaration of 20 April the parlement intoned that "this conduct reveals a planned rebellion, which could have terrible consequences for public order, and would realize the fears of the people by keeping merchants from bringing their grain to market, because they could not do so safely" (ADHG C 316; cf. Bourderon 1953: 116 and 1954: 163; Viala 1909: 58–61).

Five years later, on 7, 8, and 9 June 1778, Toulouse compounded a similar series of events into its largest struggle over subsistances since Louis XIV's reign. This time, reported the intendant on 26 June,

> grain hadn't run out; it still hasn't. But it *is* dear. That dearness is the natural consequence of a famine year, the worst I've seen in twenty-eight years, and likewise of the greed of the owners of grain, of whom a number have been accused of hoarding. The capitouls thought they should quickly raise the price of bread ... that sudden rise probably caused some grumbling. But what reinforced it, and could be the chief cause, was the civic guard. (ADHG C 316)

The trouble with the civic guard actually began as trouble with the artisans in general. Despite urging, the archdiocesan vicars general refused to cancel the last two holidays of Pentecost so that workers could earn more bread. Instead they sent out an instruction authorizing only those who "had to work to live" to do business that day—for any proud master artisan, a clear invitation to close his shop or be considered poor. As a consequence, remarked the royal prosecutor, "the helpers and workmen who live on daily wages had no work and therefore no bread" (ADHG C 316, letter of 25 June 1778).

When the parsimonious capitouls refused to authorize a bread ration for the hungry artisans who mounted the city's guard, yet insisted that the artisans go on patrol, grumbling rose to a roar. One group of dissidents attacked a patrol that had mustered and marched. The parlement sought to keep things under control by issuing another edict forbidding public gatherings. The next evening a large public gathering, featuring the wives of artisans, formed in the square by the city hall. Some troops, including the city's regular watch, lined the square. That night's patrol and the fearful capitouls sheltered themselves inside the city hall. Outside, members of the crowd shouted against the patrol, the capitouls, and the high price of bread. They spoke of breaking into the city hall. As officials consulted and maneuvered, people began to stone those who entered and left the city hall. Then they stoned the watch. Members of the watch fired, killing a young woman and wounding four other people. At least one other person died in the subsequent fighting.

Small-Town Grain Seizures

Neither of these later events in Toulouse came close to a classic eighteenth-century grain seizure. A more typical scenario occurred at St.-Denis, near Mende. On 11 December 1749 local people gathered at the ringing of the church bell, when someone saw the leaseholder of the local benefice about to cart off his grain. They stoned him and his carters, keeping them from removing carts or grain from the parish (ADH C 1304). Sometimes the action included damage to the persons or property of people holding the food. But that was not essential. No matter that these were all actions that authorities themselves might well take when food was short; to most authorities the people's doing them qualified as "pillage" and "riot."

Classic grain seizures occurred mainly in villages and smaller towns rather than in great cities. In villages and smaller towns, because grain was more likely to be leaving a producing area full of food-buying people who felt they had a prior claim to the grain. In villages and smaller towns, because members of the community—including authorities—were more likely to agree that the local poor had an enforceable right to be fed before grain departed. Where the countryside contained many wageworkers (in agriculture, industry, or both at once), the local poor were numerous and were heavily dependent on the availability of grain at a fair price.

Consider the region of Albi in 1773. There, "the riots usually occur according to the same routine: one or several wagons pass, leaving a farm; a gathering forms; the people force the drivers to go back to where they came from, so the grain won't leave the community. Now and then, they sack the wagon" (Bourderon 1953: 111). Around Carcassonne, in the same year,

> at the end of spring the situation was marked, according to the consuls, by the threat of famine, high prices, and low wages. That situation, borne with difficulty until then (there had already been "alarms" in March) became all the more untenable when the merchants . . . created an artificial shortage at the very moment of the harvest by buying grain in the fields. It was then, when grain was not short, that revolt broke out: from 11 to 13 August workers, artisans, and women of Carcassonne rioted, stopped grain wagons, didn't pillage them, but demanded the setting of a reasonable price, which the consuls had no choice but to accept. (Bourderon 1953: 111)

Both around Albi and in Carcassonne, then, local "rioters" acted in place of local authorities to enforce community rules.

We gain some insight into community claims over food supply by looking at a conflict of June 1777 in Bastide-de-Besplas, in the Pyrenees foothills. There Descuns, a notary-lawyer of Rieux, owned a house occupied by his son-in-law Deprat. Descuns customarily sold all the grain raised on his land in Bastide-de-Besplas because it was too expensive to ship it to Rieux. In 1777 he sold the lot to Laverau, a merchant of nearby Montesquieu. "M. Laverau had taken part of my grain," complained Descuns,

> and had sold almost all of it to bakers of La Bastide. He came one day to take away a bit of mixed grain and some maize and settle his account with M. Deprat . . . when the whole populace gathered in front of my house, some with stones, others with staves and other forbidden weapons, and shouted at the tops of their lungs that they wanted to kill M. Laverau and burn my house. M. Deprat, having heard the noise, came to the door and asked them what they wanted. They repeated in a threatening tone that they wanted to kill M. Laverau and have the grain in my house and burn the house. (ADA 1 C 38, 7 July 1777)

At that, Deprat offered to sell them the grain, but no one wanted to pay his price. When Deprat closed the door on them "they didn't dare do anything." In this case it was apparently legitimate for Deprat to sell Descuns's grain and for Laverau to resell it—just so long as the local bakers received the grain. The trouble began when Laverau showed signs of removing maize, the poor people's food, from the community.

Over France as a whole, the old regime collapsed in the midst of a subsistence crisis, the crisis of 1788–1790. The shortage and price rise contributed to the regime's collapse at least by increasing the burden on a fiscally overloaded government; in place after place, the current administration's inability to cope with food shortage served as context or pretext for the "revolutionizing" of a community by throwing out some or all of the old powerholders, forming a revolutionary committee, and reorganizing the local system of control over food, manpower, and good citizenship.

The crisis was severe. In the Mediterranean section of Languedoc, for example, "the poor grain harvests of 1788–1791 coincided with the overproduction of wine . . . That double crisis led to a slowdown in domestic wool production, for woolen cloth sold badly. The peasants of Villemoustaussou, who lived partly from spinning and carding, were overwhelmed. At exactly the same time they were fighting with the lord over feudal rights. In 1789 the village had twice as many deaths as the previous year" (Godechot and Moncassin 1965: 33). Late in 1788 a report from Grenade declared that "three-quarters of the inhabitants, belonging to the class of agricultural laborers, have been in dire poverty since the end of summer" (Bastier 1975: 84). In Toulouse emergency measures began in July 1788. The municipality eventually bought 6,000 setiers of wheat, inventoried the grain on hand, subsidized the price of bread, and exercised close surveillance over the market (ADHG C 303, reports of 5 January, 10 July, and 30 July 1789). Even these measures were not enough to prevent grain seizures and demands for price controls in the suburbs of Toulouse (Viala 1909: 64–66).

During the revolutionary summer of 1789, grain seizures recurred through much of Languedoc. They took the classic forms, but with two innovations. First, people coupled their intervention in the food supply with attacks on landlords and widened resistance to taxes on food. Second, "for the first time, people in many localities succeeded in imposing fixed prices for bread and other commodities" (Bourderon 1953: 112). As they saw landlords and local authorities threatened from without by the national revolutionary movement, the ordinary people of Languedoc dared to challenge them from within.

Labor against Capital

Languedoc's regional division of labor sharpened during the eighteenth century. Lower Languedoc, the hinterland of Montpellier, grew more industrial, while Upper Languedoc, the hinterland of Toulouse, built its agricultural base. Within Lower Languedoc, Nîmes, the Cévennes, and the regions in between lost ground in silk manufacturing during the century's first half but regained in the second. Lodève and its own tributary area experienced an eighteenth-century boom in wool production. With the 1690s, exports of cloth to the Levant revived handsomely. From a royal decree of 1736 onward, the boom included a quasi-monopoly of cloth for French military uniforms. In the same region during the second half of the century, villagers began to spin and weave cotton from the Near East and the American South. The province's northern reaches, including the Cévennes and Vivarais, continued to combine herding, subsistence farming, and outwork for the textile industry. An anonymous pamphlet on agriculture in Lower Languedoc, published in Nîmes in 1787, praised hill people for their wisdom: "It is good for the people of Gévaudan, Velay, Vivarais, and Cévennes to take up manufacturing; but they have the sense to become manufacturers and farmers, depending on the season . . . They work the wool they have cut from their sheep, that their wives have washed and spun" (*Lettres* 1787:

5–6). Around Toulouse, meanwhile, large landlords involved themselves more and more heavily in the growing of grain for export, and city-oriented wine production expanded as well. If anything, Upper Languedoc became more exclusively agricultural than before.

The prosperity of the annual fair at Beaucaire, on Languedoc's side of the Rhône opposite Tarascon in Provence, signaled the importance of Languedoc's trade with Switzerland, Italy, and the Mediterranean. Over the century, indeed, the province's commerce was pivoting away from Lyon and toward Marseille. Increasing shipments of Lodève's woolen fabrics to the Ottoman Empire accelerated the shift to the Mediterranean. At least equally important was the flow of Toulousan wheat to Lower Languedoc and the Mediterranean; wheat traveled via great horse-drawn barges on the magnificent Canal du Midi. Increasing traffic on the canal and a fever of road construction throughout the province reflected a great commercialization of Languedoc's economy. As the economy commercialized, capital accumulated in agriculture and industry.

Within manufacturing, Languedoc witnessed increasing conflict between those workers and owners who wanted to overthrow cumbersome constraints on the use of labor and capital, and those who tried to use established corporate privileges to their own advantage. The 1750s brought an expansion of these struggles for and against the expansion of capitalism. In Nîmes the Molines brothers found themselves blocked by other merchants when they sought to weave a new, cheaper silk. In 1749 they managed to push authorization of the new process through Nîmes's assembly of silk manufacturers, but in March 1752 their competitors got the king's council to annul the assembly's decision. The Molines promptly opened a new shop in Uzès, out of Nîmes's jurisdiction. But the merchant-manufacturers of Nîmes sent an inspection team to Uzès, where the Molines' workers fought them off. The merchants of Nîmes had the workers prosecuted and forced Louis Molines to resign as one of their syndics (ADH 1309).

In general, nevertheless, entrepreneurs such as the Molines were gaining the advantage. A familiar capitalist idiom was forming within the apparently traditional system of guilds and royal regulations. Listen to the complaint of the sieur Roques, manufacturer of Carcassonne, against the menders of his city:

> The workers employed by manufacturers of woolens for the Levant, especially those of Carcassonne, have tried to wreck the trade by their inferior work, by their insubordination, and by their perpetual ambition—contrary to reason and justice—to place themselves on the same level as the manufacturers who own the cloth, who respond to the

workers' greed with goodwill, as if the workers shouldn't be subject to them, obey them by making the goods as the manufacturers ask them to, and pay the agreed-upon price in order to avoid confiscation of their merchandise and to maintain the trade's reputation for their own advantage and that of the state. To remedy the disorder that caused these workers' mutiny, the king's council issued an order on 18 October 1740 that the manufacturers could use whatever workers they wanted, masters or not, in their homes and shops. (ADH C 1308)

The menders of Carcassonne had fought off Roques's use of cheap labor by having goods seized in his shop. But the forward-looking intendant ruled in Roques's favor, and against the menders.

Entrepreneurs were not the only ones to take the initiative. Workers sometimes defended themselves against the risks of unemployment by attempting to maintain local monopolies in their segments of the labor market. In 1775 coopers in Sète demanded the expulsion of foreign workers from the city; when authorities didn't act fast enough for them, they attacked outside workers on their own (ADH C 6665). The increasingly frequent battles between groups of journeymen from rival orders likewise involved the effort to enforce labor-market monopolies; the confrontations between the rival journeymen's guilds of Gavots and Dévorants at Annonay in August and September 1788, for instance, concerned access to textile employment in the town.

In between agriculture and industry, the same complex play of capital and privilege went on. Near Alès, the viscount Bréard had joined the merchant Tubeuf in acquiring mining rights. But in 1784 armed peasants opened up their own mines and resisted attempts to expel them. Bréard and Tubeuf called in royal troops to enforce their monopoly (ADH C 6691).

Sometimes similar struggles broke out in the capitalized (and therefore proletarianized) sectors of agricultural production, notably winegrowing. In 1778 local laborers attacked the "mountaineers" who arrived in Méze, as usual, for summer work in the vineyards. After one such attack, on 2 July, Bouliech, a consul, tried to arrest a certain Henrie. Other laborers ganged up on him and freed Henrie. When the Maréchaussée arrived, the locals somehow arranged to have the wounded mountaineer taken off to jail. In requesting the arrest of the laborers involved, Bouliech pointed out that "we pay the local laborers forty to fifty sous a day, and they have boasted that they will get rid of all the mountaineers, since then they can force us to pay them an ecu a day. That would keep us from winegrowing, which provides the chief income making it possible for local people to pay the taille" (ADH C 6666). Such an argument had obvious appeal for royal officials.

Royal officials often joined disputes over wages and capital whether they wanted to or not. At Montredon, near St.-Pons, poor local people had begun working wool for the better-paying merchants of Bédarieux in 1751. The merchants of St.-Pons, however, sent a royal inspector to force the people of Montredon to work for them, at lower wages. The inspector received a gunshot wound for his trouble (ADH C 1308).

In the agricultural sector landlords, merchants, and collectors of rents in kind gained handsomely. From the 1720s to the 1780s, the comfortable canons of Toulouse's St.-Sernin saw a doubling of their tithe and a quadrupling of their seigneurial dues from land in the surrounding area (Frêche 1974: 533). Almost everywhere, especially in agricultural areas, land moved increasingly into noble and bourgeois hands as the number of landless people grew far faster than the population as a whole. Concentration, however, went much further in the vicinity of Toulouse than around Montpellier. In Montpellier's region, peasant smallholders remained numerous; they invested an effort in olives and especially grapes, which compensated for the small sizes of their plots. While the bourgeois of Montpellier and other commercial towns became dominant landlords in the nearby plains, peasants predominated in the rougher *garrigues*. Nowhere were the clergy important landholders. Nor did nobles predominate anywhere (Soboul 1958: 23–29).

Around Toulouse, country people had a different experience. In the village of Léguevin, eighteen kilometers from Toulouse, by 1782 bourgeois—especially bourgeois of Toulouse—owned 56.5 percent of the land (Aragon 1972: 443). In a sample of seven localities spread through Upper Languedoc:

> the exodus of nobles to the cities, the growth and settlement of a resident bourgeoisie ... the concentration of trade, the decline of rural artisans, the recession of smallholding farmers in favor of sharecropping and, increasingly, of operation by stewards around the cities and along the Canal du Midi in the Lauragais, the rapid rise of agricultural wageworkers between 1695 and 1734, then their stabilization at that high level, are the fault lines of the region's evolution.   (Frêche 1974: 351)

In the region of Toulouse, landlords increasingly sought to squeeze new income from their estates by using the courts. The court of Toulouse's seneschal saw two waves of lawsuits during the eighteenth century. The first began in the 1730s, when the great lords of the parlement and other rich landholding families used the excuse of unpaid feudal dues to reorganize and expand their fiefs. After 1750, and especially in the 1780s, "the great feudal litigants were bourgeois or members of the military nobility" (Bastier 1975: 293). The bourgeois were on the offensive, expanding their holdings and insisting on their privileges. The military nobles were more often on the defensive, trying to patch together enough income to survive in a time of rising prices. Lawsuits proliferated mainly in the wheat-growing hinterland of Toulouse, rather than in the less commercialized agricultural regions of Castres or Carcassonne (Bastier 1975: 290–291).

Despite the use of feudal dues as a wedge, the increasing prominence of city-dwelling noble landlords did not depend on them. Neither as a share of seigneurial income nor as a part of peasant expenses were those dues generally substantial in the region of Toulouse (Bastier 1975: 258–279). Instead, the city dwellers—noble and bourgeois alike—drew the bulk of their land-based income from rents paid them by their tenants. Everywhere, wealthy city dwellers increased their hold on rural land.

Toulouse, especially, grew fat on the returns from its agricultural hinterland. Toulouse's merchants and rentiers built the elegant neighborhoods that remind us today of the city's eighteenth-century greatness. During the later eighteenth century, they gave the Capitole a new facade, built graceful walks and quais along the Garonne, laid out new squares, and lined them with their own townhouses. The great costs of embellishing the city and linking it to the rest of France via splendid new roads ultimately came from the labor of Languedoc's rural people. Rents and taxes paid the way.

Within the city, inequality increased. It was not so much the nobility as the bourgeoisie who gained. In samples of dowries drawn from the city's marriage records for 1749 and 1785, the average increase for the whole population was 60 percent. The "upper bourgeoisie," however, increased its dowries by 133 percent between the two dates. If we compute a simple index of inequality in wealth for the categories nobility, upper bourgeoisie, petty bourgeoisie, upper working class, and lower working class in the two years, the index is 60.8 in 1749 and 67.4 in 1785. Inequality, already sharp in 1749, increased notably between then and 1785 (computed from tables in Godechot and Moncassin 1965; the "index of inequality," roughly speaking, represents the proportion of the total wealth that would have to be moved in order to make all categories equal. Godechot and Moncassin, it is only fair to add, do not compute the index, and interpret their evidence as showing no significant change.)

Although the bourgeoisie was gaining, the landowning nobility still towered over the city's wealth. Toulouse housed "the most aristocratic parlement in France" (Wolff 1974: 346). The members of the parlement held the city's greatest fortunes and attracted other well-heeled nobles into their society. The average noble income, Robert Forster has estimated, "might be fixed at 8,000 livres, (5,000 from the land and 3,000 from offices and *rentes*). In 1789, 8,000 livres was two to three times the revenue of a prosperous merchant, a retired bourgeois, or a successful lawyer at Toulouse" (Forster 1960: 175-176). It was also, he has noted, some sixteen times the income of a skilled artisan, and sixty times the wage of a farm overseer. Yet a farm overseer (a *maître-valet*) cut a powerful, prosperous figure among the mass of poor agricultural workers.

Most likely the wealthiest person in Toulouse at the end of the old regime was the former attorney of the parlement, Jean Gabriel Aimable Alexandre de Riquet de Bonrepos. He was, as the name Riquet might suggest, an heir of the seventeenth-century entrepreneur and tax-farmer who built the Canal du Midi. Of his 1.3 million livres in wealth, a full 900,000 consisted of almost a one-fourth interest in the canal. But the rest consisted of landed property: not only the chateau of Bonrepos from which he drew his noble name, but also another chateau and seven rent-earning farms outside Toulouse (Sentou 1969: 86-87).

As the case of Riquet indicates, the distinction between "noble" and "bourgeois" wealth ultimately made less difference in Toulouse than the grand titles suggest. Toulouse's bourgeois drew their wealth from land management and agricultural commerce, not from manufacturing. If they helped to create a proletariat, that happened mainly in the country, not in the city around them. For the successful bourgeois, the path of honors led to the nobility via the Capitoulat or a purchased office. The nobles themselves drew their revenues from the growing market for grain. Nobles were, in some ways, the more active capitalists: commercializing agriculture, proletarianizing the peasantry, calculating their advantage in terms of the market price. Languedoc's fundamental divisions did not set off an "advanced" urban-industrial world from a "backward" rural-agricultural world. They set labor against capital.

Struggles over Land

Advances of capitalism and capitalists into the countryside stimulated Languedoc's greatest struggles of the later eighteenth century. Grain seizures represented one form of the conflict, resistance to landlords' profiteering and aggrandizement another. Sometimes whole communities aligned themselves against landlords or—more often—their agents. Around Sommières, the "consuls, syndics, and principal inhabitants" of eight villages pleaded against Joubert, treasurer of Languedoc and leaseholder of the barony of Montredon. Joubert wanted, they said, to use a decree he had obtained in 1786 to "deprive them of pasture for their animals in the wastes and common lands, of wood for heating . . . of bushes and useless trees for the fertilization and improvement of their plowland" despite immemorial usage and incontestable right (AN H^1 1105, letter of 19 February 1788). The royal government, however, decided to leave that touchy case to the lower courts (AN H^1 1105, notes).

In Juvinas (Vivarais), the local peasants suffered fifteen years of cheating from Gilles Arzellier, overseer for the marquise de Choisinet. Using his skills as notary and small-town lawyer, he forged documents, manipulated feudal dues, foreclosed on notes acquired at a discount from other lenders and landlords, and held on to land ceded temporarily in payment of debts. Eventually his victims began a campaign of terror against Arzellier's own tenants and succeeded in driving them away. In August 1762 a band of twenty men burned his farms, barred the doors and windows of his house, set it afire, ran him down when he escaped, cut and shot him, then buried him beneath a cairn. Unfortunately for his assassins, Arzellier was still alive; he survived to have the band's leaders broken on the wheel in Aubenas (N. Castan 1980b: 79–80).

In 1783, similarly, the people of St.-Sardos, near Toulouse, ended a decade of increasing pressure by Castera, leaseholder of the tithe and other dues owed to the chapter of Sarlat (Périgord). By threatening him, stoning his wife, surrounding his house, refusing lodging to his bailiffs and wagons to his carters, breaking wagons brought in from outside, sacking his barn, then refusing to inform on each other, the local people succeeded in blocking the collection of the tithe (N. Castan 1980b: 69–70).

This action by full-fledged peasants, however, was unusual. In Languedoc—especially in the region of Toulouse—poor farmers and landless agricultural laborers seem to have spearheaded the attacks on landlords and their agents. Restrictions on hunting rights and on use of common lands produced the sharpest grievances. In 1782 the mayor and consuls of Lacaune asked the subdelegate of Castres to enforce the provincial rules against the keeping of goats in the forest. When the subdelegate marched into the woods with the mayor, a "multitude of women and children" stoned them, "shouting all sorts of nonsense." The women's husbands, reported the official, were off hiding the goats. The next day, when he and the municipal officers went to visit the homes of the culprits, they found neither people nor goats. Eventually the intendant, the subdelegate's superior, decided that

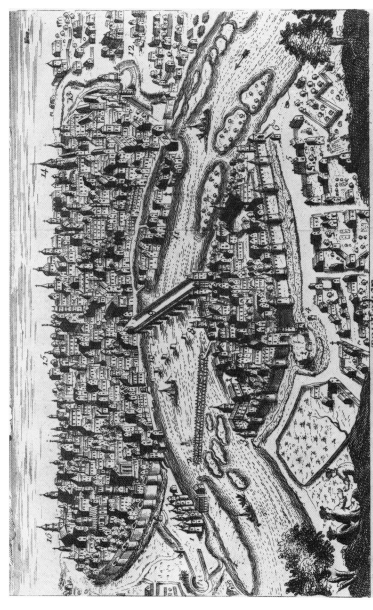

Fig. 17. Toulouse in the eighteenth century

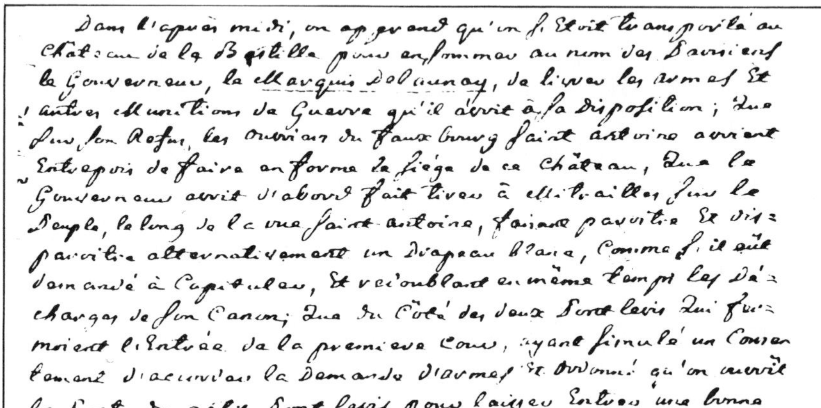
Dans l'après midi, on apprend qu'on s'étoit transporté au Chateau de la Bastille pour ensommer au nom des Parisiens le Gouverneur, le Marquis Delaunay, de livrer les armes Et autres Munitions de Guerre qu'il avoit à sa disposition; Que sur son Refus, les ouvriers du fauxbourg saint antoine avoient Entrepris de faire en forme le siège de ce Château, Que le Gouverneur avoit d'abord fait tirer à Mitrailles sur le Peuple, le long de la rue saint antoine, faisant paroître Et dis=paroître alternativement un drapeau blanc, Comme s'il eût demandé à Capituler, Et redoublant en même tems les dé=charges de son Canon; Que du Côté des deux Ponts levis qui fer=moient l'Entrée de la premiere Cour, ayant simulé un Consen=tement d'accorder la Demande d'armes Et ordonné qu'on ouvrît la Porte du petit Pont levis pour laisser Entrer une bonne partie de Ceux qui s'y trouvoient, la Porte refermée Et le Pont levis Remonté, il avoit fait fusiller toutes les Personnes qui occupoient la premiere Cour, parmi lesquelles se trouvoient trois Electeurs venus de l'hôtel de ville pour Traiter avec lui; dont le sieur abbé fauchet Prédicateur du Roi; Mais qu'alors la Milice Bourgeoise qui occupoit le dehors indignée d'un Procédé aussi Barbare envers ses Concitoyens dont Elle Entendoit les Cris, Et secondée par des Grenadiers du Régiment des Gardes françoises dont un surtout avoit eu le Courage de monter le premier à l'assaut, aussitôt des Echelles Posées Et une Breche faite du Côté des Ponts-levis, avoit Consommé la Prise du Château en moins de trois heures, Ce Château vainement attaqué par Henri IV Et Louis XIV qui n'avoient pu s'en Emparer, tué ~~deux~~ Canonniers, ~~saisi le Gouverneur le sieur Chevalier Dupujet Lieutenant de Roi~~ et le Major, Enfin saisi le Gouverneur Qu'Elle avoit Conduit en-

Fig. 18. Hardy's description of the taking of the Bastille goats in forests were the business of the forest wardens, not of his staff (AN H[1] 1102). Wherever landlords enclosed meadows and woods, they faced the rage and subversion of poor people who now had no place to pasture their animals (N. Castan 1980a: 83).

With the start of the Revolution, plenty of rural people found their chances for revenge. Languedoc had its own attacks on castles. In 1790

> crowds formed and damage occurred at Blaye, Cuq, and Rosières; a crowd armed with rifles, pistols, and staves broke into the court of the chateau of Saussenac, belonging to the marquis de La Prune–Montbrun. A farmer broke the storehouse doors with a hammer; in less than an hour, the crowd emptied the storehouse and took away 318 hectoliters of grain. A leader took people through the living areas as they seized furniture, linen, and draperies; the leader broke into the archives and used the marquis' books and papers to light a fire in the salon. He carefully unfolded a folio book marked with a red stripe, saying there were no longer any seigneurs. The following day, the rioters sacked the chateaux of La Ganterie and Mir. (Bastier 1975: 304)

The absent marquis had prosecuted one of the crowd's leaders for poaching.

Thus the nobles and bourgeois who had been closing the forests and wastes, punishing the hunting and gathering by which poor families supplemented their incomes, and pushing their estates for more and more revenue found the poor in both a mood and a position to retaliate. The poor people's Revolution did not last long. Languedoc's poor people lacked the bourgeois allies who sustained their counterparts in other, more revolutionary, regions. But while the poor people's movement lasted, it vented grievances accumulated during a century of advancing agricultural capitalism.

At the start of the century, in the time of Lamoignon de Basville, the state's conquest of Languedoc had still faced serious obstacles. If puissant Protestant patrons had disappeared, their onetime clients had kept the will to resist. Another half-century of coercion, persuasion, and conciliation brought them, too, into an uneasy modus vivendi that accepted the state's priority. Aside from the Camisards, none of the fierce fiscal, municipal, regional, or dynastic rebellions that had marked Languedoc's seventeenth century recurred in the eighteenth. Resistance to the state's expansion fragmented and declined. Although students, youth groups, and local factions continued to fight their battles, they fought within the perimeter of a well-established state.

The weight of conflict shifted toward problems posed by capitalist property relations. The grain seizure, the struggle between merchants and artisans, the attempt of workers to exclude others from their local labor markets, the resistance of smallholders and agricultural laborers to landlords came to dominate Languedoc's contention. Increasingly the development of capitalism, rather than the forced growth of the state, set the rhythms and terms of popular collective action.

7 ⌒⌒

Statemaking, Capitalism, and Contention

I N 1698 LAMOIGNON DE BASVILLE was by no means the only in
tendant to describe his province for the instruction of the duke o
Burgundy. Almost every intendant set deputies and clients in motion tc
help prepare a memoir for the king and his heir apparent. Miromesnil, intendant of the generality of Tours, had to report on its three subdivisions:
Touraine, Maine, and Anjou. Of Anjou, he observed that its trade "consists
of supplies people gather in the countryside, of cattle (of which the whole
province provides a large number to adjacent provinces), and of a few items
people make here" (AN H^1 1588^{12}). Miromesnil saw the trade of Angers—
mainly textiles—in a warmer light. Angers's woolen industry linked the city
with its sheep-raising hinterland.

City and country had other important bonds in Anjou. Production and
sale of "white wines in great abundance" connected Saumur and other Loire
Valley cities to nearby vineyards. Stock-fattening tied cattle-market towns
such as Beaupréau both to the farms of the Bocage and to larger cities outside Anjou. Finally, cottage linen production, attached small commercial
towns such as Cholet or Château-Gontier at once to daily farm life and to
the Atlantic trade of La Rochelle, Nantes, and St.-Malo. Small mines of coal
and iron dotted the landscape. Nevertheless, the Anjou of 1698 turned in
on itself more than did Languedoc, Burgundy, the Ile-de-France, or
Flanders.

From a political point of view, likewise, Anjou was less impressive than
most other provinces: no Estates, no parlement, relatively few great nobles

to protect or exploit the province. Except for the deplorable weakness of taxable trade, Anjou was a statemaker's ideal, docile province.

Ferrant, intendant of Burgundy, portrayed his region as more widely connected than Anjou. The duke of Burgundy, the prince of Condé, and their clients gave the province strong ties to the royal court. Active Estates, a moderately independent parlement, and municipalities with vestiges of autonomy gave Burgundy, in theory, the means of mounting respectful opposition to the crown.

Furthermore, the province had some commercial interest. "This beautiful province," rhapsodized Ferrant,

> produces plenty of everything essential: grain, wine, fodder. There are forests, tree farms, mines, and iron forges. The soil for grain-growing is not the same quality in all of Burgundy. The districts [*bailliages*] of Chalon, Beaune, Dijon, Auxonne, St. Jean-de-Lône, and Verdun, and more generally all the lowlands down to the Saône, consist of good wheat land, where it usually isn't even necesary to use fertilizer. Most of the land can even grow wheat, barley, and oats in alternation. There are also turnips, which are in the ground only four or five months before being harvested, thus leaving the earth free for seeding in grain. The land can therefore produce three harvests in two years.
>
> The other districts—Autun, Auxois, Brionnais, Châtillon-sur-Seine—are called mountain areas. Even the Mâconnais and part of the Charollais have only light soil and produce little but rye, albeit in great quantity.
>
> Burgundy also produces plenty of high-quality wine. Some of it goes for export: wine from Beaune goes by road to the region of Liège, to Germany, to Flanders, and even to England.   (AN H[1] 1588[16])

Like Anjou, then, Burgundy remained overwhelmingly an agricultural region. There were two basic differences: First, the province had a heavier involvement than Anjou in international markets. Second, it devoted much of its effort to just two valuable cash crops: wheat and wine.

Flanders looked different from either Anjou or Burgundy. The "Flanders" of 1698 consisted mainly of lands that Louis XIV had recently seized from the Spanish; some of the territory, in fact, later returned to the Low Countries. Three different intendants—those of Maritime (or Flemish) Flanders, of Walloon Flanders, and of Hainaut—divided the territory and the task of reporting on it. Ypres, Lille, and Mons served as capitals of the three generalities. Armies had been warring back and forth across the region for decades, and diplomats were then plotting ways to gain, or regain, permanent control of its rich resources.

Many of Flanders' people spoke Flemish. Some spoke Spanish as well. They drank beer and supported the Catholic church faithfully. These traits separated them from much of France. Yet they differed most from the people of other provinces in being active and successful in trade.

Lille acted as centerpiece to all this activity. "The city of Lille," observed intendant Dugué de Bagnols, "is the one that keeps all the others in motion. It is, so to speak, the soul of the whole region's trade, since the wealth of its inhabitants permits them to start big projects. This city's strength is hard to believe. Surely more than 100,000 people in the countryside and neighboring cities live on Lille's business" (AN H[1] 1588[22]; although Dugué de Bagnols signed the report, the principal author appears to have been Jean Godefroy, a high official of Lille's royal courts, and the intendant's frequent collaborator: Trénard 1977c: 17).

What *was* Lille's business? That was the point: it included both an active manufacturing complex (especially textiles) and the trade sustained by an agriculture the likes of which did not exist elsewhere. "The effort of country people," wrote Dugué de Bagnols and Godefroy, "plays a large part. I dare say there is hardly a land anywhere in the world where people work so hard" (AN H[1] 1588[22]). Both small-scale textile production and cash-crop agriculture occupied the bourgeois, peasants, and landless laborers of the countryside. In peacetime, furthermore, a large share of the goods produced in Lille's region flowed across the frontier to cities of the Low Countries, and thence into world markets.

To the northwest, in Flemish Flanders, dairying and stock raising involved a larger share of the population. Military and naval activity also counted. Flemish Flanders had five fortified cities: Ypres, Furnes, Dunkerque, Bergues, and Gravelines. Of them, Dunkerque was an important port, and a major base for buccaneers—although the intendant left that point unstated. Instead, he offered a character sketch:

> The Flemish are plump and good-looking, naturally slow, but rather hard-working when it comes to farming, manufacturing, or trade; no nation knows its trade better than they do. They like to drink together and to strike bargains a glass in hand. Like the ancient Belgians they are great lovers of liberty and enemies of servitude. You can win them over more easily by charm than by force. They get angry and make up easily, loving and hating in a manner quite different from our own. They aren't very sensitive in love or hate, consoling themselves in hardship by saying that something worse could have happened. They have intelligence and good sense without being witty. That is why people find them rough and stupid in conversation. Yet they are clever in business,

which they think through carefully, and sometimes fool those who think they are cleverer.   (AN H[1] 1588[20])

The intendant apparently spoke from experience.

To the southeast, in Hainaut, mining of coal and iron constituted the region's "greatest wealth" (BN Fr 22221). Here, the intendant offered one of the few complaints against the region's peasants: as mine operators, they left something to be desired; they lacked the capital to get at the less accessible seams of coal. "Richer and more intelligent people," thought intendant Voysin, could bring in machines to extract all the coal. Nevertheless he gave Hainaut's people high ratings for their devotion to work, especially in view of the repeated ravages they had recently suffered from French-Spanish wars (BN Fr 22221).

All three expert observers of Flanders in 1698 described the region as industrious, prosperous, and eminently commercial. Yet there were some differences between the two Flanders, on the one side, and Hainaut, on the other. The two intendants from Flanders could quickly dispose of clergy and nobility. They were few and unimportant in Flanders. As Dugué de Bagnols/Godefroy said for his immediate vicinity, "The province of Lille is a commercial area. It is therefore hardly surprising that there are few nobles" (AN H 1588[22]). The reasoning applied almost as well to the clergy. In Hainaut, Voysin reported more noble landlords—especially "Spanish" nobles holding land on both sides of the international frontier—as well as more substantial church property. Nevertheless even Hainaut had fairly modest landowners by national standards. These intendants were administering areas populated by commoners and run by bourgeois.

The generality of Paris also had more than its share of commerce but operated quite differently from Flanders. Intendant Phélypeaux gave the generality outside of Paris 857,000 people. Another 500,000, he said, lived in the central city. No other generality of France approached its 40 percent of city dwellers (Dupâquier 1979: 195–197; the 40 percent includes Paris). The rest of the region served the capital: truck farming close at hand, Versailles and the court at arm's length, regions of wheat growing, winegrowing, and noble residences over much of the remaining territory. Outside Paris and its immediate surroundings, manufacturing had no more than local importance. The description of Provins in 1698 will serve, *mutatis mutandis,* for all the generality: "The élection's only trade is in grain that goes by wagon to Port-Montain, on the Seine two leagues from Provins. These people load it on to boats for shipment to Paris. There used to be a woolen industry in Provins, but it collapsed because of lawsuits between the merchant drapers and the weavers. The weavers' guild is strong in Provins and makes good linsey-woolseys, which sell in nearby cities" (BN Fr 22205). In many versions, the story repeated itself throughout the generality of Paris. It came down to the consolidation of an economy committed to the great city's needs.

The generality had no Estates of its own. But it more than made up for that lack: Paris and its hinterland had the country's preeminent parlement, a proudly autonomous municipality, a massive religious establishment, and the chief instruments of national government. "The generality of Paris is the most important in the kingdom," crowed Phélypeaux (BN Fr 22205). If its nobles had long since lost most of their power as seigneurs of individual parishes in the Ile-de-France, and if they treated their many country houses as places of entertainment and recreation rather than as seats of power, the great concentration of noble, bourgeois, and ecclesiastical landlords in the capital still gave the region as a whole tremendous weight.

In drafting his report on Languedoc, intendant Basville portrayed his province as a predominantly agricultural region on its way to becoming industrial. Expanding the textile industry would, he thought, "give the peoples of Languedoc a new activity; they progress by means of this sort of work, and the province can better support itself this way than by agriculture, since the greater part of the land is sterile" (AN H^1 1588^{26}). As of 1698, the greatest recent progress had appeared in the sale of woolens, especially fine woolens, to the Levant via Marseille. Basville described the tough French competition with the English and especially the Dutch for that profitable trade. The French, he boasted, were gaining.

Inside the kingdom, woolen goods of Lodève, controlled by merchants of Lyon, clothed both soldiers and civilians. Trade in silk goods, according to Basville, was likewise relatively new—no more than sixty years old as a significant item of production—and growing. This trade, too, operated under Lyon's direction. The silk trade, commented Basville, "always decreases greatly in wartime, because people spend less on furniture and clothes, and because in peacetime we send a good deal of silk goods to England and Holland. The wool trade, in contrast, increases in wartime because of the large number of troops there are to clothe" (AN H^1 1588^{26}).

Basville even saw industry in Toulouse's future. "No city in the kingdom," he claimed, "is better located for trade and manufacturing" (AN H^1 1588^{26}). After all, he reasoned, food was cheap, supplies for manufacturing were abundant, and the city had superb access to waterways. He had to admit, however, that as of 1698 "there is little trade. The inhabitants' spirit takes them in other directions. They can't stand outsiders. Monasteries and nunneries take up half the city. The fact that becoming a capitoul makes one noble puts an additional brake on the growth of trade. The same goes for the parlement. All the children of big merchants would rather live as nobles or take on public office than continue their father's business" (AN H[1] 1588[26]). In fact only the trade in French wheat and Spanish wool kept Toulouse from being a commercial desert. One had to go to Carcassonne and to the cities of Lower Languedoc—Montpellier, Nîmes, Lodève—for the sort of commercial spirit that warmed an intendant's heart and filled his coffers.

The rich wheat production of Toulouse's plain, for all its concern to Basville in crisis years, didn't enter his vision of the future. Nor did Basville consider the influence of Lyon and Marseille, or the relative unattractiveness of the landscape for agriculture, as likely *causes* of Lower Languedoc's industrial development. Basville saw Languedoc's regional variations clearly. In thirteen years of vigorous administration he had studied his province well. But he looked hardest at the variations that affected the success of his mission, and attributed them chiefly to differences in the leading inhabitants' spirit of enterprise.

The intendants of our five regions, then, described provinces that contrasted in important ways: with respect to the importance of trade, the prominence of cities, the extent of manufacturing, the strength of the regional nobility, the autonomy of provincial institutions. At one extreme: Anjou, with fairly weak provincial institutions, no great magnates, little manufacturing, relatively little commercial agriculture. At the other: Flanders, the very emblem of commercialization in agriculture and manufacturing, just coming under the power of the French crown, still quite distinctive in administration and fiscal structure.

If Anjou and Flanders defined the limits, however, the Ile-de-France, Burgundy, and Languedoc each marked off their own special spaces: the Ile-de-France for sheer power and wealth; Burgundy for its fine wines and great nobles; Languedoc for its Protestants, its commercial involvement in the Mediterranean world, its relatively vigorous and autonomous municipal institutions, and its sharp internal divisions. In the two dimensions of involvement with capitalism and subordination to the national state, the five regions occupied very different positions.

Capital and State Power in Languedoc

The eighteenth century pushed all five regions further along both dimensions: toward increased involvement in capitalism, toward greater subordination to the state. In France as a whole, both agricultural and industrial production commercialized as they increased in volume. The share of manufacturing rose. Capital accumulated, the proportion of wageworkers grew, and—at least for such people as day-laborers and ordinary construction workers—real wages declined. Those changes summed to the general advance of capitalism.

Capitalism grew differently in each region: through the expansion of wool and wheat trades in Languedoc, through the expansion of rural textile production and winegrowing in Anjou, through wine and wheat in Burgundy, through industrial growth in Flanders, through the increasing commercial activity of Paris in the Ile-de-France. Likewise, the relations between capitalist markets and peasant communities differed from region to region. In eighteenth-century Burgundy and Languedoc landlords were actively playing the capitalist game: consolidating property, squeezing out the rights of small peasants, reestablishing old dues, shifting to the most profitable cash crops. In Flanders great landlords had disappeared. Large peasants themselves had exceptional strength, although they had to defend their strength against both the region's bourgeoisie and the local landless.

In Anjou and Ile-de-France large landlords had long since snuffed out the privileges of peasant communities; the fact that in Anjou those landlords were largely absentee nobles and in the Ile-de-France often commoners is quite secondary. The largest difference between the two regions lay in the fact that the cash-crop farmers of the Ile-de-France were producing for an immense, hungry, growing, grasping metropolis, while their Angevin counterparts continued to grow their crops largely for export from the region. The growers of the Ile-de-France's great winefield shifted perceptibly to cheaper varieties for that mass market during the eighteenth century (Lachiver 1982: 132–173).

As capital increased, concentrated, and grew in power, its advances stimulated conflict. Holders of small capital fought off manipulation by holders of large capital, workers struggled with capitalists, and—most of all—people whose lives depended on communal or other noncapitalist property relationships battled others who tried to extend capitalist property into those domains. They battled over rights to land, food, and labor. The eighteenth-century prevalence of the grain seizure expressed the struggle against merchant capital on the local scale. The rise of worker-worker and worker-owner conflicts bespoke the increasing importance of industrial capital and the increasing size of the industrial proletariat. As the eighteenth century wore on, the intensifying confrontation between landlords and peasants as well as between landlords and the rural poor followed the landlords' attempts to profit from exclusive capitalist property rights in the land.

Statemaking likewise entered a new phase: after repeated seventeenth-century challenges to the state's very survival, the eighteenth century brought consolidation. Instead of settling their troops on the land, intendants increasingly taxed the civilian population to pay for military expenses and segregated soldiers from that population. Instead of great regional rebellions and major claimants to national power, intendants found themselves facing dispersed resistance, village by village. Instead of dispatching armies to cow the people of a city or a region, intendants laid down a dense net of agents and collaborators. Louis XV felt sufficiently confident of his power in the provinces to use wholesale exile as a way of controlling uncooperative officials and parlements; in the seventeenth century, exiling powerful enemies had invited regional rebellion. Taxes themselves routinized; the crown not only built up a corps of professional revenue officers but also avoided the imposition of new taxes and eschewed taxes of dubious legality. A fortified, bureaucratized fiscal structure became the framework of the whole state. The state's very success generated illegal activity, such as the smuggling of salt, which paradoxically assumed the state's existence; without the state's effort to make money by monopolizing salt, the price would have been too low to entice smugglers.

State control grew unevenly, consolidating past gains in Anjou, Burgundy, and the Ile-de-France while extending dramatically in Languedoc and Flanders. In Anjou ordinary people witnessed the consolidation of state power in the form of tightened tax collection, increased regulation of industrial production, more stringent control of smuggling, and, supremely, promotion of the grain trade at the expense of local demands for food. In Burgundy the state likewise appeared as a promoter of marketing and collector of taxes. But there the state also made itself known as the enemy of parlementary power.

In the Ile-de-France people found the state invading everyday life. At least in Paris, police powers expanded significantly: agents of the state closed in on previously inviolable "free spaces" such as Templars' Yard (l'enclos du Temple), required householders to light their streets, arrested beggars and vagabonds as never before, organized syndicates of many trades in order better to supervise and tax them. Jean de la Mare's great handbook *Traité de la police,* published for the first time by 1720, summed up the precedents and practices of the new, intense surveillance. By the 1780s Sébastien Mercier was writing of an impressively dense and persistent spy network: "A suspect is followed so closely that his most trivial doings are known, right up to the moment when it's convenient to arrest him" (Mercier 1906 [1783]: 182). Speaking of the increasingly powerful *lieutenant de police,* however, he concluded that controlling the city's hungry masses was a thankless task: "It is a terrible and difficult job to control so many men in the grip of famine while they see others swimming in abundance; to hold back so many miserable people, pale and undone, around our palaces and splendid dwellings, while gold, silver, and diamonds fill those same dwellings, so that they are mightily tempted to break in and ease the want that is killing them" (Mercier 1906 [1783]: 195).

From the perspective of the mighty, the maintenance of public order consisted largely in the containment of desperate and hungry people. The grain seizure, in that perspective, was simply the collective version of everyday individual property crime. But the ruling-class vision of the poor had its complement in poor people's vision of the high and mighty: with the heightened royal control of grain markets grew the popular idea that high officials, perhaps including the king himself, were building a grain monopoly in order to reap the enormous profits speculation could bring. With some justice, the eighteenth-century state gained a reputation as interfering and profiteering.

Yet, among our five regions, it was in Languedoc and Flanders that state power expanded most rapidly. Languedoc's intendants strove to subordinate municipalities, the parlement, and the Estates to the crown's needs. In Flanders, royal agents sought to eliminate the privileges and special status recent conquest had given the region. On balance, the crown made great gains.

Relative to an expanding economy, however, the eighteenth-century state's demands rose much less than they had under Louis XIII and Louis XIV. Exhibit 4 expresses the national tax burden in terms of hectoliters of wheat per person per year; it divides taxes into direct and indirect (not only excise, customs, and the like, but also other incidental sources) and indicates the years in which France was involved in international wars. It was still true, on the whole, that taxes rose with international war; yet even that effect attenuated as the crown relied increasingly on longer-term loans for military expenditure. Only Napoleon's great wars after 1800 reestablished the dramatic, immediate connection between warmaking and tax increases. In real cost per capita, direct taxes actually declined slightly over the century. The fluctuations and increases concentrated on indirect sources of revenue. It is as if the king had learned how much resistance he could stir up by increasing taxes on land and property, and had shifted to taxes on trade and transactions.

Contrary to beliefs on both sides of the English Channel, French people at the end of the eighteenth century were less heavily taxed than their British neighbors. Exhibit 5 shows the evolution of taxation in Great Britain and France from 1715 to 1808, expressed as a share of income per capita. The two countries began at about the same levels. But in these terms, France's tax burden per capita declined, while—if we include Britain's enormous expenses in the Napoleonic wars—British taxes doubled their share of per capita income. During the eighteenth century the British state grew faster than the economy. In France the opposite was true.

Revenues probably came in more easily in Britain than in France; the British economy was more commercialized than the French, and the British collected a much higher share of the total as indirect taxes. Nevertheless it is worth remembering that in 1765 the Stamp Act, a tax measure designed to help pay for the debt accumulated by the Seven Years' War, not only incited widespread resistance in Britain but also precipitated the first stages of Britain's most important eighteenth-century rebellion: the American Revolution.

Then the wheel turned. Despite the relatively rapid growth of the French economy, the crown's ineffectual efforts to cope with the debt accumulated from the Seven Years' War and the American war precipitated its

Exhibit 4.   National tax revenue in hectoliters of wheat per capita, 1715–1808 (Mathias and O'Brien 1976)

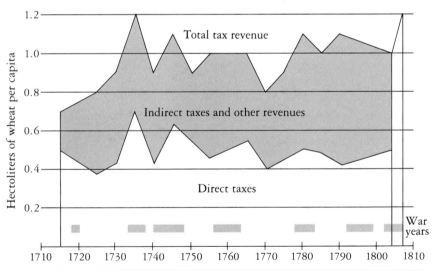

great struggles with the parlements during the 1770s and 1780s. They eventually led to the calling of the Estates General in 1789. That convocation opened the way to France's own revolution.

Economic growth and taxes obviously varied from one region to another. By the third quarter of the century, the distribution of agricultural production and tax burden was much as shown in Table 4. (By this time, war and ensuing treaties had once again changed the frontier; the generalities of Lille and Valenciennes now constituted Flanders.) The *vingtième*, a new tax keyed to estimates of revenue from the land, represented an attempt at reform rather than an accumulation of previous practices. Nevertheless, royal estimates of "ability to pay" still depended in part on political considerations, and on the sheer cost of collection. Even considering their exceptional productivity in grain, the generalities of Paris and Lille paid disproportionately high taxes. The generality of Valenciennes (roughly, Hainaut and Cambrésis) paid for being a military outpost but had some revenues from mines and metalworking to make up for it.

Exhibit 5. Percent of income per capita collected as taxes in Britain and France, 1715–1812 (Mathias and O'Brien 1976)

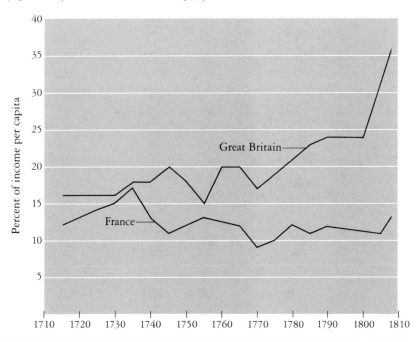

Table 4. Distribution of agricultural production and taxation around 1760

Generality	Vingtièmes per square league	Values of grain per square league	Vingtièmes per setier of grain	Vingtièmes per 100 livres of value
Paris	6,576	55,909	1.95	11.76
Tours	1,669	45,861	0.54	3.63
Dijon	1,571	77,759	0.37	2.02
Montpellier	1,439	50,728	0.58	2.84
Lille	4,888	92,921	0.83	5.26
Valenciennes	2,280	22,729	1.63	10.03

Source: Rémond 1957.

Whether measured by taxes per volume or taxes per value, the generalities of Tours, Dijon, and Montpellier clearly had the fiscal advantage.

In one respect, statemaking and capitalism worked in opposite directions. Statemaking, broadly speaking, standardized France and each of its regions: imposed a common language, a single administration, increasingly uniform systems of law, taxes, regulation, and coercion. If statemaking had an uneven impact during the eighteenth century, that was because the installation of the standard apparatus had further to go in a Flanders than in an Anjou.

The extension of capitalist property relations, on the other hand, tended to differentiate among regions and even within them. On the whole, areas of agricultural capitalism began to lose their industry, regions concentrating on a single cash crop became more common, and where industrial capital was accumulating that accumulation speeded up. Thus eighteenth-century Anjou saw Cholet emerge as the nucleus of a small region of intensive rural linen production tied closely to the Atlantic trade, while nearby Saumur played its part as the capital of wine and wheat; the contrast between the two cities, and between their hinterlands, sharpened throughout the century.

Statemakers continued to rely on holders of capital for day-to-day revenues, and the capitalists continued to profit from the alliance. Speaking of a special commission on tax-grabbers (maltôtiers) established by the regent (the duke of Orléans) shortly after his arrival in power, Angers's Canon René Lehoreau reminisced that

> people claim that the commission made those scoundrels pay back more than 300 million in the year 1716 alone. The first tax-grabber arrested in

Angers was Verrie, receiver of Ponts-de-Cé. The commissioners of Angers, by order of those of Paris, arrested him and had him taken, feet and hands bound, to the city's royal prison, where he stayed for a long time. Through the influence of his friends he was finally taken to Paris, where he found favor; they decriminalized his case and turned it into a civil suit. Thus he escaped the threat of punishment for his embezzlement. They charged him 25,000 livres. What saved him was that he had dealings with our upright intendant, who, frankly speaking, told him to steal; since [Verrie] had taken care to keep his letters, he received favorable attention. Anyway, half the city was secretly involved in tax-grabbing and working with him; their fear of getting caught likewise helped him. His post was eliminated, but he has so many friends that he is still collecting. In fact he never stopped; the only difference is that he now collects through an intermediary.   (Lehoreau 1967: 257–258)

Indeed, continued Lehoreau, it wasn't clear that Verrie would ever have to pay back the 25,000 livres. The maltôtier was indispensable; he had so much influence that royal officials could not afford to eliminate him. In this respect eighteenth-century statemakers continued the practices of the seventeenth century.

An Opposition Forms

Fiscal policy was not the only sphere in which statemakers helped capitalists exploit other people, and in which exploited people turned increasingly against royal policy. The same thing happened in regard to food supply, craft monopolies, and access to land. Eighteenth-century royal officials went even further than their seventeenth-century predecessors in promoting the nationalization of the grain trade. That meant combatting the claims of particular localities to the supply of grain currently on hand. They "freed" the grain trade as a rapidly rising share of the total population came to depend on marketed grain for everyday consumption. More and more people— especially wageworkers in agriculture, in rural industry, or both at once— therefore became vulnerable to shortages and price rises. Result: an unprecedented amount of contention over control of food.

Craft monopolies divided the crafts themselves. Large masters commonly evaded those portions of the old regulations that limited the numbers of their journeymen and apprentices and that confined them to workers duly approved by the local artisans. But large masters also held jealously to their control of the market. Small masters commonly sought to maintain the corporate structure and the restrictions on quality guaranteed, with decreasing effectiveness, by guilds. Workers fought the efforts of masters and entrepreneurs to undercut them by hiring cheaper, less well-organized, outside labor. Journeymen, expelled from the guilds by their masters, formed *compagnonnages* to defend their rights and continued to use them after the legal abolition of trade corporations in the 1770s. Small masters against large masters, compagnonnages against all masters, rival compagnonnages against each other, all local workers against outsiders—as capital concentrated, conflict intensified.

With respect to land, the crown generally acted to promote its transformation into disposable property, to strengthen the rights of owners, to discourage multiple-use rights in the same land. Customary hunting became poaching. Customary gleaning and gathering became trespassing. Customary scratching out of a corner of wasteland became squatting. All became offenses to be punished by manorial and royal courts. Landlords and their managers rationalized their estates, revived old dues, brought their rent-books up to date, pushed for or against enclosure of commons depending on whether their incomes came mainly from cultivation (commons undesirable) or grazing (commons desirable). All in all, their actions reinforced the positions of the more prosperous peasants—whether renters or owners—and pushed smallholders toward the rural proletariat. In the agrarian world, then, large landlords fought with organized communities over dues and over control of common resources. Meanwhile, poor people resisted the loss of their rights to hunt, fish, glean, pasture, gather wood, and patch together an existence from a hundred clever uses of the common ground.

For France's ordinary people, the eighteenth century fused the costs of statemaking with the burdens of capitalism. A fiscal policy favoring those who loaned their capital to the state and extracted it from the people, a food policy favoring the shipment of local supplies wherever merchants could get the highest price, a strenuous effort to break monopolies of workers over local employment, an encouragement of bourgeois property in land—all these features of government action forwarded the interests of capitalists. Among the great eighteenth-century ministers, no doubt Turgot had the clearest view of this program. He self-consciously advocated the accumulation of capital, the elimination of small farmers, and the spread of wage labor in agriculture and industry. It would be hard to make the call for capitalism more emphatic. But all French governments of the later eighteenth century helped make such a program a reality. They trampled the interests of ordinary people.

Alliances of capitalists with statemakers produced a conglomerate opposition. On the implicit principle that "the enemy of my enemy is my friend," petty producers, tradesmen, small peasants, proletarians, lawyers, officers of parlements, and Protestants all joined in resistance to royal power. During the eighteenth century, the crown took to direct attacks on the parlements and on other institutions blocking access to its potential income. Those attacks solidified the opposition. They helped the national network of lawyers and parlementary officials to become the opposition's connective tissue. Several times before 1789, large parts of the opposition reached the point of sustained defiance to royal command—reached, that is, a revolutionary situation. In 1789 the addition of a significant subsistence crisis intensified the revolutionary situation by simultaneously aligning exceptional numbers of poor people against royal officials and by displaying, yet again, the inability of those officials to put down the poor in the absence of broad support from the rich.

In all these regards the Ile-de-France had pride of place. Through the latter half of the eighteenth century, the struggle of the parlement of Paris with the crown provided the chief signal and symbol for the crown's opponents elsewhere. As the marquis d'Argenson confided to his diary for 28 November 1751:

> Yesterday morning appeared a decree of the king's council suspending a number of consumption taxes: *droits rétablis, 4 sous par livre,* and so on. That will make life cheaper in Paris. The preamble says the act is due to the dearness of bread and will last until bread prices decline. All this has made people say that the government is afraid of the people, who could rebel, seeing the parlement in revolt and giving the example; that it took the step improperly, with craven fear, that it would never have done so without the speeches against the government, without the shouts of the assembled people when the dauphin entered Paris, and so on.   (Argenson 1859–1867: VII, 47)

(When we read this analysis, it is worth remembering that the marquis's father, Voyer d'Argenson, had been chancellor—and scourge of the parlement—during the regency of Louis XV.) With the acceleration of direct taxation and governmental borrowing of the Seven Years' War, the parlements of France tightened their alliances, deepened their resistance, and lined up more solidly than ever beside the parlement of Paris.

A paradoxical situation emerged. We might expect that royal institutions and ennobling offices would have bound dignitaries to the crown ideologically, as they did financially. In fact almost the opposite occurred. On the whole, places with parlements and other courts full of officeholders mounted the most serious opposition to royal policy from the 1750s to the beginning of the Revolution. Table 5 shows the number of ennobling offices, as of 1789, in the six capitals of our five regions (Montpellier and Toulouse shared the honors in Languedoc). The numbers describe the approximate rank order of resistance to royal will. Where officeholders and institutions proliferated, three crucial things happened. First, in the process of creating offices and institutions the crown also cemented rights, privileges, and veto powers. Second, the courts, assemblies, and other institutions nominally serving the king gave their occupants means of meeting, forming common progams, and broadcasting those programs to a waiting public. Third, officeholders developed a strong interest both in limiting the crown's further indebtedness and in sustaining the ability of their institutions to bargain for the payment of their salaries. To the extent that they added matters of principle and of regional rights to these considerations, the parlements and other sovereign courts became formidable bases of opposition.

With the suspension of many parlements, including the parlement of Paris, from 1771 until Louis XV's death in 1774, their opposition became visible throughout the nation. The Paris parlement even acquired a popular following in its home territory; that following lasted until the end of 1788. At that point the parlement—restored to its functions after two more periods of exile and faced with popular demands for a thorough house-cleaning—aligned itself with the crown in defense of its own privileges. Then the Estates General, soon to become a National Assembly, took over.

Thus occurred a series of switches worthy of the Fronde. The parlements soon abandoned a revolution they had made possible; when ordinary people demanded the curtailing of privilege, popular demands began to threaten the parlements' own enormous privileges. The capitalists against whom ordinary people first directed their revolutionary action divided sharply; those

Table 5. Number of ennobling offices in six cities, 1789

City	Number of offices	1789 population	Offices per 100,000 population
Paris	1,055	600,000	176
Dijon	187	24,000	779
Montpellier	175	31,000	565
Toulouse	172	53,000	325
Lille	17	65,000	26
Angers	2	27,000	8

Source: Shapiro and Dawson 1972, supplemented by multiple sources for population.

whose strength lay in land and fiscal privilege generally clung to the threat-ened monarchy, while those who took their advantage from control of capi-tal and professional skill soon leaped over the masses to lead the opposition to the crown. Even royalty divided: the king's brother, count of Provence, maintained his Palais Royal as an island of free speech forbidden to the po-lice, while the duke of Orléans (father of the Louis-Philippe who became *roi des français* in 1830) cast his lot decisively with the opposition in 1787. The duke suffered exile for his opposition to the king before going to the guil-lotine, in 1793, for his ties to counterrevolution. Only the bloc of ordinary people remained more or less constant; ordinary people were certain that they wanted food at a feasible price, equitable and moderate taxation, checks on speculators, and guarantees of employment. Their alliances changed, but their interests remained the same.

No eighteenth-century observer saw the whole range of events that might have signaled the approach of great changes. But two observant bourgeois of Paris chronicled many of the crucial conflicts before the Revo-lution. Between them, Edmond-Jean-François Barbier and Sébastien Hardy kept detailed journals for almost every year from 1718 through 1789.

Barbier Chronicles Conflict, 1718–1762

Barbier was a lawyer who never married. He lived all his life—from 1689 to 1771—in the house his father had bought in the rue Galande. From 1718 (when he was twenty-nine) to 1763 (when he was seventy-four) he kept a journal of epigrams, songs, verses, decrees, gossip, and *faits divers* running seven volumes in manuscript and four in expurgated print (BN Fr 10285–10291; Barbier 1847–1856). He never missed a royal wedding, preg-nancy, birth, malady, or death. Bad weather, high prices, juicy scandals, ex-ceptional celebrations, and spectacular executions found their way unfailingly into his notebook. Amid the historical bric-a-brac, Barbier also reported the great conflicts and movements of the day: royal and ecclesiasti-cal attempts to put down the too-rigorous Jansenists, resistance of the par-lement to wartime taxes, chains of grain seizures.

Barbier records no substantial conflict until 1720. In May of that year came a popular rebellion against the Parisian watch. They were tramping through the city looking for vagabonds to arrest, with the strong incentive of a bounty at 100 sous per captive. The watch made the mistake of trying their skills in the faubourg St.-Antoine: "Everyone came into the streets and rose up with clubs and other weapons. They fell upon the archers, who fired the pistols they were carrying. At that, the crowd beat the archers up. A dozen of them went to the Hôtel-Dieu for trepanning" (Barbier 1847–1856: III, 139).

That same year the so-called Law System collapsed. For two years, the Scottish banker John Law had been working to convert the French national debt into shares of the Company of the Indies, and in the process to arrange a hidden devaluation of the debt. In echoes of the Fronde, petty bourgeois and parlementarians alike protested the attack on the guaranteed annuities (rentes) that constituted the mainstay of their income. Once he became comptroller general in 1720, Law made his bank the agent of the conversion and limited the amount of paper money anyone could withdraw. The run on Law's bank in the Palais Royal (where Barbier reported fifteen thousand people jammed into the narrow rue Vivienne on 17 July) first left a score of people trampled to death; then crowds milled around it with threats to break in.

For its opposition to Law's maneuvers, the parlement of Paris found itself exiled to Pontoise. On the first of September, when Barbier strolled up to the Etoile with many other people to watch the fine folks return from the Bezons Fair, he saw the "lackeys" and "populace" call attention to Law's livery and stone the carriage in which Mme. Law was passing by (I, 50). Just after Christmas Barbier noted the triumphant reentry of the recalled parlement—its popularity the more surprising because it had just given in to the king by registering the anti-Jansenist papal bull Unigenitus. He saw that the parlement was becoming the focus of popular opposition to royal power.

To be sure, Barbier missed some of the other conflicts of 1720 in Paris and its hinterland. He failed to mention, for example, a strike of Parisian journeyman printers, and the battle with tax collectors that stirred up Ville d'Auray on 21 January (Kaplan 1979: 39; AN G^7 443). The following year, on the other hand, he did note a free-for-all between the servants of great nobles and the guards at the Fair of St.-Germain (I, 77–78). In 1721 he also chronicled the vengeance of spectators at the whipping of a thief: when the thief's victim called for the hangman to whip harder, the crowd sacked the victim's house (I, 79–80). Barbier's journal likewise mentioned the arrival of a peasant delegation from St.-Cloud at the Palais Royal (the regent's seat) to ask compensation for the damage done to their fields by the crowd at a local festival; the destruction, by a crowd numbering "five or six thousand people," of the stocks set up near the house of M. d'Erlach, captain of the Swiss Guards, for the punishment of a servant who had insulted Captain d'Erlach's wife; and the throngs who went to visit the captured highwayman Cartouche in prison, then watched his breaking on the wheel (I, 95, 107–115).

Through the 1720s, we find Barbier continuing to report popular vengeance against too-zealous punishment, an occasional grain seizure or strike, and pitched battles between rival groups of young men. He neglected, for some reason, the repeated encounters of toll and tax collectors with unwilling customers. Yet he kept on noting such curious conflicts as the one besetting Big Thomas, tooth puller on the Pont Neuf, in September 1729. Thomas proposed to celebrate the birth of a dauphin by holding a free dinner for all comers on the bridge; after the police council forbade the dangerous gathering, disappointed would-be diners broke the windows of Thomas's nearby house (I, 297–298).

In the 1730s Barbier seems to have noticed rather more public demonstrations of support for the Jansenists (in the form, for example, of mass attendance at the funeral of a prominent Jansenist priest) amid the celebrations and condemnations. For all their pedigreed leadership, the rigorist Catholic Jansenists came to symbolize opposition to a corrupt regime. An unlikely but definitive fusion of Jansenism, Gallicanism, and the defense of parlementary privilege was occurring. It became a popular cause to the extent that it opposed the arbitrary power of Pope and king.

In the 1740s resistance to conscription for the militia joined the catalog of prominent conflicts. So did attacks on police sent out to pick up beggars; the police were rumored to be sending their victims—men, women, and children—off to populate Louisiana. (Indeed, Parisian police *were* receiving regular bounties for picking up youngsters who could serve as soldiers: Nicolas 1981: 53.) Small run-ins among police, vagrants, and people who came to the vagrants' defense were everyday affairs in Paris. On 28 January 1749, for example,

> G. Delacroix, brigadier of the hospital archers, was going through the rue Dauphine with his brigade this morning. They arrested a beggar, who by his shouts and resistance aroused the populace so much that for his safety, and to avoid the mistreatment they were preparing for him, [Delacroix and his brigade] had to let the beggar go. When he and his brigade were passing the shop of Auger the hatter, someone threw several potfuls of water and urine from the third story, which encouraged the populace to gather again and to throw stones.   (Farge 1979: 149)

The greatest of all such conflicts came in May 1750. On Friday the twenty-second, several Parisian crowds attacked policemen accused of seizing children and sacked the houses in which they took refuge. On Saturday people besieged a house sheltering a police spy near the Church of Saint-Roch. A member of the watch shot a man in the belly. The crowd responded by smashing the house's door and windows. Finally the police gave up their spy: "The people . . . massacred him in a trice; they dragged him by the feet, head in the gutter, to the house of M. Berryer, lieutenant general of the police, who lives near Saint-Roch . . . We haven't seen such a sedition in forty years," commented Barbier (III: 133, 136). At that point, he reported, the resistance to the "kidnapping" of beggars was spreading through the provinces and providing the occasion for a major series of battles in Toulouse. In Paris authorities tried to check popular resistance by hanging three scapegoats at the Place de Grève on 3 August 1750; two regiments of troops and a detachment of the watch protected the executioner but did not keep the crowd from crying "Pardon them" (Nicolas 1981: 57).

During the 1750s, however, Barbier's journal gave more space than before to the intensifying controversy over Jansenism and to the closely related struggle between parlement and king. He neglected the simultaneous intensification of industrial conflict, as well as multiple conflicts over the price and supply of food. Toward the end of the decade, once the Seven Years' War was under way and news of French losses in Canada coming in, Barbier was recording another triumphant return of parlement from exile and its resistance to the imposition of war taxes. He also noted the claims of some provincial parlements and pamphleteers to speak for the nation as a whole. In 1763, at war's end, he described the great struggle between the parlement of Toulouse and the king's representative, the duke of Saint-James. During the last days of the year an assembly of dukes and peers was meeting in Paris to condemn the parlement of Toulouse for its presumptuous treatment of one of their own (IV, 481–483). On that prophetic note, Barbier's accounts of conflicts ended.

Hardy Sees Conflict, 1764–1787

Barbier's neighbor Sébastien Hardy took up the chronicle in 1764 and continued to 1789. Hardy, born in Paris in 1729, entered the booksellers' guild in 1755. His shop, marked with a golden column, stood on the rue St.-Jacques near the rue de la Parcheminerie, about eighty meters from the corner of Barbier's rue Galande. As a literate and well-connected shopkeeper with *pignon sur rue* on one of Paris' major arteries, he could easily keep his eye on the city's comings and goings. That he did: his eight manuscript volumes for twenty-six years set down an even fuller account of Parisian affairs than Barbier's seven volumes for forty-five years (BN Fr 6680–6687; the one published volume contains an abridgment of the portion of the journal running from 1764 to 1773).

Like Barbier, Hardy made it a point to record rumors about public figures, seditious posters, major edicts, royal celebrations, colorful crimes, and the incessant executions at the Place de Grève. In the 1760s he had the chance to record the dastardly doings of the marquis de Sade, just as news of Beaumarchais, Voltaire, and Benjamin Franklin entered his notebooks for the 1770s. Open conflicts went into the journal only as a small part of the news.

Nevertheless Hardy caught wind of a major struggle over food in Rouen (1768) and a rebellion against kidnappers of children in Lyon (1769). He mentioned another exile of the parlement of Brittany (1769). In Paris, he paid little attention to the important industrial conflicts going on during that decade, but noted the city's occasional brawls, kidnappings, and popular rebellions against municipal and royal authorities. On 15 July 1768, for example, archers tried to arrest a young man for debts in the rue St.-Honoré, and the young man fled into a shop. The archers followed, attacking both the shopkeeper and his wife. Then: "a Body Guard who witnessed the scene was outraged to see them mistreating the woman. He took sword in hand and fell furiously upon the archers. That increased the disturbance, and many other people joined in. The battle grew, lasting three hours despite the calling of Watch squads from several neighborhoods" (BN Fr 6680).

This was one of the two basic scenarios of the Parisian brawl: either (as in this case) a struggle began with resistance to a repressive act by authorities, or members of two competing groups began battling after an encounter between them tripped a dispute about precedence, deference, and honor.

In the 1770s Hardy continued to note the brawls, but he also reported more frequent grain seizures, agitation over exile and recall of the parlements, and burnings of ministers in effigy—plus occasional news of the rebellion against England in far-off America. The 1770s did not begin auspiciously. To celebrate the marriage of Marie Antoinette of Austria to the dauphin, grandson of the king, the city put on a great show of fireworks at the Place Louis XV. The fireworks were spectacular, but according to one count 132 people died in the streets near the Place, crushed and trampled by the crowd (Musée Carnavalet 1982: 77–78). The event augured the disastrous reign of the dauphin, as Louis XVI, beginning in 1774.

Among the many struggles over food in the 1770s, Hardy reported "popular emotions" in Caudebec, Toulouse, and Reims during July 1770, then a "considerable uprising" in Besançon during August 1771 (BN Fr 6680). If no grain seizures entered Hardy's journal for 1772, the following spring made up for the omission; Aix, Toulouse, Bordeaux, Albi, and Marmande all appeared on the roster.

Yet 1774 and 1775 far surpassed the previous years. At the death of Louis XV in 1774, Turgot replaced the unpopular abbé Terray as comptroller general. True to his beliefs, Turgot tried to stimulate commerce, and therefore wealth, by freeing the grain market from local, regional, or national administrative intervention. He insisted on his principles despite the poor harvest of 1774. He took a chance, and lost.

The year of the Flour War (Guerre des Farines), 1775, brought a chain of local rebellions to the hinterland of Paris. On 15 March, Hardy noted the price of bread for the first time that year; it had risen six deniers, from 11 sous 6 deniers to 12 sous for a four-pound loaf. From that time on, Hardy recorded each price rise. For the market of 26 April he registered an increase to 13 sous 6 deniers, reported a series of provincial grain seizures, and singled out the one in Dijon. There, he said, "the populace invaded the house of the sieur de Ste.-Colombe, counselor of the late Maupéou parlement, who was known to be one of the grain monopolists; they upset and broke everything, and searched for him everywhere." Well, not everywhere: Ste.-Colombe managed to hide in a coalpile. The crowd also sacked his country house, carrying off the grain and fodder (BN Fr 6682).

Soon after followed "popular emotions" in Pontoise, St.-Denis, St.-Germain-en-Laye, Versailles, and other places near Paris. People began to say that the king's coronation, scheduled to occur in Reims on 11 June, would be postponed because of the "fermentation." In Versailles on 2 May people forced bakers to sell their bread at two sous a pound and declared "that the same thing would happen everywhere, including Paris" (AN K 1022).

The Flour War's critical battle occurred in Paris itself the very next day. At the market of 3 May, the price of a four-pound loaf rose to fourteen sous. People began to seize the bread in the market, then to break into the shops of bakers who did not open and yield their stocks freely. This time Hardy saw action close up: a crowd entered the house where Hardy lived in the Place Maubert and made him turn over the key to his storeroom so they could search for hoarded grain. They broke into the shop next door to seize the bread that a merchant from the local market had stored there. They likewise entered the nearby shop of Hardy's brother-in-law.

Hardy therefore had the chance to notice several interesting things about the "pillagers": that they were mainly women and children, that they took care to leave untouched merchandise other than bread, that at least some of them insisted on paying for their bread at two sous per pound, about three-fifths of the current market price. After a slow start, police and troops cleared the streets. Armed guards protected each bakery for about two weeks and patrolled the markets until November. In between, a number of "seditious posters" appeared on Paris' walls. One of them read (BN Fr 6682):

> Henry IV was assassinated.
> Louis XV just missed.
> Louis XVI will be massacred before he is crowned.

(Louis XV had been "just missed" by Damiens's assassination attempt in 1757.) Although grain seizures in Paris ceased with the harvest of 1775 until mid-1788, there was one last battle in the central market, over the price of eggs, in February 1776. Outside Paris, conflicts over food also declined. The large rebellion of Toulouse in 1778 was an exception—and, in any case, not so much a grain seizure as a struggle between militia and municipality.

As the storm over bread prices had grown in town after town, so had a tempest over the parlements. In his New Year's Day notice for 1772, Hardy wrote:

> Today personal letters from Rouen told me that agitation is growing from one day to the next because of the establishment of the High Council [*Conseil Supérieur*]. Almost all members of the council had to leave town for fear of being assassinated. The curé of St.-Maclou didn't dare leave his parsonage, where he was more or less held hostage by the poor of his parish, whom he couldn't help for lack of resources. The clergy, the nobility, indeed all the orders of Normandy seem ready to rebel against the policies of the chancellor, which are beginning to hurt them badly.   (BN Fr 6681)

The chancellor was Maupéou, whose high councils were supposed to become an improved alternative to the recently exiled parlements. A few days into the new year, a crowd in Rouen forced Ficquet de Wormanville, a president of the new high council, to leave his carriage, kneel in the mud, and promise never again to attend meetings of the unpopular body. About the same time, people had posted a death sentence and built a gallows to hang Ficquet and intendant Crosne (who also served as first president of the council) in effigy. The government sent troops to Rouen. The events of Rouen set off hopeful but false rumors of the chancellor's firing. Later in the year, Hardy saw graffiti on Paris walls: "Maupéou scoundrel, a chancellor for hanging, a villain to draw and quarter."

When Maupéou finally did go into exile in August 1774, the people of Compiègne (temporary seat of the government) stoned his carriage.

Soon people were burning dummies of Maupéou and Comptroller General Terray in the squares of Paris. In the Place Dauphine, the chancellor's dummy was made of a laundry can stuffed with straw, topped with a head, and bedecked with an old judicial robe; people there announced a "decision of the parlement, which sentences sieur de Maupéou, chancellor of France, to be burned alive, his ashes scattered to the winds"—a punishment immediately visited upon the dummy. Two days later the new Maupéou mannequin burned at Henry IV's statue on the Pont Neuf was stuffed with fireworks. On 12 September, yet another crowd at the Place Dauphine innovated; with grotesque funeral ceremonies, they buried an effigy of the abbé Terray.

In July 1774 the people of Compiègne and Paris had signaled as directly as they dared their opposition to the new king's apparent intention to maintain his late grandfather's policies: when the king's carriage passed by, they remained quite silent. ("My people are rather fickle," remarked the king, "but I forgive them. They have no idea what good things I plan to do for them": BN Fr 6681). But the people knew their preferences: When the king finally sacked Maupéou, crowds began to shout "Long live the king!" When the king recalled the old parlement in November 1774, Paris' fishwives gave their customary homage: they sent a delegation with bouquets of laurel to call on the returning dignitaries. As a focus of popular displays of support and opposition, the struggle of king and parlement practically disappeared until the crisis of the late 1780s.

In 1775 the Ile-de-France's Flour War combined conventional grain seizures with attacks on farmers and complaints that members of the royal family were profiting from a corner on the grain supply. Amid the many conflicts over food came news of the return of the provincial parlements to their functions. Then that struggle, too, subsided for years. During the late 1770s Hardy's journal carried more news about insurgents in North America than about any rebels in France. In 1777, for example, the closest thing Paris saw to rebellion was the arrival in Versailles of the few members of a peasant delegation from Alsace who had escaped arrest by royal troops en route; they had set out to complain of the corvées imposed by their abbot overlord. An occasional turnout, a fight over precedence in processions, attacks on customs guards, and student brawls marked the next half-dozen years.

During the early 1780s, indeed, a street-level observer would have to have been clairvoyant to know that a revolution was coming. The new decade did, to be sure, bring controversies over such subversive books as Choderlos de Lenclos's *Liaisons dangereuses,* Mercier's *Tableau de Paris,* and

Rousseau's *Confessions.* (In his entry for 17 June 1782 Hardy called the *Confessions* "singular and bizarre": BN Fr 6684.) But the great public events included the first balloon flights by the Montgolfier brothers of the Vivarais, the triumphant return of the marquis de Lafayette from the American war, the end of that war in 1783, and, the previous year, celebrations for the birth of another dauphin.

A note of governmental caution entered the planning for those celebrations. As Hardy noted:

> To divide the people and amuse them at the same time, the prévôt des marchands and échevins took the precaution of placing the dance halls with orchestras, the distribution of bread, wine, and meat as well as quarters of turkey in different parts of the capital, such as the new grain market in the St.-Honoré quarter (it was beautifully arranged), the new veal market in the Place Maubert quarter, and the old half-moon of the boulevard St.-Antoine, etc. etc.   (BN Fr 6684, 21 January 1782)

Two days later they held a masked ball in the Hôtel de Ville, with illumination and fireworks in the adjacent Place de Grève.

The open conflicts of the early 1780s likewise had an almost frivolous air. Hardy noted substantial student battles with guards in 1780, 1781, and 1784, the last of them a rebellion of rhetoric students against an unpopular examination question. In the summer of 1784, night after night, there was a charivari near the Palais de Justice on the occasion of the marriage of a sixty-year-old widow fruitseller to a younger goldsmith; she compounded the scandal by signing over to her new husband the property previously destined for her children. That winter, people snowballed the carriage of Lenoir, lieutenant general of police, after his efforts at organizing snow removal proved ineffectual.

At first glance, 1785 resembled its predecessors in frivolous variety: it began with the first crossing of the Channel in a balloon, continued with the arrest of Beaumarchais for a sassy letter printed in the *Journal de Paris,* and ended with students of the Collège Mazarin beating up a wigmaker's helper as they came out of class. But 1785 also brought conflicts recalling the popular mobilization of a dozen years earlier. That year people formed English-style "Klubes" (as Hardy spelled them) in the free zone of the Palais Royal. A round of industrial conflicts began, and continued into the next year. At the start of May, Lenoir barely averted a small rebellion when butter in the central market went to forty-two sous per pound (by November, consumers were forcing the sale of the high-priced spread below its current market value). Shortly thereafter, processions of villagers began to troop through Paris' streets to the new Ste.-Geneviève church in order to pray for the end to the terrible drought. In June a song set to the tune of the vaudeville of Beaumarchais's new *Figaro* was circulating at the expense of Lenoir's reputation. The fourth verse ran (BN Fr 6685):

> Voiez ce Ramas de Cuistres,
> Prêtres, Moines et Prélats;
> Procureurs, Juges,Ministres,
> Médecins et Magistrats;
> Ces Uniformes sinistres
> Leur tiennent lieu de Scavoir;
> Ah! Que d'ânes sous *le Noir* . . . *Bis.*

> Look at that crowd of pedants,
> priests, monks, and bishops;
> prosecutors, judges, and ministers
> doctors and judges;
> those dark uniforms
> substitute for knowledge;
> How many asses there are *sous le Noir*
> [wearing black/under Lenoir] (repeat).

All this had the breath of revolt.

Revolt likewise appeared in the reports from Couëron, near Nantes, where early in July more than a thousand inhabitants gathered to tear down hedgerows and cut all the fodder on the land leased from the crown by four or five seigneurs. The same year brought a large strike of construction workers, in the course of which the aggrieved journeymen turned out all the construction sites, held an assembly in the Place Vendôme, and marched to Lenoir's office to demand a hearing. Paris also produced a brawl among Swiss mercenaries, other soldiers, and civilians at the Palais Royal, and a forced sale of butter in the central market. It was a conflict-ridden year.

So were all the years that followed, right up into the Revolution. The year 1786 opened with concerted resistance by Parisian errand boys to a new syndicate the government had organized for package delivery; the errand boys' action included a march to Versailles on 11 January to complain directly to the king. Other workers followed: journeyman carpenters of Paris claiming their continued right to carry off wood scraps from the job; workers of Lyon protesting a new innkeepers' tax imposed by the bishop, on account of which the innkeepers had simply shut their doors; and so on.

Hardy Forecasts Revolution

Although 1785 and 1786 certainly brought plenty of tumult, in 1787 the quality of conflict took on a revolutionary edge. In convoking the Assembly of Notables for February 1787, the king and his ministers hoped to circumvent the obstructive parlements, discover ways of reducing or supporting the budget-breaking national debt, and introduce a program of administrative reform. They failed. Royal popularity declined. The fishwives of Paris, for example, canceled their customary 14 August march to Versailles to give the queen a bouquet on the eve of Assumption. Only pressure from Lieutenant General of Police Thiroux de Crosne, reported Hardy, made the fishwives go salute the king on 25 August, the feast of his namesake Saint Louis.

By mid-August the king was again exiling the parlement of Paris—this time to Troyes. Immediately afterward, he sent his brothers to hold *lits de justice* (sessions in which the king imposed his authority directly, personally, and arbitrarily on a legislative process) with the Chambre des Comptes and the Cour des Aides, in order to legitimate new taxes. When the exiled parlementaires arrived in Troyes they received heroes' welcomes.

Law clerks, as usual, moved quickly into action. They burned edicts and wrote seditious placards while other people attacked police spies in the street. While the clerks of the Châtelet talked of occupying that court and the Châtelet's general assembly sent a deputation to the king deploring the exile of parlement, troops began to patrol the courtyard and surroundings of the Palais de Justice. Meanwhile news arrived of the Bordeaux parlement's exile to Libourne, and of statements supporting the exiled parlements from their colleagues elsewhere who were still in place.

Late in September the king gave way; he suspended the contested new taxes in favor of a supplement to the old ones, then recalled the parlement to Paris. Predictably, celebrations—breaking of shopfronts, setting off of firecrackers, burning of Calonne's effigy, and so on—began around the Palais de Justice. When the special session of parlement began, people cheered and fishwives presented their bouquets to returning judges. Thus began a new series of confrontations between parlement and monarch, these over a great loan to cover the mounting debt. The king sought to weaken the parlement by excluding princes and peers from its deliberations, exiling the fractious duke of Orléans, and arresting two leading counselors. Nor did Paris have the only confrontations: as 1787 drew to a close, Hardy heard that Louis had sent troops to Libourne. The king sought to force Bordeaux's exiled parlement to choose between the unpleasant alternatives of registering the latest decrees (this time creating provincial assemblies) or dissolving.

The parlements did not give up. On 17 January 1788 the parlement of Paris sent a full, formal deputation to the king in Versailles; they were to plead for the recall of the duke of Orléans and the release of their two imprisoned colleagues. It was the first of many postulant parlementary parades, all of them rebuffed to some degree. From Toulouse early in March arrived the news that royal agents had arrested the advocate general of that city's parlement and forced an irregular registration of the latest tax law. Crowds in Toulouse showed their support for the parlement and tried to burn the house of Languedoc's military commander. Six weeks later, royal agents in Toulouse dissolved a royal regiment, many of whose officers had refused to take part in the arrest of the parlement's advocate general.

The parlement of Paris continued to send solemn remonstrances to the king, and the king continued to bypass them. Hardy began to speak of "the future revolution"—not the overturn of the monarchy, but on the contrary the monarchy's destruction of the parlement. On the night of 4 May, royal police unsuccessfully attempted to arrest two counselors in Paris. Jean Jacques IV Duval d'Epremesnil and Anne Louis Goislard de Montsabert, members of different chambers of investigation in the parlement, had long since earned reputations as leaders of the vociferous opposition to "ministerial despotism"; on 3 May, Duval d'Epremesnil had engineered the adoption of a decree outlining the kingdom's "fundamental laws" in a sense favorable to the rights of parlement (Stone 1981: 30–31, 158–169).

The following day, while the parlement's delegation was in Versailles vainly seeking to protest once more, troops surrounded the Palais de Justice. They allowed no one to enter or leave and demanded the surrender of counselors Duval and Goislard. Members of the parlement shouted "unanimously," wrote Hardy, "WE ARE ALL DUVAL AND GOISLARD. YOU'LL HAVE TO ARREST US ALL!" (BN Fr 6686). Nevertheless, after farewell speeches the two counselors gave themselves up the next day, 6 May. As they rode off in a carriage, people who were gathered near the Palais de Justice almost succeeded in liberating them. (Two days later, young people chased the arresting officer, the count of Argoult, from the Place Dauphine.) As if by reflex, the rest of the parlement immediately enacted a formal request for their liberation.

Confrontation was sharpening. At the lit de justice of Versailles on 8 May, the parlement actually refused to register royal decrees involving major reorganization of France's courts and fiscal administration. About this time, Hardy began to use the word "patriot" to describe principled opponents of the king.

News of patriotic opposition arrived from Toulouse, Rouen, Rennes,

Aix, and especially Grenoble. In Toulouse the parlement went so far as to have the intendant of Orléans, bearer of the king's orders, arrested and barred from the city. Still, the central action continued to happen in Paris: unauthorized deliberations and refusals to deliberate by lawyers at the Châtelet, cheers for subversive stanzas at the theater, a declaration by employees of the king's own Grand Council that they would not cooperate with the proposed new courts, and so on. On 25 May, Hardy mentioned a poster at the Palais de Justice reading (BN Fr 6686):

> Palace for sale,
> Counselors for rent,
> Ministers to hang,
> Crown to give away.

Ten days later, Hardy opined that "in the disorder caused by the current revolution, royal securities have lost their value, and it is impossible to carry on any commercial dealing" (BN Fr 6686, 5 June 1788). Minor battles between police and street crowds multiplied. Although law clerks continued to spearhead the attacks, they did not work alone. On 16 June, for example, a crowd made the police release a group of migrant agricultural laborers they had arrested in the rue des Lombards.

Word came of near-insurrections in Dijon, Rennes, Pau, and Grenoble, not to mention pugnacious declarations from a half-dozen other parlements. Of Grenoble, Hardy heard that 5,000 armed men had descended from the mountains to defend the members of the parlement from royal sequestration, forced open the city gates, dragged the parlement's first president back into the city, sacked part of the city, and fought royal troops in the streets. Those events, which occurred on 7 June, came to be known as the Day of Tiles. In July in Paris the king's men jailed a dozen delegates of Brittany's nobility who had come to lay their grievances before the king and had begun to organize support for their claims; the Bretons stayed in the Bastille until September. Anonymous posters in the city began to threaten a general rebellion. What is more, Hardy started to note blockage and seizure of grain or bread in the provinces; it was a dozen years since grain seizures had occurred on any scale. Armed guards reappeared in the markets of Paris. The city returned to the *qui-vive* of the mid-1770s.

In August noisier celebrations than ever before greeted the resignation of Chief Minister Loménie de Brienne and the naming of Necker as his replacement. On the twenty-seventh, people at the Place Dauphine watched a mock trial of Cardinal Brienne, complete with dummy in episcopal robes. "After having carried the mannequin to the equestrian statue of Henry IV," wrote Hardy, "and after having pushed him down on his knees before the statue, they carted him all around the square. Then, after reading him his death sentence, and making him ask forgiveness of God, the king, the judiciary, and the nation, they lifted him into the air at the end of a pole so everyone could see him better, and finally threw him onto an already lighted pyre" (BN Fr 6687). The ringleaders—no doubt mainly law clerks—likewise read a mock decree against Chancellor Lamoignon, who was responsible for the sweeping judicial reorganization the government was attempting. Late that night run-ins near the Palais de Justice between troops and youngsters produced serious injuries.

Early in the evening of 28 August the watch blocked off entries to the Place Dauphine. "La jeunesse, backed up by a numerous populace" (as Hardy described them), attacked the blockades and killed three soldiers. About fifty people left the fray wounded (BN Fr 6687). By the next night the watch had managed to align many young people against it. Hardy reported:

> Toward seven o'clock at night, the Foot Watch and the Horse Watch having been ordered not to appear in the palace quarter, the rowdy youngsters, backed by the populace, who had planned to come declare a sort of open war on the watch, were emboldened by their absence. The youngsters began to gather on Pont Neuf and at the Place Dauphine, within which people had to close all the shops and illuminate all the facades of all the houses, along with those of the rue du Harlay. Toward nine o'clock the populace of the faubourg St.-Antoine and the faubourg St.-Marcel came to swell the number of the local smart alecks. The disorder grew and grew; instead of sticking to lighting firecrackers, which were already bothersome enough to the inhabitants, they then lit a big fire in the middle of the Place Dauphine. They fed the fire with anything they could find in the vicinity, such as the sentinel's guardhouse from the Pont Neuf near the statue of the bronze horse, the stands of orange and lemon merchants in the same place, which were made of simple planks, and the grills of poultry merchants from the Quai de la Vallée, all at the risk of burning the nearby houses. On that fire they burned the effigy of Monseigneur de Lamoignon, the current French minister of justice, after having him do public penance for his wrongdoing. (BN Fr 6687)

Before the night ended a large crowd had confronted the Paris guard in the Place de Grève, and seven or eight people had died (Rudé 1959: 32).

With the threat of new gatherings, with an attack on the guardhouse of the Ile-St.-Louis, and with bread prices still rising, detachments of the watch, French Guards, and Swiss Guards were soon patrolling Paris' markets and gathering-places. Supplementary troops arrived on 5 September. Inevitably, confrontations between troops and civilians took place. A case in point is the scuffle between French Guards and a lemonade vendor at the St.-Martin Gate on 13 September; when the troops ordered him to move, he resisted, and bystanders supported him.

The next day Chancellor Lamoignon lost his job, and the festivities of the Place Dauphine began again. (Lamoignon was heir to the fief of Basville, once the seat of Languedoc's sturdy intendant Lamoignon de Basville; hence it was no great trick for the day's versifiers to turn out sarcastic eulogies dedicated "à Basville Lamoignon," which when read aloud easily sounded like "à bas, vile Lamoignon." Six months later the rejected Lamoignon took his rifle out to the middle of his Basville estate and shot himself fatally.) This time the burning dummies represented not only Lamoignon and Brienne but also Chevalier Dubois, commander of the watch. When the king recalled the parlement of Paris a week later, celebrations, parades, firecrackers, and illuminations brightened far more of the city than the Place Dauphine. At once the parlement, which had already put a ban on fireworks, issued a decree forbidding contentious gatherings.

In the days to come, nevertheless, contentious gatherings continued. News arrived of Necker's suspension of work on the controversial new customs wall ringing Paris (that suspension, for all its popularity in other quarters, put 4,000 men out of work); there was word of the return of provincial parlements to their home towns; of a new Assembly of Notables; of more popular resistance to the watch's policing of the streets; of ever-rising bread prices; but, for the rest of the year, not of grain seizures.

Seizures of grain recurred in the early spring of 1789, following struggles between nobles and Third Estate in Rennes and Fontainebleau, publication of Sieyès's temporarily anonymous pamphlet "What is the Third Estate?" which Hardy called "singularly interesting" (BN Fr 6687, 3 February 1789), and word of "revolts" in Reims, Toulon, and Nancy "caused by the price of bread" (BN Fr 6687, 17 March and 3 April 1789). It was nearly time for the long-awaited Estates General. After mid-April Paris' sixty districts met to elect their delegates and draft their complaints. Then came the turn of the citywide assembly. The Third Estate of the *prévôté* and *vicomté* of Paris assembled at the archbishop's palace as troops patrolled the city. Then and later, Paris' Third Estate rejected the efforts of nobles to join their assemblies; for the time being, they sought to keep distinct the interests of different estates.

Hardy at the Edge of Insurrection

In the midst of the meeting and negotiating arrived a near-insurrection. On the afternoon of Monday 27 April, in Hardy's account,

> Parisians had quite a scare, to the point that people closed their shops in a number of areas. There was a sort of popular insurrection that extended from the faubourg St.-Antoine to the neighborhood of Notre Dame. A considerable share of the workers supposedly from that faubourg, whipped into action by brigands, attacked *Reveillon,* a very rich manufacturer of figured paper, and another rich individual called *Hanriot,* a saltpeter manufacturer, both friends and residents of the faubourg. (BN Fr 6687)

Reveillon and Henriot had argued in their Third Estate electors' assemblies for restraint on workers' wages, coupled with controls on food prices to keep real wages constant. Reveillon was in fact engaged in the assembly's deliberations when the attack on his house occurred. It was not the first time Reveillon's name had made the news. A former worker now successfully in business for himself since the 1750s, Reveillon was well known as the buyer of La Folie Titon, a splendid house on the rue de Montreuil. With more than four hundred workers, he was one of the faubourg's greatest industrialists. In 1777 he had obtained a decree from the king's council breaking a strike by paperworkers at his shop in Courtelin-en-Brie (AN AD^{xi} 25, 26 February 1777). In October 1787 Reveillon's gatekeepers, man and wife, were said to have enlisted a helper and killed one of Reveillon's own workers (BN Fr 6686, 9 October 1787). Reveillon had, in short, gained the reputation of becoming very rich at workers' expense.

During the night of 26–27 April, angry workers gathered in the faubourg St.-Marceau, on the Left Bank, to complain of Reveillon and Henriot. The next day, Monday the twenty-seventh, a file of workers marched from St.-Marceau toward the archbishop's palace at Notre Dame, where the electoral assemblies of clergy and Third Estate were meeting. Faced with the possible threat of a popular invasion, the clergy announced they were giving up their privileges, while the Third Estate sent a delegation to intercept the marchers at the Place Maubert. Their delegates succeeded in deflecting the march.

Next reports had the workers burning effigies of Henriot and Reveillon at the Place de Grève before moving down the rue St.-Antoine to the faubourg. Blocked by French Guards from reaching Reveillon's house, they rushed off to sack Henriot's instead. On Tuesday, 28 April, gatherings of workers formed in the faubourg St.-Antoine, the lieutenant general of police stationed 350 French Guards near Reveillon's house, another detachment of workers crossed the river from the faubourg St.-Marceau, and thousands of people milled in the streets.

The duke of Orléans, returning from the races, passed through. He gave an impromptu speech and distributed money to his audience. When the duchess of Orléans appeared in her carriage, soldiers deferred to her by opening the barricades that blocked the rue de Montreuil. Assembled workers followed her through the ruptured barricade, broke into Reveillon's house, dragged out and burned much of its contents, drank the contents of the splendid wine cellar, and fought off the additional troops went to stop them. Before the workers were suppressed a dozen soldiers and several hundred invaders were dead.

Then, as night follows day, repression followed. On the morning of 29 April, Hardy breathed a bit easier. "The faubourg St.-Antoine," he wrote later,

> had finally become a little calmer, because of the precaution of filling it with troops of every sort, and of placing two artillery pieces loaded with shrapnel at the faubourg's entry near the guardhouse of the Horse Watch, in order to intimidate them. They had also stationed a substantial armed detachment of the Royal Cravatte cavalry regiment in the Place de Grève, while seven-man patrols of French Guards and Swiss Guards circulated in various neighborhoods with bayonets on their guns. (BN Fr 6687)

"They" took care to convict two looters (a blanketmaker and a longshoreman) the same day. The scapegoats were hanged in the Place de Grève, jammed with protective troops, the day after. Interrogations and trials took almost three weeks. On 18 May royal judges condemned to death Pierre Jean-Baptiste Nicolas Mary (a twenty-four-year-old scribe at the Palais de Justice) and Marie Jeanne Trumeau (a forty-year-old meat vendor, and wife of an errand boy). According to the sentence:

> On the afternoon of 28 April said Mary, at the head of a large band of people, snatched swords from two people on the main street of the faubourg St.-Antoine, saying that he wanted to use them against the troops. Armed with the two swords, he marched at the head of the band and said things to encourage the assembling, rioting, and sedition that was going on in said faubourg St.-Antoine. Then, still followed by

a large band, he went through different neighborhoods of the city and by words, deeds, and menacing gestures alarmed and frightened those he met. He is likewise seriously suspected of having taken part in the riotous gatherings of the previous day, and (along with his accomplices, armed with faggots) even of stopping people in their carriages and announcing their intention to hurt an individual whose house (and that of another individual) were wrecked as a result of the assemblies, riot, and sedition. Said Marie Jeanne Trumeau, wife of Bertin, with words of the most violent sort, encouraged people to loot and sack Sieur Reveillon's paper factory, even though (as her testimony says) she considers Reveillon to be an upright man and a friend of the poor. At the moment of the riotous assembly she handed out faggots and clubs to various people, in fact forced some people to take them, telling them to join the band, showing them a passage leading into the factory. After the pillage, finally, she distributed pieces of wallpaper rolls, shouting *A la Reveillon.* (AN Y 10530)

Both were to hang at the St.-Antoine Gate. Trumeau, certified pregnant, escaped with her life, but Mary died for his deeds. Five others went to the galleys; the twenty-six remaining prisoners went free after the Revolution accelerated in July. The frightened Henriot fled to Vincennes, then disappeared from view. Reveillon took refuge in, of all places, the Bastille. He later completed his trajectory by emigrating to England.

King versus People

One week after the crowds cursed Reveillon and Henriot in the faubourg St.-Antoine, the Estates General opened in Versailles. The atmosphere of Paris was ominous: after the sacking of Reveillon's house, according to Hardy, the authorities had tripled the guard. Squads of fourteen cavalrymen, sabers drawn, were patrolling the streets, while contingents of ten members of the watch went around on foot. As rumors of maneuvers at the Estates General filtered in from Versailles, word of food riots in distant provinces reached Paris. But the troops kept the city quiet.

The anxious calm lasted a month. On 22 May street vendors began selling copies of the sentences given Mary, Trumeau, and others convicted in the Reveillon affair. The convicts left Châtelet prison that day in carts bearing the words SEDITIEUX or PILLARDS, and followed the path of ceremonial entries to the city in reverse: first to Notre Dame for public penance, then to the Place de Grève, finally down the long rue St.-Antoine, well protected by troops, to the Place de la Porte St.-Antoine. There, next to the Bastille, the gibbet, stocks, and branding irons awaited them.

Nevertheless, no insurrection greeted the execution of Mary and the punishment of the other pillards. The closest Paris came to rebellion in those days was in the rue St.-André-des-Arts on 25 May: police spies arrested beggar women in the street, and bystanders forced the spies to give up their captives. The genuine rebellion developed in Versailles, where on 19 June the Third Estate's assembly declared itself the national assembly and later, barred from its meeting-place, gathered at the Tennis Court to swear its determination to stay together.

That brought Parisians to Versailles once again. The king, making the best of a bad job, addressed the Third Estate on 23 June. Finance Minister Necker, disapproving of the too-limited reforms the king then proposed, stayed away. Word began to spread that the king had dismissed Necker. That night "the worried people," in Hardy's phrase, rushed from Paris to Versailles, made their way into the castle, and demanded to see the king. Ordered to raise their weapons, the royal guard put them down instead. The crowd stood its ground. Only the appearance of Necker himself ended their siege.

That resistance of the military at Versailles started something. In the next few days, several companies of soldiers assigned to patrol Paris refused the duty. On 28 June a mutinous group of soldiers went to the Palais Royal (by now the headquarters of popular orators) and announced their refusal to serve. When their colonel imprisoned fourteen of them, three hundred people marched from the Palais Royal to the jail, demanded their release, and brought them back to the palace for a triumphant dinner. During the next few days, two crowds freed prisoners from the hands of the police. Although the king had been building up troops around Paris from the moment of the Third Estate's defiance, the authorities began to lose internal control of the city.

Then rumor became fact: on 11 July the king dismissed Necker. The next day, Sunday, the orators of the Palais Royal—including Camille Desmoulins—were out in force, and met enthusiastic audiences. A crowd of thousands, bearing black flags, with wax busts of Necker and the duke of Orléans, paraded through the streets. Marchers fought royal troops in the Place Vendôme and the Tuileries. More serious still, a detachment of French Guards joined the crowd in an attack on the German regiment that was attempting to clear the Tuileries. "It was not without indignation," reported a law clerk from the Châtelet,

> that the people saw all that military force. Everyone from the Palais de Justice went to the Place Louis XV with the busts of the duke of

Orléans and M. Necker and approached the troops, insulted them, threatened them, and threw stones at them. The soldiers, seeing themselves attacked in this way, lost all control, fell on the people with gunfire and swords. But the people didn't give up. The stones that were there for construction of the new bridges served them as ammunition. (BN Fr 13713)

The German mercenaries eventually withdrew. But in the meantime Paris came close to open warfare.

The alliance of French Guards and ordinary people had not ended. That night, French Guards stood watch at the Chaussée d'Antin as "poorly dressed people" sacked and burned the tollhouse; forty of the city's fifty-four tollhouses suffered a similar fate during the night (Godechot 1965: 241). Throughout the city, tavernkeepers capped their five-year fight against the new, enlarged Parisian zone for excise taxes (octroi) by leading the attack on tollgates. Many other Parisians joined them. At the Picpus Gate, according to the toll collectors there, around four in the morning of 13 July

we saw a troop of brigands coming by the rue St.-Denis . . . They asked us whether we were with the Third Estate. We said yes. They dishonestly called for us to work with them. Far from obeying them, we hurried away and took refuge in the house of M. Duret, master wigmaker and owner of a house in the faubourg St.-Antoine opposite the tollgate. Being in a room on the first floor of that house we saw all those brigands through the window. One held a sword, another a mace, and others various offensive weapons, with which they started to break the windows of the tollbooth, then went into the tollhouse and took the effects out of all the rooms and stacked them up in the street. Then two of said criminals (one of whom was Coeur de Bois, known as a smuggler, and armed with a bare sword) went, with their arms, to the house of someone inside the gate and got a light. Then the two criminals came back and set the effects they had stacked in the street on fire.

By the time the Garde Bourgeoise arrived to chase them away, the "brigands" had burned everything in the offices (AN Z^{la} 886). Although we have no report of celebrations at Picpus, at other tollgates Parisians danced around the ruins. As the festivities went on, the ever-active fishwives strode out beyond the customs wall, cut a young tree, carried it back into the city, and planted it at the very middle of the Tuileries, in sight of the royal palace (Ozouf 1977: 46).

Early the same morning, French Guards joined the group of local workers and petty bourgeois who broke into the St.-Lazare monastery, freed the prisoners detained there, drank up much of the monks' wine, carried off rich food, and took fifty-three wagonloads of grain to the central market for sale. Freeing prisoners was very much the order of the day: Hardy reported the appearance that morning of a poster calling people to break open the Bicêtre prison at five that afternoon. Around eleven that morning, he recorded, the keeper of La Force prison had to open his gates and liberate his prisoners. People were in action everywhere. The tocsin sounded in parish churches, calling citizens to their local assemblies. Many of the assemblies formed civic militias and marched them through the streets to maintain order. Militias needed weapons; many of the citizen-soldiers spent their day searching for stores of arms. A delegation from the city's main electoral assembly, at the Hôtel de Ville, went to the Invalides to ask for arms; the governor stalled by sending the request on to Versailles.

At the Hôtel de Ville itself the militiamen met with eighty deputies from the Estates General. Around eight that evening Hardy saw

> seven or eight horsemen of the Third Estate, followed by about three hundred soldiers of the French Guard, the grenadiers, and other units, armed and marching to a drumbeat, led by sergeants and without officers, followed by a considerable multitude of insurgents armed in many different ways and dressed in a great variety of uniforms; they, too, had drums. They were going, people said, to the Place de Grève, to greet the eighty deputies from Versailles when they arrived at the Hôtel de Ville. (BN Fr 6687)

The electoral assembly at the Hôtel de Ville stayed in session all night, while the popular militia patrolled the city's streets and, under their protection, groups went to demand grain from other presumed hoarders, including the monks of the Charterhouse.

The next day was the Fourteenth of July. The tocsin sounded again, recalling citizens to their district assemblies. Early in the morning another delegation—this one thousands strong, including many citizens wearing blue-and-red cockades—showed up to demand arms from the governor of the Invalides. After fruitless maneuvering, they broke in. The invalided veterans who manned the fortress made no more than a show of resistance; the invaders carried off their guns. Then, for ammunition, they went off to the other end of the city, to the Bastille. As Hardy told the story:

> people went to the castle of the Bastille to call the governor, the marquis Delaunay, to hand over the weapons and ammunition he had; on his refusal, workers of the faubourg St.-Antoine tried to besiege the castle. First the governor had his men fire on the people all along the rue St.-Antoine, while making a white flag first appear and then disappear, as if he meant to give in, but increasing the fire of his cannon. On the

side of the two drawbridges that open onto the first courtyard, having pretended to accept the call for arms, he had the gate of the small draw-bridge opened and let in a number of the people who were there. But when the gate was closed and the drawbridge raised, he had everyone in the courtyard shot, including three of the city's electors ... who had come to bargain with him. Then the civic militia, indignant over such barbarous treatment of fellow citizens, and backed by grenadiers of the French Guard ... accomplished the capture of the castle in less than three hours.   (BN Fr 6687)

The victors moved on to the nearby Arsenal, where they seized powder for their guns. Permanent Committee chairman Flesselles was leaving the Hôtel de Ville for the Palais Royal to defend himself against charges of betraying the city to royal troops. (Only three months earlier the king had appointed Flesselles prévôt des marchands to replace Le Peletier de Morfontaine. Le Peletier had resigned in protest against the king's decision to put the election of deputies to the Estates General under the direction of the royally controlled Châtelet rather than the Hôtel de Ville. Parisians, then, had some reasons for thinking of Flesselles as the king's creature.) In the Place de Grève, Flesselles received a mortal gunshot wound; the crowd paraded his severed head.

That night the bodies of the governor of the Bastille, the powderkeeper of the Arsenal, and two veterans at the Invalides hanged for firing on the people lay exhibited at the Place de Grève. By nine o'clock people throughout Paris had lighted their windows as they did for the celebration of royal births, marriages, and military victories. The militia had its arms, the people its castle, the nation its next step toward revolution.

The following day, 15 July, confirmed the popular victory. As the king made a conciliatory speech to the Estates General in Versailles, the district assemblies met again in Paris, the civic militia drilled, people began to tear down the Bastille stone by stone, and royal troops in great numbers arrived at the Place de Grève to throw in their lot with the people of Paris. Over the next few days, many troops joined them. Late on the fifteenth members of the National Assembly arrived by carriage from Versailles, climbed down, then marched to the Hôtel de Ville surrounded by militiamen and their popular following. From there, once again mimicking the solemn old routines, they went to Notre Dame for an impromptu *Te Deum*.

Only two days later the king himself followed the deputies' routine: on 16 July he had given in to the popular demand, recalled Necker, and withdrawn the troops ringing Paris. The next day he made a pilgrimage from

Versailles to Paris. He left his bodyguard at the city limits, got out of his carriage, and walked amid 100 deputies and 200 horsemen of the civic militia to the Place de Grève and the Hôtel de Ville. No *Te Deum* for the king: he left without going to Notre Dame. Louis XVI departed via the Place Louis XV, soon to be the Place de la Révolution.

"On thinking of the events that have happened since the beginning of the week," reflected Hardy, "it is hard to recover from one's astonishment" (BN Fr 6687, 17 July 1789). The insurrection, in his opinion, had saved the city from invasion and massacre by 30,000 royal troops. An uneasy alliance formed. The city's ordinary people attacked the powers of the old regime while the city's bourgeoisie built an alternative structure of government. Assemblies, committees, militias, delegations, civic ceremonies began to supplant the forms of royal power. Paris lay at the command of its assemblies and under the close surveillance of its various citizen militias. Theaters closed, and the city gates remained under tight control. Poor people saw that their victory over the tyranny of tolls was only temporary: the taxes on goods entering Paris reappeared, now under the militia's protection.

After all the excitement, the city went into its revolutionary routines: continual meetings of its district assemblies, patrols of its new military forces, speeches and debates at the Palais Royal. Parisian authorities began a search for grain in the city's hinterland. From St.-Germain-en-Laye, Corbeilles, and elsewhere in the surrounding region came word of insurrections over the food supply. In fact the Parisian law clerks' militia took part in the pacification of Corbeilles.

Another detachment of militia went off to Compiègne to fetch back Berthier de Sauvigny, intendant of Paris, who was widely accused of treason. Meanwhile residents of the village of Viry brought in Foulon, Berthier's father-in-law and former king's councillor, reputed to have said that the hungry people could eat straw. Nicolas Ruault, a bookseller who was at the Place de Grève when Foulon arrived, said that the peasants who had captured Foulon had put a rope of straw around him in place of his sash of office. When Foulon's executioners displayed his severed head to Berthier, Foulon's mouth was stuffed with straw. Then it was Berthier's turn to die. "In an instant," wrote Ruault, "his body was slashed to ribbons. His bloody head and heart were carried into the electors' meeting room. Such a spectacle made the marquis de Lafayette tremble with horror. He immediately resigned as colonel of the milice bourgeoise. But the city officials pleaded with him not to abandon them in those terrible moments; he took back his post" (Ruault 1976: 159).

For the Place de Grève, that was the end of the massacres, the start of the celebrations. The city's authorities stepped up policing around the Hôtel de Ville. When Necker came to Paris on 29 July, patriots illuminated the Palais Royal: "Under each arcade of the galleries," reported Hardy, "they had placed a chandelier surrounded by varicolored lanterns; everywhere one saw transparencies with the words VIVE LE ROI, VIVE LA NATION, VIVE M. NECKER. The eleven arcades of the Klube [*sic*] were likewise lighted, but in a more unusual way: in the middle, they had placed a transparency with the words KLUB NATIONAL and on the two sides transparent portraits of the king and M. Necker" (BN Fr 6687). A concert capped the celebration. The next day a great crowd greeted Necker at the Place de Grève, and the city as a whole illuminated its lamps.

Over the next two months, Paris and its region witnessed a remarkable contrast. On the one hand, within the city group after group publicly pledged its allegiance to the popular cause. Beginning with the second week of August, for example, many trades and parishes sent processions—militia, banners, drums, and festively clothed civilians—into the streets. Trades sent their members in marching order, while parishes commonly sent a priest with their women and girls in white, bearing blessed bread.

Just as the time-honored ceremonial march from Paris to Versailles took on a certain assertiveness, the parish processions synthesized the old penitential parades for divine intercession in drought or famine with the new declarations of popular allegiance to the movement of resistance. The processions' most common path led from the group's regular locale to Ste.-Geneviève church, to Notre Dame, and then to the Hôtel de Ville; that was, for example, the route of the fishwives of the central market on 18 August. Some of the processions combined their affirmations of faith with demands for work, food, or civil rights; thus bakers' helpers paraded to the Hôtel de Ville on 14 August calling for work, and servants went to the Palais Royal on 29 August to ask for full citizenship.

Outside the city, on the other hand, one place after another witnessed a fight over food. On 2 August a crowd in St.-Denis decapitated the deputy mayor when he resisted the sale of bread at below market price. On 25 August "brigands" (Hardy's word) kept the millers of Pontoise from grinding their grain. In Charenton on 27 August a crowd tried to burn the local mill. Versailles saw an "insurrection" against a baker on 15 September, Chaillot the capture of five wagons of grain a day later.

In Paris, meanwhile, armed guards reappeared in the markets and at bakeries. On 17 September a group of women marched to the Hôtel de Ville to complain about bakers' profiteering. On 18 September, as Belleville sent its procession to Ste.-Geneviève, a crowd at the Pont-au-Change complained of hunger and called for an insurrection, and bakers struck back by breaking into the shop of a bookseller on the rue St.-André-des-Arts who had published a pamphlet attacking them. Through it all, the Parisian militias spent much of their time on expeditions into the Ile-de-France, seeking hoards of grain. The classic struggle of city and country over the food supply had begun again.

The mixture of celebration and struggle continued, but the issues broadened. On 27 September at Notre Dame the archbishop of Paris blessed the flags of the city's newly formed national guard. Lafayette commanded and, by Hardy's estimate, eight or nine thousand people attended. On 29 September a crowd gathered at the church of St.-Jacques de la Boucherie to protest the fees asked for the burial of a journeyman carpenter, and forced the guard who tried to block them to do penance at the poor man's coffin. The next day some of the same people returned to the church with a cantor who claimed he had unjustly lost his job, and demanded that the curé rehire him.

Yet these conflicts were nothing compared with the women's rising of 5 October. Women of the markets went to the Hôtel de Ville, entered, and seized a stock of guns there before rushing off to capture the law clerks' cannon. The tocsin sounded, and national guards by the thousands gathered in the Place de Grève. Then they went their way to Versailles, demanding "bread and the constitution." Lafayette had little choice but to go with them and tell the king about the city's troubles. He and a great mass of his national guard accompanied several thousand women to Versailles. The following day triumphant women brought the royal family back to the Place de Grève. During the next few days crowds thronged the Tuileries to catch a glimpse of the captured king. On the night of 9 October, according to Hardy's journal, the national guard patrolling the streets near the Tuileries fought "fake patrols" that were preparing to sack houses and the civic pawnshop in the neighborhood.

Soon Hardy fell silent. With extracts from the king's declaration that he would live without pomp in Paris and—when things were a bit calmer—make a tour of the provinces to hear people's problems for himself, Sébastien Hardy closed his journal on 12 October 1789.

Barbier, Hardy, and Eighteenth-Century Contention

Barbier, Hardy, and other Parisian observers saw a great deal, but they did not see everything. Religious war figured prominently in France's eighteenth-century contention; Barbier and Hardy saw none. Tax rebellions and smaller-scale resistance to taxation declined from their seventeenth-century intensity, but continued nonetheless. The attacks on Paris' tollgates were only a faint echo of action against customs barriers elsewhere. Smugglers and revenue officers fought repeatedly on the provincial and national frontiers; they had little to do with each other in Paris. Conscription brought on resistance in village after village. Communal struggles—rival groups of artisans, adjacent villages, youth groups at each other's throats—loomed much larger elsewhere in France. Paris saw almost nothing of the repeated attempts of rural people to hold off landlords' encroachments on their common rights. Although food supply did figure importantly in Paris, we must go to the hinterland to appreciate the frequency with which rural people blocked the departure of grain from their territories.

During the eighteenth century as a whole, struggles of peasants and rural proletarians against landlords became more widespread and acute in Burgundy and Languedoc than in Anjou, Flanders, or the Ile-de-France. In the latter two regions capitalist agriculture had long since established its domination, and food for the rural landless was a more pressing issue than enclosure or rack rent. Anjou had split into areas of intensive cash-crop farming and semicapitalist landholding but was experiencing relatively little change in its agrarian structure; the economic news there came mainly from the growth of rural industry. Burgundy and Languedoc, on the other hand, hosted landlords who were actively expanding their control over commons, woods, wastes, and their own lands in order to increase their sales of wines and wheat. They swept aside the rights of smallholders, who fought back as best they could. Those real issues meant little to Parisians.

Furthermore, despite the absolutely crucial part played by Paris in the national revolutionary movements of 1787 to 1789, the provinces had their own grievances and forms of action. Provincial Estates and parlements certainly responded to signals from the parlement of Paris, but many of them fought their own vigorous battles with intendant and king. Not only in the Ile-de-France, but also in Languedoc and Burgundy, the parlement led popular resistance until late in 1788.

In provinces lacking their own Estates, such as Anjou, the 1787 reforms brought in provincial assemblies. The assemblies offered regional bourgeois a new forum for their views and a more direct connection with royal power than they had previously enjoyed. Although the assemblies had only limited powers and operated under the intendant's watchful eye, they rapidly became sites of contention over taxes and provincial liberties. It was not in Paris but in smaller cities that municipal revolutions occurred; in Dijon, Lille, Toulouse, Angers, and elsewhere groups of bourgeois seized power from the previous authorities within a few weeks of the Bastille's fall.

Conflicts in smaller cities, to be sure, had something in common with those of Paris: in the hard days of July, the inability of the old municipality either to supply adequate food or to suppress the protests of poor people over food shortage typically precipitated the local crises. Dijon's people rose on 15 July, before the news of the Bastille's fall reached Burgundy. Angers had its great day of popular rebellion on 17 July, Lille on 21 and 22 July, Toulouse on the twenty-seventh. In each case, a renewal of the municipality followed. Groups that seized power tended to come mainly from the local bourgeoisie, to draw some support from the local proletariat, and to proceed by organizing both an emergency committee and a militia. Revolutionary committees, in their turn, linked municipalities to the Parisian leadership.

If there was any quintessentially revolutionary act in France as a whole, it was the seizure of power in municipality after municipality by committees acting in the name of the nation. Once these committees and their militias formed a national network centered on Paris, the French had temporarily succeeded in an effort of centralization that the monarchy itself had never accomplished. They had substituted direct, centralized rule for the mediated, indirect rule of the old regime. With the eventual capture and freezing of that structure by the Directory, the Consulate, and the Empire, France created a truly centralized structure extending all the way to the smallest commune. No king had ever built such a structure. The first version of that new system of government, the shaky coalition of 1789, involved an unprecedented articulation of Paris and the provinces.

Likewise, struggles in the countryside articulated with those of Paris. After the visible weakening of the monarchy in mid-July 1789, people who had accumulated grievances against merchants and landlords finally dared to strike at presumed hoarders, to attack such scourges as nobles' dovecotes or rabbit warrens, and to burn the papers with which landlords had been backing their claims to commons, tithes, and dubious rents. Flanders and Languedoc give us our prime examples of such struggles, but Burgundy and the Ile-de-France were not far behind. Even Anjou followed, in its way. Paris was marvelous, but it was not the whole world.

What would those intendants who in 1698 described their provinces for the heir apparent to the crown have made of the condition of those provinces just ninety years later, in 1788? None, surely, could have anticipated the great struggles of 1787 and after. No doubt all would have predicted a royal victory over internal opposition rather than a face-off between a bankrupt monarchy and a fearsome coalition linking its former victims with its former allies. Yet those descriptions had at least some elements of a valid projection. As of 1698, for example, the spectacle of a financially overextended government seeking to maintain its credit and yet to keep on spending was all too familiar. Repairing that government, sustaining it, and minimizing the costs of its wrongdoing gave them their daily work.

In their zeal to maintain the crown's sources of credit and to generate new taxable income, furthermore, intendants were hesitantly promoting commercial and agricultural capitalism. Purchases of office, loans of money, bids to farm taxes, attempts to create new industries, efforts to increase grain exports all looked desirable, since they seemed to solve the monarchy's pressing domestic problems. Those very activities, however, placed restraints on the government. The monarchy acquired obligations to repay, to consult, to favor the generators of new income. Those activities also caused the hardships about which ordinary people became angry; encroachment on commons; local food shortages; threats to small, independent artisans; oppressive taxation; forced sales of inferior salt; prosecution for hunting, gleaning, or gathering wood; execution of smugglers.

France's government did not cause these evils on its own; indeed, administrators were concerned enough about all of them to mitigate their effects when they could. Of the eighteenth century's great popular grievances, only the imposition of conscription, the raising of taxes for war, and the attempt to enforce religious conformity grew mainly from royal initiatives. For the rest, commercial and agricultural capitalists bore significant responsibilities. But by collaborating with those capitalists and authorizing their profit-taking, the French monarchy took on the stigma of their misdeeds. King Louis and his agents paid the price.

8 ⌒‿

Flanders from the Revolution
to the Great War

*A*T THE END OF THE 1780s, Lille bustled with 60,000 to 65,000 inhabitants and a vast network of commercial contacts in its hinterland. Citadel, administrative center, and market, Lille epitomized the prosperous eighteenth-century city. Lille thrived on commercial capitalism. The metropolis divided sharply between the proud, sober, solid, central neighborhoods of its merchant oligarchy and the crowded, wretched, peripheral quarters of its abundant working poor. Normally Lille's rich and poor lived quite apart. But in 1789 many normal routines dissolved.

On 23 July 1789, for example, the Maréchaussée of Flanders interrogated Charles Louis Monique. Monique, a threadmaker and native of Tournai, lived in the lodging house kept by M. Paul. Asked what he had done on the night of 21–22 July, Monique replied that he had spent the night in his lodging house and "around 4:30 A.M. he got up and left his room to go to work. Going through the rue des Malades . . . he saw a lot of tumult around the house of M. Martel. People were throwing all the furniture and goods out the window." Asked where he got the eleven gold louis, the other money, and the elegant walking stick he was carrying when arrested, he claimed to have found them all on the street, among M. Martel's effects. The police didn't believe his claims. They had him tried immediately and hanged him the same day (AML 14336, 18040).

According to the account of that tumultuous night authorized by the Magistracy (city council) of Lille on 8 August, anonymous letters had warned that there would be trouble on 22 July. On the twenty-first, two members of the Magistracy went to see the count of Boistelle, the provincial military commander; they proposed to form a civic militia. Boistelle rejected the plan. "I'll make the troops obey," he declared. "I take responsibility." But soon afterward the "awful populace" began its attacks on houses of the rich, including that of grain merchant Martel (AML 17470).

In addition to Martel's house, the raiders sacked three others. The owners of all three played prominent parts in control of the food supply; in fact all were members of Lille's Subsistence Committee. Two of the victims, Madre des Oursins and de Druez, also belonged to the governing Magistracy. The third was Lagache, the intendant's subdelegate. They did not receive the respect to which the old regime had accustomed them; while Lille's people sacked their houses, most of the royal troops declined to intervene. As in Paris, many soldiers had lost commitment to the regime.

For the work of destruction, members of the crowd borrowed hammers—faithfully returned after an hour or so—from a local locksmith. People broke into the arsenal to get torches. According to one witness, a participant replied to a military officer who asked him to stop sacking a house: "Sir, how can we leave these people alone, when they went so far as to say they would make us eat straw? It's our turn to make *them* eat straw!" (Martinage and Lorgnier n.d.: 9). The words had ominous overtones; that same day, a Parisian crowd displayed the severed head of king's councilor Foulon, mouth stuffed with straw.

For Lille's burghers, the warning came clear and loud: they had to take charge, to restore order. The next day the bourgeois of Lille formed a provisional committee and established their civic militia. The only people punished for the uprising of 21–22 July were Monique, who hanged, and another accused thief, who went to the galleys.

A notary from nearby Frelinghien who visited Lille on 23 July was amazed at how fast the city had changed: "Everyone is wearing the national cockade," he reported. "Even the troops are totally committed to the Third Estate. I had to wear the cockade myself, in order to avoid being insulted" (Théry 1923: 199). Red, white, and blue now stood for popular sovereignty. The Revolution had reached Lille.

Flanders' people had been performing revolutionary acts for months. From the beginning of 1789, rural people braved game wardens and hunted on posted land. In Lille the representatives of craft guilds protested against the merchant oligarchy as early as 14 January. "The long-desired moment has come," their spokesmen declared,

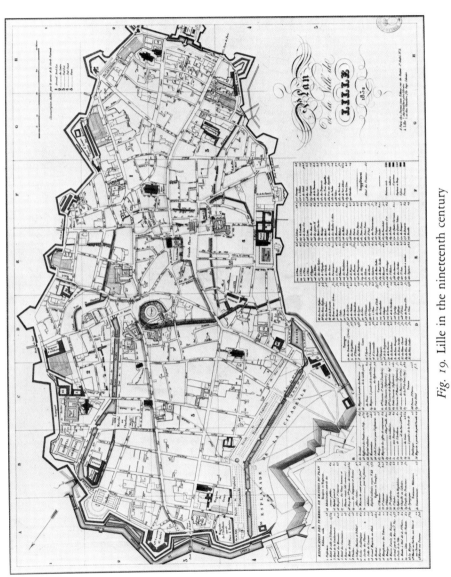

Fig. 19. Lille in the nineteenth century

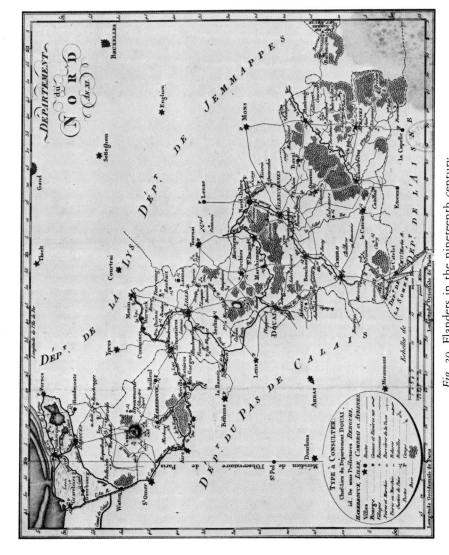

Fig. 20. Flanders in the nineteenth century

> to free ourselves from the eternal oblivion in which the ambition of our
> municipal magistrates would like to keep us, to the detriment of our
> rights, our interests, and the common good . . . It is important and es-
> sential that representatives be elected by those represented, and that the
> representatives of each order be members of that order . . . But our mu-
> nicipal magistrates want to be US, want us to have a civic identity only
> through THEM, want to represent US, plot in silence against the most
> precious of our rights. (D'Hollander 1970: 13)

No more virtual representation, they were saying; only direct representation
will do.

That spring the most frequent grievances concerned food supply. Cambrai saw its first grain seizure of the year on 13 March. Hondschoote, Hazebrouck, Valenciennes, Bergues, Dunkerque, Lille, and Douai followed close
behind. Through April, struggles over food took place mainly in urban
areas. On 6 May the people of Cambrai seized grain from local merchants'
storehouses and sold it below market. Almost immediately others in the
countryside began breaking into the grain stores of landlords, secular and
ecclesiastical alike, and selling off what they found. In some cases (such as
the abbey of Honnecourt) they burned the archives—those stores of licenses
to exploit the common people—as well. Their fellows attacked landlords'
game, refused to pay dues, started to use enclosed meadows, stopped paying
taxes and tithes.

Taken together, these acts of resistance constituted an unparalleled
challenge to authority. On 30 April the authorities of Lille deplored "the
shameful excesses that a number of malevolent individuals committed
against both farmers and other outsiders who were providing for their subsistence by bringing grain to the city's market, as well as the bakers who
took care to sell bread below its value during the winter, and are still doing
so" (AML 412). On 12 May the parlement of Flanders issued an ineffectual
edict forbidding people to break into private property; in it, the parlementarians expressed shock that people had demanded grain "in the name of the
king." About the same time, frightened municipalities began organizing
local militias to protect themselves against brigands and countrymen who
might strike against their dwindling, high-priced stores of food.

Around Lille, the annual leasing of the ecclesiastical tithe on field crops
began early in July 1789; local groups demanded that the titheholders first
allocate a portion of the tithe to the poor. Confronted with that unprecedented demand, the canons of Lille who were supervising the leasing said
they had to consult the other members of the chapter. Their stall didn't
work. On the morning of 21 July, four hundred women entered Lille, went

to the chapterhouse, and repeated a call for the canons to give a third of their tithe to the poor. Although troops drove them away before others could join them, the women's appearance in the streets sharpened the confrontation between rich and poor. That night came the attacks on the houses of Lille's well-fed elite for which Charles Louis Monique died. The following day, countrywomen returned and broke into the chapterhouse. The canons gave way, conceding a share of the tithe to the rural poor (G. Lefebvre 1959 [1924]: 378–379). The rural and urban revolutions intertwined.

Nor was Lille alone. Douai lived insurrection from 24 to 27 July, with the high point being the sacking of the city's tollgates. In Cambrai "two thousand people, led by musical instruments and drums, used violence to open the jails and free everyone in them" (Martinage and Lorgnier n.d.: 15). On 2 August, Tournai's crowd echoed Lille's; they, too, attacked the homes of bourgeois.

Unlike Paris and the Ile-de-France, Flanders had stirred rather little during the struggles of parlements and ministers in the 1770s and 1780s. Once the possibility arose that landlords and officials would lose their royal backing, however, the region's people entered the fight with a vengeance. They fought for food supplies, for access to commons, for reduction of the tithe, for the right to hunt, against feudal dues, against landlords' privileges. They mounted a sustained assault on the whole apparatus of a semicapitalist agrarian regime.

Direct attacks on landlords occurred mainly in the southeastern half of the region, in Hainaut and Cambrésis. In those regions, according to Georges Lefebvre,

> which were more similar to the rest of the kingdom, the seigneurial regime had kept all its strength. Personal dues, corvees, banalities, rights to trees, taking over of commons, suppression of use rights—nothing was missing. *Terrage* often applied in addition to the tithe. They were harder to bear because of the way in which they were collected and because the country was poorer. Lords were nowhere more eager to reestablish dues that had fallen into disuse or that produced little return; notorious lawsuits brought out fear and anger everywhere. Hate of the landlord, as much as general living conditions, unified almost all the peasants in these provinces and, in July 1789, brought them into rebellion against the old regime. (Lefebvre 1959 [1924]: 171)

In July peasants marched out from their villages to castles and especially to abbeys to demand that lords and abbots renounce, or even reimburse, the dues they had been collecting from the countryside.

In the northern half of the region—in Flanders, properly speaking—

popular action concentrated on the food supply. In those densely settled areas there were few important noble or ecclesiastical landlords, a number of substantial peasants, and a plethora of landless or land-poor workers. That northern region, crisscrossed with canals and largely Flemish-speaking, greatly resembled the Flemish and Dutch regions to the northeast. Whether in cash-crop agriculture, cottage industry, or peat cutting, its population consisted mainly of proletarians.

"Perhaps it is the overpopulation of the countryside," commented the observant English traveler Arthur Young, "to which we should attribute the fact that Flanders, with Europe's richest soil, can't feed its own cities, but must import great quantities of grain from Artois and Picardy, where large farms permit them to supply the neighboring province, whose farms are more fragmented" (Young 1976: III, 1220). Flanders' rural proletarians, heavily involved in textile production, depended on the purchase of food for survival. Within Flanders, Dunkerque, Bergues, Hondschoote, Bailleul, Hazebrouck, Armentières, Lille, and other commercial-industrial cities saw seizures of grain, price fixing, and attacks on presumed hoarders and profiteers.

Frelinghien, a village of 2,000 people about ten kilometers northwest of Lille, had its own semiofficial version of a grain seizure. Jean-Baptiste Blanquart, royal notary there, was the visitor to Lille who had felt obliged to wear the national cockade on 23 July. Blanquart reported that on 31 July at half-past four in the morning

> some women from the community came to ask me to speak to a royal captain, escorting a grain boat for the troops at Lille with fifty grenadiers under his command. Under duress, I went to the Dupire mill. There, with the boat fairly close, I asked to speak to the officer commanding the detachment. I said to him, "Captain, under duress, I have the honor to announce unhappily that the inhabitants of Frelinghien have no grain or bread. Since it is physically impossible to live without eating, and since necessity has no law, moved by their misery, I join with them in asking you to unload enough grain for the subsistence of the inhabitants. I'll guarantee that use of the grain, and will pay a reasonable price." The officer resisted, saying he had strong orders to unload nothing. As a result, I said, pointing toward the people, of whom at least eight hundred had gathered, "Well, sir, if that's how it is, let me say this: I can't hold back this multitude of inhabitants. I declare myself innocent of any bloodshed that may ensue." I added that there were probably twice as many more at Frelinghien that they couldn't see. Moved by my reasoning, he had his troops ready their arms, and offered me flour. (Théry, 1923: 201)

Blanquart was borrowing a tried-and-true tactic: portray your allies or followers as more ferocious than yourself, thereby making your terms seem a better bargain then theirs.

Blanquart made the tactic work. After more maneuvering he arranged to buy 130 sacks of grain. The next day Blanquart went to see Lille's military commander, Boistelle, for authorization to distribute the grain. Boistelle shouted and fumed but finally accepted the *fait accompli.* Around Lille and to the north, in a region swarming with landless laborers, food supply for poor people had a high priority.

Toward the south, in Hainaut, noble and church property became more significant, a few large farmers leasing large estates stood out from the mass of peasants, and the proportion of smallholders rose as well. There, peasants and agricultural workers attacked the landlords with ardor. But the attacks were not indiscriminate. In place after place, people subject to a general payment such as terrage or the tithe first demanded its remission, then forced those landlords who resisted to renounce their rights. About the same time, rural people began open and collective violations of recently established prohibitions against hunting, gleaning, gathering, and pasturing on previously common land. They began to reverse the recent advances of agrarian capitalism.

In the cities and market towns of both south and north, seizures of grain continued. Local people combined direct action against the symbols and realities of clerical or noble power with their attempts to secure an adequate food supply for the dependent poor. The great surge of action against powerholders began in mid-July 1789 and lasted until early in August. Then open conflict declined dramatically: a few minor struggles over food and common land, a last grain seizure in Lille on 23 December, but little else. The attacks and demands of July and early August, however, sufficed. Although troops intervened and people went to jail, on the whole the authorities found themselves unable to suppress such massive action. As a result, some of the old regime had crumbled in Flanders well before the formal abolition of feudalism began on the night of 4 August 1789.

Revolution in the Nord

The territory I have been calling "Flanders," with such reckless inaccuracy, became the department of the Nord in 1790. The revolutionary Nord went through two experiences that set it off from other French departments: France's enemies invaded the Nord several times in 1792, 1793, and 1794, and the later French conquests in the Low Countries temporarily took away its position on the frontier.

In other respects, however, the Nord shared the national experience. The same sorts of conflicts that shook 1789 persisted: in later years peasants continued to resist collection of the tithe, poor people continued to glean landlords' fields and to attack the landlords' own hired gleaners, while grain seizures went on more or less as before.

The urban version of the grain seizure could be just as devastating as under the old regime. On 3 Pluviose, Year IV (23 January 1796), the municipal officers of Lille wrote to the minister of the interior:

> yesterday afternoon we went through a violent crisis because, following your advice, we raised the price of bread slightly. Fifteen to twenty thousand rebels came to the Common House [*Maison Commune*, city hall] and the nearby squares and streets and ordered the municipality to rescind within an hour the decision to raise the price of bread or be massacred and see the city sacked. We did everything we could, short of force, to restore order. We have only a hundred infantrymen, who behaved well. But what could they do against that number of madmen? The mayor, surrounded by the furious horde, would have been massacred if we had resisted any longer. So we had to give in to avoid patricide.   (AML 18008)

Such rebellions had a great deal in common with their old-regime predecessors. The main difference was that the authorities' responses to these popular actions now varied with the phase the Revolution had reached: as the disestablishment of the church proceeded, for example, officials soon stopped punishing resistance to the tithe.

In the Nord and elsewhere, the Revolution did bring some new forms of collective action. When church properties went on sale, many villagers banded together to exclude outsiders from the auctions. When priests had to decide whether to accept the revolutionary Civil Constitution of the Clergy, about 85 percent of the Nord's clergy refused the crucial oath. After that, most country people shunned the priests who took over from the nonjuring clergy, and many villages protected their curés from revolutionary retribution.

The introduction and subsequent devaluation of *assignats,* paper money nominally backed by the value of nationalized properties, furthermore, excited movements of protest from peasants, merchants, and manufacturers; accepting assignats, after all, meant giving goods for dubious currency. When the call for large-scale military conscription to defend the country arose in 1793 and later, resistance to the draft became widespread. Although the struggle against military service harked back to much earlier anticonscription revolts, on the whole these actions responded to the unprecedented demands that revolutionary governments made on ordinary people.

During the early years of the Revolution, reform of the church—more exactly, replacement of the priests who refused to accept the revolutionary reforms—drove the largest wedges into local communities. In Flines, near Douai, the "constitutional" priest who replaced the old curé faced a hostile community. The fifth of October 1791 was a local holiday in Flines. Mouton, the constitutional, reported that "a large number of peasants who called themselves aristocrats and supporters of the old clergy gathered in the square across the street from the church," went into nearby cafés, and shouted "Long live the clergy! Long live the aristocrats!" "After they had drunk for a while and sung a 111-verse song they had composed about the constitutional curé and the local democrats," Mouton continued,

> they left the cafés in which they had gathered. They put white cockades in their hats and lined up behind two soldiers . . . The two soldiers, on horseback with sabers drawn, led the group of peasants with white cockades, and others with branches to which they had attached white cloths. They paraded through the village in an insulting way, shouting "Long live the clergy! Long live the aristocrats! Hang the democrats!" And they sang said song of 111 verses.   (Deschuytter 1959–1961: I, 52)

Mouton reported these counterrevolutionary doings to the district of Douai. The district eventually convicted four day-laborers for their involvement in the serenade-demonstration and in another display of hostility the following February. Elsewhere, people stoned their constitutionals or threw mud at them. In retaliation, patriotic national guard units tried to stop the ministrations of "refractory" priests by interrupting funerals and breaking up church services.

Only in cities such as Lille and Cambrai did the forms of revolutionary enthusiasm—parades, festivals, ceremonies at liberty trees, public oath-taking, meetings of revolutionary committees—prevail. There the revolutionary repertoire combined genuine innovations with clever adaptations. Political meetings and mass oath-takings had few prerevolutionary counterparts; they broke with the entertainments, processions, and solemn assemblies of the old regime by obliterating the previous line between a few participants and a great many spectators. Yet the pageantry and gaiety of the festivals borrowed from the old routines of local holidays. Even the most specifically revolutionary actions, furthermore, often built on old-regime materials. In Lille, for example, young people of different neighborhoods adapted the standard routine of collection for the maypole to new circumstances: they dunned local residents for money to erect liberty trees—those revolutionary equivalents of the maypole—in their own sections of the city.

No doubt the awesome rituals of the Terror left the old regime farthest behind. Yet only Cambrai, where Terrorist Joseph Lebon presided, built the full apparatus of revolutionary justice: tribunal, guillotine, and public humiliation of the Revolution's enemies. Only Lille, Douai, Cambrai, and Bailleul created revolutionary armies, as the militias of the Terror called themselves. Indeed, conflicts of the early Revolution often pitted the reluctant peasants and proletarians of the hinterland against the national guard, and then the revolutionary armies, of the cities, eager both to proselytize the countryside for the Revolution and to assure the urban food supply.

With these crucial exceptions, the conflicts of the Revolution generally borrowed forms that old-regime people knew well: seizures of grain, invasions of fields, and all the rest. The Revolution changed people's interests and collective-action repertoires much less than it changed their opportunities for action.

Revolutionary Reorganization

The Revolution wrought a remarkable series of administrative changes. Revolutionaries installed a single hierarchy of governmental units—commune, canton, arrondissement, department, national state—to replace a welter of overlapping and competing jurisdictions. To that nested series they attached uniform hierarchies of courts, electoral assemblies, representative bodies, and religious jurisdictions, all replacing their old-regime counterparts. That substitution introduced the most spectacular reorganization, but not the most fundamental. Two other changes reached even further into daily life.

The first profound change was the direct incorporation of local communities into the structure of the national state. Under the old regime, despite the presence of royal officers and people holding royal commissions of various sorts in most cities, towns, and villages, the monarchy had ruled local communities incompletely and indirectly; it had relied heavily on priests, lords, and other notables who had strong ties to the crown. As a result intendants, subdelegates, and other officials had to bargain incessantly with powerholders who insisted not on national law but on local privilege. For that arrangement, the revolutionary regimes first substituted a series of extraordinary committees, assemblies, and militias, dominated by the nation's bourgeoisie. Then they squeezed out the committees, subordinated the militias, and coupled each assembly with an executive tightly responsible to the next higher level of authority. As the Revolution moved toward Empire, the executives gained more power than the assemblies. In the process, French people created the first large state in world history ever to rule directly right down to the individual village.

Revolutionary authorities reinforced their incorporation of local communities into the national state by a move old-regime authorities had often dreamed of but never executed: they absorbed both the revenues and the debts of municipalities into the national fiscal structure. In the inflationary years of the early Revolution those debts evaporated.

The monopolization of tax power ended centuries of struggle at a stroke. It continued, even tightened, the dependency of municipalities on the national state. But it ended the state's dependence on the particular abilities of municipalities to raise revenues, and abolished the privileges that had aligned the municipalities against royal efforts to raise taxes. The incorporation of communities was at once a political and a fiscal *tour de force*.

Once that centralized framework started to operate, many actions by local and national authorities reinforced the incorporation of local communities into the state. As never before, the government became the employer of last resort. When wartime price controls squeezed the artisans and retail merchants of Lille and other cities, they often sought employment as clerks, policemen, concierges in government offices. As the revolutionary government built up its military strength, new jobs opened up: "Lille, a frontier fortress, offered very wide opportunities for employment, thanks to teeming military offices and huge storehouses" (Cobb 1965: 154). In fact, with the growth of governmental administration in the Nord, the government became for some people the employer of *first* resort; revolutionary committees served, among other things, as placement offices for well-connected militants.

No doubt conscription had the largest effect of all. The military drafts of 1793 and thereafter involved directly in the government's fate not only every community but also the majority of individual households. During the later Revolution and the Empire, the professionalization of government service and the continued expansion of military organization continued the absorption of local life into the national state.

The second deep change followed from the first. France's cities finally gained something their rulers had long coveted: the power to coerce their hinterlands. As landlords, titheholders, tax collectors, and merchants, city people had long exploited country people. Nevertheless, the presence in the countryside of lords, priests, and municipalities holding chartered privileges had checked the ambitions of the cities. Old-regime urban officials, for example, had few means to force outsiders to deliver them food in times of shortage. As a result they encouraged wealthy households and institutions to assure their own food supplies via tithes, rents, and direct production of crops both inside and outside the city walls.

Shortages of the early Revolution, however, brought the apparatus of committees, assemblies, administrations, and militias together in the requisition of grain and the control of its marketing throughout the hinterland. Rural people resisted and evaded those frightening controls as best they could. Yet the cities' combination of revolutionary zeal, authorized armed force, and backing from the state tipped the balance away from hapless countrymen. As city administrations lost their autonomy in relation to the state, they gained power over their hinterlands.

Flanders Faces the Nineteenth Century

At the nineteenth century's very outset, the Nord's prefect Christopher Dieudonné signed a famous *Statistique* prepared mainly by his secretary-general, Sébastien Bottin. Looking back from 1801 through a dozen years of war and revolution, Dieudonné/Bottin saw a department that had lost about 13,000 people from its 1789 total of 808,000. The cities had lost some 30,000 inhabitants, just over 10 percent of their total, while the countryside had actually gained. "It isn't hard to understand the reasons for that decline in the urban population," said the *Statistique:* "Emigration was heavier from the cities, and we know that many émigrés died. The cities supplied many more men, proportionately, to the armies. The stagnation of trade, shops, and factories for ten years paralyzed thousands of workers, most of whom went elsewhere to find work" (Dieudonné 1804: 37). The 795,000 people who remained were distributed unevenly among the department's six districts. Table 6 summarizes the division of land and people in 1801.

Dieudonné's data make the variation plain. In the reclaimed, still relatively marshy, land of the northern district of Bergues, meadows used for stock raising constitute a third of the area. Around Hazebrouck we find less water and more woods, but about the same area in pasture. Lille has the highest share of its land in houses, mills, and factories, as well as the most arable land: around its crowded cities and towns, more than three-quarters of

Table 6. Distribution of land and people in the Nord, 1801 (percent of total land by arrondissement)

Category	Bergues	Hazebrouck	Lille	Cambrai	Avesnes	Douai	Department total
Woods	2.8	8.6	4.0	5.5	21.4	12.4	10.7
Water	2.3	0.3	0.6	0.3	0.4	0.6	0.7
Swamp	3.5	0.6	1.4	0.1	0.2	1.2	1.0
Pasture	33.2	31.5	11.4	10.9	36.7	15.7	23.9
Arable	48.6	52.0	73.1	78.4	35.0	62.0	56.3
Gardens	2.0	0.9	3.4	1.1	0.7	1.9	1.6
Roads	2.0	4.4	4.2	2.5	2.5	3.2	3.1
Structures[a]	1.0	1.2	1.8	1.2	0.6	1.4	1.1
Waste	4.6	0.4	0.0	0.0	2.5	1.5	1.6
Total	100.0	99.9	99.9	100.0	100.0	99.9	100.0
Total hectares	73,706	70,818	90,410	87,361	149,510	107,884	579,689
Population	83,685	101,970	226,519	112,944	98,288	171,466	794,872
Persons/km^2	113.5	144.0	250.5	129.3	65.7	158.9	137.1

Source: Dieudonné 1804: 32–35.
a. "Houses, mills, and factories."

its area is given over to gardens and cultivated fields. The district of Cambrai resembles that of Lille, with even more land in gardens and arable. Avesnes, to the southeast, has much of its area in woods and pasture, and little in urban structures. Douai, though relatively wooded, has more than its share of arable. All districts but that of Avesnes are settled at densities twentieth-century people recognize as nearly urban; Lille, with over 250 persons per square kilometer, teems with people.

One crucial use of the Nord's land occupied too little area to show up in such a comparison: the mere 44 hectares in mines and quarries concentrated in the southeastern section of the department, including the low-density district of Avesnes. The three coal mines of Fresnes, Vieux-Condé, and Anzin produced more than any other comparable cluster in France. At the time of the Revolution, according to Dieudonné/Bottin, the Anzin mine was an "immense establishment" that had "reached a high degree of splendor" (Dieudonné 1804: I, 165). Some 4,000 workers, reported the *Statistique,* then toiled in the mines.

Similarly, the land-use data hide the very widespread digging and burning of peat in the department's northern districts—one more tie to the standard organization of the Dutch-speaking coastal regions to the northeast. Finally, charcoal-burning forges worked the iron drawn from mines in the heavily wooded region around Avesnes.

These various fuels supported metalworking industries through much of the Nord. The central and northern sections also operated an important vegetable oil industry. Nevertheless, at the start of the nineteenth century textiles dominated the department's manufacturing. Dieudonné/Bottin took it as a matter of course that rural people generally worked in agriculture, but spun and wove in the off-season. Cities such as Lille, Cambrai, and Douai not only controlled the trade in textiles but also housed their own large shops. Wool manufacturing became more prominent toward the southeastern edge of the Nord, cotton concentrated in the regions of Lille and Douai, and linen flourished through much of the department. As of 1804, all that textile activity made the Nord one of the world's great industrial areas. With textiles, oil pressing, mining, metalworking, and other industries, country and city alike buzzed with trade.

Concentration and Implosion

The Nord entered the nineteenth century an industrial and commercial powerhouse. City and country alike connected to national and international markets. The Nord already contained provincial France's greatest concentration of industrial capital. Yet its industry and commerce belonged to recognizable eighteenth-century types. The Nord's people in 1804 produced mainly for markets and often worked for wages. But most of them did their work in small producing units: shops, farms, households. In the countryside a large number of wage earners divided their time among seasonal labor on other people's farms, domestic manufacturing for local merchants, and gardening on the small plots they rented or owned. In the cities merchants, master artisans, journeymen, and domestic workers all aimed their efforts toward the market. Except for mines, almost all productive organizations operated with few workers and modest capital. Merchants, rather than capitalist entrepreneurs, provided the regional economy's connective tissue.

The next century wrought great changes: concentration of capital; movement of labor, production, and capital to cities; expansion of production based on machines and fossil fuels; shift of the prime locus of proletarians and proletarianization to urban areas. The Nord led the national implosion of capital, labor, and production itself into cities and factories. The Nord took on the lineaments of urban, industrial capitalism.

The Nord's capitalists did more than move production to cities, increase the scale of production, expand horsepower, multiply machines, and introduce full-fledged factory production. They launched a centurylong struggle to wrest control of production and of labor markets away from workers. Workers resisted where and when they could. They organized, sabotaged, went on strike, attacked strikebreakers and cheap laborers recruited from outside. The Nord became famous for its workers' militancy.

Yet over the century capitalists, usually supported by local and national authorities in the name of "order" and "freedom to work," gained enormous ground. Proletarianization and subordination of labor began in the mines but soon entered metalworking and textiles. By 1900 big capitalists, responding to signals from national and international markets, made the basic decisions concerning what to produce, how much, where, and with what labor; only the conditions under which workers would actually supply that labor remained open to bargaining.

Textiles continued to dominate the region's industry. Cotton started displacing wool and linen. Mining, metalworking, and steam-powered manufacturing increased in scope and scale. Small industrial cities such as Anzin grew large, and villages that had formerly hosted cottage industry grew into smoky factory towns. Tourcoing and Roubaix provide the obvious examples.

In and around Lille itself cotton production expanded, a garment industry organized in urban sweatshops arose, rural linen production for urban entrepreneurs and distant markets flourished, and the trade of an industrial region multiplied. Nearby Tourcoing specialized in wool weaving, while adjacent Roubaix concentrated on cotton. Not far north, Halluin worked with linen. Although the commercial crisis of 1827–1831 stimulated a move of Roubaix's manufacturers back toward wool, cotton remained king there throughout the nineteenth century. Throughout the century Belgians from nearby regions of declining cottage industry poured across the border into Roubaix, Tourcoing, and other expanding factory towns. At the century's high point, in 1872, just over half of Roubaix's population was Belgian-born (Reardon 1981: 172).

Unlike the hinterlands of smaller industrial centers elsewhere in France, the countryside around Lille, Cambrai, and other accumulators of capital in the Nord did not deindustrialize, depopulate, and turn to market gardening for the urban market. Around the great centers of cotton and wool production, handloom weaving of higher-priced cloth survived the century. Elsewhere in the Nord, lace and batistes provided work for thousands of spinners and weavers. The miners of Anzin, Fourmies, and other places in the department's southeastern half dug wider and deeper. Industrial towns and villages proliferated, and even seasonal domestic production continued. Despite its glorious agricultural history, the industrializing region came to depend more and more on imports of food from elsewhere.

Concentration and implosion occurred in the sphere of coercion as well as in the sphere of capital. Postrevolutionary governments, for all their trappings of royalty, clung to the consolidated, centralized structure built during the Revolution and fortified during the Empire. A researcher sees it in the archives—which are, after all, nothing but trimmed-down files of former governments. Before the Revolution, royal officials' correspondence shows them maneuvering to increase the central government's power, especially its fiscal power. It shows them bargaining with city authorities and regional institutions. It shows them intervening in the region's affairs with increasing power, but still as outsiders and after the fact. Intendants, subdelegates, and their fellows did acquire advance information about the doings of regional powerholders; indeed, most of them came from or joined existing networks of power. But they left the day-to-day surveillance and control of the general population to municipal authorities, regional courts, church officials, and local lords. As a result, little anticipatory intelligence about the likely actions of workers and regional powerholders flowed from Lille or Valenciennes to Versailles.

What a contrast with the postrevolutionary archives! Nineteenth-century representatives of the state still had to take the region's powerholders into account. But their correspondence and records also show them operating the governmental apparatus down to the individual community; they pumped to Paris a continuous stream of information on fiscal administration, road construction, opportunities to promote manufacturing or trade, worker organization, and political action. The old regime's intendants might have deplored the lack of autonomy that characterized the prefects, their nineteenth-century successors; but they would surely have envied the means of coercion and intelligence those prefects had at their call.

The twin concentrations of capital and coercion framed nineteenth-century contention. The holders of capital began with a decided advantage. Their control of growing capital in a time of capital intensification helped them become masters of the sphere of production. But the Revolution and Empire had also given them great power in the sphere of coercion. Their access to the state helped them establish a public definition of workers' organization as a threat to public order, of strikes as "disorders" or "troubles" or at least as "violations of the freedom to work."

Workers, furthermore, had carried over from the old regime a principle of organization and collective action that concentration made obsolete. In general, skilled workers in a trade organized at the level of a community, sought to make a common front against the workers of that community, and tried to control the entry of workers into their trade anywhere in the community. To control actual and potential workers in the trade, they deployed a variety of sanctions: sharing of rituals and secrets, pooling for mutual aid, withholding of information and support from nonconformists, plus ritual mockery and direct coercion for blacklegs, ratebreakers, strikebreakers, and other undesirables.

Early nineteenth-century workers likewise had a number of means for putting pressure on employers. The word "strike," which we now associate inevitably with firm-by-firm action, conveys badly their usual mode of action. The British word "turnout" fits better: the routine in which a group of aggrieved workers in a trade assembled to talk over their grievances, then went from shop to shop in that trade throughout the community, made a hullabaloo, called the workers inside to join them, continued their march through the streets until they had assembled as much of the trade as they could muster, moved off to a relatively secure public place (such as a field at the edge of town), debated their grievances, demands, and actions, then sent a delegation to bargain with representatives of the employers.

As employers built large plants employing may workers in different trades, and as the number of workers in a community began to number thousands, the old scale and type of organization no longer served workers well. In skilled crafts employing relatively small numbers and giving their members control of irreplaceable, crucial skills, adaptations of the old forms survived; indeed, with strikes and trade unions illegal, nineteenth-century workers' politics long depended on secret, militant organizations built on craft models. But in the growing remainder of the labor force the old organization atrophied or never formed at all. The growth of large firms and semiskilled industrial labor eventually threatened the artisans on their own ground; through competition or through their direct employment by large capitalists, artisans and skilled workers faced proletarianization.

During the nineteenth century, as capital concentrated, and as the alliance of capital and state became more obvious, workers fashioned new forms of organization and action: the politically active workers' association, the trade union, the public demonstration, the firm-by-firm strike. By the end of the century workers of the Nord had established themselves as socialists, as collectivists, as allies of political radicals. In 1893 Jules Guesde, the great socialist leader, himself went to the Chamber of Deputies from a Roubaix constituency.

Workers' Politics

The Nord took a while to recover from the rigors of the Napoleonic wars. The region bore the brunt of enemy occupation in 1815, then slowly rebuilt its industrial strength. One of the costs of losing the war was that Belgium once again became foreign territory. That result cut off merchants along the frontier from an important area of domestic production. Merchants responded by encouraging migration across the frontier into the newly forming shops and factories. By 1819 one of the century's recurrent themes of conflict had come clearly into view: cost-cutting employers recruited Belgian workers from nearby areas of declining cottage industry as native French workers attempted to maintain control of the labor market—and, to some small extent, of wages—by keeping Belgians out.

In Roubaix employers had been cutting wages on the ground that (despite protective tariffs) English competition was doing them in. At the same time they had been recruiting Belgians who were willing to cross the border and work for low wages. They had also been building high-density housing for the workers, deducting the rent from their pay, and evicting workers who proved to be troublesome. Those *courées* and *forts,* as people called them, were becoming heavily Belgian. On Bastille Day 1819, according to the royal prosecutor,

> rather serious disturbances broke out in that populous and entirely industrial city . . . Politics has nothing to do with the affair . . . it is a sort

of coalition among French workers for the purpose of expelling from Roubaix and the surrounding area the Belgian workers who have settled there, and whose competition brings down a wage that the French would like to see rise. The fourteenth of this month, between eight and nine in the evening, when the workers were leaving their shops, a crowd of four or five hundred people gathered in Roubaix. The aim of that gathering was to attack and expel the foreign workers employed in the same shops. The local police stepped in, and order was restored. (AN BB[18] 993)

On 15 July three gendarmes on horseback frightened off another gathering, but a rock hit one Belgian; he was said to have shouted, while under the protection of the gendarmes, "You Frenchmen can't do anything to us. We're the bosses here now!" (AN BB[18] 993). The gatherings continued for days.

The fact that the prosecutor ruled out "politics" meant that no organized group making claims on the national structure of power—republicans, supporters of Napoleon, or anyone else of that ilk—had a hand in the events. In fact Flemish-French hostility as such played only a small part in the local politics of Roubaix and other frontier towns. For the next two decades, workers' politics in the Nord concerned labor markets, wages, and working conditions.

The transition from the Restoration of 1815–1830 to the July Monarchy of 1830–1848 made little difference to the tone or tempo of workers' politics in the Nord. True, a moment of absorption into national politics arrived in 1830; during the July Days, as the news of insurrection arrived from Paris, workers streamed out of the factories of Lille and rushed through the streets breaking windows and shouting "Long live the Charter!" When the cavalry tried to break up the crowds, people stoned them. When the infantry fraternized, the shout changed to "Down with the cavalry! Long live the line!" (*Gazette des Tribunaux,* 2 and 3 August 1830). In Douai, young people "of the working class" went through the streets forcing people to light their lights in celebration of the Revolution (AN F[7] 6778).

The struggle with employers, however, continued to preoccupy the Nord's workers. The night of 10 August 1830, for example, workers in Roubaix gathered in large numbers and asked employers for a raise. More precisely, they demanded restoration of the four sous per yard of finished cloth employers had cut from their pay the year before. For resisting that decision by undoing the cloth then in their looms and disassembling the looms themselves, in October 1829 the merchants' court of Roubaix had sentenced several workers at the Motte Brédard plant to two days in jail and court costs (Deyon 1981: 65). Ten months later, in August 1830, Roubaix's weavers "broke the windows of the principal factories," wrote the royal prosecutor, "and entered in force to ask for written agreement to the raise" (AN BB[18] 1186). Although *Le Moniteur Universel* of Paris blamed the action on "foreign workers," the chief division clearly followed class lines (*Le Moniteur Universel* 18 August 1830).

In general, until the 1840s the Nord's workers relied on the local organization of their trades and made little effort to form unions and other special-purpose associations. More broadly, associations did not begin to play major parts as vehicles of collective action—working-class or bourgeois— until well after the July Revolution. In 1834 the prosecutor of the arrondissement of Lille provided an inventory of associations in the city. He enumerated 106 workers' mutual aid societies, providing sick benefits from pooled funds and named for saints.

The city's bourgeoisie—"merchants, rich bourgeois, and national guards"—had twelve associations whose object was to drink and play cards. The only one with a worrisome political cast, he reported, was the *salon des négociants,* which consisted of confirmed legitimists. The one republican drinking club, with twenty-two members, had recently dissolved. Finally, medical students had a society that "does not seem to involve politics" (AN BB[3] 167). Only in the 1840s did an organized republican opposition start to show up in Lille's public life.

To the thinness of formal organization among workers corresponded a near-absence of strikes. Workers in textile towns did occasionally use the informal structure of their trade to keep others away from their jobs, to sanction workers who broke ranks, and to organize an occasional turnout. But on the whole, considering their wages and working conditions, the Nord's textile workers mounted very little collective opposition to the region's capitalists during the 1820s and 1830s.

For serious, long-term strikes during those decades, we must turn to the Nord's miners, especially those who worked for the big Anzin Company in its pits at St.-Waast-la-Haut and Anzin. Citing fierce Belgian competition, the company had begun cutting wages in the early 1820s. At the same time it tightened surveillance and discipline in the mines. The economizing paid off; in 1833 the company's stockholders were receiving an 8 percent return on their investment (Guignet 1973: 351). The miners complained not only of the four sous in daily pay they had lost in 1823, but also of being treated with contempt by the Anzin Company's officials.

Periodically the miners struck back. Shortly after the July Revolution, for example, they had risen briefly and unsuccessfully (Aguet 1954: 56). In

May 1833 it was a different story. The so-called Four Sous Riot (*émeute des quatre sous*) made its mark in national labor history. When the Anzin Company's governors met in Anzin on 10 May, word spread among miners that the governors were finally going to give back the four sous they had taken away ten years earlier. Nothing of the sort happened. After the disappointing meeting, a new story went the rounds: the company was actually considering another wage cut, and Charles Mathieu (pit supervisor at St.-Waast, whose brother Joseph was mine inspector and mayor of Anzin) had been cashiered for favoring a raise. The story gained credibility from the fact that, shortly after the governors' meeting, Charles Mathieu did leave the company to take a job elsewhere.

On 17 May two or three hundred people—men, women, and children—gathered before the company offices in St.-Waast. They demanded their four sous, called for the firing of three overzealous supervisors, and sang songs whose refrain ran "Down with the Parisians, long live the Mathieux of Anzin!" (Guignet 1973: 348). Some of the miners went to the lodgings of Monnier, one of the three unpopular supervisors, where they broke furniture and tore up clothing.

After the company's general agent, Englishman Mark Jennings, met with members of the crowd, the mayor and the curé of Anzin persuaded the miners and their families to disband. In the meantime, however, company officials had called the police. That evening detachments of gendarmes, cavalry, and infantry, plus 150 national guards, converged on Anzin. During the following days gendarmes made a few arrests, and support for a work stoppage developed in a number of nearby coal mines, but few direct confrontations between miners and troops occurred. Philippe Guignet summarizes the events:

> From 17 to 22 May the miners unquestionably kept the lead; the movement spread, the "forces of order," which were numerically inferior to the massed workers, being unable or unwilling to stop the strikers. That is why the authorities decided to put a stop to the movement on the twenty-second by calling on regular army units. On the twenty-seventh, in a region placed under a state of siege, the miners decided to return to work. (Guignet 1973: 348)

The national authorities who sent in massive force were probably remembering the 1831 silkworkers' strike in Lyon, which turned into a general insurrection; they were not going to let Anzin get out of hand.

As insurgents, the miners of Anzin were remarkably nonviolent during the Four Sous Riot. But as strikers, they looked remarkably like insurgents. In fact during the 1830s the miners and their employers had no established routine—by striking or otherwise—for collective negotiation over employment, wages, and working conditions. Every work stoppage therefore took on a tinge of insurrection.

Mid-Century Mobilization

The increased tempo of industrial conflict during the 1830s and 1840s normalized the strike, at least to some degree. Miners kept up their losing battle for wages and job control. Anzin itself produced another small strike in December 1833, and standup battles in 1837, 1846, and 1848; in these confrontations miners typically tried to stop the pithead machinery, and mine owners typically called in troops to protect their property. During the same period the mines of Denain, Fresnes, Vieux-Condé, and Abscon joined the ranks of major strike producers; in most of their strikes, a walkout from one mine incited a work stoppage in at least one more.

In the later 1830s textile workers of Lille's region began to organize strikes as never before. In the spinning mills of Lille, employers cut the piece rate in 1839. The senior workers of dozens of plants started meeting to plan their defense, first establishing a pool of money to aid the unemployed, then edging toward transforming it into a strike fund. The first full-fledged work stoppage came in August. After a quick settlement of that first dispute, which ended with city officials intervening to cancel the wage reduction, the "elders" of the trade started drafting a citywide agreement.

By mid-September workers were responding to rising food prices by calling for wage increases. Paris' *Le Constitutionnel* clipped this account of the events of 20 September from the *Echo du Nord:*

> Groups of cotton spinners who had left their shops went to various spinning mills to persuade those who were still working to follow them. In some of these plants the rebels started disturbances by throwing stones at the windows. The national guard eagerly took arms; a number of patrols organized at once and spread out through the city, especially toward the threatened places. About nine o'clock that night the groups, which had previously been separated, met together in the main square; one heard incoherent yells, or rather jeers, that the national guard had the good sense to ignore. A police officer read the mayor's edict forbidding riotous assemblies. Immediately afterward, he gave the required three calls to disperse, and the national guard started clearing the square.

Heavy rain helped scatter the groups. The following morning at five the national guard was out; its mission was to assure the entry into shops of those workers who didn't want to follow their comrades in rebellion. There were still a few attempts at disorder and a few arrests. (*Le Constitutionnel* 23 September 1839)

As we might expect, the national guard drew its troops especially from Lille's bourgeoisie.

Although the spinners of Lille did not strike again on any scale until 1848, the series of conflicts in 1839 showed the substantial class division within the city as well as the capacity of its textile workers for collective action. In nearby Tourcoing, Roubaix, and Fourmies, similar strikes—most often incited by employers' attempts to cut wages, and again typically ending with the authorities' use of armed force against the workers—occurred repeatedly between 1839 and 1848.

During the same period, small signs began to appear that workers were identifying their cause with opposition politics at the national scale. In the Nord those glimmers of political opposition often took on a republican tint but sometimes colored themselves Bonapartist. In 1840 the prosecutor at the royal court of Douai began to report incidents in which people sang the semiseditious *Marseillaise* in the streets or at the theater. In 1841 republicans of Lille and Valenciennes joined the resistance to the national census, seen widely as a government maneuver to extend its control and to clear the way for tax increases.

In 1846, when workers of Roubaix gathered to protest curtailment of the Mardi Gras celebrations, they turned to attacking well-dressed young men as "sons of industrialists," shouting "Down with the industrialists!" and breaking the windows of bourgeois cafés, police stations, and homes of manufacturers. They sang the *Marseillaise* as they marched through the streets. When the radical bourgeois of Lille organized their part of the national campaign for political reform in 1847, a few workers actually joined them. With the news of the February Revolution in Paris, many of the activists in Lille's streets were workers. The theme song of those days was, of course, the *Marseillaise*.

Once a provisional republic took power in Paris, workers of the Nord underwent a remarkable mobilization. In Valenciennes, Tourcoing, and especially Lille, workers' marches through the streets became commonplace. Almost immediately after the February Revolution, furthermore, a new round of important strikes began. During 1848 Anzin, Lille, Roubaix, and Tourcoing all had significant strike movements. Then, as Louis Napoleon's government tightened its control, moved to the right, and began its deliberate dismantling of the radical republican movement in the country as a whole, the Nord's workers demobilized.

The experience of Lille shows that process of mobilization and demobilization clearly. When the news of revolution first reached Lille on 25 February 1848, groups of workers entered the prefecture, seized rugs, wall hangings, and a bust of Louis-Philippe from the prefect's dwelling, burned the household goods in the city's Grand'Place, paraded the bust through the streets like a severed head, and threw it in the canal. Groups of workers likewise burned the suburban railroad station at Fives and attacked the interim central station in Lille. Noisy gatherings in the streets continued for several days. The National Guard of Lille took on the task of containing them.

Two weeks later, Lille's workers were again marching. This time, however, they were protesting cuts in the workday (hence in total pay). The city's textile manufacturers, under pressure from the Nord's revolutionary commissioner, Delescluze, had agreed upon the cuts as a way of getting unemployed workers back on the job. A group of workers sought to organize a citywide turnout but failed to bring out all those who had accepted the reduced scale. Strikers gathered outside the working shops, shouted their call, and tried to block the entries. Workers ("accompanied by women and children," according to *Le Siècle,* 20 March 1848) set up barricades and fought the national guard in the streets. But their main business was with employers and strikebreakers. The evening of 14 March, for example, about four hundred men, women, and children had assembled in Lille's Grand'Place and marched off toward the city's spinning plants, singing the *Marseillaise.* According to Courtin, government commissioner at Lille, at about eight o'clock

> a large group of workers went through several streets of Lille to the house of M. Bonami Defresne, a spinning master. After making threats and shouting, they broke the entire front of the house with stones and staves. Windows, frames, and blinds were nearly destroyed, and large stones have been found inside the house. The disorder did not end until the police and national guard approached; without them, the crowd would most likely have entered the dwelling . . . The workers are unemployed, and unfortunately blame that terrible state of affairs on the bad will of the masters. M. Defresne is disliked because of the frequent difficulties he has had with the people he employs. The spinning mill, which is separate from his house, was left alone.   (AN BB[30] 360)

At the same time that some workers were in the streets, however, others were attending the Société des Ouvriers, which collaborated with the

Société Républicaine des Amis du Peuple in the first phases of the revolution at Lille. Although employment, salaries, and working conditions remained the centers of workers' politics, they had once again connected directly with national politics.

Lille's conflicts continued through 1848, with workers breaking into the premises of the republican *Echo du Nord* in response to its comments on workers' complaints (15 April), meeting to demand aid for the unemployed (10 May), vigorously protesting the exclusion of some workers from the workshops set up for the unemployed (22 May), demonstrating against employers who were introducing the system of two banks of bobbins per spinner (14 August), besieging the mayor to resist the substitution of piece rates for daily pay in the municipal workshops (24 August), and striking repeatedly through it all. As the struggles continued, however, the prefect sent troops to break strikes and dissolved the Société Républicaine des Fileurs de Coton de Lille as the municipality finally dissolved the municipal workshops and as it became a crime to call for the "democratic and social republic." By the end of 1848, as in the rest of France, control of the government had slipped away from the coalition of workers and radical republicans that had formed in February.

The rightward drift continued. In Lille an antirepublican association, Les Amis de l'Ordre, made its appearance. After a round of republican-worker demonstrations (one of them a Mardi Gras procession mocking the great figures of the new regime, including President Louis Napoleon) early in 1849, the city's left began to collapse. The pace of strike activity declined as well. The workers of Lille, after a year on the defensive, were demobilizing. As if to underline that demobilization, authorities forbade civic celebration of the revolution's anniversary at the end of February, called for a *Te Deum*, and once again made the singing of the *Marseillaise* a crime.

Neither workers nor bourgeois republicans managed very effective resistance to Louis Napoleon's final seizure of power. Lille became the center of articulate republicanism. As a retrospective report to the minister of justice put it:

> The newspaper *Messager du Nord* put itself at the head of the movement as its editor, M. Bianchi, began active oral propaganda. In Lille and the surrounding area even the most active vigilance could not prevent the formation of extremely dangerous secret societies. On 20 October they found at the door of the subprefecture of Avesnes an anonymous note saying: "Citizen subprefect, you dissolved the national guard . . . In 1852 you'll get yours. When the time comes, we'll burn your headquarters, and we'll know how to get rid of you." (AN BB[30] 423)

The dream of an insurrection to bring the Democratic and Social Republic in 1852 had apparently not died in Avesnes. But the dreamers had again to dream it anonymously, in dark of night.

Louis Napoleon preempted any such insurrection by his coup d'état of 2 December. Lille, Douai, and Anzin then gave the Nord's chief shows of resistance. In Lille on the evening of 3 December, a "deplorable collision" set the police against 600 republican demonstrators, who shouted "Long live the Republic!" and sang the *Marseillaise* but eventually dispersed without trying to take over the city (*Le Constitutionnel* 7 December 1851). Douai had a similar confrontation; 200 shouters of "seditious slogans" faced the police. In Anzin 40 workers broke into the city hall, grabbed guns, and went from factory to factory in Anzin, Raismes, Beuvrages, and Vicoigne, trying unsuccessfully to bring out the workers. At the approach of a cavalry detachment from Valenciennes, the would-be rebels turned tail (*Le Moniteur Universel* 10 December 1851). The newspaper reported that Anzin's raiders were not miners; of the 11 residents of Anzin formally charged with participation in resistance to the coup, one was a clerk for the Anzin Company, and the rest were artisans outside the mines (An BB[30] 396). The great workers' mobilization of 1848 had definitively ended.

Changing Repertoires

Contention in the Nord during the Second Republic combined forms of action that strongly recalled the eighteenth century with other forms that remain familiar today. Attacks on Belgian workers, for example, reached their nineteenth-century peak between 1848 and 1851. Around Denain especially, manufacturing workers tried repeatedly to force the firing and expulsion of Belgians. But Denain was not alone: in May 1848, workers in Tourcoing and in Semain called for Belgians to leave town. Where the workforce in a trade was relatively small and compact, resident workers could still hope to control the local labor market. In time of contraction, that often meant calling for the expulsion of "outsiders," even those who had been at work for a long time.

Similarly, textile workers continued to act via the communitywide turnout: trying to get the entire trade to stop work by marching from shop to shop and by blocking the entrances to unstruck shops. That tactic was becoming decreasingly effective in the towns with large shops and many workers, such as Roubaix. There, the one-firm strike was becoming common.

Struggles over food showed the combination of old and new forms most clearly. The term "food riot" gives a specious sense of continuity; in the nineteenth century, it covers routines as different as blockage of the shipment of grain, seizure of stored grain for placement in the public domain, forced sale of grain or bread below the current market price, direct attacks on presumed profiteers, and demonstrations urging public officials to control prices, distribute food, or punish profiteers. During the Second Republic all of these occurred at one time or another in the Nord.

Blockages occurred fairly often. In April 1848, for example, workers in Dunkerque stopped the departure of a shipload of grain from the port while people in Trélon, Anor, and Baives, on the Belgian border, blocked the shipment of grain out of France. In Anor people also confiscated eight sacks of flour from a merchant and deposited them in the town hall, asking that the municipality distribute the flour free. In Fourmies

> they forced the mayor to go with the workers to raid a baker. They took 170 sacks of flour from him. Those sacks likewise went to the town hall, but people were very angry because of the size of the stock. The women, especially, made a great racket, threatening to string up the baker on the liberty tree. In order to escape, that man and a co-owner of the flour said they were making a gift of the flour to the commune. (AN BB[30] 360, report of deputy prosecutor of Avesnes, 29 April 1848)

When workers from Trélon went to Baives in order to stop shipments across the border, the municipality of Baives rang the tocsin and called out the national guard, who shot at the invaders and severely wounded two. (An exaggerated account reaching *Le Constitutionnel* and *Le Siècle* in Paris reported twelve of Trélon's workers dead in that encounter.)

In addition to these classic actions, people also organized in ways that broke with the eighteenth-century grain seizure. On 19 May 1848, for instance, "troublemakers" in Villers-Outréaux, near Cambrai, "assessed a contribution in bread and money on those landowners whom they singled out as giving nothing or too little to the poor"; a detachment of gendarmes and fifty cavalrymen soon put a stop to that popular organization of charity (*Le Siècle* 29 May 1848). The demand that wages be adjusted to match the price of food, or vice versa, figured repeatedly in the workers' demonstrations in larger cities. Indeed, the price and supply of food remained crucial issues for the Nord's workers well into the twentieth century. Men and women of the Nord, for example, took an active part in the nationwide demonstrations of 1911 against high food prices.

By 1911, however, the old-fashioned blockage, seizure, and forced sale had almost faded from memory. On a national scale, the last important wave of grain seizures in the old style came in 1853–54. During that period, troops of beggars wandered through the Nord and harassed householders. In Cambrai someone circulated an anonymous handbill threatening grain merchants. In Aymeries, near Avesnes, someone tried to burn a hayrick, leaving a pole stuck in the ground bearing a chunk of bread and a notice: BREAD AT FIFTEEN SOUS OR EVERY FARM WILL BE BURNED! (AN BB[30] 432). That was as close as the hungry Nord came to a grain seizure. Despite constant struggle over wages, prices, and living conditions, the Nord never again produced a significant cluster of blockages, seizures, or forced sales. During the *vie chère* movement of 1911, women in many markets of the Nord did set prices for butter, eggs, and milk. But their action generally took the form of organized demonstrations by women's "resistance leagues" (Flonneau 1966). From its place as the most frequent form of popular contention in 1789, in sixty years the grain seizure had dwindled to insignificance.

Meanwhile the strike, the demonstration, the election rally, the public meeting had become the standard forms of popular involvement in open struggle. During 1848 and 1849 ordinary people—especially workers—of the Nord had helped combine these newer forms into their part of a national political movement. The repression of 1849 and thereafter checked that variety of popular involvement for twenty years but did not stamp it out entirely.

In the 1850s the strike itself was still evolving: the turnout and related forms of communitywide action within a trade were declining as the firm-by-firm strike came into its own. In Roubaix, for example, we see a significant contrast between the 1840s, when weavers and spinners generally tried to turn out the entire trade against the masters for the purpose of striking a collective bargain, and the 1860s, when the workers of Motte, Toulemonde, Roussel, Delfosse, and other major firms struck separately and made their own settlements—even though management and workers in each company constantly watched and aided their counterparts in the city's other firms.

The only important exception was the Roubaix general strike of 1867. Then workers from many firms joined in attacking both the homes and the shops of the capitalists who had sent out an appeal for work on two looms instead of one. Even that strike had begun as separate actions within three large firms. When the owners of the struck firms consulted with each other and with their fellow owners, that concert borught all the city's weavers together (ADN M 619). The concentration of capital and the increase in the scale of the labor market had rendered the old forms of working-class collective action ineffective; it thereby promoted workers' counterorganization at the scale of the firm.

By the 1860s, more generally, concentration and nationalization of both capital and coercion had wrought a great transformation of popular contention. At the end of the Second Empire the ordinary people of the Nord were engaged in meetings, demonstrations, electoral campaigns, associations, and trade unions in ways that look quite familiar to twentieth-century eyes.

More was to come: continuous struggles between secularizing radicals and defenders of the Catholic church against disestablishment; strikes at a scale and frequency not previously imagined, including the great Anzin conflict of 1884, fictionalized in Zola's *Germinal;* May Days marked by strikes and demonstrations, including the massacre of workers in Fourmies on 1 May 1891; the formation of a strong Marxist workers' party led by Jules Guesde; election campaigns such as the one in 1891 that made Paul Lafargue, Marx's son-in-law, deputy of Lille; fights between activists of competing parties; the 1911 protests over high food prices; in short, the full, familiar apparatus of twentieth-century contention. The apparatus rested on a clear line separating labor from capital. A song published by Roubaix barkeep, poet, and former weaver Victor Cappart in 1885 conveys the Nord's working-class rhetoric (Marty 1982: 199):

> Bankers and big owners
> Lucky in your birth,
> I see you don't want to know
> The misery of proletarians.
> You stroll comfortably
> While the workers labor
> Without fatigue, you sleep lazily
> On wool, while workers sleep on straw.

Not that all workers were fiercely militant, or that none ever collaborated with capitalists. At Roubaix itself the persistent division between French and Belgian frequently compromised working-class solidarity. During the late nineteenth century, Roubaix's employers had some success in organizing company unions to combat workers' own organizations. Industrialist Eugène Motte even wrested the mayor's position away from the local socialists. Yet in Roubaix and elsewhere, the dominant themes of popular collective action derived from class conflict.

In a sort of complaint, Robert Pierreuse once commented on workers' politics in Roubaix at the end of the nineteenth century:

> Politics didn't interest [the worker] except to the extent that the doctrines and men that sought his vote helped or wanted to help solve the social problem caused by the existence of a rich bourgeoisie owning the means of production and a proletariat that considered itself oppressed, whose existence depended heavily on bosses who gave him work and paid low wages. Workers of Roubaix aimed at only one goal: their own liberation. They joined the electoral fray only to reduce the influence of capital. (Pierreuse 1969: 250)

One reading of this situation is that Roubaix's workers had a cramped, self-interested view of politics. Another is that they had become that long-sought commodity: perceptive, class-conscious analysts with their own, autonomous organization. In either case, their organization sufficed to bring an entirely socialist municipality to power in 1892, and to elect Jules Guesde deputy the following year.

The Nord as a whole had become headquarters and prize of France's foremost Marxist party, the Parti Ouvrier Français. With over 63 percent of its 1896 labor force in manufacturing, the Nord stood as a model of large-scale capitalist production. A century after 1789, a region of merchants, peasants, day-laborers, domestic producers, and workers in small shops had turned into a complex of mines, factories, and sooty cities. In the process, the people of the Nord had entirely transformed their means of collective action.

9 〜

Revolutions and
Social Movements

URING THE FIRST HALF of the nineteenth century, the French general staff undertook the preparation of a great map of the entire country at 1:80,000. The work proceeded under the direction of professional *ingénieurs-géographes*. But at the local scale young army officers attached to the general staff did most of the legwork. In addition to preparing a detailed local map of the section assigned to him, the officer typically had to prepare a report describing the area, characterizing its people, and solving some sort of hypothetical military problem: how, for example, to hold off an invader coming from a given direction with a force of a certain size. Each officer had to tramp his part of the country, compass and notebook in hand.

Although many of the reports set down their facts with crisp precision, some authors adopted the model of the *Statistique* then in vogue among regional officials and local savants. They presented ready-made histories of the localities, singled out the military features of those histories, sketched the people's cultural peculiarities, inventoried economic activities, tabulated population figures, and described the important landmarks, if any. In addition to their contribution to the general staff map of France, each of those officers helped record the life of one small corner of his country at one moment of the nineteenth century.

As the ingénieurs-géographes parceled out the squares of the big map, most officers found themselves assigned to tracts of villages and fields. In 1846, however, Second Lieutenant Normand Dufie, of the Fifty-fifth Line regiment, received quite a different assignment: his square included the city of Lille, with 75,000 inhabitants, "a rich, hardworking, commercial poulation." "The language of the common people is a corrupt French," reported Dufie. "It is the Flemish idiom. But in Lille everyone speaks French more or less well." In the countryside, he added, "the basic food is a very thick soup with butter or lard at noon and in the evening. During the summer they add a breakfast and a snack consisting of bread, butter, and cheese."

Dufie described the people of the region as "much given to drink; the cabaret is a consuming passion for them. To define Flemish character properly, we might say they are as faithful to the cabaret as to the Mass." Unfortunately, he commented, their favorite drink was gin, "a perfidious liquor almost always mixed with dangerous, corrosive ingredients" (AA MR 1169).

His character sketch out of the way, Dufie went on to enumerate the "industrial arts" of Lille and its region: foundries for cannon and for bells, brassworks, goldsmithing, manufacturing of starch, gin, all sort of vegetable oils, leather goods, linen, cotton, and woolen cloth. "The city of Lille," he concluded, "is the center of almost all manufacturing in its arrondissement and likewise of that of the whole department and many neighboring departments. The proximity of the frontier adds to commercial prosperity by making the city an entrepôt for a great deal of trade" (AA MR 1169). Although people worked truck gardens hard in the hinterland, it was clear that the Nord's agricultural activity served mainly to support the region's manufacturing and trade.

Anjou lay far from Flanders. When Captain Testu described the region between Saumur and Cholet in 1839, he provided a very different picture. "In traveling through the southwest part," he wrote,

> one always comes to narrow, deep valleys containing brooks that become rivers in winter, local roads that are impassable eight months of the year, and that go around woods and around pastures surrounded by trees whose branches block the way, gates and stiles to open and close at every step, roads so sunken that you can see the sky only straight up, paths that cross constantly and make it easy for the traveler to lose his way, unending solitude.

That was the *bocage,* the hedgerow landscape of the region called the Mauges. Testu saw a large contrast between that forbidding countryside and the land nearer Saumur:

> The plain, richest part of the department is composed almost entirely of the arrondissement of Saumur. Its fields are open, and its wheat harvest

is very abundant. Most of the excellent wines, which are called *côteaux de Saumur,* are white; but at Champigny-le-Sec, on the left bank of the Loire, they make a small amount of exquisite red wine; people compare it to Bourdeaux wines, and that is a proper comparison. The growing of mulberry trees and the raising of silkworms in the region is an industry that deserves support.   (AA MR 1275)

On went Testu's comparison between the "backward" agriculture of the Mauges and the "advanced" agriculture of the Saumurois. The good captain's tours through the Mauges's underbrush had not revealed to him the existence in the bocage of widespread cottage production of linen and cotton or the importance of cattle-fattening for the Paris market. He had missed the modest cluster of cotton manufacturers in the city of Cholet. Furthermore, the textile workers and quarrymen of Angers fell outside his assigned zone. Nevertheless, Testu saw correctly that Anjou divided rather sharply into two different sorts of farming, and that in both parts of the region agriculture was the dominant activity.

Reconnaissances militaires from other regions place them between the extremes of industrial-commercial Flanders and heavily agricultural Anjou. In Burgundy, the military observers noted the scattering of forges in the east (especially in the hills approaching Franche-Comté) and toward the north (especially in the wooded region around Châtillon-sur-Seine), the openfield grain farming and relative rural prosperity of north and northwest, the greater importance of enclosures and stock-raising toward the south and east, the region of concentrated winegrowing below Dijon, the pockets of iron mining, coal mining, and capital-concentrated manufacturing around Châtillon and in the area from Le Creusot southward. More than one officer joined Captain Brossard, reporter on the area around Nuits in 1839, when he deplored the expanding production of cheaper, more profitable wines such as Gamay and Noirieu at the expense of the fine vintages that endeared Burgundy to connoisseurs (AA MR 1200).

Military mapmakers in Languedoc had even greater variety to contend with than their colleagues in Burgundy. They saw the grain production of the Toulousan plain, the small-scale metalworking of the Pyrenees foothills, the expanding production of cheaper wines around Narbonne, the manufacture of woolens and silks from the Cévennes down to Nîmes, the relatively concentrated textile production of a Lodève or a Carcassonne, the smuggling—a genuine industry for some wily souls—of the mountains. As Colonel Bentabole reported of eastern Languedoc and adjacent areas in his 1842 synthesis of multiple reports, the inhabitants who aren't involved in smuggling come down from the mountains at harvest time and spread out in the plain. That season is for them rather a source of enjoyment than of fatigue. Accustomed as they are to the most difficult labors, those they do in the lowlands do not bother their health or their good humor. They often spend part of the dinner hour with dances and songs that remind them of their mountains.   (AA MR 1303)

More so than in Anjou, Flanders, or Burgundy, seasonal migration played a crucial part in the economy of Languedoc.

General staff attachés who mapped the Ile-de-France found themselves in the most intensely commercialized region of all. Anywhere they went in the hinterland, they saw the vast influence of Paris: truck gardening close in, heavily capitalized grain farming farther out, manufacturing tied to that of the metropolis in such centers as Beauvais, trade and migration oriented to Paris like water to a drain. Savor these notes from various reconnaissances:

> *Road from Paris to Aulnay-sous-Bois* (*1822*): They take an enormous quantity of fertilizer from the capital; farmers go there to get it, while bringing in vegetables and other agricultural products. (AA MR 1287)

> *Valley of the Bièvre* (*1822*): The proximity of Paris, where the inhabitants take all their crops for sale, means that contacts among the communes are unimportant. (AA MR 1288)

> *Road to Vincennes* (*1822*): Connections with the surrounding cantons, communes, and parishes are unimportant. Contacts with the capital are more active; the inhabitants go there to sell their products. They also have contact with Lagny, which has an important market . . . They have no retail trade of their own, and the four villages are entirely agricultural. Many Parisians have country houses here. (AA MR 1287)

> *Road to Meaux* (*1825*): The frequency of the trips that they make to deliver .ime or to take fruits and vegetables to market, and their continual contact with the inhabitants of Paris, must cause some of their air of distrust, sometimes even of insolence. (AA MR 1289)

> *Road from Charenton to Paris* (*1827*): There is continual contact among all these populations; they are involved in business and retail trade; their main orientation is toward the capital, whose markets they supply. (AA MR 1290)

> *The Seine between Ecole Militaire and Argenteuil* (*1833*): The department of the Seine, the smallest of the kingdom, is nonetheless the rich-

est and most important because of the capital, which occupies its center ... The banks of the Seine are jammed with a mass of villages and adorned with country houses whose richness and elegance announces the proximity of a great capital.   (AA MR 1291)

Territory between Montmartre, Colombes, Courbevoie, and St.-Ouen (1833): Every village along the riverbank shows the influence of the capital's manufacturing industries.   (AA MR 1292)

Territory between Pantin, Le Pré-St.-Gervais, Romainville, Noisy-le-Sec, and Bobigny (1846): If proximity to the capital has removed some of the originality that set them off fifty years ago, it has also made them feel the benefits of our modern civilization. On visiting the area, one is surprised to hear language spoken that is so free of patois and local words.   (AA MR 1293)

Military position between the forts of Vanves and Bicêtre (1856): The proximity of Paris and of large factories has so degraded the people of the area that their very physiques show it.   (AA MR 1294)

The heavier forms of manufacturing, as this last note indicates, were building up in the suburbs; specialized trades, retail establishments, international commerce, finance, and governmental administration were taking over more and more of the central space. Although Paris, writ large, remained the country's largest single concentration of manufacturing, contrast was sharpening between the capital, with its diversified small-scale production, and coal-burning industrial monoliths such as Roubaix and Le Creusot. The identification of "industrialization" with "factory" (*usine*) was beginning to make sense.

Concentration on a National Scale

For most of eighteenth-century France, that equation was nonsensical. A few types of production characteristically took place in large establishments. That was especially true of products in which the state had a monopoly or a strong direct interest, such as arms, salt, sailcloth, or tobacco. Religious orders responsible for orphans, paupers, or moral offenders sometimes produced textiles in organizations resembling factories in their discipline and spatial segregation, if not in their reliance on hand-powered machinery. Mines, with their high capital requirements, also typically involved good-sized firms and centralized work discipline.

The great bulk of France's manufacturing, however, went on in small shops and individual households. The great industrial regions, such as those around Lyon and Rouen, contained webs of mercantile cities whose financiers and entrepreneurs guided the production of thousands of small-scale producers. Those producers had little discretion concerning what, or even how much, they would produce. Merchants often controlled them by debt, by legal pressure, and by ownership of housing, tools, and raw materials. Nevertheless the producers technically sold what they made to the merchants, instead of simply putting their time and effort at an employer's disposal for a wage. They were almost, but not quite, full-fledged proletarians.

Merchants certainly imposed exacting standards on the goods they bought from workers; much of the day-to-day bickering between merchants and ostensibly independent artisans concerned such questions as whether the finished goods met the standards for full payment, whether the workers had taken some of the raw materials the merchants had given them, and whose measure should be used in gauging the quantity of goods produced. But merchants could not specify when, where, and how a weaver, spinner, or woodworker would do the work, or with what help from other members of the household.

What is more, rural industrial workers typically spent part of their time in agricultural labor. France's manufacturing labor force of the later eighteenth century consisted mainly of quasi-proletarians producing in their own households or in small shops. Thus a heavily industrialized region was not one with many factories, but one with a large quasi-proletarian manufacturing labor force.

A clairvoyant observer of France in 1789 might have seen the structures of nineteenth-century industrial production forming. Relatively large shops relying on water power or steam power, similar to those that were proliferating in England, were beginning to take shape in Flanders, Normandy, and a few other regions. In 1788, when France's Bureau du Commerce called on provincial intendants for reports on "factories and boilers" in their jurisdictions, M. Esmangard of Flanders and Artois reported no foundries or metal-working factories in his provinces. But as power-using producers he was able to enumerate glassworks in Lille and Dunkerque, a pottery plant in Douai, a porcelain manufactory in Lille, two shops making pipes in Arras, a gin distillery in Dunkerque, 21 salt refineries, 26 soapworks, 12 sugar refineries, plus 16 other potteries and tileworks. The clerk who summarized Esmangard's report for the bureau remarked:

> We see that the majority of these plants use coal, and that those using wood are too small to cause a shortage. In Maritime Flanders coal is cheap, because it comes from England. In the countryside they burn only peat, but a great deal of wood goes into heating in Lille, Arras,

Douai, and St.-Omer. The intendant indicates that wood is very expensive in those areas, but he does not indicate the price or the amount consumed. Hainaut's coal is too expensive for use in much of the generality. The small amount they get from Hainaut and Artois could not possibly meet the need. Companies have formed to search these provinces and find coalbeds close to large cities or rivers.   (AN F^{12} 680)

Those searches succeeded; within forty years, steam-powered mills and coal-burning forges employed thousands of workers in Flanders and Artois. But in 1788 the shift to coal fires as the source of industrial power was just beginning.

At the other extreme, the report filed by the intendant of Tours concerning the "factories and boilers" of Anjou had practically nothing to discuss. The section for the subdelegation of Montreuil-Bellay, for example, said flatly: "There are no factories in this district." For the subdelegation of Saumur, the count included twenty limekilns using charcoal, but nothing else (AN F^{12} 680).

Yet other reports of the time made it clear that Angevins were producing and selling plenty of manufactured goods. As of 1781, the royal inspector of manufacturing in the little linen center of Cholet, south of the Loire, counted only 234 textile "merchants, clothiers, and workers" in the city itself. All of them were producing by hand, most of them in their own homes. Another 848—counting only the adult males, and not the hundreds of women and children in their households—worked in the surrounding villages and sold their goods to Cholet's merchants (ADIL C 114).

Cholet's linens, especially its kerchiefs, served the national market but also entered the slave trade via Nantes. As the inspector noted in his report, most of the actual producers had no capital of their own but worked for clothiers on small advances. Nevertheless, these household workers were collectively turning out around 3 million livres per year in finished goods, at a time when the national production of textiles was worth something like 1.1 billion livres (Markovitch 1966, table 6).

Although dispersed textile production in Cholet's hinterland hung on for decades, and although Cholet's merchants built small plants in the city during the nineteenth century, nothing like the urban implosion of Flanders occurred in the Choletais or elsewhere in Anjou. Indeed, Anjou as a whole *de*industrialized during and after the Revolution. Its people devoted less and less of their energy to producing manufactured goods for sale, more and more of their effort to agriculture.

In this sense, three of our five regions deindustrialized during the century after 1789. Not only Anjou, but also Languedoc and Burgundy, moved more decisively into agriculture. For Anjou, the nineteenth century brought an expansion of winegrowing along the Loire, and of grain and cattle production in the rest of the region; the largest single exception to Anjou's deindustrialization was the expansion of the slate quarries in Trélazé, southeast of Angers, close to Ponts-de-Cé and the river.

In Languedoc, similarly, the cottage textile industry of the uplands decayed. Although Lodève had decades of prosperity as a producer of woolen cloth for military uniforms, the textile production of Bédarieux, Carcassonne, and Lodève as well hardly survived the nineteenth century; Mazamet stayed in the wool business only by taking up the shearing and processing of sheep hides (Johnson 1982). Burgundy's woodburning forges went out of business like their counterparts in Franche-Comté, while winegrowing expanded in importance; only the region from Le Creusot south toward Lyon hosted concentrated manufacturing. In different ways, the Ile-de-France and Flanders industrialized as Anjou, Languedoc, and Burgundy went the other way.

Economic Fates

All three deindustrializing regions moved into winegrowing, but with varying vigor and success. In Anjou, the winefields of the Loire Valley and the nearby Layon expanded modestly, but no new and important growing areas appeared. Nor did any remarkable concentration of landholding occur; Anjou's winegrowers remained a mixture of smallholders and day-laborers. In Burgundy, the old areas of fine wine production from Pinot noir grapes—the *côtes*—retained their small scale of production and continued to sustain communities dominated by smallholders. The cheaper wines of the Gamay grape expanded in the areas adjacent to the côtes, but primarily through the multiplication of smallholdings rather than through the development of large vineyards.

Until the mid-century expansion of France's railroad network, the winegrowing regions of Languedoc did not boom either. Indeed, the hilly areas of finer wines and peasant property kept much of their character into the twentieth century. However, the arc of plains near the Mediterranean from Perpignan to Nîmes went through an enormous transformation: rapid growth of capitalist winegrowing in the 1860s, crisis of the phylloxera blight in the 1870s and 1880s, massive increase in the production of cheap wines on large properties thereafter.

The early growth, the crisis, and the renewed expansion linked to each other: phylloxera arrived on the blight-immune American vines with which capitalizing winegrowers of the 1870s had hoped to make more money; the blighting of French vines encouraged the introduction of cheap, watered, and sugared wines from Algeria, Spain, and Italy while southerners were bringing new American vines to maturity; and the recovery permitted French winegrowers to enter the expanding market for mass-produced beverages. The shift to industrial techniques, large vineyards, and mass distribution proletarianized Languedoc's wine industry.

Not all of rural Languedoc turned to vineyard. The plains near Toulouse, for example, continued to concentrate on wheat production, while the highland regions kept their mixed economies of grazing, small crafts, and seasonal migration. Likewise, the bocages of Anjou maintained their system of grain and cattle production on medium-sized rented farms—with the added fillip that a number of noble landlords began to take active interest in the management of their estates and the politics of their tenants, and even started to live in their modest castles some of the year. In Burgundy, despite the decline of rural industry and the spread of Gamay winegrowing, most regions held to peasant polyculture, with cash crops gaining ground after mid-century. The agriculture of the Nord became ever more subservient to manufacturing. And the Ile-de-France continued its pattern of intensive market gardening close in, capitalist grain production farther out.

Even in the agricultural regions, capital and manufacturing concentrated increasingly in the cities. Angers, Dijon, and Toulouse all saw their trade expand, their traders get rich, their banks grow, their small crafts give way to large plants. Angers, for example, specialized in industries based on agriculture: not only preparation and wholesaling of food and drink, but also sailcloth manufacturing and the spinning of wool, cotton, and hemp; only the important slate quarries broke the city's ties to agriculture. Until mid-century, indeed, nearly a quarter of Angers's labor force worked directly in nurseries and market gardens within the city. Nevertheless, in 1856 a full 57 percent of Angers's labor force gained their living from manufacturing (Lebrun 1975: 199). From that point on, the city grew mainly through expansion of its commercial services. Like Dijon and Toulouse, Angers specialized more and more in the coordination of trade and capital.

Lille and Paris became very different kinds of industrial cities. If we include Lille, Roubaix, and Tourcoing in the same urban cluster, that nineteenth-century metropolis epitomized France's new manufacturing centers: factories, dense and segregated working-class neighborhoods, rapid growth. Roubaix went from 9,000 people in 1806 to 121,000 in 1906, while Tourcoing grew from 12,000 to 82,000; the increase of Lille from 50,000 to 215,000 (a mere quadrupling!) contributed to the rise of the three-city complex from 71,000 to 424,000 inhabitants. Within the set, especially after mid-century, a division of labor appeared: Roubaix and Tourcoing became factory towns dominated by family firms, Lille a financial, administrative, and cultural center tied more strongly to international capital. Together, they formed France's greatest concentration of large-scale manufacturing.

In the case of Paris, we must distinguish between the old center and the newer periphery. In the center, expanding trade, finance, services, and administration squeezed out both manufacturing establishments and working-class neighborhoods. Through the industrial shifts and the building of new, elegant residential areas, the city's segregation by class became much more pronounced. Net departure of workers and workplaces was already occurring under the July Monarchy and reached its peak after 1852, with the great bustle of Haussmann and Napoleon III. Small-scale manufacturing tended to move to the edges of the built-up area, while heavy industry located increasingly outside the tollgates, where cheap land, exemption from city taxes, and easy access to canals and railways all made new sites attractive.

Metalworking plants, for example, were already relocating in Clichy, St.-Ouen, St.-Denis, and elsewhere to the north and east of Paris before 1848. (Remember the prophetic *reconnaissance militaire* for the area near St.-Ouen in 1833: "Every village along the riverbank shows the influence of the capital's manufacturing industries": AA MR 1292.) The northeastern suburbs became Paris' equivalent of Roubaix and Tourcoing—with the important difference that instead of textiles many of the workers of Belleville and environs were making railroad cars, machines, chemicals, and other products requiring large applications of capital and energy.

As Exhibit 6 shows, all five urban clusters grew at similar rates during the nineteenth century's first half; Paris led and Angers lagged, but all the cities grew. During the great period of implosion after 1851, differences sharpened: Lille, Roubaix, and Tourcoing spurted ahead, Dijon and Paris accelerated, while the growth of Angers speeded up a bit, and that of Toulouse actually slowed down. After the turn of the century—and especially with the Great War—the growth of the cities almost ceased. In fact the population of Lille-Roubaix-Tourcoing, a combat zone in World War I, fell slightly between 1901 and 1921. Table 7 summarizes the average annual percentage rates of change for our five regional capitals. All took part in France's urban implosion. But until the plateau of the early twentieth century, the two centers of manufacturing and industrial capital grew faster than the rest.

Rates of growth, however, equalize places of very unequal size. Paris began the nineteenth century with more than half a million inhabitants and ended it with 2.7 million. Throughout the century its population ran about five times that of its closest rival, Marseille, and at least six times that of Lille, Roubaix, and Tourcoing combined. The sheer difference in scale meant that Paris could be less intensely industrial than Lille–Roubaix–Tourcoing and yet have the nation's largest mass of manufacturing. In manufacturing, in trade, and, of course, in government Paris towered over the rest of France. And the concentration continued through the nineteenth century.

Exhibit 6. Total population of major cities, 1801–1921 (censuses for the period)

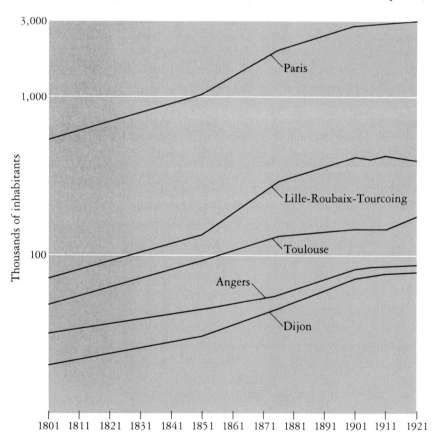

Table 7. Average annual percentage rates of change in population in five regional capitals, 1801–1921

City	1801–1851	1851–1901	1901–1921
Paris	1.3	1.9	0.3
Lille–Roubaix–Tourcoing	1.2	2.2	−0.2
Dijon	0.8	1.6	0.5
Toulouse	1.2	0.9	0.8
Angers	0.7	1.1	0.2

Source: Censuses for the period.

As a result of concentration, the great manufacturers and merchants of the industrial centers grew wealthy. Exhibit 7 provides a sense of nineteenth-century changes in wealth in Paris, Lille, and Toulouse. The evidence comes from estimates of the values of estates of persons dying in the three cities in various years from 1806 to 1911. The graph shows those values in terms of the quintals of wheat they would buy at the year's current prices— a procedure that undervalues wealth in the high-priced years of 1846 and 1847 but otherwise gives a fair idea of purchasing power (1 quintal = 100 kg = 220.5 lbs.).

Except for the disappearing day-laborers of Toulouse, all categories experienced some increase in wealth over the century. The hierarchy of wealth, by this measure, corresponds nicely to the gradations of income, with the great merchants and manufacturers of Paris generally having about five thousand times the wealth of the city's day-laborers. Shopkeepers and retailers clustered together in wealth in the three cities; toward the end of the century, the wholesale merchants of slow-growing Toulouse seem to have joined them in comfortable mediocrity. Workers in the three cities likewise ended the century fairly close together.

Yet the graph also reveals an important difference from city to city. The greater the industrial concentration, the poorer the workers and the richer the merchants. The difference in wealth between capitalists and workers therefore came out distinctly greater in Paris than in Lille, greater in Lille than in Toulouse. Within the industrial city, the trend ran to concentration and class division.

Just after the revolution of February 1848, Henri Lecouturier wrote a curious little book called *Paris Incompatible with the Republic: Plan of a New Paris Where Revolutions Will Be Impossible.* The book wrapped together the chief changes in the city—growth, concentration, and segregation—as

Exhibit 7. Mean property at death in Lille, Toulouse, and Paris, 1806–1911
(Daumard 1973: *Annuaire Statistique* 1966: 406–407)

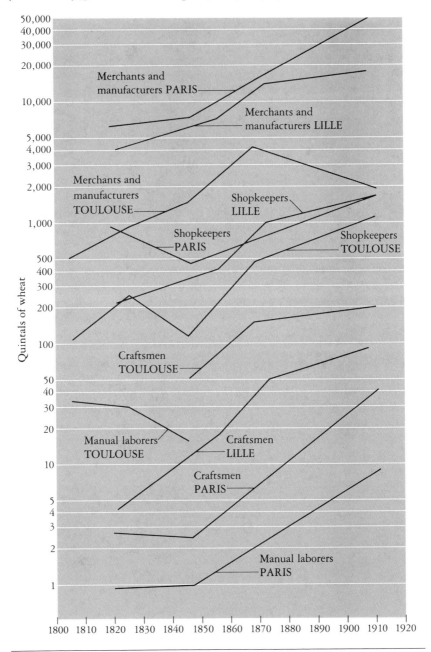

causes of revolution. "While half of Paris dies of starvation," wrote Lecouturier, "the other half eats for two. Centralization takes care of it; we are seeing the exhaustion of France, which produces, for Paris, which devours" (Lecouturier 1848: 15–16). After enumerating the city's numerous forms of decadence and immorality, he went on to complain of an anonymity that gave free reign to degenerates and criminals.

"Paris will always be revolutionary," declared Lecouturier, "so long as fragmentation isn't complete, SO LONG AS THE NUMBER OF PEOPLE WHO HAVE ENOUGH IS NOT GREATER THAN THE NUMBER OF PEOPLE WHO HAVE TOO LITTLE" (Lecouturier 1848: 65–66). Yet he did not draw a socialist conclusion from that principle. Instead, his program for Paris included these elements:

> ban on all industrial production except what is absolutely indispensable
> expulsion of all businesses beyond those necessary to serve the residents
> a census of the population, followed by expulsion of everyone without a trade
> establishment of a maximum for the labor force
> division of the entire city into four quarters separated by green space, with each quarter divided into four autonomous villages
> construction of wide, straight streets like those of Washington, D.C.
> construction of new housing easy to purchase

Except for the wide, straight streets cut through by Haussmann, Paris did not follow Lecouturier's advice. Nevertheless, Lecouturier's analysis reflects the widespread feeling in France's ruling classes that the combination of centralized power, concentrated production, rapid growth, and heightened inequality carried the threat of immorality, disorder, and rebellion.

A Changing State

Not long after Lecouturier set down his ideas about the consequences of Parisian concentration, Alexis de Tocqueville was writing his own analysis of the Revolution of 1848. Among the factors Tocqueville invoked were "the industrial revolution that in thirty years had made Paris the chief manufacturing city of France and had brought within its walls a whole new mass of workers to whom work on fortifications had added another mass of unemployed agricultural workers," and "the centralization that reduced the whole revolutionary action to seizing control of Paris and taking hold of the assembled machinery of government" (Tocqueville 1978 [1893]:

113–114). Later Tocqueville generalized this analysis into an explanation of the eighteenth-century Revolution as well.

Although Tocqueville underestimated the extent to which the revolutionaries of 1789–1799 built a new system, he saw clearly that the conjunction of a centralized state and a great metropolis made control of Paris crucial to national politics. After revolutionaries struggled their way to a centralized state structure, neither Napoleon's men nor the kings of the Restoration nor the makers of nineteenth-century revolutions undertook seriously to dismantle the structure.

The strengthening and centralization of the French state followed a remarkable sequence: establishment of revolutionary committees, militias, and provisional governments; dissolution of rival governmental structures; assumption of their fiscal powers and financial obligations; imposition of uniform principles and procedures for taxation, conscription, voting, and other forms of civic obligation from one end of the country to the other; creation of a hierarchical structure of assemblies and administrations operating continuously from nation to commune; control of the assemblies and administrations by means of roving representatives of the central power who relied on existing networks of bourgeois patriots for support; gradual but forceful substitution of the formal hierarchy for the committees and militias; elaboration of a national surveillance system strongly resembling the one Paris' old regime police had used to control the metropolis; development of armed forces reliably subservient to the central government and to no one else. Organizers of the Revolution and the Empire built the most far-reaching centralized state the world had ever seen.

Chinese and Roman emperors had, to be sure, constructed vaster systems of government. But they and their counterparts in other empires had essentially ended their administration at the regional level, stationing their own bureaucrats and soldiers in provincial capitals and relying on co-opted indigenous powerholders for routine government below that level. Old-regime France, on its much smaller scale, had not gone far beyond that arrangement. But the Revolution and the Empire, through intense struggle, established direct connections from national government to individual communes and almost—via communal councils—to local households and kin groups. Regional and local potentates who were hostile to the current national regime could still make life difficult for its representatives. Yet they had nothing like the bases of opposition afforded their old-regime predecessors by parlements, estates, corporate trades, and chartered municipalities.

The work of building the state did not end with the First Empire. Professional policing provides one indication of the state's nineteenth-century expansion. If we exclude local forces such as game wardens, the Revolution and Empire consolidated official policing into two forces. The Gendarmerie Nationale, reporting to the minister of war and responsible for the patrolling of highways and rural areas, took over the functions of the Maréchaussée, which had formed in 1720 under the same auspices and for essentially the same purposes.

The Sûreté Nationale extended to urban France in general the organization of the prerevolutionary Parisian police force, putting the system's control into the hands of the minister of the interior. The Sûreté not only patrolled streets and tracked down thieves but also pumped a regular stream of political intelligence from every department and major city to the capital. In the process, the Sûreté steadily absorbed existing municipal police forces—taking over, for example, the police of Lyon in 1851, of Marseille in 1908, of Toulon in 1918, of Nice in 1920.

The Gendarmerie and especially the Sûreté continued to grow through much of the nineteenth century. Exhibit 8 shows the fragmentary series now available concerning their forces and budgets. The curves of growth have some interesting irregularities. The trend of expenditure for the Gendarmerie already ran upward in the 1840s. Louis Napoleon accelerated the Gendarmerie's expansion during the first few years after his seizure of power, then let the force level off. After investment in the Gendarmerie declined during the last years of the Second Empire, the regime that came to power in the 1870 revolution again pumped strength into the force.

Fluctuations in Sûreté Nationale were much greater. After each nineteenth-century revolution—1830, 1848, 1870—the new regime consolidated its control over the country by vigorously expanding the police force. The significant partial exception to that rule is the Second Republic, which cut expenditures in half before Louis Napoleon, as president from the end of 1848, tightened his grip on state machinery. On the whole, policing and political repression waxed and waned together. The final effect was to lay down a uniform net of control over the entire country.

Nevertheless, not all regions participated equally in the state's nineteenth-century expansion. For one thing, strength of support for successive regimes varied dramatically from one part of France to another. Under the July Monarchy, for example, Anjou and Languedoc harbored many powerful legitimists, while Burgundy, the Ile-de-France, and the Nord had few. Anjou's legitimists consisted mainly of country-dwelling nobles and their supporters; they aligned themselves against city-dwelling Orleanists and republicans. In Languedoc, cities such as Toulouse overflowed with powerful legitimists; the legitimism of Languedoc, furthermore, had a sharp edge

Exhibit 8. Police expenditures and police personnel in France, 1825–1895 (Nicolas 1883: *Annuaire de l'Economie Politique* 1844, 1869, 1883, 1899)

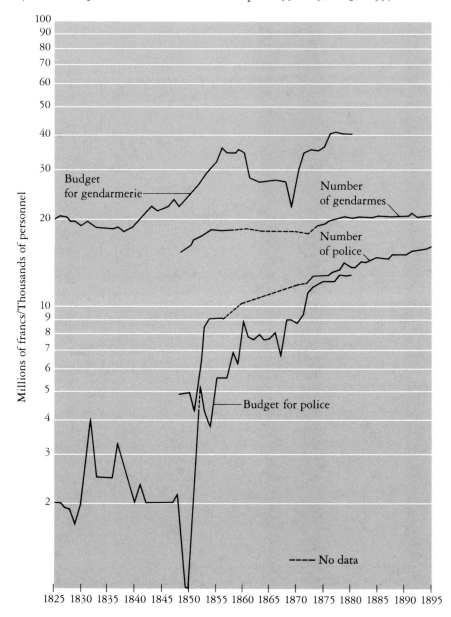

of opposition to the Protestant bourgeoisie. These variations affected both the ability of prefects to do the central government's bidding and the likelihood that a region's notables would get their share of governmental largesse.

For another thing, the government's own investment in capital-intensive projects had distinct regional biases. This time the obvious example comes from the railroads. After an early period in which railway construction followed either the needs of mineowners or the whims of the royal court, the French undertook the construction of a rail system consisting largely of links between Paris and major provincial cities. The pattern favored the Nord and, obviously, the Ile-de-France far more than it did Burgundy, Anjou, or Languedoc. Burgundy gained some advantage over Languedoc and Anjou from its location on the path from Paris to Lyon and Marseille.

Paris had its first passenger line in 1837 and established direct connections to Rouen and Orléans in 1843. Lille linked directly to Paris via a main line in 1846, Dijon in 1849, Toulouse in 1856, Angers not until 1863. The extension of railroads represents a general pattern: broadly speaking, a region's concentration of capital determined how soon and how much it received state-backed economic facilities, the favorability of its dominant classes to the current regime determined its receipt of amenities, and the strength of its opposition movements determined the extent of its repressive apparatus.

In these regards, the Revolution had made a profound difference. The shift to relatively direct rule diminished the impact of a region's economically dominant classes on its pattern of government. The consolidation and bureaucratization of the fiscal system further reduced region-to-region variability in the character and burden of taxation. The Catholic church emerged from the Revolution greatly diminished as an independent power. Although holders of land, both noble and bourgeois, continued to wield great influence in a property-qualified electorate, merchants, financiers, and manufacturers grew increasingly powerful in the national arena. Though leaving many features of local social life, production, distribution, and consumption little changed after the early flurries of experimentation with each, the Revolution transformed the national structure of rule.

Five Kinds of Revolution

Because old-regime social organization and articulation with the central government varied significantly from region to region, the Revolution took significantly different forms in our five regions. In the Nord we have already seen a strong, early movement of smallholders and rural proletarians against landlords in the southeast (Hainaut and Cambrésis), and widespread struggles of rural proletarians against landlords and merchants in the northwest (Flanders, properly speaking). In Hainaut and Cambrésis, the abolition of feudal dues and the sale of church properties helped establish a republic of smallholders.

In Flanders, rich farmers and urban bourgeois dominated the sales. The rural population, on the whole, resisted the dissolution of the church and stuck with its parish clergy. Once they saw the limits of a revolution preempted and controlled by the bourgeoisie, the Nord's rural people turned to defending whatever gains they had made. Thus the rural areas created a genuine but short-lived revolutionary movement. In the cities the already powerful mercantile and manufacturing bourgeoisie did little more than consolidate its power. During the first phase of France's revolutionary wars, the frontier province again became the scene of encampments, invasions, and battles. During that first phase, the Nord had its only large taste of Terror. In general, we see a department settling with the Revolution early, and cramping into a defense of its interests thereafter.

In Languedoc the parlement, long a defender of provincial liberties against royal aggrandizement, quickly aligned itself with the old regime when its own privileges were threatened. Rural proletarians made some efforts to redress the landlords' eighteenth-century wrongs early in the Revolution. But later they lacked the capital to take advantage of the sale of church and émigré properties.

Languedoc's Revolution concentrated in its cities. In Toulouse, the absence of a *grande bourgeoisie* independent of the great landlords opened revolutionary power to merchants, professionals, and master craftsmen. Toulouse became a national center of Jacobinism. When the Convention smashed the Girondins in June 1793, the patriots of Toulouse eventually supported the Convention. In 1793, both before and after the Federalist insurrection, cities of the zone from Toulouse to Montpellier formed major units of the volunteer revolutionary armies. Those armies actively fought the counterrevolutionaries of the south as they worked to assure the defense and feeding of their home bases.

Nîmes, however, veered toward federalism. The city divided between a powerful minority of Protestant entrepreneurs and a determined majority of Catholic workers; most of the revolution in Nîmes and its hinterland played itself out in conflicts between those two factions. At the purge of Girondins in Paris, Nîmes and its region mounted an abortive rebellion.

Languedoc's Protestants, urban and rural, supported the Revolution with vigor. A significant counterrevolutionary movement, led by landlords and manned by Catholic peasants and rural proletarians, rapidly formed in the region. Grouped around the nonrevolutionary clergy, they opposed revolutionary conscription and taxation. In 1799 their rising dislodged revolutionary authorities in a number of Languedoc's cities. But they failed to capture Toulouse and ultimately fell to republican military force. The White Terror of 1815 marked the moment of bitter Catholic and royalist revenge against the former Jacobins—Protestant, Catholic, and indifferent—of Toulouse, Nîmes, and other centers.

In Burgundy the Revolution opened with significant attacks on landlords both within and outside the winegrowing regions, as well as vigorous struggles for power in such cities as Beaune. But once the struggles of the first few years had put in place a new structure of power, the Revolution proceeded with much less open division than marked Languedoc. In 1789 and 1790 supporters and clients of the old Estates constituted an important party. In 1790 that party even managed to recapture Dijon's municipal government from the militant lawyers and merchants who had seized power in July 1789. Decimated by repression and emigration, however, the counterrevolutionary party soon disintegrated. Thenceforth lawyers, merchants, and other bourgeois held the reins.

Winegrowers of Dijon, Beaune, Mâcon, and the vineyards in between leaned toward the revolutionary left. So did the industrial workers around Châtillon-sur-Seine. Neither group, however, wielded much power. Beyond sporadic resistance to conscription and occasional demands for cheaper and more abundant foods, they mobilized rarely and ineffectively. The largely bourgeois committees, militias, and municipalities that formed throughout the region in July 1789 remained in power, *mutatis mutandis,* throughout the Revolution.

The Ile-de-France, to be sure, nurtured the national revolution, and also some of its great myths: that Enlightenment thought destroyed the monarchy, that the revolutionary movement sprang from a great subsistence crisis, that the threat of wanderers and brigands stimulated the creation of its political apparatus, that a bloodthirsty crowd smashed the old regime, that an assembly of sturdy provincials confronted a corrupt monarchy and insisted on reform. For each of these myths carries the trace of a genuine Parisian experience in 1789.

In fact the city's great concentration of journalists, publicists, clerics, clerks, and literate artisans did create a clientele for the politicized clubs and salons that proliferated in 1788 and 1789. The defenders, first of the parlements and then of the Third Estate, did indeed clothe their defenses in the language of the Enlightenment; natural rights and reason justified their opposition to arbitrary rule. Yet they were protecting genuine popular interests against real royal threats.

The second myth likewise contains a half-truth. A widespread subsistence crisis, beginning in 1788, did spur an unusually broad range of blockages and seizures of grain in Paris and its hinterland. By the middle of 1789, as the Third Estate of the Estates General was successfully declaring itself the National Assembly, emergency committees and militias were indeed forming throughout the Ile-de-France and preempting the power of the old municipalities. However, a significant part of the conflict over food in 1789 and thereafter resulted from the dispatch of official and semiofficial raiding parties from Paris into the surrounding towns. Those parties were trying to assure the great capital's food supply in the face of producers' increasing reluctance to commit their grain to the market, and villagers' increasing unwillingness to let the grain leave for Paris.

Unemployed rural workers did roam the region's roads in the spring of 1789. Many a sexton rang the tocsin to call for armed defense against the approach of brigands. But the marauders rarely came. And when they did, they usually turned out to be hapless beggars or food-hunting delegations from Paris. Aside from food blockages and scattered attacks on landlords' hunting equipment, the rural sections of the Ile-de-France experienced relatively little open conflict in 1789.

Orators, literati, clerks, and workers did gather regularly at the Palais Royal and elsewhere, calling for resistance to royal oppression, holding off or even recruiting the troops sent to disperse them. Ordinary Parisian people, furthermore, did repeatedly go to the streets, did increasingly proclaim popular sovereignty, and did occasionally take the law—even capital punishment of traitors—into their own hands. Indeed, marches of Parisian fishwives, militiamen, and officials intimidated the king and eventually, in October 1789, brought the royal family to Paris. That much might suggest the unleashing of angry mobs. But think of the context: the continuous marching, meeting, and organizing of the capital; the conversion of electoral assemblies and provisional committees into instruments of municipal government; the tense but powerful alliances developed between street people and assembly people. Those features of the early Revolution in the Ile-de-France reveal an unprecedented popular mobilization.

In point of fact, the Third Estate that met in Versailles included many provincials who found the palace town shocking. But by the time of their definitively revolutionary actions they had long since fled Versailles for Paris. There, in tacit alliance with the city's artisans and shopkeepers, augmented by dissident clergy and nobles, they braved the crown. Their actions become more comprehensible, furthermore, in the light of the royal effort to check them, to ring the capital with troops, and to dismiss the reforming Necker—in short, to engineer a coup d'état. Thus each myth refracts a reality while making its true image unrecognizable.

The myths also neglect other fundamental Parisian realities: the tension between the support for and the threat to revolutionary leaders provided by the intense local organization of artisans and shopkeepers into their own assemblies, societies, and committees; the vulnerability of a national assembly located in the capital to organized invasions by determined activists; the incessant flow of people and information to and from the country's other cities; the eventual extension throughout the country of the system of surveillance and political control pioneered in the capital, indeed modeled to some degree on the royal policing apparatus of the old regime. In all these regards, Paris and the Ile-de-France occupied a unique position in the Revolution's unfolding.

Anjou's Revolution and Counterrevolution

Anjou, too, could claim uniqueness. Although it shared with Languedoc the distinction of raising a serious counterrevolutionary movement, that movement outlasted the Revolution itself; and although its counterrevolutionaries mobilized later than those of Languedoc, they soon posed a far more serious threat to the Revolution's survival.

In 1789 and 1790 Anjou did not look much different from Burgundy or Languedoc: struggles over food supply tested authorities throughout the region. Larger cities formed their committees, clubs, and revolutionary administrations in the face of those struggles, and in the presence of new allies in big cities elsewhere, including Paris. Merchants and lawyers—essentially the same group that had entered politics in the new provincial assembly of 1787 and 1788 and had organized the province's preparations for the Estates General of 1789—established a new governing coalition. Nobles sulked, then started to emigrate in considerable numbers.

The more or less simultaneous dispossession of the church, imposition of an ecclesiastical civil service, sale of church properties, and penetration of revolutionary government to the village level sharpened the division in Anjou. On one side stood city-based bourgeois revolutionaries and their village allies; on the other, a coalition of substantial peasants, rural artisans, and parish clergy. That polarization, in turn, forced most rural people to take sides.

In a local parallel to the struggle of Paris with its hinterland, the national guards of the region's small cities sought to subjugate the fractious backcountry. They marched around trying to enforce compliance with revolutionary edicts, protect the constitutional clergy, shore up their few rural allies, and assure their own food supply. That military proselytization only accentuated the division. In the Mauges, the bocage of southern Anjou, the bulk of the population lined up against the revolutionary bourgeoisie.

Similar processes aligned much of the rural population against the Revolution in almost all the bocages of western France—not only those of Anjou, but also those of Poitou, Brittany, and Maine. "The terrain of rebellion," comments Paul Bois, "was the bocage, with its dispersed settlement; rebellion always stopped at the edge of open-field landscape" (Bois 1981: 124). But those bocages varied in the extent of their polarization, the intensity of their conflict, and their vulnerability to military and political control from the region's cities.

North of the Loire, in general, armed resistance to revolutionary authority took the form of *chouannerie*. Chouannerie involved little open warfare but plenty of ambush, harassment, individual assaults, and attacks on property—of guerrilla or terrorist activity, depending on your sympathies for or against the rebels.

South of the Loire, things developed differently. The people of the Mauges and adjacent bocages of Poitou raised more sustained and effective resistance to the efforts of revolutionaries to impose control. Several features of local social organization combined to produce that difference: the presence in villages of bourgeois who were organizing cottage textile production and administering the estates of absentee nobles; the importance of substantial peasants who typically were tenants of nobles or ecclesiastical landlords but had to deal directly with their bourgeois agents; long struggles for local preeminence between the parish clergy and the resident bourgeoisie; the weakness of national military forces and revolutionary militias in the region. In 1791 and 1792 clandestine Masses and nocturnal processions became the rallying points of counterrevolutionaries. They accelerated along with attacks on constitutional clergy; refusal to pay taxes and accept revolutionary administrative measures; boycotting of elections, assemblies, and offices; threats of violence to rural patriots.

The Mauges behaved in stunning contrast to the region around Sau-

mur. In the Saumurois, rural winegrowers and small farmers quickly cooperated with the revolutionary bourgeoisie, accepting ecclesiastical reform, in-
ducing their clergy to accept it as well, buying church properties, attending
revolutionary ceremonies, serving in the national guard, enlisting in the national armies, even joining in the forces sent to put down rebellion in the
neighboring Mauges.

After a number of attacks on patriots in 1791 and 1792, the great insurrection began in March 1793, with widespread resistance to the national
call for mass conscription, followed by attacks on local patriots and nearby
cities. Community bands of sometime soldiers soon consolidated into makeshift armies, usually commanded by local nobles with military experience.
With the armies marched priests who had rejected the revolutionary reorganization of the church, then hidden out in the countryside in defiance of
the beleaguered revolutionary authorities.

These ragged forces seized control of most of the Mauges and of adjacent sections of Poitou; made temporary conquests of Saumur, Angers,
Cholet, and other patriotic cities; and held off major revolutionary armies
for about six months. Rebellions of various sorts recurred in the region in
1794, 1795, 1796, 1799, 1815, and 1832; and the rest of the period to 1799
was full of raids and confrontations. As in Languedoc, the resistance movement that formed during the Revolution's early years subsequently changed
character considerably but took decades to disappear.

Some of the difference between the revolutionary and counterrevolutionary regions of Anjou resulted quite directly from variations in the correspondence between local material interests and revolutionary programs.
Monastic orders and external titheholders, for example, held much more of
the ecclesiastical wealth of the Saumurois than was the case in the Mauges.
In the Mauges, parish clergy held most of the church property. It was easier
and more profitable to be anticlerical in the Saumurois.

Again, many peasants in the Saumurois owned land, whereas most of
the Mauges's householders were tenants. Furthermore, the only peasants of
the Mauges with capital were the larger tenant farmers; most often they
leased their twenty-hectare farms from rentier noble landlords via the landlords' bourgeois agents, and brought their capital in the form of cattle and
tools. They had little prospect of outbidding the bourgeoisie in any auction
of church or émigré property. Thus a revolution promoting the rights of
property, restricting the power of the church, forwarding trade, and establishing relative political equality among propertyholders found ready support among the merchants and smallholders of the Saumurois and the Loire

Valley. In the Mauges, however, the tenant farmers, agricultural laborers, and textile workers who formed the great majority of the population had much less to gain from such a program.

The people of the Mauges also had something to lose from the disestablishment of the church, whose parish revenues provided a small cushion against unemployment, and whose parish clergy served as a counterweight to the local bourgeoisie. To put welfare and political power into the hands of the very merchants and lawyers who had already demonstrated their interest in cutting wages, increasing the return from leases on the land they owned or administered, and acquiring more land for their own use—that prospect threatened the well-being of most of the rural population.

Yet such a configuration did not guarantee that the peasants and artisans of the bocage would end up counterrevolutionary. That depended as well on the alliances and enmities they formed. Aligning themselves against the bourgeoisie threw the rural people of the Mauges into the arms of the clergy and the nobility. In other parts of the west, peasant communities that had maintained a certain independence of the local bourgeoisie made their peace with the Revolution (Le Goff and Sutherland 1974, 1983).

Elsewhere in France, class coalitions likewise made a large difference in alignment for or against the Revolution. Peasants and agricultural laborers of Flanders, who had long resisted the assaults of capitalizing landlords, nevertheless supported the first round of revolutionary reforms. Among Languedoc's Protestants, merchants, artisans, and peasants alike opted for the Revolution, their alliance against Catholics overriding the divergence of their other interests.

On the whole, the less wealthy peasants and agricultural workers throughout France had long been struggling to hold off the advance of agricultural capitalism. The general fit between their interests and revolutionary programs concerning the land strongly affected their orientation to the Revolution as a whole. But within those limits, whether they lined up with or against revolutionaries whose actions would ultimately advance agricultural capitalism also depended on the local play of alliances with or against the bourgeoisie.

Anjou's Postrevolutionary Contention

The century following Napoleon's defeat in 1815 created the France we know today. That truism is even truer for popular contention than for governmental structure or for character of the dominant classes.

Anjou, it is true, might seem to be a contrary case; there, after all, ostensibly counterrevolutionary movements stirred up the countryside from the early Revolution to the 1840s, and the department of Maine-et-Loire entered twentieth-century electoral politics as a right-wing bastion. In May 1815 the marquis d'Autichamp had sounded the tocsin in southern Anjou. Like his allies in neighboring Deux-Sèvres and Vendée, he raised a force of a few thousand men to march against patriotic cities and Napoleonic troops. The insurgents even managed to control the bocage for a month, and to divert 20,000 imperial soldiers from the forces fighting around Waterloo.

After Napoleon's second abdication in July 1815, royalist forces occupied Durtal and disarmed the patriot centers south of the Loire. In 1832, when the duchess of Berry debarked in Provence and made her way to the Vendée to call for a legitimist rebellion against the new July Monarchy, a few halfhearted bands again mustered to attack government forces before succumbing again. Small bands of *chouans* continued to attack government personnel and facilities from time to time over the next two years.

All this counterrevolutionary activity looks like a carryover from the eighteenth century. Indeed, its noble leaders portrayed it as a straightforward continuation of the struggle of 1793. But in fact Anjou's nineteenth-century politics were falling into place. Unlike the widespread popular insurrection of 1793, the events of 1815 and 1832 depended largely on important regional nobles' calling up of their personal clienteles in the name of the Bourbons. Returning to their estates, great Angevin landlords devoted themselves to managing their properties, building their regional political bases, and constructing the myth of a faithful royalist peasantry.

In the cities, especially in Angers, life followed a very different beat. In February 1826, for example, Mardi Gras brought a guarded critique of Anjou's nobility from the liberals of Cholet. According to the subprefect, in the Mardi Gras tableau

> a feudal lord, called Prince of Darkness, appeared with many followers. They all wore hats in the shape of candlesnuffers. They carried two signs. On one was painted a donkey carrying a torch covered by a snuffer, with bats at the four corners. On the other you could read LONG LIVE THE GOOD OLD DAYS! Others carried night birds and a gibbet. Last came a bust of Voltaire.

The maskers put on two scenes: the lord's marriage, complete with enumeration of his feudal rights; and the trial and hanging of a vassal for killing a rabbit (ADML 21 M 162). Local royalists, according to the subprefect, were not amused.

For several decades the contestation of Anjou's liberal and republican activists took mainly symbolic forms: masquerades, scattered shouts of slogans, banquets. The government made more extensive action difficult. In June 1830, for instance, Angers's liberals planned a gathering to welcome two deputies who had spoken out against the king's recent abridgments of civil rights. Maine-et-Loire's prefect forbade the gathering. When a crowd led the deputies into town anyway, gendarmes surrounded the house where the deputies were scheduled to meet with their supporters, and scattered the crowd. That ended the mild display of opposition (*Le Moniteur Universel* 15 June 1830).

So it went through the 1830s. The regional prosecutor's report on the "moral and political situation" in April 1834, a convenient indicator, dwelt on the difficulties of cleaning up the last Chouans. It devoted but a sentence to Angers's Société des Droits de l'Homme, who were "trying to indoctrinate workers on their doorsteps and in the wineshops" but had "failed in the face of the people's calm mood" (AN BB[3] 167). Angers's republicans, drawn essentially from students and the local bourgeoisie, faltered through the 1830s. Nevertheless, they started their own newspaper, *Le Précurseur de l'Ouest,* in 1840. During the following decade they began agitating for press freedom and expansion of suffrage.

What Angevin republicans did *not* do was to form alliances with organized workers or draw workers, organized or not, into their own ranks. That was not because all workers were inactive. During the 1830s and 1840s strikes became more frequent in Anjou's cities. They continued to take the form of the turnout: the initiators tried to bring out the workers in all the local shops one by one, to hold a general assembly of the trade in a protected location, and then to bargain with the city's masters collectively. Turnouts also continued to call down repression: major strikes of Angers's locksmiths (1834), tailors (1836), cabinetmakers (1841), and especially construction workers (1845) all brought arrests and convictions.

Elsewhere, likewise, authorities used the language of repression to describe and deal with workers' collective action. The prosecutor of Poitiers, for example, described a turnout of Cholet's weavers on 8 and 9 October 1840 as "troubles." The city's workers had assembled to demand an increase in the price of the goods they finished. Two hundred weavers from nearby Mortagne-sur-Sèvre joined them in the streets. When the clothiers had agreed to a new scale of payments, the troubles subsided and, in the prosecutor's words, the workers, back at home, went back to their tasks and rejoiced in concessions that seemed likely to end their misery, which is unfortunately all too real.

But the calm didn't last long. The clothiers having refused to abide by the scale they had previously accepted, the riot [*émeute*] began again on the twelfth. That day the workers of Mortagne did nothing, and the justice of the peace used his influence to make the workers do their duty.

My deputy continues to assure me that up to now politics has nothing to do with Cholet's seditious movement [*mouvement séditieux*]. He adds that in the midst of the mob [*attroupement*], the men in it declared their sincere attachment to the July dynasty and to our constitutional institutions. It is very likely that the workers mean it, and have no other fault but to be acting illegally. Still one can't help recognizing that behind them are legitimists who are watching how things go, and would not miss the chance to profit by the discontent and irritation of the inferior classes [*classes inférieures*]   (AN BB^{18} 1386)

The key words clang: *troubles, émeute, attroupement, mouvement séditieux, classes inférieures*. The search for a "political" connection—one tying the strikers to organized opponents of the regime—informs the authorities' surveillance of workers. But in the absence of that political connection, and given the local capitalists' reneging on an agreement, the prosecutor is inclined to stay his hand. Thus the system leaves a little room for workers' collective action.

Except for slate quarrymen, however, Anjou's workers took little advantage of the 1848 Revolution to organize or to connect their existing organizations to national politics. Quarrymen then launched a general union (a *syndicat*). The general union, in its turn, may well have formed the matrix in which the Marianne, a secret society with socialist leanings, took shape after 1851. The quarrymen's strike of 1852, five hundred workers strong, seemed to reflect more extensive organization than its predecessors, and very likely involved the Marianne. That secret society went so far as to organize, in 1855, an abortive armed insurrection in Trélazé, St.-Barthélemy, Ponts-de-Cé, and Angers.

Anjou's most common varieties of open struggle in the 1830s and 1840s, however, were not strikes or insurrections. They were old-fashioned efforts at diverting to local consumption food supplies that were destined for other markets. Anjou's widespread blockages of grain shipments in 1839 and 1840 occurred not in the cities but mainly in bocage villages such as Le May-sur-Evre, St.-Pierre-Montlimart, Jallais, and Coron. In those places a significant part of the population worked in cottage textile production.

Blockages of grain continued to occur in those places during crisis years for another decade or so. The years 1846 and 1847 brought the last significant cluster of blockages in Anjou, although in a few localities people blocked shipments well into the 1850s. Hunger and poverty continued thereafter, but people acted on them in other ways. In about 150 years, the various forms of open struggle for control of locally available food had run their course.

From the 1850s onward Anjou's public contention pivoted mainly on strikes, demonstrations, and public meetings. Although strikes remained illegal until 1864 and trade unions were banned until 1868, workers, employers, and political authorities began pacing out new limits for legitimate strikes and workers' organizations.

Not that authorities abandoned their conception of strikes as disorders to be repressed. When some of Angers's carpenters struck in May 1860, the city's deputy prosecutor immediately charged them with the offense of coalition. The strike revived anyway in July. Then the prosecutor began preventive detention of its likely leaders. Yet he saw the logic of their action:

> We have a good deal of construction work in Angers. We might reasonably fear that as in 1854 the various building trades would follow the carpenters' lead, and that the strike would spread to all our construction sites. That is what persuaded me to ask the deputy prosecutor to put a case in the hands of the investigative judge of this court, in order to give a healthy warning to workers who are susceptible to being drawn in.   (AN BB[18] 1609, letter of 26 May 1860)

Five days later the same prosecutor recognized that in the current upswing, "workers found that it was a good time to ask for something, and they asked for it" (AN BB[18] 1609).

Other strikes that year involved carpenters of La Flèche, slate quarriers of Trélazé, stonecutters of Angers, bleachers of Cholet, and construction tradesmen of Beaufort. Remembering the Marianne insurrection five years earlier, the prosecutor looked searchingly at Trélazé's strikes for signs of secret society activity. He found none except the presence of a few former members of the Marianne.

From the 1860s to World War I, strikes provided the main occasions on which Angevins contended publicly on a large scale. Textile workers, men in the building trades, and, as always, quarrymen led the way. Shoemakers, foundry workers, and railwaymen joined them from time to time. Even in Anjou, a latecomer to industrial concentration, the locus of strikes shifted away from whole communities toward larger firms and parts of cities.

The big strikes of 1887 and 1888 in Cholet and its region marked the last concerted effort of textile workers in small shops and domestic production to hold off concentration. Although the slateworkers of Trélazé and vicinity kept semirural sites from disappearing entirely, the characteristic Angevin strike increasingly resembled the conflict of 1903 in which 1,500 workers of the Bessonneau textile plant walked off the job. Small potatoes by the standards of Roubaix or Paris, such a strike nevertheless aligned Angers with industrial centers elsewhere in France.

As the firm-by-firm strike came into its own, so did the meeting and the demonstration. Religious issues bulked larger in Anjou than in other regions. In 1895 the Dreyfus affair provoked three days of large anti-Semitic demonstrations, involving priests and students of the Catholic university, in Angers. But the disestablishment of the church divided Anjou even more. During the first half-dozen years of the new century, the church's defenders resisted the closing of monasteries, the secularization of schools, and the inventory of church property. Their action included one of the few occasions on which the most visible "rioters" in a violent demonstration were nobles. This was the news from Angers in August 1902:

> Following a lecture on freedom of education at the Circus chaired by the comte de Maillé, senator, and organized by a majority of the departmental council to protest the dismissal of the sisters, a demonstration took place. About two thousand participants in the meeting went through the streets leading to the prefecture, where they had no authorization to go. Extensive security measures had been taken, and Gendarmerie brigades came to reinforce the gendarmes of Angers.
>
> During the demonstration a number of arrests occurred, notably those of the Marquis Henri d'Armaillé, mayor of Le Bourg-d'Iré, for refusal to move on; of Baron Pierre de Candé, mayor of Noyant-la-Gravoyère, for the same reason; of Baron Louis de Candé, brother of the preceding person, for assault on an officer; of M. Henri d'Aubigné, property owner in Le Bourg-d'Iré, for seditious shouts; and of Maximilien Nicolle and Henri Normand, for insulting an officer. (*Le Temps* 25 August 1902)

Despite elite leadership and reactionary program, then, the opponents of secularization borrowed the prevailing forms of contention: the public meeting and the demonstration. Anjou, like the rest of France, had adopted the new repertoire.

Other Voices

As represented by Flanders, Burgundy, Languedoc, and the Ile-de-France, the rest of France underwent much of the same evolution as Anjou. But on the whole it did so earlier, with more direct participation in national revolutions and in collective demands for democratization, for workers' rights, for protection against arbitrary rule. We can see the difference by means of quick comparisons of the five regions at the time of five political crises: those of 1830, 1848, 1851, 1870–71, and 1905–1907.

In 1830, when Anjou's legitimists were girding to turn back the work of the July Revolution, their cousins in Languedoc were likewise activating. But in Languedoc too a significant republican movement was forming; around Toulouse, indeed, legitimists and republicans joined in a tacit alliance against the July Monarchy. Besides turnouts and opposition to tax collectors, Languedoc's open contention of 1830 consisted largely of the display and destruction of political symbols such as the fleur-de-lis and tricolor; battles raged around the two flags in Toulouse on 4 August. Although Burgundy's winegrowers joined enthusiastically in the opposition to sales taxes, the year's big event was the insurrection of 28 July, when the people of Dijon not only hooted the princess royal but stoned the royal troops sent to maintain order. People in Lille also stoned those troops that remained faithful to outgoing King Charles X, but not until 30 July. In the Nord, the rest of the year brought more turnouts and food riots than occurred in Anjou, Languedoc, or Burgundy.

The Ile-de-France produced the critical events of the Revolution of 1830—the gatherings to protest Charles X's dissolution of the National Assembly and institution of strict press controls, the building of barricades, the popular occupation of the Hôtel de Ville, the street-fighting with troops, and so on until the king's abdication. Furthermore, after the installation of the new regime its authorities had to contend continually with workers who demanded their share of the rewards. Perhaps the peak of post-revolutionary conflict occurred on 12 October, when people recognized the old regime's ex-convict police chief Vidocq (Balzac's "Vautrin") on the street and besieged the building in which he took shelter.

In 1848 Anjou again remained peripheral to the revolution, with only a few invasions of forests, workers' brawls, and other minor conflicts. Languedoc, in contrast, sprang into action with its own republican banquet campaign, active support of the Revolution in the cities coupled with considerable opposition in the countryside, multiple invasions of forests, strikes, acts of resistance against tax collectors, and, in Toulouse, struggles between moderate and radical republicans. For Burgundy, 1848 brought a broad mobilization of workers and winegrowers in the region's cities, plus extensive efforts by peasants to even accounts with their landlords. In the Nord, republicans organized demonstrations of their opposition to Louis-Philippe almost as soon as their Parisian confreres, and rapidly joined in their own variant of the February Revolution. Throughout the region, opposition between workers and owners animated the politics of 1848. Seizures and blockages of grain occurred widely, struggles between Belgian and French workers reappeared, and strikes—sometimes insurrectionary and sometimes quite general—multiplied. Again the Ile-de-France, and especially Paris, dominated the national revolutionary movement; the action ranged from early attacks on railroad property to street-fighting in February and June to frequent workers' strikes and demonstrations.

The year 1851 presented a different pattern. On the whole, Louis Napoleon's active searching out of enemies from 1849 onward demobilized radical republicans in every region. The activity of 1851, however, clustered around the last step of that repression, his coup d'état of 2 December. In Anjou even the coup brought no more than an unarmed demonstration in Angers. Languedoc divided more sharply and actively before the coup, with small-town republicans actively asserting themselves. When the coup occurred, towns and villages sent thousands of men to defend the Republic. Languedoc's departments of Ardèche (with an estimated 3,500 participants in armed rebellion), Gard (4,000), and Hérault (8,000) raised three of the largest rebel forces (Margadant 1979: 11). In Hérault, Béziers stood at the center of a large network of small-town insurrections. Béziers was the largest city in France actually taken over by the republican insurgents of December 1851.

By comparison, resistance in Burgundy remained scattered and small in scale. Although opponents of Louis Napoleon mounted demonstrations against the coup in Châtillon-sur-Seine, Dijon, Beaune, Louhans, St.-Gengoux-le-National, and Cluny, only the area around Mâcon produced an armed rebellion. The Nord, similarly, had begun 1851 with a few conflicts between republicans and defenders of Louis Napoleon, but the coup evoked no more than minor demonstrations in Lille and Douai plus a failed attempt to raise armed rebellion around Anzin.

This time, as usual, the action began in Paris. But it did not end there. Before December, close surveillance and tight repression had squeezed the regime's opponents in Paris and vicinity. Then came the coup: Louis Napoleon's dissolution and occupation of the National Assembly, declaration of a state of siege, and arrest of opposition politicians. Within the city, it precipitated a rising of some twelve hundred republicans; there were barricades, street-fighting, and close to four hundred dead. Yet the repression had been effective: Louis Napoleon's troops swept up the Parisian rebels rapidly, and no one elsewhere in the region joined them. The great bulk of 1851's insurgents rose in small places in the southeastern third of France; of our five regions, only Languedoc contributed large numbers.

By 1870 Parisians again dominated collective action. Neither in that year nor in 1871 was Anjou heavily involved in the conflicts that shook the country; only a few slateworkers' strikes broke the silence. Languedoc, in contrast, had a republican movement that opposed the Franco-Prussian War, acted quickly to support the republican regime of September 1870, and leaned toward the Paris Commune. Toulouse and Narbonne actually declared their own communes in March 1871; neither lasted more than a week.

In Burgundy, Le Creusot likewise produced a small but militant Republican movement and briefly formed a commune. The Prussian occupation of Dijon in 1870–71 silenced the republicans of the regional capital, and the rest of the region remained relatively inactive. The Nord, too, became a war zone in 1870. It involved itself little in the great political struggles of those years, concentrating instead on strikes such as the one that brought troops to Roubaix in March 1871. The Ile-de-France marked out the most important battleground of all, for Paris and Versailles were the prizes. Paris stood out not only for the quick republican seizure of power that followed the emperor's defeat and capture in September 1870, but also for the Commune of 1871; in between, the capital shook with struggle among partisans of competing futures for France as a whole.

The period 1905–1907 has less of a reputation as a time of national political crisis than do 1830, 1848, 1851, and 1870–71. Yet those years saw the definitive disestablishment of France's state church, the arrival of socialists as a national political party, an attempt to mount a May Day general strike, a national strike wave coordinated by Parisian labor leaders and involving large numbers of semiskilled workers, open confrontation between labor leaders and the government, and a vast mobilization of southern winegrowers.

In Anjou, republicans and clericals confronted each other repeatedly over the closing of convents and the inventory of church properties. Languedoc was the chief site of the huge winegrowers' mobilization of 1907; it proceeded from local organization in vintners' towns to meetings bringing hundreds of thousands of supporters into Carcassonne, Nîmes, and Montpellier to the mass resignation of municipal councils and bloody confronta-

Fig. 21. Proclamation of the Commune at the Place de l'Hôtel de Ville, 18 March 1871

Fig. 22. Père-Lachaise demonstration, 25 May 1885

tions between troops and demonstrators. The old textile and wheat areas in the hills and around Toulouse, however, remained inactive during the winegrowers' movement and through the strike wave that overwhelmed industrial France. The Catholic towns of Languedoc's northern reaches (present-day Ardèche and Lozère), however, offered determined resistance to the inventories of church property in 1906.

In Burgundy, winegrowers avoided the national movement; the most important actions of the period came from strikers of Montceau-les-Mines, Le Creusot, and a few other centers of big industry. The Nord occupied a central position in the strike wave of 1906; miners, textile workers, dockers, machine builders, and auto workers all joined in. The region also saw considerable resistance to the inventories in Boeschepe, Halluin, Lille, and other towns. The Ile-de-France experienced numerous strikes; during the strike wave of 1906, as in the Nord, workers in Parisian automobile plants joined a national movement for the first time. The May Day demonstrations of 1906, furthermore, seemed to display the revolutionary solidarity of the Parisian working class.

In moving from crisis to crisis, we see the evolution of the basic means of collective action. From 1830 to 1907 large strikes accompanied major political crises with increasing frequency. After 1848 the once-common seizure or blockage of food disappeared as a component of major political crises. From 1848 onward the deliberately staged demonstration, complete with banners, chants, and marches, became a standard feature of big political conflicts. So did the mass meeting. By 1907 French people had clearly created their own version of the social movement, combining preplanned meetings and demonstrations with the creation of special-interest associations, promulgation of programs and demands in the names of those associations, claims of support from a mass base, staged confrontations with powerholders, and constant struggles for internal control of the movement's organizations and strategy.

Outside of major crises, other changes were occurring. After 1848 the charivari—rather an important instrument of local political struggle in the 1830s and 1840s—virtually disappeared from French politics. So did a number of other venerable forms: the invasion of fields or forests, the attack on machines, the destruction of tollgates, and more. The French repertoire of contention altered rapidly.

Broadly speaking, the alteration happened earlier in regions in which capital and coercion concentrated earlier: the Ile-de-France and the Nord moved into the era of large strikes, public meetings, rallies, demonstrations, coordinated insurrections, and social movements sooner than Burgundy,

Languedoc, or Anjou. And within the regions, areas of capital concentration generally led the way; although the artisanal winegrowers of Beaune and Mâcon remained militant for a long time, such centers as Le Creusot and Montceau-les-Mines eventually became Burgundy's prime sites of working-class action and innovation.

The differing patterns of contention in our five regions corresponded neatly to variations in the organization of production and coercion. Anjou shows us the politics of a region harboring powerful landlords and a mercantile bourgeoisie. Flanders reveals the effects of capital concentration and proletarianization. Burgundy displays the variation from artisanal winegrowing to metalworking and mining. Languedoc brings out the contrast among areas of large-scale but stagnant agriculture, areas of commercial winegrowing, and areas combining small-scale farming with small-scale textile production. The Ile-de-France exemplifies the influence of a growing national capital surrounded by rings of expanding heavy industry and, farther out, of cash-crop agriculture on a grand scale.

The scope and intensity of workers' organization, for example, increased with the extent of capital concentration; in that regard, the Nord and the Seine towered above the other departments. On the other hand, government officials also worked harder at surveillance and repression in the Nord and the Seine than in most other departments; as a result, workers' organizations and dissident political groups that did exist in the peripheral regions had a greater chance of surviving periods of tightened central control.

A Rebellious Century

The new repertoire took hold in fits and starts. At the scale of a shop or a town, the repeated shocks of reorganization in the face of concentrating capital and growing state power altered the capacities of ordinary people to act collectively, as well as the relative importance of other parties—parish priests, landlords, local employers, national political figures, and others—to their fates. The local structure of a trade, for example, lost much of its strength as a base for collective action, while leaders of national political parties gained increasing influence over decisions affecting the welfare of people in one trade or another.

Not only the repertoire but also the cast of characters shifted. Landlords lost much of their importance as actors. Agents of the national government became ever more significant—eventually, for example, figuring in almost every strike as observers, policemen, or mediators. Political parties, labor unions, and other interest associations appeared openly on the scene. Organized capital, organized labor, rivals for control of the state, and officials of the state itself emerged as the chief participants in large-scale collective action.

At the scale of a city, a region, or the country as a whole, each major political mobilization contributed to changing the character and relative efficacy of different forms of collective action. Both the process of mobilization and the strategic success or failure of different forms of action left residues affecting subsequent mobilizations.

Many mobilizations filled the years from 1789 to 1914. The most obvious were the revolutions: 1789, 1830, 1848, with 1815, 1870, and 1871 more debatable instances. In each of these cases massive popular mobilization accompanied, and helped cause, a transfer of power over the national state. In addition, a staccato of defeated rebellions sounded throughout the period 1793–1871. If by "rebellion" we mean an occasion on which at least a few hundred people seized control of some significant public space and held it for more than a day against military force, nineteenth-century France had dozens of rebellions. Under the July Monarchy alone important rebellions occurred in 1831 (Lyon), 1832 (Paris), 1834 (Lyon, Paris, St.-Etienne), and 1839 (Paris).

Later, great strikes such as those of the Nord in 1880 or of France's mining regions as a whole following the Courrières mining disaster of 1906 repeatedly took on the guise of rebellion. From the Revolution of 1870 onward, organized social movements, with their swirl of meetings, demonstrations, pronouncements, and petitions, periodically brought a hundred or more French people into public places to voice common demands and complaints; the peaking of the great movement of southern winegrowers in 1907 brought that sort of mobilization to its highest point before World War I.

None of these events was a monologue. Every one of them involved dialogue—often heated—with powerholders. In the course of the conversations, three important things happened. First, powerholders and their challengers bargained out new agreements. The agreements constrained them thereafter: agreements about the demands and grievances that had brought people to the streets, agreements about the limits and possibilities of future collective action. Thus by striking, firm by firm, workers not only reached agreements with employers and authorities about the grievances and demands they articulated in their strikes, but also acquired the right to organize and to strike. The agreements were often unsatisfactory. The rights to organize and to strike operated within stringent limits. Neither qualification denies the main point: that the agreements produced by dialogue constrained later rounds of collective action.

Second, powerholders altered their strategies of repression and facilitation, often by building up their forces for the next confrontation, but sometimes by adopting a new means of repression or abandoning an old one. Thus as the existence of the demonstration became a *fait accompli,* governmental authorities took to issuing permits to assemble or march, laying out geographic limits outside of which police or troops had the right to attack demonstrators.

Third, challengers shifted their own strategies. Thus as the right to public assembly expanded (however contingently) from 1848 on, people moved away from stating their opinions through authorized ceremonies such as banquets and funerals and chose instead to hold mass meetings, marches, demonstrations involving explicit statements of their grievances and affiliations. Again, the fact that grain seizures disappeared did not mean that shortages and high prices did likewise, or that they disappeared as political issues. A Paris that had reverberated with grain seizures during earlier revolutions saw none at all during the starvation of the Prussian siege in 1870–71. When widespread cost-of-living protests occurred in the Nord and in Burgundy during 1911, they included some price-setting and some sacking of merchants' premises, but they consisted mainly of orderly boycotts, demonstrations, and marches by determined women. People concerned about food prices had adopted new means of dealing with them.

Put together, bargaining between powerholders and challengers, alterations in the modes of repression and facilitation, and changes in challengers' strategies added up to changes in repertoires of contention. The nineteenth-century shift in repertoires went even further than that of the seventeenth century. In the seventeenth century, the rebellion linking regional powerholders to local populations had virtually disappeared, the civilian mutiny had likewise faded away, the massive tax rebellion had declined in importance, and the seizure or blockage of grain had come into its own. But many forms of popular collective action persisted through that seventeenth-century transition: charivaris, intervillage fights, artisans' brawls, invasions of fields, and expulsions of unwanted outsiders all remained in the repertoire.

Practically none of the popular repertoire of contention that prevailed at the beginning of the nineteenth century survived to its end. Invasions of fields, artisans' brawls, intervillage fights, even the seizure or blockage of grains virtually disappeared. Strikes, public meetings, rallies, demonstrations, social movements, and related forms of action took over.

Consider May Day of 1913 in Dijon. During the last week of April, the building trades union and the Confédération Générale du Travail posted handbills advocating demonstrations for a reduced work week and against the bill that obliged young men to three years of military service. Workers affiliated with the *bourse du travail* planned a concert, a meeting, and then a demonstration. Confidential reports reaching the Côte d'Or's central police commissioner, however, said that the workers would not demonstrate unless at least five hundred participants showed up. Reports from Beaune, Châtillon, Auxonne, and Sémur assured the prefect that the first of May would be calm in those cities and their arrondissements. But the prefect of Saône-et-Loire requested a detachment of gendarmes to prevent trouble at Montceau-les-Mines. His colleague in Côte-d'Or sent forty-four men to Montceau.

Acting on instructions from the minister of the interior, the Côte d'Or's prefect also asked the mayor of Dijon to forbid any demonstration against the Three Year Bill. The police commissioner noted the political problem such an instruction created for the mayor: if he forbade that demonstration but allowed the Jeunesses Catholiques to make a march they had planned for a few days later, he would appear partisan indeed. In any case, the mayor refused to comply. "The republican principles of the administration I have the honor to direct," he declared, "make it a rule to respect the freedom of our fellow citizens, including the freedom to move through the streets." He objected to the application of a double standard, pointing out that

> at the time of the festival of Joan of Arc, I authorized the supporters of religious schools and their gymnastic associations to organize a parade through the city's streets, with a concert by their bands at the Place du Peuple.
>
> Furthermore, I have already implicitly authorized the bourse du travail to organize its street demonstration for May Day, as in previous years.
>
> We are informed that the members of the bourse du travail plan to demonstrate in favor of certain working conditions, likewise in favor of the so-called English week and perhaps against the Three Year Bill.
>
> The organizers have assured us that everything will go on in the customary order; in any case, we have given our police the necessary instructions for every eventuality.
>
> Knowing the temper of our population, we think it would be impolitic and dangerous to agitate people by forbidding the demonstration of members of the bourse du travail on 1 May.
>
> That to do so could lead to reprisals, especially on 4 May against the

> supporters of religious schools, even though they are only supposed to
> cross the city with their bands. (ADCO SM 3511)

As it turned out, only a hundred-odd workers came to the May Day meeting. The organizers therefore called off the demonstration. Yet the maneuvers behind the nonevent reveal a new world and a new repertoire: a world of surveillance and tight political calculation; a world in which challengers and powerholders bargain out not only the exercise of power but also the limits within which demonstrations occur; a world in which specialized associations do a great deal of public business; a world in which orderly shows of strength make a political difference. In Dijon of 1913 we see the world of collective action we know today.

10 〜

Festivals and Fights
in the Ile-de-France

*B*Y 1906, MAY DAY WAS starting its third decade as the international festival of the working class. At its Chicago congress of 1884, America's Federation of Organized Trades had fixed on 1 May 1886 as the starting point of a great campaign for the eight-hour day. American workers had responded by turning the old feast into a giant display of workers' strength. In 1889 the Second International, convening in Paris, had designated 1 May 1890 as an international day of demonstration for the eight-hour day. Back then, the newspaper *Le Père Peinard* (the pseudonym of Emile Pouget, its author) had likened the new holiday to the great day in 1870, in the Second Empire's waning months, when "everyone" had left work to follow Victor Noir's funeral procession.

Victor Noir had worked at Henri Rochefort's muckraking paper *La Marseillaise.* Louis Napoleon's kinsman Prince Pierre Bonaparte had killed Noir in an altercation during preparations for a duel between Prince Pierre and an editor of the paper; to mourn Noir ostentatiously was to demonstrate opposition to the imperial regime, without taking the risk of a manifestly political gesture. After all, could the regime risk punishing people for mourning a man who really had been murdered? The moment was too good to miss.

May Day had some of the same appeal: a holiday stolen back from the rich and powerful. In 1890, in fact, Père Peinard had suggested taking advantage of the holiday by helping oneself at the city's bright new department stores, which so blatantly pandered to the bourgeoisie: "The Louvres, the Printemps, the Belle Jardinières, and the Potins reach out their arms and make eyes at us: It's so nice to have a new overcoat on your back, or good shoes on your feet! . . . You have to be in the street to deal with social problems," declared Père Peinard, "and to see clearly who has too much to live on and who has too little" (Pouget 1976: 33).

When the director of *Le Père Peinard* received a sentence of fifteen months in jail and a fine of 2,000 francs for publishing that issue, the paper had put out a broadside. Signed, as usual, by Père Peinard, the new text trumpeted:

> And why? Because I shot off my mouth about the May Day demonstra-tion. You can bet I'm not going to shut up. I'll keep on saying that the populo is being robbed, sacked, and assassinated, and that when a chance like the first of May comes along you'd have to be nuts not to grab it. In all this, what the big shots really don't like is when you yell at their Rothschild. He's their god, that animal. To hell with him. He's not immortal. After all, they cut off Louis XVI's head. (AN BB[18] 1816)

On May Day 1890 the demonstrations and strikes of Paris had echoed Père Peinard's rebellious theme.

That was the May Day spirit. In 1906 Jacques Turbin wrote a song called *The General Strike.* Its first two verses ran (Brécy 1969: 97):

> Let's go, men of every craft,
> Every land of the whole world
> Let's make the same effort everywhere
> At the same moment, of our own free will:
> Let's all go on strike!
>
> Tired of being driven by force
> To work hard, like mere cattle,
> And tired of living without hope
> From day to day, from night to night:
> Let's all go on strike!

The idea that workers could liberate themselves through one great effort re-sonated with daily experience.

The holiday had a longer-range political message as well. Since 1890, France's May Day had been the annual rehearsal for the general strike, the revolutionary holiday workers seized for themselves. From the start, French workers—especially those aligned with "collectivist" socialism rather than with anarchosyndicalism—had used May Day to demand the eight-hour day, voice their shared grievances, and demonstrate their strength. At its

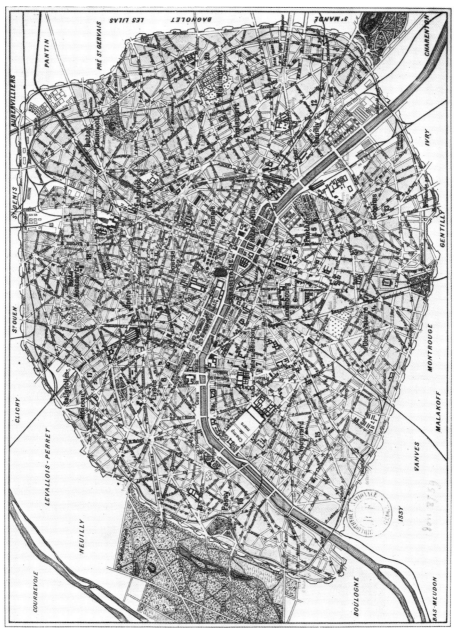

Fig. 23. Paris and the Ile-de-France in the twentieth century

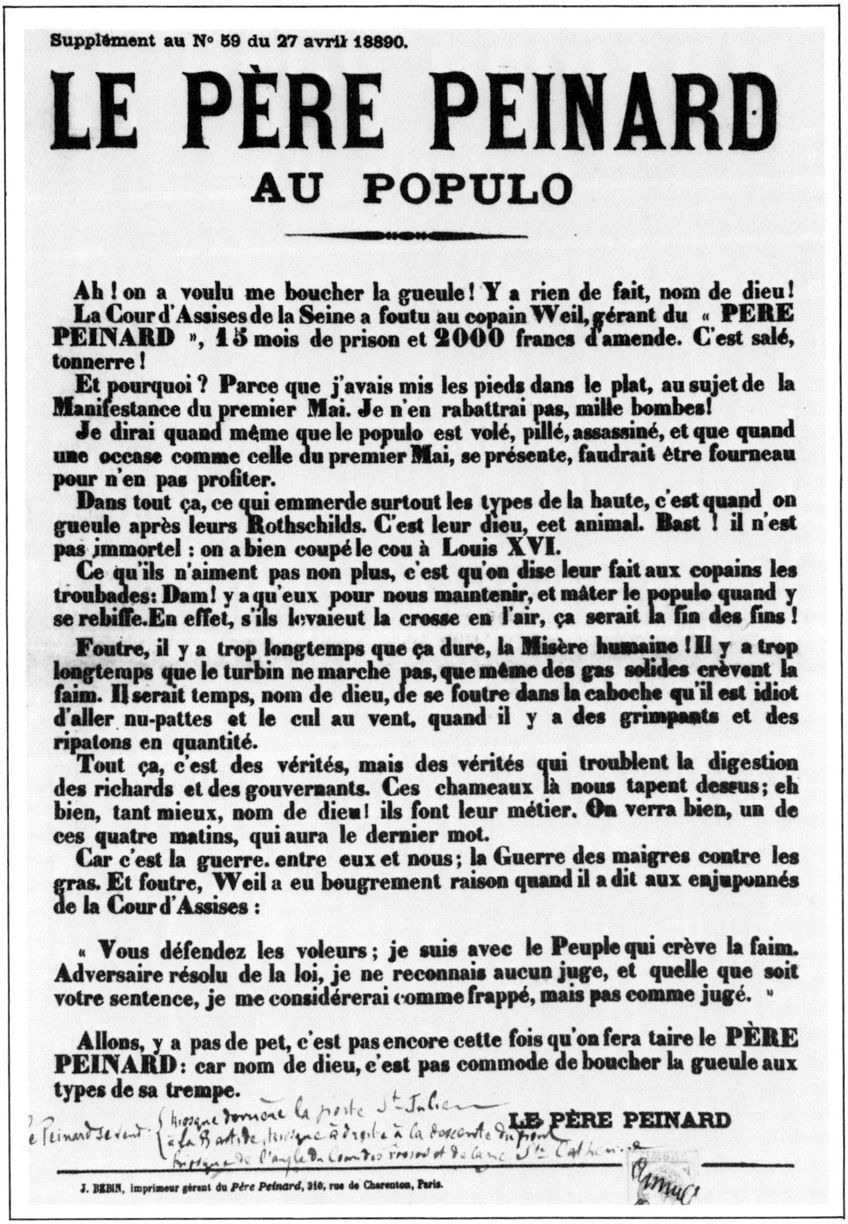

Supplément au N° 59 du 27 avril 18890.

LE PÈRE PEINARD
AU POPULO

Ah ! on a voulu me boucher la gueule ! Y a rien de fait, nom de dieu !
La Cour d'Assises de la Seine a foutu au copain Weil, gérant du « PÈRE PEINARD », 15 mois de prison et 2000 francs d'amende. C'est salé, tonnerre !

Et pourquoi ? Parce que j'avais mis les pieds dans le plat, au sujet de la Manifestance du premier Mai. Je n'en rabattrai pas, mille bombes !

Je dirai quand même que le populo est volé, pillé, assassiné, et que quand une occase comme celle du premier Mai, se présente, faudrait être fourneau pour n'en pas profiter.

Dans tout ça, ce qui emmerde surtout les types de la haute, c'est quand on gueule après leurs Rothschilds. C'est leur dieu, cet animal. Bast ! il n'est pas immortel : on a bien coupé le cou à Louis XVI.

Ce qu'ils n'aiment pas non plus, c'est qu'on dise leur fait aux copains les troubades : Dam ! y a qu'eux pour nous maintenir, et mâter le populo quand y se rebiffe. En effet, s'ils levaient la crosse en l'air, ça serait la fin des fins !

Foutre, il y a trop longtemps que ça dure, la Misère humaine ! Il y a trop longtemps que le turbin ne marche pas, que même des gas solides crèvent la faim. Il serait temps, nom de dieu, de se foutre dans la caboche qu'il est idiot d'aller nu-pattes et le cul au vent, quand il y a des grimpants et des ripatons en quantité.

Tout ça, c'est des vérités, mais des vérités qui troublent la digestion des richards et des gouvernants. Ces chameaux là nous tapent dessus ; eh bien, tant mieux, nom de dieu ! ils font leur métier. On verra bien, un de ces quatre matins, qui aura le dernier mot.

Car c'est la guerre. entre eux et nous ; la Guerre des maigres contre les gras. Et foutre, Weil a eu bougrement raison quand il a dit aux enjuponnés de la Cour d'Assises :

« Vous défendez les voleurs ; je suis avec le Peuple qui crève la faim. Adversaire résolu de la loi, je ne reconnais aucun juge, et quelle que soit votre sentence, je me considérerai comme frappé, mais pas comme jugé. »

Allons, y a pas de pet, c'est pas encore cette fois qu'on fera taire le PÈRE PEINARD : car nom de dieu, c'est pas commode de boucher la gueule aux types de sa trempe.

LE PÈRE PEINARD

J. BERN, imprimeur gérant du *Père Peinard*, 310, rue de Charenton, Paris.

Fig. 24. Père Peinard poster about May Day 1890

Bourges congress of 1904, the Confédération Générale du Travail (CGT) had committed itself to a drive for the eight-hour day, focused on May Day 1906. The official program had called for workers to walk off the job after eight hours from that day forward.

May Day 1906

In 1906 the moment seemed well chosen. Since 1886 the International had kept the eight-hour day on its own agenda. In 1905, French Socialists had joined to form the Unified Socialist Party (PSU), which became the French Section of the Workers' International (SFIO). Although Socialists had co-operated with governments intermittently since the first entry of a Socialist into the cabinet in 1898, the party had broken with the government in November 1905 over the right of schoolteachers to strike. After wielding some influence in the election of the less conservative candidate, Armand Fallières, president of France in January 1906, the party was driving for success in the legislative elections of May. Support from the CGT—which was officially apolitical, and then actually quite resistant to party control—would help the Socialists consolidate their support. Thus the party had exceptional incentives to align itself with the workers' movement.

Furthermore, the recent failed revolution in Russia offered a concrete example of a popular rising in a repressive state. The formation of soviets and the temporary success of general strikes in Moscow and St. Petersburg held out the possibility that workers in other countries could act for themselves. (The appeal of Russia's example was so great that Jean Jaurès himself felt obliged to write, in *L'Humanité* of 5 November 1905, that "when the French working class interprets the revolutionary events in Russia, it should not forget for an instant that it already has the universal suffrage which the Russian proletariat is trying to seize from tsarism": Jaurès 1976: 124.) Many labor activitists looked forward to May Day 1906 as the start of the great general strike that would destroy French capitalism. A pamphlet circulated by the Federation of Construction Trades read: "The eight-hour day will be nothing but an advance payment, an aperitif if you will, before the main course that will soon be served when workers decide to strike down the parasites of capitalism by a general strike which will be the social revolution, and which will establish a Communist regime" (Lefranc 1967: 129). Publishing his *Reflections on Violence* as a series of articles in *Le Mouvement Socialiste* from January to June 1906, Georges Sorel chose the right time for a hymn to the general strike.

The CGT actually gave its affiliates two choices: start an unlimited strike on 1 May, or begin enforcing the eight-hour day then and there. A banner hung from the Paris bourse du travail read: "STARTING ON 1 MAY, WE WILL WORK ONLY EIGHT HOURS A DAY" (Julliard 1965: 23). The CGT's national committee found itself overwhelmed with calls for help—including inspirational speakers—from union locals in Paris and elsewhere. The prefect put plainclothesmen on the trails of the committee members.

On 26 and 27 April the prefect's staff filed detailed "prognostications" of workers' intentions, first, to take May Day off and, second, to go on strike for a longer term. They based their estimates on a confidential report from a high CGT official. The advisers predicted that 8,000 lithographers, 25,000 carriagemakers, 5,000 metalworkers, and so on would begin indefinite strikes.

Those predictions were well informed. Indeed, some of them came true ahead of schedule. On 30 April, 10,000 automobile workers of the expected 25,000 in carriagemaking added themselves to the 1,200 already on strike. Nevertheless the prefect's labor-watchers properly spotted construction workers as the most active participants: 10,000 masons, 5,000 stonecutters, 20,000 painters, 2,000 carpenters and cabinetmakers, plus a full 30,000 navvies entered their calculations. "Leaving aside the typographers and the jewelers-goldsmiths, who are currently on strike," the report concluded,

> we can count on 185,000 strikers in Paris. But since the voluntary idleness of some leads to the forced idleness of others . . . the total number of strikers can be estimated at 200,000. The most troublesome will be the navvies, the bakers, the grocers, and the hairdressers; having little hope of getting benefits by means of peaceful strikes, they will try to intimidate their employers through sabotage. (AN F[7] 13267)

The prefect and his boss, Clémenceau, got the word. On 30 April they had Griffuelhes, secretary of the CGT, arrested. In jail, he joined his fellow committee member Pierre Monatte; Clémenceau had picked off Monatte earlier, at the height of the miners' strike in the north, on the charge of having incited to riot in Lens. For show, a Bonapartist leader (accused, implausibly, of subsidizing Monatte's agitation) went to jail as well. The government forbade parades and gatherings on 1 May. Then the prefect and the minister spread their forces through the city.

After the fact, it is hard to say which explanation of what actually happened was correct: that repression worked or that the government had overestimated the threat. In any case, the large crowds of workers that gathered at the bourse du travail and in the nearby Place de la République during the day cheered militant speeches but made no attempt to take over the city. Their shouts for the day were "Long live the eight-hour day! Long live May Day!" (*Le Temps* 3 May 1906). During the day, only a few scuffles between people in the street and police or dragoons broke the relative calm.

Toward the end of the afternoon, however, groups of a few hundred activists formed in the streets radiating from the Place de la République and faced off with troops or police. Some sang the *Internationale* or the *Carmagnole* as they challenged. A group of workers started to build barricades in the rue de Belleville. But the government forces clearly had the advantage. The official scorecard for the day (according to *Le Temps* 3 May 1906) ran:

> 665 people arrested, with 173 held after questioning (among the 173, 53 were foreigners who would be deported, and 35 had criminal records)
> 1 chief inspector, 12 policemen, and 3 *gardes républicains* wounded
> 12 demonstrators likewise wounded

No doubt many more demonstrators found it expedient not to report their injuries. Even if the civilian casualties ran several times the dozen reported, however, May Day 1906 would still look mainly like a peaceful show of labor's strength and determination, shadowed by the government's own display of strength and determination.

During the following days, strikes multiplied. In Paris, about 70,000 construction workers (a figure remarkably close to the prefect's predictions) laid down their tools on 2 May. Nationally, 158,000 workers—more than a third of the year's total—were on strike in May. After a high plateau from about 12 to 20 May, the national strike movement fell once more.

In national labor history, the strike wave of 1906 marked a crucial transition. Despite the importance of the northern mines in March and April, it was the first national strike wave to be coordinated in Paris and to concentrate most heavily in the Paris region. For the first time, over the country as a whole all industrial sectors including agriculture struck at higher rates than normal. Proletarian workers such as the automobilemakers of Paris played a far larger part in initiating the movement than ever before. The direct confrontation between labor's organizations and the national government—the first since the July Monarchy—set off the strike wave of April–May 1906 as a major claim of organized workers to exercise power at the national scale.

As the wave rolled on, futhermore, May's legislative elections gave the Unified Socialist Party almost 900,000 votes, and fifty-one seats in the Chamber of Deputies. Although their claims were disputed, most claimed to speak for the strikers of 1906. The passage of a Sunday rest law in July 1906 and the establishment of a separate Ministry of Labor in October reflected labor's new national strength. Likewise, the reintegration of Captain Dreyfus into the army after being declared innocent in July (not to mention the Chamber's December decision to transfer Emile Zola's ashes to the Panthéon) closed a long struggle to the advantage of the French left.

Nevertheless, many observers, including the CGT's own leaders, read the outcome of their campaign as at best a standoff. The eight-hour day did not come to pass, the definitive general strike failed to materialize, and even the show of strength in the capital went on within limits set clearly by the government's own force. That was not what many labor activists had in mind. Furthermore, when the CGT held its congress in Amiens during October 1906, its famous Amiens Charter declared its unwillingness to tie itself to any party, including the Socialists. The charter called for "complete emancipation" based on expropriation of capitalists, affirmed that today's syndicates would be tomorrow's producing units, and reiterated its faith in direct action by workers (Lefranc 1963: 151–152). The CGT's activists had not given up the effort to have labor show its own strength for its own ends.

May Day provided an occasion for muscle-flexing during each of the next few years. Although the socialist party tried repeatedly to use May Day to its own advantage, the national unions maintained control of the event. Organized labor was not, however, always able to show the same amount of muscle. As a confidential report to the minister of the interior put it just before May Day 1908:

> If 1 May 1906 was agitated, it was because the union rank and file thought they could get the eight-hour day from their bosses. The general failure of that effort, due to the withdrawal of several large organizations and the lack of agreement among the rest, made 1 May 1907 a fairly calm day: the long strikes that followed May Day 1906 had exhausted the national unions, especially in metallurgy, which still hasn't recovered from that test. (AN F^7 13267, 28 April 1908)

For 1908, the prefect of police predicted widespread observance of the unofficial holiday in metals, construction, automobiles, tobacco, matches, and machine building, with poorer showings in other industries. He also expected meetings, demonstrations, and declarations. He based his predictions on a large dossier of confidential reports from spies and informers within the labor movement.

In general, the prefect's predictions came true. The prefect's forces (backed by the army) were able to contain the holiday and to reduce the likelihood that a general strike would issue from it. In 1910, indeed, the unions had so little hope of success that they canceled the day's demonstrations.

Still, May Day had not run its course. In 1911 about four thousand marchers, red flowers in their buttonholes, showed up for the festivities. When the marchers attempted to hold a rally in the Place de la Concorde, police moved to break them up, and battles ensued; two policemen left wounded. Later, other demonstrators clashed with police near the Place St.-Paul. The same evening, when an orchestra in a Montmartre cabaret played the *Marseillaise,* "antimilitarists" in the audience replied with the *Internationale;* a brawl ensued (*Le Journal des Débats* 2 May 1911: 1). Tally for the day: sixty-odd arrests, a few dozen hurt.

World War I cramped the May Day style but did not eliminate the workers' holiday. The strike wave of 1919 and 1920 surpassed that of 1906; 2,047 officially counted strikes brought out 1.3 million workers in 1919; in 1920, 1.1 million workers joined 1,879 strikes. Both surges depended closely on the mobilization for May Day.

By May Day 1919 the CGT was once again organizing a great demonstration and general strike for the eight-hour day, and the government was again forbidding demonstrators to assemble. Under the pressure of those preparations on both sides, the Chamber passed its first enabling act for the eight-hour day. That move transformed the CGT's program into a demand for immediate application of the law in the country's workplaces. The acquittal of Raoul Villain, who had assassinated Jaurès five years earlier, added another grievance to the list. On May Day 1919, labor's marchers tried to reach the Palais Bourbon in order to address their demands to the Chamber of Deputies. Police and troops blocked them. Before the day's barricades and battles were finished, at least one worker was dead, and 600 people were injured.

In 1920 the railroad workers' union called its own strike for May Day. The CGT's appeal to miners and other transport workers for a supporting strike on 3 May persuaded relatively few workers, and the railroad employees found themselves replaced by volunteers. The dream was fading: the sequence running from workers' holiday to general strike to revolution seemed less and less likely ever to occur. From 1933 to 1936, in the heat of great struggles among left, right, and center, some Parisian Communists took 1 May as a day for challenges to the regime and its police. Then May Day virtually disappeared as an occasion for shows of strength.

Other People's Holidays

Other holidays, however, competed with May Day. The Fourteenth of July, for example, continued to symbolize the regime's revolutionary origins. Made the official national holiday by victorious republicans in 1880, Bastille Day paraded the nation's commitment, solidarity, and military might. For that very reason, it also provided a chance for different groups to act out their own relationships to the nation and its politics. During the official holiday's early years, anarchists and organized workers often boycotted the Bastille Day ceremonies as celebrations of a bourgeois revolution and glorifications of a bourgeois regime—even though the bunting and street festivals appeared mainly in working-class neighborhoods. The victory parade for World War I, on 14 July 1919, temporarily drew all but the far left into the celebration, despite the fact that the great band marched up the eminently bourgeois path from the Place de la Concorde to the Arc de Triomphe.

Then doctrinal splits reappeared: 1 May for organized workers, 8 May (Joan of Arc's feast-day) for the royalist right, 11 November (Armistice Day) for organized veterans, Bastille Day for republicans who were willing to tolerate or even support the Republic.

There were more. With the fiftieth anniversary of the Paris Commune, in 1921, the newly formed Communist party marked the division within the left by mounting its great show on Sunday, 29 May. Battling with anarchist hecklers and a Catholic procession along the way, some twenty thousand Communist supporters paraded to the Mur des Fédérés in Père Lachaise cemetery. Veterans of the Commune, now fifty years older than in 1871, went in honor to Federation Wall.

As the site of 1871's massacre of Communard leaders, the wall nicely symbolized Communist determination to right past wrongs. So much so that when leaders of the non-Communist left decided in 1926 to commemorate the Commune for themselves with a march to the wall, they took care to choose another day from the Communists' 30 May (AN F^7 13322). With the multiplication of destinations in the late 1920s (in 1928, for example, Clichy's Communists gathered at the city's war memorial), followers of competing political factions had their choice of dates, itineraries, and endpoints. Thus the relative fragmentation or unification of memorials to the Commune registered the extent of disunity on the left.

Each of the sectarian celebrations provided a welcome occasion for counterdemonstrations by opposing parties. Armistice Day became a favorite time for antimilitarist demonstrations during the 1920s, and Bastille Day a preferred occasion for Communist displays of contempt for official republicanism. In 1929, for instance, sellers of Communist periodicals appeared at many municipal ceremonies in Parisian suburbs on 14 July; they and their comrades often heckled the official parades and staged small marches of their own. In Montereau:

> toward 11:30 P.M., the band had just played the *Marseillaise* in the court-yard of the city hall after the torchlight parade when 500 Communists invaded the courtyard singing the *Internationale*. The police chief had to call gendarmes to get rid of the demonstrators. One sergeant was punched. A demonstrator named Grousselle was arrested and taken to the gendarmerie. The demonstrators having threatened to break down the doors if their comrade wasn't freed, the gendarmerie commander of Melun sent in a squad of Republican Guards, and order was restored to-ward 4:00 A.M. (*Le Temps* 15–16 July 1929: 4)

Competing shows of strength and opposition continued.

A Right, and Then a Left

During the next few years a new theme became more prominent. Increas-ingly, fascists and right-wing nationalists became the targets of organized leftists, and vice versa. At first, Italian Fascists and domestic rightists at-tracted the most attention; in fact Italian leftists often fought their right-wing countrymen. As Hitler gained power in Germany, however, his sup-porters likewise entered the fray.

In the early 1930s, nevertheless, domestic nationalists such as Croix de Feu and Action Française far outshadowed authentic fascists of Italian or German persuasion. The Croix de Feu, until then an association of aging veterans, established its Volontaires Nationaux for younger men in 1933. In 1936 it extended its political claims via the new Parti Social Français. Mem-bers of Action Française became adept at finding occasions to display their nationalism at the expense of the government or of left-wing opponents. A case in point was the French adaptation of a German play on the Dreyfus case at the Théâtre du Nouvel-Ambigu (boulevard St.-Martin) in February 1931. At the showing of 19 February, "beginning with the second act, dem-onstrators spread through all classes of seats, shouted various things, threw stinkbombs, and forced the actors to stop the play"; police finally succeeded in expelling them from the theater. They took seventy-five Action Française activists to arrondissement police headquarters (*Le Journal des Débats* 20 February 1931: 2).

On the following days, activists battled counterdemonstrators in the streets. Fights continued night after night into March. At the request of the Croix de Feu, police prefect Chiappe then banned the play. His decision scored a political victory for the right. On the rescinding of the ban under political pressure two weeks later, the right-wing coalition made the streets outside the theater so unsafe that the play closed after two more performances (Weber 1962: 298). The Camelots du Roi, shock troops of Action Française, had outmaneuvered both their leftist counterparts and the city's police.

A rhythm sounded through those turbulent years: occasion, demonstration, counterdemonstration, repression, tallying of gains and losses, new occasion. Although 1931, 1932, and 1933 brought many a battle, the following three years, 1934–1936, stand among the century's leaders for conflict in the Ile-de-France. January 1934 alone sounded a drumroll of incidents:

> *3 January:* 525 automobile workers in Nanterre went on strike against wage cuts.
>
> *5 January:* 170 foundry workers of Noisy-le-Sec likewise struck against wage cuts.
>
> *6 January:* Hawkers of left-wing and right-wing newspapers fought each other in front of the Lycée Henri IV.
>
> *9 January:* After the newspaper *Action Française* called for demonstrations outside the Chamber of Deputies to protest the ties of the "thieves" and "assassins" in the government to the swindler Sacha Stavisky (officially reported to have killed himself on the eighth, and widely believed to have been murdered to keep him quiet), Camelots du Roi assembled on the boulevard St.-Germain, blocked traffic, tore up trees, railings, and benches, and battled police, but failed to reach the Chamber.
>
> *11 January:* Camelots in larger numbers tried unsuccessfully to reach the Chamber, smashing and battling more vigorously than they had on the ninth. The same day, several hundred commuters "demonstrated" to protest the delay of a train from the Gare du Nord, and a group of suburban right-wing activists returned to Versailles from the doings in Paris, then broke into a Radical Socialist meeting there to challenge the speakers, as well as to fight with the audience (*Le Journal des Débats* and *Le Temps* 13 January 1934).
>
> *12 January:* Although heavy rain and negotiations with the police dispersed the main body of Camelot demonstrators without a fight, a group of sixty-odd activists marched from the Place de l'Opéra toward

the Place de la République struggling with policemen and shouting "Conspuez [Prime Minister] Chautemps!" Police arrested Charles Moreau (a member of Solidarité Française accused of shouting "Bandes de vaches, vous défendez les voleurs!") and Pierre Amiaud, son of a former Action Française leader, who refused to keep moving (AN F^7 12963).

14 January: As 400 Croix de Feu members gathered for a commemorative ceremony, 200 Communists appeared to demonstrate against them. Police struggled, with imperfect success, to keep the two groups apart.

18 January: In Levallois-Perret 150 bodymakers struck against wage cuts.

19 January: Camelots du Roi and Jeunesses Patriotes, shouting "A bas Chautemps, a bas les voleurs!" tried to draw passersby into a demonstration against the government.

22 January: At yet another call of *Action Française,* demonstrators once more appeared on the boulevard St.-Germain, shouting, smashing, fighting, building barricades, yet failing to reach the Chamber. Later, a reported 3,000 unionized public service workers jammed the Place de l'Hôtel de Ville to protest reductions in their benefits.

23 January: Another 2,500 right-wing activists took to the streets of the Latin Quarter with essentially the same routines as on previous outings, and saw 325 of their number arrested. On the same day about 180 Parisian metalworkers went on strike against the reorganization of work routines, and 19 mirrormakers in Courbevoie struck to call for the rehiring of a fired colleague.

24 January: 350 Parisian metalworkers went on strike against wage cuts.

27 January: In Stains, 20 foundry workers struck against wage cuts. In Paris, meanwhile, perhaps 10,000 people, called and spearheaded by Action Française, gathered to demonstrate at the Place de l'Opéra; police barely stopped them from crossing the Place de la Concorde and the Seine to the Chamber. During the day, Minister of Justice Raynaldy resigned.

28 January: The Chautemps cabinet as a whole resigned.

The right-wing crowds of Paris had helped bring down a government.

Stavisky, Chiappe, and Daladier

In fact, they soon also tumbled another one. Jean Chiappe, prefect of police, had known ties and sympathies on the right; many politicians on the left felt he had indulged the Camelots and other right-wing activists while repressing their leftist counterparts. When Radical Edouard Daladier formed a government to succeed the fallen Chautemps cabinet, one of his first acts was to name Chiappe resident-general in Morocco—a prime colonial post, but one that would remove Chiappe from Paris. Chiappe refused angrily. Daladier dismissed him. Soon the action in Paris streets began again.

On 1 February, 17,500 Parisian taxi drivers struck against a new gasoline surtax. On 3 February striking taxi drivers attacked nonstriking drivers, demonstrated at the Place de la République, and struggled with the police sent to disperse them. The evening of 4 February (the Sunday on which newspapers carried the news of Chiappe's firing), Camelots practically broke up the Comédie Française's performance of Shakespeare's *Coriolanus,* with its theme of throwing the rascals out of power. On the fifth, they returned for more of the same. But the next day made the previous month's street battles seem trivial.

In outline, the events of 6 February followed the pattern of January's antigovernment demonstrations: a published call for action in *Action Française,* preparatory gatherings on the boulevard St.-Germain and in the Place de la Concorde, attempts to reach the Chamber of Deputies, barricades, combat with police, destruction, injuries, arrests. Inside the Chamber, as often before, right and left shouted and sang each other down. Yet this time the full range of rightist groups—not only Action Française but also the Jeunesses Patriotes, the Croix de Feu, the Union Nationale des Combattants, the Fédération Nationale des Contribuables, and others—summoned their followers to the streets. And this time fourteen people died.

The Jeunesses Patriotes announced a rendezvous for "the Place de Grève, in front of the city hall, cradle of your communal liberties" and called for a march from there to the National Assembly (*Le Temps* 7 February 1934). The CGT, the Communist party, and the Communist-affiliated veterans' group Association Républicaine des Anciens Combattants called out their rank and file for counterdemonstrations against fascism. On the other hand, the Francistes—then the most openly fascist of all influential French associations—decided not to risk a public appearance.

People heeded these various calls. This time the scale exceeded anything Paris had seen since the great insurrections of the nineteenth century: the full range of right-wing groups mobilized plus a few from the far left, 120,000 people in the streets, lethal battles around the Place de la Concorde, 14 deaths, roughly 1,700 persons wounded and 600 arrested, the Daladier government brought to resign.

Daniel Guérin, himself a militant left-wing socialist, has recalled a series of vivid scenes from that evening: police and demonstrators face-to-face at the Pont de la Concorde; a burning bus in the Place; gas pipes and the Navy Ministry likewise on fire; the arrival of right-wing and left-wing veterans' groups singing, respectively, the *Marseillaise* and the *Internationale;* a counterattack of police clearing the Place de la Concorde by firing their guns; men falling with bullet wounds; rows of police blocking some of the exit routes; an older, mink-wrapped American woman drinking in the spectacle and exclaiming "I love Paris!"; a well-dressed man, bullet swelling his cheek, bellowing "Assassins!"; and, at 2:00 A.M., an intellectual leader taking the occasion to show his true colors:

> hands behind his back, beard thrust ahead, traveling the boulevards alone like a missile, angrily stepping over the debris that lies everywhere, stumbling on the cobblestones, gesturing as if he were shouting vengeance: my uncle Daniel Halévy, who, unhinged, losing all restraint, discarding any mask, publicly declares himself on the far right. (Guérin 1970: 69)

Many people aligned themselves publicly with the right at the time of the Stavisky Riots, as these events came to be known. Such rough-and-tumble rightist organizations as the Volontaires Nationaux took in thousands of new members. Yet in addition to bringing down another republican government, the events of 6 February called forth a mobilization of the left. On the seventh and ninth, Communists led major antifascist demonstrations; four more people died in the street-fighting of 9 February. On the twelfth, multiple left-wing demonstrations coupled with a widely-followed general strike throughout the region. That day marked a turning point for the Parti Communiste Français (PCF): the first time in its history that it had joined other parties in a national political strike, the beginning of its regular use of the strike as a political weapon. On 17 February the funerals of workers killed in the strikes and demonstrations of the ninth and thereafter became demonstrations of leftist determination.

Furthermore, the tempo of strikes increased throughout the Ile-de-France: after the general strike of 12 February came strikes of telegraphers (Paris) and navvies (Poissy) on the fourteenth, of plasterers (Rosny-sous-Bois) on the seventeenth, of metalworkers (Argenteuil) on the twentieth, of rubberworkers (St.-Denis) on the twenty-first, of more metalworkers (Clichy) on the twenty-sixth, of boxmakers (Paris) and navvies (Achères) on the twenty-eighth. Through it all, striking taxi drivers and their blackleg competitors bloodied each other in the streets. For the rest of 1934, organized workers, employers, leftist activists, militant rightists, and government forces interwove their many conflicts.

Popular Front versus National Front

For over two years afterward, demonstrations, counterdemonstrations, and clashes in the street joining some combination of left-wing activists, right-wing activists, and police arrived in quick succession. As anti-Semitic and profascist actions became more common on the right, left factions began to ally with one another. In June and July 1934, with the blessing of Moscow, the socialist and Communist parties worked out an agreement for unified action against the right-wing menace. By the time of the extensive leftist demonstrations of Armistice Day 1934, Socialists and Communists were talking frequently of a general strike as the way to left solidarity and political power. During 1935 a Popular Front—more clearly unified by its opposition to right extremism and governmental austerity measures than by any shared program—began to form. The Communist-led Confédération Générale du Travail Unifiée (CGTU) and the larger, nonpartisan CGT started work on a merger. After long preferring other factional holidays, a reunited left made the Fourteenth of July 1935 an immense demonstration against fascism.

With the elections of April and May 1936, a coalition of Socialists, Radical Socialists, and Communists actually came to power. In May of that year began a great national wave of sitdown strikes. Strikes in which workers took over the premises temporarily had occurred in France as far back as 1920. From 1933 to 1935, workers had occupied the premises of several major firms, including Citroen and Simca. In mid-March 1936, 380 workers of the Verduraz pasta factory in Maisons-Alfort occupied their plant for a morning (AN F^7 12964). On 10 April workers at the Boutillerie munitions plant near Amiens (with the encouragement of the manager) occupied and barricaded the factory to keep it from being seized for taxes (Prouteau 1938: 107–108). Still, France had never before seen anything like the tidal wave of May–June 1936.

Factory occupations began well outside Paris—in the Aisne, the Haute-Garonne, and the Seine-Inférieure—during the first two weeks of May. In Toulouse and Le Havre, sitdowns began when managers fired workers who had taken May Day off; in both cases, the intervention of the mayor led to reinstatement of the discharged workers. In the first occupation of the Paris region (at the Bloch aircraft factory of Courbevoie, beginning on 14 May), workers won their point in two days without direct intervention of authorities. But even there, both sides consulted extensively with government officials, and the officials watched nervously.

From then on, occupying workers commonly demanded not only the satisfaction of their immediate grievances but also the establishment of collective bargaining and regular worker representation within their plants. Metalworkers in particular and the CGT in general had been making those two broad demands since the end of World War I. Now they became urgent and widespread. With Socialists and Communists about to join Radicals in control of the national government, workers began to demand power. The annual march to Federation Wall, on 24 May, brought 600,000 demonstrators—with Communist chief Maurice Thorez and incoming prime minister Léon Blum at their head—into Parisian streets. During the following week, sitdown strikes swept through the large metalworking plants (especially those in aviation) around Paris. After a pause for the Pentecost vacation, sitdowns spread farther on 2 June. The country's largest strike wave so far had begun.

Inside the plants, occupying workers organized their daily lives and their politics. In the great Renault plant at Billancourt, which had 33,000 workers, the sitdown began on 28 May. At the behest of Communist organizers, who were bargaining with Renault's management, workers left the plant the next evening. They returned to the occupation, however, after the weekend and an abortive settlement of the strike. According to one of the participants:

> We organized food service right away. We let down baskets from the window on a rope and brought them back up full of bread, sausage, drinks, and cigarettes. After two days, we had the women leave. Inside, we organized dances and games. There were parades with Communist and Socialist flags. It was a real carnival. It lasted three weeks.
> (R. Durand 1971: 66)

During the first week of June, millions of French workers were doing the same thing as their comrades in Billancourt.

Before 1936, 1919 had been France's most strike-filled year; in 1919 about 1.3 million French workers took part in 2,047 strikes. The figures for 1936, then, had no precedent: 2.4 million workers in 16,907 strikes. Some 330,000 workers struck in the Seine alone.

Twelve thousand of the year's strikes began in June. Nine thousand involved workers' occupation of their workplaces. Every region of France had far more than its usual number of strikers. Nevertheless the strikes, especially the large sitdown strikes, concentrated in the northern band from Paris to Flanders. In France as a whole, the rates of strikes and strikers ran higher where large plants predominated and where the left had received more votes in April and May. In the course of the movement, proletarian workers in large shops rushed into the unions of the CGT. In 1936 as never before, wageworkers in factories, department stores, and big offices called for change. Agricultural and public service employees were the only large groups of wageworkers not to participate extensively.

No revolution occurred, but the movement shifted the national position of organized labor. On 6 June, Léon Blum's Popular Front government took office. Hard bargaining, and some public posturing, over the strikes began. The manufacturers' association unsuccessfully demanded evacuation of factories prior to a settlement. Chiappe, now president of the Paris city council, ostentatiously assembled its executive committee to discuss problems of "security and food supply" (Schwarz 1937: 79). In the Chamber debate of 6 June, Blum presented his plan to submit bills establishing collective bargaining and binding contracts; he received a vote of confidence, which weakened the employers' position.

By 8 June the strikes had brought industrialists, organized labor, and the government together in the Matignon Agreement, a deep transformation of the relations among the three. That agreement required management to accept collective bargaining, nondiscrimination against union members, no penalties for striking, elected union delegates to management, and increases of 7 to 15 percent in real wages. The Matignon Agreement, in short, satisfied the chief demands of major labor federations. Organized labor gained a legal standing it had never before enjoyed. *L'Humanité* ran a full-page headline: LA VICTOIRE EST ACQUISE: Victory is won!

Not quite. At that point, national union leaders discovered limits to their power. As the immediate parties to the Matignon Agreement called for strikes to end, some unions and many workers continued the struggle. They sought advantages not built into the national accord: annual vacations, special wage agreements, particular hiring procedures, amelioration of local working conditions. New sitdowns occurred in smaller shops, including retail establishments, into July. Communist chief Maurice Thorez delivered his famous declaration, "You have to know how to end a strike," on 11 June. The Chamber began passing laws enacting paid holidays, collective bargaining, and—at last—the forty-hour week the same day. Only a week or so later, however, did individual settlements start accumulating into a net decline of the national strike movement.

Aftermath

On Bastille Day 1936 workers turned out in even greater numbers than for the demonstration of unity on 14 July 1935; they had a grand victory to cel-

ebrate. Yet the great boost to the power of the political left and of organized workers neither squelched bosses, eliminated strike waves, nor silenced activists of the right. The Blum government's devaluation of the
franc, its refusal to intervene in the Spanish Civil War, and other controversial decisions weakened its connections with different parts of its constituency. Its official return to financial orthodoxy in March 1937
reassured capitalists but marked another large compromise of its initial
program.

As the Popular Front government faltered, its supporters urged it to go
further. At the same time, its enemies mobilized to regain position. Industrialists and their national association dragged their feet on the completion
and execution of the plant-by-plant contracts required by the Matignon
Agreement. Although the pace of strike activity slowed dramatically after
June, workers now occupied their plants and stores much more often than
they had before May 1936.

When the Blum government dissolved the Croix de Feu, Jeunesses Patriotes (alias Parti National Populaire), Francistes, and Solidarité Française
(alias Parti National Conjonctif Républicain) on 19 June, some went underground and some reincarnated under new names; Colonel de la Rocque's
Croix de Feu, for instance, reappeared as the Parti Social Français. As early as
the end of June 1936, militant right-wingers appropriated the tricolor as
their badge, and thus provoked leftists into attacking the national flag.
Demonstrations, counterdemonstrations, and fistfights involving the Parti
Social and the Parti Communiste again incited each other.

The government's own activities as law enforcer sometimes encouraged
its enemies and alienated its allies. In October 1936, for example, police
forcibly dislodged sitdown strikers from the Chocolaterie des Gourmets in
the rue Violet and the government requisitioned the Sautter-Harlé defense
plant. Battles between left-wing activists and groups of the right (such as
the affair in Aulnay-sous-Bois on 21 January 1937, when Communists attacked sellers of the Parti Social's paper *Le Flambeau*) likewise tended to
bring in the police on the side of reactionaries.

Rightist organizers took advantage of that fact. On 16 March 1937, four
or five hundred members of the Parti Social gathered in a Clichy cinema,
thereby taking their message to the middle of Paris' working-class Red Belt.
Five or six thousand demonstrators assembled at the city hall in response to a
call from the city's Communist officials. Riot police then protected the cinema from a thousand of the demonstrators. Police gunfire, possibly started
by shots from the crowd, killed five people and wounded three hundred
more, including Léon Blum's chief of staff. The *fusillade de Clichy* occasioned

both a CGT-called general strike and a giant funeral procession for the victims.

Nevertheless, when the Blum government resigned in June 1937, nothing like the demonstrations and strikes of its birth accompanied its demise. True, an important new round of strikes, including sitdown strikes, started in the fall of 1937. Occupation of the big Goodrich plant in Colombes (23 December) and a general strike of Paris' public services (28 December) made a return to May or June 1936 seem possible. Indeed, February 1938 brought yet another surge of occupations in the provinces.

Blum (minus his former Communist allies) returned to power in March. At once Parisian metalworkers began to recapitulate June 1936. A red flag flew over the Citroen plant in Paris. That ended the parallels: while Blum was forming his government in France, the Nazis were taking over Austria, and the prospects for war thereby sharpening. In its 1938 reprise, Blum's cabinet fell in four weeks, and the strike movement dwindled without persuading many employers to sign or honor collective contracts with their workers.

During the rest of the year, events went badly for the extreme left of the Popular Front coalition. Although scattered sitdown strikes occurred into the fall of 1938, plant owners were increasingly successful in calling the police to empty the premises. A growing share of conflicts involving workers consisted of struggles between strikers and nonstrikers, between members of rival unions. Now when department store employees paraded along the boulevard Haussmann to protest firings of their fellow workers, police easily broke up their marches.

After the Reynaud government announced its austerity measures on 12 November, workers organized wildcat strikes in major plants of the Paris region while union leaders temporized. On 24 November the management of Renault announced its own austerity plan, rescinding the gains of the Popular Front; when workers laid down their tools and occupied part of the plant, management called in the government's armed force; the evacuation of the plant was violent but successful. Then Renault shut down the plant indefinitely. By the time the CGT decided (on 25 November) to call a general strike for 30 November, most of the region's other strikes had ended. Although the big plants of the Red Belt responded well to the one-day strike call, results in Paris itself were very uneven; covered with a dense net of troops and police, the city continued to function. Politicians, employers, and labor leaders alike counted the general strike a failure. On 11 December 1938, Edouard Daladier formed a government far to the right of its predecessors. Clearly capital and armed force were joining hands.

The Popular Front heaved its last sigh on 12 February 1939, the fifth anniversary of the 1934 general strike. A week earlier, the government had refused amnesty to the hapless strikers of 30 November. On the twelfth, 25,000 marchers (fewer than in previous years) went through the motions: demonstration in the Place de la République, appearance of Léon Blum, singing of the *Internationale,* minor scuffles with the police, 40 arrests. Thereafter the rapidly changing directives from Moscow tore the Communist party from its former allies. The mobilization of French industry for war divided Socialists and absorbed workers into a temporarily expanding economy. Bastille Day 1939, unlike its popular predecessors, featured a display of French military power. Governmental repression, justified by the approach of war, tightened. Employers took advantage of the changed governmental attitude to tighten on-the-job discipline and fire union leaders. Before the Nazi conquest of June 1940, the whirlwind of the 1930s had already blown away.

Repression, Resistance, and Release

From mid-May to mid-June 1940, Paris underwent one of the most startling transformations of its history. Within a month the metropolis changed from maelstrom to mausoleum: from a great city through which millions of people fleeing the advancing German armies wheeled and dragged their movable possessions to a silenced, darkened, depopulated prize of war. By 13 June the national government had deserted Paris. So had more than two-thirds of the city's residents. The Germans who rolled in the next day rapidly imposed their own order. Under Nazi military occupation, the former capital felt the tightest grip of governmental repression it had ever experienced—even more severe than during the early empires of the two Napoleons. Just to make its commanding position clear, each day at noon the occupying army marched a detachment of troops up the Champs-Elysées to the Arc de Triomphe, where they passed in review.

If the conquering Germans were now free to tramp through the streets, almost no one else was. With German encouragement, however, a number of fascistic groups of varying tints organized and uniformed themselves; they strutted about attacking Jews, Freemasons, Communists, and other enemies. Most of these collaborating pseudo-parties were tiny and ephemeral; the only ones having much size and continuity were the Mouvement Social Révolutionnaire (reconstituted from the Cagoule by Eugène Deloncle), the Francistes (led more or less directly from the Third Republic into the Occupation by Marcel Bucard), the Rassemblement National Populaire (a new creation of Marcel Déat), and especially the Rassemblement pour la Révolution Nationale (Jacques Doriot's German-authorized version of his Parti Populaire Français). The larger groups lived on within limits set by the German administration. They survived as instruments of its control over the French population.

Although the few hundred Communists remaining in Paris toward the end of 1940 kept a semblance of their organization, at that moment of relatively cordial relations between Moscow and Berlin leading Communists were advocating a measure of cooperation with the occupier and were agitating for the liberation of comrades whom the now-dead Third Republic had imprisoned. Neither part of the program, however, lasted very long; some Communists had quickly turned to resistance at the occupation, and all plans for cooperation exploded when Germany attacked the Soviet Union in June 1941.

Soon after, both the occupying forces and the Vichy government began the active pursuit of Communists—imagined and real, past and present. In September 1941, bothered by murders of their troops in occupied France, the Nazis adopted the policy of executing 50 to 100 imprisoned Frenchmen, preferably Communists, for each German soldier killed. Both the occupying forces and the Vichy government, to be sure, used the label "Communist" freely, but their very broad use of the label tended to identify authentic Communists with opposition to the new regime. Communists soon formed the best-organized and most active nuclei of resistance to the Germans and their collaborators.

Open defiance was dangerous and difficult. Those Parisian energies that were not commandeered or snuffed out by the occupying power and its French collaborators flowed mainly into survival, individual and collective: the creation of escape routes, information channels, black markets, and networks of mutual aid. Slowly and later, however, a few of these half-hidden structures became means of collective resistance.

In the Paris of 1940, students were one of the few groups to build a collective political life that did not lie under direct German control. University authorities reopened their doors soon after the occupation began, in order to avoid having the conquerors take over their facilities. The Germans, for their part, chose to let the university and other educational institutions operate under surveillance. Students at the Sorbonne created an underground culture of resistance: jokes, slogans, rituals, anonymous tracts. At the arrest of Paul Langevin, the well-known leftist academic, on 30 October 1940, students and professors campaigned for his release; graffiti, tracts, and word of mouth spread the message. On 8 November, at the scheduled time for Langevin's course, a crowd of supporters dared to gather outside the Collège de France and demand that he be freed.

On Armistice Day 1940, groups of students and teachers gathered on the Champs-Elysées, some of them shouting "Vive la France!" and "Vive de Gaulle!" outside cafés frequented by members of fascist youth organizations. Although city police broke up those crowds, about a thousand demonstrators marched up the Champs-Elysées to the Tomb of the Unknown Soldier at the Arc de Triomphe. Later, some of them regrouped outside fascist meeting-places, shouting and singing. Police chased them but were unable to clear the streets. When German troops arrived around 7:00 P.M., they charged with clubs, guns, and grenades. It took about a quarter of an hour, three or four serious injuries, and over a hundred arrests to end the action.

In broad outline, demonstrations of this sort had been everyday occurrences in the turbulent days of the Popular Front. Now, under military occupation, that even one demonstration should occur bespoke extraordinary organization and determination. Repression raised the stakes and altered the scoring system. As repression deepened, resistance shifted to assassination, smuggling, sabotage, and protection of people threatened by occupiers and collaborators; demonstrations and similar actions virtually disappeared. In the Ile-de-France, four years of occupation brought a great decline in popular collective action.

The occasional escapes from control came as comets in a dark night. Small demonstrations occurred in 1941: near the Place de la République on Bastille Day, and at the Porte St.-Denis on 13 August. In 1942 students demonstrated at the Lycée Buffon on 10 March; on 31 May women broke into a food storehouse on the rue de Buci. For these and a few other rebellious gatherings, the Germans retaliated quickly and fiercely.

Faced with severe repression, Parisians found more subtle ways to display their solidarity. Pierre Audiat recalls what happened on 8 November 1942, when news came of a British landing in French Morocco:

> Early in the afternoon a crowd of Sunday strollers went to the major streets, spilling out into the roadways as on holidays. Montmartre had the atmosphere of a silent village fair; from Barbès-Rochechouart to the Place Clichy there was a continuous, packed parade of apparent idlers who were in fact demonstrators. People looked at each other smiling; when German soldiers went by, discreet scorn showed in their eyes and lips. (Audiat 1946: 196)

When a phalanx of blueshirts belonging to Doriot's pseudo-party rumbled down the Champs-Elysées later that afternoon, the crowds in the streets greeted them with disciplined silence. Silence could be a safe, effective weapon; students and faculty at the Sorbonne, for example, commemorated Armistice Day 1943 by means of a single minute of intense, concerted stillness (Audiat 1946: 224).

Nineteen forty-three was no doubt the darkest year of all, with students who had demonstrated at Buffon put to death on 8 February; prisoners executed almost daily at the Fresnes prison; Jews being rounded up, herded into camps, and shipped off to Germany; able-bodied Gentiles being dispatched to work in German industry; shortages and hardship intensifying throughout the year; Allied bombardment of Paris and its suburbs becoming more intense. Organized quiet stifled a scream.

Not until Bastille Day 1944, six weeks after the Allied landing in Normandy, did another major public display of opposition occur in Paris. On that day, a Communist-organized group of workers dared to march along the boulevards. They managed a forty-five-minute demonstration before German troops dispersed them, killing one demonstrator in the process. After German forces began evacuating Paris on 9 August, first railroad workers (10 August) and then police (15 August) went on strike. The next large action occurred on 19 August, when Allied troops were approaching Paris and the French puppet government had fled from Vichy to Belfort; that uprising shook off the control of the remaining Germans and their collaborators.

Gunfire rattled the capital for almost a week. By 25 August, however, Leclerc's army had entered Paris and the Germans had surrendered. Charles de Gaulle arrived late that day. For all the joy, it was a delicate moment: in the face of competing claims from the American commander and from several factions of the Resistance, de Gaulle meant to establish his own embodiment of the French state, and therefore of legitimate rule. He managed to outplay his competitors. He refused, for example, to go through the nineteenth-century routine of declaring a republic from a balcony of the Hôtel de Ville; the republic, he claimed, had never dissolved; it had merely gone into exile in his custody.

The following day, de Gaulle enjoyed a citywide celebration. This time a grand motorized parade proceeded down the Champs-Elysées from the Arc de Triomphe to the Place de la Concorde, then by the rue de Rivoli to the Hôtel de Ville, finally to Notre Dame for a Mass of victory—an itinerary whose later stages recalled great processions before the Revolution.

Paris Revives

"Is Paris burning?" asked Hitler as his troops retreated. His dreams of empire shattering, he hoped passionately for the destruction of Paris. His followers failed him. Although German occupiers packed explosives into the
Eiffel Tower, Notre Dame, and other great monuments, they never got
around to detonating them. The city went almost free. Paris had only the
wrecking of the Grand Palais and scattered damage from earlier Allied
bombing to show for its liberation. Compared with London, Berlin, and
several other European capitals, France's capital emerged from World War
II physically intact.

Yet the Ile-de-France had much rebuilding to do. The war had destroyed a great deal of the capital's political and organizational structure.
The French had to reconstitute a government of their own, restart an ex-
hausted economy, and recreate social bases for both of them. A depression
decade, four years of occupation, and another year of war at the region's
edge, furthermore, had left the physical plant itself in decay. It needed a
great deal of refurbishing. Parisians took up the work with impressive energy. Over the country as a whole, production *tripled* in the twenty years
from 1946 to 1966. The renewal of Paris played a major part in that speedy
expansion.

As Exhibit 9 shows, the postwar period changed the relationship between the Parisian population and that of the rest of France. After nearly
two centuries of very slow increases and occasional decreases, France's overall population rose rapidly from 40 million in 1946 to 50 million in 1968.
The city of Paris, however, did not share in the increase; after fluctuating at
a little under 3 million residents from the beginning of the twentieth century to around 1960, its size began to decrease rapidly: 2.8 million in 1962,
2.6 million in 1968, 2.3 million in 1975, 2.2 million in 1982. Through most
of the two centuries, Paris' share of the national population had increased
steadily—from 2 percent in 1801 to 7 percent in 1921. Now it began to
sink, reaching 4 percent in 1982.

Those numbers refer to the city of Paris, not to the whole built-up area
centering on the city. If, to make comparison possible, we take the population in the department of the Seine (or, from 1968 onward, the slightly
larger area occupied by Paris, Hauts-de-Seine, Seine-St.-Denis, and Val-de-
Marne) as an approximation of the built-up area, we see the beginnings of
strong suburbanization around 1900. We also see the slowing of suburban
growth with the Great Depression, the decrease due to World War II, a
spurt of growth from 1946 to the late 1960s, and then the start of

a decline. At that point, the agglomeration centered on Paris was still growing, but growing largely through new construction outside the old limits of the Seine.

The postwar period also altered the national position of the Ile-de-France (broadly and crudely defined as the Seine plus Seine-et-Oise, Seine-et-Marne, Oise, and Aisne before 1960; as Paris, Hauts-de-Seine, Seine-St.-Denis, Val-de-Marne, Val-d'Oise, Yvelines, Essonne, Seine-et-Marne, Oise, and Aisne thereafter). Although the region's share of the total French population has increased more or less continuously since some

Exhibit 9. Total population of Paris, Seine, Ile-de-France, and France, 1801–1982 (censuses for the period)

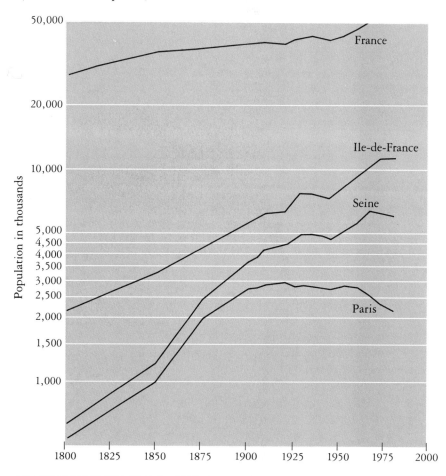

time in the eighteenth century, until World War II the region's growth resulted almost entirely from increases in Paris and the Seine. Since the war, the rest of the region—especially the section close to Paris—has increased disproportionately. A vast metropolitan complex has formed around the Parisian nucleus.

Although it looks superficially like dispersion, this process has concentrated even more of France's precious resources in and around one giant city. The logic of concentration took a while to tell, but within a few years of the war it was working as powerfully as ever. Throughout the twentieth century's first four decades France's really expensive activities—major industrial plants, scientific research, arts and entertainment, governmental administration, and a great deal more—accumulated disproportionately in the Paris region. Almost by definition these activities, with their high ratios of capital to labor, concentrated valuable facilities more rapidly than population.

After the 1950s, the appearance of tall buildings in the Paris skyline provided telling evidence of that concentration; even the apartment buildings, such as those springing up around the Place d'Italie and at the Fronts de Seine, generally replaced rundown high-density housing with lower-density housing for families with higher incomes. Those families included far more than their national share of people staffing big organizations and expensive facilities. The construction of towers for business and research, as in La Défense, Montparnasse, and Jussieu, followed the logic of concentration quite directly.

As a result of these processes, Paris' share of the national population—great though it is—has long lagged far behind its share of such critical facilities as banks, ministries, rail connections, newspapers, publishing houses, research centers, corporate headquarters, libraries, large factories, universities, or computers. Despite repeated gestures toward decentralization, most of these facilities have built up in the Paris region far faster than population. Furthermore, they have continued to build up as the city's resident population has started to decline. Facilities and income per capita have generally risen more rapidly in the Paris region than elsewhere in France. That means growing inequality.

Second, the total population of the city of Paris itself changed little during the first half of the twentieth century. In the 1960s it finally began to decline noticeably, as business, government, and transportation took over high-density dwelling areas as the relatively high-income people remaining in the city expanded their housing. In the neighborhoods of Les Halles and St.-Merri, for example, population declined more than 30 percent between

1968 and 1975. What happened? As the monumental Centre Georges Pompidou and the huge Forum des Halles went up, developers cleared small merchants and low-income households from the area. The old residents gave way to offices, shops, galleries, restaurants, and luxury apartments. Result: a substantial decrease in the stock of housing for low-income people. Another result: a great increase in the daytime, nonresident population in the area.

Over the city as a whole, the net effect of many such changes has been to reduce the total population. It has also shrunk the proportions of petty-bourgeois and working-class families, sharpened the contrast between rich and poor, increased the number of old people, decreased greatly the number of children, and swollen the foreign-born population. In contrast, the built-up area ringing the city and the satellite towns around the built-up ring continued to grow.

Planners and developers favored the new urban geography by means of a sort of radial segregation: vast, high-density housing developments for poor people along some radii outside the city, new single-family or low-density housing and shopping centers for richer people along others. Increasing numbers of Parisians commuted long distances to work in or near the center. A genuine measure of the city's evolution would have to include these voyagers in its effective population.

Postwar Struggles

The liberation of Paris did not end the war. German troops had retreated from most of France by the end of September 1944, but it took months more to dislodge them from their last toeholds. The fighting left French soil only at the end of March 1945. When the European war ended in May, about 1.8 million French citizens were still in Germany as prisoners or forced labor. France's transport system had fallen apart. Her industrial plant had suffered from almost fifteen years of decay. Factories, offices, and homes faced acute shortages of fuel. An immense black market handled distribution of food and other necessaries. A major part of France's housing had run down or disappeared. The French had all that to repair.

The French had to repair it, furthermore, at the same time as French powerholders struggled to reconstitute a government. The provisional government that formed in August 1944 faced a situation resembling that of a new revolutionary regime: its sovereignty and legitimacy uncertain; only a tattered, improvised army to back up its commands; much local administration still in the hands of people who had served the toppled power; thousands more collaborators in jails and internment camps; its own supporters determined to avenge past wrongs and get their share of influence; allies and rivals ready to struggle for a say in the state's future. Even the prestigious, forceful Charles de Gaulle, who headed the government until January 1946, encountered serious competition from Communists and from Resistance groups that had remained independent of his liberation forces.

Using that political system to restore a ruined economy challenged de Gaulle and his partners. Unlike many revolutionary rulers, de Gaulle incorporated his strongest rivals, the Communists, into the provisional government. Like the revolutionaries of 1792 and 1793, however, he adopted a number of expedients to make the existing structure produce change: installing prefects having strong ties to the new rulers, establishing or absorbing provisional departmental committees simultaneously implanted in the region and personally tied to the government, dismantling the militias those committees had commonly set up at the time of liberation, sending out specially empowered commissars to represent the central government, setting up extraordinary courts to manage the identification and punishment of former collaborators, imposing rationing and requisition.

To the array of revolutionary techniques, the provisional government of 1944 added one the Jacobins had not used: in the fall, de Gaulle made a triumphal tour through the provinces, whipping up support for the new regime and identifying it even more strongly with his person. As in 1792 and 1793, all these expedients—when they worked—substituted central authority for local autonomy.

Not all expedients worked; the government, for instance, never gained a tight enough grip on the supply and distribution of food to make rationing operate effectively. But those efforts at reasserting control precipitated the major contention of 1944 and 1945. In fact 1945 ended in a storm of complaints about food supply. On 31 December, people waiting in line at Parisian bakeries began smashing their windows and breaking up their furnishings when the stocks of bread ran out. Through 1946 and 1947, for that matter, struggles over the government's controls over wages, prices, and food repeatedly brought Parisians to the streets. It was not easy to restore a battered economy.

The restoration started slowly. France returned to its 1938 level of industrial production around the end of 1947, to its 1938 level of agricultural production around the end of 1950. During the painful recovery, Gaullists, Communists, supporters of the MRP (Mouvement Républicain Populaire, formed on the base of Catholic Resistance groups), and remnants of the pre-war parties fought for control of the government and its policy. Within the labor movement, Communists finally succeeded in their long effort to control the CGT, at the price of accepting a sharper separation between the CGT and other federations, and of contending with an internal minority, Force Ouvrière, that sought a politically-independent labor movement.

France's internal struggles coincided with the chilling of relations between the U.S. and the U.S.S.R.—and, by extension, their respective allies—into the Cold War. The international tugging and hauling made bargaining between French Communists and other parties even more difficult.

De Gaulle left the government in January 1946. He did not form his Rassemblement du Peuple Français (RPF) until April 1947. Yet his followers were taking political action long before they organized a party. After a Gaullist parade on 18 June 1946, commemorating de Gaulle's 1940 call for resistance to the Germans, participants regrouped to shout "de Gaulle to power!" Others broke the window of a Communist bookstore, grabbed the books displayed there, and burned them; the next day, Communists and unionized workers mounted an "antifascist" demonstration to protest the attack.

For the next few years the polarization of Gaullists and Communists informed political conflicts at both local and national levels. Gaullists rushed into fiercely critical opposition in January 1946. Once leaders of the old parties forced Communists out of the government in May 1947, the Gaullist-Communist struggle drastically narrowed the space in which any government could stand.

As that struggle developed, French workers returned to large-scale strike activity. The Communist departure from the cabinet, indeed, resulted from Communist support for another great strike at the newly nationalized Billancourt Renault plant; this one began on 25 April 1947 as a wildcat, but the CGT eventually took it over. The May Day celebration of 1947, which featured a march from the Place de la Bastille to the Place de la Concorde, ended in a confrontation between members of the Billancourt strike committee and the leaders of a still-hesitant CGT.

National strike waves occurred in June–July 1947 and again in November; in the November series, a national coalition demanded a 25 percent wage increase and challenged the government directly, as workers once more began to occupy their plants. During that same strike wave, Communist deputies took a leaf from the workers' book; they occupied the National Assembly itself to block a bill imposing sanctions on industrial sabotage and incitement to strike. The Republican Guard finally expelled them from the Chamber at 6:00 A.M. on 2 December.

By this time, many of the characteristics of French popular politics in the 1930s had reappeared:

> the conjunction of strike waves with national political struggles and especially with changes in the national political position of organized labor
> the difficult, contingent alliance between national labor federations and the major parties of the left, especially the Communists
> the coupling of strikes with demonstrations
> the further matching of demonstrations by political groupings with counterdemonstrations by their rivals, with frequent fighting a by-product of their confrontations
> the occupation of premises to emphasize a claim for power and forestall countermeasures of authorities

These remained standard elements of French political life from the 1930s onward.

Although French people continued to pursue plenty of their politics at the café, in the press, at peaceful meetings, and around the ballot box, with each new issue of the 1950s and 1960s the characteristic street politics reappeared. As deputies debated NATO, war in Indochina, German rearmament, the presence of American troops in France, North African independence movements, the antitax challenges of Pierre Poujade's followers, or the 1956 insurrection in Hungary, their allies and opponents outside demonstrated, counterdemonstrated, struck, occupied, and fought. Sometimes, as in the great Parisian public-sector strikes of August 1953, the action in the streets was the issue before the government. National politics and street politics intertwined.

Compared with prewar conflicts, more of the issues that now brought partisans to the streets concerned international politics. Bombings and other attacks on premises also accompanied the contention more often than they had in the 1930s. As North African independence movements mobilized in the 1950s, armed attacks by groups of North Africans on police, soldiers, and especially compatriots of different political persuasions became relatively common. Deliberate blocking of traffic and of public places likewise characterized the conflicts of the 1950s and 1960s more frequently than those before 1940. Otherwise, veterans of prewar strikes, rallies, demonstrations, street fights, and other forms of contention found much that was familiar in the struggles around the new issues.

Popular Rebellion or Coup d'Etat?

The familiar wrought the unfamiliar. Although all the terms are debatable, we can reasonably say that before 1958 Napoleon's coup of 1799 was the last time the French military as such intervened directly in national politics and played a major part in the destruction of a regime. Never before 1958 had the intervention occurred chiefly outside continental France.

By May 1958, French residents of Algeria had been complaining for months of the failure of the metropolitan government to wipe out the indigenous Algerian independence coalition, the Front de Libération Nationale (FLN). After a large demonstration by Europeans in Algiers on 26 April, the *Echo d'Alger* had published an appeal to de Gaulle on 11 May.

On 13 May two new demonstrations in Algiers—one of European civilians, the other of military men—challenged the Pflimlin government. At the end, some of the demonstrators rushed to the governor-general's palace; they took it easily. With a crowd outside, the occupants named a committee of public safety, then composed a telegram to President Coty in Paris; it proposed the naming of a national government of public safety. Many participants called for de Gaulle to take power.

On 15 May, Raoul Salan, French military commander in Algeria, hailed de Gaulle as the country's likely savior. Without committing himself openly, de Gaulle made clear in his Paris press conference of 19 May that he disapproved of the existing political system. "Now I shall return to my village," he closed, "and I shall remain there at the disposal of the country" (Maier and White 1968: 293). Five days later, another committee of public safety took over Ajaccio, capital of Corsica—not quite continental, but at least part of metropolitan France. The organizers of Algiers and Ajaccio started making plans and preparations for a coup in Paris itself. In the meantime, feverish consultations went on in and among Algiers, Corsica, Paris, and Colombey-les-Deux-Eglises (Haute-Marne), home of Charles de Gaulle.

Events in the Mediterranean had wide repercussions in mainland France. On 13 May itself, before news of the takeover in Algiers reached Paris, a veterans' march to the Arc de Triomphe had turned into a demonstration for "French Algeria," then into a fight with police who blocked access to the Chamber and other likely targets (*Le Combat* 14 May 1958). After the seizure of Ajaccio, committees of public safety formed in Lyon and other continental French cities, though not in Paris itself.

In Paris, Prime Minister Pierre Pflimlin searched for a combination and sent emissaries to all the parties. Yet Pflimlin resigned on 28 May, after de

Gaulle had issued a statement strongly implying his readiness to take over the government. That very day a military delegation from General Salan, summoned by de Gaulle, came to Colombey and briefed him on the situation in Algeria and Corsica. The same day a republican/antifascist demonstration including Pierre Mendès-France, François Mitterrand, and Edouard Daladier marched from the Place de la Nation to the Place de la République. That demonstration of the non-Communist left revealed another exceptional feature of the 1958 struggle: organized labor divided so sharply between the Communist-led CGT and the remaining federations that for once no major strike movement accompanied the crisis of government.

Negotiations with de Gaulle continued; they closed with his demanding emergency powers and a new constitution. On 29 May, President René Coty asked de Gaulle to form a new government. The next day, as the engineers of that invitation maneuvered to create the necessary majority, supporters of de Gaulle took over the Champs-Elysées and received a degree of protection from the police. Leftist counterdemonstrators who arrived shouting "Fascism will not pass!" and singing the *Marseillaise* battled police for about half an hour.

This time, however, the supporters had their way: Charles de Gaulle received full powers from a badly divided Chamber of Deputies on 1 June. That day the Communist party made its last appeal; 10,000 demonstrators gathered in different parts of Paris to oppose de Gaulle and broadcast that "fascism will not pass"; in the encounters with police that followed, 190 people were arrested and 50 wounded. Meanwhile, de Gaulle was recruiting a cabinet. His government, drawn largely from the old parties, gained the approval of both assemblies on 3 June. The very next day he was in Algiers, declaring: "I have understood you. I know what has happened here. I see what you wanted to do. I see that the road you have opened in Algeria is one of renewal and fraternity" (Maier and White 1968: 347). As it turned out, the road led to Algerian independence, and to a massive repatriation of French nationals from North Africa. But its first stretch brought France to a new regime.

Days of May and June

The institution of the Fifth Republic deflected French struggles but did not end them. For another four years all parties to the Algerian conflict—competing Algerian movements, French settlers, dissident military officers, the French government, and others—fought out their differences in the Paris region as well as in North Africa. Taking up the theme of *Algérie française,* far-right groups reappeared in public. Students again became active, both over their own local concerns and over national political problems. Vietnam reappeared, now in the context of opposition to American, rather than French, imperialism. Most of these themes converged with the problems of workers in May and June 1968.

Beginning in the mid-1960s, a postwar combination of economic expansion and baby boom brought an unprecedented number of young people into French higher education. The new suburban university at Nanterre, among others, went up to house the overflow from the Sorbonne. It summed up the expansion and its consequences: rapid construction from scratch on a former military base in the midst of an immigrant working-class area; liberal arts program with wide offerings in the social sciences; dean interested in promoting wide consultation among students, faculty, and administration; weak relationship between teaching programs and later employment of students; as of the end of 1967, no university library or research facilities; a campus consisting essentially of classrooms, offices, and dormitories; in short, an assembly plant for standardized education.

Students at Nanterre formed a number of leftist groups and gave strong support to the left-leaning National Union of French Students (UNEF). Nanterre's new school of law (an undergraduate program in France), in contrast, provided a base for a small but active group of right-wing students, centered on the Occident movement. On 16 March 1967 a Nanterre student organization dedicated to freedom of expression began a campaign for "free circulation," including the rights to hold political meetings and to circulate or post political material on campus. In the course of that campaign, 150 male students moved in with the residents of a women's dormitory. On 21 March, police called by the administration surrounded the building, and a crowd of students surrounded the police; after a long night of negotiations, the men left the dormitory unidentified and unpunished.

In the fall of 1967, clashes between leftist and rightist students intensified on the Nanterre campus. At the same time the student union launched a campaign against the government's pending reorganization of examinations and certificates. In November its members organized a strike against the application of the reforms at Nanterre and kept nonstrikers from classroom buildings. Although the strike failed, it led almost directly into a series of actions organized around educational policy, campus discipline, and the war in Vietnam. The actions included sabotage of examinations and confrontations with authorities.

When a Nanterre student was arrested on the charge of bombing the American Express building in Paris, students held an unauthorized meeting in a campus lecture hall, then occupied the university's council chamber. That was the night of 22–23 March 1968. When leaders of the "22 March Movement" called for a day of "critical university," on the German model, for 29 March, Dean Grappin shut down classes until 1 April.

From that point on, student groups multiplied meetings and counter-meetings, attacks and counterattacks; by the end of April UNEF, 22 March, and Occident were all arming themselves. In Paris on 19 April 2,000 students demonstrated to protest a recent assault on German student leader Rudi Dutschke. On 22 April 5,000 demonstrated against the Vietnam war. Raids and counterdemonstrations set Occident against its leftist foes at the Sorbonne as well as at Nanterre. The government began legal proceedings against Daniel Cohn-Bendit (a French-born Nanterre sociology student leader of German parentage who had taken German citizenship) with an eye to deporting him. On 2 May the dean, claiming that a "war psychosis" had taken over Nanterre, closed down the campus and haled eight students before the university's governing council.

Action shifted to Paris. On May Day the CGT (permitted to march on the holiday for the first time since 1954) had failed in its effort to bring out a unified demonstration of left opposition to the de Gaulle regime, but had attracted many students. The CGT's marshals had forcefully excluded far-left groups and banners from the parade. On 2 May a fire, which UNEF officials blamed on rightist students, broke out in the Sorbonne. On 3 May (the day *L'Humanité* dismissed Cohn-Bendit as a "German anarchist") student organizations at the Sorbonne held a meeting in its courtyard; at the meeting, Cohn-Bendit called for protests of fascist attacks. Citing the danger of assaults from rightist groups, the university's rector called police to evacuate the courtyard. Police arrested about 600 demonstrators as they left the Sorbonne. After the expulsion, small groups of students skirmished with police in nearby streets into the night.

On Sunday 5 May, student groups called for demonstrations the next day, and the teachers' union asked for a general strike of all university faculties. On Monday university authorities closed the Sorbonne, and four students were sentenced for participation in Friday's fighting. When police charged the file of marchers, a demonstration protesting the Sorbonne's closing gave way to street-fighting through much of the Latin Quarter. On 7 May UNEF organized a march from Denfert-Rochereau through the Latin Quarter and to the Arc de Triomphe; later, near the Sorbonne, students began throwing paving stones at police.

Meetings and demonstrations likewise started at provincial universities. President de Gaulle declared that he would not tolerate violence in the streets. For the following two days, student and union organizers sought to contain the movement and to aim it at a concerted series of demands on the government. On Friday the tenth, however, some demonstrators (saying "We have to occupy the Latin Quarter whatever it costs") began building barricades, as well as smashing or burning automobiles. Starting at two in the morning, police worked until dawn of 11 May clearing the neighborhood, barricade by barricade.

After that violent night the CGT and the Confédération Française Democratique du Travail (CFDT) called for nationwide demonstrations and a general strike on Monday 13 May, anniversary of the Algiers rebellion that started de Gaulle back to power. The demonstration in Paris brought out a possible 700,000 marchers. Although the strike itself was less than general, the appeal received a large response outside Paris. During the day Premier Georges Pompidou asked for the reopening of the Sorbonne and agreed to consider requests for amnesty to students arrested in the previous week's struggles. Arrested students did go free, and discussions went on all night in the reopened Sorbonne. For the next few days, student assemblies began debating programs for reform of their institutions, and students began refusing to take scheduled examinations. Meanwhile, on 14 May right-wing students demonstrated in Paris; they repeated their counter-demonstrations a number of times in the following weeks.

On 14 and 15 May workers in Nantes, Cléon, and Flins-sur-Seine occupied their factories. On the sixteenth, students marched from the Sorbonne to the newly struck Renault factory in Billancourt. From that point on, a massive strike movement grew to the dimensions of a general strike; in Paris strikes paralyzed transportation, public services, and supplies of goods.

Many of these strikes concerned the organization of work and worker power rather than wages and hours. Many of them, furthermore, began without union sponsorship; indeed, some strikers resisted union attempts to channel their strikes. White-collar workers and employees of high-technology industries played a larger part than in any previous strike wave. The demands looked serious. President de Gaulle, declaring "La réforme, oui, la chienlit, non" hurried home from a trip to Rumania.

When French authorities denied Cohn-Bendit reentry into France from Germany on 23 May, new demonstrations and new confrontations with police began. That same day, the Chamber voted down a motion of censure against the Pompidou/de Gaulle government. The following day de Gaulle went on the air to announce a referendum for 13 June; he was going to consult the country on the question of greater participation of students and workers in the running of their enterprises. If the referendum did not pass, promised de Gaulle, he would resign. That night, UNEF demonstrators marched toward the Hôtel de Ville, possibly with the idea of declaring a Commune there; police deflected them to the Bourse, Les Halles, and the Latin Quarter, where groups broke doors, uprooted trees, and built barricades.

On 25 May Prime Minister Pompidou invited representatives of labor and management to a general assembly at the Ministry of Labor. Two days later, national labor unions emerged from that bargaining with wage increases and shorter hours, as well as commitments to establish firm-by-firm contracts and to review the position of organized labor within firms, the organization of welfare programs, the income tax, and training for young people. During the next few days, however, most organized workers rejected that Grenelle Agreement. On 28 May about 9 million French workers were out on strike.

This was an unusual strike wave. Not only did it set records for size and draw in professionals, technicians, and white-collar workers as never before, but also it introduced new forms of action; the general assembly of the establishment and the overall strike committee elected by workers owed something to the students' example. The demands for more worker control in high-technology industries, furthermore, gave the strikes a distinctive air. Nevertheless, from early in June strikes began to end rapidly, with particular settlements following the pattern of Grenelle.

In the Latin Quarter, students continued to debate and reorganize in occupied buildings, as a student watch kept order. On 30 May de Gaulle announced the dissolution of the National Assembly and new elections for the time of the referendum. That same day, the president's supporters held a giant demonstration, similar in scale to the antigovernment march of the thirteenth. A large countermobilization was occurring.

During the first three weeks of June, students continued their work of reconstruction. Some new strikes—notably the occupation of the national radio and television by its employees—began. The police also began to clear resisting workers from occupied plants. Strike settlements accelerated as the government dissolved a number of left-wing groups and forbade demonstrations. By the time the elections of 23 and 30 June produced a Gaullist landslide, little remained of the organized movement.

One More May

Fifteen years after May 1968, May Day still brought thousands of people to Paris streets. On 1 May 1983, after four years of sharp separation, the CFDT, the CGT, and FEN (Fédération de l'Education Nationale) each sent delegations to the same parade. Force Ouvrière, by making its own morning march to Federation Wall, kept the event from being quite as "unitary" as advertised. On a chilly afternoon, perhaps 100,000 people marched or rode (on floats or sound trucks) from the Gare de l'Est to the Place de la Bastille, via the Place de la République. This time a significant proportion of the groups represented other causes than organized labor: feminists, homosexuals, pacifists, supporters of Iran's Ayatollah Khomeini, opponents of Khomeini, opponents of the Turkish regime, Palestinians, and many more. Each group found its own rationale for being there. Organized homosexuals, for example, chanted: "Heteros, homos all together—same bosses, same fight."

On the Left Bank, from the Invalides to the Panthéon, marched another parade. Its 3,000 participants were almost as heterogeneous as their Right Bank counterparts; although representatives of small business, complaining about government controls and the power of labor unions, led the march, right-wing students, members of Solidarité Chrétienne, the National Front, other anti-Communist activists, and some demonstrators with strictly personal causes joined the procession. After the left marched on the Right Bank, the right marched on the Left Bank.

Neither demonstration-parade represented the struggles of recent months as clearly as had their predecessors in 1906, 1936, or 1968. During April, medical students were on strike to oppose governmental reforms; the proposed changes installed examinations after the sixth year of medical school (like law, an undergraduate program in France) that would restrict the entry of students into popular specialties. Interns and clinic heads were likewise striking because of proposed reforms, but more for involvement in their planning than against the principles of organization they embodied. During the month, dental students (whose demonstrators chanted "Dentaire . . . en colère!") joined the movement.

In the medical schools the CGT and CFDT did not organize the strikes, but they played their part in maintaining them. Partly in response to that union presence in the movement against university reforms, law students began organizing a countermovement—similarly opposed to the reforms, but opposed to the Socialist government as well. They, too, mounted strikes and demonstrations. Their work attracted support from far-right forces such as the Groupe Union-Défense. On 27 April, when some seven thousand law students from schools throughout the region converged on the National Assembly, those who actually arrived there instead of going off in separate demonstrations faced a line of riot police. On 29 April another group of similar size went from the Sorbonne toward the National Assembly but likewise found the way blocked. On both occasions students stoned the police, who chased them from the streets with tear gas, water cannon, and nightsticks. People began to talk of another May 1968, this one from the right.

Nothing of the sort happened. As the university year dragged toward its end, and the government continued to discuss proposals for reform, the movement deflated. By May Day it was already clear that students were too divided, and too distant from the concerns of France's workers, to start anything like the movement of May and June 1968. Nor, despite the activation of right-wing forces, did they have a chance to initiate another February 1934.

Yet an observer has a strong feeling of *déjà vu*. By 1983 the essential forms of action used by Parisian students, workers, and other groups to make their claims had very long histories. The routines of forming associations and committees, meeting, demonstrating, striking, braving the police had changed relatively little in a century. All the actors—organizers, participants, police, government officials, labor unions, others—knew the routines well and had worked out standard rules for their own involvement. The press regularly (if not always accurately) reported numbers, social composition, signs of determination, slogans, arrests, injuries, responses of authorities.

Yes, there had been some changes: from the beginning of the century, organized workers tried the short national general strike as a warning to government and capital. From 1936 on, it became more common for strikers and demonstrators to occupy premises deliberately, claim rights to control those premises over the longer run, and bargain hard over their departure from the premises. Sitdown strikes provide the most obvious example. But rent strikes, squatting, hostage taking, and occupation of streets belong to the same general category.

All sides, furthermore, gradually adopted more powerful technical apparatus: bullhorns, sound trucks, printed signs, riot-police buses, and water cannon became part of the scene. Newspapers, radio, and television gave the activists of 1968 and 1983 coverage their predecessors would have envied them.

Yet the fundamental fact is continuity. As the issues and alignments have changed, the means of action have stayed largely the same. On the general principle that powerholders learn at least as fast as their challengers, and have much greater means to put their learning into practice, the probable result is this: the collective-action repertoire inherited from the nineteenth century has become less and less effective as a way of changing the structure of power, more and more effective as a signal of preferences within that structure of power. The challengers of 1968 gave some signs of breaking through those limits. They failed. The challengers of 1983 did not even try.

11 ⌒〰

Parties, Regimes, and Wars

N HIS GREAT GEOGRAPHY of France, Paul Vidal de la Blache linked the living country of 1900 or so with the experience of that corner of the earth's surface during many millennia. "The history of a people," he declared, "is inseparable from the land that it inhabits" (Vidal de la Blache 1908:1). Accordingly, he mapped out regions neither in terms of historic political divisions nor strictly according to physical features. Instead, he looked for roughly bounded niches that promoted coherent, interdependent rounds of human life.

Vidal's "Flanders," as a practical matter, covered the whole set of plains between the Ardennes and the coastal marshes—Hainaut, Cambrésis, pieces of Artois and Picardy, plus most of the historical province of Flanders. Yet when Vidal arrived at the description of Flanders, he seemed dismayed by the smoky brick towns its people had laid down. "On this terrain," he pointed out,

> each historical era has raised new ranges of cities; some of them disappeared while others began, but the creation of cities has never ended. The subsoil took its turn. It was toward 1846 that the search for coal deposits, already begun around Valenciennes a century earlier, arrived at Lens and Béthune. Beside the unified small-scale city formed a type previously unknown, the industrial agglomeration. Around the pitheads whose strange silhouettes stippled Lens's agricultural plain lined up rows of *corons* in eights or tens: sad, identical little houses, built at the

same moment to contain existences that multiplied like ciphers. Sometimes the contrast is striking: Valenciennes, identifiable from afar (as in
the paintings of Van der Meulen) by means of its elegant steeples and
major buildings, gathers its narrow streets around a central square; but
just outside its gates, like a growth, spreads an enormous unconnected
set of suburbs with their rows of houses, bars, and factories. (Vidal de
la Blache 1908: 79–80)

It was as if people had decided to deny their natural heritge.

Vidal found Languedoc less artificial. Languedoc, in Vidal's analysis, organized around a giant channel: plains and valleys that had once lain under
a sea, flanked by hills that had been its shores. "That corridor," he wrote,

> where Roman road and royal highway, canal and railway, crowd each
> other, was a passageway of peoples. To be sure, connections between
> Lower Languedoc and the rural regions of Toulouse or Albi were not
> exclusively concentrated in that passageway. Via St.-Pons, Bédarieux,
> and Le Vigan, there always were relations based on the needs of ex-
> change between mountain and plain. These small-scale connections, re-
> sulting from the juxtaposition of contrasting terrains, play a very large
> part in southern life. (Vidal de la Blache 1908: 324)

One could still, said Vidal, read the ancient landscape in the twentieth-century terrain of Languedoc.

Vidal's scheme of natural regions denied Anjou any unity: the old
province spanned the eastern and southern edges of the Breton massif, the
western edge of Paris' basin, and the Loire Valley. Approaching Anjou from
Touraine, Vidal offered a sketch that shaped many a later description:
"Down below, abundance and easy living; up above, the beginning of the
rough, poor life of the west's frontiers; a contrast whose reality the struggles
of the Revolution help us appreciate" (Vidal de la Blache 1908: 155). He
wrote again of the rolling highland to the south that

> borders the Loire Valley with a continuous shelf. Above the smiling
> valley, that stiff bluff, topped by old, high villages, forms a threatening
> wall. That was the limit of the old region called the *Mauges,* basically
> rural even in its industries, more Poitou than Anjou and, despite long
> commercial connections with the sea, hostile to the urban life of the
> river's bank. The region showed its character in 1793. (Vidal de la
> Blache 1908: 288)

Vidal believed in continuities.

Burgundy followed another passageway. It united plains and hills: a "crossroads of Europe," Vidal called the region (Vidal de la Blache 1908: 216). Connections between east and west, between the Parisian basin and the Saône Valley, between the Mediterranean and the North Sea made of Burgundy, in Vidal's estimation, a natural site for commercial agriculture, military activity, and cultural creativity. Furthermore, the distribution of rivers and good soil favored the development of dense, well-connected settlements. Once again agriculture dominated the analysis; the mining and manufacturing that were growing at Burgundy's edges almost escaped Vidal's attention. In his view, the blue-ribbon winegrowing and commercialized wheat farming of Burgundy fulfilled the region's vocation.

Facing Paris and the Ile-de-France, Vidal could not blink the importance of human intervention. "The surroundings of Paris," he observed,

> have always had an animated, lively air that Rome always lacked and Berlin lacks still. Today the great city sends out its front line of houses; they precede it like an army on the march, which invades the plain, climbs the heights, envelops whole hills. But in the old days towns and villages, of which a number have been absorbed into the growing city, led an independent existence, due to local conditions that favored the development of little groupings everywhere. (Vidal de la Blache 1908: 130)

Then Vidal gave up the effort to analyze the city. "It is enough," he concluded, "to have studied where and how the seed of the future being was planted, how a lively plant grew that no stormy wind could uproot, and to have shown that in its vitality one can feel powerful sap coming from the soil, and a knotting of roots so well established in every direction that no one can dig them up or cut them all" (Vidal de la Blache 1908: 133).

As he closed his book, however, Vidal began to wonder whether the growth of Paris had deprived provincial France of its nutriments. "Connections between Paris and the provinces abound," he mused, "but to the detriment of the ties that the provinces once had to each other. Thus the fruitful relations that existed between the east and west of our country, from the Alps to the Atlantic, have diminished so much that they are now hardly more than a historical memory" (Vidal de la Blache 1908: 348). An artificially centralized country, he thought, ran the risk of losing the tough, adaptive genius that still resided in France's peasantry.

A Population Transformed

Where was that peasantry? Vidal wrote his reflections at the start of the twentieth century. By even the broadest definition, however, peasants were then no longer France's dominant population. In 1901 France's labor force included about 19.7 million people; 8.2 million owners, renters, sharecroppers, wage laborers, and others—43 percent of the labor force—worked in agriculture. Agriculture was still the largest single sector, but a majority of the labor force worked in nonagricultural jobs. The remaining 11.5 million workers divided almost evenly between manufacturing and services, with a small number left over for mining, fishing, forestry, and a few other extractive industries. Manufacturing did not actually outstrip agriculture until the 1950s.

Yet a plurality in agriculture was not enough to make France a peasant country. In the agricultural labor force of 1901, only a minority held land as owners, renters, or sharecroppers. More than half the people in agriculture were wageworkers: hired hands, day-laborers, servants. Table 8 shows the departmental figures for the male agricultural labor force in 1901. "Heads of establishments" included owners, tenants, and sharecroppers. "Individual workers" were mainly day-laborers, while "workers in establishments" covered hired hands, overseers, and working family members. Areas of household tenant farming in Haute-Garonne and Maine-et-Loire, plus the fine-wine region of Saône-et-Loire, exceedeed the national average for heads of establishment. Areas of semi-industrial winemaking such as Aude and Hérault, on the other hand, had relatively high proportions of hired labor.

Table 8. Male agricultural labor force, 1901, by department

Department	Heads of establishments	Workers in establishments	Individual workers	Total	Heads as percentage of total
Aude	21,390	29,829	13,934	65,153	32.8
Côte d'Or	20,415	21,794	18,470	60,679	33.6
Haute-Garonne	34,204	24,680	16,003	74,887	45.7
Hérault	25,061	34,528	24,905	84,494	29.7
Maine-et-Loire	39,246	37,975	19,003	96,224	40.8
Nord	23,810	50,820	24,951	99,581	23.9
Saône-et-Loire	45,215	38,464	26,408	110,087	41.1
Seine-et-Marne	11,824	25,226	14,953	52,003	22.7
Seine-et-Oise	17,898	31,094	17,519	66,511	26.9
All France	2,028,955	2,151,623	1,396,674	5,577,252	36.4

Source: Census of 1901.

For *very* proletarian agricultural labor, we look to Flanders and the Ile-de-France; in Nord, Seine-et-Marne, and Seine-et-Oise, three-quarters of the males in agriculture worked for a wage of one sort or another.

Although some of those wage earners were children of peasants who would eventually take over farms of their own, most of them failed to qualify as peasants by any criterion. During the century (as in the latter half of the nineteenth century), wageworkers left agriculture faster than smallholders did. As a consequence, owner-operators and substantial leaseholders represented a growing proportion of a shrinking sector. Nevertheless, more and more of those owner-operators and leaseholders came to organize their lives like small—or even large—businessmen rather than like peasants. In short, according to a generous standard something like one-fifth of French households were peasants in 1901. They kept on dwindling. By 1982 fewer than one-twentieth of all households were peasants.

Following World War I, the French agricultural population stopped increasing after centuries of slow but sustained growth. In fact the whole French labor force stopped expanding in the 1920s, then contracted sharply until the 1960s. That shift accented a long-term trend in France: a decline in the share of the total population engaged in productive labor; retirement, unemployment, and increasing school enrollments, coupled with negligible natural increase and general aging of the population, all contributed to the shrinkage. By the end of the 1970s, with accelerated growth of the total population, the national labor force had returned to approximately its size in 1921. Exhibit 10 tells the story.

The graph also shows the relative growth of three large sectors from about 1785 to 1981 (although before 1856 estimates are very rough). Until the 1920s manufacturing, mining, and construction (which the French often sum up as "industry") collectively increased a bit more rapidly than services (here including trade, transport, government, the professions, rentiers, unclassifiable occupations, and other small fringes of the economy). Services began to expand faster than agriculture, forestry, and fisheries only after 1900. Following World War I, as agriculture skidded, industry and services occupied more and more of the French economy. From the 1950s onward, the size of the manufacturing labor force stabilized. It was the service sector's turn to grow. By 1981 more than half of France's labor force worked in services. A legendary country of peasants had vanished. A legendary nation of industrial workers was also fading away.

The transformation took contrasting forms in different regions. Exhibit 11 puts the evidence together in terms of the regions used in recent censuses. Translated into the departmental names and divisions of 1901 today's "Paris region" includes the Seine, Seine-et-Oise, and Seine-et-Marne. The Nord and the adjacent Pas-de-Calais form a single statistical region. The historic province of Languedoc occupies major parts of two twentieth-century census regions: Languedoc–Roussillon (Aude, Gard, Hérault, Lozère, Pyrénées-Orientales) and Midi-Pyrénées (Ariège, Aveyron, Gers, Haute-Garonne, Tarn, Tarn-et-Garonne). The Loire region combines Loire-Inférieure (now Loire-Atlantique, after the de Gaulle republic eliminated all

Exhibit 10.* The French labor force, 1780–1981 (Toutain 1963; censuses of 1962, 1968, and 1975)

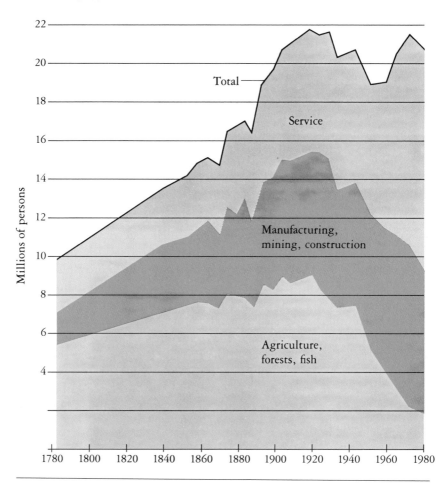

Exhibit 11.   The labor force in six regions, 1901–1975 (censuses of 1901, 1946, and 1975)

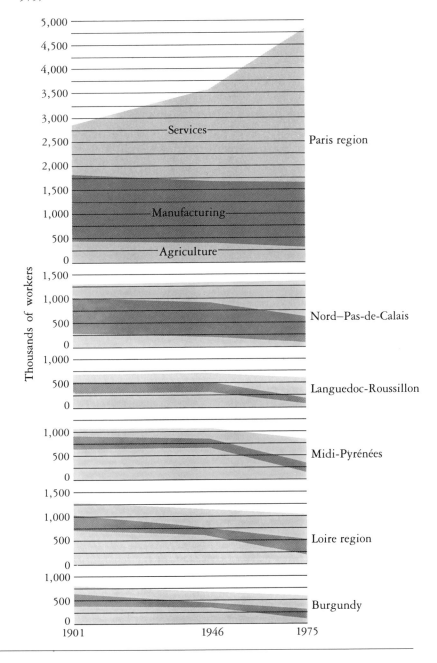

inferiority from departmental names), Maine-et-Loire, Mayenne, Sarthe, and Vendée. Finally, the Burgundy of the census comprises Côte d'Or, Nièvre, Saône-et-Loire, and Yonne.

Of these regions, only Paris saw an increase in its labor force from 1901 to 1975. The labor force of Nord/Pas-de-Calais remained more or less constant, while those of the four other regions declined. In every region the number of workers in agriculture, forestry, and fishing declined, especially after 1946. No region had a significant increase in its manufacturing labor force; in most regions, it diminished noticeably. (The numbers hide, to be sure, a substantial net movement of workers into larger, more heavily capitalized firms and into nationalized industries.)

Service industry made the great gains; in the Paris region service workers rose from about 1.1 million in 1901 to 3.2 million in 1975; services thereby became by far the dominant sector in and around the capital. In the process the Paris region captured an even larger share of the national labor force. In 1901 the region lodged 2.6 million of France's 19.7 million workers, for 13 percent of the total. The comparable area included 16 percent of the nation's labor force in 1946, and a full 22 percent in 1975.

Proportionately speaking, Burgundy, the Loire region, and the two Languedocs kept more of their labor forces in agriculture than did the Paris region or Nord/Pas-de-Calais. By the 1970s, however, the textiles and mining of the Nord were collapsing. Despite much wringing of hands about the capital's dominance and despite frequent announcements of decentralization as governmental policy, the contrast sharpened: labor, capital, manufacturing, and expensive facilities concentrated in the Ile-de-France. With a few localized exceptions (such as steel mills, aircraft manufacturing, and nuclear power plants), the rest of France specialized increasingly in services, lighter industry, and what remained of agriculture.

Strike Trends

Over the century before 1975, both in the Ile-de-France and elsewhere, French workers built more and more extensive organization. One consequence was a rising propensity to strike. From the legalization of the strike in 1864, strikes grew enormously more frequent. While strikes in the 1870s ranged from 40 to 150 per year throughout France, government reports for the 1970s—which excluded agricultural and public-sector conflicts—itemized from 3,000 to 5,000 strikes per year. In a century, strikes had become forty or fifty times more frequent.

Exhibit 12 presents annual totals of strikers from 1865 through 1981. The graph points clearly upward. Over the very long run from the 1860s to the 1960s, the annual number of strikers increased at a rate of about 5 percent per year. In the average year of the later 1860s, some 27,000 French workers went out on strike. By the later 1960s, the characteristic number was 2.5 *million* workers. Corrected for the changing size of the labor force, those numbers correspond to a rise from roughly 200 strikers per 100,000 workers to 11,000 per 100,000. In an average year of the 1870s, roughly 1 worker in 500 joined a strike. By the 1960s the equivalent of about 1 worker out of 10 was striking each year.

But the increase came amid wide year-to-year swings. The rise occurred in spurts centered on strike waves, including those of 1906, 1919, 1936, 1948,

Exhibit 12. Strikers per year in France, 1865–1981 (Perrot 1974: I, 61; *Statistique des Grèves* 1890–1935; *Annuaire Statistique* 1966, 1969, 1970, 1982; *International Labour Organization Year Book* 1951–52, 1957, 1966, 1969; Delale and Ragache 1978: 226–227; Durand and Harff 1973)

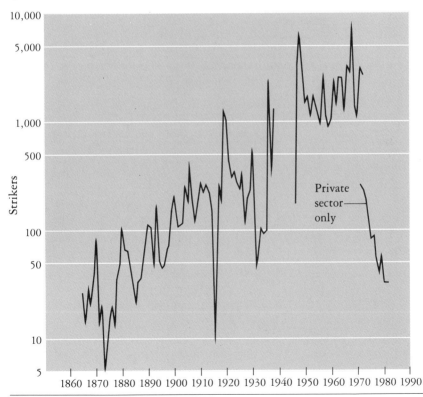

and 1968. Both repression and depression deterred strikes: times of repression such as those of the two world wars and times of depression such as
the mid-1870s and the early 1930s generally saw very few strikes.

At the departmental level comparable, continuous evidence on strike
activity is hard to find. In 1885 French governmental officials began publishing comprehensive statistics on strike activity. By the 1890s the routine
was working well; it reported the great bulk of strikes from all of France in
considerable detail. Despite lapses such as the incomplete reporting of
World War I's industrial conflicts, the system lasted until the strike wave of
1936. The great strikes of the Popular Front shattered the series. Since then,
official French strike statistics have staggered from bad to worse—fragmentary in the later 1930s, nonexistent during World War II, scattered in the
postwar years, broken again by the strike wave of 1968, confined to a dwindling private sector in the 1970s.

Exhibit 13 uses the golden half-century of strike reporting from 1885
to 1935 to compare rates of strike activity over five departments and France
as a whole. With a few interesting exceptions, Nord and Seine behaved differently from the rest of France. Anjou's textile and quarry workers occasionally raised Maine-et-Loire's rate well above the national average. To
some degree, workers of Côte d'Or, Haute-Garonne, and Maine-et-Loire all
joined the national strike movement following World War I. Yet through
most of the fifty years it was the Seine and especially the Nord that raised
the national average.

Because the Seine and the Nord had so many more workers in their
labor forces than the other departments, these higher strike propensities
meant that the Seine or the Nord, or both together, commonly brought out
a majority of the entire country's strikers. The strike movement of 1890, for
example, concentrated very heavily in the coal basin of the Nord and the
neighboring Pas-de-Calais. In 1906 the strike wave began in the north, then
enveloped the Paris region. By then, however, strike waves were becoming
national in scope. Although Flanders and the Ile-de-France still contributed
the largest numbers in 1906, high proportions of workers in the Mediterranean coastal area and the region of Lyon likewise struck.

That pattern stuck. The strike geography of 1919–20 resembled that of
1906, although overall levels of participation ran much higher. In 1936,
when the vast majority of French departments had participation rates above
2,000 strikers per 100,000 workers, France's northeast corner, including the
Nord, still led the pack. The thinness of strike statistics after World War II
makes it more difficult to follow the geography as closely as before. In the
great strike waves of 1947–48 and 1968, however, metalworkers of the Paris

Exhibit 13.   Strikers per 100,000 nonagricultural workers in five departments, 1885–1935 (*Statistique Annuelle* 1885–1889; *Statistique des Grèves* 1890–1935)

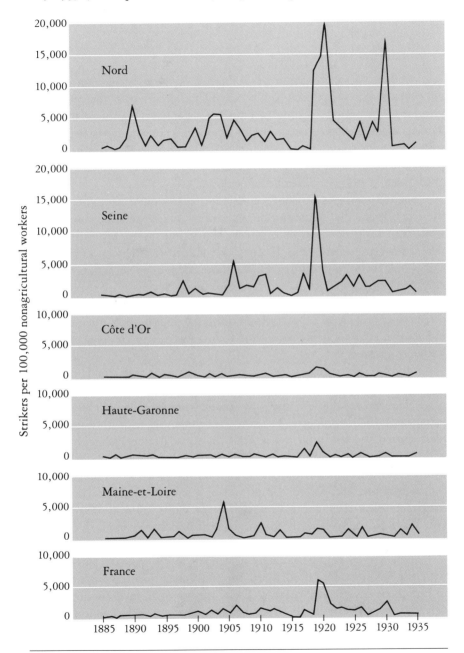

region and miners of the Nord stood out in the action. As strike waves rose and nationalized, workers along the old axis from Paris to Lille continued to play a disproportionate part.

A Concatenation of Crises

The conflicts of 1906 promoted and dramatized a nationalization of strike movements that was already under way. They occurred in the midst of a great series of national struggles. From 1905 to 1907, organized industrial workers made their presence in national politics known as never before. Despite the nonpartisan stance of the CGT, the arrival of a strong Socialist party in the Chamber of Deputies gave labor a much more direct voice in government than it had ever before enjoyed.

But the struggles of labor, capital, and government were only part of the story. From the beginning of the century on, smallholders and wageworkers in Languedoc's winefields were mounting strikes, protests, and demands for government help. In 1907 they joined together in a movement that shook the whole country. Furthermore, from 1902 on, a succession of republican governments started circumscribing the place of the Catholic church in national life: canceling the salaries the government had paid priests since Napoleon's Concordat, closing religious schools, then enacting a definitive separation between church and state. At each step, organized Catholics resisted.

Catholic resistance reached its peak in February and March 1906. To prepare for the assignment of church property to the religious associations newly required by the law, the government sent emissaries to take official inventories of that property. In town after town, the faithful occupied the local church and drove off the officials. In Paris, Action Française leagued with local people to barricade Ste.-Clothilde and St.-Pierre-du-Gros-Caillou. The occupiers of the two churches fought off the police who came to assure the inventories, and forced the unwanted visitors to chop their way in. Among those arrested at Ste.-Clothilde were Counts Louis de Bourbon and Guy de la Rochefoucauld. Artistocratic legitimists were joining the local faithful in their resistance.

Elsewhere in France the activists tended to be ordinary parishioners, with a sprinkling of local notables. The most consequential clash occurred in Boeschepe (Nord) on 6 March. There, the son of an inventorying official defended his father by fatally shooting a demonstrator. Parliamentary debate on the killing brought down the government. Ten days later the new government sent its agents instructions to suspend inventories if open resistance seemed likely. By April, toe-to-toe confrontation had become less frequent but had not disappeared.

In general, active involvement of a locality in the resistance depended on the presence of two elements: well-established Catholic practice and spirited local leadership. That combination appeared most frequently in Brittany and the adjacent areas of western France. Secondary centers of resistance, however, developed in northern Languedoc and neighboring areas (the departments of Aveyron, Lozère, and Haute-Loire) and in a few scattered departments, including the Nord. The geography of resistance anticipated later Catholic boycotting of public schools. In 1957 the twelve French departments with more than 30 percent of their primary school children in Catholic schools were Morbihan, Ille-et-Vilaine, Loire-Inférieure, Vendée, Maine-et-Loire, Mayenne, Finistère, Aveyron, Lozère, Ardèche, Haute-Loire, and Côtes-du-Nord (Mayeur 1966a: 1272). The correspondence between the maps of 1906 and 1957 is well-nigh perfect.

Among our five regions, Anjou and the Nord joined most actively in the movement. The Ile-de-France and Languedoc had a marginal involvement, and Burgundy remained indifferent. Thereafter, Anjou and the Nord went separate ways. In Anjou the struggle for and against the established church congealed into a long-term political division. There, the clericals generally kept the upper hand. The choice of schools became a bitter, visible political choice.

In the Nord as well, inventories divided communities. In Tourcoing, for example, socialist workers went through the streets breaking the windows of factories whose owners they suspected of having supplied the bales of cloth with which Catholics had barricaded local churches (Mayeur 1966a: 1265). Nevertheless, in the Nord and elsewhere the great majority of inventories proceeded peaceably. By April 1906 the Nord's great divide did not separate Catholics from Republicans. It drew the line between organized workers and capitalists.

An American Insect

The second great crisis that opened the century conformed to a very different geography. The troubles of French winegrowers between 1900 and 1910 had their origins two decades earlier. Enterprising growers of Nîmes's hinterland introduced hardy, high-production American vines in the 1880s, hoping to raise their own yields. The roots of American vines carried a microscopic insect, *Phylloxera vastatrix,* to which they were immune but French vines were not. True to its name, the blight devastated French winefields. The terrible task began: tearing up all the nation's vineyards and planting resistant American vines. To hold their markets, merchants and large producers tolerated or even encouraged two practices they would later condemn bitterly: first, the importation of cheap wine from Spain, Italy, and especially Algeria; second, the stretching of the available stock by judicious addition of water and sugar.

As the south recovered, its larger owners and merchants responded to new competition by shifting toward large-scale production of ordinary wines. Shipping wine by railroad tank car made it easier to reach the national market but gave the advantage to large producers of reliable, low-priced wine. That meant concentration of capital and proletarianization of labor. During the 1880s, for example, the Compagnie des Salins du Midi built itself from nothing into one of the country's great wine producers. By 1900 the CSM had more than 700 hectares of Hérault in grapes, and its industrial methods produced about twice the department's average yield of wine per hectare. The firm was turning out 100,000 hectoliters in good years, and averaging an annual profit of about 10 percent on its capital (Pech [1976]: 153–178).

From year to year, the prosperity of Languedoc's wine industry depended on the national market price for cheap wine, which varied mainly as a (negative) function of the previous year's national production. During most of the years from 1900 to 1906, prices were depressed and winegrowers' incomes declining. Three different conflicts overlapped temporarily with each other. First, all producers, large and small, felt the competition of cheap wines from elsewhere; organized producers protested against "fraud" (as exemplified by watering, the use of beet sugar to fortify wine, and the sale of untaxed wine) and called for governmental intervention. Second, smallholders saw themselves being squeezed by capitalist winegrowers; they complained about taxes, bankruptcy laws, and unfair competition. Finally, wage laborers were feeling the pressures of underemployment and declining wages; some of them formed unions and organized strikes.

During the concentration and proletarianization of the 1890s, scattered winegrowers' unions had formed in zones of large-scale production. In 1904 workers in southern winefields attracted national attention with a moderately successful round of strikes against major producers; in Pyrénées-Orientales (especially near Perpignan), Aude (especially near Narbonne), and Hérault (especially near Béziers and in the sections closest to Narbonne), 129 growers' strikes occurred during the year (Gratton 1917: 164).

In 1907, however, the three currents—large producers, smallholders, and wageworkers—flowed together. Deputies from winegrowing regions organized a January debate on "fraud" in winegrowing and launched a parliamentary inquiry into the question. In March the parliamentary commission came to Nîmes. Local winegrowers' committees rapidly began meeting and complaining. Grower and innkeeper Marcellin Albert of Argelliers, who had been trying to organize winegrowers' action committees for several years, now reached responsive audiences.

On 11 March a fateful series of processions began. About ninety winegrowers marched from Argelliers to Narbonne, where the parliamentary commission was sitting. Then marches multiplied. Although large growers sometimes gave their blessing and regular wageworkers sometimes joined the action, the core of the movement consisted of two overlapping groups: smallholders and those skilled vineworkers who split their effort between tending their own small plots and working for wages on other people's (Smith 1978). They organized village by village, then consolidated into regional federations.

By May the meeting-demonstrations were converging on the regional capitals—Narbonne, Béziers, Carcassonne, Nîmes, Montpellier—and attracting hundreds of thousands of participants. Sundays were the great days. On 5 May roughly 45,000 people arrived in Narbonne from 150 villages. Perhaps 150,000 came to Béziers on 12 May, 170,000 to Perpignan on 19 May, 250,000 to Carcassonne on 26 May, 150,000 to Nîmes on 2 June. On 9 June the mass meeting of Montpellier—some 500,000 participants from an estimated 430 villages—topped the series (Smith 1978: 118). The marches were among the most colorful of the twentieth century. Symbolic objects displayed during demonstrations included:

> portraits of Marcellin Albert, prophet's beard and all
> little guillotines with the words FOR CHEATERS or DEATH TO
>   CHEATERS
> little gallows with cheaters or sugarbeets hanging in them
> vines draped in black
> a scythe with threats of death to cheaters
> empty purses and turned-out empty pockets
> official notices of tax sales inscribed RESULT OF FRAUD
> a sardine labeled THE PEOPLE'S PITTANCE
> a bottle bedecked with mourning crepe
> a little coffin with the sign WINEGROWER, MY FRIEND, ARE YOU
>   READY? I'VE COME FOR YOU.
> a piece of bread on a sign draped with mourning crepe and reading
>   LOU DARNIE CROUSTET (the last crust)   (Gilbert 1970: 328)

Some of the demonstrations (such as the one at the Perpignan railroad station on 8 June) spilled over into confrontations with troops and police. Meanwhile the winegrowers' committee of Argelliers, led by Marcellin Albert, organized a tax strike backed by the resignation of hundreds of municipal councils in Aude, Hérault, and Pyrénées-Orientales. Clémenceau sent in troops.

The arrival of military forces in Narbonne, Montpellier, Perpignan, Agde, and other cities precipitated a new round of demonstrations and attacks. But these new battles were manned largely by city dwellers rather than by winegrowers (Smith 1978: 118–119). While the government was arresting Marcellin Albert and members of his committee for their advocacy of resistance, the National Assembly was passing laws against watering and undue sugaring of wines.

At summer's end, the partly successful movement began to disband. Some of the participants formed a General Winegrowers' Confederation, modeled on the CGT. (To the later chagrin of many socialists and labor leaders, it united smallholders and skilled workers in a common demand for protection of their livelihoods. A proletarian party found itself depending on a petty-bourgeois following. Nevertheless, from 1908 to 1911 organized vineworkers succeeded in a series of strikes to raise wages.)

Meanwhile a beleaguered government was releasing its prisoners and dropping its charges. Once again a movement had ended with the tacit amnesty that usually sealed success, however partial.

Proletarians and Others

Burgundy's winegrowers did not join the movement of 1907. In fact, while substantial clusters of vineyard strikes were occurring in Languedoc during the decade after 1900, not a single one appeared in Burgundy. In July 1907 the prefect of the Côte d'Or commented, rather smugly: "The events of the Midi dominated political concerns in my department during the month of June 1907. The people of Côte d'Or received the news of the troubles in those departments with more surprise and curiosity than sympathy" (ADCO 20 M 60). The difference stemmed largely from contrasting responses to phylloxera two decades earlier. On the whole, the Midi's winegrowers had moved their industry to mass production of cheap table wines from hardy American plants. In the process, wage labor became the dominant mode.

In Burgundy, smallholders and larger producers alike had chosen to reconstitute high-quality production by grafting French plants on immune American roots. The skill required for that operation and the subsequent care of the vines gave smallholders and wageworkers leverage their southern confreres lost. Swings in production, demand, and prices did not affect them so greatly. The contrast increased between industrial and artisanal forms of winegrowing.

Later and elsewhere, smallholders and skilled agricultural workers proved perfectly capable of collective action. When the winegrowers of Champagne met their crisis in 1911, for example, small producers led the attacks on big merchants, participated actively in tax strikes, and joined the demand for governmental action against "fraud." Yet thereafter, in Champagne as elsewhere, wageworkers moved toward the organization of unions and strikes, while smallholders split off in the direction of cooperatives and pressure groups.

At a national scale, to be sure, agricultural workers never played a very large part either in strike activity or in trade union federations. For as long as French strike statistics existed, agricultural workers seldom contributed more than 5 percent of all French strikes or strikers. In the years from 1890 to 1935, while the nonagricultural labor force as a whole turned out strikes at about sixty per year per million workers, agriculture produced about three per million. During the earlier decades of the twentieth century, wageworkers in relatively large mines and manufacturing firms constituted the core of French industrial conflict.

The mining and textile towns of the Nord provide some of the purest examples. Take Halluin, a factory town seventeen kilometers due north of Lille. Halluin stands on the frontier, directly across the river Lys from the Belgian fortress city of Menin. With the mechanization of linen spinning during the middle decades of the nineteenth century, the village of Halluin quickly developed into a compact city of small shops and domestic weavers. Its shops sent linen goods to merchants in Lille. In the 1880s local entrepreneurs built steam-driven weaving mills; mills came to dominate the cityscape. People flocked in from the Belgian countryside—many of them becoming permanent residents, but several thousand more crossing the border to work each day. Flemish became an everyday language.

Halluin grew to about 16,000 inhabitants, not counting the daily commuters or the dwindling number in surrounding villages on both sides of the border who wove and did other forms of outwork for the city's industry. It remained near that figure until after World War II. Most of its inhabitants lived in tight rows of low, uniform two- or three-room houses built along narrow streets, courtyards, or culs-de-sac—the very environment Vidal de la Blache deplored. Like other working-class towns in the Nord, Halluin organized a great deal of its public life around its corner bars, the *estaminets;*

in 1901 the city had one café for every eleven houses (Vermander 1978: 35). Halluin kept the appearance and condition of a nineteenth-century mill town. In 1968, for example, only 34 percent of the city's dwellings had a bath or shower, and only 19 percent had an inside toilet (Bruyelle 1976: 59).

A constant population and a fixed environment, however, did not mean a silent people. In the 1890s the strike-prone workers of Halluin and its Belgian suburbs organized a socialist union and a bourse du travail. In the next decade, local organizers followed the Belgian model by maintaining two rival labor unions, one Catholic, the other anticlerical and socialist. Now and then they cooperated. When union recognition became an issue during the big, long weaver's strike of 1909–10, for instance, the two camps joined forces and won. Over the long run, however, the secular socialists squeezed their rivals into a corner. Halluin unified to the left.

The leftward unification played itself out in local politics. Until World War I, local capitalists kept control of the municipality; the mayor was typically a textile entrepreneur. From 1919 onward, however, Socialists and Communists took charge. When the national labor federation split in 1922, the Communist affiliated CGTU became the dominant local union. During the general textile strikes of 1928–29 and 1930, the CGTU led the way. During the huge regional strike of 1930 the *Journal des Débats* ran a typical story:

> A Communist parade of 400 people took place Thursday afternoon in the main streets of Halluin. During the march, a number of incidents occurred. Mobile guards were insulted and shoved by a number of demonstrators. Two young women workers were arrested, as well as a male striker from Menen. The demonstrators left the march little by little after the arrests; the parade finally fell apart for lack of demonstrators. Following these incidents, the prefect of the Nord issued a decree forbidding all parades in the towns of the Nord. (*Le Journal des Débats* 11 September 1930)

Strike, parade, and demonstration converged.

Although the CGTU and the CGT had rejoined forces by the time of the 1936 sitdown strikes, the Communists remained strong at Halluin. Indeed, Halluin was one of the few places in the Nord (or, for that matter, anywhere else) where the Communist call for a general strike on 30 November 1938 received a wide response. The distinction between labor struggles and national politics declined. Halluin became famous as "Red City."

By the 1930s Halluin belonged to one of the country's densest clusters of red cities. Consider the nationwide strikes-demonstrations of 12 February

1934, when the left showed its strength in response to the right-wing demonstrations of 6 February in Paris, and the PCF broke out of its isolation to join other left parties. Despite the failure of the Nord's Communists and Socialists to achieve unity of action, the Nord produced more individual demonstrations than any other department of France. Not all were peaceful; in and around Roubaix, Communist strikers blocked the frontier to keep 2,000 Belgians from coming to work, stoned their buses, spread paving stones across the road, burned a truck, broke in to sack a carding plant whose workers were not striking, and fought those workers in the street. Unionized workers likewise struggled with nonstrikers in Abscon and Dunkerque. The same day, Lille, Roubaix, and Tourcoing together brought out roughly 25,000 marchers in three separate demonstrations against fascism. That number compares with perhaps 65,000 in Paris, 32,500 in Toulouse, 6,500 in Montpellier, 1,600 in Dijon, 2,000 in Angers (Lefranc 1965: 33; Prost 1966: 27).

Despite their failure to bring out a unified left in such departments as the Nord, the demonstrations-strikes of 12 February prefigured the themes and geography of the Popular Front. On the May Days of 1936, 1937, and 1938, for example, the Seine, Seine-et-Oise, and Nord again led the country for sheer numbers of demonstrations (Prost 1964: 91). Table 9 presents some further indications of the differences among departments.

One fact stands out: as the Popular Front gained momentum and strikes spread, workers rushed into unions. Throughout the country, the rate of unionization almost sextupled from one year to the next. Strike waves had always promoted union affiliation in France, but the wave of 1936 had an extraordinary mobilizing effect. Again, in France as a whole nearly one worker in ten struck in June 1936—and the base for these rates is the total labor force, including agricultural workers, professionals, executives, shopkeepers, and everyone else. Although the rates for Côte d'Or, Haute-Garonne, and Maine-et-Loire ran below those for the country as a whole, those departments still had very high strike participation by ordinary standards; from 1.2 to 6.2 percent of their work forces joined strikes in June 1936.

Practically every French department (and certainly all of these) had at least some sitdown strikes in June 1936. The Haute-Garonne, despite its relatively low strike rate in June 1936, had the distinction of helping to initiate the national movement; the sitdown strike at Toulouse's Latecoère factory (13 May) began in response to the firing of workers who had taken off May Day; from 27 May onward, many other Toulousan plants followed the example.

Table 9.　Unionization, 1936–1938, and voting and strike profiles, 1936, by department

Department	Percent of workers and officials unionized 1936	1937	Percent of metalworkers unionized, 1938	Percent voting left, 1936[a]	Strikers per 100,000 workers, June 1936
Côte d'Or	11	42	20	30	6,189
Haute-Garonne	22	58	33	46	4,678
Maine-et-Loire	16	41	34	6	1,199
Nord	15	57	84	47	37,838
Seine and Seine-et-Oise	13	78	72	43	12,639
All France	11	60	60	29	9,036

Sources: Prost 1964:214–219; *Bulletin du Ministère du Travail* 1936; census of 1936.
a. Refers to all registered voters, including those who did not vote.

With respect to unionization and strike activity, the Nord and the Paris region contrast with Côte d'Or, Haute-Garonne, and Maine-et-Loire; the combination of relatively high unionization, left voting, and extensive sitdowns mark them as bastions of working-class activism.

In the logic of French politics, working-class activism also made the Nord and the Paris region favored sites of confrontation between fragments of the left; when they were not caught temporarily in a tight alliance, both in the 1930s and later Communists and Socialists (or their union counterparts) often battled each other. By a similar logic, the Nord and the Paris region had a disproportionate share of public struggles between organized leftists and activists of the right: Action Française, Croix de Feu, and other authoritarian groupings before World War II; Gaullists, supporters of French Algeria, Poujadists, and others after the war.

Yet no region lacked for left-right clashes. During the national pulling and hauling between Gaullists and Communists during the spring of 1948, for instance, Communists tried repeatedly to sabotage public meetings of the Gaullist RPF. In Toulouse on 21 March 300 or 400 Communists managed to enter among the 1,500 in the audience. When the speaker began to attack their party, the Communists started a demonstration in the midst of the meeting, shouting and singing the *Internationale.* Gaullists naturally replied with their own shouts and the *Marseillaise.* As the meeting's marshals tried to expel the demonstrators, the predictable fight broke out. Some of the combatants used brass knuckles (*coups-de-poing américains*), blackjacks, and switchblades. By the time riot police had arrived and cleared the hall, 16 people (8 Communists, 5 RPFs, and 3 policemen) were seriously wounded, another 50 or so cut and bruised. Later the meeting resumed under police protection (*Le Monde* and *Le Figaro* 23 March 1948). Some variant of Toulouse's scenario recurred in most of France's cities for decades. Wherever fiercely rival parties recruited young activists and held public displays of their determination, the opponents sometimes came to blows.

In the first difficult years after the war, likewise, all regions saw concerted resistance against government efforts to manage the economy. In Dijon on 21 May 1947 the government's invalidation of bread-ration tickets brought a march to the prefecture. "Eight thousand storekeepers, industrialists, traveling salesmen, members of the professions and workers," the *New York Times* reported the next day, "stormed the offices of the economic control system in Dijon, burning archives and food tickets and smashing furniture and windows." *Combat,* closer to the scene, wrote of a "monstrous crowd of workers" (*Le Combat* 22 May 1947). The prefect ordered validation of the bread tickets. On 2 July of the same year, workers met in Angers at the CGT's call. They deplored the government's wage controls. After sending a delegation to see the prefect, 5,000 people went to demonstrate at the prefecture. When they broke into the courtyard, the prefect stalled them by distributing wine and butter. The prefect's move, however, did not get rid of the demonstrators. Police cleared the building (*Le Monde* 3 July 1947).

Labor-capital conflicts revived rapidly after the war, but involved state officials even more intensely than before. By the middle of 1947 France was experiencing yet another strike wave. After the Parisian metalworkers' strike of May, general strikes of railway workers, miners, and bank employees developed in June and July. In November the classic pair—Parisian metalworkers and miners of the Nord—went on strike. By the end of the month there were strikes on the railways, in the ports, and in many other industries. Sabotage and occupations of factories were widespread. Strikers took over a number of railroad stations and post offices. Around Béthune pickets stopped motorists, searched their cars, and demanded identity papers.

The movement of 1947 came close to a general strike in Alpes-Maritimes, Gard, Hérault, Haute-Garonne, Tarn-et-Garonne, Loire, and Allier—that is, in the southern departments centered on Languedoc. National and international politics hovered over the entire strike: in the organization of a strike committee based on the PCF and outside the CGT, in the resignation of Paul Ramadier's government to make way for Léon Blum, in the coalition of Communists and right-wing parties to block Blum's installation as premier, in the demand for a nationwide 25 percent increase in wages, in the symbolic destruction of English and American flags, in the settlement of the strikes by means of a national agreement between the strike committee and the government. The workers' movement resembled a revolutionary force even more than it had in 1936.

Embattled Agrarians

Despite memories of 1907 in Languedoc and of 1911 in Champagne, France's farmers almost got lost in the workers' mobilizations of the 1920s and 1930s. The exceptions were often lively. For example:

> *14 January 1933:* occupation of the departmental prefecture in Chartres by organized farmers from the Beauce
>
> *June 1933:* demonstration against the judicial seizure of property near Amiens from a Comité de Défense Paysanne activist who refused to collect social insurance payments from his employees
>
> *1934–35:* a series of protest meetings in many regions, ending in confrontations with police and counterdemonstrators
>
> *16 March 1935:* collective resistance by farmers to payment of market fees in Figeac
>
> *throughout 1935:* scattered opposition by small distillers (*bouilleurs de cru*) to fiscal controls, involving frequent resignations of municipalities in Normandy and Brittany
>
> *22 September 1935:* a bloody fight between members of the Front Paysan and Communist counterdemonstrators after a meeting in Blois
>
> *24 November 1935* and *26 January 1936:* similar affairs in Montpellier and Saint-Brieuc
>
> *fall 1936 onward:* strikes of agricultural laborers, coupled with battles between strikers and nonstrikers, in the Ile-de-France and the Nord
>
> *June 1938:* destruction of vegetables belonging to nonstriking farmers by commandos of the Comité de Défense Paysanne in Finistère

Organized farmers proved they could move and shake. Compared with the ferment surrounding industrial workers in the 1930s, however, these and a few more incidents like them added up to very little action by cultivators.

Collective action by and on behalf of French agriculture then centered on four elements that from 1934 to 1936 consolidated into the Front Paysan: the Union Nationale des Syndicats Agricoles, led by Jacques Le Roy Ladurie; the Parti Agraire of Fleurant Agricola (*nom de guerre* of Gabriel Fleurant); the Comité de Défense Paysanne of Henri Dorgères (pseu-

Fig. 25. Old workers demonstrate at the Hotel de Ville, 1947

Fig. 26. Farmers' demonstration in the Nord, 1955

donym of Henri d'Halluin); and a set of specialized producers' associations, such as the beetgrowers' Confédération Générale des Betteraviers. All four tended to take extremely conservative political lines, prefiguring Vichy's stress on work and family. As a practical matter, however, they organized lobbying and electoral campaigns around price supports and protection of the French domestic market. After the Front Paysan split in 1936, Dorgères' Jeunesses Paysannes and their paramilitary Greenshirts clearly took the lead among self-styled peasant organizations. It was they, for example, who supplied shock troops to break the harvest strikes begun by day-laborers of the Nord and Ile-de-France in 1936 and 1937. The Greenshirts paralleled in their rural sphere the antileftist activism carried on in cities and towns by the Jeunesses Patriotes, the Croix de Feu, and other protofascist formations.

None of the collaborating formations survived the Liberation. But Dorgères himself—after being tried for collaboration, convicted, and rehabilitated—returned to action in 1949. Via his newspaper *La Gazette Agricole,* he found that there still was rural opposition to government controls and taxes. His Défense Paysanne reappeared as a rival of the Parti Paysan, and then of the more formidable Fédération Nationale de Syndicats d'Exploitants Agricoles (FNSEA). Dorgères once again scored great successes in organizing small Norman distillers of apple brandy. His organizational strength concentrated heavily in the band from Bordeaux up the Atlantic coast to Anjou, Normandy, and Brittany, then along the channel coast to the Nord; that zone included the main areas for France's production and consumption of applejack (Royer 1958: 170–181).

In the early 1950s Dorgères's followers were meeting to break the seals on stills and invade the offices of the national liquor authority. In the mid-1950s Dorgères carried on an uneasy courtship with Pierre Poujade's Union de Défense des Commerçants et Artisans (UDCA). Together they blocked tax inspections, sabotaged official ceremonies, and sacked the offices of tax collectors.

Still, in the postwar years Poujade came much closer than Dorgères to building an effective national movement. Through much of France his UDCA mobilized shopkeepers to block governmental fiscal controls. Poujade first attracted national attention in July 1953, when he organized resistance to tax inspectors in his hometown of Saint-Céré, Lot. His organization started to gain a broad following in 1954, through its defense of shopkeepers in the southwest. In November 1954, for example, they managed to bring out riot police against them in Castelsarrasin, Montauban, Rodez, and Toulouse.

In January 1955 Poujade was holding a large demonstration and addressing a mass meeting in Paris, playing the electoral game with one hand as he stirred up shopkeepers' strikes and fiscal resistance with the other. By 1956, with Poujade and fifty of his collaborators sitting in the Chamber of Deputies, a significant part of the UDCA's action directly concerned national politics. In Beaune on 27 June 1956 fifty or sixty Poujadists blocked the entrance of a store owned by a rival deputy; police arrested two of the demonstrators as they cleared the way. By that time the UDCA had enough visibility to attract Communist counterdemonstrators—and thus pitched battles—to many of its meetings.

Poujadists never had much success in mobilizing farmers. That fact is mildly surprising, since the 1950s saw a great surge of rural mobilization. In common with the tactics of Dorgères and Poujade, organized farmers took to direct action on a scale rivaling that of 1907. They not only held the conventional meetings, marches, and demonstrations but also staged tractor parades, blocked roads, occupied public places, and dumped surplus produce in the streets. On 1 February 1955 some fifteen thousand farmers from the Nord and Pas-de-Calais gathered at the trade fair in Lille. They demanded government help in lowering costs and entering foreign markets and protested governmental restrictions on beet sugar. When they marched toward the prefecture from the war monument and broke through police barricades, riot police fought them, using tear gas to break up the crowd.

During the following days, farmers blocked roads in the Nord and Pas-de-Calais to dramatize their case. Outside Béthune, farmers who were blockading the city unhitched their horses and drove them against the police. Near Douai their colleagues met to pass out twelve tons of potatoes. The action in the north resonated elsewhere in France. During the first two weeks of February 1955, farmers blocked roads in the Ile-de-France, Beauce, Normandy, Brittany, and Languedoc. The demonstrators in Hérault and Gard not only stopped motorists but also gave them free wine. Soon the distribution or dumping of underpriced produce became a standard feature of farmers' actions.

Varying as a function of price swings and government policy, farmers' protests continued vigorously into the 1960s. In June 1961 meetings, demonstrations, and road blockages multiplied through rural France in a great arc from Provence to Normandy, with the Nord and Pas-de-Calais involved as well. Britanny had the most intense and concerted action. On 27 May, for instance, producers from around Pont-l'Abbé dumped hundreds of kilograms of potatoes, marinated in tractor fuel, in the city streets. Before dawn on 8 June, "at about two o'clock the order was given to all members of the farmers' union to go to Morlaix with their tractors or cars. At five 3,000 or

4,000 farmers surrounded the city and blocked all the roads. A small number of them—300 or 400—occupied the subprefecture" (Mendras and Tavernier 1962: 650). In fact the demonstrators broke down the door and chased out the subprefect.

Later both the subprefect and the prefect refused to meet with them to discuss their demands for government help in marketing their meat and vegetables. The prefect said that "although he was ready to receive leaders of the agricultural trade that wanted to defend its interests, he could not receive demonstrators who that very morning had invaded the subprefecture" (*Ouest-France* 9 June 1961). That night someone cut a dozen telephone lines serving the city. During the following days Brittany saw more phone lines severed, railroad tracks blocked, eggs dumped by the hundreds in streets, and many other acts of agrarian opposition. Farmers used a battering ram to break into the city hall of Pontivy. In far-off Moscow, *Pravda* printed a long article on French unrest featuring a photograph of that incident with the headline PAIN AND ANGER OF THE FRENCH COUNTRY-SIDE.

Meanwhile other farmers rammed their way into the prefecture at Poitiers. A thousand farmers on tractors blockaded the Vendée's prefecture at La Roche-sur-Yon. Around Toulouse, tractor parades blocked many roads. Toward the month's end, rural demonstrators surrounded Béziers while others threw beams and trees across railroad tracks in the city's hinterland.

The farmers' movements of the 1950s and 1960s stood out from their predecessors in three important ways: in their national scale and large numbers; in their repeated employment of disruptive actions such as dumping crops and blocking roads; and in their coordination by well-articulated regional and national assocations based largely on younger, more prosperous, and more entrepreneurial farmers. Farmers' movements had clearly adopted twentieth-century style. Issues and actions, to be sure, varied from one region to another; their main common grounds were an orientation to the interests of farmers who had something to market, and a direction of the action toward the national government. The movement of 1961 was the broadest rural mobilization that France had experienced since the insurrection of 1851. It changed government policy: in 1962 the so-called Pisani Charter established a series of incentives to smaller farmers who were willing to invest and innovate.

Although 1961 was a high point, it was not the end of rural action. Pinol's survey of the years 1962–1971 has cataloged an average of sixty demonstrations per year, thirteen of them violent. Throughout the decade the reliable sources of farmers' demonstrations and related actions were

Brittany, the Nord, Provence, and Languedoc. An impressive 59 percent of the events involved demands concerning government agricultural policy, and another 26 percent concerned prices. In the winegrowing regions of the south, "the struggle for a good price pairs with the fight against wine imports" (Pinol 1975: 120). The potato growers of Nord and Pas-de-Calais and the vegetable growers of Brittany worried about prices but saw a proper government agricultural policy—including a measure of protection from competitors within the Common Market—as the way to assure their well-being.

By the 1970s, variants on the planned disruption of traffic had become a specialty of rural activists. On 20 July 1973 stockraisers near Brive-la-Gaillarde dared to commit a sacrilege: to protest low wholesale meat prices, they blocked the road and delayed for an hour the departure of the great annual bicycle race, the Tour de France.

The issues and precise techniques of rural contention varied from one producing region to another. Beyond the regional variation, however, rural collective action had two remarkable things in common: first, questions of wages, tenure, or techniques of production mattered little compared with control of prices and markets; second, it went almost without saying that the national state had the means and obligation to act on rural needs.

Retaking Possession

The twentieth century brought one central innovation to France's repertoires of contention: the seizure of a space, often including the persons in it, as a means of exerting pressure on people outside that space. Collective squatting in vacant dwellings, hijackings, seizures of hostages, sitdown strikes, occupations of public buildings all had that routine in common.

To be sure, those actions shared some properties with the erection of barricades to defend a neighborhood against outsiders; that practice already existed in 1648 and temporarily became a revolutionary routine during the nineteenth century. The old agrarian practices of breaking down enclosures to pasture animals on former common land likewise acted out claims to spaces. Furthermore, the twentieth-century actions likewise often began with a defensive gesture: blocking an eviction, avoiding a lockout, and so on.

But twentieth-century activists created an aggressive, offensive version of the occupation. That version asserted the occupants' *right* to hold the premises, and used their control of the space as the basis of demands on authorities who likewise claimed rights to the same space. The combination of occupation and offensive bargaining distinguished a set of practices having few precedents before Word War I.

The sitdown strikes of 1936–1939 and the extraordinary days of May and June 1968 brought the greatest clusters of deliberate seizures of spaces. But the practice became more common outside the great moments of rebellion as well. In the 1970s people occupied their workplaces—the Lip watch factory, Titan-Coder, even the passenger liner *France*—to keep them from closing down permanently. Workers attempted to operate a number of these concerns on their own, generally without great success.

In addition to its role in the great sensational cases, the tactic of occupation was generalizing to small, local conflicts. On 17 November 1981 about 250 employees of the little Myrys shoe factory of Limoux (Aude) struck against Louis Riu, owner and operator of the firm. They had asked for a reduction of the work week to thirty-eight hours, for a slowing of the pace of production, and for early retirement at age fifty-five; Monsieur Riu had refused and proposed instead a forty-four-hour week without overtime in peak season, a thirty-six-hour week in slack season, plus some alterations in vacation pay and schedules. As employees got the news at work

> they went at once to block departmental road 118 and started turning vehicles away from the factory. At the same time, unhappy at the refusal to negotiate, they blocked the exists from the executive offices. It was then 9:50 A.M. M. Louis Riu, the boss, pushed his way through the thick picket line and got to his car, which was parked in the factory's courtyard. The car was immediately surrounded by about ten people, who kept it from leaving. M. Louis Riu got out of his car. After walking back across the courtyard, he walked out onto a local road that winds along the nearby hills. The strange parade, led by a boss with his briefcase, and consisting mainly of a colorful, noisy demonstration, continued to the middle of the vineyard, where the strikers stopped the head of their firm and started a discussion. Neither the foggy location nor the morning hour favored genuine negotiations; they made a date for later, and the odd gathering dispersed as quickly as it had formed. (Babou et al. 1981: 27–29)

That afternoon the strikers, reinforced by delegations of strikers from other plants in nearby Carcassonne and Quillan, paraded through Limoux. The parade ended at the subprefecture, where the subprefect and the strikers agreed on a three-way discussion involving workers, management, and government.

Those discussions led union representatives to call off the strike. The bulk of the workers, however, disagreed with the union; they decided to stay out and to block deliveries to the plant. Strikers blocked the vehicle entrances for two weeks, setting up a camp outside the plant. Nonstrikers continued to work inside, but no raw materials entered and no finished shoes left.

While workers occupied the delivery zone they continued to parade and sent delegations to see the prefect and the bishop. Limoux's city council voted them moral and material support. Negotiations continued. On 2 December management announced a layoff of the nonstriking employees because "it is impossible to deliver raw materials and heating fuel, or to send out finished goods" (Babou et al. 1981: 78). At the same time, management threatened legal action against those who blocked the plant. But that was a late maneuver. On the morning of 4 December, management and strikers reached a settlement—a thirty-nine hour week with forty hours' pay, plus most of the other demands. Workers had gained significantly by means of an action that was not quite a classic sitdown nor a simple picket line, but a blend of the two.

Occupying the premises, or part of them, was not always so successful. At the big Talbot automobile plant in the Paris suburb of Poissy, owned by Peugeot, management planned in 1983 to meet declining sales by laying off about 3,000 workers. Under pressure from unions and government they reduced the figure to 1,905. The threatened workers, largely African immigrants, had no guarantee of reemployment. A sitdown by a few hundred of the laid-off workers, plus some of their comrades who still held jobs, led to pitched battles in the factory. Strikers and nonstrikers hurled bolts and other auto parts at each other.

On 5 January 1984 delegates of the CFDT and CGT, unable to halt the fighting, agreed to the calling in of riot police. The plant gradually went back to work, filtering out the laid-off workers at its gates, as the government proposed lump-sum payments to immigrants who would return to their native lands. A Socialist government in a contracting economy found itself with a sharply-divided labor movement.

The occupation of space had also become a way of showing determination on behalf of a cause, without bargaining for departure from the space. About the time that the conflict at Talbot-Poissy was coming to a head, farmers in Brittany were once again demonstrating. During the first week of January Breton farmers occupied the prefecture of Vannes in Morbihan, destroyed meat in the streets, and established blockades on roads. These shows of strength backed up demands for government protection. By then, they were familiar routines.

Indeed, much of January's action had a familiar visage. In his Paris dispatch of 24 January, Paul Lewis wrote that

> social unrest is increasing in France as workers and farmers continue to protest the Government's new austerity policies ... Today, more than 3,000 workers from the Nord-Mediterranée group of shipyards marched through Paris to protest a plan that would eliminate up to 6,000 jobs. Angry farmers in northern France parked trucks and tractors on railroad tracks, blocking traffic to Paris in a continuation of their protest against low pork and poultry prices and low-priced imports. This week they have smashed local government offices, battled riot police and hijacked trucks bringing in pork sausages from Britain, the Netherlands and West Germany. In addition, five unions plan a general strike in the state-owned coal mines beginning Feb. 17 to protest 6,000 expected job losses this year and up to 20,000 over the next three years, as the Government prepares to reduce coal output. And steelworkers, angry that the Government has refused to bail out their industry, have skirmished with police in Alsace-Lorraine over the potential loss of 35,000 jobs. Even Government workers are planning a "week of action" involving work stoppages and slowdowns.   (*New York Times* 25 January 1984)

The conflicts of January followed the pattern of times of contraction: resistance to losses, demands for restitution, warnings not to touch existing rights and privileges. Contraction or expansion, however, public statements of demands and complaints repeatedly followed the same routines. By January 1984 most of those routines, in their essentials, had been operating for a century or more.

12 ᑐ~ᔌ

Four Centuries
of Struggle

N THE AFTERMATH of the turbulent 1960s, the United States was not the only country to express its national anxieties by means of a commission on the causes and prevention of violence. In April 1976 French President Giscard d'Estaing, responding to public outcry, appointed a committee to study "violence, criminality, and delinquency." The committee included such luminaries as Jacques Ellul and Jean Fourastié. Its secretary, Roger Dumoulin, was a prefect. Before the committee finished work, its chair, Alain Peyrefitte, had become minister of justice. It was visibly a blueribbon committee.

During the fifteen months of its existence, the committee held sixty-five plenary sessions and seven seminars. Testimony during the committee's hearings came from Gaston Defferre, Pierre Mauroy, Raymond Aron, Pierre Chaunu, Stanley Hoffmann, Edgar Morin, Robert Badinter, Gisèle Halimi, and many other national figures. The CGT gave political standing to the proceedings by refusing to send a witness. The committee's staff organized distinguished professional task forces and commissioned detailed reports. In short, the government was calling for serious advice on the control of violence.

The rising sense of insecurity reflected in opinion polls and in protective behavior, said the committee, resulted from the spread of individual and collective violence. It was not the first time such a crisis had seized France. "Our country," they wrote, "is periodically subjected to antisocial surges that plunge its people into anxiety, and even into anguish" (Peyre-

fitte et al. 1977: 43). Previous authorities had met those crises with repression and dissuasion; now, they suggested, was the time to worry about
prevention of violence. To that end, they made a number of recommendations: build more integrated cities, reduce abuses of public power, move capital to sites of underemployment, and so on. Their recommendations
exuded cautious liberal good sense.

   Peyrefitte's blue-ribbon committee made the classic distinction between
violence and legitimate force. Among all uses of force, they tried to single
out illegitimate abuses, which qualified as genuine violence. The bulk of
their effort dealt with individual violence, especially those forms that already
qualified as crimes. The committee excluded war, political terrorism, and
violent sports from their purview. Yet they identified part of the problem as
collective and semilegal. "In addition to criminal violence," ran the committee's general statement,

> we have ordinary violence, *as if life itself were becoming violent.* A new ag-
> gressiveness marks personal and social relations. Attacks are multi-
> plying. Insult, physical threats, taking captives, and bombing are joining
> the arsenal of conflict. Breaking and sacking, often petty and gratuitous,
> are becoming ways of expressing oneself.   (Peyrefitte et al. 1977: 32)

In the world of work, they mentioned taking captives, sitdown strikes, and
sabotage. "In other sectors of public life," the committee continued,

> violence is establishing itself as normal operating procedure. To be sure,
> violent group reactions are nothing new. But they have recently become
> almost habitual means of "social dialogue." Occupational groups no
> longer hesitate to support their chief demands by violence (road barri-
> cades, blockage of ports, sacking of administrative offices, harassment of
> public employees ...); the committee notes regretfully that in such
> cases violence often pays. Relations between offices and their clients
> sometimes take a violent turn. People challenge a department via its
> agents. These are intermittent events, but the more spectacular because
> ordinarily peaceful citizens take part. For others, violence is a means of
> attracting attention, in order to publicize cultural, moral, or religious
> demands; all this is evidence that violence threatens to become a normal
> form of social relations.   (Peyrefitte et al. 1977: 88–89)

Peyrefitte's committee could have gained from sharper definition of their
subject matter. Sometimes they were analyzing *collective action:* the array of
means people employ to act together on shared interests. Sometimes they
were discussing the narrower band of collective action we can call *contention:*
common action that bears directly on the interests of some other acting

group. Sometimes they were singling out the even narrower strip of *collective violence:* that sort of contention in which someone seizes or damages persons or objects.

The government's advisory committee did not argue that all contention was violent or becoming violent. They assumed that some forms of contention, such as electoral campaigns or the support of controversial programs by means of associations and orderly public meetings, deserved encouragement. Nevertheless, they fell into three quite debatable assumptions: (1) that violence is a coherent phenomenon with many interdependent variants, (2) that the use of one kind of violence tends to encourage the use of another, and (3) that in the France of 1968 and beyond, violence was beginning to pervade public contention.

The history of French contention makes it tempting to identify popular collective action with violence. In looking back over four centuries of French domestic conflict, we tend to recall violent moments: the seventeenth century's great civil wars, the Parisian *journées* of 1789, the uprisings of 1830, 1848, and 1871, the stifled right-wing demonstration of 6 February 1934. In 1622, when Louis XIII's judges had the severed head of rebel leader Jean de Lescun displayed at Royan's gate, its sightless eyes facing La Rochelle, they deliberately called attention to the violent side of collective action. The same is true of the workers who, on 23 February 1848, loaded wagons with the corpses of comrades massacred by soldiers of the Fourteenth Line regiment and wheeled their grisly advertisement through the city's streets for three hours. Both powerholders and rebels sometimes made death and vengeance seem central to the action.

Likewise, the sheer number of fatalities in contention occasionally approaches the level of disaster. The roughly 650 people killed in the Three Glorious Days of 1830, the 1,400 or more who died in the June Days of 1848, and the likely 20,000 Communards who perished in 1871 stain popular contention with blood. Those numbers terrify.

To Die, Contending or Otherwise

Before linking contention and violence closely, however, we should consider three lessons of the long experience we have just surveyed. First, the vast majority of events involved no significant violence. If by "violence" we mean actual damage to persons or objects, then the usual seventeenth-century assembly to seek redress, the normal eighteenth-century charivari, the standard nineteenth-century strike, and the everyday twentieth-century demonstration all tended to pass with no more than occasional pushing and shoving. Over time, furthermore, French people have moved toward forms of collective action having less likelihood of generating violence. The expulsion of a tax collector or the invasion of an enclosed field starts closer to destruction than does a public meeting or a demonstration.

Second, professional soldiers and police did the great bulk of the killing. The ratios of military to civilian deaths—for example, the 163 military and 496 civilians reported killed during the successful Parisian rebellion of 27–29 July 1830—suggest as much. When insurgents failed, they usually suffered even higher proportions of the deaths. The actions of ordinary people were less violent than the casualties make it seem.

Third, even in violent contention the scale of violence remains, with few exceptions, relatively small. B. Ts. Urlanis estimates the French troops killed and wounded during seventeenth-century wars at more than 500,000 (Urlanis 1960: 44). For the eighteenth century, his estimate is 1.4 million casualties, for the Napoleonic wars 226,000 (Urlanis 1960: 63, 91). For the years 1816–1980, Small and Singer count all interstate wars producing 1,000 battle deaths or more. By their reckoning, France led the world in number of wars fought (twenty-two) and proportion of time (3.71 months per year) at war. Only Germany and Russia had more battle deaths; Small and Singer estimate France's battle deaths during that period at 1,965,120, about 12,000 per year (Small and Singer 1982: 168).

These numbers dwarf the likely figures for casualties in France's internal struggles. Small and Singer's tabulation for civil wars in the same period involving 1,000 or more deaths (military and civilian alike) includes France's combats of 1830, 1848, and 1871. That tabulation shows France with 24,700 battle deaths (Small and Singer 1982: 276). According to those figures, from 1816 to 1980 *eighty times* as many French people died in international wars as in major civil wars.

Why concentrate on deaths? We have good practical reasons for doing so. So long as a rough correlation exists between the number of deaths and the extent of other destruction, deaths provide one of the more reliable indicators of the general extent of violence. Deaths are less ambiguous than injuries or property damage. They are also more likely to be reported with care.

Aside from rebellions and other forms of popular contention, violent deaths occur in war, legal execution, homicide, suicide, and accident. Assignments of deaths to one category or another always leave room for argument, but rough estimates exist for each of these categories back into the nineteenth century (Chesnais 1976).

In 1830, for example, about 1,000 French people died in popular contention—some 650 of them in the Parisian uprising of 27–29 July. That year France was officially at peace; only the 400-odd troops killed in the conquest of Algeria weigh in the category of war. We lack homicide figures for 1830. But the official statistics include 1,756 deaths through suicide that year, and 4,478 from accidents. Popular contention—including the killing of civilians by troops—accounted for no more than 1 violent death in 8.

In 1848, when popular contention brought approximately 1,900 deaths (1,400 or so in the June days alone), France was again officially at peace, and her recently victorious troops suffered negligible losses in Algeria. That year, by government report, 3,301 French people killed themselves. Another 8,-218 died in accidents. Indeed, the 3,554 drownings in that total amounted to almost twice as many deaths as those caused by the conflicts of the revolution.

Reverse the picture; take a year with a war but no revolution. During the years 1854–1856 France was very much at war in the Crimea. Just over 10,000 French troops died violent deaths in that period. Another 85,000 died of cholera, typhus, lingering wounds, or some combination of the three. Meanwhile, the national statistics for the same three years reported 11,700 suicides and 28,500 accidental deaths. During the Crimean War, under Napoleon III's tight control, metropolitan France saw little popular contention of any kind. Not one person died in a collective confrontation.

In 1871 there were more than 21,000 deaths—probably France's all-time high—in popular contention. Almost all of them occurred in the bloody liquidation of the Paris Commune. But in 1871 France also lost about 77,000 of its citizens to the Franco-Prussian war, not to mention about 4,000 suicides and 14,000 accidental deaths. Even the crushing of the Paris Commune did not bring the share of civil contention up to one-fifth of all France's violent deaths.

Despite the rapidly increasing pace of strikes and demonstrations, the twentieth century brought a decisive decline in fatalities from civil conflict. Yet war killed more than ever before. Some 1.3 million French people died in World War I and 600,000 in World War II. The French lost about 26,000 troops and police in the postwar liberation struggles of Indochina and Algeria, plus thousands more in deaths outside of combat. As automobiles proliferated in France, road deaths alone rose from around 2,500 per year at the start of the century to around 15,000 per year in the 1970s. In short, thousands of French people died violent deaths in every year of the twentieth century, yet rarely did anyone die in popular contention.

Perhaps a significant share of the extraordinary 6,455 homicides in the

Liberation year 1944 (compared with a "normal" level of 336 per year from 1946 to 1950) should count as outcomes of popular contention. If so, 1944 probably qualifies not only as France's all-time record year for homicide, but also as the twentieth century's most lethal year for popular contenders.

Similarly, the 1,009 homicides in 1961—the second highest total for 1930–1972—surely include some settling of accounts concerning the French withdrawal from Algeria. That was also a turbulent year for collective contention, with widespread farmers' movements, numerous demonstrations concerning North Africa, large brawls at rock concerts, and strikes, including occupations of mines. Yet during the year only 7 or 8 people died in collective confrontations. At the same time, official statistics reported 7,300 suicides, 11,000 traffic deaths, and 18,000 accidental deaths of other sorts.

During the vast mobilization of May–June 1968, at most a dozen deaths resulted directly from the thousands of strikes, demonstrations, and occupations. By adopting a fairly broad definition of "direct victim," Delale and Ragache manage to get these twelve people onto their death register (Delale and Ragache 1978: 230):

24 May, Paris: A grenade hit Philippe Mathérion, a housing manager, at a barricade in the rue des Ecoles.

24 May, Lyon: A truck pushed by demonstrators truck René Lacroix, a police officer.

30 May, Montpinçon (Calvados): A gendarme fired a shell that struck René Trzepalkowski, a worker.

7 June, Grenoble: Someone shot Mathieu Mathei, a barkeeper, in the back; this may have been an underworld execution.

10 June, Flins: Gilles Tautin, a lycée student, drowned while fleeing a charge by riot police.

11 June, Sochaux and Montbéliard: Riot police shot Pierre Beylot, an auto worker. The same day, Henri Blanchet, another auto worker, fell to his death from a ledge during a grenade attack.

28 June, Vernon (Eure): A deserter from the Foreign Legion assassinated Jean-Claude Lemire, a delivery truck driver who has been a leading *Katangais,* or right-wing thug, at the Sorbonne in May.

30 June, Arras: Right-wing commandos killed Marc Lanvin, warehouse worker and Communist, as he posted election bills.

1 July, Guadeloupe: Molotov cocktails burned Gaetan Popotte and Rémy Lollia as they were returning from an electoral rally.

A slightly tighter definition would reduce the roster to five or six of these deaths. In either case, the number is tiny by comparison with the 9 million strikers and even more demonstrators who made the events of May and June 1968. The significance of these events clearly does not lie in the sheer quantity of violence they entailed.

How Contention Matters

Yet the events matter. Somehow they matter more than the accidents that cost so many lives. They matter because French people—of all political persuasions and powers—themselves scanned contentious events for political messages. The deaths themselves were incidental. But people interpreted the readiness of participants to commit themselves and to risk harm as signs concerning the probability of new struggles for power, or new outcomes to old struggles for power. Open contention produced information about the intentions and capacities of all claimants to power—governmental authorities, opponents and rivals of the government, contenders for some particular interest, groups of ordinary people seeking just enough space in which to live their lives peacefully.

In any particular confrontation, existing powerholders tended to retain their power; existing inequalities and injustices were likely to stay in place. Yet in a significant minority of trials, ordinary people made gains or avoided losses: the harassed tax collector actually left town for a while, the seizure of grain produced a modest increase in the local food supply, the sitdown strike exacted concessions from management.

For us, too, they matter. The record of popular contention provides us with one of our surer guides to the experiences of ordinary people who faced great changes. Did French people react to the massive proletarianization of the eighteenth and nineteenth centuries? Consult the poor cultivators of Languedoc who, in the waning eighteenth century, fought the private appropriation of forests and common fields. Ask the Parisian artisans and skilled workers of 1848 who demanded the "organization of work" to maintain a semblance of workers' autonomy and control.

Did the enormous growth of the French state make much difference to the lives of ordinary people? Consider the 5,000 citizens of the privileged Boulonnais who rose against the king's illegal "regularization" of their taxes in 1662. Reflect on the rebellion of some 100,000 people in southern Anjou and nearby regions against the revolutionary state during 1793. Popular contention sends political messages other channels do not carry.

Let us not exaggerate. Among people outside the great centers of power, not everyone has equal access to the microphone. When we look closely at "popular" contention, we repeatedly find local leaders, agitators,

animators, organizers. In general, with equal interests at stake, skilled workers tend to be better prepared to act than unskilled workers, propertied farmers better positioned to pool their efforts than their migrant workers. Furthermore, because collective action rests on organization and often costs
plenty, many people bear injustices, deprivations, and broken dreams with
resignation or silent anger. The record of French popular contention brings
us closer to the continuous experience of ordinary people than do the pronouncements of politicians and philosophers. Still it underrepresents the
experience of those who mobilize least easily—who are very likely those
who suffer most. Within these limits, over the very long run the story of
French popular contention broadcasts how much the growth of the state
and the development of capitalism occurred at the expense of ordinary
people.

Transformations of Contention

Neither reactions to capitalism nor responses to the state remained constant, however. Although twentieth-century winegrowers have demanded
action and twentieth-century shopkeepers have organized against taxes, no
events remotely resembling the Boulonnais' Lustucru rebellion of 1662 or
Languedoc's eighteenth-century invasions of enclosed commons have occurred. Why?

    If we look back from 1984 to 1598, we see a seventeenth century filled
with struggles of Protestants and regional powerholders to maintain their
autonomy in the face of an aggressively expanding crown, battles of local
people to resist the rising demands for resources of a warmaking state, and
that network of conflicts we call the Fronde.

    Next we observe an eighteenth century replete with contests for con-
trol of food, of land, of labor. We find capitalists, who figured in seventeenth-century struggles largely as fiscal agents for the state, playing an
independent part as accumulators of land and capital; at the century's close,
we also discover a series of fights for control of the state that temporarily
altered the whole tempo and timbre of popular collective action and permanently changed the relative power of major social classes with respect to the
state as well as the state's own penetration into everyday life.

    Continuing, we witness a nineteenth century in which the divisions
between labor and increasingly concentrated capital, as well as between
those groups enjoying the state's protection and those the state held in
check, became fundamental to a wide range of contention. In the course of
that century, we follow a series of challenges to the national structure of

power from shifting coalitions of bourgeois and organized workers. The challenges ended in the partial incorporation of organized workers into the national structure of power, and in the near-elimination of the Catholic church from that structure of power.

In our own century the involvement of national, politically active associations in the pursuit of shared interests—already visible in the nineteenth century—has become overwhelming. Amid the incessant activity of organized workers and organized capitalists, besides the increasing tendency of people to organize their demands in national strike waves and social movements, we notice the widening activity of students, intellectuals, government employees, independent farmers, shopkeepers, and service workers. If the changing organization of capital and the expanding power of the state set the main terms of popular contention throughout the four centuries, the move from one century to the next certainly did not bring more of the same.

Bins labeled "seventeenth century," or "twentieth century," however, do not contain these many changes neatly. Considering the forms and actors in popular collective action, we can make out major accelerations of change around the Fronde and the Revolution of 1848, as well as secondary accelerations during the eighteenth-century Revolution and at the beginning of the twentieth century.

Around the time of the Fronde, the regional powerholders who had long been crucial to popular collective action began to withdraw from popular alliances and to accept (at a handsome price) subordination to the crown; in the process, local assemblies lost importance as vehicles for popular collective action, mutinies of various sorts lost much of their efficacity, and urban or regional rebellions faded rapidly.

If we needed a single date to mark that transition, 1661 would serve even better than 1648; in 1661 the great statemaking duo of Colbert and Louis XIV took on the task of making the French state unchallenged in its own domain and feared throughout the world. Colbert's successors, in collaboration with great merchants and capitalist farmers, pressed to give the national market and mobile capital priority over local claims to commodities, land, and labor; as that happened, grain seizures and related forms of resistance to the dominance of capital multiplied.

With the Revolution of 1789 and beyond, two contradictory changes occurred. On the one hand, the massive popular mobilization against the claims of capitalists and the state from 1787 to about 1793 churned out a remarkable set of innovations in popular collective action: committees, mi-

litias, assemblies, clubs, participatory festivals, parades, ceremonies, invasions of legislatures, symbolic destruction, people's courts; in one way or
another, they acted out the idea of popular sovereignty.

On the other hand, the relatively small number of organized bourgeois
who actually seized control of the state apparatus soon acted to contain and
channel popular collective action; in so doing they first extended state
structure into direct rule at the level of the individual community and then
built a centralized apparatus of surveillance and control. The new state
structure would have been the envy of any so-called absolute ruler. The reshaping of the state checked the wave of collective-action innovation and
returned France to the forms of struggle that had prevailed before the Revolution.

Around the Revolution of 1848 and Louis Napoleon's seizure of power
in 1851, the largest transformations of the forms and personnel of popular
collective action worked themselves out. As capital imploded and state centralization speeded up, contention itself shifted toward national arenas.
Local forms of resistance to capitalist claims such as the grain seizure and
the collective invasion of posted forests virtually disappeared. Local mocking routines such as the charivari and the tendentious Mardi Gras pageant
lost their *raison d'être*. Popular judicial proceedings, destruction of tollgates,
forced illuminations, attacks on machines, pulling down and sacking of private houses, and intervillage battles rapidly became antique. More slowly, but
just as definitively, the communitywide turnout gave way to the firm-by-firm
strike. Electoral campaigns, strikes, planned insurrections, demonstrations,
and public meetings quickly came to dominate popular collective action.

Lesser transformations swung on the hinge of 1905–1907. With the displacement of the state church, the partial establishment of labor as an organized political force at a national scale, the national strike wave of 1906, and
the southern winegrowers' mobilization of 1907, changes that had partially
emerged in the nineteenth-century transition appeared in full light: the
great place of parties, unions, and other national associations in the organization of popular collective action; the increasing prominence of wageworkers in large organizations as participants in contention; the deliberate
creation of social movements spanning large regions or the country as a
whole; the development of countrywide strike waves strongly involving
agents of the state.

Has another transition come upon us? Three kinds of evidence might
make us think so: (1) the heightened importance in recent decades of plant
occupations, taking of hostages, urban guerrilla activity, hijacking, road

blockades, crop dumpings, takeovers of public buildings, collective squatting, mass picketing, and other deliberate occupations of spaces and the people in them; (2) the extraordinary innovations—internal assemblies, strike committees, graffiti, and so on—of May–June 1968; (3) the greatly increased use of mass media by all parties to popular collective action.

Looked at closely, however, almost all of the cases in point involve forms of action that already have histories. The novelty consists in the differences among groups or demands. In industrial conflict, for example, the strike continues to dominate workers' collective action, but white-collar and high-technology workers become more involved, and some groups of workers demand a say in decisions concerning production and investment. Again, demands for regional autonomy, sexual rights, or freedom to pursue a distinctive style of life have become more prominent since World War II, yet the proponents of those demands have typically presented them by means of demonstrations, marches, and similar routines that were already prominent in the later nineteenth century.

Repertoires of Collective Action

The great change, then, occurred in the nineteenth century. It is convenient to call what happened a change in *repertoire*. Any population has a limited repertoire of collective action: alternative means of acting together on shared interests. In our time, for example, most people know how to participate in an electoral campaign, join or form a special-interest association, organize a letter-writing drive, demonstrate, strike, hold a meeting, and build an influence network. These varieties of action constitute a repertoire in something like the theatrical or musical sense of the word; but the repertoire in question resembles that of *commedia dell'arte* or jazz more than that of a strictly classical ensemble: people know the general rules of performance more or less well and vary the performance to meet the purpose at hand. Every performance involves at least two parties—an initiator and an object of the action. Third parties often get involved; even when they are not the object of collective action, for example, agents of the state spend a good deal of their time monitoring, regulating, facilitating, and repressing different sorts of collective action.

The existing repertoire constrains collective action; far from the image we sometimes hold of mindless crowds, people tend to act within known limits, to innovate at the margins of existing forms, and to miss many opportunities available to them in principle. That constraint results in part from the advantages of familiarity, partly from the investment of second

Fig. 27. May Day 1983, Paris

Fig. 28. Peace march, Paris, June 1982

and third parties in the established forms of collective action. Although it may seem otherwise, even government officials and industrial managers of our own time generally behave as though they preferred demonstrations and strikes to utterly unconventional forms of collective action.

The fullest available accounts of French collective action dwell on its more discontinuous and public forms: striking, demonstrating, occupying, and so on rather than building influence networks or operating special-interest organizations. Although changes in continuous and private forms of collective action have also been profound, they are harder to document than the relatively discontinuous public forms.

The main reasons for that difference in documentation are simple and important. First, in most of the discontinuous and public forms of action the *point* is to make a statement of some kind. Deliberate public statements tend to leave behind more documentation than do other varieties of collective action. Second, authorities generally monitor and seek to control discontinuous and public forms because of their implicit claims on the existing structure of power. Hence surveillance reports, instructions to spies and police, memoranda to interior ministers and the like fill the archives of former authorities.

What do those archives tell us? Sometime in the nineteenth century the people of France shed the collective-action repertoire they had been using for about two centuries and adopted the repertoire they still use today. A definitive shift to the new repertoire did not become complete until the 1850s.

Table 10 summarizes the difference. Broadly speaking, the repertoire of the mid-seventeenth to mid-nineteenth centuries had a *parochial* scope: it addressed local actors or the local representatives of national actors. It also relied heavily on *patronage*—appealing to immediately available powerholders to convey grievances or settle disputes, temporarily acting in the place of unworthy or inactive powerholders only to abandon power after the action. Despite being labeled as "riots" and "disorders," seizures of grain, invasions of fields, destruction of machines, and similar actions had a common logic and an internal order.

The repertoire that crystallized in the nineteenth century and prevails today is, in general, more *national* in scope: though available for local issues and enemies, it lends itself easily to coordination among many localities. Compared with the older repertoire, its actions are *autonomous:* instead of staying in the shadow of existing powerholders and adapting routines sanctioned by them, people using the new repertoire tend to initiate their own statements of grievances and demands. Strikes, demonstrations, electoral

Table 10. Characteristics of repertoires of popular collective action in France, 1650–1980

1650–1850: Parochial and patronized

General characteristics

Use of the authorities' normal means of action, either as caricature or as a deliberate though temporary assumption of the authorities' prerogatives in the name of the local community

Tendency to participate as members or representatives of constituted corporate groups and communities rather than of special interests

Tendency to appeal to powerful patrons for redress of wrongs and especially for representation in relation to outside authorities

Extensive use of authorized public celebrations and assemblies to present grievances and demands

Repeated adoption of rich, irreverent symbolism in the form of effigies, dumb show, and ritual objects to state grievances and demands

Convergence on the residences of wrongdoers and the sites of wrongdoing, as opposed to seats and symbols of public power

Examples

Seizures of grain ("food riots")
Collective invasions of forbidden fields, forests, and streams
Destruction of tollgates and other barriers
Attacks on machines
Charivaris, serenades
Expulsions of tax officials, foreign workers, and other outsiders
Tendentious holiday parades
Intervillage battles
Pulling down and sacking of private houses
Forced illuminations
Acting out of popular judicial proceedings
Turnouts

rallies, and similar actions build, in general, on much more deliberately constructed organization than used to be the case.

The social movement as we know it came into being with the new repertoire. The social movement consists of a series of challenges to established authorities, especially national authorities, in the name of an unrepresented constituency. Its concrete actions combine various elements of the newer repertoire: public meetings, demonstrations, marches, strikes, and so on; leaders attempt to link these actions organizationally and symbolically, as well as to bargain with established authorities on behalf of their claimed constituency.

1850–1980: National and autonomous

General characteristics

Use of relatively autonomous means of action, of a kind rarely or never employed by authorities

Tendency to participate as members or representatives of special interests and named associations or pseudo-associations (e.g., Coalition for Justice, People United Against————————)

Tendency to challenge rivals or authorities, especially national authorities and their representatives, directly rather than appeal to patrons

Deliberate organization of assemblies for the articulation of claims

Display of programs, slogans, signs of common membership

Preference for action in visible public places

Examples

Strikes

Demonstrations

Electoral rallies

Public meetings

Petition marches

Planned insurrections

Invasions of official assemblies

Social movements

Electoral campaigns

Although it does not have the official standing of an electoral campaign or a petition drive, the deliberately organized social movement occupies a recognized place in France's contemporary array of means for acting collectively. The vast, linked demonstrations of Languedoc's winegrowers in 1907 and the coordinated road-blocking and potato-dumping of Brittany's farmers in 1961 illustrate vividly the operation of social movements.

Those who claim to speak for the same social movements often divide and compete. Their actual relationship to the constituencies they boast varies enormously. In the 1950s and 1960s, such closely linked organizers as Henri Dorgères and Pierre Poujade never could adjudicate who spoke for whom. Yet on public occasions they often managed to put up a common front. Social movements focus precisely on manufacturing the appearance of unified, simultaneous challenge by means of disparate, shifting coalitions.

This complex of action was virtually unknown in Western nations until the nineteenth century. Before then, although rebellions great and small occurred repeatedly, practically no one tried to combine seizures of grain, invasions of fields, turnouts, and the like into visibly sustained challenges to established authorities. Then the social movement became commonplace. On balance, its action was national in scope and autonomous with respect to powerholders.

The dichotomies parochial/national and patronage/autonomy simplify radically in two different ways. First, each cuts a genuine continuum into just a pair of categories. In fact real strikes, demonstrations, and the like are more or less national and autonomous, not clearly one or the other. Second, the transition to more national and autonomous forms of action did not occur instantly and simultaneously. It was the net effect of many moves and countermoves, occurring at different times for different places and types of collective action.

Turnouts, for example, were the routines by which workers in a given craft who had a grievance against the employers of their locality went from shop to shop within the locality, calling out the workers to join them in a march through the town, ended the circuit with a meeting at the edge of town, voted to make a certain set of demands, sent a delegation to the employers, declared a work stoppage, and enforced it as best they could throughout the town until they reached an agreement with the employers. The turnout was relatively local in scope. It put pressure on nearby patrons—both the employers and the local authorities.

The firm-by-firm *strike,* as we know it, covers a whole town, a whole industry, or even a whole country in exceptional circumstances. Yet the main action generally occurs within and just outside a single workplace. Larger French strikes, it is true, often incorporate a routine reminiscent of the turnout: a parade through all shops, sweeping up (if possible) workers who have remained at their posts. Yet that action aims at a single employer, not at the owners of the trade as a whole. Strikes also allow workers to state their grievances and hopes independently of conversations with their immediate employers; by striking, they can send messages to the government or to the citizenry at large.

On the average, though only on the average, routines in the newer rep-

ertoire such as strikes, demonstrations, and public meetings involve less dependence on existing powerholders and greater scope than routines such as
turnouts, field invasions, and seizures of grain. That is the point of calling
the "new" repertoire relatively autonomous and national. Exhibit 14 lays
out the contrast and transition between the old and new repertoires.

Why the Repertoires Changed

Why did the prevailing repertoire of popular collective action undergo
the change from relatively parochial and patronized to relatively national and
autonomous? The answer is simple to state in principle and complex to
show in practice. In principle, the shift occurred because the interests and
organization of ordinary people shifted away from local affairs and powerful
patrons to national affairs and major concentrations of power and capital.
As capitalism advanced, as national states became more powerful and cen-

Exhibit 14. "Old" and "new" repertoires of contention in France

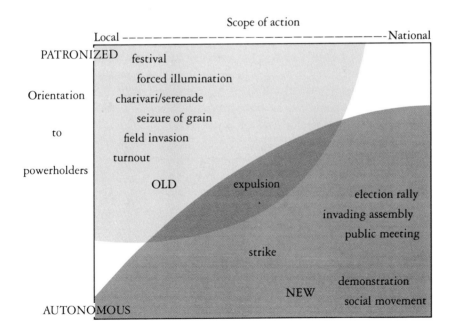

tralized, local affairs and nearby patrons mattered less to the fates of ordinary people. Increasingly, holders of large capital and national power made the decisions that affected them. As a result seizures of grain, collective invasions of fields, and the like became ineffective, irrelevant, obsolete. In response to the shifts of power and capital, ordinary people invented and adopted new forms of action, creating the electoral campaign, the public meeting, the social movement, and the other elements of the newer repertoire.

Although the shift in repertoires followed the logic of change in power and capital, each form and each actor had a particular history. The firm-by-firm strike took on its recognizable characteristics in concrete labor-management struggles as capital concentrated in locality after locality. Because the particular histories are quite different, the common processes creating the demonstration and the strike appear only in perspective, at a distance. Nevertheless, in case after case it is clear that the common processes involved concentration—concentration of capital, concentration of political power. Those concentrations altered the possibilities and forms of popular collective action. From the perspectives of individual actors, it altered their internal organization and their opportunity to act collectively.

Statemaking and capitalism did not merely shape organization and opportunity. They also dominated the fluctuating interests of different groups in collective action. The French state grew immensely in bulk and complexity; it grew in spurts such as the periods of the Revolution and the Empire, but it almost never stopped growing. Nor did it ever stop extending its power to coerce and extract. Great state-builders such as Richelieu, Napoleon, and de Gaulle left no heritage more obvious than the state's enlarged capacity to enter the lives of its citizens.

The process of statemaking affected French people's interests, and therefore stimulated popular collective action, when organization and opportunity permitted, in three ways: (1) by making direct claims on valued resources, as when the revolutionary state seized church properties in 1791 and thereafter; (2) by competing with rival governments and quasi-governments, as when Richelieu, Mazarin, and Colbert erased the liberties of cities and towns in the king's name; (3) by fostering competition among contenders for its favors, resources, and protections, as when employers and workers simultaneously sought to bend the Popular Front government of 1936. Since the rhythm of these processes was uneven—those who controlled the state were, after all, also responding to fluctuations in their own organization, opportunity, and interest—popular contention in response to statemaking rose and fell like the waves in a narrow, wind-stirred channel.

The process that eventually produced today's state-mediated capitalism in France passed through many stages. Its master trends ran toward the concentration of capital, toward the proletarianization of the labor force, and therefore toward a sharpening polarization between capital and labor. The resulting conflicts of interest generated popular collective action in three different ways. First, there was the sharpening division of interest between capital and labor itself, as when nineteenth-century textile manufacturers cut wages to meet foreign competition, and workers fought to maintain their incomes. Second, there was the competition between capitalists and other claimants on commodities and on factors of production, as when merchants stimulated grain seizures by attempting to ship grain to distant and profitable markets or to withhold grain from local markets until the price was advantageous. Third, there was competition among participants in the same factor markets, as when organized local workers attacked outsiders brought in to cut wages or break strikes.

Such conflicts of interest endure over long periods but do not produce continuous streams of open contention; contention comes sporadically. That is partly because organization and opportunity fluctuate as the parties to conflicts of interest lead their regular lives. It is partly because the parties constantly make strategic adjustments to each other's moves. It is partly because third parties—for example, the state in management-labor conflicts—likewise make moves that affect the organization and opportunity of the parties. It is also because *change* in the behavior of one of the parties has an exceptional power to attract response from another party. Although seventeenth-century French people avoided taxes whenever they could do so safely, they were especially inclined to band together for resistance when the monarchy or its tax farmers imposed a *new* illegal tax that would require yet another round of sacrifices and improvisations.

Considered from the most simplified perspective, the four centuries we have been examining break into two very broad phases of struggle. In the first we find capitalist property being created as statemakers struggled to extract resources—especially resources for making war—and to quell their rivals. In that phase, the dominant issues of popular collective action were expropriation, imposition of state control, laying down of capitalist control, and resistance to all of them.

In the second phase, within the framework of capitalist property and a strong state, we find the major themes of popular contention to be struggles between labor and capital, competition within markets, and collective efforts to control the state and its resources. Speaking very generally, the "old" repertoire belongs to the first phase, the contemporary repertoire to the second.

The Five Regions

The Ile-de-France, Languedoc, Anjou, Flanders, and Burgundy all experienced the growth of the French state and the development of world capitalism. All five regions underwent the great transformation of popular collective-action repertoires during the nineteenth century. All of them, in their ways, survived Louis XIII's military expansion, the Fronde, the struggles between Catholics and Protestants, the Revolutions of 1789, 1830, and 1848, the formation of nationwide strike movements, the Popular Front, the Occupation and Liberation, the days of May–June 1968. Yet each region underwent a different combination of capitalism, statemaking, and popular contention.

In the Ile-de-France we witness the enormous work of concentration most directly. Throughout the four centuries after 1598, Paris remained the chief prize of French political struggle; unless rooted out quickly, those who mastered Paris controlled France. From the seventeenth century onward the concentration of capital and of coercive power only increased the stakes.

Most of the struggle for possession of the capital pitted one group of national powerholders against another. Nevertheless, from time to time a coalition of relatively powerless people and dissidents from the national power structure managed to seize the city, even to topple those who controlled the state. During th Fronde, the journées of 1789, the Three Glorious Days of July 1830, the February Revolution of 1848, the Revolution of 1870, the Commune of 1871, and (to a lesser extent) the general strike of May–June 1936 or the mass occupations of May–June 1968, national power balanced on popular collective action in Paris and the Ile-de-France.

We see changes: the Fronde was the last occasion on which a coalition of regional lords seriously threatened to wrest control of the national state away from its current holders. The threat of the parlements in 1787 or 1788 pales by comparison. If the Parisian movement had been entirely independent and successful on one occasion or another, France might have had a government of great lords in 1653; of magistrates, merchants, master artisans and shopkeepers in 1788; of bourgeois, shopkeepers, and masters in 1793; of artisans, skilled large-shop workers, intellectuals, and professionals in 1848 or 1871; of organized large-shop workers, intellectuals, and professionals in 1936; of a similar set plus students and government employees in 1968.

Although from the eighteenth century onward Parisian workers mobilized with exceptional effectiveness, the contention of eighteenth-century shopworkers, with its reliance on semiclandestine craft guilds, wineshop gatherings, ceremonies, blacklists, and turnouts, bears little resemblance to twentieth-century negotiating among competing unions, government officials, political party executives, and half-organized factory workers having their own grievances and conditions for action. The main common properties are that in both centuries proximity to national powerholders and the ability, on occasion, to shut down the capital gave workers of Paris and its vicinity leverage they shared with no one else. In the twentieth century, social-movement organizers from elsewhere in France recognized that primacy regularly: to cap their challenges, they brought demonstrators and symbols of distress from provincial capitals to Paris itself.

Languedoc certainly shared in national struggles for power: Louis XIII's steely insistence on the beheading of the rebel duke of Montmorency in Toulouse, back in 1632, testifies to the importance of that province's rebellions. Languedoc also had its own distinctive existence. Big Languedoc contained several different kinds of economy, each of which experienced the state's growth and the development of capitalism in a distinctive way. In southwestern (Upper) Languedoc, we see the growth of agrarian capitalism during the seventeenth and especially eighteenth centuries. There, the division of the population into a few substantial landlords and a mass of smallholders or wage laborers, the alliance and overlap of landlords with officeholders, the containment of urban powerholders by the agrarian and official elites shaped popular politics for two centuries or more.

In northeastern (Lower) Languedoc, smaller-scale and less prosperous agriculture accompanied the proliferation of cottage industry centered on small but active commercial centers. The large Protestant population clustered disproportionately along the cottage-industry network, among poor rural outworkers and rich urban entrepreneurs. In Lower Languedoc, swings in the economic viability of textile manufacturing strongly influenced the rhythms of popular contention. The region's long, irregular deindustrialization meant that small entrepreneurs and workers were often on the defensive. The division between Protestants and Catholics added bitterness to many of Lower Languedoc's struggles—especially when the national state undertook to protect, destroy, or disestablish one religious group or the other.

The nineteenth- and twentieth-century growth of large-scale wine production further proletarianized the rural population, reshaped all Languedoc's social geography, and laid the basis for new varieties of popular politics. From the later nineteenth century onward Languedoc became France's prime region of organized agrarian radicalism, as well as the source of repeated large challenges to national agricultural policy. Although the wageworkers on the capitalist farms in Paris' hinterland sometimes organized in alliance with national labor federations based in the capital, they never rivaled the scale of Languedoc's agrarian collective action.

Anjou? In that little province the historic divisions operated on a smaller scale than in Languedoc. But the divisions were more tenacious. Through most of the four centuries after 1598, large landholders dominated the bocage and looked to Angers as their social base. Acting as rentiers rather than as full-blown agricultural capitalists, they let substantial peasants generate their incomes from medium-sized farms with the help of smallholders and day-laborers. Meanwhile, with the rise of the slave trade small merchants built up an extensive rural linen industry; after many vicissitudes, household and small-scale rural manufacturing remain important sources of income for the region's people today. The Loire Valley and connected areas supported a very different economy; industrial crops and winegrowing sustained a dense population of smallholders, wageworkers, merchants, and— until the Revolution—ecclesiastics.

Anjou's popular collective action reflected its enduring divisions. In a region long subordinated to the crown, there was little opportunity for urban rebels to garner support from local elites; the Fronde, with its divisions among the region's great powerholders, offered only a temporary exception. The artisanal and mercantile populations of Angers found few allies elsewhere in the region but managed to act on their own. The people of the bocage raised a great rebellion against the agents of the Revolution, then accepted the patronage of landlords who returned to their estates after the Revolution. That agrarian alliance underlay the region's resistance to the disestablishment of the Catholic church.

In the valley and adjacent areas, moderate and republican politics established a small base. National political struggles echoed in those areas. Local clashes involving people from the bocage, from the valley, and from Angers (not to mention the long-active quarry workers in Angers's hinterland) likewise informed Anjou's collective action. On the whole, however, during the twentieth century Anjou has remained divided from the Ile-de-France, Languedoc, Flanders, and Burgundy by its people's relative *in*action.

Flanders, on the other hand, remained hyperactive. Through the seventeenth, eighteenth, nineteenth, and twentieth centuries, Flanders experienced the construction and deconstruction of the French state through war far more often and more directly than the other four provinces. Beginning as Habsburg property, changing hands time after time, fortified and occupied over and over again, echoing repeatedly to the boots of marching armies, paying at least thrice—in destruction, in confiscation, in taxation—for every war, Flanders learned the connections between warmaking and statemaking first hand.

Flanders also became France's densest site successively for commercialized agriculture, cottage textile production, large-scale coal mining, and capital-intensive manufacturing. The region served as a proving ground for French capitalism. Proletarian collective action, both rural and urban, reached greater heights there than in any of the other regions. With the twentieth century, we find Flanders fostering militant working-class politics and consistently joining the Paris region at the head of national strike movements. Lille, Roubaix, Halluin, Douai, Valenciennes, and other cities of Flanders helped write the history of French working-class politics.

Burgundy stood aloof. On their own ground, Burgundy's winegrowers acted repeatedly to defend their interests. During the nineteenth century such wine centers as Beaune became hotbeds of republican politics. Workers of Montceau-les-Mines and Le Creusot connected well with national workers' movements. (Le Creusot, after all, organized its own commune in 1871.) Yet with the steady deindustrialization of the Châtillonnais and other sections of Burgundy, workers in the isolated centers of capital-intensive production had few potential allies within the region. Nor did winegrowers maintain militancy into the twentieth century. As Languedoc's winegrowers were pressing their demands by the hundreds of thousands in 1907, those of Burgundy tended their vines.

Back to Burgundy

It was not always so. In the 1620s Dijon and Burgundy prospered enough to attract the interest of Cardinal Richelieu and Louis XIII. Their campaign to reimpose royal rule on the cities and grandees of provincial France was succeeding; many Protestant strongholds of Languedoc, for example, had lost their near-autonomy. Now their plans were turning to the possibility of gaining ground in the great war involving their neighbor states. That would take even more money than their domestic military campaigns.

From 1628 on, the king's chief minister sought to raise royal revenue from Burgundy in two connected ways: by demanding direct grants for particular expenses such as maintaining troops in the province, and by substituting nicely cooperative élections for the reluctant tax-gathering activity of the Estates. The élections had the additional attraction, from the crown's point of view, of permitting the sale of a number of expensive offices. On the first count, individual communities pleaded repeatedly that having lodged, fed, and transported troops out of their own resources, they should not also be taxed. The Estates (with the cooperation of the duke of Bellegarde, royal governor) put pressure on the communities. But they also tried to foil the demands for payment with legal maneuvers such as challenging the form of the request or the manner of its delivery.

On the question of élections, the Estates cheered Louis XIII and Richelieu when they came to Dijon on 31 January 1629, but sought thereafter to block the impending royal decree. In February 1630, for example, they were insisting on having the original of the decree instead of a certified copy. They were also calling for an assembly of Burgundy's cities to resist the installation of the élection. By that time, however, the decree's enactment looked imminent. Word spread that the new officials would impose a tax on wine.

Dijon's Mardi Gras celebration of 1630 took place in the midst of that contest between province and crown. On 19 February the civic militia dispersed crowds that had gathered to complain about the impending increase in taxes. Dijon's people elected winegrower Anatoire Changenet (or Champgenet) their King of Fools. He led the festival. At the end of the celebrations, according to an eighteenth-century account,

> on the evening of 28 February 1630 there began in the city of Dijon a sedition carried out by a troop of winegrowers who first smashed the main gate of a private house, then went away threatening to come back the following morning. On Friday, 1 March, easily and without resistance, they attacked the houses of many of the king's officers, including that of the parlement's first president, opened them up, burned the furniture inside, and continued until the parlement and the chief officials and burghers regained courage as they saw their own danger, and put down the rebels. They acted late, having long been able to foresee said sedition because they knew the plans of the rebels, and because they had received the warning of the previous night's attack.   (AMD I 118)

The "private house" stoned and smashed by the winegrowers belonged to a royal financial officer.

Changenet had worn his garish King of Fools costume into the fray. He and his subjects-for-a-day had marched to the offender's house with drums and sharpened vine-stakes. They had sung the *Lanturelu* as they came. The following morning they had sounded the tocsin in workers' neighborhoods and helped allies from outside the city to enter by climbing over the walls. Only then did the attacks on royal officers' houses begin. Later the crowd besieged the homes of city officials—many of whom owned the vineyards in which the city's winegrowers worked. The authorities did, indeed, have ample warning that popular contention was taking a violent turn.

The winegrowers and their working-class allies sustained their rebellion until about 8 March. Then the municipality, under dire threats from the king, began serious repression. Within a few days the winegrowers' leaders had fled, and the streets lay quiet.

After the fact, Dijon's officialdom apparently worried about their tardiness; as soon as troops had put down the insurrection, they took measures to punish the culprits and to seek pardon from the king. Richelieu and Louis XIII, however, knew a good opportunity when they saw one. The king would come to accept the city's apologies, announced the duke of Bellegarde, but only with these stipulations: (1) all the city's cannon would be locked up in the castle; (2) the city could not sound its bells at the king's entry; (3) the city could not send a delegation out to greet the king; (4) royal troops, not municipal guards, would man the city's gates; (5) all winegrowers would leave the city.

Equally important, the royal decree establishing an élection went into effect almost immediately. From that point on, the Estates sent delegations asking for cancellation of the edict. Their negotiations got them nowhere until May 1631, when they finally arranged to buy back the decree for 1.6 million livres—a tidy sum at a time when a bushel of wheat sold for a livre and a laborer earned half a livre for a day's work; 1.6 million bushels of wheat would pay a lot of troops.

Meanwhile royal agents sustained the pressure for revenues. On 17 August 1630 the duke of Bellegarde refused to divert troops on their way to Piedmont from the province; he threatened to have them live on the land. The Estates promptly agreed to borrow 20,000 livres for the expenses of troops. That was a standard seventeenth-century negotiation, the Lanturelu an extreme case of a very common routine. The city's bourgeoisie did what they could do to shrug off royal demands or pass them on to the poor.

Dijon's ordinary people felt the pressure of royal aggrandizement directly. They acted against it when they could. Royal finance, provincial administration, city security, winegrowers' everyday life, and popular insurrection converged in a single event. That connection of the largest processes transforming France and the collective action of ordinary people exposes the fallacy of treating "violence," "protest," or "disorder" as a world apart, as a phenomenon distinct from high politics, as a mere reaction to stress. There lies the most important teaching of popular collective action: it is not an epiphenomenon. It connects directly and solidly with the great political questions. By the actions that authorities call disorder, ordinary people fight injustice, challenge exploitation, and claim their own place in the structure of power.

A Note on the Evidence

Bibliography

Index

A NOTE ON
THE EVIDENCE

MOST OF THE WORK for this book consisted of good old-fashioned digging in archives, reading through contemporary periodicals and scholarly
literature, and reassembling the material by time and place. Some parts of
the preparation, however, took the old-fashioned procedures to obsessive
extremes. Well into the research, I established a number of files describing
"contentious gatherings"—occasions on which a number of people gathered in a publicly accessible place and made visible claims that, if realized,
would have affected the interests of someone outside their number.

My ideal was this: For each of the five regions in each year from 1600 to
1984, find at least two continuous sources that (whatever else they contained) regularly included information about contentious gatherings over a
substantial block of time. Give preference to sources covering France as a
whole, but check them against local and regional sources. Try to estimate
their bias and degree of incompleteness. Go through each source from beginning to end, abstracting all reports of contentious gatherings. Establish a
chronological file for each region, and collate multiple mentions of the same
event. Use those files as the central description of contention in the five
provinces. Use material from other sources and descriptions of events outside Anjou, Burgundy, Flanders, the Ile-de-France, and Languedoc as background material and as means of checking or amplifying the accounts in the
central sources.

I never hoped to have a complete or unbiased catalog of contentious
gatherings in the five provinces. (Applied to Great Britain as a whole, a similar procedure identifies about 1,000 events per year in the 1830s—and the
inventory is demonstrably incomplete.) Notwithstanding its bias and incompleteness, I hoped to draw from the compilation a reasonable picture of

variation in popular involvement in contention from period to period and region to region.

That was the ideal. In practice, I had to contend with incomplete sources and limited energy. In the period from about 1680 to 1720, for example, my chief continuous source is the correspondence of the intendants of Burgundy, Flanders, Maritime Flanders, Hainaut, Languedoc, and the generalities of Paris and Tours (Archives Nationales, series G^7). Reading and abstracting that correspondence took almost all of my time in French archives for several years. The intendants' correspondence contains a great deal of information about contention but omits small events and those handled exclusively by other authorities.

In going through G^7, I had an indispensable tool. From 1874 to 1896, Arthur de Boislisle published a fat three-volume edition of the contrôleur-générals' correspondence, drawn essentially from G^7 itself. Boislisle's edition summarized or quoted about a fifth of the letters that interested me. It also provided numerous cross-references and included material from the contrôleur's general papers that I did not examine. I photocopied every page of Boislisle containing a reference to Anjou, Burgundy, Flanders, the Ile-de-France, or Languedoc, as well as other items concerning fiscal policy, food supply, and similar matters bearing on my analysis. I took the photocopies with me to the archives and checked Boislisle's references as I went through the corresponding dossiers.

For the years 1680–1720, the only other remotely feasible national source with which I am familiar is the correspondence of the Ministry of War in the Archives Historiques de l'Armée, series A^1. Having spent plenty of effort reading military dispatches for the period 1630–1671, I could not find the time to go through that source for 1680–1720.

To be sure, I examined many other more fragmentary sources from the period in municipal archives, departmental archives, the Bibliothèque Nationale, and the Archives Nationales. Some of the events and background information in my files for 1680–1720 come from Clément's edition of Colbert's papers; from Depping's compilation of state papers; from the *Gazette de France;* from series AD^{xi}, H^1, K, and Z^{1a} of the Archives Nationales; from such sources as police commissioner la Reynie's papers at the Bibliothèque Nationale; from material in numerous municipal and departmental archives; and from contemporary articles, theses, and monographs, cited in the bibliography. Nevertheless, my picture of change and variation in popular contention in the period 1680–1720 relies disproportionately on the information intendants chose to send to the contrôleur général—their superior and patron—in Paris.

For the period from 1830 onward, in contrast, I drew a significant share of information from periodicals. I did not try to make a continuous inventory of contentious gatherings. I did try to prepare uniform descriptions of two sorts of events: collective violence—occasions on which fifty or more people gathered in a single formation, and someone seized or damaged persons or objects; and strikes.

For that purpose, my many collaborators and I went through every issue of two national newspapers from 1830 to 1860 and from 1930 to 1974, plus three randomly selected months per year from 1861 through 1929. We also transcribed every description of a strike or lockout in the *Statistique des Grèves et des Recours à la Conciliation* from 1890 to 1935, as well as those reported in a number of other monographs and serials. I went through thousands of reports on the nineteenth and twentieth centuries in various archives, consulted many periodicals, and read widely in the secondary literature. Each time one of these sources mentioned a contentious gathering, I pounced on it. But none of that work involved a long, continuous, homogeneous series of reports.

So the realization falls short of the ideal. My information on other contentious gatherings since 1830 is abundant, but less continuous and complete than the documentation on strikes and larger violent events. The list of manuscript and periodical sources provides the details.

Manuscripts

A series of numbers without qualification means I have gone through each item in the series. A series of numbers followed by "passim" means that I have neglected some items.

Archives Départementales de l'Ariège (Foix). 1 CC 6, 38, rebellions and conflicts over food supply, 1691-1777.

Archives Départementales de la Côte d'Or (Dijon). B² 335, Maréchaussée de Sémur, 1661-1788; C 80-81, food supply, 1694-1789; C 112-114, military affairs, 1697-1789; C 396-543 passim, police, 1667-1790; C 3079-3140 passim, registers of Estates, 1628-1695; L 373-486 passim, general police, 1790-Year VIII; M⁸ II 1-5, food supply, 1816-1848; 8 M 10-51 passim, surveillance, Year VIII-1922; SM 2996-3530 passim, surveillance, 1913-1938.

Archives Départementales de l'Eure-et-Loir (Chartres). M 193, 216, 799, political police, 1848-1851.

Archives Départementales de la Haute-Garonne (Toulouse). C 91, police, 1702-1787; C 303-316 passim, administration, 1740-1790; L 262-275 passim, surveillance, 1789-Year VIII; 4 M 49-50, surveillance, 1832-1833.

Archives Départementales de la Haute-Vienne (Limoges). 4 M 7-8, prefectoral reports,

1831–1910; 4 n 16–21, gendarmerie reports, 1824–1848; 4 M 105–128 passim, surveillance, 1830–1871; 15 M 93, strikes, 1853–1858.

Archives Départementales de l'Hérault (Montpellier). C 162, Roure rebellion, 1670; C 234, prosecution of Protestants, 1752; C 626 battle between grenadiers and municipal watch, 1690; C 1178–1319 passim, Royal Council dispatches to the intendant, 1712–1763; C 2875, grain trade, 1678–1734; C 6564–6889 passim, military government, 1730–1789.

Archives Départementales de l'Indre-et-Loire (Tours). C 97–744 passim, provincial administration, 1761–1789.

Archives Départementales de l'Isère (Grenoble). 52 M 27, political police, 1831–1847; 52 M 55, political police, 1874–1875; 52 M 61, political police, 1901–1906; 52 M 83–89 passim, political police, 1909–1934.

Archives Départementales de la Loire-Atlantique (Nantes). L 165–1508 passim, revolutionary administration, 1790–1799.

Archives Départementales de Maine-et-Loire (Angers). 1 B 203, judicial affairs, 1720–1736; 1 B 1112–1113, criminal affairs, 1713; II B unnumbered, elections to Estates General, 1788; VII B passim, fiscal affairs, 1742–1790; VIII B passim, seigneurial justice, eighteenth century; C 20–343 passim, provincial administration, 1695–1790; 1 L 202–1310 bis passim, 2 L 45–85 passim, 6 L 19–27 passim, 7 L 97–237 passim, 9 L 32–88 passim, 142 L 1, 147 L 1, 148 L 1, 151 L 1, 152 L 1, revolutionary administration and political control, 1789–1799; 20 M 2–50 passim, 21 M 14–217 passim, political surveillance, Year VIII–1896; 24 M 230, armed gatherings, 1815; 54 M 1, description of Maine-et-Loire, 1802; 59 M 4–34 passim, reports on economic activity, 1811–1880; 67 M 1 & 5, industry and trade, 1811.

Archives Départementales de la Mayenne (Laval). M 892–940 passim, surveillance, 1827–1870.

Archives Départementales de Morbihan (Vannes). M 680–681, political police, 1847–1853; M 780, political police, 1841–1846; M 1526, strikes, 1880–1904; M 2151, commerce and industry, 1876–1935; M 2517, political affairs, 1850–1890; U 655–673 passim, correspondence of prosecutor, 1830–1854.

Archives Départementales du Nord (Lille). C 3750, surveillance, 1790; C 11226–20104, passim, police, 1680–1790; Placards 8505–8509 passim, decrees and pamphlets, 1695–1793; M 619, 625, 626, strikes, 1862–1906.

Archives Départementales des Pyrénées-Orientales (Perpignan). C 1270–1273, police, 1757–1789; C 1366–1395 passim, police, 1669–1671; 3 M^1 50–161 passim, surveillance, 1819–1833.

Archives Départementales de la Seine (Paris; now incorporated in Archives de la Ville de Paris). VK^3 26–65 passim, compensation, Revolutions of 1830 and 1848.

Archives Départementales de la Somme (Amiens). Mf 80793–107027 passim, policing, 1815–1851; Mfv 80926, police, 1825–1840; Mh 80344, food supply, 1830–1834.

Archives Départementales de la Vendée (La Roche-sur-Yon). L 138–1727 passim, revolutionary administration, 1790–1799.

Archives Historiques de l'Armée (Vincennes). A^1 11–163 passim, correspondence of Ministry of War, 1600–1660; A^1 237–265, correspondence, 1669–1671; A^1 3834–3843, inventories of correspondence, 1630–1672; AA A, B, June Days of 1848; E^1–E^5 159, general correspondence, 1830–1849; F^1 1–55 passim, general correspondence, 1848–1851; G^8 1–190 passim, routine reports and general correspondence, 1851–1860;

X^d 385-386, Revolution of 1848; X^m 42, National Guard, 1848-1849; MR 1047-1303 passim, reconnaissances militaires, 1675-1851.

Archives Municipales, Amiens. BB 64, municipal deliberations, 1638-1642; FF 910-912, police, 1645-1649; FF 1275, 1289, police ordinances, 1601-1608; FF 1289, police ordinances, 1766.

Archives Municipales, Angers. BB 53-134 passim, municipal deliberations, 1607-1790; FF 7-37 passim, municipal police, 1784-1789; I 146, political policing, 1798-1913.

Archives Municipales, Dijon. B 337-426 passim, municipal deliberations, 1698-1790; I D, extracts from municipal deliberations, 1789-1800, I 37-119 passim, policing, 1524-1789.

Archives Municipales, Lille. 385-18098 passim, (especially 385-403, 412, 413, 701, 14336, 14337, 17470, 17763, 17883, 17887, 17888, 17896, 17973, 17982, 18008, 18023, 18040, 18098), general administration, 1599-1817.

Archives Municipales, Toulouse. 1 I 1-2 I 63 passim, policing, 1756-1858; BB 40-43, municipal deliberations, 1673-1697; BB 181-188 passim, provincial administration, 1631-1791; FF 613-614, police, 1656-1789; FF 692, affaire Combécaut, 1724; GG 784, religious affairs, 1789-1814.

Archives Nationales (Paris). AD^{xi} 25, communautés d'arts et métiers, 1676-1773; AD^{xi} 48, pamphlets from Anjou, 1789-1791; BB^3 167, surveillance, 1834-1835; BB^{18} 993-1816 passim, repression and surveillance, 1819-1890; BB^{30} 360-460 passim, surveillance, 1847-1860; C 936^B, surveillance, 1848; C 3019, industrial survey, 1872-1875; D IV 1-67 passim, revolutionary reorganization of communities 1790-91; D IV bis 9-97 passim, revolutionary creation of departments, 1790-91; D xxix 22-58 passim and D xxix bis 21-39 passim, revolutionary reorganization of the church; F^{1a} 548, "Etat des Sociétés Populaires de la République, acheté en juillet 1849," 1790-91; F^{1C} I* 39-F^{1C} III Maine-et-Loire 10 passim, departmental administration, 1790-1870; F^{1d} III 33-37, compensation for participants in Revolution of 1830; F^2 I 1201-1206, rural police, 1790-1834; F^7 2585-13268 passim, political police, 1782-1938; F^9 1154-1182 passim, military police, 1830-1851; F^{12} 12-4689 passim, trade and industry, 1670-1914; G^7 156-170, correspondence of intendant of Burgundy with contrôleur général, 1678-1740; G^7 257-268, correspondence of intendant of Flanders with contrôleur général, 1678-1738; G^7 269-275, correspondence of intendant of Maritime Flanders with contrôleur général, 1681-1715; G^7 294-336, correspondence of intendant of Languedoc with contrôleur général, 1669-1739; G^7 425-447, correspondence of intendant of Paris with contrôleur général, 1681-1732; G^7 518-531, correspondence of intendant of Tours with contrôleur général, 1678-1730; G^7 1630-1728 passim, correspondence on food supply; G^7 1902, memoirs by intendants, 1716-1728; G^7 1905, plans of Paris, eighteenth century; H^1 53-1588^{47} passim, provincial administration, 1600-1793; K 1002-1719 passim, administration of Paris, 1600-1791; M 669 memoirs on insurrections in the West, 1793; Y 10530, policing of Paris, 1786-1790; Z^{1a} 884-890, criminal procedures, 1663-1790.

Archives de la Préfecture de Police (Paris): Aa 366-434 passim, political police, 1830-1851.

Bibliothèque Nationale (Paris): Fonds Français [Fr] 4152, miscellaneous essays, 1645-1664; Fr 6595, police of First Empire; Fr 6680-6687, memoirs of Hardy, 1753-1789; Fr 6731, papers of prince of Condé, 1649-1659; Fr 6732, autograph memoirs of Louis XIV; Fr 6791, Paris police, 1708-1791; Fr 6828, papers of duke of Fitz-

James, 1763-1764; Fr 6877-6879, papers of President Lamoignon, 1762-1782; Fr 6880-6907 passim, papers of Michel Le Tellier, 1640-1678; Fr 8118, deliberations of Paris Conseil de Police, 1666-1668; Fr 8121-8125 passim, policing of Paris, 1666-1721; Fr 10273-10274, anonymous journal on events of 1648-1651; Fr 10281, journal of Jean Brivat, 1715-1723; Fr 10285-10291, journal of Barbier, 1718-1763; Fr 10329, autograph memoirs of Louis XIV; Fr 11347, memoirs on trade, eighteenth century; Fr 11356, minutes of Paris Police assemblies, 1728-1740; Fr 11357-11360, Paris police reports, 1759-1777; Fr 11870, description of Saumur, c. 1723; Fr 12498, songs, satires, and epigrams, c. 1700; Fr 13679-13690, anonymous journal, 1711-1722; Fr 13713, anonymous journal, 1789; Fr 15596, miscellaneous papers on seventeenth-century rebellions; Fr 17355-18938 passim, papers of Chancelier Séguier, 1633-1660; Fr 21545-21722 passim, papers of Delamare, c. 1680-1720; Fr 22200, memoirs on provinces, 1697-1698; Fr 22387, description of Paris, 1684; Nouvelles Acquisitions Françaises [NA] 3573, police papers from Consulate and Empire; NA 5222, miscellaneous historical essays, 1636-1642; NA 5247-5249, papers of la Reynie, 1689-1698; NA 13003, journal of Godard, 1789-1817; Collection Languedoc-Bénédictins 2, descriptions of Languedoc, eighteenth century; Collection Vexin 64, policing, 1725-1790; Vexin 65, correspondence with parlement, 1778-1790; Collection Dupuy 467, papers on Burgundy, 1636; Dupuy 754, papers, 1649-1650; Mélanges Colbert 101-172 bis, papers of Colbert, 1649-1675; Cinq Cents de Colbert 3, letters and memoirs on French history, 1648-1665; Cinq Cents 103, Poitou insurrection, 1643; Cinq Cents 219, seventeenth-century rebellions; Collection Joly de Fleury [JF] 1074, policing, 1674-1776; JF 1103, crowds and riots in Paris, 1788-1789; JF 1159-1165, conflicts over food, 1775-1787.

Contemporary Periodicals and Government Publications

Almanache de Gotha. 1844, 1847, 1849-1854, 1856-1858, 1860-1870, 1872, 1874-1877, 1891-1901.

L'Année Politique. 1874-1960.

L'Année Politique Française et Etrangère. 1925-1932.

Annuaire des Deux Mondes. 1850-1932.

Annuaire Diplomatique. 1852, 1871.

Annuaire de l'Economie Politique. 1844, 1869, 1883, 1889.

Annuaire Historique. 1825-1861.

Annuaire Statistique de la France. 1872-1982.

Annuaire des Syndicats Professionels, Industriels, Commerciaux, et Agricoles. 1889-1914.

Le Combat. All issues, 1941-1947.

Le Constitutionnel. All issues, 1830-1835, 1848-1860; selected months, 1861-1873.

Le Droit. All issues, 1836-1841.

La Gazette de France. All issues, 1631-1651.

La Gazette des Tribunaux. All issues, 1830.

L'Humanité. Selected months, 1920-1929; all issues, 1930-1974; selected issues, 1975-1984.

International Labor Organization Year Book of Labor Statistics. 1951-52, 1957, 1966, 1969.

Le Journal des Débats. All issues, 1830; selected months, 1874-1915.

Le Mercure de France. All issues, 1721-1731.

Le Mercure François. All issues, 1605-1644.

Le Mercure Galant. Selected issues, 1679–1715.

Le Monde. All issues, 1946–1974; selected issues, 1975–1984.

Le Moniteur Universel. All issues, 1830–1860.

La Muze Historique. All issues, 1650–1665. Edited by M. Ravenel and Ed. V. de la Pelouze. 4 vols. Paris: Janet, 1857.

Revue Française du Travail. 1945–1967. Paris: Ministère du Travail. Statistics on strike activity.

Le Siècle. All issues, 1848.

Statistique Annuelle. 1885–1890. Paris: Imprimerie Nationale.

Statistique des Grèves et des Recours à la Conciliation. 1893–1935. Paris: Imprimerie Nationale. Strike figures for 1890–1892 come from France, Direction du Travail, *Notices et Comptes Rendus,* nos. 3 (1891) and 7 (1893).

Le Temps. All issues, three randomly selected months per year, 1861–1929; all issues, 1930–1942.

In addition to the annual government publications included in the list above, I have made extensive use of the censuses from 1801 to 1982, published with various titles at varying intervals until 1936 by the Bureau de la Statistique Générale and since 1946 by the Institut National de la Statistique et des Etudes Economiques. For information on wages I used the bulletins issued yearly by the Ministère du Travail (BMT) or its analogue for 1894–1939, especially those for 1904 (in the 1906 issue), 1916, 1929, and 1931. The same bulletins provided information on strikes after 1914; although they provide much less information than the *Statistique des Grèves,* the official statistics in the BMT for 1936 to 1938 are the only ones available. For criminal statistics, I have gone to the Ministère de la Justice, *Compte Général de l'Administration de la Justice Criminelle pendant l'Année . . .* (generally an annual, and sometimes published as part of the *Compte Général de l'Administration de la Justice Civile et Commerciale et de la Justice Criminelle*) from 1831 to 1961.

BIBLIOGRAPHY

Adam, Gérard, and Jean-Daniel Reynaud. 1978. *Conflits du travail et changement social.* Paris: Presses Universitaires de France.

Ado, A. V. 1971. *Krest'ianskoe dvijhenie vo frantsii vo vremiia velikoi burjhuaznoi revoliutsii kontsa XVIII veka* [The peasant movement in France in the time of the great French bourgeois revolution at the end of the eighteenth century]. Moscow: Izdatel'stvo Moskovskovo Universiteta.

Aguet, Jean-Pierre. 1954. *Contribution à l'étude du mouvement ouvrier français. Les grèves sous la Monarchie de Juillet.* Geneva: Droz.

Agulhon, Maurice. 1950. "L'opinion politique dans une commune de banlieue sous la Troisième République. Bobigny de 1850 à 1914." In Pierre George, M.

Agulhon, L. A. Lavandeyra, N. D. Elhai, and R. Schaeffer, eds., *Etudes sur la banlieue de Paris: Essais méthodologiques.* Cahiers de la Fondation Nationale des Sciences Politiques, 12. Paris: Colin.

——— 1970. *La république au village. Les populations du Var de la Révolution à la Seconde République.* Paris: Plon.

——— 1977. "Fête spontanée et fête organisée à Paris, en 1848." In *Les Fêtes de la Révolution. Colloque de Clermont-Ferrand (juin 1974)*, edited by Jean Ehrard and Paul Viallaneix. Paris: Société des Etudes Robespierristes.

Alatri, Paolo. 1977. *Parlamenti e lotta politica nella Francia dell'700.* Bari: Laterza.

Alberoni, Francesco. 1968. *Statu nascenti.* Bologna: Il Mulino.

d'Aldéguier, J. B. A. 1830–1835. *Histoire de la ville de Toulouse depuis la conquête des romains jusqu'à nos jours.* 4 vols. Toulouse: Paya.

Aminzade, Ronald. 1981. *Class, Politics, and Early Industrial Capitalism: A Study of Mid-Nineteenth-Century Toulouse, France.* Albany: State University of New York Press.

Amiot, Michel, et al. 1968. *La violence dans le monde actuel.* Paris: Desclée de Brouwer for Centre d'Etudes de la Civilisation Contemporaine.

Antoine, Michel. 1970. *Le Conseil du Roi sous le règne de Louis XV.* Geneva: Droz.

Appolis, Emile. 1945. "Les biens communaux en Languedoc au XVIIIe siècle." In *Assemblée Générale de la Commission Centrale et des Comités Départementaux, 1939, 2.* Paris: Tepac.

Aragon, J.-M. 1972. "Un village de Gascogne toulousaine au XVIIIe siècle: Leguévin." *Annales du Midi* 84: 439–458.

Ardant, Gabriel. 1965. *Théorie sociologique de l'impôt*. 2 vols. Paris: SEVPEN.

———— 1975. "Financial Policy and Economic Infrastructure of Modern States and Nations." In *The Formation of National States in Western Europe*, edited by Charles Tilly. Princeton: Princeton University Press.

Marquis d'Argenson. 1859–1867. *Journal et mémoires du marquis d'Argenson*, edited by E. J. F. Rathéry. 9 vols. Paris: Renouard.

Armengaud, André. 1954. "La question du blé dans la Haute-Garonne au milieu du XIXe siècle." *Bibliothèque de la Révolution de 1848* 16: 109–123.

———— 1961. *Les populations de l'Est-Aquitain au début de l'époque contemporaine*. Paris: Mouton.

Armogathe, Jean-Robert, and Philippe Joutard. 1972. "Bâville et la guerre des Camisards." *Revue d'Histoire Moderne et Contemporaine* 19: 44–67.

Aron, Robert. 1954. *Histoire de Vichy*. 2 vols. Paris: Fayard.

———— 1959. *Histoire de la libération de la France, juin 1944–mai 1945*. Paris: Fayard.

Asher, Eugene L. 1960. *The Resistance to the Maritime Classes: The Survival of Feudalism in the France of Colbert*. Berkeley: University of California Press.

Aubert, G. 1923. "Le problème des subsistances et le Maximum à Douai (1792–1794)." *Revue du Nord* 9: 233–254.

Audiat, Pierre. 1946. *Paris pendant la guerre (juin 1940–aout 1944)*. Paris: Hachette.

Augustin, Jean-Marie. 1972. "Les capitouls, juges des causes criminelles et de la police à la fin de l'Ancien Régime." *Annales du Midi* 84: 183–211.

Auvray, E. 1945. "L'administration municipale de Dourdan (Seine-et-Oise) et les boulangers, de 1788 à l'an IV." *Assemblée Générale de la Commission Centrale et des Comités Départementaux, 1939*, vol. 2. Paris: Tepac.

Babelon, Jean-Pierre. 1965. *Demeures parisiennes sous Henri IV et Louis XIII*. Paris: Editions du Temps.

Babou, Didier; Pierre Davy; Jean-Pierre François; Alain Imhof; Michel Tarrius; and Jean-Pierre Trail. 1981. *Myrys, usine occupée*. Villelongue-d'Aude: Atelier du Gué.

Badie, Bertrand. 1972. "Les grèves du Front Populaire aux usines Renault." *Le Mouvement Social* 81: 69–109.

———— 1976. *Pour une approche fonctionnaliste du parti communiste français. Stratégie de la grève*. Paris: Presses de la Fondation Nationale des Sciences Politiques.

Badie, Bertrand, and Pierre Birnbaum. 1979. *Sociologie de l'état*. Paris: Bernard Grasset.

Baker, Robert P. 1967. "Socialism in the Nord, 1880–1914: A Regional View of the French Socialist Movement." *International Review of Social History* 12: 357–389.

Barbier, Edmond-Jean-François. 1847–1856. *Journal d'un bourgeois de Paris sous le règne de Louis XV*. 4 vols. Paris: Renouard.

Barennes, Jean. 1913. "Un document sur les troubles survenus en 1789 à Aire-sur-la-Lys." *Revue du Nord* 4: 236–238.

Barral, Pierre. 1968. *Les agrariens français de Meline à Pisani*. Cahiers de la Fondation Nationale des Sciences Politiques, 164. Paris: Colin.

Barrière-Flavy, Casimir. 1926. *La chronique criminelle d'une grande province sous Louis XIV*. Paris: Editions Occitania.

Bastier, Jean. 1975. *La féodalité au siècle des Lumières dans la région de Toulouse (1730–1798)*. Commission d'Histoire Economique et Sociale de la Révolution Française, Mémoires et Documents, 30. Paris: Bibliothèque Nationale.

Baudrillart, H. 1888. *Les populations agricoles de la France.* Paris: Gillaumin.

Baulant, Micheline. 1968. "Le prix des grains à Paris de 1431 à 1788." *Annales: Economies, Sociétés, Civilisations* 23: 520–540.

——— 1971. "Le salaire des ouvriers du bâtiment à Paris, de 1400 à 1726." *Annales: Economies, Sociétés, Civilisations* 26: 463–483.

Baxter, Douglas Clark. 1976. *Servants of the Sword: Intendants of the Army, 1630–70.* Urbana: University of Illinois Press.

Bazin, A. 1838. *Histoire de France sous Louis XIII.* 4 vols. Paris: Chamerot.

Beaubernard, R. 1981. *Montceau-les-Mines. Un "laboratoire social" au XIXe siècle.* Avallon: Civry.

Beaujeu-Garner, Jacqueline. 1976. *La population française.* Rev. ed. Paris: Colin.

Beaujot, E. 1939–1943. "Le département du Nord sous la Restauration. Rapport du préfet de Villeneuve-Bargemont en 1828." *Revue du Nord* 25: 243–277; 26: 21–45.

Beik, William H. 1974a. "Magistrates and Popular Uprisings in France before the Fronde: The Case of Toulouse." *Journal of Modern History* 46: 583–608.

——— 1974b. "Two Intendants Face Popular Revolt: Social Unrest and the Structure of Absolutism in 1645." *Canadian Journal of History* 9: 243–262.

Beloff, Max. 1959. "The Sixth of February." In *The Decline of The Third Republic,* edited by James Joll. London: Chatto & Windus.

Bercé, Yves-Marie. 1964. "De la criminalité aux troubles sociaux: La noblesse rurale du sud-ouest de la France sous Louis XIII." *Annales du Midi* 76: 41–60.

——— 1974a. *Croquants et Nu-Pieds. Les soulèvements paysans en France du XVIe au XIXe siècle.* Paris: Gallimard/Julliard.

——— 1974b. *Histoire des Croquants. Etude des soulèvements populaires au XVIIe siècle dans le sud-ouest de la France.* 2 vols. Paris: Droz.

Berger, Patrice. 1978. "French Administration in the Famine of 1693." *European Studies Review* 8: 101–128.

Birnbaum, Pierre. 1982. *La logique de l'état.* Paris: Fayard.

Blanchard, Raoul. 1906. *La Flandre. Etude géographique de la plaine flamande en France, Belgique, et Hollande.* Lille: Danel.

Blin, Ernest. 1945. "Le prix du blé à Avallon, de 1756 à 1790." *Assemblée Générale de la Commission Centrale et des Comités Départementaux, 1939,* vol. 2. Paris: Tepac.

——— 1968. "Notes sur une disette de grains en Bourgogne (1770–1771)." *93e Congrès National des Sociétés Savantes, Tours, 1968. Histoire Moderne* 1: 245–266.

——— 1976. "La face administrative d'une crise frumentaire en Bourgogne (1747–1749)." *Annales de Bourgogne* 48: 5–43.

Bloch, Marc. 1952. *Les caractères originaux de l'histoire rurale française.* Paris: Colin.

Boislisle, Arthur de. 1873. *Note sur les mémoires dressés par les intendants en 1697 pour l'instruction du duc de Bourgogne.* Paris: Lahure.

———, ed. 1874–1896. *Correspondance des contrôleurs généraux des finances avec les intendants des provinces.* 3 vols. Paris: Imprimerie Nationale.

———, ed. 1881. *Mémoires des intendants sur l'état des généralités dressés pour l'instruction du duc de Bourgogne.* Paris: Lahure.

——— 1903. "Le grand hiver et la disette de 1709." *Revue des Questions Historiques,* n.s. 29: 442–509 and 30: 486–542.

Bois, Paul. 1954. "Dans l'ouest, politique et enseignement primaire." *Annales: Economies, Sociétés, Civilisations* 9: 356–367.

——— 1960. *Paysans de l'ouest.* Le Mans: Imprimerie Vilaire.

———— 1961. "Réflexions sur les survivances de la Révolution dans l'ouest." *Annales Historiques de la Révolution Française* 33: 177–186.

———— 1981. "Aperçu sur les causes des insurrections de l'ouest à l'époque révolutionnaire." In *Vendée-Chouannerie*, edited by J.-C. Martin. Nantes: Reflets du Passé.

Bonnefous, Edouard, and Georges Bonnefous. 1956–1967. *Histoire politique de la Troisième République*. 7 vols. Paris: Presses Universitaires de France.

Bonney, Richard. 1978a. "The French Civil War, 1649–53." *European Studies Review* 8: 71–100.

———— 1978b. *Political Change under Richelieu and Mazarin, 1624–1661*. Oxford: Oxford University Press.

———— 1981. *The King's Debts: Finance and Politics in France, 1589–1661*. Oxford: Clarendon Press.

Bonnier, Jean-Claude. 1980. "Esquisse d'une évolution sociale: Roubaix sous le Second Empire (1856–1873)." *Revue du Nord* 62: 619–636.

Bordes, Maurice. 1949. *Deux mouvements populaires en Gascogne au milieu de XVIIIe siècle*. Auch: Cocharaux.

Bosher, John. 1968. "French Administration and Public Finance in Their European Setting." In *The New Cambridge Modern History*. Vol. 8: *The American and French Revolutions, 1763–93*, edited by A. Goodwin. Cambridge: Cambridge University Press.

———— 1970. *French Finances, 1770–1795: From Business to Bureaucracy*. Cambridge: Cambridge University Press.

Bouju, Paul M.; Georges Dupeux; Claude Gérard; Alain Lancelot; Jean-Alain Lesourd; and René Rémond. *Atlas historique de la France contemporaine, 1800–1965*. Collection U. Paris: Colin.

Bourderon, H. 1953. "Recherches sur les mouvements populaires dans la généralité de Languedoc au XVIIIe siècle." *Actes du 78e Congrès des Sociétés Savantes, Toulouse*, 103–118.

———— 1954. "La lutte contre la vie chère dans la généralité de Languedoc au XVIIIe siècle." *Annales du Midi* 25–28: 155–170.

Bourdé, Guy. 1977. *La défaite du Front Populaire*. Paris: Maspéro.

Boutier, Jean. 1979. "Jacqueries en pays croquant. Les révoltes paysannes en Aquitaine (décembre 1789–mars 1790)." *Annales: Economies, Sociétés, Civilisations* 34: 760–786.

Bouvier, Jean. 1964. "Mouvement ouvrier et conjonctures économiques." *Le Mouvement Social* 48: 3–28.

Braure, Maurice. 1932. *Lille et la Flandre wallonne au XVIIIe siècle*. 2 vols. Lille: Raoust.

Brécy, Robert. 1969. *La grève générale en France*. Paris: Etudes et Documentation Internationales.

Brelot, J. 1932. *La vie politique en Côte-d'Or sous le Directoire*. La Révolution en Cote-d'Or, n.s. 8. Dijon: Rebourseau. [La Révolution en Côte d'Or sometimes functions like a series, as here, sometimes like a periodical, as in Delaby 1926, using consecutive volume numbers throughout.]

Briggs, Robin. 1977. *Early Modern France, 1560–1715*. Oxford: Oxford University Press.

B[rocher], Victorine. 1976. *Souvenirs d'une morte vivante*. Paris: Maspéro.

Bron, Jean. 1968–1970. *Histoire du mouvement ouvrier français*. 2 vols. Paris: Editions Ouvrières.

Brower, Daniel R. 1968. *The New Jacobins: The French Communist Party and the Popular Front*. Ithaca: Cornell University Press.

Bruchet, Max. 1925. "Le coup d'état de 1851 dans le Nord." *Revue du Nord* 11: 81–113.

Brunet, Jean-Paul. 1980. *Saint-Denis, la ville rouge. Socialisme et communisme en banlieue ouvrière, 1890-1939.* Paris: Hachette.

Brunet, Roger. 1965. *Les campagnes toulousaines, étude géographique.* Toulouse: Boisseau.

Brustein, William. 1983. "French Political Regionalism, 1849-1978. In *The Microfoundations of Macrosociology,* edited by Michael Hechter. Philadelphia: Temple University Press.

Bruyelle, Pierre. 1976. *Lille et sa communauté urbaine.* Notes et Etudes Documentaires, 4297, 4298, and 4299. Paris: Documentation Française.

Caillard, Michel. 1963. "Recherches sur les soulèvements populaires en Basse-Normandie (1620-1640) et spécialement sur la révolte des Nu-Pieds." In *A travers la Normandie des XVIIe et XVIIIe siècles,* edited by Michel Caillard, Marcel Duval, Philippe Guillot, and Mary Claude Gricourt. Caen: Annales de Normandie.

Caire, Guy. 1978. *La grève ouvrière.* Paris: Editions Sociales.

Cameron, Iain A. 1977. "The Police of Eighteenth-Century France." *European Studies Review* 7: 47-75.

Canfora-Argadona, Elsie, and Roger-H. Guerrand. 1976. *La répartition de la population, des conditions de logement des classes ouvrières à Paris au 19e siècle.* Paris: Centre de Sociologie Urbaine.

Cantaloube, C. 1951. *La réforme en France, vue d'un village cévenol.* Paris: Editions du Cerf.

Carré, Jean-Jacques; Paul Dubois; and Edmond Malinvaud. *La croissance française. Un essai d'analyse économique causale de l'après-guerre.* Paris: Seuil.

Castan, Nicole. 1980a. *Les criminels de Languedoc. Les exigences d'ordre et les voies du ressentiment dans une société pré-révolutionnaire (1750-1790).* Association des Publications de l'Université de Toulouse-Le Mirail, series A, 47. Toulouse.

——— 1980b. *Justice et répression en Languedoc à l'époque des Lumières.* Paris: Flammarion.

——— 1981 "Contentieux social et utilisation variable du charivari à la fin de l'Ancien Régime en Languedoc." In *Le Charivari,* edited by Jacques Le Goff and Jean-Claude Schmitt. Paris: Ecole des Hautes Etudes en Sciences Sociales and Mouton.

Castan, Yves. 1974. *Honnêteté et relations sociales en Languedoc (1715-1780).* Paris: Plon.

Castells, Manuel; Eddy Cherki; Francis Godard; and Dominique Mehl. 1974. *Sociologie des mouvements sociaux urbains. Enquête sur la région parisienne.* 2 vols. Paris: Centre d'Etude des Mouvements Sociaux, Ecole des Hautes Etudes en Sciences Sociales.

Cazals, Rémy. 1978. *Avec les ouvriers de Mazamet dans la grève et l'action quotidienne, 1909-1914.* Paris: Maspéro.

——— 1983. *Les révolutions industrielles à Mazamet, 1750-1900.* Paris: La Découverte/Maspéro; Toulouse: Privat.

Cella, G. P., ed. 1979. *Il movimento degli scioperi nel XX secolo.* Bologna: Il Mulino.

Centre d'Etudes de Lille. 1956. "Aspects industriels de la crise: Le département du Nord." In *Aspects de la crise et de la dépression de l'économie française au milieu du XIXe siècle, 1846-1851,* edited by Ernest Labrousse. Bibliothèque de la Révolution de 1848, 19. La Roche-sur-Yon: Imprimerie Centrale de l'Ouest.

Chaleur, Andrée. 1964. "Le rôle des traitants dans l'administration financière de la France de 1643 à 1653." *XVIIe Siècle* 65: 16-49.

Challamel, Augustin. 1879. *Les revenants de la Place de Grève.* Paris: Lemerre.

Chanut, A. 1956. "La crise économique à Tourcoing (1846-1850)." *Revue du Nord* 38: 77-105.

Châtelain, Abel. 1956. "Evolution des densités de population en Anjou (1806-1936)." *Revue de Géographie de Lyon* 31: 43-60.

Chaunu, Pierre, and Richard Gascon. 1977. *L'etat et la ville. Histoire économique et sociale de la France,* edited by Fernand Braudel & Ernest Labrousse. Paris: Presses Universitaires de France.

Chesnais, Jean-Claude. 1976. *Les morts violentes en France depuis 1826. Comparaisons internationales.* Institut National d'Etudes Démographiques, Travaux, et Documents, Cahier 75. Paris: Presses Universitaires de France.

——— 1981. *Histoire de la violence en Occident de 1800 à nos jours.* Paris: Laffont.

Chevrier, Monique. 1974. *Structures sociales des quartiers de Grève, St. Avoye, la Verrerie, et Saint-Antoine, 1738-1740.* Mémoire de maîtrise, University of Paris. Paris: Hachette. Microfiche.

Chirot, Daniel. 1977. *Social Change in the Twentieth Century.* New York: Harcourt Brace Jovanovich.

Cholvy, Gérard. 1974. "Recrutement militaire et mentalités languedociennes au XIXe siècle. Essai d'interprétation." In Centre d'Histoire Militaire et d'Etudes de Défense Nationale, *Recrutement, mentalités, sociétés. Colloque international d'histoire militaire.* Montpellier: Université Paul Valéry.

Chombart de Lauwe, Paul-Henry. 1965. *Paris. Essais de sociologie, 1952-1964.* Paris: Editions Ouvrières.

Christman, William J.; William R. Kelly; and Omer R. Galle. 1981. "Comparative Perspectives on Industrial Conflict." In *Conflict and Change.* Vol. 4 of *Research in Social Movements,* edited by Louis Kriesberg. Westport, Conn.: JAI.

Christophe, Robert. 1960. *Les Sanson. Bourreaux de père en fils pendant deux siècles.* Paris: Arthème Fayard.

Clamagéran, J.-J. 1867-1876. *Histoire de l'impôt en France.* 3 vols. Paris: Guillaumin.

Claverie, Elisabeth. 1979. " 'L'honneur': Une société de défis au XIXe siècle." *Annales: Economies, Sociétés, Civilisations* 34: 744-759.

Clément, Pierre, ed. 1861-1869. *Lettres, instructions, et mémoires de Colbert.* 6 vols. Paris: Imprimerie Nationale.

——— 1866. *La police sous Louis XIV.* Paris: Didier.

Cléray, Edmond. 1932. *L'affaire Favras.* Paris: Editions des Portiques.

Clout, Hugh D. 1977a. "Agricultural Changes in the Eighteenth and Nineteenth Centuries." In *Themes in the Historical Geography of France,* edited by Hugh D. Clout. New York: Academic.

——— 1977b. "Industrial Development in the Eighteenth and Nineteenth Centuries." In *Themes in the Historical Geography of France,* edited by Hugh D. Clout. New York: Academic.

Cobb, Richard. 1965. *Terreur et subsistances, 1793-1795.* Paris: Clavreuil.

Cochin, Augustin. 1921. *Les sociétés de pensée et la démocratie.* Paris: Plon-Nourrit.

Codaccioni, Félix-Paul. 1976. *De l'inégalité sociale dans une grande ville industrielle. Le drame de Lille de 1850 à 1914.* Lille: Université de Lille III.

Collot, Jean. 1934-1935. "L'affaire Reveillon." *Revue des Questions Historiques* 121: 35-55; 122: 239-254.

Combe, Paul. 1956. *Niveau de vie et progrès technique en France (1860-1939). Contribution à l'étude de l'économie française contemporaine. Postface (1939-1949).* Paris: Presses Universitaires de France.

Communay, A., ed. 1893. *Audijos. La Gabelle en Gascogne.* Paris: Champion.

Constant, Jean-Marie. 1974. *Structures sociales des quartiers de Saint-Avoie, du Marais, de Saint-Antoine, et de la Grève, à l'époque du système de Law.* Mémoire de maîtrise, University of Paris. Paris: Hachette. Microfiche.

Convert, Bernard; Pierre Jakubowski; and Michel Pinet. 1976. "Mobilité professionnelle, mobilité spatiale, et restructuration économique. Le cas du bassin minier Nord-Pas-de-Calais." *La Vie Urbaine,* nos. 52–54: 115–124.

Coppolani, Jean. 1963. *Toulouse au XXe siècle.* Toulouse: Privat.

Coquelle, P. 1908. "La sédition de Montpellier en 1645, d'après les documents inédits des Archives des Affaires Etrangères." *Annales du Midi* 20: 66–78.

Cordani, Yves. 1974. *Structures sociales des quartiers de la Grève, Saint-Avoie, de la Verrerie, et de Saint-Antoine, 1660–1662.* Mémoire de maîtrise, University of Paris. Paris: Hachette. Microfiche.

Courthéoux, Jean-Paul. 1957. "Naissance d'une conscience de classe dans le prolétariat textile du Nord, 1830–1870." *Revue Economique* 8: 114–139.

Crapet, A. 1920. "La vie à Lille, de 1667 à 1789, d'après le cours de M. de Saint-Léger." *Revue du Nord* 6: 126–322.

Croquez, Albert. 1912. *La Flandre wallonne et les pays de l'intendance de Lille sous Louis XIV.* Paris: Champion.

Crozier, Michel. 1970. *La société bloquée.* Paris: Seuil.

Crubellier, Maurice. 1974. *Histoire culturelle de la France, XIXe–XXe siècle.* Paris: Colin.

Dakin, D. 1968. "The Breakdown of the Old Regime in France." In *The New Cambridge Modern History.* Vol. 8: *The American and French Revolutions,* edited by A. Goodwin. Cambridge: Cambridge University Press.

Dalotel, Alain; Alain Faure; and Jean-Claude Freiermuth. 1980. *Aux origines de la Commune. Le mouvement des réunions publiques à Paris, 1868–1870.* Paris: Maspéro.

Dansette, J. L., and J. A. Roy. 1955–1958. "Origines et évolution d'une bourgeoisie. Le patronat textile du bassin lillois (1789–1914)." *Revue du Nord* 37: 199–216; 39: 21–42; 40: 49–69; 41: 23–38.

Daumard, Adeline. 1963. *La bourgeoisie parisienne de 1815 à 1848.* Paris: SEVPEN.

———— 1975. "Le peuple dans la société française à l'époque romantique." *Romantisme* 9: 21–28.

Daumard, Adeline, ed. with Felix Codaccioni; Georges Dupeux; Jacqueline Herpin; Jacques Godechot; and Jean Sentou. 1973. *Les fortunes françaises au XIXe siècle. Enquête sur la répartition et la composition des capitaux privés à Paris, Lyon, Lille, Bordeaux, et Toulouse d'après l'enregistrement des déclarations de succession.* Paris: Mouton.

Daumas, Maurice. 1982. "La géographie industrielle de Paris au XIXe siècle." In *Villes en mutation XIXe–XXe siècles. 10e Colloque International.* Brussels: Crédit Communal de Belgique.

Daumas, Maurice; Caroline Dufour; Claudine Fontanon; Gérard Jigaudon; Dominique Larroque; and Jacques Payen. *Evolution de la géographie industrielle de Paris et sa proche banlieue au XIXe siècle.* 3 vols. Paris: Centre de Documentation d'Histoire des Techniques.

Davies, C. S. L. 1973. "Peasant Revolt in France and England: A Comparison." *Agricultural History Review* 21: 122–134.

Dawson, Philip. 1972. *Provincial Magistrates and Revolutionary Politics in France, 1789–1795.* Cambridge: Harvard University Press.

Débidour, Antonin. 1877. *La Fronde angevine. Tableau de la vie municipale au XVIIe siècle.* Paris: Thorin; Angers: Lachèse, Belleuvre & Dolbeau.

Delaby, Raymond. 1926. "La survivance des dimes et des droits féodaux en Côte-d'Or pendant la Révolution." *La Révolution en Côte d'Or,* n.s. 2: 21–35.

Delale, Alain, and Gilles Ragache. 1978. *La France de 68.* Paris: Seuil.

Delefortrie, Nicole, and Janine Morice. 1959. *Les revenus départementaux en 1864 et en 1954.* Recherches sur l'Economie Française, 1. Paris: Colin.

Delsalle, Paul. 1982. "Les tisserands à domicile de la région de Roubaix (France). Relations professionnelles et conflits du travail au XIXe siècle." In *La protoindustrialisation: Théorie et réalité. Rapports,* edited by Pierre Deyon and Franklin Mendels. Lille: Université des Arts, Lettres, et Sciences Humaines.

Dent, Julian. 1973. *Crisis in Finance: Crown, Financiers, and Society in Seventeenth-Century France.* Newton Abbot: David & Charles.

Depping, G. B., ed. 1850–1855. *Correspondance administrative sous le règne de Louis XIV.* 4 vols. Paris: Imprimerie Nationale.

Derode, Victor. 1975. *Histoire de Lille et de la Flandre wallonne.* 4 vols. Marseille: Laffite Reprints. First published in 1848–1877.

Deschuytter, Joseph. 1959–1961. *L'esprit public et son évolution dans le Nord de 1791 au lendemain de Thermidor an II.* 2 vols. Gap: Imprimerie Louis-Jean.

———— 1964. "Cambrai sous la Révolution." *Revue du Nord* 46: 525–543.

Dessert, Daniel. 1984. *Argent, pouvoir, et société au Grand Siècle.* Paris: Fayard.

Dessert, Daniel, and Jean-Louis Journet. 1975. "Le lobby Colbert: Un royaume ou une affaire de famille?" *Annales: Economies, Sociétés, Civilisations* 30: 1303–1336.

Devic, Claude, and J. Vaissète. 1872–1896. *Histoire générale de Languedoc.* 17 vols. Toulouse: Privat.

Deyon, Pierre. 1964. "A propos des rapports entre la noblesse française et la monarchie absolue pendant la première moitié du XVIIe siècle." *Revue Historique* 88: 341–356.

———— 1967. *Amiens capitale provinciale.* Paris: Mouton.

———— 1979. "La diffusion rurale des industries textiles en Flandre française à la fin de l'Ancien Régime et au début du XIXe siècle." *Revue du Nord* 61: 83–96.

———— 1981. "Un modèle à l'épreuve, le développement industriel de Roubaix de 1762 à la fin du XIXe siècle." *Revue du Nord* 63: 59–66.

Deyon, Pierre, and Jean-Pierre Hirsch. 1980. "Entreprise et association dans l'arrondissement de Lille 1830–1862." *Revue du Nord* 62: 603–618.

D'Hollander, P. 1970. "La composition sociale de l'échevinage lillois sous la domination française, 1667–1789." *Revue du Nord* 52: 5–15.

Dieudonné, Christophe. 1804. *Statistique du département du Nord.* 3 vols. Douai: Marlier.

Diné, Henri. 1976. "Quelques paniques postérieures à 'la grande peur' de 1789." *Annales de Bourgogne* 48: 44–51.

Dion, Roger. 1934. *Le val de Loire. Etude de géographie régionale.* Tours: Arrault.

Druot, H., and J. Calmette. 1928. *Histoire de Bourgogne.* Paris: Boivin.

Dubois, Pierre. 1970. "Nouvelles pratiques de mobilisation dans la classe ouvrière." *Sociologie du Travail* 12: 338–344.

———— 1971. "La séquestration." *Sociologie du Travail* 15: 410–427.

———— 1978. "New Forms of Industrial Conflict, 1960–1974." In *The Resurgence of Class Conflict in Western Europe since 1968,* edited by Colin Crouch and Alessandro Pizzorno. Vol. 2. London: Macmillan.

Dubois, Pierre; Renaud Dulong; Claude Durand; Sabine Erbès-Seguin; and Daniel Vidal. 1971. *Grèves revendicatives ou grèves politiques? Acteurs, pratiques, sens du mouvement de mai.* Paris: Anthropos.

Duby, Georges, ed. 1980-1983. *Histoire de la France urbaine.* 4 vols. Paris: Seuil.

Duby, Georges, and Armand Wallon, eds. 1973-1976. *Histoire de la France rurale.* 4 vols. Paris: Seuil;.

Dugrand, Raymond. 1963. *Villes et campagnes en Bas-Languedoc. Le réseau urbain du Bas-Languedoc méditerranéen.* Paris: Presses Universitaires de France.

Dumas, F. 1907. "Une émeute d'étudiants à Toulouse en 1740." *Revue des Pyrénées* 1907: 23-43.

Dumay, Jean-Baptiste. 1976. *Mémoires d'un militant ouvrier du Creusot (1841-1905),* edited by Pierre Ponsot. Paris: Maspéro.

Dupâquier, Jacques. 1979. *La Population rurale du Bassin Parisien à l'époque de Louis XIV.* Paris: Ecole des Hautes Etudes en Sciences Sociales.

Dupeux, Georges. 1959. *Le Front Populaire et les élections de 1936.* Cahiers de la Fondation Nationale des Sciences Politiques, 99. Paris: Colin.

——— 1972. *La société française, 1789-1970.* Paris: Colin.

——— 1981. *Atlas historique de l'urbanisation de la France (1811-1975).* Paris: Editions du Centre National de la Recherche Scientifique.

Durand, Claude. 1971. "Revendications explicites et revendications latentes." *Sociologie du Travail* 15: 394-409.

Durand, Claude, and Pierre Dubois. 1975. *La grève. Enquête sociologique.* Paris: Colin.

Durand, Michelle. 1977. *Les conflits du travail. Analyse structurelle.* Sceaux: Centre de Recherches en Sciences Sociales du Travail, Université "Paris-Sud."

Durand, Michelle, and Yvette Harff. 1973. "Panorama statistique des grèves." *Sociologie du Travail* 15: 356-375.

Durand, Robert. 1971. *La lutte des travailleurs de chez Renault racontée par eux-mêmes, 1912-1944.* Paris: Editions Sociales.

Duranthon, Marc. 1978. *La carte de France. Son histoire, 1678-1978.* Paris: Solar.

Durost, H. 1960. "Un récit de l'émeute dijonnaise de 1775." *Annales de Bourgogne* 32: 191-192.

Edwards, Stewart. 1971. *The Paris Commune, 1871.* London: Eyre & Spottiswoode.

Egret, Jean. 1962. *La pré-Révolution française.* Paris: Presses universitaires de France.

——— 1970. *Louis XV et l'opposition parlementaire, 1715-1774.* Paris: Colin.

Elkaïm, Jean. 1970. "Les subsistances à Auxonne de 1788 à l'an V. Dijon: Archives Départementales de la Côte d'Or." *La Révolution en Côte-d'Or,* n.s. 12: 1-69.

Erbès-Seguin, Sabine. 1970a. "Relations entre travailleurs dans l'entreprise en grève: Le cas de mai-juin 1968." *Revue Française de Sociologie* 11: 339-350.

——— 1970b. "Le déclenchement des grèves de mai: Spontanéités des masses et rôle des syndicats." *Sociologie du Travail* 12: 177-189.

Erpeldinger, Manne, and Claudine Lefebvre. 1974. "Les misérables sous la Révolution (districts de Lille et de Douai)." *Annales Historiques de la Révolution Française* 46: 164-186.

Esmonin, Edmond. 1964. *Etudes sur la France des XVIIe et XVIIIe siècles.* Paris: Presses Universitaires de France.

Evenson, Norma. 1979. *Paris: A Century of Change, 1878-1978.* New Haven: Yale University Press.

Evrard, Fernand. 1947. "Les paysans du Mâconnais et les brigandages de juillet 1789." *Annales de Bourgogne* 19: 7-39, 97-121.

Fallachon, Philippe. 1972. "Les grèves de la Régie Renault en 1947." *Le Mouvement Social* 81: 111-142.

Farge, Arlette. 1979. *Vivre dans la rue à Paris au XVIIIe siècle.* Paris: Gallimard/Julliard.

Farge, Arlette, and André Zysberg. 1979. "Les théâtres de la violence à Paris au XVIIIe siècle." *Annales: Economies, Sociétés, Civilisations* 34: 984-1015.

Faure, Alain. 1974. "Mouvements populaires et mouvement ouvrier à Paris (1830-1834)." *Le Mouvement Social* 88 :51-92.

———— 1978. *Paris Carême-Prenant. Du Carnaval à Paris au XIXe siècle.* Paris: Hachette.

Fizaine, Simone. 1931. *La vie politique dans la Côte-d'Or sous Louis XVIII. Les élections et la presse.* Paris: Les Belles Lettres.

Flonneau, Jean-Marie. 1966. "Crise de vie chère 1910-1914. Réactions populaires et réactions syndicales." Diplôme d'études supérieures, Institut d'Histoire Economique et Sociale, Université de Paris.

Fohlen, Claude. 1951. "Esquisse d'une évolution industrielle. Roubaix au XIXe siècle." *Revue du Nord* 33: 92-102.

———— 1953. "Crise textile et troubles sociaux: Le Nord à la fin du Second Empire." *Revue du Nord* 35: 107-123

———— 1963. "La décadence des forges comtoises." In *Mélanges d'histoire économique et sociale en hommage au professeur Antony Babel,* vol. 1. Geneva: Privately published.

Foisil, Madeleine. 1970. *La révolte des Nu-Pieds et les révoltes normandes de 1639.* Paris: Presses Universitaires de France.

Fondation Nationale des Sciences Politiques. 1967. *Léon Blum chef de gouvernement, 1936-1937.* Cahiers de la Fondation Nationale des Sciences Politiques, 155. Paris: Colin.

Fontvieille, Louis. 1978. "Dépenses publiques et problématiques de la dévalorisation du capital." *Annales: Economies, Sociétés, Civilisations* 33: 240-254.

Forbonnais, F. Veron Duverger de. 1758. *Recherches et considérations sur les finances de France depuis l'année 1595 jusqu'à l'année 1721.* Basel: Frères Cramer.

Forestier, Henri. 1941. "Le 'droit des garçons' dans la communauté villageoise aux XVIIe et XVIIIe siècles." *Annales de Bourgogne* 13: 109-114.

———— 1945. "Les villageois et les milices paroissiales (1692-1771)." *Annales de Bourgogne* 17: 268-274.

Form, William. 1981. "Working-Class Divisions and Political Consensus in France and the United States." *Comparative Social Research* 4: 263-296.

Forster, Robert. 1960. *The Nobility of Toulouse in the Eighteenth Century.* Baltimore: Johns Hopkins University Press.

Fourastié, Jean. 1969. *L'évolution des prix à long terme.* Paris: Presses Universitaires de France.

Fournier, Georges. 1975. "Traditions municipales et vie politique en 1789." In *Droite et Gauche de 1789 à nos jours.* Montpellier: Centre d'Histoire Contemporaine du Langue-doc Méditerranéen et du Roussillon, Université Paul Valéry.

France. 1889-1914. *Les associations professionnelles ouvrières.* 4 vols.

France. Documentation Française. 1982. *La France en mai 1981. Forces et faiblesses.* Paris: Documentation Française.

France. Institut National de la Statistique et des Etudes Economiques [INSEE]. 1966. *Annuaire statistique de la France, 1966. Résumé retrospectif.* Paris.

——— 1973. *Données sociales.* Paris.

——— 1977. *Principaux résultats du recensement de 1975.* Collections de l'INSEE, 238. Paris.

——— 1980. *Tableaux de l'économie française, édition 1980.* Paris.

France. Ministère du Commerce. Office du Travail. 1894-1904. *Les associations profession-nelles ouvrières.* 4 vols. Paris: Imprimerie Nationale.

Franchomme, Georges. 1969. "L'évolution demographique et economique de Roubaix de 1870 à 1900." *Revue du Nord* 51: 201-248.

Frêche, Georges. 1974. *Toulouse et la région Midi-Pyrénées au siècle des Lumières (vers 1670-1789).* Paris: Cujas.

Freyssenet, Michel. 1979. *Division du travail et mobilisation quotidienne de la main-d'oeuvre. Le cas Renault et Fiat.* Paris: Centre de Sociologie Urbaine.

Fridenson, Patrick. 1972. *Histoire des usines Renault.* Vol. 1: *Naissance de la grande entreprise, 1898/1939.* Paris: Seuil.

Friedmann, Georges, ed. 1970. *Villes et campagnes. Civilisation urbaine et civilisation rurale en France.* 2d ed. Paris: Colin.

Gabory, Emile. 1923. *Les Bourbons et la Vendée d'après des documents inédits.* Paris: Perrin.

Gaillard, Jeanne. 1971. *Communes de province, Commune de Paris.* Paris: Flammarion.

——— 1977. *Paris, la ville, 1852-1870.* Paris: Champion.

Gamson, William A. 1968. *Power and Discontent.* Homewood, Ill.: Dorsey.

Gamson, William A.; Bruce Fireman; and Steven Rytina. 1982. *Encounters with Unjust Authority.* Homewood, Ill.: Dorsey.

Garidou, Jean-François. 1970. "Les mouvements ouvriers agricoles dans l'Aude (1900-1910)." In *Carcassonne et sa région. Actes des XLIe et XXIVe congrès d'études régionales tenus par la Fédération historique du Languedoc méditerranéen et du Roussillon et par la Fédération des Sociétés académiques et savantes de Languedoc-Pyrénées-Gascogne, Carcassonne, 17-19 mai 1968.* Montpellier: Centre d'Histoire Contemporaine du Languedoc Méditerranéen et du Roussillon, Université Paul Valéry.

Garlan, Yvon, and Claude Nières. 1975. *Les révoltes bretonnes de 1675. Papier Timbré et Bonnets Rouges.* Paris: Editions Sociales.

Garnot, Benoît. 1981. "Délits et châtiments en Anjou au XVIIIe siècle." *Annales de Bretagne et des Pays de l'Ouest (Anjou, Maine, Touraine)* 88: 283-304.

Gaudin, Gilbert. 1973. *Géopolitique et structures urbaines à Narbonne.* Paris: Maisonneuve & Larose.

Gauthier, Florence. 1977. *La voie paysanne dans la révolution française. L'exemple picard.* Paris: Maspéro.

——— 1978. "Sur les problèmes paysans de la Révolution." *Annales Historiques de la Révolution Française* 232: 305-314.

Gendarme, René. 1954. *La région du Nord. Essai d'analyse économique.* Paris: Colin.

Georges, Bernard. 1966. "La C.G.T. et le gouvernement Léon Blum." *Le Mouvement Social* 54: 49-68.

George, Pierre; Pierre Randet; and Jean Bastié. 1964. *La région parisienne.* 2d ed. Paris: Presses Universitaires de France.

Gibert, Urbain. 1970. "Quelques aspects populaires des manifestations viticoles de 1907." In *Carcassonne et sa région.* See Garidou 1970.

Gillet, Marcel. 1973. *Les charbonnages du Nord de la France au XIXe siècle.* Paris: Mouton.

———, ed. 1975. *La qualité de la vie dans la région Nord-Pas-de-Calais au 20e siècle*. Villeneuve d'Ascq: Université de Lille III.

——— 1979. "Industrie et société à Douai au XIXème siècle." *Revue du Nord* 61: 417–426.

Girard, Georges. 1921. "Le logement des gens de guerre à Montpellier à la fin du XVIIe siècle." *Carnet de la Sabretache*, 3d s., 4: 369–403.

Girod, P.E. 1906. *Les subsistances en Bourgogne et particulièrement à Dijon à la fin du XVIIIe siècle*. Dijon: La Revue Bourguignonne.

Godechot, Jacques. 1965. *La prise de la Bastille*. Paris: Gallimard.

——— 1966. "L'histoire sociale et économique de Toulouse au XVIIIe siècle." *Annales du Midi* 78: 363–376.

——— 1978. "Aux origines du régime représentatif en France: Des Conseils politiques languedociens aux conseils municipaux de l'époque révolutionnaire." In *Vom Ancien Régime zur Französischen Revolution. Forschungen und Perspektiven*, edited by Ernst Hinrichs, Eberhard Schmitt, and Rudolf Vierhaus. Göttingen: Vandenhoeck & Ruprecht.

Godechot, Jacques, and Suzanne Moncassin. 1965. *Démographie et subsistances en Languedoc (du XVIIIe au début du XIXe siècle)*. Paris: Imprimerie Nationale.

——— 1967. "Structures et relations sociales à Toulouse en 1749 et en 1785." *Annales Historiques de la Révolution Française* 37:129–306.

Goetz-Girey, Robert. 1965. *Le mouvement des grèves en France, 1919–1962*. Paris: Sirey.

Gossez, A.M. 1904. *Le département du Nord sous la Deuxième République, 1848–1852*. Lille: Leleu.

Gossez, Rémi. 1953. "La résistance à l'impôt: les quarante-cinq centimes." *Bibliothèque de la Révolution de 1848* 15: 89–132.

——— 1956. "A propos de la carte des troubles de 1846–1847." In *Aspects de la crise et de la dépression de l'économie française au milieu du XIXe siècle, 1846–1851*, edited by Ernest Labrousse. Bibliothèque de la Révolution de 1848, 19. La Roche-sur-Yon: Imprimerie Centrale de l'Ouest.

——— 1967. *Les ouvriers de Paris*. Vol. 1: *L'organisation, 1848–1851*. Bibliothèque de la Révolution de 1848, 24. La Roche-sur-Yon: Imprimerie Centrale de l'Ouest.

Goubert, Pierre. 1960. *Beauvais et le Beauvaisis de 1600 à 1730*. Paris: SEVPEN.

——— 1967. *L'avènement du roi-soleil*. Paris: Julliard.

——— 1969–1973. *L'Ancien Régime*. 2 vols. Paris: Colin.

——— 1982. *La vie quotidienne des paysans français au XVIIe siècle*. Paris: Hachette.

Gratton, Philippe. 1971. *Les luttes de classes dans les campagnes*. Paris: Anthropos.

Greenberg, Louis M. 1971. *Sisters of Liberty: Marseille, Lyon, Paris, and the Reaction to a Centralized State, 1868–1871*. Cambridge: Harvard University Press.

Grundy, Kenneth W., and Michael A. Weinstein. 1974. *The Ideologies of Violence*. Columbus, Ohio: Charles E. Merrill.

Guérin, Daniel. 1970. *Front Populaire, révolution manquée. Témoignage militant*. Paris: Maspéro.

Guéry, Alain. 1978. "Les finances de la monarchie française sous l'Ancien Régime." *Annales: Economies, Sociétés, Civilisations* 33: 216–239.

Guignet, Philippe. 1973. "L'émeute de quatre sous, ou les voies de la protestation sociale à Anzin (mai 1833)." *Revue du Nord* 55: 347–364.

——— 1977. *Mines, manufactures, et ouvriers du valenciennois au XVIIIe siècle*. 2 vols. New York: Arno Press.

——— 1979. "Adaptations, mutations, et survivances proto-industrielles dans le textile

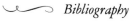

du Cambrésis et du Valenciennois du XVIIIe au début du XXe siècle." *Revue du Nord* 61: 27–60.

Gurr, Ted Robert, ed. 1980. *Handbook of Political Conflict.* New York: Free Press.

Guthrie, Christopher. 1983. "Reaction to the Coup d'Etat in the Narbonnais: A Case Study of Popular Political Mobilization and Repression during the Second Republic." *French Historical Studies* 13: 18–46.

Halebsky, Sandor. 1976. *Mass Society and Political Conflict: Toward a Reconstruction of Theory.* Cambridge: Cambridge University Press.

Hamscher, Albert N. 1976. *The Parlement of Paris after the Fronde, 1653–1673.* Pittsburgh: University of Pittsburgh Press.

Hanagan, Michael P. 1980. *The Logic of Solidarity: Artisans and Industrial Workers in Three French Towns, 1871–1914.* Urbana: University of Illinois Press.

Hardin, Russell. 1983. *Collective Action.* Baltimore: John Hopkins University Press for Resources for the Future.

Harding, Robert R. 1978. *Anatomy of a Power Elite: The Provincial Governors of Early Modern France.* New Haven: Yale University Press.

Hardy, S. P. 1912. *"Mes loisirs." Journal d'évènements tels qu'ils parviennent à ma connaissance (1764–1789).* Edited by Maurice Tourneaux and Maurice Vitrac. Paris: Picard.

Hasquin, Hervé, ed 1975. *L'intendance du Hainaut en 1697.* Paris: Bibliothèque Nationale.

Haumont, Antoine. 1973. *Paris. La vie quotidienne.* Notes et Etudes Documentaires, 3982, 3983. Paris: Documentation Française.

Hauser, Henri. 1907. *Les compagnons d'arts et métiers à Dijon aux XVIIe et XVIIIe siècles.* Dijon: Damidot, Nourry. Reprinted from *Revue Bourguignonne* 17.

Hausser, Elisabeth. 1968. *Paris au jour le jour. Les évènements vus par la presse, 1900–1919.* Paris: Editions du Minuit.

Haut, Michèle. 1974. *Structures sociales des quartiers de la Grève, Saint-Avoye, Saint-Antoine à la fin du 17e s., 1697–1700,* Mémoire de maîtrise, University of Paris. Paris: Hachette. Microfiche.

Héliot, Pierre. 1935. "La guerre dite du Lustucru et les privilèges du Boulonnais." *Revue du Nord* 21: 265–318.

Henriot, Marcel. 1933. *Le Club des Jacobins de Sémur, 1790–1795.* La Révolution en Côte d'Or, *n.s.* 9. Dijon: Rebourseau.

——— 1947. "Le partage des biens communaux en Côte d'Or sous la Révolution. L'exemple du district d'Arnay-sur-Arroux." *Annales de Bourgogne* 19: 262–274.

Herbert, Edward. 1976. *The Life of Edward, First Lord Herbert of Cherbury, Written by Himself.* Edited by J. M. Shuttlesworth. London: Oxford University Press.

Hesse, Ph.-J. 1979. "Géographie coutumière et révoltes paysannes en 1789." *Annales Historiques de la Révolution Française* 51: 280–306.

Heylyn, Peter. 1652a. *Cosmographie, in four Bookes. Containing the Chorographie and Historie of the Whole World and all the principall Kingdomes, Provinces, Seas, and Isles thereof.* London: Henry Seile.

——— 1652b. *Cosmographie: the Second booke: Containing the Chorographie and Historie of Belgium, Germanie, Denmark, Swethland, Russia, Poland, Hungarie, Sclavonia, Dacia, and Greece, with the* ISLES *thereof.* London: Henry Seile.

——— 1656. *France Painted to the Life by a Learned and Impartial Hand.* London: William Leake.

Heywood, Colin. 1981. "The Role of the Peasantry in French Industrialization, 1815-80." *Economic History Review,* 2d ser. 34: 359-376.

Hibbs, Douglas A., Jr. 1978. "On the Political Economy of Long-Run Trends in Strike Activity." *British Journal of Political Science* 8: 153-175.

Higonnet, Patrice L.-R. 1971. *Pont-de-Montvert: Social Structure and Politics in a French Village, 1700-1914.* Cambridge: Harvard University Press.

Hilaire, Yves-Marie. 1966. "Les ouvriers de la région du Nord devant l'église catholique (XIXe et XXe siècle)." *Le Mouvement Social* 57: 181-201.

Hillairet, Jacques. 1970. *La rue Saint-Antoine.* Paris: Editions de Minuit.

Hinrichs, Ernest; Eberhard Schmitt; and Rudolf Vierhaus, eds. 1978. *Vom Ancien Régime zur französischen Revolution. Forschungen und Perspektiven.* Göttingen: Handenhoeck & Ruprecht.

Hirschman, Albert O. 1970. *Exit, Voice, and Loyalty: Responses to Decline in Firms, Organizations, and States.* Cambridge: Harvard University Press.

Hobsbawm, E. J. 1971. "Class Consciousness in History." In *Aspects of History and Class Consciousness,* edited by Istvan Meszaros. London: Routlege & Kegan Paul.

——— 1974. "Peasant Land Occupations." *Past & Present* 62: 120-152.

Hoffmann, Stanley. 1956. *Le mouvement Poujade.* Cahiers de la Fondation Nationale des Sciences Politiques, 81. Paris: Colin.

Holton, Robert J. 1978. "The Crowd in History: Some Problems of Theory and Method." *Social History* 3: 219-233.

Hood, James N. 1971. "Protestant-Catholic Relations and the Roots of the First Popular Counterrevolutionary Movement in France." *Journal of Modern History* 43: 245-275.

——— 1979. "Revival and Mutation of Old Rivalries in Revolutionary France." *Past & Present* 82: 82-115.

Houssel, J.-P., ed. 1976. *Histoire des paysans français du XVIIIe siècle à nos jours.* Roanne: Horvath.

Huard, Raymond, 1975. "Montagne rouge et Montagne blanche en Languedoc-Roussillon sous la Seconde République." In *Droite et Gauche en Languedoc-Rousillon, Actes du Colloque de Montpellier, 9-10 juin 1973.* Montpellier: Centre d'Histoire Contemporaine du Languedoc Méditerranéen et du Roussillon, Université Paul Valéry.

——— 1979. "La préhistoire des partis. Le parti républicain dans le Gard de 1848 à 1881." *Le Mouvement Social* 107: 3-14.

——— 1982. *Le mouvement républicain en Bas-Languedoc, 1848-1881.* Paris: Presses de la Fondation Nationale des Sciences Politiques.

Huber, Michel; Henri Bunle; and Fernand Boverat. 1965. *La population de la France, son évolution et ses perspectives.* 4th ed. Paris: Hachette.

Hunt, David. 1984. "Peasant Politics in the French Revolution." *Social History* 9: 277-299.

Hunt, Lynn A. 1976a. "Committees and Communes: Local Politics and National Revolution in 1789." *Comparative Studies in Society and History* 18: 321-346.

——— 1976b. "Local Elites at the End of the Old Regime: Troyes and Reims, 1750-1789." *French Historical Studies* 9: 379-399.

——— 1978. *Revolution and Urban Politics in Provincial France: Troyes and Reims, 1786-1790.* Stanford: Stanford University Press.

——— 1984. *Politics, Culture, and Class in the French Revolution.* Berkeley: University of California Press. 1984.

Index-atlas des départements français. 1968. Rennes and Paris: Oberthur.

Isherwood, Robert M. 1978. "Popular Musical Entertainment in Eighteenth-Century Paris." *International Review of the Aesthetics and Sociology of Music* 9: 295–310.

―――― 1981. "Entertainment in the Parisian Fairs in the Eighteenth Century." *Journal of Modern History* 53: 24–47.

Jacotin, A. 1941. "Notes sur le coup d'état du 2 décembre 1851 en Côte d'Or." *Annales de Bourgogne* 13: 73–96.

Jacquart, Jean. 1956. "Une paroisse rurale de la région parisienne: Morangis aux XVIe et XVIIe siècles." *Mémoires de la Fédération des Sociétés Historiques et Archéologiques de Paris et de l'Ile-de-France* 8: 187–211.

―――― 1960. "La Fronde des princes dans la région parisienne et ses conséquences materielles." *Revue d'Histoire Moderne et Contemporaine* 7: 257–290.

Jaurès, Jean. 1976. *La classe ouvrière,* edited by Madeleine Rebérioux. Paris: Maspéro.

Jeanneau, Jacques. 1974. *Angers et son agglomération.* Notes et Etudes Documentaires, 4065, 4066, 4067. Paris: Documentation Française.

Jehan de la Cité [F. Lavergne]. n.d. *L'Hôtel de Ville de Paris et la Grève à travers les âges.* Paris: Firmin-Didot.

Johnson, Christopher H. 1982. "Proto-industrialization and De-industrialization in Languedoc: Lodève and its Region, 1700–1870." In *La protoindustrialisation: Théorie et réalité. Rapports,* edited by Pierre Deyon and Franklin Mendels. Lille: Université des Arts, Lettres, et Sciences Humaines.

Josse, Raymond. 1962. "La naissance de la Résistance à Paris et la manifestation étudiante du 11 novembre 1940." *Revue d'Histoire de la Deuxième Guerre Mondiale* 12: 31.

Jousselin, Mathurin. 1861. "Journal de M. Jousselin, curé de Sainte Croix d'Angers." In *Inventaire analytique des archives anciennes de la mairie d'Angers,* edited by Célestin Port. Paris: Dumoulin.

Joutard, Philippe. 1965. *Journaux camisards, 1700/1715.* Paris: Union Centrale d'Editions.

―――― ed. 1976. *Les Camisards.* Paris: Gallimard/Julliard.

―――― 1977. *La légende des Camisards. Une sensibilité au passé.* Paris: Gallimard.

Julliard, Jacques. 1965. *Clémenceau briseur de grèves.* Paris: Julliard.

Kaplan, Steven. 1979. "Réflexions sur la police du monde du travail, 1700–1815." *Revue Historique* 261: 17–77.

―――― 1981. "Note sur les commissaires de police de Paris au XVIIIe siècle." *Revue d'Histoire Moderne et Contemporaine* 28: 669–686.

―――― 1984. *Provisioning Paris: Merchants and Millers in the Grain and Flour Trade during the Eighteenth Century.* Ithaca: Cornell University Press.

Kergoat, Danièle. 1970. "Une experience d'autogestion en mai 1968 (émergence d'un système d'action collective)." *Sociologie du Travail* 12: 274–292.

Kettering, Sharon. 1978. *Judicial Politics and Urban Revolt in Seventeenth-Century France: The Parlement of Aix, 1629–1659.* Princeton: Princeton University Press.

―――― 1982. "The Causes of the Judicial Fronde." *Canadian Journal of History* 17: 275–306.

Kleinclausz, Arthur Jean. 1909. *Histoire de Bourgogne.* Paris: Hachette.

Korpi, Walter. 1974. "Conflict, Power, and Relative Deprivation." *American Political Science Review* 68: 1569–1578.

Korpi, Walter, and Michael Shalev. 1980. "Strikes, Power, and Politics in the Western

Nations, 1900–1976. In *Political Power and Social Theory,* edited by Maurice Zeitlin. Greenwich, Conn.: JAI Press.

Kossmann, Ernst Heinrich. 1954. *La Fronde.* Leiden: Pers Leiden.

Kozhokin, E. V. 1982. "K probleme stanovlieniia klassovo soznaniia frantsuzskovo pro-lieteriata" [On the problem of the growth of class consciousness of the French proletariat]. *Vopros' i Istorii* January: 57–66.

Kravetz, Marc. ed. 1968. *L'insurrection étudiante, 2–13i mai 1968.* Paris: Union Générale d'Editions.

Kriegel, Annie. 1966. "Structures d'organisation et mouvement des effectifs du parti communiste français entre les deux guerres." *International Review of Social History* 11: 335–361.

Labrousse, Ernest; Pierre Léon; Pierre Goubert; Jean Bouvier; Charles Carrière; and Paul Harsin. 1970. *Des derniers temps de l'âge seigneurial aux préludes de l'âge industriel (1660–1789).* Vol. 2 of *Histoire économique et sociale de la France,* edited by Fernand Braudel and Ernest Labrousse. Paris: Presses Universitaires de France.

Lachiver, Marcel. 1982. *Vin, vigne, et vignerons en région parisienne du XVIIe au XIXe siècles.* Pontoise: Société Historique et Archéologique de Pontoise, du Val d'Oise, et du Vexin.

La Mare, Nicolas de. 1792. *Traité de la police.* 3d ed. 4 vols. Paris: Brunet. See also BN Fr 21545–21722 for inventories, notes, sources, and original manuscript.

Lamorisse, René. 1975. *Recherches géographiques sur la population de la Cévenne languedocienne.* Montpellier: Imprimerie du "Paysan du Midi."

Landes, David S. 1976. "Religion and Enterprise: The Case of the French Textile Industry." In *Enterprise and Entrepreneurs in Nineteenth- and Twentieth-Century France,* edited by Edward C. Carter II, Robert Forster, and Joseph N. Moody. Baltimore: Johns Hopkins University Press.

Lane, Frederic. 1958. "Economic Consequences of Organized Violence." *Journal of Economic History* 18: 401–417.

Langeron, Geneviève. 1929. "Le Club des Femmes de Dijon pendant la Révolution." *La Révolution en Côte d'Or,* n.s. 5: 5–71.

Lasserre, André. 1952. *La situation des ouvriers de l'industrie textile dans la région lilloise sous la Monarchie de Juillet.* Lausanne: Nouvelle Bibliothèque de Droit et Jurisprudence.

Laurent, Robert. 1931. *L'agriculture en Côte-d'Or pendant la première moitié du XIXe siècle.* La Révolution en Côte-d'Or, n.s. 7. Dijon: Rebourseau.

——— 1957. *Les vignerons de la "Côte d'Or" au dix-neuvième siècle.* 2 vols. Paris: Les Belles Lettres.

——— 1975. "Droite et Gauche en Languedoc. Mythe ou réalité." In *Droite et Gauche.* See Huard 1975.

Lebrun, François. 1965. "Les grandes enquêtes statistiques des XVIIe et XVIIIe siècles sur la généralité de Tours (Maine, Anjou, Touraine)." *Annales de Bretagne* 72: 338–345.

——— 1966. "Les soulèvements populaires à Angers aux XVIIe et XVIIIe siècles." *Actes du quatre-vingt-dixième Congrès National des Sociétés Savantes. Nice 1965,* I, 119–140. Paris: Bibliothèque Nationale.

——— 1971. *Les hommes et la mort en Anjou aux 17e et 18e siècles.* Paris: Mouton.

———ed. 1975. *Histoire d'Angers.* Toulouse: Privat.

Le Clère, Marcel. 1979. "La police politique sous la IIIe République." In Jacques Aubert

et al., *L'état et sa police en France (1789-1914)*. Centre de Recherches d'Histoire et de Philologie de la IVe Section de l'Ecole Pratique des Hautes Etudes Médiévales et Modernes, 33. Geneva: Droz.

Lecouturier, Henri. 1848. *Paris incompatible avec la République. Plan d'un nouveau Paris où les révolutions seront impossible.* Paris: Desloges.

Ledrut, Raymond. 1968. *L'espace social de la ville. Problèmes de sociologie appliquée a l'aménagement urbain.* Paris: Anthropos.

Lefebvre, Bernard. 1979. "Argent et révolution: Esquisse d'une étude de la fortune à Douai (1748-1820)." *Revue du Nord* 61: 403-416.

Lefebvre, Bernard, and Louis Thbaut. 1979. "Evolution démographique et développement industriel: Le douaisis de 1750 à 1870." *Revue du Nord* 61: 165-180.

Lefebvre, Georges. 1914-1921. *Documents relatifs à l'histoire des subsistances dans le district de Bergues pendant la Révolution (1788-an V).* Lille: Robbe.

——— 1959. *Les paysans du Nord pendant la Révolution Française.* Bari: Laterza. First published in 1924.

——— 1970. *La Grande Peur de 1789.* Paris: Colin. First published in 1932.

Lefebvre, Pierre. 1973. "Aspects de la 'fidélité' en France au XVIIe siècle: Le cas des agents des princes de Condé." *Revue Historique* 250: 59-106.

Lefevre, Pierre. 1925. *Le commerce des grains et la question du pain à Lille de 1713 à 1789.* Lille: Robbe.

Lefranc, Georges 1963. *Le mouvement socialiste sous la Troisième République (1875-1940).* Paris: Payot.

——— 1965. *Histoire du Front Populaire (1934-1938).* Paris: Payot.

——— 1966a. *Juin 36: L'explosion du Front Populaire.* Paris: Juilliard.

——— 1966b. "Problématique des grèves françaises de 1936: Bilan provisoire d'une quête de témoignages." *Bulletin de la Société d'Histoire Moderne* 65: 2-8.

——— 1967. *Le mouvement syndical sous la Troisième République.* Paris: Payot.

——— 1969. *Le mouvement syndical sous la Troisième République.* Paris: Payot.

——— 1969. *Le mouvement syndical de la Libération aux évenements de mai-juin 1968.* Paris: Payot.

Le Goff, T. J. A., and D. M. G. Sutherland. 1974. "The Revolution and the Rural Community in Eighteenth-Century Brittany." *Past & Present* 62: 96-119.

——— 1983. "The Social Origins of Counter-Revolution in Western France." *Past & Present* 99: 65-87.

Leguai, A. 1965. "Les 'émotions' et séditions populaires dans la généralité de Moulins aux XVIIe et XVIIIe siècle." *Revue d'Histoire Economique et Sociale* 43: 44-65.

Lehoreau, René. 1967. *Cérémonial de l'Eglise d'Angers (1692-1721).* Edited by François Lebrun. Paris: Klincksieck for Institut de Recherches Historiques de Rennes.

Lemoine, Annick. 1974. *Structures sociales des quartiers de Grève, Saint-Avoye, Saint-Antoine, 1684-1688.* Mémoire de maîtrise, University of Paris. Paris. Hachette. Microfiche.

Lentacker, Firmin. 1974. *La frontière franco-belge. Etude géographique des effets d'une frontière internationale sur la vie des relations.* Lille: Imprimerie Morel & Corduant.

Léon, Pierre; Maurice Lévy-Leboyer; André Armengaud; André Broder; Jean Bruhat; Adeline Daumard; Ernest Labrousse; Robert Laurent; and Albert Soboul. 1976. *L'avènement de l'ère industrielle (1789-années 1880).* Vol. 3, pt. 1 of *Histoire économique et sociale de la France,* edited by Fernand Braudel and Ernest Labrousse. Paris: Presses Universitaires de France.

Lequeux, André. 1933. "L'industrie du fer dans le Hainaut français au XVIIIe siècle." *Revue du Nord* 19: 5–28.

Le Roy Ladurie, Emmanuel. 1966. *Les paysans de Languedoc*. 2 vols. Paris: SEVPEN.

———— 1974. "Révoltes et contestations rurales en France de 1675 à 1788." *Annales: Economies, Sociétés, Civilisations* 29: 6–22.

———— ed. 1975. *L'âge classique des paysans*. Vol. 2 of *Histoire de la France rurale*, edited by Georges Duby and Armand Wallon. Paris: Seuil.

———— 1981. *La ville classique*. Vol. 3 of *Histoire de la France urbaine*, edited by Georges Duby. Paris: Seuil.

Le Roy Ladurie, Emmanuel, and Michel Morineau. *Paysannerie et croissance*. Vol. 2 of *Histoire économique et sociale de la France*, edited by Fernand Braudel and Ernest Labrousse. Paris: Presses Universitaires de France.

Letellier, Gabriell; Jean Perrett; and H. E. Zuber. 1938. *Le chômage en France de 1930 à 1936*. Institut Scientifique de Recherches Economiques et Sociales, Enquête sur le Chômage, 1. Paris: Sirey.

Lettres sur l'agriculture du Bas-Languedoc. 1787. Nîmes: Castor Belle.

Levasseur, Emile. 1907. *Questions ouvrières et industrielles en France sous la Troisième République*. Paris: Rousseau.

Lévêque, Pierre. 1980. *La Bourgogne de la Monarchie de Juillet au Second Empire*. 5 vols. Lille: Service de Reproduction des Thèses, Université de Lille III.

Lewis, Gwynne. 1978. *The Second Vendée: The Continuity of Counter-Revolution in the Department of the Gard, 1789-1815*. Oxford: Clarendon Press.

Liagre, Charles. 1934. "Les hostilités dans la région de Lille." *Revue du Nord* 20: 111-130.

Linhart, Robert. 1978. *L'établi*. Paris: Minuit.

Lissagaray, Prosper-Olivier. 1969. *Histoire de la Commune de 1871*. Paris: Maspéro.

Liublinskaya, A.D. 1966. *Vnutriennaya politika frantsuskovo absolutismo* [The domestic policy of French absolutism]. Moscow and Leningrad: Izdatel'stvo "Nauka."

Locke, John. 1953. *Locke's Travels in France, 1675-1679, as related in his Journals, Correspondence, and Other Papers*. Edited by John Lough. Cambridge: Cambridge University Press.

Lofland, John. 1981. "Collective Behavior: The Elementary Forms." In *Social Psychology: Sociological Perspectives*, edited by Morris Rosenberg and Ralph Turner. New York: Basic Books.

Loirette, F. 1966. "Une émeute paysanne au début au gouvernement personnel de Louis XIV: La sédition de Benauge (déc. 1661–janv. 1662)." *Annales du Midi* 78: 515-536.

Lorwin, Val R. 1954. *The French Labor Movement*. Cambridge: Harvard University Press.

Lottin, Alain. 1979a. "Les vivants et les morts au XVIIIe siècle. Les incidents de Lille (1779) et de Cambrai (1786) lors des translations de cimetière." *Actes du XVIIIe Congrès de la Fédération des Sociétés Savantes du Nord de la France*. Lille: Commission Historique du Nord.

———— 1979b. *Chavatte, ouvrier lillois. Un contemporain de Louis XIV*. Paris: Flammarion.

Louvet, Jehan. 1854-1856. "Journal, ou récit véritable de tout ce qui est advenu digne de mémoire tant en la ville d'Angers, pays d'Anjou et autres lieux (depuis l'an 1560 jusqu'à l'an 1634)." *Revue d'Anjou* 3, pt. 1: 257-304; 3, pt. 2: 1-64, 129-192, 257-320; 4, pt. 1: 1-65, 129-192, 257-320; 4, pt. 2: 1-64, 29-192, 257-320; 5, pt. 1: 1-64, 129-192, 285-332; 5, pt. 2: 1-64, 133-196, 281-370.

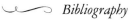

Lucas, Colin. 1973. *The Structure of the Terror: The Example of Javogues and the Loire.* London: Oxford University Press.

Lüdtke, Alf. 1980. "Genesis und Durchsetzung des modernen Staates: Zur Analyse von Herrschaft und Verwaltung." *Archiv für Sozialgeschichte* 20: 470–491.

Luxardo, Hervé; Jean Sandrin; and Claude-Catherine Ragache. 1979. *Courrières—1906, 1,100 morts: Crime ou catastrophe?* Evreux: Floréal.

Lyons, Martyn. 1980. *Révolution et Terreur à Toulouse.* Toulouse: Privat.

Machiavelli, Nicolò. 1969. "Sopra la primi deca di Tito Livio." In *Opere,* edited by Ezio Raimondi, Milan: Mursia.

Machu, Léon. 1949. "L'importance du banquet de Lille dans la campagne de réforme (7 novembre 1847)." *Revue du Nord* 31: 5–12.

——— 1956. "La crise de l'industrie textile à Roubaix au milieu du XIXe siècle." *Revue du Nord* 38: 65–75.

——— 1964. "Deux aspects de la répression policière dans le Nord à l'époque du Second Empire." *Revue du Nord* 46: 385–394.

Magne, Emile. 1960. *Paris sous l'échevinage au XVIIe siècle.* Paris: Editions Emile-Paul.

Maier, Charles S, and Dan S. White, eds. 1968. *The Thirteenth of May: The Advent of de Gaulle's Republic.* New York: Oxford University Press.

Malotet, A. 1910–1912. "L'industrie et le commerce des toiles fines à Valenciennes dans les temps modernes." *Revue du Nord* 1: 281–320; 3: 329–394.

Mandrou, Robert. 1973. *Louis XIV en son temps, 1661–1715.* Paris: Presses Universitaires de France.

Mann, Michael. 1973. *Consciousness and Action among the Western Working Class.* London: Macmillan.

Marcet, Alice. 1974. "Les conspirations de 1674 en Roussillon. Villefranche et Perpignan." *Annales du Midi* 86: 275–296.

——— 1977a. "Une révolte antifiscale et nationale: Les Angelets du Vallespir, 1663–1672." *Actes du 102e Congrès National des Sociétés Savantes, Limoges 1977. Histoire Moderne* 1: 35–48.

——— 1977b. "Le Roussillon, une province à la fin de l'Ancien Régime." In *Régions et régionalisme en France du XVIIIe siècle à nos jours,* edited by Christian Gras and Georges Livet. Paris: Presses Universitaires de France.

Marczewski, Jean. 1965. "Le produit physique de l'économie française de 1789 à 1913 (comparaison avec la Grande-Bretagne)." In *Histoire quantitative de l'économie française.* Cahiers de l'Institut de Science Economique Appliquée, no. 163, series AF, 4. Paris.

Margadant, Ted. 1979. *French Peasants in Revolt: The Insurrection of 1851.* Princeton: Princeton University Press.

Markovitch, T. J. 1966. *L'industrie française de 1789 à 1964. Conclusions générales.* Cahiers de l'Institut de Science Economique Appliquée, no. 179, series AF, 7. Paris: L'Institut de Science Economique Appliquée.

——— 1976. *Les industries lainières de Colbert à la Révolution.* Geneva: Droz.

Marres, Paul. 1935–1936. *Les grands Causses. Etude de géographie physique et humaine.* 2 vols. Tours: Arrault.

Marseille, Jacques, and Martine Sassier. 1982. *Si ne veulent point nous rinquérir in va bientôt tout démolir! Le nord en grève, avril/mai 1880.* Paris: Privately published.

Martin, A. 1929. *Les Milices provinciales en Bourgogne, 29 novembre 1688-4 mars 1791.* Dijon: Pernigaud & Privat.

Martin, Germain, and Paul Martinot. 1909. *Contribution à l'histoire des classes rurales en France au XIXe siècle. La Côte d'Or. Etude d'économie rurale.* Paris: Rousseau.

Martinage, Renée, and Jacques Lorgnier. n.d. [1980?]. "La répression des séditions et émotions populaires de 1789 par la Maréchaussée de Flandres." Reprint from *Collection des Travaux de la Faculté des Sciences Juridiques, Politiques, et Sociales de Lille.*

Marty, Laurent. 1982. *Chanter pour survivre. Culture ouvrière, travail, et techniques dans le textile. Roubaix 1850-1914.* Liéven: Atelier Ethno-Histoire et Culture Ouvrière Léo Lagrange.

Marwell, Gerald. 1981. "Altruism and the Problem of Collective Action." In *Cooperation and Helping Behavior,* edited by V. Derlega and J. Grzelak. New York: Academic Press.

Masanelli, J. C. 1981. *En Languedoc sous l'Ancien Regime. Gaujac à l'époque de Louis XIV.* Nîmes: Imprimerie Bernier.

Mathias, Peter, and Patrick O'Brien. 1976. "Taxation in Britain and France, 1715-1810: A Comparison of the Social and Economic Incidence of Taxes Collected for the Central Governments." *Journal of European Economic History* 5: 601-650.

Mathiez, Albert. 1926. "Dijon en 1789 d'après les lettres inédites de François Nicolas Bertheley, Commis aux Etats de Bourgogne." *La Révolution en Côte d'Or,* n.s. 2: 1-20.

Mayeur, Jean-Marie. 1966a. "Religion et politique: Géographie de la résistance aux inventaires (février-mars 1906)." *Annales: Economies, Sociétés, Civilisations* 21: 1259-1272.

——— 1966b. *La séparation de l'église et de l'état (1905).* Paris: Julliard.

Mazoyer, Louis. 1947. "Les origines du prophétisme cévenol (1700-1702)." *Revue Historique* 197: 23-54.

McPhail, Clark, and Ronald T. Wohstein. "Individual and Collective Behavior within Gatherings, Demonstrations, and Riots." *Annual Review of Sociology* 9: 579-600.

Mendras, Henri, and Yves Tavernier. 1962. "Les manifestations de juin 1961." *Revue Française de Science Politique* 12: 647-671.

Menétra, Jacques-Louis. 1982. *Journal de ma vie.* Edited by Daniel Roche. Paris: Montalba.

Mercier, Louis Sebastien. 1906. *Tableau de Paris.* 3 vols. Paris: Bibliothèque Nationale. First published in 1783.

Meuvret, Jean. 1977. *Le problème des subsistances à l'époque de Louis XIV.* 2 vols. Paris: Mouton.

Meyer, Jean. 1975. "Le XVIIe siècle et sa place dans l'évolution à long terme." *XVIIe Siècle* 106-107: 23-57.

Michel, Georges. 1891. *Histoire d'un centre ouvrier (les concessions d'Anzin).* Paris: Guillaumin.

Michel, Henri. 1981. *Paris allemand.* Paris: Albin Michel.

Michel, Louise. 1970. *La Commune, histoire et souvenirs.* 2 vols. Paris: Maspéro.

Millot, H. 1925. *Le comité permanent de Dijon, juillet 1789-février 1790.* La Révolution en Côte d'Or, n.s., 1. Dijon: Rebourseau.

Minces, Juliette. 1967. *Le Nord.* Paris: Maspéro.

Mitchell, Harvey. 1968. "The Vendée and Counterrevolution: A Review Essay." *French Historical Studies* 5: 405-429.

Mollat, Michel, ed. 1971. *Histoire de l'Ile-de-France et de Paris.* Toulouse: Privat.

Mommsen, Wolfgang J., and Gerhard Hirschfeld, eds. 1982. *Social Protest, Violence, and Terror in Nineteenth- and Twentieth-Century Europe.* New York: St. Martins.

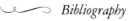

Monchicourt, Marie-France. 1974. *Structures sociales des quartiers de Grève, Saint-Avoye, Saint-Antoine, la Verrerie, 1670-1675.* Mémoire de maîtrise, University of Paris. Paris: Hachette. Microfiche.

Monin, Henri. 1884. *Essai sur l'histoire administrative du Languedoc pendant l'intendance de Basville (1685-1719).* Paris: Hachette.

Monin, Hippolyte. 1889. *L'état de Paris en 1789. Etudes et documents sur l'Ancien Régime à Paris.* Paris: Jouanot, Noblet & Quantin.

Monnier, Raymond. 1981. *Le faubourg Saint-Antoine (1789-1815).* Paris: Société des Etudes Robespierristes.

Montchrestien, Antoine. 1889. *Traité de l'économie politique.* Paris: Plon. First published in 1615.

Moore, Barrington, Jr. 1966. *Social Origins of Dictatorship and Democracy.* Boston: Beacon.

Moote, A. Lloyd. 1971. *The Revolt of the Judges: The Parlement of Paris and the Fronde, 1643-1652.* Princeton: Princeton University Press.

Morineau, Michel. 1971. *Les faux-semblants d'un démarrage économique: Agriculture et démographie en France au XVIIIe siècle.* Paris: Colin.

Mottez, Bernard. 1966. *Systémes de salaire et politiques patronales. Essai sur l'évolution des pratiques et des idéologies patronales.* Paris: Editions du Centre National de la Recherche Scientifique.

Mousnier, Roland. 1951. "L'évolution des finances publiques en France et en Angleterre pendant les guerres de la Ligue d'Augsbourg et de la Succession d'Espagne." *Revue Historique* 205: 1-23.

———— ed. 1964. *Lettres et mémoires adressés au Chancelier Séguier (1633-1649).* 2 vols. Paris: Presses Universitaires de France.

———— 1971. *La vénalité des offices sous Henri IV et Louis XIII.* 2d ed. Paris: Presses Universitaires de France.

———— 1978. *Paris capitale au temps de Richelieu et de Mazarin.* Paris: Pédone.

Müller, Klaus-Jurgen. 1980. "Protest—Modernisierung—Integration. Bemerkungen zum Problem faschistischer Phänomene in Frankreich 1924-1934." *Francia* 8: 465-524.

Musée Carnavalet. 1975. *L'ancien Hôtel de Ville de Paris et la Place de Grève.* Paris: Imprimerie Municipale.

———— 1982. *De la Place Louis XV à la Place de la Concorde.* Paris.

Nadaud, Martin. 1976. *Léonard, maçon de la Creuse.* Paris: Maspéro.

Napo, Felix. 1971. *1907: La révolte des vignerons.* Toulouse: Privat.

Nef, John U. 1940. *Industry and Government in France and England, 1540-1640.* Ithaca: Cornell University Press.

Neveux, Hugues. 1983. "Dimension idéologique des soulèvements paysans français au XVIIe siècle." *Bulletin de la Société d'Histoire Moderne* 82: 2-8.

Nicolas, Charles. 1883. *Les budgets de la France depuis le commencement du XIXe siècle.* Paris: Berger-Lévrault.

Nicolas, Jean. 1980. "Le tavernier, le juge, et le curé." *Histoire* 25: 20-28.

———— 1981. "La rumeur de Paris: Rapts d'enfants en 1750." *Histoire* 40: 48-57.

Noin, Daniel. 1973. *Géographie démographique de la France.* Paris: Presses Universitaires de France.

Oberschall, Anthony. 1978. "Theories of Social Conflict." *Annual Review of Sociology* 4: 291-315.

Olson, Mancur. 1965. *The Logic of Collective Action.* Cambridge: Harvard University Press.

O'Reilly, E. 1882. *Mémoires sur la vie publique et privée de Claude Pellot.* 2 vols. Paris: Champion.

Ozouf, Mona. 1971. "Le cortège et la ville: Les itinéraires parisiens des fêtes révolutionnaires." *Annales: Economies, Sociétés, Civilisations* 26: 889–916.

——— 1975. "Du mai de liberté à l'arbre de la liberté: Symbolisme révolutionnaire et tradition paysanne." *Ethnologie Française* 5: 9–32.

——— 1976. *La fête révolutionnaire, 1789–1799.* Paris: Gallimard.

——— 1977. "Innovations et traditions dans les itinéraires des fêtes révolutionnaires: L'exemple de Caen." *Ethnologie Française* 7: 45–54.

Pagès, Georges. 1937. "Autour du grand orage, Richelieu et Marillac: Deux politiques." *Revue Historique, Mémoires et Etudes,* January–March: 67–73.

Patouillet, Xavière. 1971. "L'émeute des Lanturelus à Dijon en 1630." Mémoire de maîtrise, Unité d'Enseignement et de Recherche, Sciences Humaines, Dijon.

Paul-Levy, Françoise. 1984. *La ville en croix. De la révolution de 1848 à la rénovation haussmannienne. Eléments pour une problématique générale.* Paris: Librairie des Méridiens.

Pavie, Eusèbe. 1899. *La guerre entre Louis XIII et Marie de Médicis, 1619–1620.* Angers: Germain & Grassin.

Pech, Rémy. 1975. "Les thèmes économiques et sociaux du socialisme ferrouliste à Narbonne (1880–1914)." In *Droite et Gauche. See* Huard 1975.

——— [1976]. *Entreprise viticole et capitalisme en Languedoc Roussillon du phylloxéra aux crises de mévente.* Association des Publications de l'Université de Toulouse–Le Mirail, series A, 27. Toulouse.

Perrot, Michelle. 1974. *Les ouvriers en grève. France 1871–1890.* 2 vols. Paris: Mouton.

Perrot, Michelle and Annie Kriegel. 1966. *Le socialisme français et le pouvoir.* Paris: Etudes et Documentation Internationale.

Péter, J. 1925. "Le pays d'Avesnes pendant les années d'invasion, 1793–1794." *Revue du Nord* 11: 161–212.

Péter, J., and Ch. Poulet. 1930–1933. *Histoire réligieuse du département du Nord pendant la Révolution (1789–1802).* 2 vols. Lille: Facultés Catholiques.

Petitfrère, Claude. 1974. *Blancs et Bleus d'Anjou (1789–1793)* 2 vols. Lille: Atelier de Reproduction des Thèses, Université de Lille III.

Peyrefitte, Alain, and Comité d'Etudes sur la Violence, la Criminalité, et la Délinquance. 1977. *Réponses à la violence.* 2 vols. Paris: Presses Pocket.

Pickles, Dorothy. 1965. *The Fifth French Republic.* 3d ed. London: Methuen.

Pierrard, Pierre. 1965. *La vie ouvrière à Lille sous le Second Empire.* Paris: Bloud & Gay.

——— 1967. *Lille et les lillois. Essai d'histoire collective contemporaine (de 1815 à nos jours).* Paris: Bloud & Gay.

——— 1975. "Habitat ouvrier et démographie à Lille au XIXe siècle et particulièrement sous le Second Empire." *Annales de Démographie Historique* 1975: 37–48.

——— 1976. *La vie quotidienne dans le Nord au XIXe siècle.* Paris: Hachette.

——— 1978. *Histoire du Nord. Flandre–Artois–Hainaut–Picardie.* Paris: Hachette.

Pierreuse, Robert. 1969. "L'ouvrier roubaisien et la propagande politique (1890–1900)." *Revue du Nord* 51: 249–273.

——— 1972. "La situation économique et sociale à Roubaix et à Tourcoing de 1900–1914." Thesis, Université de Lille III.

Pieyre, Adolphe. 1982. *Histoire de la ville de Nîmes depuis 1830 jusqu'à nos jours.* Marseille: Laffite Reprints.

Pilbeam, Pamela. 1976. "Popular Violence in Provincial France after the 1830 Revolution." *English Historical review* 91: 278–297.

Pillorget, René. 1975. *Les mouvements insurrectionnels de Provence entre 1596 et 1715.* Paris: Pédone.

Pinchemel, Philippe. 1969. *La France.* 2 vols. Paris: Colin.

Pinkney, David. 1972. *The French Revolution of 1830.* Princeton: Princeton University Press.

Pinol, Marc. 1975. "Dix ans de manifestations paysannes sous la Cinquième République (1962–1971)." *Revue de Géographie de Lyon* 50: 111–126.

Platelle, Henri. 1964. "Un village du Nord sous Louis XIV: Rumégies." *Revue du Nord* 46: 489–516.

Plouin, Renée. 1953. "L'Hôtel de Ville de Paris sous Haussmann." *La Vie Urbaine/Urbanisme et Habitation,* n.s., nos. 3–4: 241–250.

Plumyène, J., and R. Lasierra. 1963. *Les fascismes français 1923-63.* Paris: Seuil.

Poëte, Marcel. 1931. *Une vie de cité. Paris de sa naissance à nos jours.* Vol. 3 of *La spiritualité de la cité classique, les origines de la cité moderne (XVIe–XVIIe siècles).* Paris: Picard.

Poggi, Gianfranco. 1978. *The Development of the Modern State: A Sociological Introduction.* Stanford: Stanford University Press.

Poirier, Louis. 1934. "Bocage et plaine dans le sud de l'Anjou." *Annales de Géographie* 43: 22–31.

Poitrineau, Abel. 1961. "Aspects de la crise des justices seigneuriales dans l'Auvergne du dix-huitième siecle." *Revue Historique du Droit Français et Etranger,* 4th s. 38–39: 552–570.

Polet, Jean. 1969. "Les militants anarchistes dans le département du Nord au début du XXe siecle." *Revue du Nord* 51: 629–640.

Porchnev, Boris. 1963. *Les soulèvements populaires en France de 1623 à 1648.* Paris: SEVPEN.

Porot, Jean-François. 1974. *Structures sociales des quartiers de Grève, Saint-Avoye, et Saint-Antoine, 1789-1795.* Mémoire de maîtrise, University of Paris. Paris: Hachette. Microfiche.

Port, Célestin. 1861. *Inventaire analytique des archives anciennes de la Mairie d'Angers.* Paris: Dumoulin; Angers: Cosnier & Lachèse.

——— 1874–1878. *Dictionnaire historique, géographique, et biographique de Maine-et-Loire.* 3 vols. Paris: J.-B. Moulin; Angers: Lachèse & Dolbeau.

Pouget, Emile. 1976. *Le père peinard.* Edited by Roger Langlais. Paris: Editions Galilée.

Price, Roger D. 1973. "The French Army and the Revolution of 1830." *European Studies Review* 3: 243–267.

——— 1982. "Techniques of Repression: The Control of Popular Protest in Mid-Nineteenth-Century France." *Historical Journal* 25: 859–887.

Prost, Antoine. 1964. *La C.G.T. à l'époque du Front Populaire, 1934-1939. Essai de description numérique.* Cahiers de la Fondation Nationale des Sciences Politiques, 129. Paris: Colin.

——— 1966. "Les manifestations du 12 fevrier 1934 en province." *Le Mouvement Social* 54: 7–28.

——— 1967. "Les grèves de juin 1936, essai d'interprétation." In *Léon Bum chef de gou-*

vernement, 1936-1937. Cahiers de la Fondation Nationale des Sciences Politiques, 155. Paris: Colin.

Prouteau, Henri. 1938. *Les occupations d'usines en Italie et en France (1920-1936).* Paris: Librairie Technique et Economique.

Przeworski, Adam. 1977. "Proletariat into a Class: The Process of Class Formation from Karl Kautsky's *The Class Struggle* to Recent Controversies." *Politics and Society* 7: 343-401.

Przeworski, Adam; Barnett R. Rubin; and Ernest Underhill. "The Evolution of the Class Structure of France, 1901-1968." *Economic Development and Cultural Change* 28: 725-752.

Puls, Detlev, ed. 1979. *Wahrnehmungsformen und Protestverhalten. Studien zur Lage der Unterschichten im 18. and 19. Jahrhundert.* Frankfurt am Main: Suhrkamp.

Rancière, Jacques. 1981. *La nuit des prolétaires. Archives du rêve ouvrier.* Paris: Fayard.

Rascol, Pierre. 1961. *Les paysans de l'Albigeois à la fin de l'Ancien Régime.* Aurillac: Imprimerie Moderne.

Reardon, Judy. 1981. "Belgian and French Workers in Nineteenth-Century Roubaix." In *Class Conflict and Collective Action,* edited by Louise A. Tilly and Charles Tilly. Beverly Hills, Calif.: Sage.

Rebouillat, Marguerite. 1964. "Les luttes sociales dans un village du Mâconnais. Sercy pendant la Révolution." *Annales de Bourgogne* 36: 241-269.

Reboul, Pierre. 1954. "Troubles sociaux à Roubaix en juillet 1819." *Revue du Nord* 36: 339-350.

Reinhard, Marcel. 1971. *Nouvelle histoire de Paris. La Révolution 1789-1799.* Paris: Hachette.

Reinhard, Marcel; André Armengaud; and Jacques Dupâquier. 1968. *Histoire générale de la population mondiale.* Paris: Editions Montchrestien.

Relation de tout ce qui s'est passé à la Réception de Monseigneur le duc de Bourgogne et de Monseigneur le duc de Berry et pendant leur séjour à Toulouse et de leur navigation sur le Canal de communication des deux Mers. 1701. Toulouse: Boude.

Rémond, André. 1957. "Trois bilans de l'économie française au temps des théories physiocrates." *Revue d'Histoire Economique et Sociale* 35: 416-456.

Restif de la Bretonne, N. E. 1930. *Les nuits de Paris, la semaine nocturne, vingt nuits de Paris.* Edited by Henri Bachelin. L'Oeuvre de Restif de la Bretonne, 1. Paris: Editions du Trianon.

———— 1931. *Le paysan et la paysanne pervertie.* Edited by Henri Bachelin. L'Oeuvre de Restif de la Bretonne, 2. Paris: Editions du Trianon.

Reynaud, Jean-Daniel, and Yves Grafmeyer, eds. 1981. *Français, qui êtes-vous? Des essais et des chiffres.* Paris: Documentation Française.

Richard, Jean. 1956. "Le 'droit des garçons' dans la région de Saint-Jean-de-Rosne." *Annales de Bourgogne* 28: 264-266.

———— 1961. "La levée des 300,000 hommes et les troubles de mars 1793 en Bourgogne." *Annales de Bourgogne* 33: 213-251.

Rioux, Jean-Pierre. 1980-1983. *La France de la Quatrième République.* 2 vols. Paris: Seuil.

Robbe, Marie-Agnès. 1937. "La milice dans l'intendance de la Flandre wallonne au XVIIIe siècle." *Revue du Nord* 23: 5-50.

Robert, Daniel. 1967. "Louis XIV et les Protestants." *XVIIe Siècle* 76-77: 39-52.

Robin, Régine. 1970. *La société française en 1789: Sémur-en-Auxois.* Paris: Plon.

Roche, Daniel. 1978. *Le Siècle des Lumières en province. Académies et académiciens provinciaux, 1680-1789.* 2 vols. Paris: Mouton & Ecole des Hautes Etudes en Sciences Sociales.

——— 1981. *Le peuple de Paris.* Paris: Aubier Montaigne.

Rokkan, Stein, and Derek W. Urwin. 1982. "Centres and Peripheries in Western Europe." In *The Politics of Territorial Identity: Studies in European Regionalism,* edited by Stein Rokkan and Derek Urwin. Beverly Hills, Calif.: Sage.

Roubaud, François. 1983. "Partition économique de la France dans la première moitié du XIXe siècle (1830-1840)." *Institut d'Histoire Economique et Sociale de l'Université de Paris I (Panthéon-Sorbonne), Recherches et Travaux* 12, 33-58.

Rougerie, Jacques. 1964. "Composition d'une population insurgée. L'exemple de la Commune." *Le Mouvement Social* 48: 31-47.

——— 1971. *Paris libre 1871.* Paris: Seuil.

——— 1972. "L'A.I.T. et le mouvement ouvrier à Paris pendant les évènements de 1870-1871." *International Review of Social History* 17: 3-101.

——— 1977. "Recherche sur le Paris du XIXe siècle. Espace populaire et espace révolutionnaire: Paris 1870-1871." *Institut d'Histoire Economique et Sociale de l'Université de Paris I (Panthéon-Sorbonne), Recherches et Travaux* 5, 48-83.

Roupnel, Gaston. 1955. *La ville et la campagne au XVIIe siècle. Etude sur les populations du pays dijonnais.* Paris: Colin.

Royer, Jean-Michel. 1958. "De Dorgères à Poujade." In *Les paysans et la politique,* edited by Jacques Fauvet and Henri Mendras. Cahiers de la Fondation Nationale des Sciences Politiques, 94. Paris: Colin.

Ruault, Nicolas. 1976. *Gazette d'un parisien sous la Révolution. Lettres à son frère 1783-1796.* Paris: Perrin.

Rudé, George. 1959. *The Crowd in the French Revolution.* Oxford: Clarendon Press.

——— 1964. *The Crowd in History: A Study of Popular Disturbances in France and England, 1730-1848.* New York: Wiley.

Ruttan, Vernon W. 1978. "Structural Retardation and the Modernization of French Agriculture: A Skeptical View." *Journal of Economic History* 38: 714-728.

Saché, Marc. 1930-1931. "Trente années de vie provinciale d'après le journal de Toisonnier. Angers (1683-1713)." *La Province d'Anjou* 5: 167-177, 224-239, 262-272, 301-311; 6: 19-34.

Sagnes, Jean. 1980. *Le mouvement ouvrier en Languedoc. Syndicalistes et socialistes de l'Hérault de la fondation des bourses du travail à la naissance du Parti Communiste.* Toulouse: Privat.

Saint-Germain, Jacques. 1962. *La Reynie et la police au Grand Siècle.* Paris: Hachette.

Saint-Jacob, Pierre de. 1947. "La fin des impositions directes d'Ancien Régime en Bourgogne." *Annales de Bourgogne* 19: 249-259.

——— 1948. "La situation des paysans de la Côte d'Or en 1848." *Etudes d'Histoire Moderne et Contemporaine* 2: 231-242.

——— 1960. *Les paysans de la Bourgogne du Nord.* Paris: Les Belles Lettres.

——— 1962. *Documents relatifs à la communauté villageoise en Bourgogne du milieu du XVIIe siècle à la Révolution.* Paris: Les Belles Lettres.

Saint-Léger, Alexandre de. 1900. *La Flandre maritime et Dunkerque sous la domination française (1659-1789).* Paris and Lille: Cassette.

——— 1942. *Histoire de Lille des origines à 1789.* Lille: Raoust.

Duc de Saint-Simon. 1873. *Mémoires du duc de Saint-Simon.* Edited by Mm. Chéruel and Ad. Régnier fils. 21 vols. Paris: Hachette.

Salert, Barbara, and John Sprague. 1980. *The Dynamics of Riots.* Ann Arbor: Inter-University Consortium for Political and Social Research.

Sanson, Rosemonde. 1976. *Les 14 juillet, fête et conscience nationale, 1789-1975.* Paris: Flammarion.

Sauvageot, Jacques; Alan Geismar; Daniel Cohn-Bendit; and Jean-Pierre Duteil. 1968. *La révolte étudiante. Les animateurs parlent.* Edited by Hervé Bourges. Paris: Seuil.

Sauvy, Alfred. 1965-1972. *Histoire économique de la France entre les deux guerres.* 3 vols. Paris: Fayard.

Schmid, Alex P., and Janny de Graaf. 1982. *Violence as Communication: Insurgent Terrorism and the Western News Media.* Beverly Hills, Calif.: Sage.

Schneider, Robert A. 1982. "Urban Sociability in the Old Regime: Religion and Culture in Early Modern Toulouse." Ph.D. diss., University of Michigan.

Schnerb, Robert. 1923-1924. "La Côte d'Or et l'insurrection de juin 1848." *La Révolution de 1848* 20: 155-170, 205-221.

——— 1973. *Deux siècles de fiscalité française, XIXe-XXe siècle. Histoire, économie, politique.* Paris: Mouton.

Schultz, Patrick. 1982. *La décentralisation administrative dans le département du Nord (1790-1793).* Lille: Presses Universitaires de Lille.

Schwarz, Salomon. 1937. "Les occupations d'usines en France de mai et juin 1936." *International Review of Social History* 2: 50-100.

Seale, Patrick, and Maureen McConville. 1968. *Drapeaux rouges sur la France.* Translated by Jean-René Major. Paris: Mercure de France.

Ségrestin, Denis. 1975. "Du syndicalisme de métier au syndicalisme de classe: Pour une sociologie de la CGT." *Sociologie du Travail* 17: 152-173.

Seidman, Michael. 1981. "The Birth of the Weekend and the Revolts against Work: The Workers of the Paris Region during the Popular Front (1936-38)." *French Historical Studies* 12: 249-276.

Sentou, Jean. 1969. *Fortune et groupes sociaux à Toulouse sous la Révolution (1789-1799), Essai d'histoire statistique.* Toulouse: Privat.

Shapiro, Gilbert, and Philip Dawson. 1972. "Social Mobility and Political Radicalism: The Case of the French Revolution of 1789." In *The Dimensions of Quantitative Research in History,* edited by William O. Aydelotte, Allan G. Bogue, and Robert William Fogel. Princeton: Princeton University Press.

Siauve, Gustave. 1896. *Roubaix socialiste, ou quatre ans de gestion municipale ouvrière (1892-1896).* Lille: Delory.

Siegfried, André. 1911. "Le régime et la division de la propriété dans le Maine et l'Anjou." *Annales du Musée Social* 1911: 195-215.

Singer-Kérel, Jeanne. 1961. *Le coût de la vie à Paris de 1840 à 1954.* Recherches sur l'Economie Française, 3. Paris: Colin.

Small, Melvin, and J. David Singer. 1982. *Resort to Arms: International and Civil Wars, 1816-1980.* Beverly Hills, Calif.: Sage.

Smith, J. Harvey. 1978. "Agricultural Workers and the French Wine-Growers' Revolt of 1907." *Past & Present* 79: 101-125.

Snyder, David. 1976. "Theoretical and Methodological Problems in the Analysis of Government Coercion and Collective Violence." *Journal of Political and Military Sociology* 4: 277-293.

Soboul, Albert. 1958. *Les campagnes montpelliéraines à la fin de l'Ancien Régime. Propriété et cultures d'après les compoix.* La Roche-sur-Yon: Potier.

———— 1962. *Précis d'histoire de la Révolution française.* Paris: Editions Sociales.

———— 1970. *La civilisation et la Révolution française.* Vol. 1: *La crise de l'Ancien Régime.* Paris: Arthaud.

Sonenscher, Michael. 1983. "Work and Wages in Paris in the Eighteenth Century." In *Manufacture in Town and Country before the Factory,* edited by Maxine Berg, Pat Hudson, and Michael Sonenscher. Cambridge: Cambridge University Press.

Spuhler, Hans. 1975. *Der Generalstreik der Eisenbahner in Frankreich von 1910. Das Scheitern des Revolutionären Syndikalismus und die repressive Politik Briands.* Berlin: Duncker & Humblot.

Stearns, Peter N. 1968. "Against the Strike Threat: Employer Policy toward Labor Agitation in France, 1900–1914." *Journal of Modern History* 40: 474–500.

Stevenson, Robert Louis. 1926. *Travels with a Donkey in the Cévennes.* New York: Scribner's.

Stone, Bailey. 1981. *The Parlement of Paris, 1774–1789.* Chapel Hill: University of North Carolina Press.

Strong, Ann Louise. 1971. *Planned Urban Environments: Sweden, Finland, Israel, the Netherlands, France.* Baltimore: Johns Hopkins University Press.

Tapié, Victor L. 1952. *La France de Louis XIII et de Richelieu.* Paris: Flammarion.

Tarrow, Sidney. 1983. *Struggling to Reform: Social Movements and Policy Change during Cycles of Protest.* Western Societies Program Occasional Papers, 15. Ithaca: Center for International Studies, Cornell University.

Tavernier, Yves. 1962. "Le syndicalisme paysan et la politique agricole du gouvernement (juin 1958–avril 1962)." *Revue Française de Science Politique* 12: 599–646.

Thbaut, Louis. 1979. "Les voies navigables et l'industrialisation du Nord de la France." *Revue du Nord* 61: 149–164.

Théry, Louis. 1923. "Une commune rurale de la Flandre française au début de la Révolution: Frelinghien." *Revue du Nord* 9: 193–205.

Thomas, Alexandre. 1844. *Une province sous Louis XIV. Situation politique et administrative de la Bourgogne de 1661 à 1715.* Paris: Joubert.

Thompson, Edward P. 1972. " 'Rough Music': Le charivari anglais." *Annales: Economies, Sociétés, Civilisations* 27: 285–312.

Thompson, J. K. J. 1982. *Clermont-de-Lodève, 1633–1789: Fluctuations in the Prosperity of a Languedocian Cloth-Making Town.* Cambridge: Cambridge University Press.

———— 1983. "Variations in Industrial Structure in Pre-Industrial Languedoc." In *Manufacture in Town and Country before the Factory,* edited by Maxine Berg, Pat Hudson, and Michael Sonenscher. Cambridge: Cambridge University Press.

Tilly, Louise A. 1972. "La révolte frumentaire, forme de conflit politique en France." *Annales: Economies, Sociétés, Civilisations* 27: 731–757.

Tocqueville, Alexis de. 1978. *Souvenirs.* Paris: Gallimard. Written in 1850–1851, first published in 1893.

Torsvik, Per, ed. 1981. *Mobilization, Center-Periphery Structures, and Nation-Building: A Volume in Commemoration of Stein Rokkan.* Bergen: Universitetsforlaget.

Toulemonde, Jacques. 1966a. "Notes sur l'industrie roubaisienne et tourquennoise dans la première moitié de XIXe siècle." *Revue du Nord* 48: 321–336.

——— 1966b. *Naissance d'une métropole. Histoire économique et sociale de Roubaix et Tourcoing au XIXe siècle.* Tourcoing: Frère.

Touraine, Alain. 1955. *L'évolution du travail ouvrier aux usines Renault.* Paris: Centre National de la Recherche Scientifique.

——— 1968. *Le mouvement de mai ou le communisme utopique.* Paris: Seuil.

——— 1981. *The Voice and the Eye: An Analysis of Social Movements.* Cambridge: Cambridge University Press.

Touraine, Alain; Michel Wieviorka; and François Dubet. 1984. *Le mouvement ouvrier.* Paris: Fayard.

Toutain, J.-C. 1963. *La population de la France de 1700 à 1959.* Cahiers de l'Institut de Science Economique Appliquée, no. 133, series AF, 3. Paris: L'Institut de Science Economique Appliquée.

Traugott, Mark. 1978. "Reconceiving Social Movements." *Social Problems* 26: 38–49.

Trénard, Louis. 1972. "Pauvreté, charité, assistance à Lille, 1708–1790." *97e Congrès National des Sociétés Savantes, Nantes 1972. Histoire Moderne* 1: 473–498.

——— 1974. "La crise révolutionnaire dans les pays-bas français. Etat des recherches." *Annales Historiques de la Révolution Française* 46: 292–316.

——— 1975. *Les mémoires des intendants pour l'instruction du duc de Bourgogne (1698). Introduction générale.* Paris: Bibliothèque Nationale.

———, ed. 1977a. *Histoire d'une métropole. Lille–Roubaix–Tourcoing.* Toulouse: Privat.

——— 1977b. "Provinces et départements des Pays-Bas français aux départements du Nord et du Pas-de-Calais." In *Régions et régionalisme en France du XVIIIe siècle à nos jours,* edited by Christian Gras and Georges Livet. Paris: Presses Universitaires de France.

———, ed. 1977c. *L'intendance de Flandre wallonne en 1698.* Paris: Bibliothèque Nationale.

——— 1977d. "Les fêtes révolutionnaires dans une région frontière. Nord–Pas-de-Calais." In *Les fêtes de la Révolution,* edited by Jean Ehrard and Paul Viallaneix. Paris: Société des Etudes Robespierristes.

——— 1978. "Lille au siècle des Lumières." *De Franse Nederlanden* 1978: 193–207.

——— 1981. "Notables de la région lilloise au seuil du XIXème siècle." *Revue du Nord* 63: 169–187.

——— 1983. "D'une culture régionale à une culture française: Lille de 1667 à 1715." In *Pouvoir, ville, et société en Europe 1650-1750,* edited by Georges Livet and Bernard Vogler. Paris: Ophrys.

Truquin, Norbert. 1977. *Mémoires et aventures d'un prolétaire à travers la révolution.* Paris: Maspéro.

Tudesq, André-Jean. 1964. *Les grands notables en France (1840-1849). Etude historique d'une psychologie sociale.* 2 vols. Paris: Presses Universitaires de France.

——— 1967. "Les influences locales dans l'administration centrale en France sous la Monarchie de Juillet." *Annali della Fondazione Italiana per la Storia Amministrativa* 4: 367–386.

Tulard, Jean. 1976. *Paris et son administration (1800-1830).* Paris: Commission des Travaux Historiques, Ville de Paris.

Union National des Etudiants de France and Syndicat National de l'Enseignement Supérieur. 1968. *Le livre noir des journées de mai.* Paris: Seuil.

Urlanis, B. Ts. 1960. *Voin'i i narodo-naselienie Evrop'i. Liudskie poteri vooruzhienn'ix sil evro-*

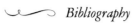

peiiskix stran v voinax XVII–XX vv {Wars and European populations: Losses of life in the armed forces of European countries, seventeenth to twentieth centuries}. Moscow: Izdatel'stvo Sotsial'no-ekonomicheskoi literatur'i.

Vallès, Jean. 1975. *L'insurgé.* Paris: Gallimard. First published as articles in 1883–1884, and as a book in 1886.

Van Doersen, Arie Theodorus. 1960. *Professions et métiers interdits. Un aspect de l'histoire de la révocation de l'Edit de Nantes.* Groningen: J. B. Wolters.

Vauthier, Gabriel, 1921. "Cérémonies et fêtes nationales sous la Seconde République." *La Révolution de 1848 et les Révolutions du XIXe Siècle* 18: 51–63.

Vermander, Dominique. 1978. *Un siècle d'histoire ouvrière à Halluin (1840–1940).* Halluin: La Maison pour Tous.

——— 1982. "La cité pré-industrielle d'Halluin au milieu du XIXe siècle." *De Franse Nederlanden* 1982: 33–61.

Viala, Louis. 1909. *La question des grains à Toulouse au dix-huitième siècle (de 1715 à 1789).* Toulouse: Privat.

Vidal de la Blache, Paul. 1908. *La France, tableau géographique.* Paris: Hachette.

Viennot, J.-P. 1969. "La population de Dijon d'après le recensement de 1851." *Annales de Démographie Historique* 1969: 241–260.

Walton, John. 1984. *Reluctant Rebels: Comparative Studies of Revolution and Underdevelopment.* New York: Columbia University Press.

Weber, Eugen. 1962. *Action Française: Royalism and Reaction in Twentieth-Century France.* Stanford: Stanford University Press.

Weir, David R. 1976. "Collective Action in Winegrowing Regions: A Comparison of Burgundy and the Midi." Working Paper 137, Center for Research on Social Organization, University of Michigan.

Wemyss, Alice. 1961. *Les Protestants du Mas-d'Azil. Histoire d'une résistance (1680–1830).* Toulouse: Privat.

Willard, Claude. 1965. *Le mouvement socialiste en France (1893–1905). Les Guesdistes.* Paris: Editions Sociales.

Williams, Philip. 1958. *Politics in Post-War France: Parties and the Constitution in the Fourth Republic.* 2d ed. London: Longmans.

Wilson, Kenneth L., and Anthony Orum. 1976. "Mobilizing People for Collective Political Action." *Journal of Political and Military Sociology* 4: 187–202.

Wolfe, Martin, 1972. *The Fiscal System of Renaissance France.* New Haven: Yale University Press.

Wolff, Philippe, ed. 1967. *Histoire du Languedoc.* Toulouse: Privat.

——— 1974. *Histoire de Toulouse.* Toulouse: Privat.

Wood, James L., and Maurice Jackson. 1982. *Social Movements: Development, Participation, and Dynamics.* Belmont, Calif.: Wadsworth.

Wright, Gordon. 1964. *Rural Revolution in France: The Peasantry in the Twentieth Century.* Stanford: Stanford University Press.

Young, Arthur. 1976. *Voyages en France. 1787, 1788, 1789.* Translated and edited by Henri Sée. 3 vols. Paris: Colin.

Zeeuw, J. W. de. 1978. "Peat and the Dutch Golden Age. The Historical Meaning of Energy-Attainability." *A.A.G. Bijdragen* 21: 3–32.

INDEX

Abscon: strikes in, 265, 369

Action Française, 321, 322, 323, 324, 362, 370

Administration, 130, 136, 142, 259-260, 266-267, 338-339, 395-396; of Burgundy, 13-14, 18, 39-40, 208, 401-403; of Languedoc, 72, 170-171, 172, 191, 209, 401; of Anjou, 95, 100, 109-114, 115; of Brittany, 147; of Flanders, 209

Administrative reform, 227, 228, 230, 239, 253-255

African workers, 378

Agricultural laborers, 279, 296, 298, 328, 354-355, 358, 364; contention by, 200, 250; strikes by, 362, 366, 367, 372, 373

Agricultural policy, 374, 376. *See also* Food supply control

Agricultural production, 22, 109, 207, 211

Agriculture, 60, 65, 66, 67, 212, 244, 298, 354; in Anjou, 110, 201, 206, 242, 275-276, 281, 282; in Languedoc, 183, 185-186, 191-197, 205-206, 242, 276, 280-282, 308, 358, 376, 399-400; in Burgundy, 202, 207, 242, 276, 280-281, 282, 353, 358; in the Ile-de-France, 204, 242, 277, 282, 308, 355, 358; in Flanders, 242, 257, 259, 275, 282, 355, 358, 401. *See also* Winegrowing

d'Aguesseau, intendant of Languedoc, 154, 155

Aides. See Pancarte

Aix, contention in, 222, 229

Albert, Marcellin, 365, 366

Albi, contention in, 190, 191, 222

Algeria, 342, 343-344, 364, 370, 384, 385

Alsace, 224

Alsace-Lorraine, 379

American war (1776-1783), 47, 171, 210, 224

Angelets, contention by, 146, 147, 150-151

Angers, 71, 72, 103, 213, 282, 291, 297, 400; description of, 70-80; contention in, 84-90, 92, 93-98, 139, 146, 243, 299-302; celebrations in, 87, 89, 106, 299-300; city council of, 101-102, 104, 107, 110-112, 114; population of, 283, 285; strikes in, 302-303; demonstrations in, 305, 369, 371

Anjou, 89, 201-202, 206, 212, 289, 291, 308, 400; description of, 68, 71, 275-276, 352-353; contention in, 80-83, 84, 242, 243, 295-303, 304, 306, 363, 386

Anor, 270

Antimilitarist demonstrations, 320

Anti-Semitism, 303, 326, 331, 334

Antiwar demonstrations, 36-38, 344, 345

Anzin, 257; strikes in, 263-265, 272; contention in, 269, 305

Ardèche, 305, 307. _See also_ Languedoc

d'Argenson, marquis, 215

Argenteuil, contention in, 137, 325

Armistice Day, 320, 326, 333

Army, 117, 126, 128, 129–131, 342. _See also_ Soldiers; War

Artisans, 279, 288; contention by, 138–139, 189, 200, 295, 386

Artois, 279, 280, 351

Assemblies, 117, 160, 237, 238, 242–243. _See also_ Parlement; Protestant assemblies

Assembly of Notables, 227

Association Républicaine des Anciens Combattants, 324

Aubenas, contention in, 138, 151

Aude, 355, 356; strikes in, 364

Audiat, Pierre, 333–334

Audijos rebellion, 147, 149–150

Aulnay-sous-Bois, 329

d'Autichamp, marquis, 299

Automobile workers, 317; strikes by, 307, 316, 322, 323, 326, 327, 340, 378

Avesnes, 257, 269

Aveyron, 356, 363

Aymeries, 271

Bachelors' guilds, 30–31

Bakers, 240; attacks on, 22–23, 109, 157–158, 191, 222–223, 247, 270, 339; contention by, 86, 241

Barbier, Edmond-Jean-François, 217–220

Bastide-de-Besplas, 191

Bastille, fall of, 237–238, 243

Bastille Day, 59, 320–321, 328–329, 331, 333, 334

Basville, Lamoignon de, intendant of Languedoc, 155–156, 164–171, 172, 173–176, 186, 187, 188, 205

Beaune: contention in, 35, 36, 293, 305, 308; demonstrations in, 374

Belgian workers, 272; attacks on, 261–262, 269, 302, 369

Bellegarde, duke of, 402, 403

Bénauge, 147, 148

Bergues, 255; contention in, 247, 249

Berry, duchess of, 299

Berry, duke of, 162, 163–164

Bessan, 179–180

Berthier de Sauvigny, intendant of Paris, 239

Béziers: contention in, 305; demonstrations in, 365, 375

Blanquart, Jean-Baptiste, 249–250

Bleachers, strikes by, 302

Blois, 372

Blum, Léon, 327, 328, 329, 330, 331, 371–372

Bocage, 275–276, 296, 298, 301, 400

Boeschepe, 362–363

Bois, Paul, 296

Boistelle, count of, 246

Bonaparte, Prince Pierre, 313

Bonnets Rouges. _See_ Révolte du Papier Timbré

Bordeaux: contention in, 94, 95, 143, 148, 152, 222; parlement of, 227

Bottin, Sébastien, 255, 257

Bouchu, intendant of Burgundy, 16, 19

Boulogne and Boulonnais, contention in, 147, 148–149

Bourgeois, 195–197, 239, 242, 263, 273, 292, 403; contention by, 218, 243, 268, 293, 295–297, 388, 389; attacks on, 248, 291

Bourg-sur-Aisne, 137

Bourse du travail, 311

Boxmakers, strikes by, 325

Bread: prices, 23, 222, 230, 231, 240, 251; rationing, 371

Brienne, Loménie de, 229, 231

Brittany, 147, 229, 296, 376; contention in, 151–153, 363, 372, 374–375, 378, 393

Bucard, Marcel, 331

Burgundy, 202, 289, 291, 308, 358, 363; contention in, 17–24, 29, 139, 242, 243, 293, 304, 305, 306, 310, 401–404; description of, 69, 70, 276, 353

Burgundy, duke of, 162, 163–164, 166, 201, 202

Cabet, Etienne, 33, 35

Cabinetmakers, strikes by, 300, 316

Cagoule, 331

Cambrai, 253, 257; contention in, 246, 248, 271

Cambrésis, 211, 351; contention in, 248, 292

Camelots du Roi, 322–323

Camisards, 147, 156, 174–178, 186, 199

Capestan, 172

Capitalist development, 60–61, 73, 182, 206–208, 257–261, 387–388, 395–397, 401; and contention, 5–8, 9, 11, 16–17, 20–24, 397–398

Capitation, 165, 175, 185

Carcassonne, 193–194, 276, 281; contention in, 138, 146, 190–191, 306, 365

Carpenters: contention by, 226; strikes by, 302, 316

Castres, 177–178

Catalans, contention by, 150

Catholic church, 128, 185, 186, 278, 291, 293, 362, 368, 388, 389; supporting resistance, 25, 29, 92–93, 95–96, 223, 363; attacks on, 138, 152, 174, 204, 236–237; disestablishment of, 251, 272, 295–296, 298, 303, 306, 400; reorganization of, 252, 297; power of, 291, 297, 388. *See also* Church property; Tithe

Celebrations, 117, 139, 310, 389; in Burgundy, 2, 30–31, 402–403; in Anjou, 87, 89, 106, 299–300; in Languedoc, 163–164, 180; in Flanders, 252–253, 266, 268

Céret, 150

Cévennes, 165, 168, 182, 183–184; contention in, 155, 174–175, 176. *See also* Languedoc

CFDT. *See* Confédération Française Democratique du Travail

CGT. *See* Confédération Générale du Travail

CGTU. *See* Confédération Générale du Travail Unifiée

Chalon[-sur Saone], 146

Chamber of Deputies, 317–318, 319, 328, 343, 346, 374; demonstrations against, 322, 323, 324

Champagne, 29, 367

Champmoron Wood, 15–16

Charenton, 240

Charivari, 30–34, 199, 225, 310, 382, 389

Charles X, 304

Charmois, 24

Chassecoquins, 2

Châtillon-sur-Seine, 34, 276, 293, 305

Chaulnes, duke of, 152

Chiappe, Jean, 322, 323, 324, 328

Cholet, 212, 276, 280, 297; strikes in, 300–301, 302, 303

Chouannerie, 296, 299, 300

Church property, 205–206, 250, 292, 307, 396

Civil wars, 80–83, 84, 119–127, 155, 383. *See also* Fronde; Wars of Religion

Class divisions, 5, 273, 283, 298

Class war, 151, 161, 263, 266

Cléon, 346

Clichy, 282; strikes in, 325; demonstrations in, 329–330

Cohn-Bendit, Daniel, 345–346

Colbert, Charles, 103

Colbert, J. C., 13, 115, 132, 148, 152, 388, 396

Coal mining, 201, 204, 276, 351–352, 360, 379, 401

Collective action, 3–4, 10, 74–78, 116–117, 381–382, 390–395

Collective bargaining, 271, 327, 328, 377

Comité de Défense Paysanne, 372, 373

Commarin, 146

Common interests, 25, 74–75, 76, 77

Common rights, 25, 40, 73, 74–75, 146–147, 242

Commune. *See* Paris Commune

Communists, Communist party, 320, 324, 326, 327, 331, 332, 339, 340–341, 372; demonstrations by, 319, 323, 325, 334, 368–369, 370–371, 374

Compagnies de garçons. See Bachelors' guilds

Compiègne, 224

Condé, prince of, 17, 91, 94, 95, 122, 126, 143–145, 202

Confédération Française Démocratique du Travail (CFDT), 346, 347–348, 378

Confédération Générale des Betteraviers, 373
Confédération Générale du Travail (CGT), 311, 326, 340, 343, 348, 362, 371, 378, 380; program of, 315–316, 318, 319, 327; demonstrations by, 316, 319, 324, 345, 346; strikes by, 330, 346
Confédération Générale du Travail Unifiée (CGTU), 326, 368
Conscription, 254, 288; resistance to, 180, 219, 242, 251–252, 293, 297
Construction industry, 355
Construction workers, 55, 315; strikes by, 226, 300, 302, 316, 317
Consumption taxes. *See* Excise taxes
Contention, 3–4, 381–382, 386–390; historical analysis of, 9–12
Coopers, contention by, 194
Corsica, 342, 343
Côte d'Or, 358, 366; strikes in, 360, 369, 370. *See also* Burgundy
Coty, René, 343
Couëron, 226
Courbevoie, strikes in, 323, 326
Courts, 102, 128, 195–196, 229, 262–263. *See also* Sentences
Crafts. *See* Guilds
Crimean War, 384
Croix de Feu, 321, 322, 323, 324, 329, 370, 373. *See also* Parti Social Français

Daily routines, 10, 11, 75, 76
Daladier, Edouard, 323–324, 330, 343
Day of Tiles, 229
Déat, Marcel, 332
Deaths, 191; from contention, 189–190, 272, 329, 382, 383–385. *See also* Executions
Deloncle, Eugène, 331
Demonstrations, 307, 310, 328–329, 341, 342, 382–383, 385–386, 391; in Flanders, 270, 305, 310, 368–369; in Anjou, 303; in the Ile-de-France, 305, 344–346, 348–349; in Languedoc, 393. *See also* Police: and demonstrators; Troops: and demonstrators
Denain, 269; strikes in, 265

Dieudonné, Christopher, 255, 257
Dijon, 36, 72, 212, 282, 291, 401–402; celebrations in, 2, 402–403: demonstrations in, 2–3, 305, 310–312, 369, 371; municipal council of, 13–14; contention in, 14–17, 18, 20–23, 26–29, 139, 140, 229, 243, 293, 304, 402–404: parlement of, 20–21; grain seizures in, 222
Dorgères, Henri (pseudonym), 372, 373, 374, 394
Doriot, Jacques, 332, 334
Douai, 253, 257, 2790–280: contention in, 247, 248, 266, 269; demonstrations in, 252, 262, 305
Dreyfus affair, 303, 318, 321–322
Droit annuel, 83
Dufie, Normand, 274–275
Dugué de Bagnols, intendant of Flanders, 203–204
Dumoulin, Roger, 380
Dunkerque, 203, 279; contention in, 247, 249; strikes in, 369
Durtal, 299
Dutch War, 127, 152
Duval d'Epremesnil, Jean Jacques IV, 228

Edict of Nantes, 121–122, 154, 155, 156
Eight-hour day, demand for, 313, 314–319, 328
Elbeuf, duke of, 149
Élection, 89, 139, 172, 204, 402–403
Elections, electoral campaigns, 271, 272, 317–318, 347, 389, 396
Ellul, Jacques, 380
Enclosure, 214, 276; resistance to, 23–24, 25, 199, 226, 246, 247, 383, 389
Enlightenment, 293–294
Entry taxes, 104
Errand boys, contention by, 226
Estates, 205, 242; of Languedoc, 170; of Burgundy, 202, 402, 403.
Estates General, 211, 216, 231, 234, 237, 238, 295. *See also* Third Estate; National Assembly
Etampes, 137
Excise taxes, 35, 152, 215, 236

Executions, 137, 139, 149, 178, 182, 188, 239; in Paris, 46, 48–50, 53, 220, 233, 234, 235; in Angers, 86, 102; in La Rochelle, 124
Exile, as punishment, 208, 221, 227

Factories, 5, 258, 278, 279–280, 283. *See also* Sitdown strike
Fallières, Armand, 315
Famine, 109, 110, 156–157
Farmers, 292, 388; attacks on, 224, 247; contention by, 297, 372–376, 378, 379, 393
Farmers' movements, 375, 385
Fascism, 321; demonstrations against, 324, 325, 326, 333–334, 343, 369
Fatalities from contention. *See* Deaths
February Revolution (1848). *See* Revolution of 1848
Fédération de l'Education Nationale (FEN), 348
Fédération Nationale des Contribuables, 324
Fédération Nationale de Syndicats d'Exploitants Agricoles (FNSEA), 373
Federation of Construction Trades, 315
Federation Wall, 320, 327, 348
Ferrant, intendant of Burgundy, 158–159, 202
Feudal dues, 195, 196, 248, 292
Feudal rights, 25, 73, 74–75, 191
Fifth Republic, 343
Figeac, 137
Financiers, 129, 132, 279
Firewood, right to cut, 15–16, 18–19, 198
Firm-by-firm strike, 6, 10, 271, 303, 309, 389, 394, 396
First Empire, 288
Fiscal administration, 228, 260, 291, 330, 371. *See also* Public finance
Fiscal policy, 213, 214, 251, 329, 372, 373. *See also* Taxation; War: financing of
Fiscal power, 254, 259, 288
Fishing industry, 354, 355, 358
Fishwives, contention by, 227, 236, 240, 294
Fitz-James, duke of, 180–181

Flanders, 206, 207, 250–251, 279, 289, 291, 308, 358, 360; war in, 13, 143, 146, 158; description of, 69, 71–72, 202–204, 211, 275, 351–352, 356; contention in, 94, 146, 158, 242, 243, 292, 298, 304, 363, 374, 376, 400–401
Flemish Flanders, 202, 203–204
Fleurant, Gabriel, 372
Flines, 252
Flins-sur-Seine, 346
Flour War, 222, 224
Foix, 181
Fontainebleau, 231
Food prices, 157, 185, 213, 220, 225–226, 232, 249, 265, 270–271, 272, 310. *See also* Bread: prices
"Food riots," 20, 156, 234, 270, 304
Food supply control, 78, 156–159, 213, 214, 220, 221, 339, 387; in Anjou, 107–114, 115, 117–118, 208, 295, 301; in Languedoc, 184–187, 191–192; in Flanders, 246, 248, 249, 269–271; in the Ile-de-France, 294, 296. *See also* Grain seizures; Grain trade
Force Ouvrière, 340, 348
Foreign workers, 263; contention against, 194, 262. *See also* African workers; Belgian workers
Forestry industry, 354, 355, 358
Forster, Robert, 197
Foundry workers, strikes by, 302, 322, 323
Fourastié, Jean, 380
Fourmies, 272; contention in, 266, 270
Four Sous Riot, 263–265
Fourteenth of July. *See* Bastille Day
Franche-Comté, 13, 281
Francistes, 324, 329, 331
Franco-Prussian War, 306, 384
Frêche, Georges, 183
Frelinghien, contention in, 249–250
French Morocco, 333
French Section of the Workers' International (SFIO), 315
Fronde, 17, 40, 91–101, 115, 134, 140–145, 387, 388, 398, 400
Front de Libération Nationale (FLN), 342

Front Paysan, 372, 373

Gabelle. *See* Salt tax
Garancière, 137
Gard, contention in, 305, 356. *See also*
    Languedoc
Gasoline surtax, 324
de Gaulle, Charles, 334, 339, 340,
    342–343, 345–347, 396
Gaullists, 339, 340, 370–371
Gendarmerie Nationale, 289
General strike, 306, 314, 318, 349, 379,
    398; in Flanders, 271, 368, 371; in the
    Ile-de-France, 325, 330, 371
General Winegrowers' Confederation, 366
Gimon, 137
Giscard d'Estaing, Valéry, 58, 380
Glassworkers, demonstrations by, 37
Godefroy, Jean, 203, 204
Goislard de Montsabert, Anne Louis, 228
Grain, 107; prices, 183; taxes, 23, 188
Grain blockages, 21, 114, 270, 294, 301,
    302, 305, 307
Grain seizures, 207, 209, 221–222, 229,
    231, 305, 307, 310, 388, 389, 397; in
    Burgundy, 20–23, 24, 34, 40, 222; in
    Anjou, 108, 111, 113–114, 116; in the
    Ile-de-France, 157–158, 222–223, 224,
    241, 294; in Languedoc, 158, 186,
    188–189, 190–192, 200; in Flanders,
    247, 249–250, 251, 253, 270–271
Grain trade, 20–22, 109, 112, 115–116,
    158, 182, 209, 213, 222, 224; in Bur-
    gundy, 156–157, 158–159, 208; in Lan-
    guedoc, 166–167; in the Ile-de-France,
    204; in Anjou, 208
Grand Council, 229
Greenshirts, 373
Grenade, 192
Grenelle Agreement, 347
Grenoble, 229
Groupe Union-Défense, 348
Guérin, Daniel, 324–325
Guerre des Farines. *See* Flour War
Guesde, Jules, 272, 273
Guignet, Philippe, 264

Guilds, 101, 193, 194, 205, 213–214, 246
Guillaume Gate, 15, 18–19

Hainaut, 202, 204, 211, 280, 351; conten-
    tion in, 248, 250, 292
Halluin, 259, 367–368; strikes in, 368–369
d'Halluin, Henri, 373. *See also* Dorgères,
    Henri
Hardy, Sébastien, 51–52, 217, 220–226,
    227–234, 240
Haute-Garonne, 354, 356; strikes in, 326,
    360, 369, 370, 371. *See also* Languedoc
Haute-Loire, 363
Haussmann, Georges Eugène, baron, 43,
    56–57, 283, 297
Hazebrouck, 255; contention in, 247, 249
Henry IV, 2, 48, 64, 80, 121, 127
Hérault, 355, 356, 364; contention in,
    305, 371
Herbert, Sir Edward, 120, 122
Heylyn, Peter, 67–69, 133–134, 135
Hondschoote, contention in, 247, 249
Hôtel de Ville (Paris), 43, 44–47, 51–61,
    95, 225, 237, 238, 240, 304, 334, 347
Huguenots, *See* Protestants

Ile-de-France, 11, 70, 136–137, 202–205,
    206, 208–209, 211, 215, 289, 291, 308,
    356, 358; contention in, 94–95, 137,
    139, 143, 144, 224, 242, 293–295, 304,
    305, 306, 363, 398–399; description of,
    277–278, 353
Industrialization, 60, 65, 205, 278, 279,
    280, 287, 308
Industrial conflict, 220, 221. *See also*
    Workers: contention by
Industrial production, 208, 339
Innkeepers' tax, 226

Jacobinism, 292, 293
Jansenists, 219, 220
Jaurès, Jean, 315, 319
Jeunesses Patriotes, 59, 323, 324, 329, 373
Jews. *See* Anti-Semitism
Joyeuse, 181
July Days (1830), 262, 382, 398

July Monarchy, 32, 54, 283, 289, 291, 299, 304, 309
June Days (1848), 56, 382, 384
Juvinas, 198. *See also* Vivarais

La Boulaye, marquis de, 98
La Bruyère, Jean de, 161
Lafargue, Paul, 272
Lafayette, marquis de, 55, 239, 241
La Flèche, 302
La jeunesse (unmarried men), contention by, 179-180, 230
La Mare, Jean de, 208
Landlords, 193, 195-197, 214, 242, 282, 297, 299, 308, 399, 400; attacks on, 23-25, 34, 197-200, 207-208, 247, 248, 250, 251, 270, 292, 298, 305
Land tax. *See* Taille
Langevin, Paul, 332-333
Languedoc, 72, 137, 166-169, 170, 172, 175, 205-206, 207, 289, 291, 305; description of, 68-69, 276-277, 352, 356; contention in, 93, 147, 178-182, 199-200, 242-243, 292-293, 297-298, 304, 306-308, 363, 380
Lanturelu, 14-15, 18, 139, 140, 403
La Rochelle, 123-124
Latin Quarter, 323, 345-346, 347
La Trémouille, duke of, 98
Lavardin, marquis de, 152
Law, John, 218
Law clerks, 239; contention by, 229
Lawyers, 295, 298: contention by, 88, 215, 293
Lecouturier, Henri, 285, 287
Le Creusot, contention in, 306, 307, 308
Lefebvre, Georges, 248
Left Bank, 348
Léguevin, 195
Le Havre, 326
Le Mas-d'Azil, 154
Le Roy Ladurie, Jacques, 182, 372
Les Amis de l'Ordre, 268
Lescun, Jean-Paul de, 123-124
Lescure, 185
Les Sables-d'Olonne, 123, 147

Levallois-Perret, 323
Lewis, Paul, 378-379
Libourne, 227
Lille (region), 204, 211, 255-257
Lille (city), 202, 203, 245, 253, 254, 257, 258-259, 263, 279, 291; description of, 71-72, 275; contention in, 243, 246-248, 249-250, 262, 266, 268, 269, 304; celebrations in, 253, 268; strikes in, 265, 266, 267-268; population of, 282-285; demonstrations in, 305, 374
Limoges, contention in, 126-127
Locke, John, 105, 154
Locksmiths, strikes by, 300
Lodève, 205, 276, 281
Loire, 71, 356, 358, 400; contention in, 29, 371
Loire River, 71, 79-80
Lorraine, war in, 127-128
Louis XIII, 80-83, 84, 87, 93, 119-127, 134, 135, 136, 399, 401, 402, 403
Louis XIV, 16, 46, 93, 100, 110, 115, 127, 135, 136, 148, 149-150, 170, 171, 388; and war, 13, 19, 103, 143, 162; and rebellion, 17, 40, 95, 143-144, 145, 154
Louis XV, 180, 208, 216, 221, 222, 223
Louis XVI, 52-53, 221, 222, 223, 238-239, 240, 241
Louis Napoleon. *See* Napoleon III
Louis Philippe, 55, 305
Louvet, Jehan, 81-82
Lozère, 356; contention in, 307, 363. *See also* Languedoc
Lustucru rebellion, 146, 148, 387
Luynes, duke of, 122
Lyon, 289; contention in, 221, 226, 309; strikes in, 264, 360

Mâcon, 293, 308
Magne, Emile, 45
Maine, 296
Maine-et-Loire, 299, 354, 358, 360; contention in, 300; strikes in, 369, 370. *See also* Anjou
Maisons-Alfort, 326
Maltôtiers, 129, 212-213

Mantes, 137

Manufacturing, 65, 207, 278–279, 354, 355, 358; in Languedoc, 183–184, 193–194, 197, 205; in Flanders, 203, 258, 275, 279–280, 282–285; in Anjou, 206, 276, 280, 400; in the Ile-de-France, 277, 282–285

Mardi Gras, 117, 266, 268, 299–300, 389, 402

Maréchaussée, 175, 289

Marianne (secret society), 301, 302

Marie Antoinette, 221

Marie de Medici, 80–83, 84, 139

Maritime Flanders. _See_ Flemish Flanders

Marmande, 222

Marseillaise (song), 58, 266, 267, 268, 269, 319, 321, 325, 343, 370

Marseille, 284, 289

Marxist parties, 272, 273. _See also_ Communists, Communist party; Socialist party

Masons, 55; strikes by, 316

Mass meetings, 302, 303, 306, 307

Matignon Agreement, 328, 329

Mauges, 298; description of, 275–276, 352–353; contention in, 296–297

Maupéou, sieur de, 223–224

May Day, 272, 306, 320; (1890), 313–314; (1906), 307, 313, 315–318; (1907), 318; (1908), 318; (1910), 319; (1911), 319; (1913), 310–312; (1919), 319; (1920), 319; (1936), 369; (1937), 369; (1938), 369; (1947), 340; (1968), 347, 349–350; (1983), 347–348, 349–350

Mayenne, 358

Mazamet, 281

Mazarin, cardinal, 93, 94, 95, 100, 110, 129, 132, 145, 148, 396; opposition to, 97, 101, 103, 143, 146

Mende, 138, 175

Mendès-France, Pierre, 343

Merchants, 258, 261, 279, 388, 397; political power of, 91, 285, 293, 295, 297, 298, 308; attacks on, 271, 292, 293

Mercier, Sébastien, 208–209

Metalworkers, 330; strikes by, 323, 325, 327, 360, 362, 371, 379

Metalworking industries; in Flanders, 257, 258; in Languedoc, 276; in the Ile-de-France, 283; in Burgundy, 308

Meursault, 34

Michel, Louise, 57

Militia, 51, 237–241, 243, 288, 294, 339; in Burgundy, 28, 402; in Anjou, 94, 97, 106; in Languedoc, 188, 223; in Flanders, 246, 247, 253, 254

Miners, 354; strikes by, 263–265, 307, 309, 316, 319, 360, 362, 371, 379

Mining, 355, 379; in Languedoc, 194; in Anjou, 201; in Burgundy, 202, 276, 308; in Flanders, 204, 211, 257, 258, 259, 263–265, 307, 309, 351–352, 358, 360, 362, 367, 371, 401

Miromesnil, intendant of Tours, 201

Mitterrand, François, 60, 343

Mirrormakers, strikes by, 323

Monatte, Pierre, 316

Mons, 202

Montceau-les-Mines: strikes in, 307, 308

Montchrestien, Antoine, 121

Montereau, 321

Montgaillard, 180

Montmorency, duke of, 139

Montpellier, 195, 212, 216; contention in, 93, 137, 138–139, 140; demonstrations in, 306, 365, 366, 369, 372

Montredon, 195

Montreuil, 149

Montreuil-Bellay, 280

Morlaix, 374–375

Mortagne, 301

Moulins, 93

Mouvement Républicain Populaire (MRP), 339–340

Mouvement Social Révolutionnaire, 331

Music, and contention, 26–27, 58, 226, 248, 272, 317. _See also_ Serenade

Nancy, 231

Nanterre, 344

Nantes, contention in, 152, 346

Napoleon I, 298, 299, 342, 396

Napoleon III, 266–267, 268–269, 283, 289, 305–306, 384, 389

Napoleonic wars, 209–210, 383
Narbonne, contention in, 306, 365, 366
National Assembly, 216, 235, 238,
    294–295, 340–341, 366; dissolution of,
    304, 305, 347; demonstrations against,
    340, 348–349
National Front, 348
National guard, and strikers, 265–266,
    267, 270
Nationalism, 6, 73, 321
National Union of French Students
    (UNEF), 344–346, 347
Navvies, strikes by, 325
Necker, Jacques, 229, 231, 235–236, 238,
    240, 295
Nemours, 137
New Converts, 167–168, 169–170, 177
Newspapers, 14, 35, 122–123, 300, 304,
    313–314, 322, 329, 373
Nice, 289
Nîmes, 363, 365; contention in, 137, 138,
    175–176, 292, 293, 306
Nobles, 126, 142, 160, 161, 171–172, 174,
    196–197, 204, 206, 229, 231, 282, 295,
    298, 299; rebellion by, 101, 122–123,
    125–126, 130–131, 145, 146, 223, 398;
    demonstrations by, 303, 362. *See also
    specific names, e.g.,* Lafayette, marquis
    de
Noir, Victor, 313
Nord. *See* Flanders
Normandy, 372; contention in, 142

Occident movement, 344, 345
Octroi. *See* Excise taxes
Offices, 216; sale of, 18, 130, 132, 172,
    402; control of, 125, 131
Organizations, 16, 23, 74, 78
Organized labor. *See* Unions
Orléans, duke of, 212, 227, 228, 233,
    235–236
d'Orléans, Gaston, 139
Ormée, 95, 143

Painters, strikes by, 316
Palais de Justice, 225, 227, 228, 229, 230,
    235

Palais Royal, 217, 218, 225, 235
Pamiers, 125
Pancarte, 86, 93, 96, 102, 133, 304
Panthier, 24
Paris (generality). *See* Ile-de-France
Paris (city), 70–71, 72, 157, 207, 277–278,
    282, 287, 291, 328; description of,
    43–44, 56–57, 353, 356; celebrations in,
    47–48, 58, 59, 218, 221, 225, 227,
    229–230, 231, 236, 240–241, 334; dem-
    onstrations in, 59, 60, 321–323, 324,
    331, 342–343, 345–349, 369, 374;
    strikes in, 59, 218, 226, 314, 316–317,
    324, 325, 371, 374; Protestants in,
    124–125; grain seizures in, 157–158,
    222–223, 294; contention in, 217–220,
    221, 224, 228–233, 235–241, 293–294,
    305–306, 309, 383; taxation in, 239,
    324; population of, 283, 284–285,
    335–338: German occupation of,
    331–335
Paris Commune (1871), 57–59, 306, 320,
    382, 383, 384, 398
Parlement, 211, 215, 216, 223, 227, 242,
    293–294, 398; of Anjou, 92, 142, 227;
    of Paris, 94, 101, 103, 162, 205, 218,
    220, 224, 227, 228, 293–294; rebellion
    of in Paris, 96–98, 137, 142–143; of
    Languedoc, 125, 180, 229, 292; of Bur-
    gundy, 202; of Brittany, 221; of
    Flanders, 247
Parti Agraire, 372
Parti Communiste Français (PCF), 325,
    329, 369, 371
Parti National Conjonctif Républicain,
    329. *See also* Solidarité Française
Parti National Populaire, 329. *See also*
    Jeunesses Patriotes
Parti Ouvrier Français, 273
Parti Paysan, 373
Parti Populaire Français, 332
Parti Social Français, 321, 329. *See also*
    Croix de Feu
Pas-de-Calais, 356, 358; contention in,
    360, 374
Pau, 229
PCF. *See* Parti Communiste Français

Peasants, 183, 195, 218, 297, 353, 354, 355, 373; contention by, 24, 111, 191, 207. *See also* Agricultural workers

Perpignan, 365, 366

Perroy de la Forestille, Claude, 25

Peyrefitte, Alain, 380–381

Pflimlin, Pierre, 342

Phélypeaux, intendant of Paris, 204–205

Phylloxera vastatrix, 364

Picardy, 351

Pierreuse, Robert, 273

Pisani Charter, 375

Place Dauphine, 224, 228, 229, 230, 231

Place de Grève, 42–43, 44–50, 54–57, 60–61, 221, 225, 239–240; contention at, 51–54, 57–59, 230, 233, 237, 238

Place de la Concorde, 324–325

Place de la République, 316–317, 323, 324

Place de l'Hôtel de Ville, 42, 43, 57, 58, 59, 323

Plasterers, strikes by, 325

Ponts-de-Cé, 79–83; contention in, 95, 99–100, 114, 301

Poitiers, 375

Poitou, contention in, 93, 147, 296, 297

Police, 1–2, 108, 175, 288–289; and demonstrators, 36–37, 317, 319, 325, 329–330, 342, 344, 348–349, 371, 373, 374; attacks on, 219–220, 225, 227; and strikers, 329, 330, 347, 378, 379; strikes by, 334

Police powers, 208–209

Police surveillance, 32–33, 36, 38, 54–56, 208–209, 311, 316

Political parties, 308–309. *See also specific parties, e.g.*, Parti Communiste Français

Pompidou, Georges, 346, 347

Pontoise, 240

Popular Front, 326, 328, 330–331, 360, 369, 396

Population, 64, 65, 66–67, 183, 184, 255, 282–285, 355

Pouget, Emile, 313–314

Poujade, Pierre, 341, 373–374, 394

Poujadists, 370

Power, 136, 142, 161, 260, 310, 388, 391, 404; struggle for, 10–11, 386; central-ization of, 29, 75–76, 122, 128–129, 288, 387, 395–396. *See also* Catholic church: power of; Fiscal power; Police powers; State power

Prats-de-Mollo, 150

Printers, strikes by, 218

Prisoners, freeing of, 28–29, 174, 219, 228, 236, 237–238

Proisy, 137

Proletarianization of population, 5, 61, 109, 183, 207, 249, 258, 308, 386, 397. *See also* Rural proletariat

Property, 16–17, 40, 200, 212; rights, 73, 74–75, 297; contention over, 23, 198–199, 207–208, 214, 246–248, 250–251, 253, 304, 307, 310, 386, 389. *See also* Landlords

Property tax. *See* Taille

Protestant assemblies, 137, 138, 146, 155, 160, 177

Protestants, 136, 215, 387; in Anjou, 106–107, 118; in Languedoc, 154, 165, 167–170, 171, 172–178, 199, 206, 291, 292–293, 298, 399. *See also* Wars of Religion

Provence, 376

Provence, count of, 217

Provins, 204–205

Public finance, 132, 209, 214, 215, 227, 244

Public gatherings, 10, 139, 302, 370, 382, 396; forbidden, 14, 21, 189–190, 316, 319, 368; right to, 310, 311. *See also* Demonstrations; Mass meetings

Public service workers, 323, 328; strikes by, 330, 341

Pyrénées-Orientales, 356; strikes in, 364

Quarriers, 301, 360, 400; strikes by, 302, 303, 306

Quarries, 257, 281, 282

Radical Socialists, 322, 326, 327

Railroads, 281, 291; attacks on, 305

Railroad workers: contention by, 38; strikes by, 302, 319, 334, 371

Rassemblement du Peuple Français
   (RPF), 340, 370–371
Rassemblement National Populaire,
   331–332
Rassemblement pour la Révolution Na-
   tionale, 332, 334
Reformed Religion. *See* Protestants
Reims, contention in, 29, 221, 231
Rennes, contention in, 93, 152, 228, 229,
   231
Resistance groups, 339, 340
Restif de la Bretonne, 46, 50, 53
Reveillon Riots, 50–51, 232–235
Révolte du Papier Timbré, 147, 151–152
Revolt of the Armed Masks, 182
Revolution (1789–1799), 39, 40, 50–56,
   288, 291–298, 398
Revolution (1830), 262, 304, 382, 383,
   384, 398
Revolution (1848), 39, 40, 266, 287–288,
   301, 305, 383, 388, 389, 398
Revolution (1970), 57, 398
Ribaute, 137
Richelieu, cardinal, 121, 129, 134, 140,
   171, 396, 401, 402, 403
Rights, 10, 131, 132, 136, 146–147, 191,
   216, 243, 294. *See also* Communal
   rights; Property: rights; Public gather-
   ings: right to
Rohan, duke of, 95, 98, 99–100
Roquelaure, duke of, 173, 186–187
Roubaix, 258, 259; contention in,
   261–263, 272–273; strikes in, 266, 306,
   369; population of, 282, 283–285
Rouen, 291; contention in, 221, 223, 228
Roure rebellion, 147, 151
Roussillon, 147, 356; contention in, 146;
   Sovereign Council of, 150
Royal power. *See* State power
RPF. *See* Rassemblement du Peuple
   Français
Rubberworkers, strikes by, 325
Rural proletariat, 183, 184, 194, 214
Russian Revolution, 36

Sabotiers, 147
St.-Antoine (faubourg), contention in,
   232, 233

St.-Barthélemy, 301
Saint-Brieuc, 372
St.-Cloud, 218
St.-Denis, 283; contention in, 137, 190,
   240; strikes in, 325
St.-Etienne, 309
Ste.-Foy, 123
St.-Germain-près-Montargis, 137
Saint-Jacob, Pierre de, 24
Saint-James, duke of, 220
St.-Nicholas parish, 14–15
St.-Omer, 280
Saintonge, 93
St.-Philibert, 27
St.-Pons, 195
St.-Sardos, 198
Saint-Simon, duke of, 166, 170
St.-Thibéry, 179–180
St.-Waast-la-Haut, 263–264
Salan, Raoul, 342, 343
Sales tax. *See* Pancarte
Salt tax, 13, 86, 89, 98–99, 104–105, 108,
   133, 147, 149–151
Samain, 269
Saône-et-Loire, 354, 358. *See also* Bur-
   gundy
Saumur, 110, 118, 212, 275–276, 280; con-
   tention in, 98–99, 113, 296–297
Second Empire, 272, 289, 313
Second International, 313
Second Republic, 270, 289
Seine, 356, 360; contention in, 327, 369.
   See also Ile-de-France
Seine-et-Marne, 355, 356. *See also* Ile-de-
   France
Seine-et-Oise, 355, 356; demonstrations
   in, 369. *See also* Ile-de-France
Sentences, 106, 177–178, 218, 262–263;
   for contentious activities, 15, 19, 31,
   89, 96, 113, 158, 176–177, 179, 182,
   234–235. *See also* Executions
Serenade, 29–30, 33, 252
Service industry, 354, 358
Sète, 194
Seven Years' War, 171, 210, 215, 220
Shoemakers, strikes by, 302, 377–378
Sitdown strike, 371, 377–378, 381, 385,
   398; in the Ile-de-France, 326–328, 329,

Sitdown strike (*cont.*)
330, 340, 346, 347; in the Nord, 368; in Languedoc, 369
Skilled workers, 260–261, 386, 387
Slateworkers. *See* Quarriers
Smuggling, 181, 208, 242, 276–277; of salt, 104–106, 108, 150–151, 176; of grain, 112
Social classes, 74–75, 146. *See also* Class divisions
Socialism, 73–74, 301, 314, 315, 368
Socialist party, 326, 362
Socialists, 327, 331, 368, 369, 370, 378
Social movement, 76, 307, 392–394, 396
Société des Droits de l'Homme, 300
Société des Ouvriers, 267–268
Société Républicaine des Amis du Peuple, 268
Société Républicaine des Fileurs de Coton de Lille, 268
Soissons, count of, 93
Soldiers, 123, 208, 235, 237, 246, 403; billeting of, 92, 93, 100, 101, 104, 106, 115, 137, 402; and civilians, 94, 106, 117, 131, 139, 143–144, 230–231, 235–236, 304, 305–306; and demonstrators, 230, 270, 307, 366; and strikers, 268, 366. *See also* Veterans
Solidarité Chrétienne, 348
Solidarité Français, 323, 329
Sologne, 147
Sorel, Georges, 315
Soubise, duke of, 123
Stains, 323
State, 128–129, 208, 212, 288, 386; resistance to, 5–8, 11
State power, 40, 161, 163–166, 170, 387. *See also* Power: centralization of
Stavisky, Sacha, 322
Stavisky Riots, 324–325
Stonecutters, strikes by, 316
Strikes, 42, 358–362, 370–372, 382, 385–386, 389–390, 391, 401; in Flanders, 263–265, 306, 307, 309, 360, 362, 370, 373; in Anjou, 300, 301, 306; in the Ile-de-France, 305, 307, 319, 325, 340–341, 346–347, 360, 370, 373; in

Burgundy, 307, 367; as a political weapon, 325, 340–341. *See also* Firm-by-firm strike; General strike; Sitdown strike; Turnout
Students: contention by, 178–179, 225, 344–346; demonstrations by, 3, 332–333, 334, 348–349
Subsistances (tax), 91, 139
Sunday rest law, 318
Sûreté Nationale, 289
Surveillance, 259, 301, 305, 308, 312, 332. *See also* Police surveillance

Taille, 14, 94, 133, 142, 171, 175–176, 185, 194
Taillon, 133
Tailors, strikes by, 300
Tanners, contention by, 88
Tardanizats, 147
Tarn-et-Garonne, 356; strikes in, 371
Taxation, 13, 61–63, 103–104, 128, 133–136, 159, 208, 209–213, 244, 254, 388, 291; in Burgundy, 18, 401–402; in Anjou, 89, 208; in Languedoc, 171–172, 175. *See also specific taxes, e.g.,* Salt tax
Tax collection, 14, 98, 101–102, 132, 156, 158, 208, 211
Tax collectors, 99, 123, 148–149, 219; attacks on, 14–15, 90, 94, 108, 137, 139, 144, 146, 218, 304, 383
Tax exemptions, 89, 96, 102, 131, 133, 134, 147, 148–149, 172, 186
Tax-farmers, 128, 129, 132, 133, 134–135; contention involving, 102, 136, 138, 139, 150, 181
Tax-grabbers. *See* Maltôtiers
Taxi drivers, strikes by, 324, 325
Tax rebellion, 40, 144, 156, 160, 242, 310, 366, 386, 387, 397; in Burgundy, 14–15, 34–35, 146; in Anjou, 85, 86–91, 92–95, 98, 102, 107–108, 139, 146; in the Ile-de-France, 137, 140, 146, 324; in Languedoc, 137–140, 158, 172, 178, 180–182, 293; in Flanders, 247
Teachers: strikes by, 315, 345; contention by, 332–333, 334

Telegraphers, strikes by, 325

Terrage, 248, 250

Terray, abbé, 222, 224

Textile industry, 397; in Languedoc, 166–167, 181, 184, 192–194, 195, 205, 207, 276, 281, 308, 399; in Anjou, 201, 212, 276, 280, 282, 296, 301, 360, 400; in Flanders, 203, 249, 257, 258–259; 262–263, 267, 358, 367–369, 401; in the Ile-de-France, 204–205

Textile workers, strikes by, 264, 265–266, 267–268, 269, 271, 302, 303, 307, 360, 367–369. *See also* Weavers

Third Estate, 28, 170, 231, 232, 235, 237, 246, 294–295. *See also* National Assembly

Third Republic, 331, 332

Thorez, Maurice, 327, 328

Three Glorious Days (1830). *See* July Days (1830); Revolution (1830)

Three Year Bill, 311

Tithe, 176, 185, 195; contention over payment of, 198, 247, 248, 250, 251

Tocqueville, Alexis de, 287–288

Tollhouses, attacks on, 236, 242, 248, 307, 389

Torrében. *See* Révolte du Papier Timbré

Toulon, 231, 289

Toulouse, 72, 163–164, 170–172, 177–178, 195–197, 205–206, 216, 282, 289, 291; contention in, 140, 158, 178, 179, 220, 223, 228–229, 243, 292–293, 304–305, 306; celebrations in, 163–164; parlement of, 178–179, 181, 182, 187, 189, 196–197, 206, 220, 228, 229; population of, 183; grain seizures in, 187–190, 192, 221, 222; strikes in, 326, 369; demonstrations in, 369, 370–371, 375

Tourcoing, 258, 259; strikes in, 266, 269; population of, 282, 283–285; demonstrations in, 363, 369

Tournai, 248

Tours, 212

Trade: promotion of, 121, 158, 159, 244, 297; in Languedoc, 166–169, 193, 197, 205–206, 282; in Anjou, 201, 282; in Flanders, 203, 245; in the Ile-de-France, 204, 207; in Burgundy, 282. *See also* Grain trade

Trade unions. *See* Unions

Traffic, blocking of, 322, 341, 374–375, 376, 379, 393

Transport workers, strikes by, 319

Trélazé: contention in, 301; strikes in, 302, 303

Troyes, 29, 227

Tuileries, 235, 236, 241

Turbin, Jacques, 314

Turgot, Anne-Robert-Jacques, 214, 222

Turnout, 260, 263, 267, 269, 300, 304, 389, 394

22 March Movement, 345

UDCA. *See* Union de Défense des Commerçants et Artisans

UNEF. *See* National Union of French Students

Unified Socialist Party (PSU), 315, 317–318

Union de Défense des Commerçants et Artisans (UDCA), 373–374

Unionization, 309, 328, 369, 370

Union Nationale des Combattants, 324

Union Nationale des Syndicats Agricoles, 372

Unions, 261, 301, 309, 318, 330, 331, 347, 364, 368, 370; and politics, 341, 363, 388

Urbanization, 66, 67, 109, 282–287

Urlanis, B. Ts., 383

d'Usson, marquis, 181–182

Ustensile, 104

Uzès, 154, 175

Valenciennes, 211, 352; contention in, 247, 266

Vannes, 378

Vendée, 29, 358

Vermersch, Eugene, 58–59

Versailles, 58, 70, 235, 240, 306

Vesles, 137

Veterans, 321; demonstrations by, 324, 342

de Viau, Théophile, 48, 119–120

Vichy government, 332, 334
Vidal de la Blache, Paul, 351–353, 367
Vietnam war, 36, 344, 345, 384
Villain, Raoul, 319
Ville d'Auray, 218
Villemoustaussou, 191
Villers-Outréaux, 270
Villy-le-Brûlé, 24
Vingtième, 211
Violence, committee to study, 380–382
Viserny, 24
Vivarais, 168, 176, 185, 186–187, 198; contention in, 146, 151, 155, 182. _See also_ Languedoc
Volontaires Nationaux, 321, 325

Wage controls, 371
Wage cuts, 261, 263, 297, 298; strikes against, 265, 266, 267, 322, 323
Wage increases, 328, 347, 366; demands for, 340, 372
Wages, 5, 50–51, 61, 105, 183, 207, 232, 262, 265; disputes over, 195, 270, 300–301, 397
Walloon Flanders, 202
War, 16, 64, 65, 87, 89–90, 93, 121, 125, 128, 142, 159–160, 202, 383, 384; financing of, 103–104, 123, 128–136, 144, 171, 172, 209–210. _See also_ Civil wars
War of the Camisards, 156, 174–178, 186
War of Devolution, 13, 127
War of the Mother and the Son, 80–83, 84
War of the Spanish Succession, 64, 162–163, 172
Wars of Religion, 118, 119–120, 121–127, 139, 140, 154–156, 159, 171, 241–242
Wars with Spain, 13, 104, 121, 126, 127, 134, 142, 147
War taxes, 87, 103–104, 121, 144, 180–181, 215, 220
Wealth, 196, 197, 285. _See also_ Wages
Weavers, 101, 205; contention by, 102, 263; strikes by, 271, 300–301, 368

White Terror (1815), 293
Wildcat strike, 440, 450
Wine, 206, 276, 376; tax on, 181, 402
Winegrowers, 15–17, 28, 140; demonstrations by, 34, 365–366, 393; contention by, 35, 78, 293, 297, 304, 305, 306–308, 309, 387, 401, 402–403; strikes against, 362, 364–365
Winegrowing, 354–355, 363–366; in Burgundy, 29, 202, 276, 281, 282, 308, 353, 366–367, 401–403; in Languedoc, 194, 281–282, 308, 362, 364, 399, 401; in Anjou, 207, 281, 400
Women, 271; contention involving, 14–15, 21, 188–190, 198, 222, 247–248, 270, 333; complaints to officials, 86, 138, 187, 188–189, 249; punishment for contentious activities, 139, 158, 176–177, 188, 233–234. _See also_ Fishwives
Wood, tax on, 19. _See also_ Firewood
Workers, 42, 45, 54–56, 57, 192–195, 200, 279, 285, 354–358; contention by, 50–51, 55, 85, 232–233, 237, 294–295; seasonal migration of, 277, 282; representation in management, 327, 328. _See also specific occupations, e.g.,_ cabinetmakers
Workers' movements, 36, 54, 371–372
Workers' organizations, 56, 261, 263, 272, 309. _See also_ Unions
Workers' politics, 261–265, 272–273
Working conditions, 262, 263, 267, 311, 318, 347, 377. _See also_ Eight-hour day
World War I, 36–37, 319, 320, 360, 384
World War II, 330, 331–335, 338–339, 360, 384

Young, Arthur, 249
Ypres, 202

Zola, Emile, 272, 318